READINGS FOR SOCIAL RESEARCH

Theodore C. Wagenaar

Miami University
Oxford, Ohio

Wadsworth Publishing Company
Belmont, California
A Division of Wadsworth, Inc.

Sociology Editor: Curt Peoples
Production Editor: Helen Sweetland
Designer: Janet Wood
Copy Editor: Amanda Frost

Printed in the United States of America

1 2 3 4 5 6 7 8 9 10—85 84 83 82 81

Library of Congress Cataloging in Publication Data

Main entry under title:

Readings for social research.

Includes bibliographies.
1. Social science research—United States—Addresses, essays, lectures.   I.   Wagenaar, Theodore C.
H62.5.U5R4   300'.72073   80-20183
ISBN 0-534-00740-6

Preface

Decision-makers and citizens alike are constantly confronted with data and scientific conclusions. Newspapers and popular magazines report daily on the latest research on cancer, pollution, support for the president, causes of delinquency, changing attitudes toward divorce, and similar topics of popular interest. The federal government is increasingly involved in the role of data collection, and we occasionally hear about attempts to develop centralized data files on large numbers of Americans. Even in your social science courses you are constantly presented with research findings in support of particular conclusions. In short, our society is becoming increasingly dependent on and responsive to scientific findings.

As a result of these developments, it is important for college graduates to become competent consumers of research. Whatever your future occupation may be, you will undoubtedly find yourself confronted with numerous research reports and perhaps you may be asked to convert these reports into policy implications. Doing so will in part be contingent on your knowledge of research methods and their implications. Reading this volume (preferably in conjunction with a methods text) will, I hope, contribute to your ability both to understand and use social science research.

THE RESEARCH PROCESS

The process of social scientific research is primarily that—a process. This process is neither sophisticated nor new, but it is a very logical orientation for developing answers to research questions. In fact, it could almost be described as common sense. Virtually all research studies follow a similar pattern. The problem is first clarified: exactly what is the research question to be examined? Variables are identified as being cause or effect, and the nature of the relationships between variables is specified. The particular hypotheses developed are linked to a larger body of relevant knowledge and theory. Concrete measures must then be developed in order to deal more accurately with concepts and their interrelationships. With these measures in hand, a researcher then selects an appropriate research strategy for gathering the data required to assess the hypothesis. The data are then analyzed in terms of the hypotheses and research questions and both conclusions and inferences are made so that the findings of the specific study can be integrated with the larger body of knowledge on the topic.

To illustrate this process, let's examine the issue of living arrangements and performance among college students. The research question is: What is the relationship between these two concepts? This question could be transformed into a hypothesis: students living in dorms will perform at a lower rate than students living in an off-campus arrangement. This hypothesis may be developed through perusal of the literature on social environments of student living groups and their effects on student behavior. Explicit measures of both living groups and college performance are then developed and an appropriate (preferably random) sample of college students is selected for interviewing. The results are punched onto computer cards and analyzed with the use of a few statistics. The hypothesis is either supported or not supported and the results are analyzed in terms of the previous theoretical and empirical work on the topic. Perhaps our results add a new dimension to this literature or substantiate a particular theory.

This process of doing research is not a unilateral progression from one step to another. In fact, researchers typically work on several steps simultaneously and often backtrack to previous steps. Decisions made at any one stage may directly or indirectly influence decisions made at prior or subsequent stages. Each stage, as well as the process as a whole, involves a series of constraints that must be recognized and choices that must be made in response to these constraints. Yet there is an underlying logic that pervades this entire research process, a logic that reflects the scientific approach to understanding reality. This logic provides a framework for both the research process and the structure of this volume.

ABOUT THIS VOLUME

My principal goal in this volume is to contribute to your ability to understand and use social science research. This goal is best accomplished in conjunction with a good social research methods text and a competent instructor. Assuming that you have both of these, I have chosen two strategies for maximizing this goal. First, I have selected many examples of research studies to provide concrete examples of designs and issues discussed in your text and in your class. The use of examples in teaching has been demonstrated to be an effective learning technique; these examples will provide you with an opportunity to see applied in real studies many of the concepts learned from your text and class. In addition to their instructional purpose, these articles were selected for their diversity and interest to students; topics include the homosexual identification process, transracial adoption, sex-role orientation, danger in underground mining, homicide, and friendship and self-disclosure among college students. I have deliberately avoided the "classics" and the typical hard-to-read articles found in many social science journals. An additional function of these examples is to demonstrate that social research does not always occur as neatly as some textbooks portray. Several researchers' personal accounts of how they actually did their research (written especially for this volume) demonstrate this aspect of social research.

Second, in addition to examples of social research, I have included several articles that provide additional coverage of basic concepts and issues. One article, for example, presents a credibility scale for assessing sampling designs and then applies this scale to several studies (Section 2.3). Another article reviews the limitations of generalizability from social psychological experiments (Section 3.3). Another provides guidelines for reading and assessing social science research reports (Section 1.1), something omitted from most texts. Student reflections on the interviewing process are included in another pertinent article (Section 3.5).

Both of these strategies are designed to strengthen your knowledge of social research and to improve your analytical skills. Both attempt to make you more critical, even skeptical, about research studies you may encounter. And, I hope, both will convince you of the complexities of doing social research.

This volume is organized in four parts, each with two to five sections. Part 1 serves an introductory function and covers the logic of scientific inquiry, ethical considerations, and guidelines for reading and assessing social science research reports. Part 2 deals with the initial stages of the research process: theory, research design, measurement, and sampling. These issues assist in clarifying and structuring the inquiry process. Part 3 builds upon Part 2 in its coverage of the basic strategies for gathering data to answer the already developed research questions. These data-gathering strategies include field research; content analysis, historical analysis, unobtrusive measures, and ethnomethodological research; experiments; evaluation research; and survey research. Once the inquiry process has been structured and the research design selected and executed, the data must be analyzed and this analysis related to the issues raised in the first three parts. Hence, Part 4 contains a review of statistics (without formulas) and examples of causal analysis.

Several articles were solicited especially for this volume. Authors were asked to keep you, the student, in mind in writing these articles. The remaining articles were selected on the basis of three criteria: illustration of several aspects of social science research, interest to students, and a minimal display of complex techniques and statistics. Diversity of topics and social science disciplines were additional criteria applied. In short, I selected or solicited the articles on the basis of interest level (several students helped in the selection process) and pedagogical utility.

In terms of structure, this volume parallels the popular Babbie text more closely than other texts. Yet I have made a deliberate attempt to provide articles and a structure that will serve as a useful supplement for any social research text. To that end, I provide brief introductions to each section, plus an appendix correlating these sections to chapters in each of sixteen popular research texts.

Finally, although my principal goal involves your becoming a knowledgeable consumer of social science research, I also hope that through this volume you will see the excitement, even the fun, involved in the process of doing social science research and learning more about human interaction.

ACKNOWLEDGMENTS

Ronald Corwin is most responsible for my interest in social research. He skillfully played the role of mentor by providing me with a unique opportunity to observe the inner workings of a creative social scientist. Through countless discussions with him, I learned a great deal about the process, the intricacies, and, most important, the excitement of doing social research.

I would also like to thank the authors of the articles that appear here, particularly those whose articles were solicited especially for this volume. I also acknowledge with gratitude the various publishers who have granted permission to reprint their articles.

Several students assisted me in selecting interesting and readable articles for this volume: Sr. Joyce Parris, Linda Murphy, Randy Gans, and Michele Charlton. Other people provided suggestions for the organization of the volume and carefully reviewed my articles: Sr. Kristin Wenzel, Barbara Wagenaar, Karen Smith, Carol Smith, Carla Howery, and Earl Babbie. In addition, the volume was reviewed at various stages by Edgar Webster, Oklahoma State University; Roger Trent, West Virginia University; James Robbins, Tufts University; Thomas Koebernick, Wright State University; and Reed Geertsen, Utah State University.

Several people at Wadsworth have played key roles in the birth of this volume. Both Curt Peoples and Steve Rutter have provided useful advice and constant support and have demonstrated acute sensitivity to the social sciences. Helen Sweetland competently supervised the production phase of the work, and Barbara Cuttle excellently played the role of interloper between manuscript and text.

Clara Haag typed numerous drafts of articles and introductions in her usually skillful and efficient manner. Additional typing assistance was provided by Carol O'Malley, Nancy McGary, and Cindy Brown.

I also wish to acknowledge with appreciation all of my research methods students. They have contributed considerably to my approach to teaching research methods and have provided me with both ideas and feedback on the articles.

Finally, I dedicate this book to my daughter, Keri Anne, who in her own way has taught me a great deal about human interaction and the process of social research.

Contents

PART ONE: AN INTRODUCTION TO INQUIRY   1

Section 1.1: Social Scientific Inquiry   2

The Logic of Science in Sociology, Walter L. Wallace   4

Of Drooling Dogs and Periwinkles, Jonathan Kellerman   14

Some Guidelines for Reading and Assessing Research Reports in the Social Sciences,
Theodore C. Wagenaar   15

Section 1.2: The Ethics of Social Research   30

Social Scientists Ought to Stop Lying, Donald P. Warwick   33

Jokers Wild in the Lab, Zick Rubin   38

PART TWO: THE STRUCTURING OF INQUIRY   43

Section 2.1: Theory and Research Design   44

What Is Theory? Gerald S. Ferman and Jack Levin   48

Research Methods for the Study of Conflict and Cooperation,
William F. Whyte   53

Bold but Irrelevant: Grow and Shapiro on Transracial Adoption,
Amuzie Chimezie   61

Not So Bold and Not So Irrelevant: A Reply to Chimezie,
Deborah Shapiro and Lucille J. Grow   68

Section 2.2: Measurement   72

Measuring Sex-role Orientation: A Normative Approach,
Donna Brogan and Nancy G. Kutner   76

. . . Answer Yes or No, Adam Yarmolinsky   86

Section 2.3: The Logic of Sampling   88

Small-scale Sampling with Limited Resources, Seymour Sudman   90

PART THREE: MODES OF OBSERVATION   103

Section 3.1: Field Research   104

Research as Process: The Human Dimension of Social Scientific Research,
Richard R. Troiden   108

Reflections on Being a Complete Participant, John S. Fitzpatrick   118

Section 3.2: Content Analysis, Historical Analysis, Unobtrusive Measures, and Ethnomethodological Research   130

Criminal Homicide as a Situated Transaction, David F. Luckenbill   134

Researching Murder Transactions, David F. Luckenbill   143

The Social Scientist as Historian: How Important Is It to Look Back? Douglas Klegon   152

Unobtrusive Measures: An Inventory of Uses, Thomas J. Bouchard, Jr.   161

Ethnomethodology, Kenneth D. Bailey   178

Section 3.3: Experiments   191

Boundaries around Group Interaction: The Effect of Group Size and Member Status on Boundary Permeability, Eric S. Knowles   195

Hot and Crowded: Influences of Population Density and Temperature on Interpersonal Affective Behavior, William Griffitt and Russell Veitch   199

Some Limitations on Generalizability from Social Psychological Experiments, Edgar F. Borgatta and George W. Bohrnstedt   206

Section 3.4: Evaluation Research   211

Getting Started with Evaluative Research, Janet P. Moursund   215

An Experiment in Parole Supervision, John J. Berman   228

Some Problems in Experimentation in a Legal Setting, H. Laurence Ross and Murray Blumenthal   238

Section 3.5: Survey Research   244

Friendship, Proximity, and Self-disclosure, Zick Rubin and Stephen Shenker   248

The Role of the Interviewer, Jean M. Converse and Howard Schuman   261

Factors Affecting Response Rates to Mailed Questionnaires: A Quantitative Analysis of the Published Literature, Thomas A. Heberlein and Robert Baumgartner   273

PART FOUR: ANALYSIS OF DATA   279

Section 4.1: Social Statistics and Data Analysis   280

Social Statistics without Formulas, Theodore C. Wagenaar   281

Section 4.2: Causal Analysis   302

Race, Daughters and Father-loss: Does Absence Make the Girl Grow Stronger? Janet G. Hunt and Larry L. Hunt   305

Secondary Analysis: A Personal Journal, Janet G. Hunt and Larry L. Hunt   317

Music to Get Pregnant By, Mike Royko   323

Appendix: Readings Correlated with Chapters of Widely Used Social Research Texts   325

Contributors   327

PART ONE

An Introduction to Inquiry

SECTION 1.1

Social Scientific Inquiry

Social scientific inquiry is very much like detective work in its search for causes. In both approaches there exists a desire to describe the phenomenon being investigated and to determine possible alternative explanations for the phenomenon. Both social scientific inquiry and detective work are in search of answers; only the focuses of inquiry differ. Both involve possible false leads, constant reformulation of the question, the use of a variety of investigative methods, and careful attention to conceptualizing the relevant factors. Furthermore, both approaches emphasize the role of empirical data, objectivity, and the use of logical thought processes. Ultimately, all such inquiry involves a considerable amount of common sense and reliance on the investigator's creative abilities to "break" a case.

ASSUMPTIONS OF THE SCIENTIFIC APPROACH

Like the detective approach to inquiry, the scientific mode of inquiry relies on several basic assumptions. Fundamentally, social scientists assume that a certain order exists in the universe. Social regularities exist, very much like regularities of the physical world such as the law of gravity. For example, individuals tend to marry persons of a similar background, men tend to earn more than women, and large social groups experience more formalized social interaction than small social groups.

Social scientists assume that this reality is knowable and that one of the best approaches for understanding this reality is through the use of the scientists' senses; this practice is known as empiricism. Empiricism involves the collection of data for purposes of imposing order on the reports of the senses so that explanations can be developed. Moreover, these explanations must be testable through the use of empirical methods so that different scientists using the same methods will arrive at essentially the same results.

Another assumption is that causes exist to explain most social phenomena. Social scientists assume, for example, that there are causes for discrimination, sex-role stereotyping, interpersonal conflict, and other social phenomena. Very few, if any, social phenomena are caused by one factor alone. Because social scientists do assume that causes exist for social phenomena, the job of the social scientist is to determine (1) the

2

possible causes, (2) the relative importance of each of the possible causes, and (3) how the potentially causal factors may interact with each other to produce an outcome that may not occur as a result of any one of the factors alone.

ARE THE SOCIAL SCIENCES REALLY SCIENTIFIC?

This question has long been debated in the social science literature. Generally the debate involves a comparison of social science with natural science. Pro arguments assert that social scientists, like natural scientists, employ empiricism, strive for general theories, emphasize the elimination of personal values (objectivity), investigate regularities, and use mathematical techniques. Con arguments include such assertions as many social concepts (such as attitudes) cannot be observed and therefore cannot be measured; measuring social concepts may change them; behavior may not correspond with attitudes; too many factors are at work to be able to make causal assertions; replicability is difficult given the dynamic nature of social phenomena; and true experimentation involving control over the cause and the effect (the hallmark of causal analysis) is difficult to perform for most social phenomena. I personally believe that the scientific process reflects a frame of mind more than a specific set of procedures, so that it is pointless to argue about whether social science is really science. I see the use of the scientific approach as a useful strategy for objectively increasing the body of social scientific knowledge.

THE READINGS

The readings in this section focus on the social scientific inquiry process and the reporting of results obtained through this process. The first article, by Walter L. Wallace, has become a classic in terms of formulating the research process in the social sciences. Wallace emphasizes the reciprocal relationship between theory (general knowledge based on compilations of research findings and logical methods) and research (the empirical data-gathering process applied to hypotheses derived from theories). A central theme in his book is that theory and methods are closely related when the goal is building cumulative knowledge. Wallace also emphasizes the role of what he calls "observational effects." He thus places heavy reliance on sensory observation. And finally, Wallace emphasizes the role of logical methods in both deriving testable hypotheses from theories and transforming raw empirical conclusions into an integrated body of knowledge in a given area.

The Wallace diagram of the scientific process is a popular depiction of the basic steps involved in social scientific research. Note his distinction between "information components" and "methods"; the methods steps permit the transition from one information component to another. The model is a good one for describing the ideal way to approach social scientific research. Unfortunately, as Wallace himself notes, the process generally does not operate in such a predetermined manner, and each step itself can involve a number of false starts. Backward steps also occur almost as frequently as forward steps; in fact, the phrase "two steps forward and one step backward" quite accurately describes the process. But this developmental feature is exactly what makes social scientific research exciting to do while increasing the validity of the results.

In the second article, Jonathan Kellerman makes some observations on the "payoff" of scientific investigations. The article is a response to Senator William Proxmire's

"Golden Fleece" awards for highly specialized (and, in his view, meaningless) research studies that do not have a direct and obvious payoff. Kellerman argues that one goal of scientific investigation is the pursuit of knowledge, regardless of any direct policy relevance. He notes, however, that such "pure" research often has unexpected policy relevance.

The last article in this section contains a set of guidelines for reading and assessing social science research articles. Published accounts of research are often the distillation of an entire research project and may omit much of what actually happened or what was actually found. This article includes suggestions for reading social science articles so that they make sense and for assessing their quality. Since you are just beginning your research methods course and have not yet encountered all the details of doing social scientific research, you may wish to reread this article upon completion of the course. The article is placed in this first section to provide a general framework for analyzing the research articles you will be reading in this book and elsewhere while studying research methods. Be sure to look over the Appendix before reading the article so that you will be sensitized to the range of issues to consider when reading social science articles.

THE LOGIC OF SCIENCE IN SOCIOLOGY
Walter L. Wallace

SCIENCE AND THREE ALTERNATIVES

Whatever else it may be, science is a way of generating and testing the truth of statements about events in the world of human experience. But since science is only one of several ways of doing this, it seems appropriate to begin by identifying them all, specifying some of the most general differences among them, and thus locating science within the context they provide.

There are at least four ways of generating, and testing the truth of, empirical statements: "authoritarian," "mystical," "logico-rational" and "scientific."[1] A principal distinction among these is the manner in which each vests confidence in the *producer* of the statement that is alleged to be true (that is, one asks, *Who* says so?); in the *procedure* by which the statement was produced (that is, one asks, *How* do you know?); and in the *effect* of the statement (that is, one asks, What *difference* does it make?).

In the authoritarian mode, knowledge is sought and tested by referring to those who are socially defined as qualified producers of knowledge (for example, oracles, elders, archbishops, kings, presidents, professors). Here the knowledge-seeker attributes the ability to produce true statements to the natural or supernatural occupant of a particular social position. The procedure whereby the seeker solicits this authority (prayer, petition, etiquette, ceremony) is likely to be important to the nature of the authority's response, but not to the seeker's confidence in that response. Moreover, although the practical effects of the knowledge thus obtained can contribute to the eventual overthrow of authority, a very large number of effective disconfirmations may be required before this happens.

The mystical mode (including its drug- or stress-induced hallucinatory variety) is partly related to the authoritarian, insofar as both may solicit knowledge from prophets, mediums, divines, gods, and other supernaturally knowledgeable authorities. But the authoritarian mode depends essentially on the social position of the

---

knowledge-producer, while the mystical mode depends more essentially on manifestations of the knowledge-consumer's personal "state of grace," and on his personal psychophysical state. For this reason, in the mystical mode far more may depend on applying ritualistic purification and sensitizing procedures to the consumer. This mode also extends its solicitations for knowledge beyond animistic gods, to more impersonal, abstract, unpredictably inspirational, and magical sources, such as manifest themselves in readings of the tarot, entrails, hexagrams, and horoscopes. Again, as in the case of the authoritarian mode, a very large number of effective disconfirmations may be needed before confidence in the mystical grounds for knowledge can be shaken.

In the logico-rational mode, judgment of statements purporting to be true rests chiefly on the procedure whereby these statements have been produced; and the procedure centers on the rules of formal logic. This mode is related to the authoritarian and mystical ones, insofar as the latter two can provide grounds for accepting both the rules of procedure and the axioms or "first principles" of the former. But once these grounds are accepted, for whatever reasons, strict adherence to correct procedure is held infallibly to produce valid knowledge. As in the two preceding modes, disconfirmation by effect may have little impact on the acceptability of the logico-rational mode of acquiring knowledge.

Finally, among these four modes of generating and testing empirical statements, the scientific mode combines a primary reliance on the observational effects of the statements in question, with a secondary reliance on the procedures (methods) used to generate them.[2] Relatively little weight is placed on characteristics of the producer *per se*; but when they are involved, achieved rather than ascribed characteristics are stressed—not for their own sakes, but as *prima facie* certifications of effect and procedure claims.

In emphasizing the role of methods in the scientific mode, I mean to suggest that whenever two or more items of information (for example, observations, empirical generalizations, theories) are believed to be rivals for truth-value, the choice depends heavily on a collective assessment and replication of the procedures that yielded the items.[3] In fact, all of the methods of science may be thought of as relatively strict cultural conventions whereby

the production, transformation, and therefore the criticism of proposed items of knowledge may be carried out collectively and with relatively unequivocal results. This centrality of highly conventionalized criticism seems to be what is meant when *method*[4] is sometimes said to be the essential quality of science; and it is the relative clarity and universality of this method and its several parts that make it possible for scientists to communicate across, as well as within, disciplinary lines.

Scientific methods deliberately and systematically seek to annihilate the individual scientist's standpoint. We would like to be able to say of every statement of scientific information (whether observation, empirical generalization, theory, hypothesis, or decision to accept or reject an hypothesis) that it represents an *unbiased* image of the world—not a given scientist's *personal* image of the world, and ultimately not even a *human* image of the world, but a *universal* image representing the way the world "really" is, without regard to time or place of the observed events and without regard to any distinguishing characteristics of the observer. Obviously, such disembodied "objectivity" is impossible to finite beings, and our nearest approximation to it can only be *agreement* among individual scientists. Scientific methods constitute the rules whereby agreement about specific images of the world is reached. The methodological controls of the scientific process thus annihilate the individual's standpoint, not by an impossible effort to substitute objectivity in its literal sense, but by substituting rules for intersubjective criticism, debate, and, ultimately, agreement.[5] The rules for constructing scales, drawing samples, taking measurements, estimating parameters, logically inducing and deducing, etc., become the primary bases for criticizing, rejecting, and accepting items of scientific information. Thus, ideally, criticism is not directed first to what an item of information says about the world, but to the method by which the item was produced.

But I have stressed that reliance on the *observational effects* of statements purporting to be true is even more crucial to science than is its reliance on methodological conventions. By this I mean that if, after the methodological criticism mentioned above, two information components are still believed to be rivals, the extent to which each is accepted by the scientific community tends to depend heavily on its resistance to repeated attempts to refute it by observations. Similarly, when two methodological procedures are believed to be rivals, the choice between them tends to rest on their relative abilities to generate, systematize, and predict new observations. Thus, Popper says: "I shall certainly admit a system as empirical or scientific only if it is capable of being tested by experience. . . . It must be possible for an empirical scientific system to be refuted by experience" (1961:40–41).

Assuming that observation is partly independent of the observer (that is, assuming that he can observe something other than himself, even though the observation is shaped to greater or lesser degree by that self—assuming, in short, that observations refer, partly, to something "out there," external to any observer), it becomes apparent that reliance on observation seeks the same goal as reliance on method: the annihilation of individual bias and the achievement of a "universal" image of the way the world "really" is. But there is an important difference in the manner in which the two seek this goal. Reliance on method attacks individual bias by subjecting it to highly conventionalized criticism and subordinating it to collective agreement. It thus seeks to overpower personal bias with shared bias. Reliance on observation (given the "independence" assumption mentioned above), however, introduces into both biases an element whose ultimate source is independent of all human biases, whether individual and unique or collective and shared. In a word, it seeks to temper shared bias, as well as individual bias, with *un-bias*.

Therefore, the scientific mode of generating and testing statements about the world of human experience seems to rest on dual appeals to rules (methods) whose origin is human convention, and to events (observables) whose origin is partly nonhuman and nonconventional. From these two bases, science strikes forcibly at the individual biases of its own practitioners that they may jointly pursue, with whatever falter and doom, a literally superhuman view of the world of human experience.

Finally, in this brief comparison of modes of generating and testing knowledge, one should remember that neither the scientific, nor the authoritarian, nor the mystical, nor the logico-rational mode excludes any of the others. Indeed, a typical effort will involve some scientific observation and method, some authoritarian footnoting and documentation, some invocations of ritually purified (that is, trained) imagination and insight, and some logico-rational induction and deduction; only relative emphasis or predominance among these modes permits classifying actual cases. It is perhaps just as well so, since none of the modes can be guaranteed, in the long run, to produce any more, or any more accurate, or any more important, knowledge than another. And even in the short run, a particular objective truth discovered by mystical, authoritarian, or logico-rational (or, indeed, random) means is no less true than the same truth discovered by scientific means. Only our confidence in its truth will vary, depending on which means we have been socialized to accept with least question.

Given this initial perspective on science as compared to other ways of testing the truth of statements about the world of human experience, a more focused approach to it can be made.

OVERVIEW OF ELEMENTS IN THE SCIENTIFIC PROCESS

The scientific process may be described as involving five principal information components whose transformations into one another are controlled by six principal sets of methods, in the general manner shown in Figure 1. This figure is intended to be a concise but accurate map of most of the discussion in this book; for this reason, parts of it will be reproduced at appropriate points. However, the reader may wish to turn back to the complete figure occasionally in order to keep clearly in mind its full perspective. In brief translation, Figure 1 indicates the following ideas:

Individual observations are highly specific and essentially unique items of information whose synthesis into the more general form denoted by empirical generalizations is accomplished by measurement, sample summarization, and parameter estimation. Empirical generalizations, in turn, are items of information that can be synthesized into a theory via concept formation, proposition formation, and proposition arrangement. A theory, the most general type of information, is transformable into new hypotheses through the method of logical deduction. An empirical hypothesis is an information item that becomes transformed into new observations via interpretation of the hypothesis into observables, instrumentation, scaling, and sampling. These new observations are transformable into new empirical generalizations (again, via measurement, sample summarization, and parameter estimation), and the hypothesis that occasioned their construction may then be tested for conformity to them. Such tests may result in a new informational outcome: namely, a decision to accept or reject the truth of the tested hypothesis. Finally, it is inferred that the latter gives confirmation, modification, or rejection of the theory.[6]

Before going any further in detailing the meaning of Figure 1 and of the translation above, I must emphasize that the processes described there and throughout this book occur (1) sometimes quickly, sometimes slowly; (2) sometimes with a very high degree of formalization and rigor, sometimes quite informally, unself-consciously, and in-

tuitively; (3) sometimes through the interaction of several scientists in distinct roles (of, say, "theorist," "research director," "interviewer," "methodologist," "sampling expert," "statistician," etc.), sometimes through the efforts of a single scientist; and (4) sometimes only in the scientist's imagination, sometimes in actual fact. In other words, although Figure 1 and the discussion in this book are intended to be *systematic* renderings of science as a field of socially organized human endeavor, they are not intended to be inflexible. The task I have chosen is to set forth the principal common elements—the themes—on which a very large number of variations can be, and are, developed by different scientists. It is not my principal aim here to analyze these many possible and actual variations; I wish only to state their underlying themes. Still,

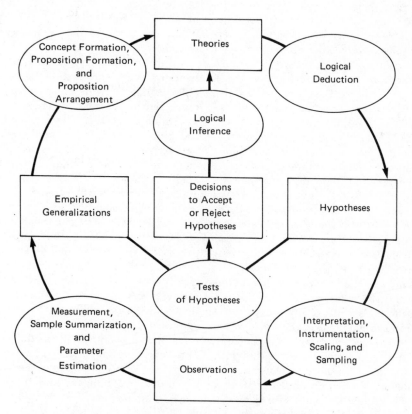

Note: Informational components are shown in rectangles; methodological controls are shown in ovals; information transformations are shown by arrows.

Figure 1   The principal informational components, methodological controls, and information transformations of the scientific process

it seems useful to discuss briefly the types of variation mentioned above (particularly the last type), if only to defend the claim that my analysis of themes is flexible enough to incorporate, by implication, the analysis of variations as well.

Each scientific subprocess (for example, that of transforming one information component into another, and that of applying a given methodological control) almost always involves a series of preliminary *trials*. Sometimes these trials are wholly imaginary; that is, the scientist manipulates images in his mind of objects not present to his senses. He may think, "If I had this sort of instrument, then these observations might be obtained; these generalizations and this theory and this hypothesis might be generated; etc."; or perhaps, "If I had a different theory, then I might entertain a different hypothesis—one that would conform better to existing empirical generalizations." When these imaginary trials, sometimes running several times through the entire sequence of scientific transformations, seem to be accomplished all in one instant (and when, of course, these imaginary trials turn out, when actualized, to be correct and fruitful), the scientist's performance is said to be "insightful." It is here, in making imaginary trials, that "intuition," "intelligent speculation," and "heuristic devices" find their special usefulness in science.

For maximum social acceptance as statements of truth by the scientific community, trials must not be left to imagination alone; they must become actual fact. The actualization of scientific processes (for example, actually constructing a desired instrument) usually brings about a reduction in speed and an increase in the rigor and formalization with which trials are carried out, because it subjects the entire trial process to the constraints and intransigences of the material world. An increase in the role specialization of the scientists who carry out the trials is also likely to result.

It is important to note that in the trial process just referred to (whether imaginary or actualized), directions of influence opposite to those shown in Figure 1 are often taken temporarily.[7] For example, the first formulation of a hypothesis deduced from a theory may be ambiguous, imprecise, logically faulty, untestable, or otherwise unsatisfactory, and it may undergo several revisions before a satisfactory formulation is constructed. In this process, not only will the deduced hypothesis change, but the originating theory may also be modified as the implications of each trial formulation reveal more about the theory itself.

Similarly (to move further around Figure 1), the process of transforming a hypothesis into observations may involve several interpretation trials, several scaling trials (in which new scales may be invented and alternative scales selected), and several sampling trials. In each trial (at this point in the scientific process, trials are often called "pretests" or "pilot studies"), new observations are at least imagined and often actually made; and from them the investigator judges not only how relevant to his hypothesis the final observations and empirical generalizations are likely to be, but how appropriate his hypothesis is, given the observations and generalizations he can make. He may also judge how appropriate his methods are, given the information he is seeking to transform. Thus, the invention and trial of a new scaling, or instrumentation, or sampling, or interpretation technique may result in the deduction of new hypotheses rather than the reverse process shown in Figure 1.

Despite these retrograde effects that may be seen for every information transformation indicated in Figure 1, the dominant processual directions remain as shown there. When counterdirections are taken, they are best described as background preparations and repairs prior to a new advance. Thus, the invention of a new instrument for taking observations may occasion the deduction of new hypotheses, so that when new observations are actually and formally taken with the new instrument, they will be scientifically interpretable (that is, transformable into empirical generalizations that will be comparable with hypotheses, etc.) rather than mere extra-scientific curiosities. Similarly, a particular formulation of a theoretically-deduced hypothesis may react on its parent theory or on the method of logical deduction, and the theory may react on its supporting empirical generalizations, decisions, and on the rules of logical induction; so that when the next step is actually taken (that is, when observations are made, via interpretation of the hypothesis, scaling, instrumentation, and sampling), it will rest on newly-examined and firm ground.

But as C. Wright Mills implied, such careful background preparation does not always occur, and in practice any element in the scientific process may vary widely in the degree of its formalization and integration with other elements. Mills argued specifically that the relationship of theorizing to other phases in the scientific process can be so tenuous that theory becomes distorted and enslaved by "the fetishism of the Concept." Similarly, he claimed, the relationship of research methods to hypotheses, observations, and empirical generalizations can be so rigid that empirical research becomes distorted by "the methodological inhibition."[8] It may be added that the distinction between researches that "explore" given phenomena and researches that "test" specific hypotheses is another manifestation of the same variability in degree of formalization and integration; "exploratory" studies, precisely because they probe new substantive or methodological areas, may rest on still unformalized and unintegrated theoretical, hypothetical, and methodological arguments. Understanding a published report of such a study often depends on inferring the theory that "must have" undergirded the study, or on guessing the empirical generalizations, or hypotheses, or observations, or tests, etc., that the researcher "must have" had in mind. "Hypothesis-testing" studies,

however, are likely to have more explicit, more formalized, and more thoroughly integrated foundations in all elements of the scientific process.[9]

Finally, in this preliminary description of elements in the scientific process, it seems useful to note that sociologists (and other scientists, as well) often refer simply to "theory" (or "theory construction") and "empirical research" as the two major constituents of science. What is the relation of these familiar terms to the more detailed elements just outlined?

Figure 2 is designed to answer this question by suggesting that the left half of Figure 1 represents what seems to be meant by the inductive construction of theory from, and understanding of, observations; whereas the right half represents what seems to be meant by the deductive application of theory to observations and the knowledge of observations.[10] Similarly, the top half of Figure 1 represents what is often referred to as theorizing, via the use of inductive and deductive logic as method; whereas the bottom half represents what is often meant by doing empirical research, with the aid of

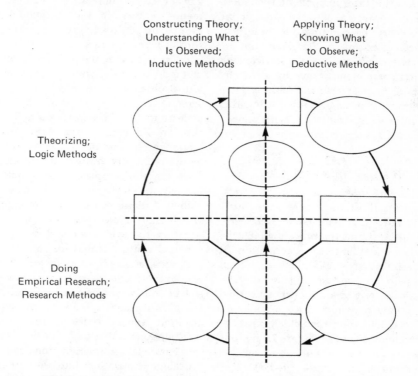

Figure 2 Classification of the principal components, controls, and transformations of the scientific process according to some conventional terms

what are called "research methods." The manifold interrelations between these segments of the scientific process should be clear from Figure 1, which also suggests that the process may be as readily divided along many other lines.[11]

It will be noted in Figure 2, however, that all five information components, and two of the methodological control sets, are shown in marginal positions. The marginality of information components is meant to signify their ability to be transformed into each other, under the indicated controls, and thus to play at least dual roles in the scientific process. Of special importance is the transformational line up the middle. This line represents the closely related claims that tests of congruence between hypotheses and empirical generalizations depend on the deductive as well as the inductive side of scientific work and are as essential to constructing as to applying theory; that decisions to accept or reject hypotheses form an indispensable bridge between constructing and applying theory and also between theorizing and doing empirical research; and that the logical inference controlling the incorporation of such decisions into theory is marginal between constructing and applying theory. By pointing out these marginalities, I mean to emphasize the paramount importance of this series of methodological controls and information components, wherein "concrete" observations made on the world and "abstract" theories made within the mind are brought together in their most intimate confrontation, with inevitably profound consequences for both.

AN ILLUSTRATION BASED ON DURKHEIM'S *SUICIDE*

The formulations presented so far are relatively abstract. An illustration based on Durkheim's famous study (first released in 1897) may convey the overall sense of the process which the rest of this book dissects for closer examination. (It must be emphasized that in this illustration I am not concerned with how empirically true my statements about suicide are, nor am I much concerned with how accurately they reproduce Durkheim's statements; instead, I am concerned chiefly that the form of my statements illustrates Figure 1, and thus illustrates how scientific statements about suicide *would* be generated and their truth tested.[12])

Suppose a scientist became interested in explaining why suicide rates are higher among some people than others. Such an interest is almost certain to be generated by prior theory and hypotheses (Durkheim indicated in the Preface to *Suicide*, pages 35–39, that his own interest was so generated), even though they may be vague, implicit, and unconsciously held. But the first explicit step in satisfying one's research interest would be to interpret the concept "suicide" in terms of phenomena on which observations can actually be made.[13]

Following that, one might choose or construct the scales that are to be applied to these observations. Durkheim used the ratio scale of counting; the nominal scales of religious affiliation, sex, nationality, etc.; the interval scale of calendar year; and the (obviously) ordinal scale of marital status.

Next, the instruments whereby observations will be made are determined. Durkheim relied on official documents (which he accepted as accurately recording observations on suicide as he interpreted the term) and the published works of others.

Then, decisions regarding sampling procedures are made. Durkheim sampled suicides presumably committed during given years of the nineteenth century, in various geopolitical units of Europe, by persons in given age categories, by persons of given sex, etc.

Finally, by acting in accord with the above methodological decisions, a large number of individual observations would be collected. These observations would be measured by the appropriate scales and the measures would then be summarized in the form of rates, averages, totals, maps, tables, graphs, and the like. Since these summaries would refer only to the observations that were actually in the samples, some estimate would be made of the corresponding true (that is, error-free) values of these measures in the populations from which the samples were drawn. Durkheim does not seem to have considered this question explicitly, and simply treated his sample statistics as if they were population parameters.

At this point, the large number of observations so laboriously collected might be reduced to a brief but informationally heavy-laden empirical generalization: "suicide varies with Catholic and Protestant religious affiliation."

The next information transformation (of empirical generalization into theory) involves four entirely mental steps: (1) forming a concept (explanans) that identifies some characteristic that the examined religious affiliation populations, together with other populations still unexamined, may have in different degree, and that may logically or causally account for their having different suicide rates; (2) forming a concept (explanandum) that identifies some characteristic that suicide rates have in common with other conceivable rates, by virtue of which they might all be logical or causal consequences of the explanans; (3) forming a proposition in which the explanans and explanandum are related in a way consistent with the relationship stated in the originating empirical generalization; and (4) forming several such propositions, all sharing a common explanandum or a common explanans, and arranging them in such a way that further hypotheses can be deduced and tested.

To continue the Durkheim-based example, the first step (forming the explanans) means that one might arrive at a statement such as, "Suicide rates vary inversely with the *social integration of individuals* in its very-low-to-moderate range." Here only religious affiliation—the independent variable of the originating empirical generalization—has been theoretically conceptualized. After the second step, one might say, "The *incidence of deviant behavior* varies inversely with the social integration of individuals in its very-low-to-moderate range," thus adding a more abstract conceptualization of suicide rate[14]—the original dependent variable. The third step might yield a theoretic proposition of the following kind: "The social integration of individuals, in its very-low-to-moderate range, causes, in inverse ratio, the incidence of deviant behavior." Here the explanans and explanandum are related as cause and effect—a relationship consistent with that in the original empirical generalization, but going beyond observable "covariation" to the more abstract "causation."[15]

Finally, in the fourth step, through reiterations of the above process (beginning with the transformation of observations into empirical generalizations) one might develop three other Durkheim-like propositions. Then, all four propositions (together with necessary definitions) might be arranged into the following concatenated theory:

Definitions:
(1) "Deviant behavior" refers to individuals' violations of particular behavioral prescriptions or proscriptions promulgated by others.

(2) "Social integration" refers to the degree to which individuals objectively receive benefits and injuries provided by others, and so are integrated into the latter's social system.

(3) "Normative integration" refers to the degree to which individuals subjectively accept behavioral prescriptions and proscriptions promulgated by others, and so are integrated into the latter's normative system.

Propositions:
The incidence of deviant behavior is caused:
(1) In inverse ratio by social integration in its very-low-to-moderate (egoism) range;
(2) In direct ratio by social integration in its moderate-to-very-high (altruism) range;
(3) In inverse ratio by normative integration in its very-low-to-moderate (anomie) range; and
(4) In direct ratio by normative integration in its moderate-to-very-high (fatalism) range.

From such a theory, one could deduce, interpret, and finally test new hypotheses purporting to explain the incidence of kinds of deviant behavior other than suicide by referring to manifestations of social and normative integration other than those actually examined in the process of generating the theory. For example (again drawn from Durkheim), if it could be shown that unmarried persons experience less social integration than married persons, and that both are in the very-low-to-moderate range of social integration, then the theory predicts that the unmarried will have a higher suicide rate, and a higher incidence of other deviant behavior, than the married. New observations and new empirical generalizations to test the truth of this new hypothesis could be generated as before, by interpreting the hypothesis into directly observable terms, scaling, instrumentation, and sampling; and by measurement, summarization, and parameter estimation. Then the new empirical generalizations could be compared with the hypothesis; and if the comparison were judged favorable, a decision to accept the hypothesis would be made and confirmation for the theory would be inferred (or, more precisely, no disconfirmation would be inferred). If the theory were to remain unchanged, results of tests of many such hypotheses would describe the limits of the theory. That is, such results would indicate which varieties of "deviant behavior," "social integration," and "normative integration" fall within its explanatory scope, and which varieties do not. But since scientists are usually more interested in expanding than in describing the limits of a theory, it would almost certainly be modified under the impact of each test that did not give positive results.

NOTES

[1]The outlines of the following discussion were suggested by Montague (1925).

[2]For a classic discussion of some sociological relations between the mystical, scientific, and authoritarian modes, see Malinowski (1948); and for classic experiments, essentially comparing the authoritarian and the scientific modes (that is, group influence on individual perception), see Asch (1958) and Sherif (1958). Betsy Barley (private communication) recalls Groucho's summary line in *Duck Soup*: "Who are you going to believe—me or your eyes?"

[3]To say this is a distinguishing tendency of the scientific mode is not to say that this tendency is never opposed. Political pressure has been brought to bear, at various times and places, on the ideas of Galileo, Marx, Darwin, and many others.

[4]My use of "method" probably incorporates some of what Nagel calls "technique," since he restricts scientific method to "the general logic employed ... for assessing the merits of an inquiry" (1967:9).

[5]See Nagel (1967:10).

[6]Compare Bergmann's similar, but more abbreviated, formula: "The three pillars on which the house of science is built are observation, induction, and deduction" (1957:31). For other capsule descriptions of the scientific process, see Popper (1961:111), Bohm (1957:5–6), Kaplan (1964:9–10), Stinchcombe (1968:15–18), Blalock (1969:8), and Greer (1969:4).

[7]I am indebted to Richard J. Hill for pointing this out to me; the "temporarily" and the "trial" ideas are my own interpretations, however.

[8]Mills dubbed these two distortions "grand theory" and "abstracted empiricism" (1959:25–75). Glaser and Strauss also derisively contrast "logico-deductive theory, which ... was merely thought up on the basis of *a priori* assumption and a touch of common sense, peppered with a few old theoretical speculations made by the erudite," with "grounded" theory—theory generated "from data systematically obtained from social research" (1967:29,2).

[9]Diana Crane (1972) suggests that exploratory studies, and the variant of the scientific process that they represent, are typical of an early stage of growth in a scientific discipline (Kuhn's "preparadigm" period, 1964), whereas hypothesis-testing studies are typical of a more mature ("paradigm-based") stage.

[10]I use "application" in its scientific, rather than its engineering, sense.

[11]For a more detailed discussion of some interdependencies based on the "theory-versus-research" distinction, see Robert K. Merton, "The Bearing of Sociological Theory on Empirical Research," and "The Bearing of Empirical Research on Sociological Theory" (1957:85–117). Figure 1 also embraces the factors that Kuhn indicates are meant by his term "paradigm." Kuhn says: "By choosing [the term] paradigm I mean to suggest that some accepted examples of actual scientific practise—examples which include law, theory, application, and instrumentation together—provide models from which spring particular coherent traditions of scientific research" (1964:10); although at one point (1964:77) Kuhn identifies "theory" alone with "paradigm."

[12]For his statements, see Durkheim, *Suicide* (1951); and for summaries of the present state of knowledge about suicide, see Gibbs (1966 and 1968), and Douglas (1967).

[13]For his part, Durkheim interpreted suicide as "cases of death resulting directly or indirectly from a positive or negative act of the victim himself, which he knows will produce this result" (1951:44). The extent to which this is an interpretation that refers to phenomena that were in actual nineteenth century practise *observable* (particularly considering the last clause of Durkheim's interpretation) is, of course, questionable.

[14]In the main body of *Suicide*, Durkheim did not conceptualize suicide rate at any higher level of abstraction, and for this reason, his theory remains somewhat asymmetrical. In the Preface to *Suicide*, however, he did suggest that high suicide rates were symptomatic of "the general contemporary maladjustment being undergone by European societies" (1951:37).

[15]See Blalock (1968:155).

REFERENCES

Asch, Solomon E.
1958   "Effects of group pressure upon the

modification and distortion of judgments." Pp. 174–183 in Eleanor E. Maccoby, Theodore M. Newcomb, and Eugene L. Hartley (eds.), Readings in Social Psychology. New York: Holt, Rinehart and Winston.

Bergmann, Gustav
1957 Philosophy of Science. Madison: University of Wisconsin Press.

Black, Max
1967 "The justification of induction." Pp. 190–200 in Sidney Morgenbesser (ed.), Philosophy of Science Today. New York: Basic.

Blalock, Hubert M., Jr.
1969 Theory Construction. Englewood Cliffs: Prentice-Hall.

Blalock, Hubert M., Jr., and Ann B. Blalock
1968 Methodology in Social Research. New York: McGraw-Hill.

Bohm, David
1957 Causality and Chance in Modern Physics. London: Routledge and Kegan Paul. Reprint, New York: Harper, 1961.

Crane, Diana
1972 Invisible Colleges: Diffusion of Knowledge in Scientific Communities. Chicago: University of Chicago Press.

Douglas, Jack D.
1967 The Social Meanings of Suicide. Princeton: Princeton University Press.

Durkheim, Emile
1951 Suicide. New York: Free Press.

Gibbs, Jack P.
1966 "Suicide." Pp. 178–195 in Robert K. Merton and Robert A. Nisbet (eds.), Contemporary Social Problems. New York: Harcourt, Brace and World.

Gibbs, Jack P. (ed.)
1968 Suicide. New York: Harper & Row.

Glaser, Barney G. and Anselm L. Strauss

1967 The Discovery of Grounded Theory. Chicago: Aldine.

Greer, Scott
1969 The Logic of Social Inquiry. Chicago: Aldine.

Kaplan, Abraham
1964 The Conduct of Inquiry. San Francisco: Chandler.

Kuhn, Thomas S.
1964 The Structure of Scientific Revolutions. Chicago: University of Chicago Press.

Malinowski, Bronislaw
1948 Magic, Science, and Religion and Other Essays. Glencoe: Free Press.

Merton, Robert K.
1957 Social Theory and Social Structure. Glencoe: Free Press.

Mills, C. Wright
1959 The Sociological Imagination. New York: Oxford University Press.

Montague, William P.
1925 The Ways of Knowing. New York: Macmillan.

Nagel, Ernest
1967 "The nature and aim of science." Pp. 3–13 in Sidney Morgenbesser (ed.), Philosophy of Science Today. New York: Basic.

Popper, Karl R.
1961 The Logic of Scientific Discovery. New York: Science Editions.

Sherif, Muzafer
1958 "Group Influences upon the Formation of Norms and Attitudes." Pp. 219–32 in Eleanor E. Maccoby, Theodore M. Newcomb, and Eugene L. Hartley (eds.), Readings in Social Psychology. New York: Holt, Rinehart and Winston.

Stinchcombe, Arthur L.
1968 Constructing Social Theories. New York: Harcourt, Brace and World.

OF DROOLING DOGS AND PERIWINKLES

Jonathan Kellerman

After his hair transplants and ingenious way of fending off muggers, Sen. William Proxmire is perhaps best known for his well-publicized attacks upon Federal extravagance, including government-funded scientific research that appears ambiguous, fatuous, not immediately practical or downright silly. He has received praise in this role, as a kind of people's hero in the fight against excess government spending.

Proxmire's ridicule of spurious-sounding research is just part of a fast-growing tendency on the part of legislators and laymen to express their distrust of scientific research, and science, in general. Gone are the days when Sputnik 1 created a national paranoia that led to two decades of productive research and achievement. The emphasis now is upon careful evaluation of research projects and accountability. One must show what one is going to accomplish in order to get funding, as a *first* step.

This emphasis, though understandable in light of our current economic woes, is a dangerous one, in that it ignores the pattern of scientific accomplishment in a historic perspective.

SERENDIPITIES

When one reviews the history of major scientific accomplishments, it is interesting to find how many great discoveries occurred either purely by accident, or as unpredictable side benefits of apparently unrelated research efforts. The discoveries of smallpox vaccine, bacteria and X-rays are just a few of these. In more recent times, one can point to the development of birth-control pills as a result of research into fertility, and to the widespread use of anti-cancer drugs that were originally developed as antibiotics (and were quite poor in this regard). Similarly, Pavlov's scholarly attempts to learn more about learning and conditioning have led to important advances in the field of mental health relating to the treatment of sexual dys-

function, phobias, headaches and numerous other emotional-behavioral problems. This is not to say that all scientific discovery is serendipitous, merely that a good chunk of it is.

This is not surprising if one considers scientific accomplishment as one form of creative achievement. Psychologists have known for years that creativity flourishes best where there is an emphasis upon freedom, novelty and diversity. Thus, attempts to narrowly define a scientific goal and to mechanically channel efforts toward a well-specified end, be it a cancer cure or a better mousetrap, may not bear fruit. As Elie Shneour has noted in *Science* magazine, had today's narrow standards of funding been applied to polio research, the result may well have been not a vaccine but rather a compact, efficient, computerized, portable iron lung. Similarly, Baruch Blumberg, the 1976 Nobel Prize co-winner in medicine, has said that his research started out as quite esoteric and impractical and would probably not have been funded under today's standards.

SILLY PROJECTS

Another point should be made with regard to Proxmire's attacks. The senator has a tendency to latch onto titles of projects that may sound silly, but not to delve into the content of these studies in depth. This is something of a cheap shot, as it is very easy to make anything sound silly and thus dismiss it out of hand.

To a layman the study of something as esoteric as sexual attraction in the boll weevil may appear fatuous at best and perversely voyeuristic at worst. But to biologists interested in developing sterile strains of the bug as a nonpolluting alternative to chemical insecticides, this kind of information can be invaluable.

One can just see Pavlov being laughed out of Congress for wanting to fool around with bells and drooling dogs. Similarly, Harlow's work on infant deprivation in primates, which has had broad implications for human psychology and psychiatry, could very easily be brushed off as playing pointless games with orphan monkeys. One last example is that of the development of the drug vincristine, used to fight cancer. This alkaloid comes from the Vinca plant—the lowly periwinkle. Can you imagine the scientist who discovered it being refused funds because he was toying with garden flowers?

The point, of course, is not that everything and anything should be funded under the heading of research but that the criteria should be those of scientific validity, not apparent practicality. Ironically, the mass of rules and regulations developed in the name of program evaluation has created a monstrous bureaucracy that is self-propagating. This has grown to such an extent that now it often costs as much to evaluate a program as to conduct it. If we are seeking ways of trimming fat, let us slice away at the layers of bureaucrats who, once ensconced in civil-service positions, never die, fade away or otherwise disappear.

Just think of the savings that can be had by eliminating the staggering piles of typed-in-quadruplicate government forms that seem to proliferate almost magically at the sound of the word "accountability." Another way to save money would be to stop encouraging waste. Under current government practices, if a scientist is given $1,000 for the first year of his study, he must spend every penny of that $1,000 to receive comparable funds the second year. Thus, last minute "fill-up" spending is encouraged and thrift is punished.

A TRUSTING ATTITUDE

Perhaps the answer is to train scientists, while still in graduate school, in the art of glossy, deceptive packaging. After all, we have seen how successful many attempts at glamorous labeling have been in eliciting political support and funds. (Think of all the cooks, bodyguards and go-fers who were hired as special administrative assistants, not to mention undeclared wars labeled as technical operations and soldiers employed as advisers.) One would hope that it doesn't come to this, and that an open, trusting attitude is taken toward scientists and their endeavors so that the United States will remain the international leader in technical and creative achievement. Otherwise we may have to wait for another sputnik.

SOME GUIDELINES FOR READING AND ASSESSING RESEARCH REPORTS IN THE SOCIAL SCIENCES

Theodore C. Wagenaar

Research texts too frequently emphasize the "how to do" dimension of research at the expense of the "how to assess" dimension. But both dimensions are crucial for a more complete understanding of social science research methods. Increasing your knowledge and skills in one will contribute to your knowledge and skills in the other. Although few of you will actually be completing research studies in the future, as social workers, personnel managers, nurses, executives, teachers, organizational employees, or citizens, you will be constantly confronted with research reports.

The major objective of this article is to enable you, as a student of social science research, to become more analytical, even skeptical, about the research you read. By the time you complete this article, you will be convinced that the appearance of research in print is no guarantee that it is reliable and valid. Moreover, you will have both a general guide for reading and analyzing research studies and a series of specific questions and criteria that you can apply to most research studies (these questions and criteria are outlined in the appendix to this article).

Unfortunately, most published social science research reports are written for the peers of the researcher, not for students. Hence, articles are often difficult for the student to comprehend. Fortunately, most studies do follow a similar organization, which will make our task of developing general criteria somewhat easier. The analytical scheme and criteria described in this article are designed to work for most types of research and for most topic areas.

Studies in the social sciences generally have one of four focuses: explanation, description, exploration, or evaluation. Explanatory studies emphasize causal analysis and the relationship of research results to the larger body of knowledge in the area. An example is a study of the causes of delinquency. Descriptive studies emphasize portrayals of a given concept or group of persons. A study reporting the percentage of Americans who support abortion under differing circumstances would be a descriptive study. Exploratory studies often reflect first attempts in a new area of research. An open-ended survey used to determine what factors may be associated with singleness as a lifestyle might be such an exploratory study. Finally, evaluation studies emphasize determination of the effect an intervention may have had. A good example might be a study reporting on two alternative teaching techniques in order to determine which is more effective. Research studies also incorporate a variety of designs, most notably survey, experiment, observation, or available data designs.

Based on your knowledge of social science research in general and of focuses and designs in particular, you will have to decide if and when to apply a certain principle or criterion. If the author notes that she is doing an *exploratory* study of factors associated with childlessness (see Goodbody, 1977), it would be inappropriate to criticize the nonrandomness of the sample (although you should definitely treat the reported results as tentative). In short, you should apply the principles of assessment according to the stated purpose of the research.

I should note that you will not be able to assign a research quality score to an article using the assessment guide. To do so would mean that very clear standards exist for judging according to each criterion, that each criterion carries approximately equal weight (or that weights could be assigned), and that no subjectivity on the part of the assessor

enters. Obviously, these conditions cannot be met (at least not yet). Neither should you assume that the guidelines presented here are comprehensive. Although they include the major criteria that should be applied for assessing research, I do not pretend that they are exhaustive (for book-length assessment guides, see Katzer, Cook, and Crouch, 1978; Millman and Gowin, 1974; and Tripodi, Fellin, and Meyer, 1969). In sum, use this article as a guide for making an initial judgment regarding the soundness of the research and the extent to which that research is reliable and can be validly applied.

You will note that one essential question informs all elements in the assessment process: What aspects of a study reduce the confidence you can place in the results? Related to this central focus, how many different sources of error can be identified in the study? How seriously does each source distort the results? Did the author identify possible sources of error at various stages of the research? How adequately were these error sources reduced? What about possible sources of error *not* mentioned by the author—how might they influence the results? Picture in your mind the components of the ideal research study. Then use this assessment guide to determine as best you can how well the study measures up to your conception of the ideal study. Please keep in mind that no study will ever meet all the criteria suggested. Your job is to analyze the study to determine how seriously the principles have been violated. Now let's turn to a general scheme for *reading* research articles. After that, we'll discuss the assessment guidelines themselves.

A GENERAL SCHEME

Most social science research reports follow a basic format: statement of the problem, methods, and results. Knowledge of this format will make it easier for you to read and assess an article. This outline often corresponds to the overall stages of the research process, although you are reminded of a point made earlier and illustrated in the authors' personal journals included in this volume: the way research is reported is seldom the way the research was actually conducted.

Authors usually start with a section that can be labeled *Statement of the Problem* (or *Introduction*). In this section, the author usually accomplishes several objectives. First, the general research question is outlined. In the Hunt and Hunt article on father absence (Section 4.2), for example, the authors state the problem early: What is the effect of father absence on girls? Second, the general research question is frequently placed in the context of the larger body of knowledge in the subject area. Authors typically note similarities to previous research to support their position; they also criticize previous research to highlight their contribution. The Hunts discuss their research question in terms of the literature on early socialization, sex-role socialization, and racial differences regarding socialization (and they criticize the popular belief in the matriarchal nature of black families). Third, the author cites specific references in the literature. In addition to citations to the areas just mentioned, the Hunts reference their own previous study on father absence among boys. And fourth, the author

may present specific hypotheses. In the Knowles study (Section 3.3), for example, three specific hypotheses are listed, one of which proposes that the more members an interacting unit has, the more impenetrable the boundary becomes.

In reading the introductory section of an article, be sure that you understand both the general research question *and* how it fits into the larger body of knowledge in that area. You should also have a clear idea as to the specific research questions or hypotheses. Make marginal notes on points that are not clear to you now but that may be explained later in the article. I often find it useful at this point to diagram what I perceive to be the major concepts and their interrelationships. The Knowles study on group interactions could be diagrammed as follows (↑ means "increases" and ↓ "decreases"):

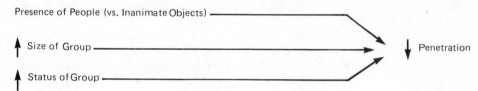

There is no set guideline for developing a diagram; use what works best for you in terms of clarifying the concepts and their interrelationships.

The second section usually found in research articles is one that could be labeled *Methods*. Several items are included in this section. One is discussion of the data employed: who or what was studied, how many cases were included in the initial sample, how many cases were in the usable sample, when the data were collected, what sampling or selection procedure was used and why, and other similar questions regarding the data. A second item covered is operationalization: Exactly how was each concept measured? For example, Knowles operationalized the status of interactors by manipulating age and dress of the experimenters. A third item found in many methods sections is discussion of the research design. In the case of experiments, pretests and posttests as well as timing of the stimulus should be described. And fourth, there will usually be some discussion of the analytical tools. Authors may note that they are using multiple regression, tabular analysis, or some other advanced mode of analysis. In reading through the methods section of an article, be sure that all of your questions on design and data have

been at least partially answered; if they haven't, make marginal notes. These notes will prove useful when you go through the article again for assessment purposes.

The third section covered by most researchers can be labeled *Results* (or *Discussion*, or *Results and Conclusions*). While reading this section, refer back to the diagram or outline you developed when reading the Statement of the Problem section. Begin to fill in the relationships and to determine if the hypotheses were supported. Don't routinely skip the tables. In fact, it is a good idea to read and interpret the tables before reading the author's analysis in order to compare your own analysis with the author's. Trace the results reported for each hypothesis and for the effects of control variables, if they are used. In this section (or often in a separate final section), the author may also discuss the limitations of the study and the implications of the study for the larger body of knowledge on the topic. Do the comments seem appropriate? Do they correspond with your own observations? Again, marginal notes may be useful.

In sum, when reading a research article, try to keep a mental outline in your mind as you proceed (your diagram will be useful). Students have noted that reading an article twice is useful. In the first reading, read the abstract and spend about five or ten minutes skimming the article to create your mental outline and to recall what you've learned about that particular design. Resist the temptation to get bogged down in the details of the study. The second time through, emphasize assessment: read the entire article, making marginal notes where relevant. In this reading pay careful attention to the details of design, operationalization, and analysis.

ASSESSMENT GUIDELINES

Both general and specific criteria can be applied to most social science research articles. Such criteria will not apply to all articles, but they can be used as guidelines. The quality of the assessment, however, will ultimately depend on the knowledge and diligence of the assessor.

For simplicity's sake, I have posed most guidelines in the form of questions. Since I have not provided response categories, you may wish to use a scale such as 1 to 3 or 1 to 5 to permit comparison across articles. In the previous section I organized the general scheme for reading around three broad categories: statement of the problem, methods, and results. In this more detailed assessment guide, I shall use five categories: statement of the problem, conceptualization, research design, results, and conclusions.

Statement of the Problem

1. *How clearly and simply is the research problem stated?*
   The author should state the basic research question early in the article before going into the theoretical background. In the article on sex-role orientation, for example, Brogan and Kutner note early the problem with sex-role orientation scales (Section 2.2).

2. *How completely is the research tied to the larger body of theory and knowledge in the area?*
   Grounding the research problem in existing literature assures some continuity in knowledge production. By connecting the research question with the existing knowledge, the researcher is in a better position to contribute new knowledge in an area and is less likely to repeat the mistakes made by previous researchers. Two

recent articles investigated the division of labor in couples (Stafford, Backman, and Dibona, 1977; Berheide, Berk, and Berk, 1976). The first is well grounded in the literature (50 citations were made), tying the research issue to the literature on division of labor, sex roles, feminism, decision-making, effect of wife's participation in the labor force, socialization, and similar topics. The second presented a more cursory review of the literature (14 citations were made), making no attempt to discuss the various theoretical and conceptual approaches to the problem or to tie the research issue to this literature. I am reasonably sure that the former researchers benefited from the strengths and weaknesses of previous work and I am willing to attach more credibility to their efforts.

3. *Based on what you know of other works in the area, how accurately does the author reference previous works?*
   This criterion really derives from the preceding one but is worthy of special attention. Far too often authors will list a series of references, only some of which are relevant to the topic analyzed. If an author lists 15 references after a one-sentence theoretical statement, it is likely that he or she paid insufficient attention to integrating the research issue into the larger literature. Authors themselves frequently do not read the originals of the works they are citing, which may result in distortions such as treating a small exploratory study as if it were a well-executed experimental design study. If you have the time, you might go back and read a few of the studies referenced to ascertain the accuracy of the author's literature review. I recently reviewed a work that cited a study concluding that career women are more sexually active than more traditional women. In going back to the original article, I discovered that the authors of that study surveyed *only* career women, which makes it difficult to make conclusions about career women in comparison to traditional women.

4. *How well is the purpose of the research explained?*
   It is important to identify the purpose of a study so that you can apply appropriate standards in reading the rest of the study and in determining the usefulness of the results. If the goal of a study is an initial exploration of an area, then you can expect a less tightly developed theoreti-

cal analysis and a less rigorous design. Too frequently authors label their studies as exploratory but later in the article make explanatory analyses with high levels of implicit generalization. Your job is to determine the consistency between the purpose and the results of the study. Berheide, Berk, and Berk (1976), for example, in their article on division of labor between couples (noted in question 2 above) introduced their study as an initial exploratory analysis of a larger study in progress, which may mean that less attention will be paid to the careful development of hypotheses and to sophisticated statistical analysis of causal relationships.

5. *How clearly are hypotheses stated?*
Not all authors state their research question(s) in the form of specific, testable hypotheses. A lack of hypotheses may mean one of two things. First, it may mean that the current knowledge in the field under investigation is so preliminary that explicit hypotheses cannot be developed. Statement of specific hypotheses is contingent on sufficient previous work and conceptual analysis; a brand-new field may lack such resources. Second, the lack of hypotheses may indicate insufficient attention to integration of the current investigation with previous studies. Your job is to determine (1) if hypotheses are stated; (2) if so, how clearly they are stated (direction of relationship?); and (3) if the hypotheses are linked to previous work in the area.

6. *How extensively do the author's biases influence the statement of the problem and its definition?*
Authors generally have various sorts of biases. One researcher may adopt the Marxist approach to theory; another researcher may emphasize the use of surveys. It is important to realize that biases influence the perception of the research problem, the identification of independent and dependent variables, the research design, and even what is defined as a significant finding. The identification of implications of theoretical biases requires some familiarity on your part with the major theoretical orientations in your field. At the very least you must recognize that even an identified theoretical perspective may or may not affect the execution and the reporting of a study. You may also identify bias by looking for such things as the exclusive use of one statistical technique (such as tables) when

other techniques would be more appropriate (such as correlations).

Conceptualization

1. *How completely are the relevant concepts identified?*
Before discussing the operationalization of concepts, the author should clearly identify all the relevant concepts in the theoretical framework, as opposed to merely stating a general research question. In a study of teacher militancy, for example, the inclusion of personal characteristics of teachers only would be less theoretically useful than the inclusion of personal characteristics of teachers, teacher orientations, school characteristics, and community characteristics.

Occasionally a researcher will select only a few concepts in order to elaborate on basic relationships. Such an approach, if it has been defined and justified in the statement of the problem, is entirely reasonable. But if an author states that a study involves a comprehensive analysis of worker morale and then identifies only a few job-related concepts, be alert to the limitations of such a study. One way to assess this item is to compare your diagram of the concepts and their interrelationships with the discussion of the results; if concepts emerge in the discussion that are not on your diagram, then the author failed to identify all of the relevant concepts (or else you overlooked them). Once again, the overall emphasis is on how adequately the author formulated the basis for the study.

2. *How clearly are the interrelationships among the concepts identified?*
An author who explicitly outlines the interrelationships among concepts has done a more thorough analysis of the existing literature in a field than one who merely states that concepts X, Y, and Z will be examined. More important, the author who pays attention to concept interrelationships makes it easier for the reader to follow the subsequent empirical relationships. In the Rubin and Shenker article on friendship (Section 3.5), for example, specific statements are made about linkages between concepts (e.g., "It was predicted that friendship would be positively related to self-disclosure in all areas"). Most research that you read will report in some

manner—simple or complex—on the linkages among several independent variables and one or more dependent variables. What matters is how clearly the author has identified and justified the interrelationships suggested.

3. *How adequately have concepts been operationalized?*
Social science researchers often limit the scope of their conceptual definitions in the quest for measurability and quantification. For instance, consider this equation: marketability of college students equals dating experience plus grade point average (Stafford, Backman, and Dibona, 1977:49). In this example the authors were attempting to develop the concept of marketability as a measure of the personal resources of students. They reasoned that a student's most important personal assets are sexual attraction (measured by dating experience) and academic achievement (measured by GPA). (It is interesting to note that the authors found a positive correlation between GPA and dating experience for men, but a negative correlation for women.)

The most important point regarding operational definitions is this: Read them. The results must be interpreted in terms of the operational definitions used. As an example, a study using absentee rates to measure alienation among high school students must be interpreted differently from one using a 30-item scale measuring powerlessness, normlessness, or meaninglessness.

Several basic points may help in determining operational adequacy. First, a general rule of thumb is that operational definitions reflecting many separate dimensions of a concept are better than those reflecting only one or two dimensions. Hence, an operational definition of marital happiness employing only one global question ("Overall, how happily married are you?") is not as well operationalized as one employing various dimensions, such as communication quality, shared goals, sexual compatibility, decision-making, ideas on children, and shared time. Second, the more items used to measure a concept (or dimension of a concept), the more sound the operational definition. In the example just mentioned, an operational definition employing five questions for each dimension is more sound than one employing only one question per dimension. And third, the larger the number of different methods used to measure a concept, the more sound the operational definition. Hence, an operational definition of marital happiness employing both questionnaires and in-the-home observation is more dependable than a definition employing only questionnaires. Similarly, someone doing an observation study in social work agencies would be in a better position to develop sound operational definitions by relying on official documents in addition to observation than by relying on observation alone. In short, sound operational definitions are clear, specific, and complete both in terms of method and items.

Be advised, however, that not all concepts can be clearly, specifically, and completely operationalized. Such concepts as social structure and ecosystem have yet to meet these criteria for operationalization. Your job is to determine (1) how well the concept has been operationalized, given the background the author provides, and (2) how these operational definitions influence the methods used and the results obtained.

4. *How adequately have the reliability and validity of the operational definitions been determined?*
This criterion is related to the one immediately preceding; both refer to sound operationalization techniques. Reliability refers to consistency and repeatability of a measure, whereas validity refers to accurately measuring the concept you wish to measure. Both are fundamental aspects of measurement (see the introduction to Measurement, Section 2.2, for further discussion). Your job in assessing articles with this criterion is twofold. First, note if any mention is made of techniques employed for testing the reliability and validity of the concepts. Second, note how high the measures are (you should remember that values are more easily calculated for reliability than validity). Coefficients should exceed .90 to be considered highly reliable, or valid, for the few techniques that allow calculation of validity coefficients. Note, for example, that Brogan and Kutner calculated a reliability coefficient of .95 for their sex-role orientation scale and also assessed the validity of the scale by examining relationships previously supported by the literature (Section 2.2).

Research Design

1. *How adequately is the research design described?*
   This item is quite simple, but it is very important. All you have to do is determine how completely the author describes all aspects of the design (basic design type, sampling, instruments, data collection procedures, data analysis procedures, precautions, and the like). If you are reading an article that devotes one short paragraph to the design of the research, proceed to the results with caution. Brief discussion of the design does not automatically mean a poor study, but it does mean that you have little basis on which to assess the study. Conversely, a complete discussion of the design does not automatically mean a quality study; that conclusion depends on your evaluation of what has been described.

2. *How appropriate is the design, given the author's statement of the problem and conceptualization?*
   Using this criterion, you must assess the suitability of the research design. If the author has outlined in the statement of the problem a carefully described set of specific hypotheses and then proceeds to use a case study of one small group of persons, be alert to how this design may limit a definitive test of the hypotheses. Your assessment of the appropriateness of the design must consider the researcher's purpose in doing the study (explanatory, exploratory, descriptive, evaluative), for the selection of a research design is contingent on and influences the other dimensions of the research process.

3. *How appropriate are the sampling procedures?*
   The sampling design determines to a large extent the usability and generalizability of the results. A sample of one (a frequent characteristic of case studies) has limited generalizability, whereas a random sample of 1,000 has high generalizability. As with the general design, the purpose of the study influences the type of sampling procedures used; an exploratory study of singles may preclude the use of a large random sample.
   Several aspects of the sampling design deserve your attention. First is sample size. Quite simply, the smaller the sample size, the higher the rate of possible bias and error (sampling er-

ror) and the lower the generalizability. Conversely, the larger the sample size, the lower the sampling error and the more you can be sure that sample values resemble population values (assuming random sampling). In a study of the implications of voluntary childlessness, for example, Goodbody selected her sample of six childless women through contacts with an organization for nonparents (Goodbody, 1977). She noted that the study was exploratory and that the group of women was "highly particularized." These are appropriate precautions. But she also emphasized the role an unhappy childhood played in the women's decision to remain childless because four of the six women reported unhappy childhoods. As an assessor of such an article, you should immediately question the generalization of the results, particularly since Goodbody did not study women with children. It is possible that two-thirds of a sample of women with children would have reported unhappy childhoods as well.

Another implication of sample size is the use of statistics. Many advanced statistical procedures require large sample sizes for valid results. How large is large enough? Opinions vary on required sample size, but you may wish to use the rule of thumb requiring an absolute minimum of about 50 subjects and preferably at least 100, particularly if advanced statistics are used.

Perhaps more important than sample size is sample design. The primary criterion here is randomness of selection, for random sampling allows more generalizability than nonrandom sampling. Recall also that sampling error, a measure of how accurately the sample resembles the larger population, can only be calculated with random samples. A random sample of 100 will generally afford a higher level of generalizability than a nonrandom sample of 1,000. Let me illustrate with two studies done recently on our campus. One sample involved a systematic random sample of 110 students using the student handbook; the other involved a sample of 1,025 students nonrandomly. The selection process for the larger sample favored introductory classes and sociology classes. The actual proportion of the entire student body that was female was 51 percent. The small random sample produced 56 percent female students, whereas the large nonrandom sample produced 64 percent female students. Although neither sample was exactly equal to the larger population value, the random sample was closer, even though it was much smaller than the nonrandom sample.

Another example may be useful, this time from two published reports on attitudes toward extramarital sexual relations (the articles appeared next to each other in the journal). Maykovich (1976:694) used "a quota sampling method" to select 100 white American women between 35 and 40 years old, married, middle class, residing in medium-sized cities in the metropolitan area. Singh, Walton, and Williams (1976) used a nationally based random sample of about 1,500 persons (National Opinion Research Corporation data). Maykovich reported that 56 percent of her sample approved of extramarital sexual relations, while Singh et al. reported that only 14 percent viewed extramarital sexual relations as "wrong only sometimes" or "not wrong at all." Even though the Singh et al. study reports on all people, the difference in approval levels is sufficient to question the validity of the nonrandom quota sample used in the first study. These examples also make another point: You should note how specifically and completely an author describes his or her sampling procedure. The Maykovich study, for example, gives no description of how the women were actually selected.

Randomness is a particular problem for experiments since most experiments rely on volunteers. In reading an experimental study, carefully read the section describing subject selection. If subjects were all introductory psychology students, then generalizability must be limited to introductory psychology students of professor X at Z university.

You should also be particularly alert to randomness of sample selection in studies reported in the popular literature. Samples of 10,000, 25,000, or 100,000 are not uncommon in studies reported in such magazines as *Psychology Today*, *Redbook*, and *McCall's*. But most of these studies rely on questionnaires printed in the magazine that readers are asked to fill out and mail to the magazine (at the respondent's expense). A study on masculinity summarized in *Psychology Today* reported results on a study of 28,000 men and women (Tavris, 1977). About 50 percent of the

sample consisted of persons who had never been married, about 30 percent held more than a college degree, and over 50 percent reported themselves as "very liberal" or "liberal." These figures are very different from those describing American adults in general (the corresponding figures are approximately 15 percent, 5 percent, and 30 percent respectively). It follows that such conclusions as "more women describe their lovers as aggressive, physically strong, competitive, self-confident, and successful at work than the men describe themselves" (Tavris, 1977:36) should not be assumed to apply to Americans in general. This is not to say that the results are incorrect; in fact, they may be correct. It is only to say, in the words of the author, that "volunteer surveys are rarely representative of the American public" (Tavris, 1977:35), which is a warning to the reader to exercise caution in accepting what is generalizable. Read the sample description carefully before making your assessment of generalizability.

I wish to emphasize, in light of the preceding discussion, that a random sample is not always possible. There are no master lists from which to randomly sample such people as parachutists, homosexuals, and battered wives. Your job as assessor, then, is to determine (1) the appropriateness of the design, given the topic and types of cases studied, and (2) the implications the sampling design has for generalizability. Studies using nonrandom or otherwise limited samples should report this clearly; an example is quoted here from a battered wives study (Carlson, 1977:455–56):

Generalizations can only be made to a population of abused women who appeal for assistance to a voluntary nonprofessional women's organization. Substantial amounts of data are missing for certain variables, especially those pertaining to the assailants.

This statement is located early in the article so that readers can exercise appropriate caution when reading the results.

You should also realize that a random sampling design may not always result in a random sample for data analysis. This is particularly true for multistage sampling designs. Howard, Royse, and Skerl (1977), for example, reported on a study of attitudes toward transracial adoption employing a random sampling design with four stages (census tracts, blocks, households, and individuals). Because they selected only one person per household (generally the person at home and the first to answer the door), the sample constituted about 75 percent women. Another complicating factor in using random designs is the nonresponse rate. Nonrespondents may be quite different from respondents on a number of variables and this may limit the generalizability of the results. In a study of the elderly Goudy (1976) found that nonrespondents were less likely to be married, had lower levels of education, and had lower-level incomes. Hence, generalizations about all elderly persons from the results compiled from those who responded must be made with caution. Unfortunately, most studies do not afford the opportunity to compare nonrespondents with respondents.

Similar in its effects to nonresponse bias is dropout bias, particularly for experiments. The authors of the article on parole supervision in this volume (Section 3.4) note that during the interim between pretest and posttest many of the subjects had to be dropped for one reason or another. It is always possible that dropouts will be substantially different from those who remain in a study, which may bias the results and limit the generalizability of the study. In short, focus your attention on the sample actually used, not the initial cases sampled. For further discussion of sample credibility, see Seymour Sudman's article in Section 2.3.

4. *How extensively does the researcher deal with possible sources of error?*
The researcher should at least note possible sources of error. If these are not mentioned (few researchers like to point out weaknesses in their own designs), you should make marginal notes on conceivable sources of error. Such sources of error include:

researcher bias

sampling effects

use of volunteers, their ability to "psych out" a study

characteristics of persons running the experiment or doing the interviewing (see Smith, 1975:88 for a review of experimenter effects)

the effect of the study setting, such as interview setting or experimental lab

the time of day, month, or year (particularly relevant for attitude surveys on popular issues, although this type of error may influence an experiment done at the end of a semester or an observation study done just after a change in command)

bias in the measurement instruments

the effect of violation of ethical principles

the effect of confidentiality and anonymity or the lack thereof

the effect of large amounts of "missing data"

the effects of pragmatic constraints, such as time, money, or computer limitations

the use of available data, with unknowns regarding reliability and validity

the failure to rule out the effects of "extraneous" as well as relevant control variables

To be sure, most research reports will not contain thorough analyses of these and other possible sources of error. Your job is to be alert to their possible effects and to judge the results accordingly.

5. *How appropriate are the analytical techniques used?*
Applying this criterion most effectively would require a course in social statistics. I mention it here only to call attention to its importance and to urge you to evaluate the statistical techniques as carefully as you can (see Section 4.1). A few of the more important criteria are listed here:

Are the statistical techniques appropriate for the level of the data—nominal, ordinal, interval, or ratio? You should not see t tests used with ordinal level dependent variables, for example.

Are the techniques used appropriate for the nature of the data? The use of a statistic requiring two categories of cases will be inappropriate for an experimental design without a control group.

Are the assumptions of statistical techniques being met? For example, regression analysis generally requires the presence of linear relationships, and path analysis requires the researcher to formulate a time-ordered causal model.

Are levels of statistical significance reported only when random samples are used? Random sampling is required for the use of such tests.

The basic point is to ascertain whether the techniques used are appropriate for both the design and the nature of the data.

6. *How much attention is paid to ethical considerations?*
Ethical considerations should emerge in the design phase of the research. The following principles should be considered:

> voluntariness of participation
> confidentiality
> protection of persons participating in the study
> informed consent

Ethical considerations are particularly important in experimental and observation designs, although they exist for other types of designs as well. As an example of an ethical violation in survey research, Sabatini and Kastenbaum (1973) reported on the use of the "do-it-yourself death certificate" in their research on death attitudes. This technique involved having students completely fill out their own death certificates. The authors did not discuss the ethical implications of such a technique, although they did note that one student destroyed her death certificate because the task upset her. Undoubtedly the process of filling out the certificate may influence both the respondents and their death attitudes. Although this criterion is less specific and probably has less direct impact on the results than the other criteria in this section on research design, this is nonetheless an important problem to consider. (See the introduction to Section 1.2 for further discussion of these principles.)

Results

1. *How adequately are data reported?*
If no actual data are reported, you must rely solely on analysis. Hence, you do not have the opportunity to check interpretations. For example, in a study of the effect of sex composition on an intensive group experience (Carlock and Martin, 1977:29) the authors noted that

> *Women in the all-female group were slow to develop group involvement, and the intensity of their involvement never exceeded a moderate level. In contrast, women in the male-female group demonstrated*

a high level of emotional intensity early in the life of the group.

But since no statistics were provided, we have no indication of how large the differences were or how statistically significant the results were. My point is that an article should at minimum report the measures of association and associated tests of statistical significance. A good research report will also report means, standard deviations, tables, complete correlation matrices, F values, and similar statistics if such figures are appropriate for the study.

2. *How consistent are interpretations of the data with the raw data?*
Assuming that the data are reported, examine the interpretations made on the basis of the data. For example, in the Goudy study of the elderly the author concluded that nonrespondents "were generally similar to deceased dropouts on marital status, income ..." (Goudy, 1976:363). But an examination of the data indicates that 66 percent of the nonrespondents had incomes below $8,000, while only 55 percent of the deceased category had such incomes. Once the data have been presented, you the reader can decide if the two categories are similar or different.

Newspaper articles are notorious for presenting conclusions without data or conclusions that go beyond the data presented. An Associated Press wire service story ("Stanford Notes More Pregnancies," 1975), for example, began by noting that "the pregnancy rate among Stanford University women this year is 150% higher than the 1974 rate...." Reading further, we see that 12 pregnancy tests were positive in 1974 and 30 in 1975. These figures represent a shift from .3 percent of all female students to .8 percent, hardly as alarming as the quoted sentence might lead you to believe.

Researchers are often under considerable pressure to establish differences or relationships, and as a result moderate differences or relationships are often overinterpreted in the results section. In addition, a researcher's results may be quite significant but conflict with his or her biases. In such a case, the comments made by the author may not adequately and accurately reflect the data. Your job as assessor is to examine the data presented and then review the author's analysis and interpretation of the data in order to determine the congruence between data and interpretation.

3. How adequately does the author distinguish statistical from substantive significance?

Recall from our previous discussion that sample size will influence the statistical significance of the results. Thus a relatively high correlation of about .50 will not be statistically significant in a sample of 20, whereas even a relatively low correlation of about .15 will be statistically significant in a sample of 1,000. Your task is to assess both statistical and substantive significance in light of sample size and other design considerations to make sure that an author is neither understating nor overstating the results.

Consider as an example a study (Wake and Sporakowski, 1972) that compared parents with students in terms of "filial responsibility"—the responsibility children have to support their aged parents. Using a scale of possible scores ranging from 18 to 90, the authors reported mean scores for parents and students as 42.06 and 43.77, respectively, and noted that the results were statistically significant. But one can question whether this difference in scores was *substantively* significant. The results do not suggest a large difference in attitude, at least not a large enough difference to warrant placing a great deal of confidence in the results for policy considerations.

The reverse can also happen. A reasonably large difference (or relationship) may exist, but the sample size may be so small as to suggest caution in interpreting the results. For example, a researcher may examine the impact of an early release program on prisoners' subsequent violations of the law. The researcher may find that 20 percent of the prisoners in the early release program and 40 percent of those not in the program later violated the law, a sizable difference. But since perhaps there are only ten persons in each group, this difference may not be significant statistically. Perhaps this is the best study on the topic to date. If so, the results should be taken for their implications in terms of policy recommendations rather than categorically dismissed as not attaining statistical significance. In sum, study the design and sampling procedures carefully and weigh the relative strengths of statistical and substantive significance in terms of what the author says about the data and the relevance of the data for your purposes.

4. To what extent does the author consider control variables?

Failure to consider control variables may lead to unquestioning acceptance of such conclusions as smoking causes sexual experience, sexual experience causes high GPAs, and kissing leads to financial success. You may recall that the three prerequisites for establishing causality are (1) a clear time ordering of the variables, (2) the existence of a relationship between the independent and dependent variables, and (3) ruling out for other possible causes of the dependent variable. The third prerequisite is the most problematic since there is always the possibility that variables other than the hypothesized independent variable may cause the dependent variable as well. In fact, possible rival variables may influence both the independent and dependent variables in such a manner that no *real* relationships exist between the hypothesized independent variable and the dependent variable. I shall demonstrate the importance of considering possible control variables with a few examples.

A few years ago a newspaper article proclaimed "Teen Users of Cigarettes 'Rebellious' " (*San Diego Union*, March 27, 1976:A-10). I have reconstructed the data reported in Table 1.

Table 1. Relationship between Smoking and Sexual Experience among 500 Teenagers

		Smoking Experience	
		Yes	No
Sexual	Yes	44%	15%
Experience	No	56%	85%
		100%	100%

The article concluded that teenage smokers were more sexually active than nonsmokers and left the impression that cigarette smoking caused sexual experience among teenagers. Certainly a relationship exists, giving some credence to the causal supposition. Time order, however, was difficult to establish. It is possible that sexual experience occurred before the smoking experience and may have been the cause of smoking, rather than vice versa. Even more important was the article's failure to rule out for other possible explanatory factors. Undoubtedly such variables as religion, peer involvement, and liberalism could explain sexual experience as well as smoking experience.

Consider another example, again from the newspaper (as I noted earlier, newspapers are notorious for making these kinds of errors of analysis). An article entitled "Colleges Reach 'Sexual Utopia'" (*Cincinnati Enquirer*, Sept. 19, 1976:A–16), made the following statement: "The longer you have been having sex, the more likely you are to be an A student. A full 67% of the people who made A's have been making love for more than two years." Note first that no comparison figures were given for the percentage of students not making A's who have also been making love for more than two years; it could be just as high as the other group. More important, however, the assertion that sexual experience caused high grades is inappropriate given the failure to control for such variables as year in college. Generally, upper-level students have both higher GPAs and more sexual experience than lower-level students; hence, college class level may explain both sexual experience and grades such that no real relationship exists between sexual experience and grades.

I add one more newspaper report, this time for you to determine rival explanations. *The Oregonian Forum* reported that "men who kiss their wives before leaving for work in the morning enjoy better health, live longer and earn more money" ("Study Indicates Benefits of That Morning Kiss," July 27, 1977: D–11). The data: 83 percent of 100 executives whose careers were slipping seldom or never kissed their wives. The article suggested to wives that they "grab him [husband] and give him a big kiss that will cause him to quiver with emotion all day long" to ensure good health and financial success. (One wonders if the reverse is true for employed wives!) What are the possible control variables that should be considered?

Failure to consider control variables occurs in journal research studies as well. Many statistics and reports on sex discrimination fail to rule out the effects of experience when noting salary and other differences between men and women. Knapman (1977:463), for example, presented data indicating that the mean number of months for promotion of social workers from level one to level two is 51.4 months for women and 17.7 for men; the average salary for women is $11,154 and for men $12,140. The charge of discrimination would have been more convincing if age and experience had been controlled.

A related issue is the presence of control groups. Be cautious of an author who draws comparative conclusions without specifying the comparison groups (like the conclusion noted earlier on sexual experience as related to grades). For a researcher to make any definitive conclusions about the effect of a given variable, a control or comparison group must exist. A control group is particularly necessary if an experimental design is used. Random assignment of subjects to experimental and control groups reduces the effect of rival explanations. Since assignment to treatment and control groups is less feasible in survey research, it is important that you be alert to rival explanations when reading survey research reports.

5. *Given the statement of the problem, how adequately do results deal with issues raised?*
Go back to the statement of the problem and your assessment of it. Look at your diagram of all the hypothesized relationships. Have data and interpretations been presented for each one? Have modifications been made as a result of design or analysis considerations? The author may have hypothesized a relationship between X and Y but then discovered that the operational definition did not attain sufficient reliability to enable a conclusive test of the relationship. Was this finding noted? In sum, make sure that (1) all the originally suggested hypotheses or research questions have been dealt with (at least in some fashion) and (2) the results provide an adequate test of the hypotheses or questions (i.e., the data gathered and analytical techniques used were appropriate).

Conclusions

1. *How adequately does the author summarize results?*
The author should present a brief summary of the results of the study in the "Conclusions" section, paying particular attention to how the

results compare with the original hypotheses or research questions. Any qualifications or outstanding findings should be noted. This summary should incorporate all major findings, even if they do not support the hypotheses. Having reviewed the data and the results section, you should be able to assess the adequacy and accuracy of the summary.

2. *How completely does the author discuss implications of the study?*

Implications of the study can be examined in three ways. First, the author can discuss the implications of the study in terms of previous knowledge about the topic. The reader should check to see if results confirm, disconfirm, or modify previous research. Try to think particularly of research on topics with which you are familiar but which have not been cited by the author. Second, there may be a discussion of the implications for future research. Are weaknesses and strengths noted so that future researchers may capitalize on them? Perhaps future researchers should pay more attention to a particular variable not included in the reported study but later thought to be significant. In the Knowles article on boundary penetration in this volume (Section 3.3), suggestions for future research could include the effects of such status variables as age and height. The author may also suggest that future researchers should emphasize a different theoretical perspective or a different population.

Third, policy implications may be discussed. Not all studies are amenable to policy suggestions, and many social scientists do not think it relevant to discuss policy implications. But increasingly social scientists are assuming the role of policy advisors. The Hunts, for instance, contemplate the effects of the lack of a social policy "designed to alter the opportunity structure for females" (Section 4.2). The author of the parole supervision evaluation study offers policy suggestions for improving parole supervision (Section 3.4).

3. *Does the author overgeneralize from results?*

While reading the concluding section, constantly keep in mind the nature of the design and sample and the limitations they place on generalizations that can be made from the data. Are minimal relationships indiscriminately concluded to apply to all subpopulations, including those not examined?

4. *Does the author make causal analyses based only on correlation data?*

Be alert for conclusions and policy recommendations assuming causality on the basis of correlations only, especially if few or no control variables were used. If a researcher reports a high negative correlation between rules emphasis and achievement in schools and then suggests widespread deemphasis on rules as a means for increasing achievement level, you should immediately question the validity of this conclusion (again, particularly if no other variables were controlled).

CONCLUSIONS

I have attempted to provide in this article an introduction to the world of reported research. (A summary of the questions I suggested as assessment guidelines has been reproduced in the appendix to this article for handy reference.) I have emphasized particularly the following sources of error:

> inadequate measurement of the concepts
> failure to build a case for the theoretical logic of a study
> failure to specify the exact population studied
> the use of nonrandom sampling
> inadequate presentation of data on which to base conclusions

Remember that this is an introductory guide—coverage of more advanced assessment strategies would require completion of a research methods course. (If you desire more advanced reading, see Katzer, Cook, and Crouch, 1978; Millman and Gowin, 1974; or Tripodi, Fellin, and Meyer, 1969). Remember also that these are guidelines, not inflexible rules. Not all of the criteria apply equally well to all topic areas or research designs. Moreover, you should not feel bound by my organization—analysis of control variables could take place just as easily in the research design section as in the results section.

I would like to close with one point not mentioned earlier: Your personal reaction is an essential criterion in assessing any research. Research articles must have some relevance for you if they are to be useful. Only you can determine this level of relevance. If a title catches your eye but the variables examined do not fit your purpose, then the quality of the research design or writing obviously will not matter. But when an article does seem to suit your needs, this guide should prove useful to you, not only as a tool to assist you in evaluation of research but also as a contributor to your development as an informed, skilled, and skeptical consumer of research reports in the social sciences.

APPENDIX: LIST OF QUESTIONS TO USE IN ASSESSING SOCIAL SCIENCE RESEARCH ARTICLES

A.   Statement of the Problem
  1. How clearly and simply is the research problem stated?
  2. How completely is the research tied to the larger body of theory and knowledge in the area?
  3. Based on what you know of other works in the area, how accurately does the author reference previous works?
  4. How well is the purpose of the research explained?
  5. How clearly are hypotheses stated?
  6. How extensively do the author's biases influence the statement of the problem and its definition?

B.   Conceptualization
  1. How completely are the relevant concepts identified?
  2. How clearly are the interrelationships among the concepts identified?
  3. How adequately have concepts been operationalized?
  4. How adequately have the reliability and validity of the operational definitions been determined?

C.   Research Design
  1. How adequately is the research design described?
  2. How appropriate is the design, given the author's statement of the problem and conceptualization?
  3. How appropriate are the sampling procedures?
  4. How extensively does the researcher deal with possible sources of error?

5. How appropriate are the analytical techniques used?
  6. How much attention is paid to ethical considerations?

D.   Results
  1. How adequately are data reported?
  2. How consistent are interpretations of the data with the raw data?
  3. How adequately does the author distinguish statistical from substantive significance?
  4. To what extent does the author consider control variables?
  5. Given the statement of the problem, how adequately do results deal with issues raised?

E.   Conclusions
  1. How adequately does the author summarize results?
  2. How completely does the author discuss implications of the study?
  3. Does the author overgeneralize from results?
  4. Does the author make causal analyses based only on correlation data?

REFERENCES

Berheide, C. W., S. F. Berk, and R. A. Berk
  1976 "Household work in the suburbs: the job and its participants." Pacific Sociological Review 19(October):491–517.

Carlock, Charlene J. and Patricia Y. Martin
  1977 "Sex composition and the intensive group experience." Social Work 22(January):27–32.

Carlson, Bonnie E.
  1977 "Battered women and their assailants." Social Work 22(November):455–60.

"Colleges reach 'sexual utopia' "
  1976 Cincinnati Enquirer, September 19, A–16.

Goodbody, Sandra Toll
  1977 "The psychosocial implications of voluntary childlessness." Social Casework 58(July):426–34.

Goudy, Willis J.
  1976 "Nonresponse effects on relationships between variables." Public Opinion Quarterly 40(Fall):360–69.

Howard, Alicia, David D. Royse, and John A. Skerl
 1977 "Transracial adoption: the black community perspective." Social Work 22(May):184–89.

Katzer, Jeffrey, Kenneth H. Cook, and Wayne W. Crouch
 1978 Evaluating Information: A Guide for Users of Social Science Research. Reading: Addison-Wesley.

Knapman, Shirley Kuehnle
 1977 "Sex discrimination in family agencies." Social Work 22(November): 461–65.

Maykovich, Minako K.
 1976 "Attitudes versus behavior in extramarital sexual relations." Journal of Marriage and the Family 38(November):693–99.

Millman, J. and D. Bob Gowin
 1974 Appraising Educational Research: A Case Study Approach. Englewood Cliffs: Prentice-Hall.

Sabatini, Paul and R. Kastenbaum
 1973 "The do-it-yourself death certificate as a research technique." Life-threatening Behavior 3(Spring):20–32.

Singh, B. Krishna, Bonnie L. Walton, and J. Sherwood Williams
 1976 "Extramarital sexual permissiveness: conditions and contingencies." Journal of Marriage and the Family 38(November):701–12.

Smith, H. W.
 1975 Strategies of Social Research. Englewood Cliffs: Prentice-Hall.

Stafford, R., E. Backman, and P. Dibona
 1977 "The division of labor among cohabiting and married couples." Journal of Marriage and the Family 39(February):43–57.

"Stanford notes more pregnancies"
 1975 Cincinnati Enquirer, November 30, A–7.

"Study indicates benefits of that morning kiss"
 1977 The Oregonian Forum, July 27, D–11.

Tavris, Carol
 1977 "Men and women report their views on masculinity." Psychology Today 10(January):35–42 ff.

"Teen users of cigarettes 'rebellious'"
 1976 San Diego Union, March 27, A–10.

Tripodi, Tony, Phillip Fellin, and Henry J. Meyer
 1969 The Assessment of Social Research. Itasca: F. E. Peacock.

Wake, Sandra B. and Michael J. Sporakowski
 1972 "An intergenerational comparison of attitudes towards supporting aged parents." Journal of Marriage and the Family 34(February):42–48.

SECTION 1.2

The Ethics of Social Research

Social scientists increasingly are paying attention to the ethical implications of their research. Several factors may account for this concern. Certain published studies have raised serious ethical questions. Examples include such studies as Milgram's (1965) study involving a subject's giving electric shocks to a confederate of the researcher for failure to learn word associations and Humphreys' (1970) observation study of homosexual activity in a public place (which also involved securing participants' identities with license number identification). In addition, the last decade has seen a dramatic increase in both the number of social science research investigations and the number of persons involved in such studies. To these can be added the general atmosphere of skepticism and reduced confidence in the government that has developed in the wake of Watergate. Individuals are now more reluctant to participate in official studies, particularly government-sponsored studies. One result of federal concern for ethics in social research has been the formation of committees on most campuses to review all studies involving human subjects for conformity with ethical principles.

WHERE DO ETHICS ENTER?

Ethical issues enter at all phases of the research process, from inception of the problem to publication of the results. Take data-gathering as an example. Middlemist et al. (1976) performed a study of 60 college men to determine the relationship between interpersonal distance and both the delay of onset of urination and the duration of urination. An observer stationed in an adjacent stall used a periscope prism hidden in a stack of books lying on the floor of the stall and a stopwatch to gather the data. A case could be made that the subjects' privacy was being invaded with such a procedure, a fundamental ethical principle. The authors devoted virtually no space in their article to possible violations of ethical principles. In a subsequent issue of the journal, however, Gerald Koocher raised the possibility of potential harm to "unsuspecting or unstable individuals who might discover that they were being observed" (Koocher, 1977:120). He also raised the issue of the journal editor's responsibility to reconsider publication of a study employing possibly unethical procedures, an interesting but generally ignored issue.

Consider the study of a small town published some years ago. Vidich and Bensman (1958) describe in considerable detail the events and people of the community.

30

Although they did not identify individuals by name, they presented a sufficient number of details so that people could be identified. Ethical issues in the research dissemination stage are not limited to publications only. In a case I am familiar with, a researcher informed the news media that a high proportion of the students in a public school system were taking drugs to control hypertension (the proportion was incorrect). The ethical issue of confidentiality applies to both these studies. Similar examples could be given for the other stages of the research process.

THE READINGS: ETHICAL PRINCIPLES AND EXAMPLES

Both readings in this section reveal many instances of violation of ethical principles. Implicitly, the authors identify several ethical principles. Among the most relevant principles are the following:

1. Minimal Harm to Participants

This principle involves the reduction or elimination of physical and psychological harm to participants. Physical harm is not prevalent in social research, but psychological harm may be inflicted by an experiment involving degradation, an evaluation research study involving withholding treatment from a control group, or an interview involving sensitive exploration of such topics as rape experiences or sexual feelings. Harm may also be inflicted by deception and violation of confidentiality.

Harm must be balanced against the benefits of the study. Zick Rubin, for example, believes that the social importance of the Milgram shock study justifies the harm that may have resulted to the participants. The self-fulfilling prophecy study noted by Rubin also raises the harm/benefit issue: Were the results (demonstration of the self-fulfilling prophecy) worth the possible harm done to some of the students (deprivation of high expectations)? Since the control students probably received treatment similar to what they would have experienced without the experiment, it is doubtful whether the harm done outweighed the study benefits.

2. Deception

It may be argued that a certain degree of deception is necessary to protect the validity of the study. Certainly Milgram would have encountered very different results had he told his subjects the real purpose of his experiment. Similarly, telling respondents the exact nature of a survey study may result in biased answers. But deception can go too far; there's a big difference between not telling respondents the exact hypotheses of a study and posing as a watchqueen in a public restroom for the purpose of observing homosexual activities (and, via license plates, later interviewing the participants as part of a "social health study"). Perhaps we could distinguish two aspects of this principle: withholding information versus actually giving false information. Whether one is worse than the other depends on your values.

Both articles in this section emphasize this ethical principle. Rubin emphasizes the dehumanizing aspect of deception, although he does not take a stand against all deception. Donald Warwick identifies four types of deception in his example-filled article and concludes that it is doubtful if deception aids human welfare, a rationale often espoused by social researchers. He suggests, tongue-in-cheek, that we develop a "Gross National Deception" index to quantify the total amount of deception occurring in social research.

3. Privacy and Confidentiality

This principle states that the privacy of the individual must be respected and that any information gathered must be kept strictly confidential. Proposed national data banks and longitudinal studies may involve invasions of privacy. Fields (1977:1) notes other examples:

An anthropologist investigating an urban Hispano-American community encountered a number of problems that threatened the confidentiality of the research—difficulties in concealing the site of the study and his observations of illegal behavior which, if reported, could cause problems for some research subjects. He decided not to report his findings.

A newspaper editor apologized to readers after a subscriber who had participated in a readership survey accidentally discovered that the supposedly anonymous questionnaire had been coded with invisible ink so the respondents could be identified. The editor investigated and found that many market researchers secretly coded their questionnaires.

Regarding confidentiality, it is important to note that social scientists do not enjoy the same legal protection as doctors and lawyers. In fact, their research records may be subpoenaed in a court of law. Recently, a Harvard economist and a research assistant were subpoenaed to produce field notes and act as witnesses in a civil case regarding a company they had studied during research on decision-making by public utilities (Fields, 1977:1)

As an example of how confidentiality may be maintained, review Troiden's procedures in his article in the field research section (Section 3.1); he had a fool-proof method for protecting confidentiality by giving the respondent the sheet with the respondent's name and address, leaving Troiden only with an identification number. In addition, interviews were taken by hand instead of taped and questionnaire answers were recopied so that handwriting could not be identified.

4. Informed Consent

Informed consent means (1) that the participants are informed of the study goals, possible benefits, and possible dangers and (2) that the participant agrees willingly to participate. In special cases, this principle may involve explaining the study in the participant's native language or securing permission from parents or guardians. Students are often required to participate in studies conducted by their professors; such a practice may be a violation of the principle of informed consent. Informed consent generally involves written agreement by the participant and often involves the right to withdraw from the study at any time. Informed consent does not end with the preliminaries of a study; it should also include appropriate debriefing and removal of harmful aftereffects.

These four basic ethical principles pertain primarily to a participant's rights and welfare. But researchers also have responsibilities to their colleagues, to research sponsors, and to the larger public. These obligations include truthful reporting of results, reporting all results instead of just parts, making appropriate use of statistics, citing sources where appropriate, and treating sponsors fairly but refusing to participate in a sponsor's concealing of the purpose of the research.

Concrete ethical standards are difficult to develop. Unlike the rules for applying various statistical procedures, ethical principles remain only guidelines. As both Troiden and Fitzpatrick note in their personal journals (field research section, Section 3.1), it is important to apply the principles within a particular context. For example, deciding how much deception is permissible depends primarily on the researcher's familiarity with the situation. Hence, after ten minutes of conversation with a homosexual subject, Troiden informed the subject that he was doing research on homosexuality in order to reduce the possibility of the subject's regarding Troiden as a potential partner.

You should note that many studies could not be done if these principles were followed stringently, particularly in terms of the informed consent principle. It is doubtful, in fact, whether Milgram's shock study could be done today, given current ethical standards and existing human subjects committees.

In sum, it is impossible to answer yes or no to the question: Is this procedure ethical? It depends on the context, and for each principle a range from "completely ethical" to "completely unethical" exists. In the final analysis, ethics brings values into play more than do other aspects of the research process.

REFERENCES

Fields, Cheryl M.
  1977 "A growing problem for researcher: protecting privacy." The Chronicle of Higher Education 14(May 2):1 ff.
Humphreys, Laud
  1970 Tearoom Trade: Impersonal Sex in Public Places. Chicago: Aldine.
Koocher, Gerald P.
  1977 "Bathroom behavior and human dignity." Journal of Personality and Social Psychology 35(2):120–21.
Middlemist, R. Dennis, Eric S. Knowles, and Charles F. Matter
  1976 "Personal space invasions in the lavatory: suggestive evidence for arousal." Journal of Personality and Social Psychology 33(5):541–46.
Milgram, Stanley
  1965 "Some conditions of obedience and disobedience to authority." Pp. 243–62 in Ivan D. Steiner and Martin Fishbein (eds.), Current Studies in Social Psychology. New York: Holt, Rinehart and Winston.
Vidich, Arthur J. and Joseph Bensman
  1958 Small Town in Mass Society. Princeton: Princeton University Press.

SOCIAL SCIENTISTS OUGHT TO STOP LYING

Donald P. Warwick

Nearly every moral code in human history has condemned lying as evil and destructive of mutual trust. Yet deception is common in social science research and, in some areas, virtually the norm. In order to facilitate the collection of data, or to advance man's knowledge, or to help the oppressed, researchers condone deception in the laboratory, on the streets, and in our social institutions. They deliberately misrepresent the intent of their experiments, assume false appearances, and use other subterfuges as dubious means to questionable ends. These tactics are unethical and unjustified. They are also dangerous, because they may spread to other segments of society.

The problems posed by lying and deceit differ according to how, where, and why they are used. Essentially, sociologists and psychologists practice four types of deception.

The first and most damaging is deliberate public deception, where scientists lie to members of the community and to individuals in organizations. To learn, for instance, how teacher expectations affect student achievement, Robert Rosenthal and Lenore Jacobson (1968) lied to 18 elementary-school teachers. They told them that certain children in their classes would bloom academically while others probably would not. They said they had predicted the children's success on the basis of their scores on an "intellectual-blooming" test. Actually, it was a nonverbal IQ test and there were no intellectual differences in the children.

At the end of the school year, when Rosenthal and Jacobson measured the students' progress, they found what they had predicted; the children who were expected by their teachers to succeed scored higher than those who weren't. There was evidence, said the researchers, for a Pygmalion effect.

A SELF-FULFILLING PROPHECY

The research team received national attention for their experiment (Rosenthal, 1968). They had proved that when teachers expect failure they'll get it, and vice versa. Since 1968, at least 242 other researchers have repeated the experiment in many different settings. Hundreds, perhaps thousands, of people have been duped for the sake of scientific progress and academic promotions.

Albert Reiss, Jr. and Donald J. Black ran a series of surveys in which they lied to policemen in three cities. They told the officers they were studying how citizens react to police, when in fact they were measuring the reverse interaction.

These deceptive experiments are only two among thousands. One wonders how this kind of chicanery affects researchers, research participants, students, and the public. The teachers who were deceived in the Pygmalion studies must have had many misgivings about themselves and more about Rosenthal's methods. Few would knowingly allow such scientists in their classrooms. Some parents must have been furious when they found their children were used as guinea pigs, particularly when bright children failed to do well because the teachers didn't expect it. And by now these studies are required reading and standard lecture material in dozens of social science and education courses. With about three quarters of a million high-school and college students taking psychology courses each year just in the U.S., and many of these exposed to Pygmalion and other deceptive research, the impact is great.

Accounts of the experiment in the press and on television undoubtedly left a bad taste in many other mouths. Through many channels social scientists tell the public that lying is justified when it is for the right ends. In this way they undermine mutual trust and make it easier for others to follow suit. They also reinforce a cavalier attitude toward truth in their own professions.

"BLEEDING" STOOGES ON THE SUBWAY

Scientists can destroy public trust by deed as well as by word. Jane and Irving Piliavin (1972), for instance, conducted an experiment in Philadelphia in which they had a confederate collapse in a moving subway train. They were trying to test people's inclination to help their fellow human beings. As the stooge fell, he released a trickle of "blood" from an eyedropper in his mouth. Sometimes the experimenters placed another confederate near the impending drama. He wore an intern's jacket, priest's attire or ordinary street clothes. These variations were used to see what effect they would have on the passengers' reactions. The Piliavins staged this gory melodrama about 50 times on the same subway line.

Stanley Milgram is so clever at devising his experiments that their ingenuity blinds us to their manipulative and condescending nature. He dubbed one famous deception "The Lost-Letter Technique" (Milgram, 1969). Here researchers walked around a city dropping several hundred stamped letters. The envelopes were addressed to organizations such as "Friends of the Nazi Party" or "Friends of the Communist Party." On the basis of whether people ignored the letters, mailed them, destroyed them, opened them, or whatever, Milgram judged how the citizens felt about diverse organizations. Those who found these letters were unwitting participants in social research.

Recently, Milgram devised a "lost-child technique." He turns a nine-year-old youngster out on the street, and the lost child tries to enlist adult aid to telephone home. Milgram has staged fights between husbands and wives on the Massachusetts Turnpike, and concocted other schemes of public deception.

This type of research is not only devious, it is irresponsible. As the news spreads that bloody victims are only research stooges, that lost children are in fact part of an experiment, and that lost letters are really props to test political attitudes, the already scant propensity for one person to help another seems likely to diminish.

SOCIAL SCIENTISTS CRY WOLF

I would not be surprised if eventually the public fails to respond to cries of wolf in the name of scientific progress. These tricks simply strengthen the growing conviction that you can't trust people you don't know. If a mugger doesn't hit you, a credit checker doesn't spy on you, or a salesman doesn't take you to the cleaners, a social scientist will dupe you. Deceptive research may well play a role in creating the present climate of distrust in America.

The laboratory is another arena for scientific deviousness. Here researchers delight in creating artificial situations and environments to elicit and measure specific human actions. The most common ploy is to use stooges who pose as fellow subjects in the experiment. They give the real subjects prearranged instructions or react to their behavior with planned responses.

Diana Baumrind (1971) tells about how one student was humiliated and embarrassed by a laboratory ruse. The subject said she was "embarrassed at having been manipulated into feeling pride at nonachievement and gratification at praise I didn't deserve. . . . The devastating blow was struck by a psychologist, whose competence to judge behavior I had never doubted before" (1971:890). Baumrind reminds us that the most serious effect of deception may be that "the subject is taught that he cannot trust those who by social contract are designated trustworthy and whom he needs to trust in order not to feel alienated from the society" (1971:894).

HOW TO SUCCEED IN ACADEME

It is naive to assume that a short debriefing after an experiment will wipe out these effects. Even college freshmen become jaundiced and quickly learn how experimentalists operate. They know that those who "make it big" do so on the basis of deceptive research; that the profession gives its greatest rewards to those who are ingeniously amoral; and that a good researcher does not allow public sensitivities to get in the way of a good piece of research.

The third ruse is covert observation. Here scientists gather data while participating in the daily lives of their subjects. They go into factories, schools, mental hospitals, under false pretenses. William Caudill (1958), for instance, faked symptoms to be admitted to a mental hospital. Leon Festinger, Henry Riecken, and Stanley Schachter (1956) posed as true believers to study an apocalyptic religious group. John Lofland and his associates feigned alcoholism to study members of Alcoholics Anonymous (1960). I would place these practices close to deliberate public deception.

When sociologists justify this sort of behavior as necessary for gathering data, it should be no surprise that the FBI condones similar tactics for gathering political intelligence. Justice Louis Brandeis once argued that while we can never be sure about the value of ends, whether political, social, or economic, we can be clear about means: "Lying and sneaking are always bad, no matter what the ends."

The least serious type of deception takes place when researchers give a generally accurate but incomplete statement of the purposes and uses of the research. Some would argue that if participants aren't fully informed about the study, they are being deceived. It is my feeling that we can distinguish between a deliberate lie or ruse and a situation in which a survey interviewer gives an honest statement about the purposes of the study without going into detail about its sponsorship, hypotheses, and applications. Ethical problems arise only when relevant details are left out or misrepresented.

Outright lies and misrepresentations abound in social research. Julius Seeman (1969) reports that from 1948 to 1963, the number of studies using deception in personality and social psychology rose from 18 to 38 percent. But, with a plethora of excuses, practitioners go on deceiving.

THE ENDS JUSTIFY THE MEANS

The highest god of the researcher is science. And the scientist insists that he only uses deception to advance man's understanding of himself and society, and thus to promote human welfare. If he can't conduct his work without deception, he says, then the subject's right to truth is outweighed by the higher goal of advancing knowledge.

Where there are no ethical-review committees, he becomes the sole judge.

I challenge this stance on both empirical and ethical grounds. First of all, it is highly doubtful that any study involving deception ultimately promotes human welfare. Certainly the Pygmalion research increased our knowledge, but it is fallacious to equate knowledge with welfare. As Cicero put it: "Knowledge that is divorced from justice should be called cunning rather than wisdom."

Secondly, if it is all right to use deceit to advance knowledge, then why not for reasons of national security, for maintaining the Presidency, or to save one's own hide? Who is to decide which gods merit a sacrifice of the truth?

DECEPTION TO HELP THE UNDERDOG

In the 1960s, social scientists began touting a new excuse for deception. They said that social science must serve the underdog, and that deception for this cause is morally acceptable. Laud Humphreys (1970) used this defense to justify the way he gathered data about homosexuals. He passed as gay at private gatherings; posed as a lookout or "watchqueen" to observe fellatio in public restrooms; used a concealed tape recorder to summarize his observations and to note the license-plate numbers of homosexuals; and told the police he was doing "market research" so they would give him access to license registers. Finally, a year after he observed these men, he donned "straight" clothes and interviewed them at home under the guise that he was doing a "social-health survey of men in the community." I cannot believe that such data will really improve the lot of homosexuals. Even if it did, Humphreys' chain of lies was not morally justified.

A variant of the last justification is that scientists should employ deception to expose the rotten dealings of the "power elite." Sociologist John Galliher argues that "every person is entitled to equal privacy and dignity of treatment as a private citizen. However, equal protection may require unequal treatment of different types of subjects. . . . When actors become involved in Government and business or other organizations where they are accountable to the public, no right of privacy applies to conduct in such roles." He goes on: "Confidential information provided by a research subject must be treated as such by the sociologist unless it is evident that the gain by society and/or science is such that it offsets the probable magnitude of the individual discomfort" (1973:97, 98).

CIVIL RIGHTS: SOME HAVE THEM, SOME DON'T

Galliher's reasoning smacks of the values espoused by Richard Nixon and the Watergate squad. In Galliher's code, the poor and ignorant have civil rights; others, especially businessmen and Government officials, enjoy them only at the sufferance of the social scientist. Thus, while the White House Plumbers were ransacking Lewis J. Fielding's office, Galliher's ethical view would have allowed social scientists to pilfer files from the psychiatrists of civil servants to study their role conflicts in office. In his terms, violating promises of confidentiality for the good of science and society would "offset the probable magnitude of individual discomfort." The dangers in bracketing the civil liberties of some citizens seem too obvious to deserve comment.

Finally, some scientists practice deception simply because it is the best way to gather data. Their god is expedience, and their high priests often the local promotion and tenure committee.

Just as we now have truth-in-lending laws, so we need truth-in-research laws to protect an otherwise vulnerable public. Police officers, teachers, and other subjects who have been told outright lies should have legal redress for their grievances. I would prefer to have the professions police themselves, but they will not. The laissez faire ethic in sociology and psychology is too strong for a code of ethics with teeth. Government must step in to prevent the most flagrant abuses, especially public deception.

We might also develop a new social indicator, the GND. It would measure Gross National Deception. First we would define the realms of deception, such as politics, advertising, social research. Then, for the latter category, analysts would simply add up the total number of deceptive studies, and tally the number of individuals involved and affected. The annual numbers would rise and fall, hopefully stimulating debates comparable to those generated by figures on unemployment or the GNP.

At present we too often dispose of ethical questions quickly so that we can get on with the real business of theory and research. The time has come to examine not only the techniques, but the moral implications of social research. Watergate was the latest example of a corrosive deceit in America. In the social sciences, as in politics, the truth is often sacrificed on the altar of some higher principle. The cumulative results are a pervasive suspicion of Government and an increasing wariness in dealing with our fellow man. These are the natural fruits of a deceiving society. Social scientists who do not hesitate to point an accusing finger at the White House are too quick to shrug off their own complicity in this moral decay. We should now put our own house in order with a permanent moratorium on deceptive research.

REFERENCES

Baumrind, Diana
  1971 "Principles of ethical conduct in the treatment of subjects." American Psychologist 26(10):887–896.

Caudill, William
  1958 The Psychiatric Hospital as a Small Society. Cambridge: Harvard University Press.

Festinger, Leon, Henry W. Riecken, and Stanley Schachter
  1956 When Prophecy Fails. Minneapolis: University of Minnesota Press.

Humphreys, Laud
  1970 Tearoom Trade: Impersonal Sex in Public Places. Chicago: Aldine.

Galliher, John F.
  1973 "The protection of human subjects: a reexamination of the professional code of ethics." American Sociologist 8(3):93–100.

Lofland, John F. and R. A. Lejeune
  1960 "Initial interaction of newcomers in Alcoholics Anonymous." Social Problems 8(2):102–111.

Milgram, Stanley
  1969 "The lost-letter technique." Psychology Today 3(1):30–33, 66, 68.

Piliavin, Jane A. and Irving M. Piliavin
  1972 "Effect of blood on reactions to a victim." Journal of Personality and Social Psychology 23(3):353–361.

Reiss, Albert J., Jr., and D. J. Black
  1967 "Interrogation and the criminal process." American Academy of Political and Social Science Annals 347(November): 47–57.

Ring, Kenneth, Kenneth Wallston, and Michel Corey
  1970 "Mode of debriefing as a factor affecting subjective reaction to a Milgram-type obedience experiment: an ethical inquiry." Representative Research in Social Psychology 1(1):67–88.

Rosenthal, Robert
  1968 "Self-fulfilling prophecy." Psychology Today 2(4):44–51.

Rosenthal, Robert and Lenore Jacobson
  1968 Pygmalion in the Classroom. New York: Holt, Rinehart and Winston.

Seeman, Julius
  1969 "Deception in psychological research." American Psychologist 24(11): 1025–1028.

Warwick, Donald P.
  1973 "Tearoom trade: means and ends in social research." Hastings Center Studies 1(1):27–38.

Warwick, Donald P. and John F. Galliher
  1974 "Who deserves protection?" (An exchange between Warwick and Galliher) American Sociologist 9(3): 158–160.

JOKERS WILD IN THE LAB

Zick Rubin

Two young men, college sophomores, sit at a table facing a screen, electrodes clamped to their wrists. A tall young man explains to them that he is a graduate student in psychology and that he is investigating homosexual arousal: the students are to watch pictures of men projected on the screen while a galvanometer hooked to the electrodes monitors subtle changes in their skin conductivity. These responses will measure the extent of their homosexual arousal. The more the needle jumps, the more homosexual they are. And, as the students watch photographs of seminude men, they find to their dismay that the needles do a lot of jumping . . .

The tall young man was indeed a graduate student—named Dana Bramel—then working on his Ph.D. thesis at Stanford. But nothing else Bramel told the sophomores was true. The electrodes were not connected to the galvanometer. Bramel controlled it from a hidden switchboard. And he was *not* studying homosexual arousal, but rather the mechanisms underlying the defensive projection of undesirable traits to others. (One conclusion: students who thus "learn" that they are homosexual often decide that their friends are too.)

The sophomores, serving as experimental subjects to meet a requirement of their introductory psychology course, invariably fell for Bramel's story. Afterward, of course, he told them what he was really up to. Some of his subjects thought it was a good joke. Others probably did not.

TRICKS

This experiment typifies a popular mode of social-psychological research that many psychologists don't like to talk about. It centers on trickery that ranges from harmless clownery to the downright diabolical.

Take an example from Ohio State: the trusting subject sits in front of a large steel machine with an impressive array of push buttons, lights, and toggle switches. The experimenter says he is studying motor learning and that the subject's task will be to turn lights on and off consecutively by pushing appropriate buttons. After demonstrating the procedure the experimenter explains that "All my research money is tied up in this contraption and I'll never get my master's degree if it doesn't function properly." Forewarned, the subject starts pushing buttons carefully—but, as the script dictates, never carefully enough. Soon he hears a deafening bang followed by a shrieking whistle and swirling clouds of thick white smoke. The experimenter now speaks in a broken voice, "I'll never get my master's now . . . (choke) . . . What did you do to the machine? . . . (sob) . . . Well, I guess that ends the experiment . . . (long pause and then solemnly) . . . The machine is broken."

On this tragic note, the subject mumbles his apologies and prepares to leave. But before he can do so the experimenter suddenly brightens and asks a favor. "I'm a member of the Young Democrats and have to circulate this petition," he says. "As long as you're here, would you sign it?" The petition reads: "The tuition at Ohio State University should be doubled to improve the quality of the faculty and the physical condition of the university." It is a safe bet (which was confirmed with control subjects) that virtually no sane Ohio student would sign such a declaration. But 56 per cent of the guilt-stricken experimental subjects did.

BIAS

Some social psychologists argue that such techniques are essential in studying such phenomena as persuasion, conformity, aggression, and embarrassment. One cannot simply ask people about

Reprinted from *Psychology Today* Magazine. Copyright © 1970 Ziff-Davis Publishing Company. References added.

such things and expect objective answers. It is to counteract these biasing effects that the experimenter resorts to deception. By creating a believable cover story and catching the subject off guard, the experimenter increases the likelihood that his results will reflect real social behavior.

There is little doubt that trumped-up laboratory happenings can yield valuable information. A classic example is the series of psychodramas staged in the late 1940s by Solomon Asch (1958) at Swarthmore. The studies pretended to deal with visual acuity but they were in fact concerned with conformity. In one variant of the script, seven students were asked in turn which of three lines was identical in length to a comparison line. Actually only one of the students was really a subject and he was maneuvered into the next-to-last position. The other six were paid confederates instructed to make judgments that were clearly, often ludicrously, incorrect. The key question was: How often would the subject go along with the crowd?

CRITICS

Asch's experiments were widely applauded by social scientists. But during the 1950s and particularly the 1960s, laboratory playwrights proliferated. As they have gained in popularity, the productions have evolved from unexciting skits into dazzling—often terrifying—extravaganzas.

And they have been criticized. Members of the profession decry what they consider to be a move from science to fun and games. Kenneth Ring (1967) of the University of Connecticut has noted that "There is a distinctly exhibitionistic flavor to much current experimentation, while the experimenters often seem to equate notoriety with achievement." Also, the deception involved has been called dehumanizing and some experimenters have been accused of doing serious psychological harm to unsuspecting and unconsenting subjects.

The theater where the dramas take place is usually a suite of soundproof rooms equipped with one-way mirrors, an intercom system, and an assortment of electrical gadgetry. The cast includes experimenter, subject, and often an additional performer popularly known as a stooge. The stooge is an assistant of the experimenter who advances the plot in the guise of a fellow subject or an uninvolved bystander.

In Asch's studies, for example, the stooge's major task was to keep a straight face while making ridiculous perceptual judgments. In recent years stooge assignments have become more diverse. They have had to insult subjects (while the subjects watch through a one-way mirror), to impersonate deaf people (in a study of attitudes toward the deaf), and to exhibit spontaneous and unrestrained euphoria (in a study dealing with the contagion of emotion), among other chores.

DATE

Other stooges are cast in more melodramatic roles. The drift toward soap opera is illustrated by an experiment conducted by Elaine Walster (1970), now a professor at the University of Wisconsin. Walster wondered whether a young woman's self-esteem affects her propensity to fall in love.

The cast consisted of 37 Stanford and Foothill Junior College coeds, and the romantic lead was played by Gerald Davison, a matinee-idol-type graduate student. As the drama opened, each girl arrived at an empty reception room where a sign asked her to wait for the experimenter. Then Davison, smooth and well-dressed, came out and explained that he was waiting for another experimenter. After a few moments of silence, Davison casually began a conversation, and in 32 out of 37 cases was able to make a date with the subject.

The experimenter then arrived and escorted each happily deluded subject to another room, where she explained that the purpose of the study was to compare various personality tests. The subject had previously taken a test and now she saw an evaluation of her own personality prepared by a "therapist" in San Francisco. Half of the girls got the great news that they possessed, among other things, "sensitivity to peers, personal integrity, originality and freedom of outlook." The remaining girls received far-less-glowing reports, such as, "Although she has adopted certain superficial appearances of maturity ... her basically immature drives remain. ... She shows a weak personality, antisocial motives, a lack of flexibility and originality, and a lack of capacity for successful leadership ... Her feelings of inadequacy led her constantly to overestimate many of her own characteristics." (If these girls hadn't had feelings of inadequacy before the experiment began, they surely had at this point.)

Next the girls were asked to rate how much they liked certain persons, including a teacher, a friend, "and, since we have one space left, why don't you also rate that fellow from Miss Turner's study whom you were waiting with?" This evaluation was the point of all the preceding rigamarole. The result: subjects with lowered self-esteem (the ones told that they were immature, etc.) reported that they liked Davison more than did the girls with raised self-esteem.

CURTAIN

In the final act of the melodrama, Walster confessed to the young innocents that the personality appraisal was phony, that they were not really all that bad or all that good, and finally—the crushing blow—that the date must be broken. "I was just so upset," Walster told me when I discussed the experiment with her. "It wasn't just breaking the date, but that they might be embarrassed that a guy could con them to that extent." To reassure her subjects she stressed the fact that *nobody* turned Gerry down, and that even if he wanted to, Gerry was forbidden to date any subject. Finally, the girls were sworn to secrecy. According to Walster, virtually all of them went away happy.

I asked Davison, who is now a professor at the State University of New York at Stony Brook, how he felt about his stooging experience. His answer: "I have regretted ever participating in it. Looking back on the study now, I have concluded that the importance of the results did not justify the magnitude and/or the quality of the manipulations."

SHOCK

Equally troubling questions are raised by the widely reported studies of obedience done at Yale by Stanley Milgram (1965). His subjects were men from a wide range of occupations who were told that they were to take part in a study of the effects of punishment on memory.

First a pair of subjects drew straws to decide who was to be the teacher and who was to be the learner. The learner was then taken into an adjacent room (out of the teacher's sight) and strapped into the laboratory version of an electric chair, where electrodes were attached to his arms. The teacher, meanwhile, was seated behind a precision-made shock generator, ostensibly capable of delivering painful jolts to the learner. The generator had 30 clearly marked voltage levels with switches ranging from 15 to 450 volts, and with labels ranging from "Slight Shock" to "Danger: Severe Shock." Two additional switches were designated only as "XXX."

The learner's task was to memorize a list of word pairs. Whenever he made a mistake the teacher was to punish him by administering a shock, increasing the intensity one step each time. Before they began, the teacher himself was given a "mild" shock of 45 volts to make it painfully clear that the shocks were real. As the session went on, the learner made many mistakes and had to be given increasingly severe shocks. The pain seemingly became excruciating. As the level of the shocks increased, the learner grunted, moaned, and hollered, demanding to be released. After 315 volts the learner no longer answered, but groaned whenever a shock was administered and finally stopped making any sounds at all.

The learner was, of course, a stooge. The shock generator was phony and the learner's protests were really on tape. The teacher, who was the only real subject (the drawing was fixed), didn't know this. The object of the study was to find out at what point he would refuse to obey the experimenter's commands.

WRECK

For many subjects, the experience was terrifying. "I observed an initially poised businessman enter the laboratory smiling and confident," one of Milgram's observers reported. "Within 20 minutes he was reduced to a twitching, stuttering wreck, who was rapidly approaching a point of nervous collapse. He constantly pulled on his earlobe and twisted his hands. At one point he pushed his fist into his forehead and muttered, 'Oh God, let's stop it.' And yet he continued to respond to every word of the experimenter, and obeyed to the end." (Sixty per cent did so.)

Some psychologists contend that Milgram's procedures may have caused severe psychological harm. Herbert Kelman of Harvard suggests that "at least some of the obedient subjects came away from this experience with lowered self-esteem, having to live with the realization that they were willing to yield to destructive authority to the point of inflicting extreme pain on a fellow human being" (1966:21).

Many experiments have been at least as ghoulish as Milgram's. For example, a group of Army psychologists at the then-called Leadership Human Research Unit in Monterey, California has studied reactions of new recruits to extreme stress. Unwitting subjects were made to believe, among other things, that they were on a plane about to make a crash-landing, and that they were personally responsible for an explosion that had seriously injured a soldier.

VALUE

Milgram's work has a social importance that, in my view, vastly overweighs any psychological harm it may have inflicted, and which was probably minimal. He carefully screened his subjects before the experiment, painstakingly dehoaxed them afterward, and had a psychiatrist follow up on them.

There is a question, however, whether much of the work of laboratory manipulators is science at all. The orientation toward fun-and-games, as Ring (1967) has noted, is often antithetical to the proper scientific goals of increasing knowledge and, ultimately, serving the public good. Worse, many experimental social psychologists have taken deception for granted. They have assumed that the moral value of honesty, which they subscribe to in virtually all other contexts, is simply irrelevant to their behavior in the laboratory. This, in my view, is an unjustified conceit.

Kelman has argued cogently that tricks in the laboratory help to create an image of man as "an object to be manipulated at will." As he puts it, "Deception has been turned into a game, often played with great skill and virtuosity. . . . In institutionalizing the use of deception in psychological experiments we are contributing to a historical trend that threatens values most of us cherish" (1966:20).

"PRETEND"

To eliminate all deceptive experiments would be a mistake. I am convinced that many are of potentially great scientific and social importance. However, psychologists should first consider more straightforward methods of gathering data—even if they seem to be less fun.

Such reflection has recently come into vogue, and there has been a discernible trend toward nondeceptive role-playing procedures. In such studies, subjects are asked in effect to *pretend* that they are taking part in an experiment. The procedures of the pseudoexperiment are carefully explained to them, and they are asked to behave as they think they would if they were really in the experimental situation.

Many social psychologists doubt the validity of such an approach, however. A characteristic opinion is that of Columbia's Jonathan Freedman, who calls most role-playing studies "a return to the prescientific days when intuition and consensus took the place of data" (1969:107). Although Freedman may be right, the potential value of such procedures certainly deserves to be explored systematically.

At the same time that they are being beset by a storm of ethical criticism, social psychologists have also been required to refine their methods in response to pragmatic concerns. Students on many campuses have become increasingly alert to deceptive techniques. As a result, experimenters have been resorting to increasingly complex deceptions and double-deceptions. "It's like bugs and DDT," one researcher told me. Others seek new sources of uncorrupted subjects, including nursery-school students, mental patients, and church groups.

REAL

Still another way to combat subject sophistication is to stage experiments in real-life settings. The New York City subway stretch from 59th Street to 125th Street in Manhattan was the scene of a naturalistic study of altruism conducted recently by Irving and Jane Piliavin of the University of Pennsylvania and Judith Rodin of New York University (1969). A young male rider simulated collapse on the subway-car floor, while observers recorded who came to his aid and how quickly they did so. And James Bryan of Northwestern and Mary Ann Test of Mendota State Hospital in Wisconsin (1967) set up shop on a Los Angeles thoroughfare to study the role of imitation in altruistic behavior—in this case, helping a stooge change a flat tire. Such real-life experiments are becoming increasingly popular, and they are of potentially great value in helping to span the gulf between studies of social behavior in the laboratory and in real life.

Nevertheless the vast majority of laboratory playwrights continue to stage their performances in the soundproof rooms with the flashing lights and the one-way mirrors, and their stars continue to be unsuspecting—they hope—college students. As ethical criticism intensifies and the credibility gap widens between experimenter and subject, some observers foresee an early end to psychology's theater of the absurd. "It might just die," Milgram said ruefully, "like acupuncture and bloodletting." But others are convinced (and they are probably right) that the battle of wits between experimenter and subject will go on—like bugs and DDT.

REFERENCES

Asch, Solomon E.
   1958   "Effects of group pressure upon the modification and distortion of judgment." Pp. 174–183 in T. M. Newcomb and E. L. Hartley (eds.), Readings in Social Psychology. New York: Holt, Rinehart and Winston.

Baumrind, Diana
   1964   "Some thoughts on ethics of research: after reading Milgram's behavioral study of obedience." American Psychologist 19(6):421–423.

Bryan, James H. and Mary A. Test
   1967   "Models and helping: naturalistic studies in aiding behavior." Journal of Personality and Social Psychology 6(5):400–407.

Freedman, Jonathan L.
   1969   "Role playing: psychology by consensus." Journal of Personality and Social Psychology 13(2):107–114.

Kelman, Herbert C.
   1966   "Deception in social research." Transaction 3(July-August):20–24.

McGuire, William J.
   1967   "Some impending reorientations in social psychology: some thoughts provoked by Kenneth Ring." Journal of Experimental Social Psychology 3(2):124–139.

Milgram, Stanley
   1965   "Some conditions of obedience and disobedience to authority." Pp. 243–262 in Ivan D. Steiner and Martin Fishbein (eds.), Current Studies in Social Psychology. New York: Holt, Rinehart and Winston.

Piliavin, Irving, Judith Rodin, and Jane Piliavin
   1969   "Good samaritanism: an underground phenomenon?" Journal of Personality and Social Psychology 13(4):289–299.

Ring, Kenneth
   1967   "Experimental social psychology: some sober questions about some frivolous values." Journal of Experimental Social Psychology 3(2):113–123.

Walster, Elaine
   1970   "Effects of self-esteem on liking for dates of various social desirabilities." Journal of Experimental Social Psychology 6(5):248–253.

PART TWO

The Structuring of Inquiry

SECTION 2.1

Theory and Research Design

A close relationship exists between theory and research in the social sciences. Theory can be seen as providing a framework within which to do research; theory provides a way to think about and approach a topic. Similarly, research design allows the testing and reformulation of theories. Theory contributes to the cumulativeness of social science, whereas research design provides a strategy for executing the studies suggested by theory. The type of design selected is largely contingent on the nature of the phenomenon to be investigated. In this section we will examine and exemplify some of the characteristics of theory and research design.

THEORY

Unfortunately, the term *theory* has many definitions: It has been used to describe untested ideas ("I can give you my theory of . . . "), the ideas of classical scholars (such as Durkheim and Weber), major schools of thought (such as structural functionalism), and deductive sets of propositions (if A, then B; if B, then C; therefore, if A, then C). Theory generally refers to a summary of knowledge in a subject field, arranged in the form of interrelated statements. Theories provide both explanations and predictions of social phenomena by causally relating one or more concepts to one or more other concepts. For example,

several studies report that status disintegration (persons occupying positions that make conflicting demands and expectations) covaries with suicide rates. It has also been shown that the observed covariation is nonspurious, and one can hardly dispute the argument that status disintegration precedes suicide. The role of theory in this case is to interpret the covariation. An established interpretation is that conflicting demands and expectations lead to emotional stress, which in turn leads to suicide (Nachmias and Nachmias, 1976:9–10).

Hence, the researcher, on the basis of previous research and theory on a topic, formulates the topic in terms of general interrelationships between a given dependent concept and selected independent concepts. Theory thus serves as a cumulative summary of knowledge in an area such that new hypotheses can be derived to test the theory. My introduction to theory is purposively brief given the excellent introduction found in the first reading in this section.

CONCEPTS

A theory is constructed with concepts; the theory structures and provides meaning for the concepts. In the example noted above, status disintegration theory provides a possible explanation for such dysfunctional behavior as suicide.

A concept may be defined as a mental abstraction associated with a term or symbol. The symbol may represent any type of phenomenon, ranging from the very concrete, such as marital status or age, to the very abstract, such as ecosystem or love. Concepts serve to impose order on and to classify social phenomena, thereby affording communication among social science researchers. For example, the concept of androgyny has been developed in recent years to foster research and communication regarding persons exhibiting characteristics traditionally ascribed to both sexes. According to this concept, a person can be both masculine and feminine, both aggressive and gentle, both active and passive, depending on the specific situation. Masculinity and femininity are conceptualized as two separate dimensions rather than as two ends of the same continuum. The development of the concept of androgyny arose in part out of a rejection of the idea that sex-typing is beneficial for the individual and society (see Walum, 1977:100ff). With the development of this new concept and its associated theory, research on sex roles can advance further. Concepts, then, are the elementary building blocks of hypotheses and, indirectly, of theories as well, and they aid the researcher in establishing the generalizations so sought after in social science research.

There are two levels of definition for concepts. One level is the nominal (or conceptual) level, which involves stating in simpler concepts what the concept means. Feminism, for example, may be defined at this level as a belief in the equality of women and men. The second level is the operational level, which consists of an explicit description of the procedures to be followed in measuring a concept. Feminism may be operationally defined with a ten-item scale measuring opinions on equality in various areas and behavioral support for such feminist issues as the Equal Rights Amendment (e.g., signing a petition for the ERA). Both definitions of a concept are relevant for communication and replicability by other researchers. Note in subsequent articles in this volume how authors define their concepts and the implications these definitions have for their research. The next section on measurement will further develop operational definitions for concepts.

HYPOTHESES

Hypotheses simply relate two or more concepts, typically in a causal manner. The relationship is often suggested by theory. For example, in the article on father absence in Section 4.2, Causal Analysis, the Hunts develop hypotheses regarding the effect of father absence on girls on the basis of socialization and sex-role formation theories. Similarly, in Section 3.3, Experiments, Knowles develops some specific testable hypotheses from the general theoretical literature on group boundaries. Hypotheses are tentative testable statements derived from theory. Since theory is more general and cannot be directly tested, hypotheses are employed to indirectly test theory.

Hypotheses may also help suggest theories for further testing, especially if the hypotheses are the product of the researcher's immersion in the data. For example, research examining hypothesized correlates of androgyny may suggest modifications of traditional sex-role socialization theories.

Hypotheses need not be causal, although this characteristic is predominant, given the usually explanatory focus of social science research. Causal hypotheses are either explicitly or implicitly stated in an "if . . ., then . . ." structure. The "if" part of the hypothesis specifies the conditions or the independent variable, whereas the "then" part specifies the consequent or dependent variable. Alternatively, hypotheses may be stated directionally: the higher the level of status disintegration, the higher the suicide rate; or, the older a person becomes, the more conservative he or she becomes.

Hypotheses may also be descriptive, such as those suggesting that sociology majors tend to be other-directed or that the birthrate is decreasing. Both causal and descriptive hypotheses, however, should be clearly linked to theory and contain clearly defined concepts.

RESEARCH DESIGN

The theory and hypotheses must now be tested. To do so requires selecting an appropriate research design. Three basic designs are employed by social scientists: surveys, experiments, and field research. Other designs less frequently used include content analysis, historical research, unobtrusive measures, and ethnomethodology. The particular design selected depends largely on the research problem and the researcher's preferences. A researcher interested in attitude formation, for example, would probably employ the survey design, whereas a researcher interested in conflict-management behaviors would probably employ the experimental design. The survey design is by far the most popular among social scientists, perhaps as a result of the desire for generalizability and ease of data access. It may be that problems selected by social scientists are best analyzed by survey research.

Each of the basic designs is examined in depth in Part 3. Here I only wish to note that each design has its own advantages and disadvantages. The survey design maximizes generalizability, the experimental design maximizes control over the independent variable and the construction of experimental and control groups, and the field research design maximizes the naturalness of the research situation. On the other hand, the survey design lacks control over the relevant variables, the experimental design lacks generalizability, and the field research design lacks control over the research setting. At this point, you may find it useful to reread Wallace's discussion of the famous Durkheim study of suicide (Section 1.1) in light of the points we have just covered concerning theory and research design.

THE READINGS

The readings in this section focus on theory and research design and the interplay between the two. In the first of article Gerald Ferman and Jack Levin consider various definitions and characteristics of social science theory. Note the progression in specificity as they go through their definitions. Note too the distinction between inductive and deductive reasoning as general approaches to building theories. The former involves going from concrete observations to more general conclusions, the latter from more general, abstract principles to more specific and testable hypotheses. The authors' distinction is described as verifying theory (more deductive) or developing theory (more inductive). Their pyramid analogy is useful in the literature on social science theory.

The article by William Whyte on conflict and cooperation illustrates two points. First, the dialogue between theory and research design is cogently presented. Whyte develops in step-by-step format the developmental formulation of his theoretical model. Note also how the development of his theoretical model occurred before, during, and after the research; too often social scientists give the impression that theories are developed only before a study begins.

Second, Whyte's article illustrates how the use of multiple research designs enhances the validity of research findings. Note his conclusion that he would have overlooked certain findings had he employed only one design instead of the two he did employ—survey and field research. Note how the nature of his research topic dictated which questions could best be answered by the survey design and which questions could best be answered by the observation design. Even more important, note how the development of his theoretical model was dependent on the results of *both* designs. If either design had not been used, the theoretical model would not have been as complete.

The last two articles in this section reflect a rather common occurrence in social science research: a dispute over the appropriateness of research design. Such disputes can arise because individual researchers often have their own favorite designs and criticize other researchers whose designs differ from their own. Research on "hot" social issues is also likely to engender criticism of research design, particularly when the results are not consonant with the criticizer's values.

In the first of these Amuzie Chimezie criticizes a study on transracial adoption by Lucille Grow and Deborah Shapiro and very clearly defines his own values on the topic. Focus on his comments on research design when reading the critique. Note particularly the remarks about the lack of a control/comparison group. Grow and Shapiro studied black adoptees in white homes but did not study black adoptees in black homes or black children similar to the adoptees but not adopted. They argued that the former was not necessary since no one questions the preferability of within-race adoption and the latter was not feasible. Note also Chimezie's comments about the selection of variables and the operationalization of these variables (even the definition of blackness was problematic). And note carefully Chimezie's suggested design—does it answer all of his criticisms?

Grow and Shapiro respond to Chimezie's critique in the following article. Note their comment that no control group was necessary given the descriptive emphasis of the study. And note their responses to his comments about the measurement of variables. One wonders if the study would have received such criticism had the topic been less emotional.

No one design is best for all research topics. It is important for you to be aware of the various designs and their characteristics so that you can better assess the congruence between topic and design as well as the congruence between theory and design.

REFERENCES

Nachmias, David and Chava Nachmias
    1976   Research Methods in the Social Sciences. New York: St. Martin's Press.
Walum, Laurel Richardson
    1977   The Dynamics of Sex and Gender: A Sociological Perspective. Chicago: Rand McNally.

WHAT IS THEORY?

Gerald S. Ferman
Jack Levin

Thus far, we have examined the nature of concepts, variables and propositions, the basic elements of theoretical analysis. We now turn our attention to larger questions of *theory:* What is it? What can be done with it? How is it used in the context of social science research?

Like other complex terms, "theory" has been used in several different ways to indicate several different things. Despite this diversity of usages, however, we can identify three widely employed meanings of theory as found in the literature of social science: (1) Theory as Concept, (2) Theory as Conceptual Scheme, and (3) Theory as Consummation of Explanation.

1. Theory as Concept

Theory is used by many to mean the expression of a concept which represents the nature of social or political reality. In this rather vague and general usage, theory is viewed as "philosophizing" about phenomena of interest to the social scientist, regardless of the particular form that it takes. Thus, we find sociologists addressing themselves to reference group "theory" or to role "theory," though these terms can properly be regarded only as concepts—albeit important concepts—around which a sizable body of research has accumulated.

2. Theory as Conceptual Scheme

In a more precise meaning, theory is frequently treated as a set of *somewhat* related concepts which represent the nature of social or political reality. In political science, for example, the display of concepts in Figure 1 is sometimes regarded as a theory of voter decision making or choice.

Figure 1 identifies three concepts and, by means of arrows, indicates that each concept is related to the voter's choice to support one or another of the major political parties. However, this conceptual scheme does not specify *how* each concept is related to voter choice; nor does it specify whether these concepts are related to one another. Instead, it simply indicates that each concept by itself has some influence of an unspecified nature on the individual's voting decision. *Note:* As we shall see below, the scheme in Figure 1 could be given greater explanatory power by clearly specifying the relationships among concepts. For example: The more one identifies with a political party, the greater the probability that one will vote for the candidates of that party.

A second example of "theory as conceptual scheme" can be found in the well-known communication model: "Who says what to whom in which channels with what effect?" (Lasswell, 1960). In this "theory," the important elements of the process of communication are identified but remain unexplained. That is to say, we are left with a set of "empty boxes" to be filled in by the researcher who seeks to understand the nature of communication. For example, the source of a communication (the "who?" box) might be treated as a variable in the prediction that a highly credible source generates better acceptance of a communication message than does a source having low credibility.

3. Theory as Consummation of Explanation

To this point, we have defined "theory" with reference to a set of concepts. Unlike previous conceptions, theory as *Consummation of explanation* consists of a set of interrelated propositions, at least one of which is testable by means of research. Any proposition subjected to empirical test is referred to as a *hypothesis* (Phillips, 1971).

Much of the work of social science research is concerned with testing hypotheses about the na-

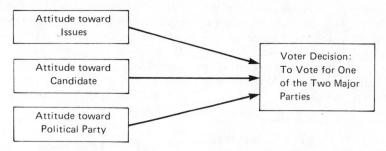

Figure 1 A "theory" of voter decision making

ture of social or political reality as derived from theory. Some hypotheses are supported by the results of investigation; others are disconfirmed by the data and discarded or revised as needed. Illustrative of some commonly tested social science hypotheses are the following: (1) "The greater the level of frustration, the greater the aggression." (2) "Interpersonal attraction is enhanced to the extent that participants are similar with respect to important values or attitudes." (3) "The more credible or trustworthy the communicator is perceived to be, the greater the tendency to accept his communication." (4) "Those individuals who benefit most from a system of social stratification are most likely to accept it." (5) "The greater the perceived opportunity for upward social mobility, the less radical the political attitude." (6) "The greater the sexual freedom, the less prostitution." (7) "The more decentralized the governmental system, the greater the impact of special interests on policy."

Social scientists typically justify their hypotheses in a loosely structured theoretical rationale which takes the form of a few paragraphs to several pages in which the reasons for their hypothesis are given. At least partial justification for a given hypothesis usually can be found in the existing literature of social science, either in earlier theoretical analyses or in previous research. As a result, the theoretical analysis of a problem almost invariably will include some related literature.

To illustrate, let us consider the hypothesis "Parent-child attractiveness is enhanced to the extent that they are similar with respect to important values." The theoretical analysis of the foregoing hypothesis might well include (1) earlier theories in which the more general relationship between value consensus (or attitude similarity) and interpersonal attraction has been discussed, and (2) pre-

vious research in related areas wherein this relationship has already been tested such as mate selection, friendship choice, and ethnic group relations.

GENERATING THEORY

The intellectual processes involved in generating theory as consummation of explanation can be identified as (1) inductive reasoning and (2) deductive reasoning.

1. Inductive Reasoning

Inductive reasoning can be conceived as the process of building up from the concrete to the abstract; that is to say, as moving from the base of a pyramid of specific observations and facts to its pinnacle as represented in abstract concepts and propositions. For instance, a student who wishes to study voting behavior examines the voting data in his community. As a result of these observations, he generates a series of questions for which he produces tentative answers in the form of a few systematically related propositions.

As illustrated in Figure 2, this reasoning might proceed in the following way: "Most people where I live vote Republican. Why is this so? That is, what characteristic of these people influences them to vote Republican?" Answer: "They are relatively affluent." Assuming that affluence affects voting behavior, Proposition 1 (P1) becomes: Affluent people tend to vote Republican. "Why?" Answer: "Because affluence is a type of reward in the context of industrialized socio-political systems. But why would "rewarded" people vote Republican?" Answer: "Because the Republican party more than the Democratic party stands for the status quo." Thus, a more general proposition in terms of which P1 can be incorporated and explained: Individuals rewarded in industrialized socio-political systems tend to support the political group that represents the status quo (P2). "Why is this so?" Answer: "This is a case of self-interest being expressed." If so, an even more general proposition can be derived (P3): In regard to political preference, individuals tend to act in terms of their self-interest.

2. Deductive Reasoning

As we have seen, the student who uses inductive reasoning proceeds by a continuous chain of questions and answers, beginning at the base of a pyramid consisting of concrete observation and ending with an abstract proposition in which less abstract propositions can be explained. By contrast, *deductive reasoning* starts at the abstract pinnacle of the pyramid in Figure 2 and systematically proceeds to its concrete base. In this process, the student initially identifies a general interest or problem, focusing on broad concepts and assumptions. He then moves from this abstract level to derive a set of increasingly more concrete propositions, culminating in at least a single testable hypothesis. Deductions:

To illustrate: A student might ask, "Is man's political behavior motivated by self-interest?" Answer: "To a large extent, yes. Assuming that man is so motivated (P3), how will he behave when making a voting decision?" Middle-level proposition

(P2): Individuals rewarded in industrialized socio-political systems tend to support the political group that represents the status quo. Observations: (1) The Republican party more than the Democratic party stands for the status quo. (2) Affluence is a type of reward in the context of industrialized socio-political systems. Thus, (P1) Affluent people tend to vote Republican.

THE STRUCTURE OF THEORY

Social scientists do not always carry out the intellectual processes of induction and deduction to their logical conclusion; nor do they frequently make explicit reference to the nature of the links between their propositions and underlying assumptions. As noted earlier in this chapter, social scientific theories generally take the form of loosely structured rationales in which the reasons for hypotheses are stated, though not as a series of ordered propositions.

Before moving on, however, we should at this juncture examine some of the more systematic forms which theory is capable of taking—forms which are becoming more widely employed by social scientists concerned with increasing their understanding of social or political behavior. The theoretical structures discussed here are (1) the postulate form and (2) the chain form.

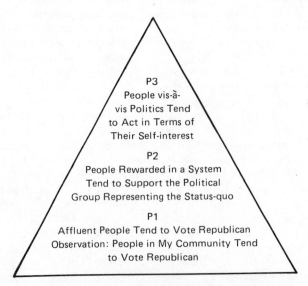

Figure 2   A "pyramid" of propositions regarding voting behavior

1. The Postulate Form

In the *postulate form* of theory, the investigator assumes or postulates at least one abstract proposition from which more concrete propositions can be derived and tested. By application of logic and appropriate definitions, if the postulate is true, then propositions A, B, C, and D should be true. Moreover, if proposition D is tested and confirmed, the entire theoretical structure including the postulate and untested propositions can be regarded as being more tenable. Consider the following example of the postulate theoretical structure:

Postulate: Individuals who are rewarded in a system tend to support that system; whereas individuals who go unrewarded tend to reject it.

Proposition A: The more discrimination by a system against a group, the greater the likelihood that members of that group will resort to rebellion (e.g., riots).

Proposition B: The more a nation is condemned by an international system (e.g., the United Nations), the stronger the probability that it will reject that system.

Proposition C: The more a worker is paid by an organization, the more he tends to identify with that organization.

Proposition D: The greater the affluence, the stronger the tendency to vote.

Proposition E: The more respect and positive recognition an individual receives from his family, the stronger his identification with that family.

Another example of the postulate form of theory can be found in the well known study of suicide by Durkheim (1951). A basic postulate in Durkheim's theory is that "the greater the integration of a group, the less suicide within that group." From this assumption, it is possible to derive numerous testable hypotheses which predict for example that suicide is more likely (A) among Protestants than among Catholics, (B) among the single, divorced, and widowed than among the married, (C) among children of broken homes than among children of stable homes, and (D) among city dwellers than among rural dwellers.

2. The Chain Form

As a chain connects its component parts, so a theory in *chain form* links a set of propositions by means of shared variables. From this structure, it is

possible to derive an additional but limited set of propositions, any of which might be tested by the researcher. Confirmation of a derived proposition has implications for the entire theory including other derived as well as original propositions.

To illustrate this form of theory, consider the following "chain" of propositions having to do with the so-called "Democratic dilemma of developing countries":

A. The more a political system stresses egalitarianism, the more civic participation is valued.
B. The more civic participation is valued, the greater the civic participation.
C. The greater the civic participation, the greater the demand for short-term rewards.
D. The greater the demand for short-term rewards, the greater the allocation of system resources for consumer items.
E. The greater the allocation for consumer items, the less ability for long-range economic development.

Deductions:

A. The more a political system stresses egalitarianism, (1) the greater the civic participation, (2) the greater the demand for short-term rewards, (3) the greater the allocation of system resources for consumer items, (4) the less ability for long-range economic development.
B. The more civic participation is valued, (1) the greater the demand for short-term rewards, (2) the greater the allocation of system resources for consumer items, (3) the less ability for long-range economic development.
C. The greater the civic participation, (1) the greater the allocation of system resources for consumer items, (2) the less ability for long-range economic development.
D. The greater the demand for short-term rewards, (1) the less ability for long-range economic development.

As shown in the foregoing example, five interrelated propositions produce 10 testable deductions. By tradition, the derived proposition which relates the first and last variables of the original set of propositions (in this case, Deduction A4) is tested.

It should be noted that other variations of this basic chain form of theory are possible. For instance, the theoretical structure known as a *model* is held together by a common factor, the dependent variable. However, the independent variables of a model may be separately related to its dependent variable by means of chain-like substructures which specify the linkages in the casual relationship. Detailed discussion of theoretical models lies beyond the scope of this book.

EVALUATION OF THEORY

How can a theory be evaluated? Having conducted a theoretical analysis, on what basis do we decide whether it is worthwhile or ineffective? The following general criteria are frequently applied for this purpose: (1) explanation (and prediction), (2) scope, (3) parsimony, and (4) fruitfulness.

1. Explanation (and Prediction)

An effective theory is capable of *explaining* social or political phenomena. In connection with social science research, explanation has two important meanings. In the first place, to explain is to increase our *understanding* of the causes of a phenomenon under investigation. This means that the answers generated by a theory are tentatively accepted based upon the rationale of the theory by a community of social scientists who seek to better understand a phenomenon. In its second meaning, explanation refers to the *empirical test* of a hypothesis. If a hypothesis is supported by the results of research, the underlying theory is said to explain some part of the data. If, however, a hypothesis is disconfirmed, then the theory is not regarded as an effective explanation.

The ability of the social scientist to accurately predict the occurrence of an event is related to this second meaning of explanation—that meaning which depends upon the empirical test of a hypothesis. For instance, if a theory indicates that frustration produces increased aggression, it should be possible to predict the level of aggression from observing the level of frustration (assuming, of course, that other relevant variables have been controlled). Moreover, in the context of a laboratory experiment, it should be possible to *create* aggressive behavior by manipulating the level of frustration experienced by the subjects. In this way, we explain the occurrence of aggression.

It should be noted that the explanatory power of social scientific theories is relatively weak especially in terms of prediction. At best, present-day theories account for slight differences in behavior. As social scientific explanations develop, however, we should be able to increase the accuracy of our predictions as well.

2. Scope

What happens when competing theories predict the same outcome? In such cases, *scope* or level of generality becomes an important criterion for choosing between them. It was earlier noted that abstract concepts tend to be more useful than their concrete counterparts. In a similar way, we can now suggest that theories which explain a larger number of phenomena—that have greater scope—are more effective theories. The reason is clear: the researcher who uses an abstract theory gets more for his effort, in so far as he explains a wider range of phenomena. It is something like the fisherman who uses a fishing rod to catch fish, when he could have used a large net. The result is greater output for the same expenditure of effort.

3. Parsimony

Any theory may be evaluated with respect to *parsimony*. A parsimonious theory is a simple theory; it employs a small number of assumptions and propositions in order to explain a given phenomenon. Holding other considerations constant, the simpler theory is always preferable to the more complex theory. For example, a theory in which juvenile delinquency is explained with three independent variables may be superior to a theory which explains juvenile delinquency with ten independent variables.

4. Fruitfulness

To the list of criteria for judging the effectiveness of theory including explanation, scope, and parsimony, we must add a final item. This criterion, *fruitfulness*, refers to the capacity of theory to generate new inquiries and discoveries.

Suppose for example, that our efforts to explain the rules of international law lead . . . to the theory that, by and large, the influence of a state . . . rests on two factors: (1) its reputed or actual ability to impose its desires through coercive measures, and (2) its reputed or actual willingness to employ such measures. In other words, international law is a function of the relative power and interest of the states concerned. The very enunciation of the theory leads to questions concerning circumstances in which it does or does not hold true ... [and] even more, suggests questions and hypotheses concerning the factors shaping the development of law within countries. If international law reflects a combination of power and interest, what of assumption that domestic law reflects the common good or the public interest or justice? ... that government ... constitutes a sort of impartial arbiter serving to "adjust" conflicting claims ... (Van Dyke, 1960, pp. 107–108).

One of the more fruitful theories in social science can be found in Festinger's (1957) Theory of Cognitive Dissonance, according to which making a decision per se creates dissonance ("nonfitting relations" among cognitions) as well as the pressure to reduce dissonance. Despite its essentially social psychological nature, this theory has been applied to explain such diverse phenomena as race relations in the United States, the onset of rumors in the aftermath of a disaster, and reactions to disconfirmation among true believers, to mention just a few. The many hundreds of studies which have been devised in order to test or examine the implications of the theory of Cognitive Dissonance attest to its unusual fruitfulness. In such research, a variety of relevant questions and answers beyond the original focus of the theory have been generated, the ultimate result being greater output for an initial research investment.

REFERENCES

Durkheim, Emile
　　1951　Suicide. New York: Free Press.
Festinger, Leon
　　1957　A Theory of Cognitive Dissonance. Stanford: Stanford University Press.
Lasswell, Harold D.
　　1960　"The structure and function of communication in society." Pp. 117–130 in W. Schramm (ed.), Mass Communication. Urbana: University of Illinois Press.
Phillips, Bernard S.
　　1971　Social Research: Strategy and Tactics. New York: Macmillan.
Van Dyke, V.
　　1960　Political Science: A Philosophical Approach. Stanford: Stanford University Press.

RESEARCH METHODS FOR THE STUDY OF CONFLICT AND COOPERATION

William F. Whyte

This paper is a response to my frustration with the standard ways of categorizing research methods in sociology. Even the format of the 1975 [ASA] program aggravated my frustration. We had one series of meetings entitled "Quantitative Methods" and another series entitled "Qualitative Methods." What is one to do if he/she feels that this dichotomy represents an extremely counterproductive misrepresentation of both existing realities and potentialities of development of more effective methodologies in the future?

Revised version of a paper presented at the 1975 ASA meeting.

Things have not changed much in sociology since I last appeared on an ASA program five years ago. At that time I participated in a panel discussion focusing on observational and interviewing methods in field research. At the end of that session, a graduate student came up to me, shook my hand and said, "I want you to know that your talk has been an inspiration to me." When I asked what had been so inspiring, he replied, "Your talk will be most helpful to me in a campaign I am organizing to eliminate the required course in statistics from our sociology curriculum."

I was dumbfounded. I asked myself what I could have said that might be misinterpreted as a

---

From *The American Sociologist,* November 1976. Reprinted by permission. References updated.

condemnation of statistics since I could remember making no reference to that subject. If I mentioned the survey or questionnaire method at all, it was simply a passing reference to my belief that it is not an all-purpose method. Apparently, since I had been advocating interviewing and observational methods, it must have followed that I was against the survey and therefore against statistics.

Later in the same meeting, I encountered the opposite point of view. Peter Rossi was conducting a didactic session on survey research methods. He was proceeding with the systematic and competent presentation we would expect of him when, in response to a question from the floor, he said, "It is very difficult to bring the survey method to bear upon the problem you raise."

His questioner asked further, "Then why not use another method?"

Rossi replied, "What other method is there?"

Of course, this remark was meant as a joke; indeed we all did laugh. On the other hand, the remark was simply a caricature of a widely held view in sociology these days. And perhaps the remark did not seem so funny to the questioner, for, a few minutes later, while Rossi was still continuing with his didacting, she got up and left the session.

As I reflect upon these experiences, I recognize that they represent points of view that have persisted in sociology for a long time. Almost a quarter of a century ago, George Strauss (1952) wrote a paper on the methods he had used to study a union local. In addition to interviewing many of the members, he had attended the biweekly local meetings over a period of a year. After he had got acquainted with many of the members of the local, he found that he could identify everyone who attended meetings. For each meeting he drew a map of the hall and recorded where each member sat. He also observed that, while most members remained in their chairs throughout the meeting, several members from time to time would get up and move about, whispering to some of the sedentary members. Of course, these turned out to be influential members: leaders of the opposition, or key activists supporting the administration, whose officers sat on the platform.

Strauss also noted that, with hardly any exceptions, supporters of the administration sat on one side of the hall and opponents sat on the other side. When he observed, over a period of months, a

thinning out of the ranks on the administration side and an increase in the number on the other side, he made the prediction, later confirmed, that the next election would bring about a change in the local union administration.

Strauss submitted the article to a major journal and it was accepted for publication. But it was no doubt a difficult decision, for the editor felt called upon to write Strauss at length to point out that, while the article was certainly of interest, Strauss had been guilty of using primitive research methods. The editor went on to explain what a modern, scientific researcher would do: he would carry out one or more surveys, in which he would ask the members whom they would like to sit next to in union meetings, and so on.

When I saw this letter, I felt as if I had been led by Alice through the looking glass. I had been assuming that the purpose of the methods we use in sociology is to make possible systematic descriptions and analyses of human behavior. Here was a man who presented solid, systematic, and quantitative data directly upon behavior, yet he was informed that he was not really being scientific because he had not used a survey.

The problem is that in sociology "quantitative methods" have become code words for survey research—as if only the survey could yield legitimate quantitative data.

VILLAGE STUDIES IN PERU

In some of the research with which I have been associated in Peru, students, through interviewing, observation, and examination of records, gathered the following types of data on two villages in the same culture area: amount of land owned by each family, number of cows and sheep per family, income from crops sold, attendance at monthly community meetings, and attendance at *faenas* (community work bees for which each family is required to provide a male member). They also had exact information on the fines levied on nonattendants and the percentage of fines collected in each of the two villages.

Now the laymen would assume that these students were using quantitative research methods, but the well-socialized sociologist would know that this was not the case, for these were students of anthropology and they did not use the questionnaire. Since the survey is the only quantitative method, our students should have gone around with a questionnaire and asked people point blank how much land they owned, how many animals, how often they attended community meetings and *faenas*, and how often they paid the fines levied on them for nonattendance. We did not use a questionnaire for these specific questions because we felt we could not trust the answers we would get, and furthermore we felt that point-blank questioning by our students in these sensitive areas might result in our getting thrown out of the community.

Not to mislead my readers in concluding that I am engaging in a polemic against the questionnaire, I must add that, although I had a rather late start in survey research, I can now claim to have accumulated more IBM cards and tapes from surveys in which I participated than the average professor of sociology. I am not against the survey method; I am only against the prevailing view in sociology that the survey is the only really scientific method. However, I am not simply making a plea for a live-and-let-live attitude in the choice of research methods; I am claiming that the value of the survey can be greatly enhanced, in certain types of studies, when it is not used alone but in combination with the intensive interviewing and observational methods which are more characteristic of social anthropology.

I shall support this statement by drawing upon recent work, which enabled us to make a theoretical advance, which would have been impossible without the use of both of these methods. The illustrations came out of a ten-year collaborative research program between Cornell University and the Institute for Peruvian Studies, with Jose Matos Mar being co-director for the Institute and Lawrence K. Williams and me being co-directors for Cornell. (While we both have worked with the range of methods utilized in our program, I am especially indebted to Professor Williams for most of what I have learned regarding survey research and data analysis.)

We were engaged in a number of other studies in Peru, ranging from industry to peasant movements, but we concentrated particularly upon research on development and change in rural communities. Along with interview/observational research we carried out surveys of 23 communities and three haciendas in 1964 and, in 1969, resurveyed twelve of these same communities (along with the three original haciendas and three addi-

tional ones). In this paper, I shall utilize data only from the twelve communities for which we have survey data from 1964 and 1969. While I could give numerous examples here showing how our description and analysis of the communities were enhanced by the combined use of these two methods, it seems more important to concentrate on how utilization of this combination enabled us to push ahead in theorizing regarding the nature of peasant communities. For this purpose, I shall go through the steps I myself followed in this analysis as well as I can reconstruct them.

THE RESEARCH PROBLEM

We began with a review of the anthropological literature regarding the nature of the peasant community, focusing particularly on the controversy between (1) Robert Redfield (1930), supported by Julian Pitt-Rivers (1960–61), and (2) Oscar Lewis (1951) and George Foster (1960–61). Redfield had presented a rather idyllic picture of the peasant community as a *gemeinschaft* type of organization in which people were bound together by common understandings and mutual goodwill. Studying the same community some years later, Lewis found it riven by strife, envy, and mutual suspicion. He went on to assume that peasant villages tended to be that way. This point of view received strong support some years later when Foster (1966) published his influential article "Peasant Society and the Image of the Limited Good." He argued that peasants tend to regard all the good things in life, from land to health, as existing in short supply so that one family's gain would be another family's loss. With this world view goes a high degree of envy and interpersonal mistrust.

Our own studies tended to support the Lewis-Foster view in general, for we found in our surveys a high degree of mistrust and envy, along with informant reports on friction and conflict. At the same time, we noted that there were substantial variations among our communities in the level of trust and envy, with several communities evidencing a high degree of trust and a low level of concern with envy.

When we published our first report on this research program (Matos Mar *et al.*, 1969), we had not gone beyond the variations we found among peasant communities.

INTEGRATING METHODS
FOR PROGRESS IN THEORY

The next steps forward did not come until 1973, but then one particular "discovery" triggered the momentum and led us rapidly onward, as indicated in the following sequence:

1. I was rereading an anthropology student's report on the village of Mito in preparation for writing a chapter about Mito and two other communities in the Mantaro Valley of the central highlands of Peru when I found my attention arrested by a point I had previously overlooked. The student described Mito as being low in both conflict and cooperation. That struck me as strange.

2. I asked myself: could it really be so? To check on this interpretation, I studied a set of marginals for 1969 to examine responses to two questions: "When it comes to cooperating on some project for the community, how well do the people cooperate? Would you say the cooperation is good, fair, or poor?" and "Is there much conflict or division among the people of this village?" (much, some, little, or none). To my mounting excitement, I found indeed that respondents in Mito perceived the level of both cooperation and conflict lower than did respondents in the two other Mantaro Valley communities.

3. Now I asked myself: why was I surprised in finding a community that apparently was really low in both conflict and cooperation? I suddenly realized that, while Lewis and Foster differed sharply with Redfield on the amount of conflict and cooperation in the peasant community, all of these men were making the same implicit assumption that I had previously made myself. They were thinking in terms of what I now call a single continuum model with cooperation at one end and conflict at the other. These anthropologists were debating whether the typical peasant community should be placed toward the conflict or the cooperation ends of the continuum, but they were all implicitly assuming that if the community was high in conflict, it must be low in cooperation, and vice versa.

4. When I had questioned the validity of the single continuum model, alternative models came to my mind almost immediately. The simplest model, of course, is that shown in Figure 1, where we set up two parallel continua, one for cooperation and one for conflict, with high and low being indicated at opposite ends of each continuum. In other words, one assumed that the two variables may be independent of each other so that location of a community in terms of one variable will not predict its location for the other. When I had drawn the parallel lines, in accordance with these assumptions, it then became obvious that if I placed the two lines perpendicular to each other, it would be possible to place each community in both conflict and cooperation with a single point, as indicated also in Figure 1.

5. The next step was to test this new model against the empirical data. I noted that the high-low and low-high communities in conflict and cooperation would fit either the single continuum or the two continua or four-box model. I had found, in the case of Mito, a low-low community, which did not fit the single continuum model but did fit the evolving new model. Would I also find high-high cases? The single continuum model implicitly assumed a high negative correlation in respondents' perceptions of the level of cooperation and conflict in the community. The two continua or four-box model assumed little if any correlation between perceptions on conflict and cooperation. What correlations would we in fact find? And so far the theoretical reformulation was based only upon examination of the 1969 data. Would the same pattern emerge in an analysis of the 1964 data? In other words, would this evolving theoretical framework hold for both years, thus providing a stable data base for theorizing? With the collaboration of Lawrence K. Williams and Larry French, I found the two continua or four-box model supported at every point. There were indeed two communities falling in the high-high box in 1969 and one community in that box in 1964, with another just barely outside it. The correlation between the perceived cooperation and perceived conflict items were $-.08$ and $+.06$ in 1964 and 1969 respectively—just about as close to zero correlation as one can get without cooking the data. As we located the communities in our four-box framework for both years and checked these conflict-cooperation correlations for both years, we found the stable pattern that indicated we were on firm ground with our theorizing.

In drawing the diagram shown in Figure 2, we first noted the mean value of the responses for each of the two items for both years. To avoid giving extra weight to the larger communities, where our sample sizes were larger, to calculate the mean

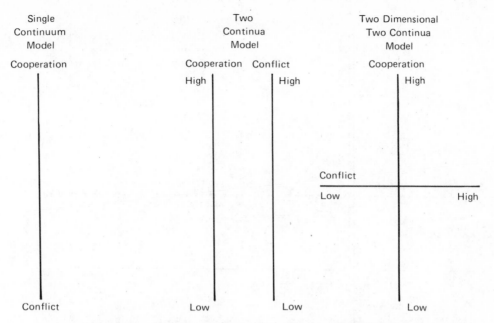

Figure 1 Theoretical models for conflict and cooperation
in peasant communities (reprinted from *American Ethnologist* 2:2 [May 1975]:376)

score of the total of the twelve communities together, we simply added the means for each community and divided the total by 12. In Figure 2, the solid lines indicate the mean scores of the 12 villages taken together for cooperation and conflict and also the placement of each village for 1969. The mean scores of the 12 villages together for 1964 are shown in the dotted lines. To avoid cluttering up the diagram, we have shown in dotted lines the 1964 placement of only those villages which shifted from one box to another in this five-year period. The mean scores for each village for both years, along with other statistical data, are reported in detail in another publication (Whyte: 1975).

6. While it is gratifying to find a consistent pattern in the survey responses, it would be more satisfying if we could state, at least roughly, what this pattern seems to mean. I went on to ask myself what the communities that fell within a given box have in common and how they differ from those that fell into other boxes. Here I had to rely primarily upon the reports of the anthropological studies. As I pondered these reports, it seemed to me that a rather consistent pattern did emerge. The villages in the low-conflict–high-cooperation box

seemed to be highly cohesive units, moving ahead on community projects on which there was general agreement regarding the equitable sharing of costs and benefits. The high-high communities appeared to be those characterized by factional strife and widespread complaints about the equity of distribution of costs and benefits of community projects but where nevertheless some projects were moving forward. The high-conflict–low-cooperation communities appeared to be those where the divisions were too sharp to permit much progress and yet the factional leaders were still struggling. The low-low communities seemed to be those which were going nowhere in terms of common village projects and where potential leaders had given up the struggle.

7. Next I shifted my attention from the grouping of communities in the four boxes to the shifting of communities from one box to another. In Figure 2, we see that five out of twelve had indeed made such a shift. Four had moved from a high-conflict–low-cooperation box over to the low-low box, which seemed, on the face of it, a natural progression. We might assume that in a community sharply divided within, but with neither faction making progress in realizing its objectives, the

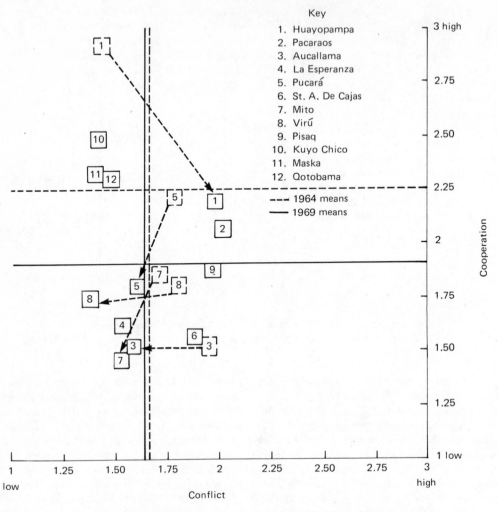

Key
1. Huayopampa
2. Pacaraos
3. Aucallama
4. La Esperanza
5. Pucará
6. St. A. De Cajas
7. Mito
8. Virú
9. Pisaq
10. Kuyo Chico
11. Maska
12. Qotobama

--- 1964 means
— 1969 means

Figure 2   Perceived cooperation and conflict, 1964
and 1969 (reprinted from *American Ethnologist* 2:2 [May 1975]:377)

community might well shift over to low-low, as the factional leaders gave up the struggle.

The most striking and interesting change was evidenced by Huayopampa, which had not only been in the high-cooperation–low-conflict box for 1964 but had shown a much higher level of perceived cooperation than any other community. By 1969, Huayopampa had dropped sharply in perceived cooperation (though still remaining above the mean of 1969 for that variable) and had shifted over so as to manifest the second highest level of conflict among the twelve villages. In late 1969, in comparing the marginals for Huayopampa be-

tween 1964 and 1969, I had noted a number of rather marked changes including the drop in perceived cooperation and the increase in perceived conflict. At the time, I found these changes interesting, but not interesting enough to compel me to drop other plans to give sole attention to Huayopampa. Now, when I had before me the pattern of placement of all of these communities in the four-box framework, I saw clearly the strikingly different movement of Huayopampa, compared to the other communities. That demanded an explanation. Explanation required not only re-examining our field data in anthropological reports of studies carried out as late as 1967, but it also required a new (although brief) field trip to Huayopampa by one of our research groups.[1]

8.   Next I reviewed our studies that focused on issues and lines of social cleavage in our communities. In high cooperation situations we may think (in an oversimplified way) of the whole community moving together, but in cases of conflict it is clear that the community is not fighting against itself. There must be some lines of cleavage dividing the community into two or more factions. I did find, on reviewing these cases, examples of the prevalent source of conflict among Marxist theorists: differences in wealth and social class; but we also found other communities where cleavages could not be explained along these lines at all. As laid out elsewhere (Whyte: 1975), we found cases where conflict fell along the lines of age-grading or generational divisions; we noticed differences in economic and social-cultural activities, neighborhood divisions, religion and religious organizations, and political party membership. Thus I feel that while the measurement of perceived conflict has been essential to our theorizing, that is only a beginning of exploration of the nature of conflict within communities.

9.   Because our analysis and theory have moved well beyond the point reached at the time the data were gathered, we now see serious deficiencies in our research. Although I do not expect ever again to become involved in such an extensive research program, it may be useful to others contemplating community studies to review the deficiencies we ourselves recognize, so that they may go beyond us in both methodology and theory.

The most obvious deficiency is that our whole argument rests upon just two survey items, one for conflict and one for cooperation. Of course, any future researcher focusing upon conflict and cooperation at the community level would use more than a single survey item to assess community perceptions regarding each of the two variables. Furthermore, it is not good enough to focus simply at the community level. Cooperation at that level is built upon smaller groups of people who somehow manage to work together, and we need to study the structure of those groups and their relations to the larger whole. Regarding conflict, for each community we need to establish the lines of social cleavage, along with the issues that tend to focus the conflict. Future researchers can certainly devise

good survey items to enable us to determine the quality of relations across the categories of people listed earlier (old versus young, rich versus poor, and so on). And we can put more substance on the nature of these cleavages as we observe and interview in the community.

ON THE NEED FOR METHODOLOGICAL INTEGRATION

However important this reformulation of conflict and cooperation in communities will turn out to be in the perspective of future research, I would argue that the researcher who remains within the single continuum model of conflict-cooperation is bound to confuse himself-herself and anyone who listens to him/her. While the two-dimensional or four-box model will undoubtedly appear crude in the future, I hope I have gone far enough to show the possibilities for methodological and theoretical advances that are opened up by this theoretical reformulation.

Could this reformulation have occurred without the combined use of the two methods? If we had depended upon anthropological studies alone, this idea surely would not have occurred to me. When we have in the literature cases of drastically different interpretations of the same peasant community given by well-known anthropologists, it seems unlikely that I would trust the interpretation of a young student who reported Mito as being low in both conflict and cooperation. Given the past record by the experts, it would have been much easier to assume that the student was simply mistaken. I began to move beyond the old single continuum model—only when it was possible to verify the anthropological report with survey data.

Could the theoretical reformulation have arisen out of survey analysis alone? That is conceivable because the reformulation builds primarily upon the survey data, but such a theoretical advance with survey data alone seems to me highly unlikely. In the first place, it would be folly to base what I claim to be a major theoretical reformulation simply upon two survey items. I have been emboldened to present this reformulation because the pattern of responses to these two survey items is strongly supported by reports from intensive anthropological studies. Furthermore, even had I been able to lay out the pattern of survey responses, as shown in the four-box model, I would not have known what to make of it. I could only have reported that I had found an interesting statistical pattern, but, without the data from the anthropological field studies, I would have been at a loss for explanations of the differences in social structure and social processes that underlay the statistical pattern.

Before concluding, let me refer back once more to the community where we started: Mito. Even the combination of survey data and anthropological field studies was not enough to explain for us how Mito came to be so different from the other two communities we studied in the Mantaro Valley. It was only when Giorgio Alberti and his associates dug into the history of these three communities that it became apparent why the Mito that we studied was such a stagnant community. But the use of history makes up another story well beyond the bounds of this paper. (See Alberti: 1974, and Whyte and Alberti: 1976.)

CONCLUSION

This paper is *not* about Peru. Readers who have questions regarding the Peruvian communities which we studied should look elsewhere for possible answers (Alberti, 1974; Matos Mar *et al.*, 1969; Whyte, 1975). This paper is about the gains to be achieved, both in substantive findings and in theory building, through combining research methods that are often thought to be in competition with each other.

One critic sees this paper as suggesting that "the relationship of ethnographic observation to survey research is linking theory generation to theory testing. The thought process described starts with the ethnography as a source of ideas and then tests them against survey data."

In other words, research is a two-step process: the researcher begins with "soft" methods to develop ideas, and then moves on to the "hard" science methods of testing those ideas. After that, he/she starts over, with another project, and goes through the same old one-two.

That is the conventional wisdom in sociology—and it is dead wrong. It distorts reality and understates the value of *both* research methods.

While I did indeed get the germ of a theoretical idea from reading the anthropological report on Mito, it was only when I checked the marginals for the surveys on the three Mantaro Valley communities that I realized I might have an idea worth developing as well as testing. Indeed, while the 1969 survey data provided a replication of the 1964 statistical pattern of conflict-cooperation, and thus a powerful scientific test of our theoretical reformulation, it is important to note that the re-survey also served to focus our attention upon communities that had changed markedly in perceived conflict-cooperation. Finding that the shift for Huayopampa was unique both in direction and magnitude led us back to that community for further anthropological field work.

We need also to question the common belief that verification is only possible through surveys. In the early stages of their field projects, researchers got the impression that the *junta comunal* (local government) in Pacaraos was weak and ineffective and that the *junta comunal* in Huayopampa was powerful and effective. Our 1964 survey included the following item: "To solve the problems of this community, how much power do you think the *junta comunal* has?" We found the alternative, "all the power necessary," chosen by 90% of the respondents in Huayopampa, and by 23% in Pacaraos.

The enormous difference in marginals is one verification of the field workers' impressions, but it is not the only possible verification. Our anthropological field worker compiled records of the attendance at obligatory monthly community meetings and *faenas* and found large and consistent differences in favor of Huayopampa. Furthermore, we found that for fines levied for failure to comply with community obligations, Huayopampa collected 100% and Pacaraos fell below 30%.

We must also distinguish between verification and explanation. The survey tells us that the differences in perceptions of *junta comunal* power are statistically significant far beyond the .01 level, but the survey alone does not tell us what events and social processes have led people in these two communities to view their local governments in such drastically different ways. If we are really interested in discovering and analyzing the behavior and social processes underlying the attitudes and perceptions which we measure with surveys, then we must rely upon the field methods of interviewing and observation.

This conclusion requires us to abandon exclusive use of surveys and also the rigid two-step progression from "soft" to "hard" science. My strategy calls for a weaving back and forth among methods through the various stages of research, from design to field execution to data analysis.

Finally, it is counterproductive to file methods and theory in separate mental compartments. I have sought to demonstrate that the reformulation of theory presented in this paper would have been impossible without the particular combination of research methods utilized in our program.

NOTE

[1]While what happened to Huayopampa is beyond the scope of this presentation, readers interested in the point will find some discussion of this case in a recent paper (Whyte, 1975).

REFERENCES

Alberti, Giorgio
    1974   Poder y Conflicto Social en el Valle del Mantaro. Lima: Instituto de Estudios Peruanos.
Foster, George
    1960–1961   "Interpersonal relations in peasant society." Human Organization 19:174–178.
    1966   "Peasant society and the image of the limited good." American Anthropologist 67:293–315.
Lewis, Oscar
    1951   Life in a Mexican Village: Tepoztlán Restudied. Urbana: University of Illinois Press.
Matos Mar, Jose, William F. Whyte, Julio Cotler, et al.
    1969   Dominacion y Cambios en el Peru Rural. Lima: Instituto de Estudios Peruanos.
Pitt-Rivers, Julian
    1960–1961   "Comment on Foster: interpersonal relations in peasant society." Human Organization 19:180–183.
Redfield, Robert
    1930   Tepoztlán: A Mexican Village. Chicago: University of Chicago Press.
Strauss, George
    1952   "Direct observation as a source of quasi-sociometric information." Sociometry XV (February-May):141–145.
Whyte, William F.
    1975   "Conflict and cooperation in Andean communities." American Ethnologist 2 (May):373–392.
Whyte, William F. and Giorgio Alberti
    1976   Power, Politics, and Progress: Social Change in Rural Peru. New York: Elsevier.

BOLD BUT IRRELEVANT:
GROW AND SHAPIRO ON TRANSRACIAL ADOPTION

Amuzie Chimezie

As a way of meeting the needs of black children waiting for adoption, transracial adoption has been objected to by some individuals and groups, most black [11; 1:100–105; 7:156–164]. The basis of this objection is the belief that, given the condition of blacks and the strained relation between blacks and whites in this society, a white home is inappropriate for rearing a black child and detrimental to the development of certain indispensable characteristics.

Such characteristics include ethnic awareness, identification with "blackness," and possession of survival strategies in a racially hostile environment. Chestang expressed concern over the prob-

From *Child Welfare*, Vol. LVI, No. 2 (February 1977), pp. 75–86. Reprinted by permission of the Child Welfare League of America and the author.

ability of the transracially adopted black child's growing up without these characteristics when he asked:

Can white parents equip a black child for the inevitable assaults on his personality from a society that considers his color to be enough reason to reject him? Can they learn to do this without having internalized the duality of character so necessary for survival? How can the black child learn the necessary maneuvering, seduction, self-enhancement through redefinition, and many other tactics taught by black parents, by word and deed, directly and indirectly? [1:100–105]

Many of these characteristics are generally subsumed under the term "identity."

What happened in the history of black Americans and what happens in the socialization of children can help in the understanding and appreciation of the fear that black children reared in white homes will not develop appropriate and healthy characteristics in terms of relating to themselves and other blacks. Hare points out the difficulty that many "high-yellow" blacks (mulattoes) had in relating to other blacks [6:9–14]. Furthermore, it is a fact that children acquire most of the psychological and social characteristics of the families and communities in which they are being reared. It is therefore possible that black children reared in white families and communities will develop anti-black psychological and social characteristics. One reaction to the issue was an insistence upon current "hard data" [2:369–371; 10:109; 12:109–110]. Although the demand for current empirical data was initiated to counter the opposition to transracial adoption, such data are also necessary to justify the practice of transracial adoption.

This was the state of the controversy when Dr. Lucille J. Grow and Dr. Deborah Shapiro launched their study of transracial adoption, *Black Children— White Parents: A Study of Transracial Adoption* [5]. Readers were given the impression that it would provide the needed data to settle the controversy [2:369–371]. The aim of this paper is to look critically at the Grow-Shapiro study to see whether it has provided the relevant "hard data" that could validly be used to make a responsible decision on the practice of having black children adopted transracially. The critical-evaluative comments that follow are based on the assumptions that readers expected the study to provide relevant data; that

the authors were aware of the fears and hypotheses of the objectors to transracial adoption; that they set out on the study knowing what the arguments on both sides of the "debate" were; and that the crucial questions to be answered revolved around identity in all its dimensions [5:ii–iii].

THE GROW-SHAPIRO STUDY
The Subjects

Roughly 125 adopted children (subjects) were studied. "At least 17% of the study children were light enough to pass (as white) and still others were not conspicuous in their communities" [5:194]. Elsewhere, the authors state that according to the parents, it was only in 55% of the cases that the child's being black was obvious to others [5:28]. This means that 45% of the subjects were really white. Though probably genotypically partly black, such children were so phenotypically white that most of the data based on their responses and teacher and parental evaluations of them must have confounded the results. Since they were not different from whites in color and other physical features, they must have perceived themselves and been treated by others as white. How one is treated is a factor in one's behavior and attitude.

In one instance, the authors realized the seriousness of the problem of phenotypical whiteness. "An analysis (of the data on the frequency of social cruelty against the children) was done in which the white-appearing children were omitted from consideration [5:194]." In most of the analyses of other variables, however, the "white-appearing" children (with no black features whatsoever) were regarded as black children. This was a serious fault. No such children should be included in a study of the effects of transracial adoption on black children.

The Design

No control groups were used in the study. The subjects were merely described on the basis of their scores on the California Test of Personality and the Missouri Children's Behavior Checklist. Other descriptions of the subjects were based on subjective evaluations (by interviewers, teachers, and parents), physical and neurotic symptoms, peer relations, and attitude toward blackness—all based on subjective parental responses to questions asked by interviewers. Since the design did not use any control group, there is no way of determining whether the main identity score of the subjects was adequate.

The way the subjects' "attitude toward blackness" was measured was most inappropriate. The white adoptive parents were asked by interviewers to say whether they thought their black adoptees had positive or negative attitudes toward blackness. It is necessary to point out that the authors fully realized that their study called for the use of control groups. They admitted: "Whether negative feelings are more common among the transracial adoptees than among black children of comparable age reared in black families could be determined *only* (italics added) by study of an appropriate comparison group of black children in black families" [5:181–182]. One of their aims was to provide data relevant to the position taken by the critics of transracial adoption of black children, who fear or hypothesize that the transracially adopted black child will "lose his identification with his racial and cultural heritage" [5:iii]. Why then were control groups not used?

The fault in the design of the study makes the finding on the subjects' "attitude toward blackness" virtually useless as a basis for the resolution of the controversy over the transracial adoption of black children, since the all-important hypothesis about identity was not validly or reliably tested. What the reading public has, in this study, is the adoptive white parents' word about the black adoptees' identity against the critics' word. Now, who is right about the black adoptees' identity—the white adoptive parents or the critics?

Methodology

The most serious methodological fault of the study is the use of the white adoptive parents—a group that is biased in favor of transracial adoption[1]—to evaluate transracial adoption and its effects on the black adoptees' identity. One does not expect those who adopt transracially and support the practice of transracial adoption to easily admit that it has adverse effects on the adoptees' identity. This is simple common sense. Moreover, although most of the adoptive parents were reported as seeing the need for their black children to develop black identity, some did not see any need for their black adoptees to identify with the black community or be aware of the contributions of black he-

roes [5:60]. The latter group of adoptive parents cannot be expected to be sensitive to any loss of identity on the part of the black children under their care. Therefore, it is not valid to ask such individuals to evaluate the children's sense of identity; but in the Grow-Shapiro study they were asked.

In addition to white adoptive parents, interviewers and teachers were used as evaluators in the study. The interviewers evaluated the adoptive families, covering such dimensions as the relations of the adoptive parents to the black child, the parents' "degree of comfort when responding to race-related questions," etc. All these evaluations were subjective. Moreover, the authors did not say whether the interviewers were for, against, or neutral to transracial adoption prior to their interview assignments. Their attitude, definitely, would make a difference.

Of the 37 interviewers used in the study, about 73% were white. But the reader was not told whether the black and white interviewers had similar attitudes toward the transracial adoption of black children. The answers given to the interviewers by the adoptive parents were actually influenced by the race of the interviewer. For example, more black than white interviewers were told by the adoptive parents that "their (black) child did not know of her or his black background and that they did not anticipate that their child would have special difficulties due to race." There were many other discrepancies in the responses elicited from the parents by the black and the white interviewers. It appears that the white adoptive parents told the black interviewers what they thought they wanted to hear, but shared some "classified" information with the white interviewers. This racial factor should have been anticipated and obviated by ruling out the interview method of data collection in this particular study.

The use of evaluation by teachers as a source of data is another methodological fault of the Grow-Shapiro study. White teachers as a group are notorious for perceiving black children negatively [3:7–14; 9]. That, of course, is consistent with the modal white attitude toward blacks in the larger society outside the school. Any person who is aware of the racism in this society would not, in the particular evaluation under discussion, ask an average white teacher, as Grow and Shapiro did [5:3], to say whether she thinks a given black child "is likely to get along in life." The typical white teacher's rating is a foregone conclusion. Some even assign mentally retarded IQ scores to black children without actually testing them [4:36–40]. In spite of these social realities, white teachers were asked to make such evaluations of black children in the Grow-Shapiro study. The result, of course, was an overall negative evaluation that the authors described as "somewhat less positive than those on school performance." The teacher evaluations, especially those in the affective domain, were subjective. It is doubtful whether teacher evaluations (black or white) were really necessary in this study. Moreover, the kind of teacher evaluation that was asked for was not even relevant to the black child's identity, which is the central issue in the transracial adoption controversy.

It was an appropriate gesture on the part of the authors to have thought of using standardized tests at least for some parts of the study. In view of the confounding variables inherent in the interview method, a standardized test administered directly to the children would be more valid, though that would eliminate very young children from such a study. The investigators used three tests, but only one, the California Test of Personality, was administered directly to the children. The other two tests were turned into subjective tests in the sense that the adoptive parents and the children's teachers were merely asked to state their impressions or opinions about the children by responding to test items drawn from these two tests.

The investigators, however, did not say how these tests were validated, that is, whether black children were part of the validation or standardization sample on whom the norm of behavior or adjustment was based. If black children did not participate significantly in the establishment of the norm (standardization), which is probable, it is not valid to assess them with the instruments. One could argue that these black adoptees were being given white values and that they might as well be assessed with instruments based on white norms. Any instrument based on white norms would definitely be very useful to those white adoptive parents who might want to know the extent to which they have succeeded in making their black adoptees white; but it is improbable that culturally conscious blacks would use an instrument standardized on white children to assess the personal-

ity and adjustment of black children reared in the black culture and community. How would one interpret, for example, a "good" score on the affective tests used in the Grow-Shapiro study? Would a black child with a "good" score on these tests be deemed a normal black child, a normal "white" child, or just a normal child?

Another fault with the tests is that some of the items were not valid for assessing black children in a white community. For example, one of the tendencies measured by the Social Adjustment subtest of the California Test of Personality was "community relations," which indicates whether the child "mingles happily with neighbors, (and) takes pride in community improvements." It is difficult for most black children to "mingle happily with neighbors" in an all-white community that is cruel to them. About 69% of the black children who were light brown or dark with "Negroid features" were reported by Grow and Shapiro to have experienced social cruelty in the white neighborhood where they were being reared. None of the children who were white in complexion and Caucasian in other physical features experienced any social cruelty from whites.

This means that the frequency of experienced social cruelty for black children was not the norm for white children in the same environment. It also means that such an environment means one thing to white children and a different thing to black children, both phenomenologically and in terms of stimulus value. In light of this, it should not be surprising that the black children lashed out against their aggressors—a reaction that probably can explain the investigators' finding that "a disproportionately high number of study children showed more than usual (*usual* perhaps for white children in a friendly, white environment) difficulty in the area of social adjustment."

Assuming that a "disproportionately high number" of adoptive black children have problems relating to their cruel white environment, what conclusions should one draw about such children? Maladjusted? One is tempted to make such a conclusion, but on second thought one wonders whether it would not be more valid to suspect that perhaps something is probably wrong with a child who would be at peace—well adjusted, if you will—with an uncomfortable, cruel environment. It is not certain whether the black children's Social

Adjustment score should be interpreted as maladjustment or as an index of the social pathology of the white environment. Perhaps what the authors should have investigated is the behavior of the adoptees toward other blacks after they (the adoptees) have been through white upbringing. This would have been more relevant to the crucial question of identity and acceptance of other blacks.

Most seriously, the standardized tests used in this study had nothing to do with the children's identity. That crucial dimension, identity, was measured subjectively. One wonders whether the light treatment that the investigators accorded this variable is an index of its insignificance to them.

In categorizing the adoptive parents on the basis of their attitudes toward blacks, the investigators had a problack but no antiblack category. Is the reader expected to believe that there are no antiblack whites among those who adopt black children? Was this category purposely left out, or was the omission attributable to the nature of the measuring instrument? In this connection, it is revealing that whereas 14% of the adoptive mothers were opposed to the adoption of *all-white* children by black parents, only 10% were opposed to the adoption of *all-black* children by white parents. The difference between 14% and 10% might or might not be significant, but it does say something about this dimension of the racial attitudes of these adoptive mothers. Not that the data per se are necessarily reliable (the figures could be higher or lower; how they were arrived at was not reliable), but the authors should have brought out this discrepancy in their discussion of the attitudes of the white adoptive parents toward blacks. One could be simultaneously a liberal and a racist.

GENERAL COMMENT ON THE GROW-SHAPIRO STUDY

Grow and Shapiro unveiled numerous correlations between variables such as mother's church attendance and child's personal adjustment; parents' reason for adoption and child's social adjustment; etc. Most of the correlations, however, were not relevant to the critical issue of the black child's identity and attitude and behavior toward himself as a black person, toward black people, black culture, black behavior, and other black characteristics. Coping mechanisms were not investigated. At this time, these central issues should receive

greater investigative attention than other dimensions of life under adoption because they underlie the controversy between the opposers and the supporters of transracial adoption of black children.

Other issues have been touched on here and there in the literature on transracial adoption, but only as factors that help or hinder the development of a healthy identity. For example, the adoptive parents' attitude toward blacks; their lack of knowledge of what it takes to survive oppression; the neighborhood where the adoptive parents try to rear the black child—these are all secondary issues that have been mentioned in the literature as factors that affect the child's identity and mastery of necessary survival strategies [8:180–187; 7:156–164]. Therefore, studying them without seriously studying the child's identity, ethnic awareness, and coping strategies is evading the major issues.

The authors did indicate something about identity (attitude toward blacks), but it was neither reliably nor completely measured. For example, the children's knowledge of black culture, experience, and "history" was not measured. The quality of their interaction with and behavior toward other blacks was not measured. These were serious omissions.

Not only did the investigators underemphasize and unrealiably measure the crucial variable; they also burdened the study with "nonissues," such as the child's health, academic performance, and level of aggression. Practically no published argument against transracial adoption contends that transracial adoption adversely affects the child's physical health or academic performance. It appears that the investigators merely planned and executed a "traditional" study of adopted children, paying primary attention to the standard variables covered in such a study, regardless of their irrelevance to the present controversy.

SUGGESTED APPROACH
Design

In order to relate to the current controversy over transracial adoption, any study that purports to provide data that are useful in discussing the problem must seriously deal with the issue of identity and its correlates. For this, an appropriate design and valid, reliable instruments and methodology would be necessary.

Such a study would need at least four groups of black adoptees:

1. living with white parents in a white community (WPWC);
2. living with white parents in a black community (WPBC);
3. living with black parents in a black community (BPBC); and
4. living with black parents in a white community (BPWC).

This design would make it possible to assess the effects of "parentage" and community both separately and in combination. If the objectors to transracial adoption are right, adopted black children reared by black parents in a black community (BPBC) should score significantly higher than adopted black children reared by white parents in a white community (WPWC) on any test of black identity and its correlates. More groups could be added for a more elaborate study. For example, groups made up of adopted black children reared in integrated communities could be added. Black children living with their natural parents in a black community could also be used as a control group.

Subjects

The black adoptees for this kind of a study should be those who are phenotypically black enough not to pass for white. Adoptees who are so phenotypically white that practically nobody could mistake them for black should not be included in such a study, irrespective of the genotypical blackness. This point has been mentioned earlier.

Another category of adoptees that should be excluded from such a study is that of very young children who cannot take a pen-and-paper type of test. Since no interviews or subjective assessments would be used, it is necessary that all of the subjects be able to read and comprehend simple statements.

Methodology

The demerits of interviews and subjective, "indirect" assessments (for example, asking teachers and adoptive parents to evaluate the children's attitudes and other affective traits) have been discussed earlier in this paper. Whatever is being tested in this suggested study on transracial adop-

tion should be tested through the use of objective, written items that the subjects would answer in writing by making simple marks on the paper. In this way, no interviewers, no teachers, no parents, no subjective evaluation would be involved. The idea is to eliminate all social and vested interest variables that could confound the results, as they definitely did in the Grow-Shapiro study.

The "Blackness" or Identity Test

The "blackness" or identity test should include, but not be limited to, the following dimensions:

1. knowledge of black life, culture, and history;
2. knowledge of the racial situation in this society;
3. familiarity with the names, lives, and bases of importance of black heroes;
4. ability to appreciate, participate in, and feel at home with black culture;
5. possession of coping mechanisms, personality, and skills necessary for survival under oppressive conditions;
6. positive attitude toward blackness (self, other blacks, black behavior, and black culture in general); and
7. ethnic awareness.

The knowledge and abilities to be measured in this test are those acquired through informal education or in the ordinary process of growing up in the black family and community. The test, therefore, should not include items based on school curricula, except where such curricula overlap the knowledge and abilities acquired through natural interaction with the sociopsychological environment of the black community.

Such a test would have to be one devised by black psychometricians or psychologists and standardized on black children before being used in the transracial adoption study. An impromptu test, hastily assembled and carelessly administered, would not do. It is necessary that such a test be constructed by blacks who have a feeling for black culture and survival, and who know what black identity means in terms of attitude and behavior. It would be advisable to consult black individuals and groups who either have the resources (human and/or ideational) or have actually had some experience in constructing similar or related tests.[2] It would not be a bad idea to consult those blacks who have, in their writings on transracial adoption, warned against its possible adverse effects on the black child's identity. The idea is to have a pool of items, relevant to the dimension of blackness being measured, from persons who have had the relevant experience and have the relevant academic expertise.

In the administration of the test and analysis of the data, the opposers and supporters of transracial adoption must be represented. In fact, it would not be out of order to duplicate the subjects' answer papers, immediately after the test is over, for separate analyses by the parties involved. This is a controversial issue. The two parties to the controversy must be satisfied. There should be no room for suspicion of possible manipulation of data.

SUMMARY

This paper evaluated the Grow-Shapiro study of transracial adoption of black children by white parents and assessed its relevance to the controversy over transracial adoption. It has been observed in this paper that the study failed to address itself seriously to the question of black identity and its correlates—the crux of the adoption controversy. The children's "attitude toward blackness" was subjectively and unreliably measured. "Nonissues" and the variables related to them dominated the study. Most of the measures used in the study were subjective. Nonblacks (virtually white children) were included in the sample studied—a factor that must have confounded the data. The design did not include necessary control groups; it was therefore inappropriate and unsatisfactory. The use of interviewers seriously invalidated some of the data. In view of these shortcomings, the assertion by the investigators, on the basis of the results of the study, that the sample they studied had "a success rate of 77%" is misleading [5:224]. Moreover, what should be the most important basis for any statement on rate of success—the children's identity—was neither studied in all its dimensions, nor reliably measured. As a basis for settling the controversy over transracial adoption, the value of the study is practically nil.

Some suggestions were made in this paper about how to go about designing and executing a study that would be relevant to the transracial adoption controversy, covering such dimensions as design, subjects, tests, and methodology. These suggestions do not purport to be exhaustive; they essentially point to where attention should be directed, and identify faults and pitfalls to avoid, leaving the details and other modifications to the investigator. It is hoped that future studies of this problem will focus on, and regard more seriously, the central issues in this controversy. Both parties to the "debate" need the data that would be provided by an appropriately designed and reliably executed study.

NOTES

[1]The finding that white adoptive parents favor transracial adoption of black children is hardly surprising; it merely confirms what has been common knowledge derived from common sense and the expressed opinions of certain adoptive parents' organizations, for example, the Open Door Society.

[2]The Association of Black Psychologists, the National Association of Black Social Workers, Dr. Robert L. Williams of Washington University, St. Louis, and William E. Cross, Jr. are examples. Williams constructed the BITCH test, a culture-relevant black intelligence test. Cross has studied the process of becoming "black" in America.

REFERENCES

1. Chestang, Leon. "The Dilemma of Biracial Adoption," Social Work, XVII (May 1972).

2. Child Welfare. "Readers' Forum," LI, 6 (June 1972).

3. Clark, Kenneth B. "Clash of Cultures in the Classroom," Integrated Education, I (August 1963).

4. Cottle, Thomas J. "...Faked...," Learning (November 1974).

5. Grow, Lucille J., and Deborah Shapiro. Black Children—White Parents: A Study of Transracial Adoption. New York: Child Welfare League of America, 1974.

6. Hare, Nathan. The Black Anglo-Saxons. New York: Macmillan, 1965.

7. Jones, Edmond D. "On Transracial Adoption of Black Children," Child Welfare, LI, 3 (March 1972).

8. Katz, Linda. "Transracial Adoption: Some Guidelines," Child Welfare, LIII, 3 (March 1974).

9. Kozol, Jonathan. Death at an Early Age. New York: Bantam Books, 1967.

10. Lien, Margaret. "Biracial Adoption," Social Work, XVII (September 1972).

11. National Association of Black Social Workers' Conference. "Position Paper Developed from Workshops concerning Transracial Adoption." Conference in Nashville, 1972.

12. Short, Carolyn R. "Biracial Adoption," Social Work, XVII (September 1972).

NOT SO BOLD AND NOT SO IRRELEVANT: A REPLY TO CHIMEZIE

Deborah Shapiro
Lucille J. Grow

Why Dr. Amuzie Chimezie credits us with boldness in his title at the same time that he charges us with irrelevance is somewhat puzzling, since he makes no reference to boldness in the content of his paper. The Child Welfare League's study of transracial adoption was made in response to a concern expressed by the Office of Child Development about children involved in what was, in 1971, a relatively new practice. Since this was an appropriate professional concern for both organizations, neither merits credit for boldness in studying it, but that the content of the study is irrelevant to those concerned with the issues involved seems highly debatable.

Any critic of any study may decide that the investigators chose the wrong goals, and it is legitimate for a critic of this study to contend that it should have focused entirely on the issue of black identity. However, if it had been so focused, it would have been an entirely different study and probably done under different auspices. A detailed critique of a research effort involves recognition of the investigators' goals and frame of reference. The study was not entitled "Black Identity in Children Adopted by White Parents." It was concerned with a form of adoption practice and carried out in the research center of a child welfare organization with a constituency of professionals concerned with children. The success of any adoptive placement, transracial or otherwise, is judged on the basis of the total experience of the child and the family. It is virtually inconceivable that the League would have done a study of any group of adoptees without examining, in some way, that total experience.

The June 1972 issue of Child Welfare to which Chimezie refers contained an editor's note announcing that the League was "currently engaged in a study of adoption by white families of children of black or part-black parentage." This was followed by a brief description of some of the characteristics of the study sample. No assertions were made, nor could they have been made, that this study would "settle the controversy." In fact, one is hard put to think of any single study that served to "settle" a controversy. Research reports provide evidence, in varying degrees of strength, on the questions they examine. Any policy decisions that may be indicated are usually based on the cumulative evidence of a number of studies. For this reason, the comparability of the findings of this study of transracial adoption with the findings of other adoption studies is highly relevant.

RELEVANCE OF THE STUDY

For the social worker reader who may not be so convinced as Dr. Chimezie that the study was irrelevant, the following comments are in order.

1. Chimezie's view on who is to be considered black seems somewhat different from that of

From Child Welfare, Vol. LVI, No. 2 (February 1977), pp. 86–91. Reprinted by permission of the Child Welfare League of America.

other blacks who have commented on this issue. The more common view seems to be that children with any degree of black parentage are to be considered black, regardless of appearance. Some agencies responsible for black children do not designate any as "racially mixed," but consider them black if they have one black parent. As was indicated in the report, many of the children placed with white parents were the offspring of one black parent. To have included only the children of obvious black appearance would have been a distortion of adoption practice, even had it been possible to know, in advance of the interview, just what these children looked like. In any case, feelings about blackness were certainly relevant for all the children and their families.

2.   The reasons for the absence of a control group were explained in the preface to the study. There is nothing magical about the presence or absence of control groups in the analysis of any descriptive study; some poor studies have had them and some good studies have not. The essential question for the investigator is whether he has an appropriate and accessible sample for comparison. In this instance, the decision was made against a control group of black adopted children in black homes because it was and still is accepted that the inracial adoption, when feasible, is preferable to transracial adoption. The basic question about transracial adoption was whether it worked at all and to what extent. A control group of black children similar to those in the sample but not placed for adoption would have been very difficult to identify within the limits of this study.

The prevalence of a problem or its absence in any given group is instructive with or without a comparison with another group. The paragraph of the report cited by Chimezie is preceded by the statement that in most questions related to attitudes toward blackness, one-quarter to one-third of the children were reported as having some sort of negative feeling about being black. Allowing for parental understatement, the true proportion may be somewhat higher, but the figure still means that most of the children studied showed no evidence of negative feelings about blackness. Given the racist elements in American society, it seems unlikely that any group of black children, adopted or otherwise, would have shown a significantly lower degree of negative feelings about blackness as reported by their parents.

3.   Chimezie asks the reader to choose between the white adoptive parents' word on the identity problems of their children and the word of the "critics." The parents reported on the behavior and feelings of specific children with whom they had been in daily contact, for the most part, from 5 to 9 years. Critics speak in general terms, based on general knowledge. There are certainly ample grounds for the fears expressed by the critics of transracial adoption, but fears and facts are not the same. Social workers directly concerned with the problem do have to make a choice when the conclusions to be derived from two different sources of knowledge are not the same. But the preferred choice is not so self-evident to the social workers as it is to Chimezie.

Eliminating parents as a source of information would make impossible or at least severely handicap any study involving questions of child adjustment. That parents are usually biased in favor of their children does not invalidate the findings. "Bias" is not a monolithic phenomenon. The total data collected by any study will have some variables that the investigator disregards because of the likelihood of strong bias, others where the bias will be taken into account in interpreting the data, and still others that can be considered unbiased. For this study, suffice it to note that the motivation of these parents to present themselves and their children favorably did not prevent substantial numbers from giving detailed information on a wide range of problems, including racial identification.

4.   The interviewers hired for the study were trained professionals. Most were apparently reasonably neutral about the issue under examination. Two of the black social workers were openly opposed to transracial adoption, but there was no evidence that their interviews were affected by their convictions.

Chimezie's reaction to the section of the report that deals with the effects of the interviewer's race is to say that the interview method should not have been used at all. The more usual response to the discovery of the biasing effects introduced by using interviewers who do not match their respondents on significant characteristics is to avoid such mismatching in future research, not to eliminate interviewing as a method of data collection. The effect of the race of the interviewer was examined in relation to every variable on which it could conceivably have an effect. The 10 variables showing significant differences were reported in the study, but they represented a small proportion of the total number of possibilities. Since the number of interviews in which interviewer and respondent were not matched by race was small, the effect on the overall direction of the findings was minimal.

5.   In relation to the comments on the use of teacher's evaluations, the reader may note the data on pages 30–31 of the report. The large majority of the children were considered to be doing average (as well as their peers) or above average school work. The more global ratings on the Weinstein Scale of Well-Being were *relatively* less positive than the specific ratings on school performance; nevertheless, most children in the sample were rated as likely to get along well in life. If white teachers are universally biased against black children, how did so many of these children manage to get positive ratings? The presence of some white-appearing children in the sample does not account for it. The studies Chimezie cites involve white teachers working in black communities. Perhaps the response of white teacher toward individual black children in nonghetto schools is less stereotyped than that of white teachers in black communities.

6.   Buros' *Mental Measurements Yearbook* (fifth, sixth, and seventh editions), the standard reference in the field, lists at least nine studies, based on samples of black children and youth, that used the California Test of Personality. More basic, however, was the question of what kind of test would have been appropriate for this study. Efforts to reduce the white middle class bias inherent in many intelligence and personality tests have been made in the interests of children living within a minority subculture. Why, for example, would one test the intelligence of black children reared in white middle class homes on tests designed for children living in black communities? Tests measuring a sense of black identity that would be appropriate for any group of blacks are still in the process of development. Certainly none was available when the study was planned. If Chimezie had cited an adequately tested measure of black identity appropriate for the age range of children in the study and available in 1971, his criticism of the choice of tests would have been well taken. His own comments indicate that such a test is still very much in need of development.

The fact that one of the subtests of the California Test of Personality indicates whether or not the child "mingles happily with neighbors and takes pride in his community" is precisely what makes it a relatively good test for transracially adopted children. Those having serious problems in the community would be expected to score low on this subtest, reducing the overall adjustment score. It was reported that 60% of the children tested had average or high social adjustment scores. In analyzing the differences between those who scored low and the others, all important variables were considered, including the child's appearance and the reported experiences with social cruelty. The white-appearing children did not have higher social adjustment scores than the visibly black. In fact, none of the variables that contributed to the low social adjustment score was racial in nature.

The parents' perception of incidents of cruelty was an entirely different variable fraught with complications that were described in the report, which the reader can examine for himself. One does not underestimate the potential of racial cruelty for damage to children, but in itself it does not represent a complete explanation of the variations in their ability to adjust socially.

7.   Chimezie's suggestion that the study should have investigated the behavior of adoptees after they have been through a white upbringing is generally valid, but not for the time the study was made. Finding a sample of transracial adoptees over the age of 6 was difficult enough; finding an adult sample would have [been] close to impossible. It would also have been of little value to the staffs of agencies concerned with the fate of children currently in their care to wait for the results of a study that could not be known for a decade or more.

8.   Chimezie equates subjective measurement with "light treatment." Unfortunately, there is no direct relationship between the importance of any given variable and the availability of a good instrument with which to measure it.

Even when acceptable instruments are available, the subjective feelings of the parties most directly concerned are relevant data and on many issues, the key data. In any case, the reader of the full report may judge for himself whether the issue of black identity was given light treatment.

9.   Chimezie's suggested research design is theoretically interesting but far from practical. It

ignores, for example, the critical variables of age. Even if preschool children are excluded from the study, one would not compare the sense of black identity of a 6-year-old with that of a 16-year-old. To find children in each of the categories named and meet the necessity of controlling for age in a population of widely scattered adoptees would be an extremely difficult task. If data collection follows, as Chimezie indicates it should, the development of a sophisticated, well tested instrument, it constitutes a 10-year effort at the least, and again, does not help workers who must make decisions now.

Finally, a major difficulty with these and other similar comments that have come to our attention is the sense that answering them may be an exercise in futility. Those who have come to the conclusion that transracial adoption is wrong usually hold convictions as strong as Chimezie's. One is hard put to imagine any feasible research project that would change this position. We agree with Chimezie that both parties need good data, but note the quotation marks he placed around the word "debate." Is there really a debate?

For the social workers involved, the key issue is still how best to achieve permanence for children. For those whose mind is open regarding transracial adoption, perhaps reading the study, Chimezie's critique, and this reply will help clarify many of the issues.

SECTION 2.2

Measurement

Measurement is perhaps the most fundamental feature of the social scientific investigation process. Recall the centrality of empiricism to the scientific method. Without the measurement of concepts, we are unable to answer the questions we may have about social phenomena and we are unable to definitively test our hypotheses. In addition to promoting empiricism, measurement contributes to such other features of the scientific method as objectivity, reliability, and validity.

CONCEPTUALIZATION AND OPERATIONALIZATION

The process of measurement generally involves conceptualization and operationalization, although the two should be seen more along a single continuum of generality-specificity than as entirely separate processes. Conceptualization generally precedes operationalization and involves thinking through the meanings of concepts. Let us say you select social isolation as a concept. Conceptualization of this concept will involve a great deal of thought and reading to clarify what is meant by this concept. You may decide to include an individual's relationship to friends, social groups, social institutions, and integration into predominant cultural values. Additional reading and thinking will undoubtedly lead to further clarification in your own mind as to what social isolation really is.

Having refined the conceptual definition, you then begin with the operationalization process, which involves a more exact specification of the measurement procedures to be used. Specific indicators must be developed that reflect the concept; each will represent some aspect of the concept so that a combination of all the indicators represents a valid operational definition of your concept. Continuing with the social isolation example, you may choose to measure relationships with friends with three questions, one on the number of friends, one on the frequency of visits with friends, and one on the closeness of the friendships.

I have portrayed the measurement process as being quite simple. In reality, simplicity applies only to the most concrete concepts, such as age or sex. The more complex or abstract the concept, the more difficult the measurement process. A great deal of time and work is required to conceptually and operationally define an abstract concept so as to have a reliable and valid measurement of that concept. An example is the concept of love. Zick Rubin (1976), noting that social psychologists have virtually ignored this concept, reviewed the theoretical literature on romantic love and then focused on three major components that emerged from his review: affiliative and dependent need, predisposition to help, and exclusiveness and absorption. This phase of his work reflects the conceptualization process. He then developed indicators for each of the three components; examples include "It would be hard for me to get along without ---" (affiliative and dependent need), "I would do almost anything for ---" (predisposition to help), and "I feel that I can confide in --- about virtually everything" (exclusiveness and absorption). This second phase reflects the operationalization process. Rubin also developed a liking scale to further clarify his measurement of love.

PRINCIPLES OF MEASUREMENT

Your methods text undoubtedly treats in depth the various principles of measurement, but I wish to emphasize a few of the basic principles. First, carefully tease out the various possible dimensions of a concept. The concept marital happiness might include such dimensions as satisfaction with interpersonal communication, shared activities, and sexual compatibility. The point is to consider all the various aspects of the concept. Be sure to exclude possible independent variables. Length of marriage, for example, would be a possible cause of marital happiness, not an inherent dimension of marital happiness.

Second, begin to develop as many specific indicators per dimension as possible. Indicators may include attitude statements, behaviors, or content analysis. Indicators for the concept marital happiness might include questionnaire items (e.g., "How satisfied are you with the decision-making process in your marriage?"), observing behavior (e.g., observing the number of disagreements between a husband and wife), self-reported behaviors (e.g., "In the last three weeks, how many arguments did you have with your spouse?"), or content analysis (e.g., examining diaries kept by husband and wife). The point is to ask yourself: What would I accept as a valid indicator of my concept (or dimension of the concept)?

Dimensions and indicators should represent as much of the concept as possible. Hence, the selection of dimensions must represent all or a reasonable sampling of all the possible dimensions of the concept. The selection of indicators for each dimension must similarly represent an adequate sampling of all possible indicators for that dimension. Increasing the number of dimensions and indicators included in the measure increases the likelihood that the concept has been adequately measured. Using only one dimension, or worse, using only one indicator can seriously undermine conceptual adequacy.

Third, attempt to reduce the number of indicators to a group that most accurately and reliably reflects your concepts. This can be done by pretesting your operational definition on a small sample of people (or groups, organizations, or magazines, whatever your unit of analysis is). In the Rubin and Shenker article on friendship in the survey research section (Section 3.5), an initial pool of 60 items was given to 50 freshmen who were asked to rate the items. From this pool 32 items were selected. By using item analysis and other techniques to see how well a given item correlates to the total index, you can eliminate those indicators that detract from the soundness of your operational definition.

Fourth, consider using the various specific indexing and scaling procedures described in your text. Perhaps the use of "strongly agree–strongly disagree" indicators is in order (the Likert technique). Or perhaps you may wish to order your indicators according to some underlying structure among your indicators and attach scores accordingly (the Guttman technique). Or you may wish to ask people whom they prefer to associate with or in fact do associate with (the sociometric technique; a modification of this technique is used by Rubin and Shenker in their friendship study, Section 3.5). Or you may wish to use other, less frequently used techniques such as the semantic differential or the Thurstone technique.

RELIABILITY AND VALIDITY

At base level, measures must be both reliable (repeatable and consistent) and valid (accurate). Several procedures can be used to assess validity. The *face validity* approach involves a judgment made by an expert in the field regarding the extent to which the indicators logically reflect the concept. For example, a marriage counselor would be an excellent source to review a marital happiness scale. *Predictive validity* techniques involve correlating a measure with either a subsequent behavior manifesting the concept or with a well-known measure of the concept. As an example of the former, Rubin correlated love scale scores with mutual eye-gazing in a separate laboratory study; an example of the latter would be correlating a newly developed short love scale with scores on Rubin's love scale. The *known groups* approach involves comparing two or more groups of persons that we definitely know differ on our measure. For example, we could give a feminism scale to a group of National Organization for Women members and a group of "Total Woman" graduates. *Construct validity* involves the testing of hypotheses that we have derived from existing theory and literature. If the hypotheses are supported, then we have support for the validity of our measures.

Several procedures can be used to assess reliability. The *test-retest* method simply involves giving the same measure to the same people at different times; the higher the correlation between the two scores, the higher the reliability. *Parallel forms* involves two similar measures of the same concept; the correlation between the two forms indicates reliability. The *split-half* technique involves correlating any one-half of the items with the other half. *Item analysis* involves an assessment of how each indicator correlates with the sum of the remaining indicators.

ERROR EVERYWHERE

Thus far I have concentrated on error that may develop in the measurement phase of the research process. Error of this type may reduce the reliability and/or validity of measures (such as poorly worded indicators, indicators that do not reflect the concept, and inconsistency among the indicators). But error may also enter at other phases of the research process. At the hypothesis stage hypotheses may incorrectly or incompletely represent a theory. The researcher's biases may also contribute to error at this stage. At the sampling stage inaccurate, incomplete, or nonrandom sampling strategies may produce error, especially in terms of generalizability. At the data collection stage error may creep in because of poorly trained interviewers or observers, problems with the setting (e.g., someone present during an interview), errors in coding the data, and errors in analyzing the data (e.g., violating assumptions of statistics or making an error in calculating scale scores). Be constantly alert to possible sources of error and do whatever is possible to reduce them. This point is discussed in my article in Section 1.1 on assessing research articles.

THE READINGS

Both readings in this section illustrate the measurement process. The article by Donna Brogan and Nancy Kutner details the rationale and procedures for the development of a sex-role orientation scale. Their careful review of previous scales led them to conclude that few scales covered the entire spectrum of sex-role orientation (many are limited to marriage and family situations), that many were dated (given the rise of the women's movement), that many focused on behaviors as opposed to attitudes, that few applied equally well to both males and females, and that few focused on the normative conceptions of appropriate male and female behavior.

Note too Brogan and Kutner's discussion of the conceptualization and operationalization processes they employed. After reviewing the dimensions underlying some of the previously developed scales, they outline the six dimensions they used. After developing indicators for each dimension, they then reduced the number of items from 53 to 36 with the use of both item analysis and the split-half method to assess reliability. To assess validity they used both face validity and construct validity techniques. Face validity was attained by using several items from existing measures and by using previous studies as guides. Construct validity was attained by correlating their measure with various other independent and dependent variables shown in the literature to be related to sex-role orientation.

The article by Adam Yarmolinsky is included primarily for fun. But it does illustrate how questionnaires can be constructed without much thought given to theoretical issues (that is, for descriptive purposes only), how difficult it can be to develop questions equally meaningful for all respondents, how difficult it can be to operationalize such abstract concepts as social philosophy, and the problems with using only "yes-no" response categories. Parenthetically, consider the measurement problems in Yarmolinsky's "counter-questionnaire."

REFERENCE

Rubin, Zick
    1976   "Measurement of romantic love." Pp. 495–507 in P. Golden (ed.), The Research Experience. Itasca: Peacock.

MEASURING SEX-ROLE
ORIENTATION: A NORMATIVE APPROACH

Donna Brogan
Nancy G. Kutner

Arlie Hochschild (1973:1023) has recently called the issue of sex roles "the single biggest blind spot in existing sociology." Her concern was primarily with gaps in the body of research to date on sex roles. In our own research in this area, we have encountered a methodological "gap" as well: the lack of an up-to-date scale with which to measure normative conceptions of appropriate sex roles for both males and females. In this paper we present a new scale for measuring sex-role orientation and describe the relation of a number of variables to the scale.

OVERVIEW OF
EXISTING SEX-ROLE SCALES

Numerous scales which tap dimensions of sex roles can be found in the psychological and sociological literature.

The main focus of sex-role scales in the psychological literature is the concept of masculinity-femininity. Some of the best known scales which purport to tap masculinity-femininity are the Terman-Miles Attitude-Interest Analysis Test, the Masculinity-Femininity Scale of the Strong Vocational Interest Blank, the Masculinity-Femininity Scale of the Minnesota Multiphasic Personality Inventory (MMPI), and the Gough Femininity Scale. Because it was suspected that the traditional notions of sex-appropriate behaviors and interests on which these scales are based may no longer be relevant, five psychologists (Rosenkrantz et al., 1968) recently developed a new sex-role questionnaire which they claim measures "perceptions of 'typical' masculine and feminine behavior" (Broverman et al., 1972:60–61).

Masculinity-femininity scales have recently been strongly criticized on the grounds that they tend to confound items relating to sex-role prefer-

ence, sex-role adoption, and sex-role identity[1]—thereby making the concept of masculinity-femininity, as measured by such scales, essentially meaningless (Constantinople, 1973). It is not the purpose of this paper to enter into a debate over the utility of masculinity-femininity tests. It does seem important, however, to recognize the possible problems associated with masculinity-femininity scales. In addition, it is our opinion that such scales, because of their typical concentration on measuring personality attributes (aggressiveness, independence, emotionality, etc.) and individual interests ("home-oriented," "dislikes math and science very much," "enjoys art and literature," etc.) neglect the aspect of sex roles which is of most importance for sociologists, that is, normative prescriptions for the behavior of males and females. Moreover, in our own earlier work we found that a subject's score on a personality and interest oriented masculinity-femininity scale failed to correlate with the subject's score on a scale focusing on conceptions of appropriate male and female role behavior (Kutner and Brogan, 1974:477–478).

The main focus of sex-role scales in the sociological literature has been on marital and family roles. One example is Motz's Role Conception Inventory (Motz, 1952), which measures personal and public attitudes about sex roles in the context of marriage and family. If, however, one is interested in attitudes about appropriate sex roles in a broader context, few scales are available. Kammeyer (1964) has developed a normative role

Research was conducted in Fall, 1974, and was supported by a Faculty Research Grant-in-Aid from Emory University, 1974–75. This is a revision of a paper presented at the annual meeting of the Southern Sociological Society, Washington, D.C., April, 1975.

attitudes scale which measures attitudes toward "the proper kinds of behavior for women in various spheres of life," but it consists of only five statements and deals only with female role behavior.[2] Women's liberation, or feminist, scales also exist (*e.g.*, Kirkpatrick, 1936), but, again, these do not tap attitudes concerning appropriate behavior for males.

The most useful set of sex-role attitude items that we have found is contained in Levinson and Huffman's (1955) Traditional Family Ideology, or TFI, Scale. The scale has four sections, two of which are labeled: (1) items measuring husband and wife roles and relationships, and (2) items measuring general male-female relationships and concepts of masculinity and femininity. (The remaining two sections, which deal with views of appropriate parent-child relationships and child-rearing techniques, and with general values and aims regarding the family, are not relevant for measuring sex-role ideology.) These two sections of the TFI Scale tap what Levinson and Huffman call "ideological orientations" regarding sex roles and permit a differentiation of respondents along an autocratic-democratic continuum. However, many of the items in these sections of the TFI Scale, developed around 1950, appear outdated (*e.g.*, the item "It is a reflection on a husband's manhood if his wife works") given the economic need of many families for two incomes and the fact that approximately 40% of American wives are in the labor force. When we administered the adapted TFI Scale (the two sections described above) to 166 male and female university students, almost all subjects scored within the "non-traditional" or democratic half of the scale (Kutner and Brogan, 1974). Although university students are probably less traditional in sex-role orientation than the general population, a more up-to-date scale would undoubtedly be preferable. A related problem with the TFI items is that the meaning of some is ambiguous at this point in time (*e.g.*, the meaning of "well" in the statement "A man who doesn't provide well for his family ought to consider himself pretty much a failure as husband and father").

For the most part, Levinson and Huffman's items focus on behavioral expectations rather than on alleged masculine or feminine attributes or traits. We view the mixing of these two types of items in one scale as undesirable because we believe that it is useful to separate "sex-role orienta-tion" (defined as attitudes about what is "right" for males and females to do) from "sex difference stereotypes" (perceptions of "typical" traits, interests, and behavior of males and females—*i.e.*, views of what males and females "are like"). For example, the view that "in general, men are better drivers than women" is a sex difference stereotype; it is (usually) not a view of how things "should be" in a moral sense.

A recent study of the relationship between role orientation and achievement motivation in college women (Alper, 1973) utilized an original measure of sex-role orientation (the Wellesley Role-Orientation Scale, or WROS) containing a 7-item "feminine trait" subscale, a 7-item "feminine role activities" subscale, and a 7-item "male-oriented careers" subscale. A subject's role orientation score in this study was the total number of "feminine" responses to all 21 items. The author (Alper, 1973:30) is puzzled by the fact that the scale "fails to correlate with some of the other seemingly relevant measures" such as the sex-role measure developed by Rosenkrantz *et al.* (1968). We suggest that the explanation may lie in the confounding of dimensions within the scale. A set of items such as the WROS provides a general overview of issues relevant to differential male and female options and expectations, but it does not conform to the model of a unidimensional attitude scale.

The scale which we present in this paper is designed to focus exclusively on sex-role orientation, which we define as normative conceptions of appropriate behavior for males and females. We conceptualize sex-role orientation as a continuum ranging from traditional to nontraditional and including beliefs about appropriate behavior for *both* sexes.

A NEW SEX-ROLE ORIENTATION SCALE

Construction of the Scale

Fifty-three Likert-type attitude statements constituted the pool of items used in constructing the scale. Many of the items were adapted from earlier scales and research questions, following a thorough review of related literature. The two investigators collaborated in writing additional items to cover issues not previously included in sex-role attitude studies. Our objective was to reflect options available to males and females at this point in time in American society, within the following content areas:

1. attitudes toward the traditional sex-based division of labor in marriage: the notion that a wife's place is in the home while the husband's place is in the "outside" world of work;
2. attitudes toward the traditional sex-based power structure: the notion that men should be in positions of authority over women in the work world and in the family;
3. attitudes toward traditional and nontraditional employment of women and men;
4. attitudes toward traditional and nontraditional political status of women;
5. attitudes toward appropriate sex-role socialization of male and female children;
6. attitudes toward existing stereotypes of appropriate sex-role behavior not covered by above areas (standards of dress, morals, etc.).

Almost 300 subjects completed questionnaires containing the sex-role orientation items in the fall of 1974. Subjects were contacted in three ways: (1) Seventy of the subjects were first-year graduate students in Emory University School of Nursing (69 females, 1 male), enrolled in a required research course. Although these subjects were homogeneous with respect to their chosen profession, they varied in age (early 20's to middle 50's) and marital status. Sixty-six subjects were white; the remaining four were black; (2) fifty-four subjects were undergraduates at Emory University, enrolled in a family sociology course. There were 42 females and 12 males in this sample. All were white and had a middle-class background; most were never married and were between 18–22 years old; (3) additional subjects were 45 married couples and 42 dating couples who, independent of their partners, completed questionnaires containing the sex-role orientation items. These subjects were contacted by the undergraduate students in the family sociology class. Like the undergraduates, these subjects were white and middle-class. The dating couples, many of whom were also undergraduate students at Emory, were generally in their early 20's. Married couples, however, represented a wide age range. All subjects completed the sex-role orientation items and provided basic demographic information such as sex, age, marital status, religion, and occupation. From Emory graduate student nurses and undergraduates, information was re-

quested about the work experience of the subject's mother during the subject's childhood, subject's parents' occupations, and which parent had the most influence on the subject's attitude development; five attitude items concerning parent-child relationships were also included as a measure of authoritarianism. In addition, Emory undergraduates were questioned about their current college major and anticipated career plans.

Responses from all subjects (N = 298) to the 53 sex-role orientation items were used to perform an item analysis. Response to each item was correlated with subject's total score for the set of 53 items. Forty of the items had an item-to-total correlation coefficient of .50 or above. We decided to discard 4 of these items, however, because of their somewhat ambiguous phrasing, which had been noted by several subjects.

The remaining 36 items were subjected to further analysis by dividing subjects into six subgroups according to their response to the item (strongly agree to strongly disagree), and comparing the average total score across the six subgroups. All 36 items appeared to satisfactorily discriminate among subjects by this criterion. The 36 items are listed in Table 1. As a safeguard against response set, twenty of the items are phrased in a traditional way; the remaining 16 (marked by asterisks in Table 1) are phrased in a nontraditional way.

Scoring Procedure

Subjects were asked to respond to each item by selecting one of the following answers: strongly agree, moderately agree, agree slightly more than disagree, disagree slightly more than agree, moderately disagree, strongly disagree. For starred items, the response categories of strongly disagree to strongly agree were assigned values of 1 to 6. Responses to the remaining items were scored in reverse order (i.e., strongly agree = 1 and strongly disagree = 6).

A subject's total score was the sum of the numerical value of responses to all 36 items, thus total scores could range from 36 to 216. The lower the total score, the more traditional the subject's sex-role orientation (SRO); the higher the total score, the more nontraditional the subject's SRO.

Internal Validity Check on Responses

Two items included in the scale provided a check on the consistency of a subject's responses.

Table 1. Sex–Role Orientation Scale Items

Item/Total r

.61   1. It is more important for a wife to help her husband's career than to have a career herself.

.61   2. The idea of young girls participating in Little League baseball competition is ridiculous.

.54   *3. The relative amounts of time and energy devoted to a career on the one hand, and to home and family on the other hand, should be determined by one's personal desires and interests rather than by one's sex.

.52   4. It is more important for a woman to keep her figure and dress becomingly than it is for a man.

.74   5. The old saying that "a woman's place is in the home" is still basically true and should remain true.

.66   6. A woman should refrain from being too competitive with men and keep her peace rather than show a man he is wrong.

.64   7. A woman whose job involves contact with the public, e.g., salesperson or teacher, should not continue to work when she is noticeably pregnant.

.65   8. The husband should take primary responsibility for major family decisions, such as the purchase of a home or car.

.71   9. In groups that have both male and female members, it is appropriate that top leadership positions be held by males.

.68 10. Unless it is economically necessary, married women who have school-aged children should not work outside the home.

.57 11. If there are two candidates for a job, one a man and the other a woman, and the woman is slightly better qualified, the job should nevertheless go to the man because he is likely to have a family to support.

.50 *12. Marriage is a partnership in which the wife and husband should share the economic responsibility of supporting the family.

.53 13. A woman should not accept a career promotion if it would require her family to move and her husband to find another job.

.50 *14. A married woman who chooses not to have children because she prefers to pursue her career should not feel guilty.

.53 15. Unless it is economically necessary, married women who have preschool-age children should not work outside the home.

.66 16. It is generally better to have a man at the head of a department composed of both men and women employees.

.60 *17. A husband should not feel uncomfortable if his wife earns a larger salary than he does.

.52 *18. It is all right for women to hold local political offices.

.51 19. A male student and a female student are equally qualified for a certain scholarship; it should be awarded to the male student on the grounds that he has greater "career potential."

.51 *20. The use of profane or obscene language by a woman is no more objectionable than the same usage by a man.

.60 *21. It is certainly acceptable for boys, as well as girls, to play with dolls.

.63 22. Girls should primarily be counseled to enter "feminine" vocations such as nursing, public school teaching, library science, etc.

.51 *23. Women should not feel inhibited about competing in any form of athletics.

.55 *24. Parents should encourage just as much independence in their daughters as in their sons.

.70 *25. Women should be able to compete with men for jobs that have traditionally belonged to men, such as telephone lineman.

.61 *26. It is O.K. for a wife to retain her maiden name if she wants to.

.66 *27. There is no reason why a woman should not be president of the United States.

.61 28. Career education for boys should have higher priority with parents and teachers than career education for girls.

.69 29. Even though a wife works outside the home, the husband should be the main breadwinner and the wife should have the responsibility for running the household.

Table 1. Continued

Item/Total r		
.53	30.	In elementary school, girls should wear dresses rather than slacks to school.
.54	*31.	It is acceptable for a woman to become a member of the church clergy.
.54	*32.	It is acceptable for women to hold important elected political offices in state and national government.
.68	33.	It is not a good idea for a husband to stay home and care for the children while his wife is employed full-time outside the home.
.59	34.	The only reason girls need career education is that they may not marry or remain married.
.58	*35.	There is no particular reason why a man should always offer his seat to a woman who is standing on a crowded bus.
.60	*36.	Men should be able to compete with women for jobs that have traditionally belonged to women, such as telephone operator.

Note: Items are listed in the order in which they appeared on the questionnaire.
*These items are phrased in a nontraditional way.

The two items are #10, "Unless it is economically necessary, married women who have school-aged children should not work outside the home," and #15, "Unless it is economically necessary, married women who have preschool-age children should not work outside the home." Answers to these two items were clearly related, although, as expected, greater importance was attached to mothers of preschool-age children not working outside the home.

Reliability of the Scale

Reliability of responses by the 298 subjects to the 36 items was calculated by means of the split-half method. Alternate items were used to construct two halves, each consisting of 10 items phrased in a traditional way and eight items phrased in a nontraditional way. The split-half reliability coefficient was .95.

Construct Validation of the Scale

To obtain an indication of the validity of our 36-item SRO scale, we examined a series of relationships for which support has been found in previous research on factors related to sex-role attitudes:

(1) *Sex and educational status.* Mason and Bumpass (1975) report that women's educational attainment has a greater effect on "sex-role modernity" and favorable attitudes toward equality of opportunity for women than do any of the other de-

mographic variables they investigated. Our own previous research experience (Kutner and Brogan, 1974) with two sections of Levinson and Huffman's TFI scale, described above, indicated that graduate student nurses were more nontraditional in sex-role orientation than either female or male undergraduate students at Emory University. Female undergraduate students were more nontraditional than male undergraduate students, although the difference was not statistically significant. Because similar groups of subjects at Emory University were contacted in the present study, we anticipated the same rank ordering of the three groups on SRO if our scale was measuring a dimension similar to that measured by the TFI items. The data did indicate the same rank ordering, as shown in Table 2; moreover, the three groups were significantly different in average SRO scores.

As noted above, the majority of dating couples who completed the SRO items were also undergraduate students. A comparison of SRO scores for females and males in this sample provides a useful check on the sex differences reported in Table 2, because the male undergraduate N in Table 2 is small. The average SRO scores of female ($\bar{x} = 180.4$) and males ($\bar{x} = 153.4$) in the sample of dating couples differed significantly ($\alpha = .05$), using the Student-Newman-Keuls test.

(2) *Age.* Although little research attention has been directed to this relationship, it seemed reasonable to expect that age would also be related

Table 2. SRO Scores, by Sex and Graduate/Undergraduate Status

Sample	N	Mean SRO Score*	s.d.	SRO Score Minimum	SRO Score Maximum
				Range	
Female graduate student nurses	69	186.8	16.5	151	216
Female undergraduates	42	178.2	25.5	90	215
Male undergraduates	12	162.6	27.9	128	208

*An analysis of variance was performed, using all 7 subject groups: female graduate student nurses, dating females, female undergraduates, married females, male undergraduates, married males, and dating males. Differences in mean SRO score for these 7 groups were significant [$F (6,290) = 8.95$; $p < .001$]. Using the Student-Newman-Keuls procedure for multiple comparisons, the three groups described in Table 2 differed significantly from eac ι other ($\propto = .05$).

to sex-role orientation scores, since older persons are generally thought to be more traditional than younger persons.[3] Two of our subject groups, graduate student nurses and married couples, varied sufficiently in age distribution to allow us to examine this relationship as a validity check. As reported in Table 2, there was relatively little variation in SRO scores among the nurses. Married couples, however, had the largest amount of variation in SRO scores (for married females, $\bar{x} = 169.2$, s.d. $= 33.0$, score range $= 78-216$; for married males, $\bar{x} = 159.7$, s.d. $= 35.2$, score range $= 76-214$). The relationship of age to SRO was therefore investigated for females and males in the sample of married couples, after dividing subjects into three age-groupings of approximately equal size. Results are reported in Table 3. As we anticipated, for both females and males, younger persons were most nontraditional in SRO and older persons were most traditional in SRO. Age differences were significant for males, but not significant for females, at $\propto = .05$.

(3) *Religious affiliation.* Lipman-Blumen (1972) found a relationship between present religious affiliation and sex-role ideology among females, with women espousing Judaism, Eastern religions, atheism, or no formal religion being least traditional, and Catholics and Protestants being most traditional. Similarly, Levinson and Huffman (1955) found that Catholics had the highest TFI mean, followed in order (decreasing traditionalism) by Protestants, Jews, the unaffiliated, and Unitarians. This suggested another validity check on our data. For all female subjects (N = 182), a

Table 3. SRO Scores of Females and Males in Married Couple Sample, by Age

Age	N	Females Mean SRO Score*	s.d.
22 or younger	14	184.9	22.7
23–42	16	166.4	40.2
43 or older	15	157.7	28.5

Age	N	Males Mean SRO Score**	s.d.
23 or younger	15	175.3	26.5
24–45	15	160.3	41.6
46 or older	15	143.5	30.2

*$F (2,42) = 2.77$; $p = .07$
**$F (2,42) = 3.40$; $p = .04$

comparison was made of mean SRO scores among Catholics, conservative Protestants, ⌐iberal Protestants,[4] Jews, Unitarians, and those with no religious affiliation. The last two categories were significantly more nontraditional in SRO than the other categories; results are given in Table 4.

Our findings are similar to those of Levinson and Huffman and Lipman-Blumen, with the exception that Jewish females in our study are more

Table 4. SRO Scores of Female
Subjects, by Religious Affiliation

Religious affiliation	N	Mean SRO Score*	s.d.
Catholic	31	173.9	30.5
Conservative Protestant	24	176.3	30.2
Liberal Protestant	68	176.8	22.9
Jewish	37	179.3	24.1
Unitarian	4	198.0	3.9
None	18	200.8	13.8

*$F (5,176) = 3.66; p < .01$

similar, on the average, to Protestants and Catholics than to Unitarians or those with no religion (although their mean SRO score *is* higher or more nontraditional, than the scores of Protestants and Catholics). We suggest that this may reflect variation in religious orthodoxy or traditionalism within the Jewish samples in the three studies. Levinson and Huffman (1955:265–266), who found much variation in TFI scores *within* their Jewish sample and within their Catholic and Protestant samples as well, note that "a group will show ideological uniformity only to the extent that its members have in common other, psychologically related characteristics." We recognize that religious group membership *per se* is unlikely to be a primary determinant of sex-role attitudes.[5]

(4) *Authoritarian child-rearing ideology.* Finally, we examined the relationship between degree of authoritarian childrearing ideology (measured by 5 Likert-type items) and SRO scores for female graduate nurses and male and female undergraduates. Following Levinson and Huffman's argument that traditional family ideology is part of a larger syndrome of autocratic ideology, it seemed reasonable to expect degree of authoritarian childrearing ideology to be directly related to degree of traditional sex-role orientation. The 5 items used to measure authoritarian childrearing ideology[6] were taken from an extensive study of family living patterns (Project NC-90, Cooperative State Research Service, U.S.D.A.). Correlations between authoritarian childrearing ideology as measured by these items and SRO scores were significant for both graduate nursing students and undergraduate stu-

dents (for nurses, $r = +.43$, $p < .001$; for undergraduates, $r = +.53$, $p < .001$), with more authoritarian persons tending to be more traditional in sex-role orientation as predicted.

To summarize the results of our efforts at construct validation of our scale, predicted relationships were found between SRO scores and the demographic variables of sex, educational attainment, age, and religious affiliation (with the exception of Jewish females). In addition, the predicted relationship was found between SRO and authoritarian child-rearing ideology.[7]

RELATION OF SRO TO SELECTED ADDITIONAL VARIABLES AMONG FEMALE UNDERGRADUATES

Data reported in this section are for female undergraduate students only. The data were also obtained from undergraduate male students and graduate student nurses, but the small sample size ($N = 12$) of the former and the small variability in SRO scores among the latter mean that these data are not very useful for investigating correlates of SRO. The dating and married couples' questionnaires did not elicit these particular data.

Mother's Education, Employment, and Attitudinal Influence

The three variables examined first in relation to SRO are all logically antecedent to the development of an individual's sex-role orientation. Relationships between these three variables and sex-role attitudes have been investigated in prior studies, but findings have been inconsistent.

(1) *Mother's education.* In Lipman-Blumen's (1972:37) study of over 1,000 college-educated, married women, "obvious socioeconomic indexes, such as parents' income, education or occupation, surprisingly had no bearing on the daughter's sex-role ideology." On the other hand, Meier (1972) found, among male and female college students, a marked positive relationship between "feminine social equality (FSE) orientation" and mother's (but not father's) educational attainment.

We have noted above the positive relationship found in our own previous research (Kutner and Brogan, 1974) and in that of Mason and Bumpass (1975) between a female subject's own level of education and her sex-role outlook. It seems quite likely that among undergraduate female students, the "educational attainment model" furnished by the student's mother would be related to the student's SRO. The reasoning here is that more highly educated mothers are also likely to be more nontraditional in sex-role outlook and will tend to transmit this orientation to their daughters. Our data for female undergraduates parallel Meier's (1972) findings; the higher her mother's level of education, the more nontraditional the undergraduate female's SRO. Mean SRO of subjects whose mothers completed high school or vocational training beyond high school was 159.4; of subjects whose mothers completed some college or graduated from college the mean was 181.8; and of subjects whose mothers had graduate or professional school training it was 187.6 [F (2,39) = 3.08; p = .05].[8]

(2) *Mother's employment.*   Meier (1972) reports, for the college students he surveyed, a marked positive relationship between FSE orientation and extent of mother's involvement in occupational roles outside the home during the student's school years. This is consistent with Nye and Hoffman's (1963:301) conclusion that daughters of mothers who work outside the home tend to be less traditional in sex-role outlook than are daughters whose mothers do not work. However, in Lipman-Blumen's (1972) study of college-educated, married women, mother's employment showed no relationship to daughter's sex-role ideology.[9]

The female undergraduates in our sample whose mothers had been employed one or more of the subject's school years (grades 1–12) were more nontraditional in SRO than those whose mothers had not worked or who had worked less than one year, but the difference was not significant [F (2,39) = 0.66].

(3) *Salience of mother in attitudinal socialization.*   A third relationship reported by Meier (1972) is between FSE orientation and salience of mother rather than father in attitudinal socialization. We included in our questionnaire Meier's (1972:117) measure of parental salience in attitudinal influence:

Thinking back to your childhood and up through your high school years, which of your parents seems to have been most influential, on the whole, in shaping your attitudes and your general outlook on life? Decide between your mother and father, even if the difference was slight.

Two-thirds of the undergraduate females in our sample reported more influence by their mothers; however, those who reported more influence by their fathers were similar to the former in average SRO score. Thus, our data do *not* conform to the pattern reported by Meier for his college student sample.

Lipman-Blumen's (1972) findings with respect to parents' influence also indicated no clear trends. She found a slight tendency for women who admired their *fathers* more than their mothers to be less traditional in sex-role ideology than those who admired their mothers more than their fathers. On the other hand, a *mother's* encouragement to attend graduate school enhanced the tendency toward a nontraditional outlook more than did a father's encouragement (but encouragement by both parents was most related to nontraditionalism).

Career Aspirations of Female Undergraduates

Female graduate student nurses in our study were significantly less traditional in SRO than undergraduate females, even though the former represent a traditionally "female" vocational field. We were interested, therefore, to see if SRO was related to career aspirations of female undergraduates.

Two researchers have recently reported a relationship between sex-role attitudes and educational/occupational aspirations among females. Lipman-Blumen (1972) found that a majority of the nontraditional women in her sample aspired to graduate studies, while a majority of the traditional women did not. Alper (1973) reports that the more "feminine" college women among her subjects (as measured by her role-orientation scale) were less likely to be planning on graduate school or a career. In addition, her projective measure of achievement motivation was significantly related to the sex-role orientation measure among undergraduate women.

Our female undergraduate subjects were asked, "Do you have any particular career(s) or occupation(s) that you plan to enter? If yes, please indicate what they are." The majority (71%) did have a career goal in mind, but their average SRO score was almost identical to the average SRO score of female undergraduates who did not have such a goal. Among those who indicated a planned occupation, those aspiring toward a high level professional career (e.g., doctor, lawyer, college professor) were slightly more nontraditional (SRO $\bar{x}$ = 180.5) than those listing other occupations (SRO $\bar{x}$ = 176.2), but the difference was not statistically significant [F (1,26) = 0.26]. Thus, among the undergraduate females in our study, SRO differences do not predict aspirations as clearly as was the case in Lipman-Blumen's and Alper's studies.

Differences from study to study in the instrument used to measure sex-role orientation may be involved in the discrepancy between the findings of this study and earlier studies. Two other explanations can also be suggested. First, undergraduate females may express nontraditional attitudes about husband/wife relationships, women holding political office, etc., without having committed themselves to pursuing a particular career. Typically, there is less pressure on females than on males to make early career decisions. A second possibility is that females who hold nontraditional sex-role attitudes are reluctant to pursue a career because of the obstacles which they perceive to confront "career women."

CONCLUSION

We have argued that a need exists for a sex-role orientation scale which is both up-to-date in item content and phrasing and focuses on normative views of appropriate male and female behavior. We have presented a scale which we believe meets these criteria and which appears to be reliable and valid. Finally, we have discussed relationships between sex-role orientation, as measured by our scale, and selected antecedent and dependent variables. These relationships are consistent with some prior research, although this is more true with respect to mother's educational attainment and daughter's SRO than in the case of the other relationships considered.

In particular, the relationship between sex-role orientation and female aspirations merits further study. It is our hope that the scale presented here will facilitate and stimulate research in this important area, and in others as well.

NOTES

[1]Constantinople (1973) defines *sex-role preference* as the activities or traits an individual would prefer to engage in or possess, while *sex-role adop-*

tion refers to activities or traits actually manifested by an individual. *Sex-role identity* is more complex, including "both cognitive and affective factors which reflect both self-evaluation and the evaluation of others as to one's adequacy as a male or female ... one's definition of adequacy would probably vary with the kinds of standards of sex role appropriateness to which one had been exposed in the process of development" (1973:391).

[2]Lipman-Blumen (1972) and Mason and Bumpass (1975), similarly, have utilized short (5- or 6-item) female-role-ideology scales.

[3]Mason and Bumpass (1975), in their study of sex-role ideology among never-married women, examined the relation of age to sex-role modernity and to favorable attitudes toward equality of opportunity for women. They found no relationship.

[4]Liberal Protestant includes Presbyterian, Episcopalian, Methodist, and Congregational. Conservative Protestant includes Baptist, Christian Scientist, Lutheran, United Church of Christ, Seventh Day Adventist, and Christian. This categorization was taken from Anderson (1970:116).

[5]In addition to identifying an individual's religious group membership, it is important to determine degree of religious involvement. Although such a measure was not included in this study, we have found (Kutner and Brogan, 1973) that females with high religious involvement (frequent church attendance, numerous church organization memberships, and/or large amount of time spent per month in church affairs) are significantly more traditional in SRO than females characterized by medium or low religious involvement. Among males, however, we found no significant difference in average SRO among the three religious involvement groupings.

[6]The five items, to which subjects were asked to respond in terms of 6 categories (strongly agree to strongly disagree), were: (1) Respect for parents is the most important thing that children should learn; (2) Most children should be toilet trained by 15 months of age; (3) Most kids should be spanked more often; (4) A child should be taken away from the breast or bottle as soon as possible; (5) The most important goal of the parent is to see that the kids stay out of trouble.

[7]It would have been desirable to investigate also the relationship between race and SRO; Mason and Bumpass (1975) found substantial differences between the responses of black and white women

to sex-role statements. Our sample contained only four black persons, all graduate nursing students, and we therefore did not include race as an identifying variable in the research.

[8]Perhaps Lipman-Blumen's findings are not consistent with Meier's or ours because her sample was older (median age 23.4) than a typical college student sample. In our own study, there was no relationship between mother's educational attainment and SRO among the female graduate student nurses.

[9]Similarly, we found no relationship between extent of mother's employment and SRO among the female graduate student nurses in our study.

REFERENCES

Alper, Thelma G.
1973 "The relationship between role orientation and achievement motivation in college women." Journal of Personality 41 (March):9–31.

Anderson, Charles H.
1970 White Protestant Americans. Englewood Cliffs: Prentice-Hall.

Broverman, Inge K., Susan Raymond Vogel, Donald M. Broverman, Frank E. Clarkson, and Paul S. Rosenkrantz
1972 "Sex-role stereotypes: a current appraisal." Journal of Social Issues 28 (2):59–78.

Constantinople, Anne
1973 "Masculinity-femininity: an exception to a famous dictum?" Psychological Bulletin 80 (5):389–407.

Hochschild, Arlie Russell
1973 "A review of sex role research." American Journal of Sociology 78 (January):1011–1029.

Kammeyer, Kenneth
1964 "The feminine role: an analysis of attitude consistency." Journal of Marriage and the Family 26 (August):295–305.

Kirkpatrick, Clifford
1936 "The construction of a belief pattern scale for measuring attitudes toward feminism." Journal of Social Psychology 7:421–437.

Kutner, Nancy G., and Donna Brogan
1973 "The relationship of sex, age, and orientation toward sex roles to knowledge of selected slang." Paper presented at annual meeting of the Southern Sociological Society, Atlanta, Ga.
1974 "An investigation of sex-related slang vocabulary and sex-role orientation among male and female university students." Journal of Marriage and the Family 36 (August):474–484.

Levinson, Daniel J., and Phyllis E. Huffman
1955 "Traditional family ideology and its relation to personality." Journal of Personality 23 (March):251–273.

Lipman-Blumen, Jean
1972 "How ideology shapes women's lives." Scientific American 226 (January):32–42.

Mason, Karen Oppenheim, and Larry L. Bumpass
1975 "U.S. women's sex-role ideology, 1970." American Journal of Sociology 80 (March):1212–1219.

Meier, Harold C.
1972 "Mother-centeredness and college youths' attitudes toward social equality for women: some empirical findings." Journal of Marriage and the Family 34 (February):115–121.

Motz, Annabelle B.
1952 "The role conception inventory: a tool for research in social psychology." American Sociological Review 17 (August):465–471.

Nye, F. Ivan, and Lois W. Hoffman
1963 The Employed Mother in America. Chicago: Rand McNally.

Rosenkrantz, Paul S., Susan Raymond Vogel, Helen Bee, Inge K. Broverman, and Donald M. Broverman
1968 "Sex-role stereotypes and self-concepts in college students." Journal of Consulting and Clinical Psychology 32:287–295.

...ANSWER YES OR NO

Adam Yarmolinsky

One of the rewards of a Harvard education is that every few years you get to fill out a questionnaire. The basic reunion questionnaire is pretty straightforward, and requires only a little memory exercise (What year was Matthew born?) and lower mathematics (Ben will graduate in the Class of Seventy-which?). But there is usually a more wide-ranging anonymous questionnaire as well, offering some opportunity to exercise one's powers of imagination and introspection.

Accordingly, I turned with pleasant anticipation to the anonymous questionnaire (light blue, as compared to the plain white report form) in my thirtieth reunion materials. What I found seemed to have been prepared by and for the late George Apley—if not for the graduates of General Beadle College or Bob Jones University.

It began by asking whether I liked my job and how much money I made; but only those who were self-employed or owned their own businesses were asked, "Are you happy?" Is it assumed that the satisfied organization man must be a happy organization man? Then it inquired (still under the cover of anonymity, of course) how many times I had married and how many children and grandchildren I had. After that, the questionnaire got down to business by inquiring whether I believed in God (answer Yes or No). I resisted the temptation to reply with the punch line from the story about the astronaut who was asked if he had seen the Deity ("Well, to begin with, She's black ..."), and I faced the next problem: "Do you believe organized religion has a significant value in today's world?" Here, despite a refreshing third option, "No opinion," I began to feel trapped. What kind of value, for whom? If I say Yes, do I forgo the distinction between religion and religiosity? If I say No, do I deny the enormous impact of Pope John? And, in a somewhat different direction, of the brothers Berrigan? Or shall I deny any opinion, at least that

I am willing to share with my classmates on a Yes or No basis?

But my eye moved to the next question, which asks whether I or any of my immediate family now or ever have been drug users. Heroin? Marijuana? It's all the same to the questioner—although he takes care to explain that he is excluding "prescription drugs" and "social drinking."

Lest I find this line of questioning too specific, I need only turn the page to be given a broader scope. "What is your social philosophy?" I am asked, with four convenient answers to choose from: cynical, optimistic, conservative, and liberal, plus an escape hatch—"Other (name it)." My instinct at this point is to take the escape hatch, and color myself bewildered.

But in case there is any doubt about the questionnaire's social philosophy, I have only to read down the page to "Do you think the Courts are too lenient?" Just answer yes or no, buddy. "How would you cut down waste in government?" Of course that's where the waste is, silly.

The questionnaire is interested in other social issues as well—but somewhat selectively. It wants to know to what I attribute the increasing crime rate in the United States, but it is incurious about the causes of the increasing unemployment rate in the United States—or the enormous persistent casualty rate among Southeast Asians. It wants to know my view on civil rights legislation (not enough—about right—too extensive), but not my view on civil rights enforcement. It wants to know whether I approve of today's "permissiveness"— but not whether I approve of today's authoritarianism. And it wants to know how often I attend religious services, but not how often I read a book, or encounter a new idea, or shed a tear, or laugh out loud.

Now, the reader may complain, this begins to sound as if I ought to go off and write my own

From the *Harvard Bulletin*, February 1973, pp. 30–31. Reprinted by permission.

questionnaire. Why not? It's an ancient political maxim that you can't beat something with nothing. What follows here is offered to my classmates, and others, in the best contemporary tradition as a counter-questionnaire. Replies, anonymous or otherwise, may be addressed to me in care of the *Bulle-*

tin. If the results reveal anything that seems useful, interesting, or amusing, I'll pass them on to the editor of the *Bulletin.*

Meanwhile, I must complete the blue form and the white form so they get in before the deadlines.

COUNTER-QUESTIONNAIRE

How often are you astonished these days? _____

   By yourself? _____ By others? _____

Do you laugh much? _____ About what? _____

Do you cry ever? _____ About what? _____

What do you think about when you wake up at 3 in the morning? _____

When did you last forget yourself? _____

   Under what circumstances? _____

What is the most interesting thing about your life? _____

_____ The most boring? _____

If you had it to do over again, would you be a different person? _____

   In what ways? _____

If you had to be someone else, who would you be? _____

Are you more likely to be the victim or the perpetrator? _____

Do your children understand you? _____

What do you hope for your children? _____

_____ What do you fear? _____

_____ What do you

expect? _____

Does God love you? _____ Do you care? _____

Where are you likely to spend eternity? _____

What's most wrong with this world? _____

   Is it anybody's fault? _____ Whose? _____ Can it be fixed? _____

   Is it likely to be? _____ What, if anything, are you likely to do about it? _____

Why do you drink so much? _____

Why doesn't this question apply to you? _____

As between polygamy and polyandry, which would you prefer? _____

Does space exploration excite you? _____ Bore you? _____

How do you feel about your dreams? _____

   How do the people in your dreams feel about you? _____

What has been your greatest disappointment? _____

Whom are you trying to impress? _____

   Whom are you trying to show up? _____

What are you really curious about? _____

Which of these questions was the hardest to answer? _____

_____ Which was the easiest? _____

_____ Are there any questions you'd like to ask? _____

_____ Or answer? _____

SECTION 2.3

The Logic of Sampling

Sampling involves selecting a segment of a larger group of elements for study. Studying such a subset affords considerable savings in time and money and often affords a higher level of accuracy than studying everyone or everything in the larger group. Consider all the practical difficulties and the length of time it would take to study all 15,000 students on a campus; the use of 250 interviewers (each interviewing 60 students) and the passage of time (with intervening events) may severely reduce the accuracy of the study. Hence, sampling procedures are used to increase the efficiency, reliability, and validity of a study.

RANDOM VERSUS NONRANDOM SAMPLING

Sampling procedures can be classified as being either random or nonrandom. Random samples are those in which every element (person, organization, etc.) has an equal and known chance of being selected, whereas nonrandom samples do not employ this principle. A variety of designs exist for both approaches. Considering first the random designs, the *simple random* design usually involves the use of a table of random numbers, although the principle is like the names-in-the-hat procedure. The *systematic* design involves selecting every element falling at a predetermined interval; simply divide the number of elements you need into the number in the population to determine the interval for selection. The *stratified* design involves grouping the elements on such characteristics as sex or grade level before selecting the sample. The *cluster* design involves sampling collectivities of elements, such as cities or blocks, before selecting the elements.

Turning now to nonrandom designs, the *quota* design allows the interviewer to fill predetermined quotas of certain characteristics of the elements, such as specifying that 50 percent are male or 15 percent are black. The *judgment* design involves purposive selection of elements according to the researcher's knowledge about the subject. For example, marketing researchers have concluded that Columbus, Ohio, is one of the most typical cities in the United States in terms of population mix. The *convenience* design involves sampling whatever elements are convenient to sample, such as students walking out of the library. The *snowball* design involves asking people to name other possible individuals to be included in the study. For example, Troiden (Section 3.1) describes how he used this design to secure the names of additional male homosexuals from several homosexual acquaintances.

A crucial implication of sampling design is the level of generalizability the design affords. Random designs allow the researcher to make inferences about the larger population within certain limits; this is accomplished using probability theory. For example, the random samples selected by the Gallup Poll researchers allow generalizability to all adult Americans within certain limits. Nonrandom designs allow virtually no such inferences about the larger population; a sampling of students walking out of the library cannot be generalized to all the students of a particular school. The importance of generalizability is contingent on the researcher's goals and topic. An exploratory study of spouse-beating would not mandate the use of a random sample.

A second important point regarding generalizability is that the sample can be only as accurate as the sampling frame, the list from which the sample elements are actually taken. A highly sophisticated random sample of the university student directory will have limited generalizability if that directory excludes the 20 percent of the students who registered late or requested exemption from the directory.

A word on random sampling versus random assignment: in the section on experiments (Section 3.3), we note the importance of randomly assigning subjects to the experimental and control groups to make sure the two groups are reasonably similar. But random assignment to either of these two groups says nothing about the selection of the subjects prior to assignment. If all the subjects are introductory psychology students of Professor Y, then in essence we have a nonrandom convenience sample. No matter how rigorous the experimental design, generalizability is extremely limited with such samples. Generalizability could be enhanced by first drawing a random sample of the student body and then randomly assigning those persons selected to either the experimental or the control group. Even then, generalizability could only be extended to the student body at that school since that is the population originally sampled.

OTHER CONSIDERATIONS

Sampling design is a highly refined and highly statistical topic in research methods. Fortunately, it is not always necessary for the researcher to be an expert in the nuances of sampling. There are two reasons for this assertion. Many research studies involve analysis of an entire population or involve populations that are extremely difficult to sample randomly. For example, no sampling is required if you intend to study all the elementary schools in Wichita or all the parachutists who are members of a national parachuting organization. Troiden found it impossible to develop a master list of all homosexuals in the nation (or even in a community) in his study included in the field research section of this volume (Section 3.1). Luckenbill (in the section on less obtrusive measures, Section 3.2) used all the murder files for one county for one decade, again not requiring extensive knowledge of sampling procedures. Most social science research articles, in fact, use either a nonrandom sample or a random sample of a rather restricted population.

Complete familiarity with sampling design is also not always necessary because a sampling specialist is often hired for a study of large size and budget. If the study is to be a major one and if it is well funded, it is wise to bring in such a sampling consultant. In comparison to data-analysis procedures, which are recurrent throughout a study and require a fairly extensive knowledge base on the part of the researcher, sampling is generally done only once in a study and can frequently be left to a sampling expert (you can always reanalyze the data after getting advice but you cannot redraw the sample). This is not to say the researcher can leave it all to the consultant; he or she must have a good working knowledge of sampling to both advise the consultant and interpret recommended procedures and to execute studies of lesser scope and budget.

THE READINGS

Applied Sampling by Seymour Sudman is the best book on sampling for those with limited resources and limited statistical expertise. The selection included here presents a credibility scale for assessing the quality of a sampling procedure used in a study (assuming the procedures are described; if not, be doubly careful). The scale includes four criteria—generalizability, sample size, sample execution, and use of resources—with generalizability comprising 20 of the possible 35 points. Obviously, Sudman judges generalizability as the most crucial aspect of sample quality. He then presents several examples illustrating how the scale can be applied. You might use his scale when reading other studies in this volume to assess the quality of the sampling procedures used.

Two comments are in order regarding this reading. First, the use of Sudman's scale can result in low scores for many student samples, given the typically low budget of such studies. Such studies, however, should still be undertaken as long as Sudman's major point is remembered: the sampling design largely determines the generalizability of the study. Second, his examples focus primarily on individuals as the units of analysis. But the sampling designs noted above and Sudman's credibility scale can be applied to subjects other than people. For example, you could take a random (or nonrandom) sample of schools, churches, letters to the editor, issues of *Redbook*, nations, communities, communes, sororities, suicide notes, murder files, or presidential speeches. Similarly, sampling designs can be applied to observation, experiment, and other designs besides survey design. Hence, in an observation study of one or two organizations, you could randomly or nonrandomly select time periods, events, locations within the organizations, or positions. It all depends on what you wish to study. Once again, the topic of inquiry influences the sampling and research designs selected.

SMALL-SCALE SAMPLING WITH LIMITED RESOURCES

Seymour Sudman

INTRODUCTION

Most social scientists who have no training in sampling get their ideas on what to do from reading other people's research in scientific journals. The reviewers of journal articles, however, are themselves not always experts in sampling and are primarily concerned with the substance of the article and the analytic procedures used. Thus, the quality of sampling in published studies varies enormously. Many of the studies reported are based on small-scale samples that have serious limitations, which are sometimes recognized and often ignored.

Abridged from *Applied Sampling*, Academic Press, 1976. Reprinted by permission. Some references added.

In this chapter, we look at studies selected from recent issues of the *American Sociological Review*, the *American Journal of Sociology,* and *Public Opinion Quarterly*, and comment on the quality of sampling used in them. This is by no means a random sample of studies. Very large national and cross-national studies have been omitted since they are discussed later in this book. Where multiple studies were found using the same sampling methods, only one or two were chosen for illustration. Also, while some of these studies have inappropriate sample designs, the editorial screening process has prevented most of the studies with really bad samples from ever seeing the light of day. The purpose of this chapter is to alert researchers with limited resources to procedures for improving the quality of their samples as well as to suggest criteria for reader evaluation of sample credibility of published research.

In criticizing some of these studies, we are not concerned with their theoretical or analytical procedures. A poor sample design should not lead the reader to believe that the findings of a study are necessarily invalid or that contrary results are indeed correct. Rather, concern about sampling methods should lead to reduced credibility of the findings and an increase in the uncertainty about their generalizability. The refutation of study findings must come from other studies with greater credibility.

A CREDIBILITY SCALE

To formalize the notion of credibility and organize the discussion in this chapter, a credibility scale has been developed for judging small-scale samples. The credibility scale includes the factors that samplers would generally consider in looking at a sample: the generalizability of the findings, sample size, the execution of the sample design, and the use of the available resources. The items included in the scale and the weights assigned are given in Table 1.

The weights assigned and the scoring of individual studies are personal judgments, so that different samplers might assign different weights and might rank samples somewhat differently from the way they are listed here. These weights should not be used uncritically to distinguish between samples with similar levels of quality. Nevertheless, readers should be able to detect the differences between the best and worst sample designs and be able to apply them in their critical reading as well as in their planning and write-ups of their own sample designs. It should also be noted that even the best of the designs discussed in this chapter have serious flaws and do not compare to the larger standard samples discussed in later chapters.

Geography

Before turning to a discussion of the specific studies, a brief discussion of the factors in the scale may be helpful. Greatest emphasis is placed on how well the data may be generalized. Unless one is dealing with a small special population in a single location, a limited sample does not usually represent the total universe. If one observes the same results in several locations with widely differing populations, however, one has a great deal more confidence in their generality than if the sample is only of a single location. The greatest relative increase in quality is achieved by increasing the number of locations from one to two, and comparing the results from the different sites. Combining the results of several locations could conceal important site effects and should be done only after a careful analysis has indicated no significant site differences.

The researcher with limited funds may feel that control of the field work and quality of the data collection will be improved by limiting the sample to a single location, but this assumption should be examined very carefully. Frequently, it will be found that tighter control can be maintained over small crews in several locations than over a larger interviewing group in one location, although it may require more effort by the field supervisor or project director.

Another alternative, which is observed in Example 1, is for two researchers in widely scattered locations to collaborate. The results obtained by combining resources are substantially better than the sum of two separate studies. Still another helpful method for increasing sample credibility is to compare the results of a study to those of earlier studies. If the results replicate those of earlier studies, both the old and new studies gain in credibility, even if the methodologies and questionnaires differ. If, however, the results of a study contradict the results of earlier ones, the researcher is faced with serious problems of deciding whether the dif-

Table 1. Credibility Scale for Small Samples

	Score
A. Generalizability	
1. *Geographic spread*	
Single location	0
Several locations combined	2
Several locations compared	
Limited geography	4
Widespread geography	6
Total universe	10
2. *Discussion of limitations*	
No discussion	0
Brief discussion	3
Detailed discussion	5
3. *Use of special populations*	
Obvious biases in sample that could affect results	−5
Used for convenience, no obvious bias	0
Necessary to test theory	5
General population	5
B. Sample size	
Too small, even in total, for meaningful analysis	0
Adequate for some but not all major analyses	3
Adequate for purpose of study	5
C. Sample execution	
Poor response rate, haphazard sample	0
Some evidence of careless field work	3
Reasonable response rate, controlled field operations	5
D. Use of resources	
Poor use	0
Fair use	3
Optimum use	5
Total points possible	35

ferences are caused by sample differences, different measurement procedures, or something else.

Discussion of Limitations

A careful discussion of the study's sample limitations is useful, especially for readers with limited sampling backgrounds. Thus, a study that carefully states and explores its possible sample biases gains rather than loses credibility.

As an example consider the following excerpts from Lenski's *The Religious Factor* (1963: 1, 33–34):

The study was carried out in the Midwestern metropolis of Detroit, fifth largest community in America today, and probably eleventh largest in the world. Here, by means of personal interviews with a carefully selected cross-section of the population of the total *community (i.e., suburbs as well as central city), we sought to discover the impact of religion on secular institutions.*

Strictly speaking, the findings set forth in this volume apply only to Detroit. However, in view of the steady decline of localism and regionalism in America during the last century, it seems likely that most of these findings could be duplicated by similar studies in other communities. This is a matter to which we shall return later in this chapter. . . .

In its economics, politics, ethnicity, and religion, Detroit most closely resembles Cleveland, Pittsburgh, Buffalo, and Chicago. In common with these communities, Detroit is noted for heavy industry, high wages, a large industrial population, a large proportion of eastern European immigrants of peasant background, and a rapidly growing Negro minority recently arrived from the rural South. Among the major metropolitan centers it bears least resemblance to New York and Washington, both of which differ markedly in terms of economics, ethnicity, and religion, and, in the case of voteless Washington, in terms of politics as well.

Despite these local peculiarities it seems probable that most of our findings in Detroit can be generalized and applied to other major metropolitan centers throughout the country, with the possible exception of the South. This appears likely for two reasons. In the first place, the issues we investigated are basically national in character, and not local. Advances in transportation and mass communication mean that people all over the country are nowadays subject to similar pressures and influences. Local and even regional peculiarities have been progressively eroded. More and more the nation is becoming a political, economic, religious, and social unit. Secondly, Americans are becoming more and more mobile. Of those now living in greater Detroit, nearly two thirds were born elsewhere. More than half were born outside of Michigan, and therefore outside the sphere of Detroit's direct influence, and within the orbit of some other metropolitan center. This constant movement of population also hampers the development of regional peculiarities, and promotes the homogeneity of the national population.

In the last analysis, however, the only sure test of the generalizability of the findings of a study based on a single community can come from similar studies conducted elsewhere. For this reason, throughout this book references will be made (usually in footnotes) to earlier studies which have dealt with similar problems elsewhere. In this way the reader will be better able to judge to what degree the findings of this study are unique to Detroit, and to what degree they may apply to other communities.

While the extended discussion of sample limitations possible in a book or monograph must be condensed in a journal article (if not by the author, then by the editors) some discussion of the critical differences between the sample and universe should be included.

Use of Special Populations

The use of special populations may sometimes be a powerful tool for testing a theory. In a study of the socialization of children, samples of school children are highly appropriate. For testing organizational effects on managers or workers, the firm is the logical place to begin. In Example 5, cadets at a military academy are used to study professional socialization.

In some cases the use of a special population may lead to obvious or potential biases. Thus, the use of college students to represent the total population leads to major education and social class biases. In addition, the authority relation between the students and the researcher may be such that response effects are greatly magnified.

A common use of special populations is in secondary analyses when data initially collected for one purpose are reanalyzed for a different purpose. If the initial data were from a general population sample, then, of course, there are no problems. Potential biases arise when a special population is treated as a regular population sample in the reanalysis. This procedure is sometimes justified because it makes very efficient use of limited resources; in this case, it is especially important that the sample be critically examined by the researcher for all possible biases.

Sample Size

...The adequacy of the sample depends on the details of the analysis. Few studies seen in the literature have samples that are too small when only the total sample is used. For most analyses, however, breakdowns of the sample are required; for many breakdowns, the observed samples are inadequate. A general rule is that the sample should be large enough so that there are 100 or more units in each category of the major breakdowns and a minimum of 20 to 50 in the minor breakdowns.

Sample Execution

The quality of a sample depends not only on its design but also on its execution. Low cooperation rates may indicate sloppy field work and lack of follow-up procedures. A frequent example of this is seen in mail surveys that use a single mailing and obtain low cooperation rates when additional mailings could increase cooperation to the generally accepted level of about 80%. The biases in mail samples are toward those respondents with more education and those who are most interested in the topic.

Even worse are personal samples in which the interviewer is allowed to select the respondents or households to be interviewed. Here no measure of cooperation is possible and the biases are likely to be toward the most accessible respondents. These are more likely to be women, unemployed, middle-aged or older, and middle-class.

Use of Resources

Although this factor is independent of judgments about the absolute quality of a sample, it seems appropriate to consider how well the sample was designed and executed with the resources that were available. Several of the examples to be given later report studies that were conducted in response to a specific news event. In these cases, the researchers rushed into the field with very limited resources. If they had waited to obtain funds and select a careful sample, the timeliness of the research would have vanished. Even here, however, some sampling methods are far better than others. A quick phone sample, for example, is far superior to street-corner interviewing, since it is far less biased and no more costly.

The use of natural clusters, such as classrooms when the study deals with children or college students, is also an efficient use of limited resources. On the other hand, if the study is to be conducted by mail, heavy clustering is an inefficient use of resources, since it reduces the generalizability of the results without reducing costs.

EXAMPLES

The examples listed here are in decreasing order of credibility, based on the credibility scale of Table 1 and on my judgment. A brief discussion of the aim of the study and the sampling method used is given, as well as the scores on the individual components of the scale. For additional information about the studies, readers are urged to consult the original articles, which should be readily accessible.

Example 1   "Effects of Vertical Mobility and Status Inconsistency: A Body of Negative Evidence" (Jackson and Curtis, 1972) and "Community Rank Stratification: A Factor Analysis" (Artz et al., 1971)

Both these studies are based on the same sample of six communities, three in Indiana and three in Arizona. Male heads of households were drawn randomly from the street address sections of city and suburban directories. The sample size was 686 males in Phoenix and between 300 and 400 in the other cities. In Indianapolis, the interviewing was part of the Indianapolis Area Project, a training program similar to the Detroit Area Study. In the other cities, interviewing was done by Elmo Roper Associates, a well-known research firm.

The first study attempted to determine whether dimensions of social rank combine addi-

tively, or interactions appear to support the notions of status inconsistency or vertical mobility. The results favored the additive models. The second study, a factor analysis of rank measures, suggested that stratification systems vary by community context.

Credibility Score. $31/35 = .89$.

Generalizability 6. The use of six locations widely separated and of different sizes is very useful. As Jackson and Curtis (1972:702) put it:

> *Analyzing our problem in several rather different communities allows us to estimate whether mobility and/or inconsistency effects are more or less general, or whether they appear only in certain social settings. It also allows us to see which effects do not replicate across cities in any fashion and hence should possibly be labeled chance fluctuations.*

The results reported in the first study are used to disconfirm a theory. As is well-recognized, the requirements for confirming a theory are substantially stronger than those for disproving one. Here the absence of positive evidence of status inconsistency and vertical mobility in six different communities would lead most readers to accept the research and reject the theory.

Discussion of Limitations 5. A careful discussion of the selected communities.

Use of Special Populations 5. The universe is limited to male household heads, which seems appropriate given the aims of the study. Households are selected at random from city directories.

Sample Size 5. It is clear that the sample sizes here are ample for the analysis.

Sample Execution 5. Although the completion rates are not given, and it would have been useful to have them, all evidence is that the study was done very carefully.

Use of Resources 5. This sample has two excellent examples of the careful use of resources. First, it combines research with training of students; second, it combines the resources of researchers in Indiana and Arizona.

While this is not a national study, some readers may feel that the sample size is too large for this study to be considered small-scale. The quality would not suffer very much, however, if the samples were considerably smaller, or if only four instead of six communities had been used. Thus, many of the techniques seen here could be used by researchers with more limited funds.

Example 2 "Social Position and Self-Evaluation: The Relative Importance of Race" (Yancey et al., 1972)

This study evaluates the effects of race, sex, city, age, education, marital status, and employment on self-esteem and stress: Race has minimal effects when other variables are controlled. The study was conducted with 362 blacks and 350 whites in Nashville, Tennessee, and 215 blacks and 252 whites in Philadelphia, Pennsylvania.

Employing 1960 census information and any information available on subsequent neighborhood change, residential areas in both cities were selected which were thought to hold lower-, working-, and middle-class blacks and whites. Within each residential area, blocks were randomly chosen. Specific dwellings were selected by systematically interviewing in every fifth dwelling unit. Within each dwelling unit, the interviewer attempted to interview the head of the household, but interviewed some second adult when it became clear that the household head was unavailable. The nonresponse rate, given three callbacks, was under 5% in each city. An effort was made to match race of interviewer with race of respondent, but approximately 35% of black respondents were interviewed by white interviewers. An analysis indicated no effects of the interviewer's race on the results related to stress.

Credibility Score. 30/35 = .86.

Generalizability 5. Here is another example of researchers, one in Philadelphia, the others in Nashville, combining their resources to give the results in two locations. While slightly less convincing than the results in six locations, these results are far better than if only one city had been used. Note also that this research was intended to disconfirm a theory, so fewer locations were needed.

Discussion of Limitations 5. There is a discussion of the differences between the two sites and the general effects of city and region.

Use of Special Populations 5. It is a general population sample with the head of the household interviewed.

Sample Size 5. The size is clearly adequate.

Sample Execution 5. The sample was carefully done with a very low noncooperation rate.

Use of Resources 5. The resources for this study were obviously less than for Example 1, but they were well utilized by combining researchers from two locations.

Example 3 "Employment Opportunities for Blacks in the Black Ghetto: The Role of White-owned Businesses" (Aldrich, 1973)

A study of black- and white-owned businesses in black ghettos in Boston, Chicago, and Washington, D.C., indicates that white-owned businesses are much larger than black businesses, dominating the labor market of the ghetto, and that white owners are much more likely to hire "outsiders" and whites. For comparison, ghetto areas are compared to nonghetto areas in the three cities. Of the total of 512 business sites, interviews were obtained from 431, giving a completion rate of 84%. This study was a follow-up to an earlier study of crime and law enforcement in the same neighborhoods.

Credibility Score. 28/35 = .80.

Generalizability 6. While three sites were used, the reader is troubled by the lack of locations in the West and South, although it may be argued that Washington, in some ways, is a Southern city.

Discussion of Limitations 5. There is a detailed discussion of the six neighborhoods. The fact that patterns of ownership and operation are quite comparable in all the neighborhoods studied is used to defend the generality of the findings, although occasional differences are observed.

Use of Special Populations 5. This is a study of small businesses, which is the population used.

Sample Size 3. The sample sizes are adequate when all cities are combined, but they become small in the individual neighborhoods, especially the black-owned businesses. There are only 18 black-owned businesses in the two neighborhoods in Boston, and 25 in Chicago. Since all the businesses in the neighborhood were sampled, the only way to increase the sample size would be to add more neighborhoods.

Sample Execution 5. There was a high cooperation rate within neighborhoods.

Use of Resources 4. Although the use of neighborhoods used earlier for another purpose is efficient since the location of businesses already had been done and interviewers were available, the firms chosen in these neighborhoods are not evenly distributed between black and white ownership. This results in a sample of 377 white-owned and 134 black-owned firms. For comparison, it would have been better to increase the number of black-owned firms and reduce the number of white-owned firms until the sample sizes in the two groups were about equal. This would have required additional neighborhoods plus subsampling of white-owned firms.

Example 4 "The Structure of Scientific Fields and the Functioning of University Graduate Departments" (Lodahl and Gordon, 1972)

Four academic fields—physics, chemistry, sociology, and political science—were studied and it was found that the relatively high paradigm development in the physical sciences facilitated agreement over field content as well as greater willingness to interact with graduate students than in the social sciences. A stratified random sample of 20 university departments in each field was chosen. The sample did not represent all graduate schools, only those listed in the Cartter Report of high-quality schools; within departments, all faculty members were surveyed. The overall response rate was 51% and a total of 1161 responses were received.

Credibility Score. 26/35 = .74.

Generalizability 6. There are two major concerns with the generalizability of this sample, although it involves 80 randomly selected departments. The first is the omission of schools not named in the Cartter Report. There is no discussion of why this procedure was adopted rather than using all schools that offer graduate training. The second is the selection of the fields. While there is a careful discussion of why these fields were selected, one might wonder if the results would have been the same had the biological sciences or other physical

sciences, such as astronomy and geology, been included.

Discussion of Limitations 3. There is a brief discussion of possible sample biases indicating no differences by age or rank of respondents.

Use of Special Populations 5. The use of faculty members is appropriate for this study.

Sample Size 5. The sample is large enough for comparison between the four fields.

Sample Execution 3. The low response rate in this study is due to the fact that only a single mailing was used. Two follow-up mailings probably would have increased the cooperation to 80% or higher and removed concerns that respondents most interested in the topic were more likely to respond.

Use of Resources 4. The use of mail for contacting faculty members is an efficient way to gather data when there are limited resources. It would have been better to put some of the funds into follow-up mailings to reduce bias, even if this meant that fewer schools could be sampled.

Example 5 "Power and Ideological Conformity: A Case Study" (Garnier, 1973)

This is a study of professional socialization at Britain's Sandhurst Military Academy, indicating that conformity to the staff's goals is achieved. The sample size of 883 comprised 92% of the cadets at the academy during 1967.

Credibility Score. 26/35 = .74.

Generalizability 1. Although this is only at a single location, some effort is made to generalize by discussing other studies. If resources were available, one could attempt to extend this study to other military academies in the United States or to officer candidate schools and other military training programs.

Discussion of Limitations 5. Given the limited nature of this study, the discussion of limitations is excellent. In addition to calling it a case study, the author concludes the paper with the following remark:

> It must be noted that these findings stem from a case study. While the findings presented here seem reasonable, they are never-

theless based on limited evidence. If the study of socialization, and particularly socialization taking place within organizations, is going to proceed further, the time may have come to manipulate the variables isolated here in the laboratory. If the laboratory is too artificial a setting, then future researchers should make sure that the variables described in the literature are systematically manipulated. Only then can reasonable findings become scientific [p. 362].

Use of Special Populations 5. Military academies are appropriate settings for studies of power.

Sample Size 5. Since all cadets were included, the sample size is clearly sufficient for this case study. For broader generalization, the sample could be increased by using more sites.

Sample Execution 5. The 92% cooperation rate is very good and indicates careful field work and follow-up procedures.

Use of Resources 5. The use of self-administered forms for all cadets indicates a careful use of resources.

Example 6 "Managerial Mobility Motivations and Central Life Interests" (Goldman, 1973)

Using 489 middle managers and specialists in seven American industries, the study relates "career anchorage points" and central life interests. The data indicate that, regardless of age, education, level of labor force entry, and present position, "upwardly anchored" managers and specialists are more work-oriented.

Credibility Score. 24/35 = .69.

Generalizability 3. The study was conducted in seven firms: two steel companies; a vertically integrated lumber and paper firm; a maker of paints, waxes, and wallpaper; a firm producing large plastic signs; a big city bank; and a mattress and box spring manufacturer. Although this is quite an assortment, the criteria for choosing these specific firms are not given; we can only speculate that possibly the investigator knew someone in each firm. Also, the data for firms are never shown separately so that one can determine something about the variability among firms.

Discussion of Limitations 4. Although a discussion of how the firms were selected is omitted, there is a discussion of the selection of individuals within firms and a careful discussion of other studies on the same topic.

Use of Special Populations 5. The use of middle-management executives and specialists is necessary to test the theory.

Sample Size 3. The total sample size is adequate, but the interesting comparisons are between "upward career anchorages" and the rest. There are only 66 respondents in the "upward" category, making many of the analyses very shaky.

Sample Execution 5. A mail-back system with two follow-ups produced an overall cooperation rate of 85%, with the lowest rate from any company being 82%. This is very satisfactory.

Use of Resources 4. The use of mail is an efficient procedure for contacting business executives once they have been located. The major problem with this study is that only 13% of the sample fell into the most interesting category, "upward career anchorage." A possible procedure for increasing the sample size of this group would have been to use some sort of screening questionnaire with a larger initial population and then to take all those with "upward career anchorages" and a subsample of the remainder. While this general procedure is usually very efficient, it might have been impossible to do any screening for this study.

Example 7 "Race, Class, and Consciousness" (Hurst, 1972)

This study relates race, class, size of birthplace, and age to class consciousness, race consciousness, and interest in politics. The data come from a sample of 1870 whites and 434 blacks in four cities in Connecticut. The findings indicate that both race and class are important and reinforce each other in their effects on feelings of exploitation or privilege, but that race is somewhat more important.

Credibility Score. 24/35 = .69.

Generalizability 2. The major problem with generalizing the data from this study is that all four cities are combined so that there is no way to tell if there are variations between cities. Also, blacks in Northern industrial cities may not feel the same as blacks in the South and in rural areas.

Discussion of Limitations 5. There is a careful discussion of the sampling and field methodology as well as a detailed comparison to earlier research.

Use of Special Populations 5. This is probability sample of white and black households in the selected cities.

Sample Size 4. While the sample is large enough for classification by a single variable within race, it is too small among blacks for any further breakdowns.

Sample Execution 5. The completion rate varied from 85% to 89% indicating, as does the discussion, that the field work was done carefully.

Use of Resources 3. For the purposes of this study, the sample would have been more efficient if half the sample were white and half black. This study, however, is one of a series based on results from the same locations; it may be that the other studies did not require as large a sample of black households.

Example 8   "How Fast Does News Travel?" (Schwartz, 1973-74)

The shooting of Governor George Wallace on May 15, 1972 provided an opportunity to measure how fast nationally significant news travels. Interviews were conducted by phone in New York City between 5:00 and 10:00 P.M. on the day of the shooting. Six interviewers completed 312 three-question interviews.

Credibility Score. 23/35 = .66.

Generalizability 0. The study was of a single location, with no discussion of other studies of the spreading of news.

Discussion of Limitations 3. There is a discussion of the study's limitations—that it was done in New York City, that only persons home between 5:00 and 10:00 P.M. were interviewed, and that households with unlisted numbers were omitted. It would have been useful to know the completion rate, the number of refusals, the number not at home, and the number of men and women in the sample. Comparisons to other studies, such as the Kennedy assassination, also would have been valuable in interpreting these results.

Use of Special Populations 5. The use of a phone sample of the general population is appropriate here because of the need for speed. Random digit dialing might have been possible.

Sample Size 5. About 60 interviews per hour were obtained. For the purposes of this study, this seems sufficient since the key question was merely "Have you heard the news . . . ?"

Sample Execution 5. Although the details are sketchy, the brevity of the questionnaire suggests that very few of the persons who were reached refused to answer the three questions. Obtaining more than 300 interviews in an evening is an accomplishment.

Use of Resources 5. Although this obviously is not a perfect sample, it is a very good example of the optimum use of limited resources to collect timely data when a significant event has occurred.

Example 9   "Ministerial Roles and Social Actionist Stance: Protestant Clergy and Protest in the Sixties" (Nelsen et al., 1973)

This study reports the results of a factor analysis of Protestant clergymen in five cities to items on the role of the clergy. Two roles—traditional and community problem solving—are especially related to protest orientation. Of the 960 respondents selected in Atlanta, Boston, Los Angeles, Minneapolis, and Pittsburgh, 443 returned mail questionnaires.

Credibility Score. 19/35 = .54.

Generalizability 2. Although five cities are used here, all the results are combined, so that one has no notion of the variability between a Southern city, such as Atlanta, and the others, all with their own special characteristics.

Discussion of Limitations 2. While there is a general discussion of cooperation rates by location and denomination, there is no discussion of why the specific cities were chosen or how they might differ from other cities.

Use of Special Populations 5. The use of Protestant clergy is a direct function of the purpose of the study.

Sample Size 5. The sample size of 443 is large enough for the analyses of this study but would be thin if there were separate analyses by denomination or city.

Sample Execution 2. The 46% cooperation rate could easily have been raised above 80% with two additional mail follow-ups. Although there are probably no education biases, there are obvious biases by city (cooperation ranged from 32% to 60%) and denomination (cooperation ranged from 40% for Baptists to 64% for Lutherans), and possibly by social action variables also.

Use of Resources 3. The use of mail is a good idea for this study, but there is no obvious reason for the study's having been limited to only five cities. Assuming directories were available for several hundred cities, a sample of 20 or more cities would not have required any additional mailing expenses, and would have required only a little extra for sampling. The results would have had far greater generalizability; also, some of the resources should have been retained for additional mailings.

Example 10   "A Test of Lindesmith's Theory of Addiction: The Frequency of Euphoria among Long-Term Addicts" (McAuliffe and Gordon, 1974)

Data are presented to show that long-term addicts experience euphoria frequently, crave it, and act to obtain it. The sample consists of 64 addicts in Baltimore—47 white and 17 black, 4 female and 60 male.

Credibility Score. 18/35 = .51.

Generalizability 0. The study is in only one city, with no comparisons to other studies.

Discussion of Limitations 4. A fairly good discussion of the characteristics of the sample is provided, but no discussion of how the sample might differ from the population of addicts. Thus, one suspects the sample is low on women, older addicts, and possibly blacks.

Use of Special Populations 5. The use of addicts is required by the theory being tested.

Sample Size 2. The data are adequate to prove that addicts experience euphoria, but the sample sizes are too small for most of the other analyses.

Sample Execution 2. This is really the most difficult aspect of the sample to criticize. On the one hand, it is evident that no list of addicts exists and that no screening procedure could produce a prob-

ability sample of addicts. On the other hand, this sample is clearly biased, in many ways, toward addicts most like the three male interviewers and most involved in drug-using social networks. It would be useful to add other kinds of users to the sample, such as those currently undergoing medical treatment and those in prison or awaiting trial. If the results were confirmed for these other groups, the study would be substantially more credible.

Use of Resources 5. The use of personal interviews with addicts seems to be the optimum procedure, although it would have been valuable to extend the sample to other locations by cooperating with other investigators, if this were possible.

Example 11   "Aspirations of Low Income Blacks and Whites: A Case of Reference Group Processes" (Lorenz, 1972)

A sample of 67 blacks and 110 whites in public housing in New York City are analyzed to determine whether their aspirations are a function of their position in their own racial group or of the position of the racial group in the society.

Credibility Score. 14/35 = .40.

Generalizability 0. This is a special sample of low-income households in only one location, with no discussion of results from other studies.

Discussion of Limitations 4. The study includes a rather complete discussion of the characteristics of this sample, without any discussion of population characteristics.

Use of Special Populations 2. The use of public housing residents as representing low-income households is primarily for convenience and not because it is necessary for the theory. To find other low-income households would require screening the general population, a difficult task.

Sample Size 1. For many of the key analyses in this study, there are fewer than 20 respondents, and seldom ever are there more than 50 or 60. Thus, the detailed analysis is subject to very large sampling variability.

Sample Execution 5. The data for this study are a secondary analysis of data collected earlier by Caplovitz. As far as can be determined, the field work on the original study was done carefully.

Use of Resources 2. This study is an example of the secondary analysis of data initially intended for another purpose. The initial study was intended to prove that low-income households in New York pay more for furniture and other goods. The current study omitted about 60% of the initial sample because data for these respondents were not applicable or available. Although secondary analysis is very inexpensive, the small size and special character of the secondary analysis sample make broad generalizations very risky. One suspects that there are other sources of data for secondary analysis of low-income households that, if added to these results, could greatly increase generalizability and credibility.

Example 12   "Measuring Individual Modernity: A Near Myth" (Armer and Schnaiberg, 1972)

A sample of 156 white males in the "Uptown" neighborhood of Chicago was used to study individual modernity. The results indicate that modernity scales tend to predict scores on anomia, alienation, and socioeconomic status as well as predict other measures of modernity. Conversely, measures of anomia and alienation appear to predict modernity scores almost as well as do the modernity scales.

Credibility Score. $13/35 = .37$.

Generalizability 3. This sample is in a single neighborhood in a single city. There are, however, comparisons to studies in Africa, Brazil, Mexico, and Turkey.

Discussion of Limitations 3. There is a brief discussion of the characteristics of "Uptown."

Use of Special Populations 0. The use of white married males is not a function of the theory but, rather, a convenience for the researchers. (The study had another purpose—the study of family-planning norms.) There is no reason, however, to believe that using this population introduces special biases.

Sample Size 5. All the analyses are based on the total sample, so the sample size is adequate.

Sample Execution 0. The sample of white married males is a haphazard sample, so nothing can be said about response rate or representativeness of the sample, even for the single neighborhood.

Use of Resources 2. Personal interviews were used, which seems an optimum procedure. The cost of conducting interviews in several Chicago neighborhoods and of using probability procedures would not have been substantially greater than the haphazard method actually employed.

Example 13   "Race, Sex, and Violence: A Laboratory Test of the Sexual Threat of the Black Male Hypothesis" (Schulman, 1974)

Data from a laboratory experiment with 84 white male students at the University of California at Santa Barbara are used to support the psychoanalytic view of racism—that it is a function of the sexual threat of the black male.

Credibility Score. $7/35 = .20$.

Generalizability 0. The study makes use of data for students at only one school, and there is no discussion of similar findings elsewhere.

Discussion of Limitations 2. The characteristics of the students participating in the experiment are given, but no comparison is made to the population of all college students or to the general population.

Use of Special Populations −5. Clearly, the college students are selected here for convenience, not to support a theory. Although the author believes that the theory is supported because the students are generally liberal and educated, my judgment is that this is just the sort of situation in which students will respond to the authority of the experimenter and give the expected results. Thus, I find these results totally unconvincing. The same results on a general population sample, even if limited geographically, would make a substantial difference in credibility for this kind of study.

Sample Size 2. The sample is split into four treatment groups for analysis, and because of an error in operation, one group has only 14 subjects while the other three groups have 27, 23, and 20 subjects.

Sample Execution 5. There is no evidence of bias in the class that was selected for this experiment— 20 subjects were eliminated because they indicated an awareness of other similar experiments or because of an error in conducting the experiment.

Use of Resources 3. The ready availability of college students makes them the subjects for most experiments conducted by university researchers. Yet, as this example indicates, this procedure may seriously affect the credibility of results. The use of noncollege populations instead of, or in addition to, college students can greatly improve the quality of a sample.

It should be obvious to readers that there are very substantial differences in the quality of the samples presented in these examples; those given first are clearly better than those described later. There seems to be no value in arbitrarily assigning words like "good" and "poor" to the studies at the top and bottom of the list, since the changes in quality are continuous rather than discrete. As anyone who has ever graded examinations knows, it is far easier to recognize high quality than to decide how much poor quality should be penalized.

It should also be evident from the examples that limited resources need not necessarily lead to low-quality samples. The imaginative use of special populations when applicable, collaboration with other researchers, and comparisons with other studies all help to improve the quality of a sample. The appropriate use of mail and phone methods should always be considered. As is stressed throughout the remainder of this book, some careful thinking early is always better than later regrets and apologies.

SUMMARY

In this chapter are described a group of studies, none of which use standard national probability samples. There are, however, major differences in the quality of these studies, based on the following criteria:

1. How well can the data be generalized?
2. How complete is the discussion of the sample and its limitations?
3. Is the use of a special population necessary to test a theory or is a special population used only for convenience?
4. Is the sample size adequate for the analysis reported?
5. How well was the sample design carried out?
6. How well were the limited resources used?

Several procedures are suggested for maximizing limited resources—working with colleagues at other geographic locations, comparing results to other published work, and using special populations and mail and phone methods where applicable. The discussion of sample limitations should include not only a description of the sample but of the population that the sample is intended to represent.

Small samples, of necessity, limit the depth of analysis. The solution is not to ignore these limits in discussing the data but, rather, to oversample critical groups that otherwise would be underrepresented. There should always be a description of how the study was conducted, the methods used, and the cooperation rate achieved. These results are, of course, meaningful only if a careful design and not a haphazard sample is used.

Ingenuity and careful planning can overcome many of the problems associated with limited resources and can produce samples with high credibility.

REFERENCES

Aldrich, Howard E.
  1973 "Employment opportunities for blacks in the black ghetto: the role of white-owned businesses." American Journal of Sociology 78(May):1403–1425.

Armer, Michael and Allan Schnaiberg
  1972 "Measuring individual modernity: a near myth." American Sociological Review 37(June):301–316.

Artz, Reta, Richard Curtis, Dianne Fairbank, and Elton Jackson
  1971 "Community rank stratification: a factor analysis." American Sociological Review 36(December):985–1001.

Caplovitz, David
  1967 The Poor Pay More. New York: Free Press.

Garnier, Maurice
  1973 "Power and ideological conformity: a case study. American Journal of Sociology 79(September):343–363.

Goldman, Daniel R.
  1973 "Managerial mobility motivations and central life interests." American Sociological Review 38(February):119–125.

Hurst, Charles E.
  1972 "Race, class and consciousness." American Sociological Review 37(December):658–670.

Jackson, Elton F. and Richard F. Curtis
    1972   "Effects of vertical mobility and status inconsistency: a body of negative evidence." American Sociological Review 37(December):701–713.

Lenski, Gerhard
    1963   The Religious Factor. Garden City: Doubleday.

Lodahl, Janice B. and Gerald Gordon
    1972   "The structure of scientific fields and the functioning of university graduate departments." American Sociological Review 37(February):57–72.

Lorenz, Gerda
    1972   "Aspirations of low income blacks and whites: a case of reference group processes." American Journal of Sociology 78(September):371–398.

McAuliffe, William E. and Robert A. Gordon
    1974   "A test of Lindesmith's theory of addiction: the frequency of euphoria among long-term addicts." American Journal of Sociology 79(January): 795–840.

Nelsen, Hart M., Raythna Yokely and Thomas Madron
    1973   "Ministerial roles and social actionist stance: protestant clergy and protest in the sixties." American Sociological Review 38(June):375–386.

Schulman, Gary I.
    1974   "Race, sex, and violence: a laboratory test of the sexual threat of the black male hypothesis." American Journal of Sociology 79(March):1260–1277.

Schwartz, David A.
    1973–74   "How fast does news travel?" Public Opinion Quarterly 37(Winter): 625–627.

Yancey, William L., Leo Rigsby and John D. McCarthy
    1972   "Social position and self-evaluation: the relative importance of race." American Journal of Sociology 78 (September):338–370.

PART THREE

Modes of Observation

SECTION 3.1

Field Research

Close interrelationships exist between the problem selected, the research design selected, and the data and their interpretation. In this section we will demonstrate these interrelationships for field research, a strategy involving direct observation of social behavior.

ADVANTAGES AND DISADVANTAGES

The major advantage of field research is that it allows the researcher to discover the subject's own definition of reality, that is, the framework by which the subject makes sense out of the world. For example, a field reseacher may wish to observe in maternity wards to understand how mothers-to-be define the delivery process. The researcher attempts to understand this definition of reality by observing and applying analytical tools appropriate to the situation. In comparison, other research designs require the subjects to respond to a prior construction of reality developed by the researcher through such instruments as questionnaires. Hence, we could say that the field research design is a more valid portrayal of the situation.

Field research maximizes naturalism. Both survey and experimental designs disrupt the normal flow of events to some degree and thus may reduce the validity of the results. But most field research designs involve minimal or no disruption of the normal flow of events; an observer in a preschool will only minimally affect the behavior of the children. Field research is also the only appropriate design for certain topics and subjects, such as an analysis of sex-role behavior among nursery school children. Another advantage is that the researcher can incorporate the context of the behavior in the attempt to explain certain social phenomena; the same behavior may have different meanings or consequences in different settings. Field research also allows greater in-depth analysis because research is usually done over a longer time period. And because the researcher is actually present, less reliance need be placed on the subject's account of the social setting.

Field research has several disadvantages as well. The researcher's lack of control over the situation makes causal assertions difficult. Because most field researchers study only one or a few settings, generalization becomes difficult; one cannot generalize to all nursery schools on the basis of a study in only one nursery school. Measurement of the variables is also more problematic than with other designs, which contributes to the difficulty of both data analysis and the establishment of causal relationships. For example, a researcher may have difficulty measuring ambivalence in an observation study of the birthing process. Finally, the time commitment required for field research results in severe constraints on numbers of subjects, settings, and concepts to be analyzed.

VARIATIONS OF THE BASIC DESIGN

Field research involves designs that vary in terms of the naturalness of the setting and the degree of structure imposed by the observer (Bailey, 1978:219). Hence, the setting may range from a highly controlled setting such as a laboratory to a completely undisturbed natural setting such as a cocktail party. The observer may utilize highly structured analytical techniques (such as the famous Bales group interaction technique) or more loosely structured techniques (such as just "hanging around" and developing concepts and categories as they emerge). Typically, the more artificial the setting, the more highly structured the observation technique.

Raymond Gold (1958) describes four roles an observer can play, based on a continuum of the degree of researcher involvement. In the *complete participant* role, neither the identity nor the purpose of the researcher are known. For example, a researcher may become a church member to study the church's members and structure. This role provides unique insights available only to members of a group, but may be difficult to execute over time. In the *participant-as-observer* role, the researcher's identity is known but the researcher still participates fully in the normal activities of the group. For example, a researcher may play the role of assistant in a nursery school although he or she is known to be a researcher. Knowledge of the researcher's presence, however, may alter the normal behavior of the persons being studied. In the *observer-as-participant* role, the researcher's identity is known, and the researcher interacts with members of the group without becoming fully involved in all the activities of the group. For example, a researcher may observe in a high school and occasionally become involved in classroom and social activities. Because of less participation, the researcher obtains a less complete view of the members' activities. In the *complete observer* role, the researcher simply observes and does not participate in the activities of the group. For example, the researcher may simply sit in a classroom without becoming involved or may observe students through a one-way mirror. The researcher's identity may or may not be known to the subjects. Each of these roles has unique advantages and disadvantages and each role influences both the data collection procedures and data analysis. Generally, the observer role maximizes objectivity, whereas the participant role maximizes comprehensiveness.

THE BASIC STEPS

The first step in field research is to decide on the goals of the study. Is the goal to test or to generate hypotheses? For example, a researcher may wish to observe in hospitals to develop hypotheses regarding nurses' reactions to dying patients and their families. Also, is the goal descriptive or explanatory or exploratory? The nature of the goal influences the execution of the study. The second step is to decide whom to study, being careful to select a group that is not overstudied and that has relevance for your theoretical emphases. A study of dental students, for example, would be relevant to test professional socialization theories.

Third, clarify exactly what you wish to examine. The focus may be on attitudes, on participants' definition of the situation, on the effect of the context, on actions as compared to attitudes, or on interpersonal relationships. The fourth step is to gain entry, often a difficult step. Focus on legitimizing yourself as a researcher with persons at various levels in the structure of the group or organization being studied. Then rapport must be established, particularly if the culture and language of the group are different from your own. Consider the importance of reciprocity at this point—what can you provide the persons you are studying in exchange for their willingness to be studied?

Next comes the actual observing and recording. Note-taking should be done carefully with attention to developing categories for analysis. Separate description from interpretation from evaluation. After exiting from the setting, the rather difficult process of making sense of the data must begin. The importance of filing and cross-filing will become evident. At this stage, pay attention to analyzing the sequence of events and the interrelationships between variables. You may wish to focus on apparent similarities and dissimilarities. Using a diagram or flowchart may prove helpful. You may also want to relate your data analysis to other studies on similar topics. (For an excellent, more detailed treatment of field research, see Bailey, 1978.)

THE READINGS

This section contains the personal reflections of two field researchers. Troiden's study involved extensive observation and interviews with homosexuals in an attempt to uncover relevant factors associated with the acquisition of gay identity among men. Fitzpatrick's goal was to identify the relevant dimensions of an occupational subculture of danger among underground miners. Both researchers spent a great deal of time in the field, Troiden to secure an understanding of the homosexual experience so that he could develop a series of relevant questions to be asked in later interviews on gay identity and Fitzpatrick to "become one of them" so that he might learn by experience how miners cope with the ever-present threat of danger. Both used the field technique for its main advantage: a comprehensive analysis of the interaction effect of people in social situations—what is also called a contextual analysis. Both used this technique to get as close as possible to an "insider's" definition and experience of a situation.

Since one emphasis in this volume is how methodological strategy influences the entire research process, I would like to compare the implications of the roles played by Fitzpatrick and Troiden: complete participant versus observer as participant. Since Fitzpatrick was a complete participant in the mine, his research role was unknown to those whom he studied. Troiden's subjects knew his researcher role. Fitzpatrick had no entry problems (apart from a prior futile attempt to secure entree at a different mine by explaining his research role), while Troiden was constantly questioned by gay respondents about his reasons for the study. Troiden therefore had to develop justifications for the study, whereas Fitzpatrick did not.

As a miner, Fitzpatrick had to meet all the obligations of being a miner, whereas Troiden only partially engaged in the activities of homosexuals. As a result Fitzpatrick had difficulty in examining a wide sampling of mining activities, whereas Troiden deliberately sampled widely in his attempt to represent homosexuals in different geographical areas and with various demographic characteristics. Troiden was able to openly take notes and share some of his notes with informants to establish their validity, but Fitzpatrick had to settle for memorizing key points or hastily scratching a few notes with the aid of his mining light only.

Although both experienced ethical dilemmas, Fitzpatrick had to deal with the issue of being a disguised researcher. Troiden, on the other hand, had explicit procedures for informing his gay informants of his researcher role. But then Troiden had to be concerned with how his presence affected his subjects' behavior and verbalizations, a problem Fitzpatrick did not face. As a result of their different research roles, Troiden, unlike Fitzpatrick, felt a need to meet reciprocity demands of informants. And last, Fitzpatrick relied more on sensitizing concepts and nonquantitative means of data analysis, while Troiden emphasized the development of forced-choice and other questions in his desire to use quantitative analysis. These two studies illustrate well the influence of methodological strategy on data collection and analysis.

Since both authors used the observation technique, similarities in their experiences also exist. Observation research is often used for exploratory or theory-generating purposes (see their discussions of "grounded theory"). Fitzpatrick used observation to develop an explanatory approach to understanding occupational danger and Troiden to develop a list of questions to be asked in a later interview study. Neither had precisely defined hypotheses prior to completing the study; instead, each researcher was looking for relevant concepts to analyze the characteristics of social reality reflected in the data. Observation research involves constant reformulation of data and analytical categories; both authors speak of making such reformulations. Any form of participant observation also involves ethical dilemmas; the sections of the personal journals dealing with ethics are particularly informative. Both emphasize how such dilemmas must be resolved within the context of the particular research project.

Observation research by necessity means studying a limited number of cases. Fitzpatrick studied only one mine and Troiden only a few dozen homosexuals (for the observation phase of his study). Generalizability is thus limited. Because generally only one researcher is involved in observation research and because that researcher is frequently intimately involved with the subjects, the problems of bias and reliability arise. These twin problems of low generalizability and reliability constitute the major disadvantages of observation research.

In the first article Troiden "tells all," or at least more than most observation researchers do. Note his personal reactions to completing the study, particularly how he responded to questions about his credibility as a researcher and his sexual orientation. At one point he even questioned his humanity; at another he reports being alienated from the respondents. Note too the crucial role his friend played in establishing contacts and coping with the demands of the research. Note the implications of his high level of involvement in the research; he explains that such involvement yields a higher level of sensitivity to the phenomenon under investigation, but such involvement may also influence the researcher's objectivity. And, last, note his insightful analysis of the ethical dilemmas he encountered, particularly with regard to honesty, exploitation, and confidentiality.

When reading Fitzpatrick's article, notice his emphasis on *scientific* observation as opposed to everyday observation. The former is more systematic, precise, objective, and analytical than the latter. Fitzpatrick discusses several issues to consider when choosing a unit or setting: careful preliminary investigation, personal strengths and characteristics, and analysis of potential roles to be filled. He emphasizes the importance of locating oneself where the action is and developing a balance between generating data with questions and simply letting the data evolve. Note particularly his injunction to pay attention to the unique; such phenomena often aid considerably in understanding the ordinary. Fitzpatrick describes some of the elements of "going native" and the steps he took, such as leaving the mine for a short time, to prevent loss of objectivity. It is interesting that Fitzpatrick does not spend much time discussing ethics, particularly given his disguised role in the mine. He notes that few ethical concerns were relevant for him, particularly since he was not studying topics such as explanations of or blame for mine danger. Furthermore, he met all of the demands of his position as a miner. Finally, note his suggestions for analyzing data gathered in the complete participant mode, particularly his development of concepts to explain the social regularities observed and to impose conceptual order on the data.

REFERENCES

Bailey, Kenneth D.
    1978   Methods of Social Research. New York: Free Press.
Gold, Raymond L.
    1958   "Roles in sociological field observations." Social Forces 36(March):217–23.

RESEARCH AS PROCESS:
THE HUMAN DIMENSION OF SOCIAL SCIENTIFIC RESEARCH

Richard R. Troiden

This paper describes the observational phase of a study I conducted to determine the gay identity acquisition process among male homosexuals. Technically my study qualifies as an instance of "between methods triangulation"—that is, I used two methods, observation and formal interviews, to obtain the data (Denzin, 1978). I engaged in fieldwork primarily to determine what questions I should include in the formal interview schedule and to gain access to potential interviewees.

John M. Johnson (1975) and John Lofland (1971) have argued that few researchers tell all that transpired during their research when discussing how the study was done. Indeed, Lofland has remarked:

One of my mentors has commented that what typically goes into "how the study was done" are "the second worst things that happened." I am inclined to believe that his generalization is correct. What person with an eye to his future, and who wishes others to think positively of him, is going to relate anything about himself *that is morally or professionally discrediting in any important way? This is especially the case since field work tends to be performed by youngish persons who have longer futures to think about and less security about the shape of those futures. We delude ourselves if we expect very many field workers actually to "tell all" in print (1971:132–33).*

Whether it is discrediting or not, in this report I shall attempt to share with you a sense of what it is actually like to engage in observational research. I shall discuss (1) how I prepared for the observational phase of this research and gained access to potential informants; (2) the strategies I employed to include as large a cross section of the homosex-

Author's note: I wish to thank Professors Kenneth Feldman, Erich Goode, Charles Lippy, Ned Polsy, Myer Reed, June Starr, and Theodore C. Wagenaar for their criticisms of an earlier draft of this paper. This paper is based in part on research aided by a grant from the National Institute of Mental Health, grant number 1 RO1 MH 28155–01.

---

ual population in my sample as possible; (3) how I gained the acceptance of informants and dealt with the reactions of more conventional persons to the topic of my research; (4) how I made sense of the data I gathered during the fieldwork phase of my investigation; (5) the ethical considerations that confronted me and how I attempted to resolve them; (6) some of the more interesting results of my study; and (7) the impact this research has had on my personal life.

PREPARATION AND GAINING ACCESS

During the preparatory stage of research before fieldwork began, I spent nearly all of my time with a friend, a fairly well-known member of a gay community in the Midwest, who later served as my guide and vouched for my credibility during my initial excursions into the gay world. Most of the problems I faced during this period were self-generated. For instance, I was uncertain as to what I should say or do if sexually propositioned, groped, or asked to dance. I was also unsure as to how friendly I dared become with informants. I was fearful that some males would misinterpret my attentions as indicating sexual interest and that other men would view my behavior as playing favorites. Either way, I ran the risk of alienating potential informants, something I wished to avoid at all costs.

These dilemmas and others like them were for the most part resolved through discussions with my friend. He cautioned me against announcing to the world at large that I was on the scene engaged in observational research. Such behavior, he argued, would almost certainly make some of the men feel "uptight," ill at ease, and possibly resentful because they were present not to be studied but to relax and enjoy themselves. At the same time, however, he emphasized that if asked to explain my presence, I should do so immediately and with absolute honesty.

After my friend had supplied me with what I saw as the rules of decorum for the gay community, he then introduced me to his friends and acquaintances as "my friend Rick from New York who is interested in researching homosexuality." Not surprisingly, the nature of the introduction sparked the curiosity of these men. They almost always asked me which aspects of homosexuality I wished to investigate. When I told them I was in-

terested in compiling a list of questions that gays themselves thought should be included in any study of homosexuality, most were flattered and volunteered to assist me.

At this time I did not "go public"—my presence was unknown to most of the gay community. I avoided gay bars, parties, and the like until I had a clear sense of exactly what I wanted to accomplish. My interactions therefore were confined primarily to my friend and his close friends during the initial stage of observation. Our meetings usually took place in their homes or apartments.

Since I cultivated friendships with members of the gay community as a means of determining the questions male homosexuals themselves thought should be included in any study of homosexuality and since I used these opportunities to seek out potential interviews with these men, I adopted the "participant-as-observer" role. Following Gold (1958), when a researcher uses this strategy, both the informant and the investigator are aware that theirs is a research relationship. The informant, then, is aware that he or she is providing the investigator with information he or she plans to use and perhaps publish. As Gold has stated, the researcher who adopts this role is apt to spend as much time participating as observing:

> At times he observes formally, as in scheduled interview situations; and at other times he observes informally—when attending parties, for example (Gold, 1958:220).

Once my friend and his friends and acquaintances had supplied me with a list of questions they felt I should include in my interview schedule, I decided to spend as much time as I could with these men during their leisure time in order to become relaxed and comfortable both in the gay world itself and in the company of gay men. Once comfortable, I was ready to enter the field.

MAXIMIZING
VARIATION IN THE SAMPLE

Heeding the advice of Rosalie Wax (1957), once I went public I tried to avoid partisan identification with any specific clique structure lest this result in other cliques being closed to me. In addition, following Weinberg and Williams (1972:172), I sought to avoid "being overly identified with the least accepted members of the group because they are most available for social engagement."

The avoidance of overidentification with any one person or clique posed a serious problem for me. At large social gatherings I often tend to act remote or withdrawn. Even in settings peopled mainly with friends and acquaintances, my interaction (if any) is usually confined to a small group of very close friends. By temperament, then, I am suited for "Polsky-style" field research: I have little or no difficulty in keeping my mouth shut and my eyes open (Polsky, 1967). But this personal style is disastrous if one's goal is to penetrate as many friendship networks as possible to obtain interviews with a wide cross section of the homosexual population. With the help of informants, a relatively straightforward method was devised to circumvent the problem of my reticence and maximize the variation within my sample.

As social groupings, many homosexual friendship groups overlap and those that do not often contain members who, although they may not socialize, know one another. Informants I knew and felt comfortable with agreed to introduce me to acquaintances in friendship groups other than their own. Hence, my sampling technique was that of the "snowball sample." Such a sampling strategy is particularly useful for populations for which no master list exists (see Section 2.3 in this volume on sampling).

The snowball sampling procedure had three benefits. First, it placed me in a social role in which I felt comfortable—that of researcher as opposed to socializer. Second, it minimized the extent to which my own personal preferences and biases guided the selection of source persons. And third, it assisted me in maximizing the types of persons included in my study.

GAINING ACCEPTANCE AND CONVENTIONAL REACTIONS

Not unlike others who have conducted observations in natural settings, once I was in the field on a regular basis and started asking men if they would be willing to take part in a formal interview session, I found my acceptance by them put to the test (Carey, 1972; Goode, 1970; Polsky, 1967; Weinberg and Williams, 1972; Whyte, 1955). In addition to the problem of acceptance, my competence to do research, my credibility as genuine investigator, and my sexual identity were repeatedly challenged even though I was introduced to potential informants by people I had already interviewed. The problems I encountered nearly led me to abandon the project.

Like Gans (1968), I found the task of establishing myself as a credible and competent researcher far more difficult and time-consuming than I had anticipated. In addition to anticipated questions as to anonymity and confidentiality, nearly all of the men to whom I was introduced asked me to spell out my operational definition of homosexuality, demanded to know the steps I had taken or planned to take in order to interview a cross section of the homosexual population, asked me to list the sources from which I had obtained the interview schedule items, and so forth. I used such discussions to my own advantage by emphasizing the important role their referrals and introductions would play in helping me gain access to a broad spectrum of the homosexual population.

Once satisfied that I had developed clear-cut strategies to cope with methodological issues, many of the men insisted I level with them and declare what I expected to gain from the research. Not surprisingly, the answers "I want to make life easier for homosexuals in American society" or "It is my hope to enlighten society at large by presenting a portrait of gay life as it really is" would not have been accepted as valid motives (even if these had *actually* been my motives). Indeed, on numerous occasions I was told so. My claim that the project had initially been conducted to obtain data for a social deviance term paper and later expanded into a dissertation research project was met with skepticism. I was extremely upset by these responses. I took them as challenges to my honesty and professional integrity.

Fortunately, time spent in the gay world convinced me there were very valid reasons why neither my honesty nor professional integrity should have necessarily been assumed. During the course of my fieldwork, for instance, I observed ten to fifteen different young men in varied situations introduce themselves as persons doing research for a term paper for social problems or a social deviance course. Without exception, several drinks later near evening's end, these men declared themselves gay and/or allowed themselves to be "seduced."

I nevertheless remained deeply troubled when my credibility was called into account. This distressed me far more than the challenges I received regarding the nature of my own sexual orientation. If my own research experience was in any way typical (and at this time I have no reason to believe otherwise), I should find it extremely difficult to take seriously any male researcher's claims that his sexual identity was not called into account while conducting an investigation of gay men. I can think of no instance in which my sexual orientation went *unchallenged!* I was invariably viewed in one or more of the following ways: (1) as a person who was genuinely gay but a professional, unwilling to allow his homosexuality to interfere with his research; (2) as a person uncertain of his own sexuality and fighting an intrapsychic battle against openly recognizing, acting on, and accepting his homosexuality; (3) as an individual who was fully aware of his homosexuality but unwilling to act on it for fear of endangering his professional standing; (4) as a latent homosexual, completely unaware of the repressed homosexual component in his personality; (5) as a gay who was using the interview session either as a means of meeting potential sexual partners or as a vehicle for making a "perfect match"—that is, locating a lover.

I was neither surprised nor upset when informants classified me in any one of the first four categories. Such categorizations did not strike me as unwarranted. When asked about my sexual identity, I always stated that, given the Kinsey (1948) data, I believed that most men, including myself, given an ideal opportunity, would have sex with the right man at an opportune time during their lives. I also stated that at rock bottom my own sexual orientation and behavior had nothing to do with my presence in the gay world. This argument satisfied many—but by no means all—of the informants. The unsatisfied invariably accused me of using the research to obtain "tricks" (sexual partners) or meet a potential lover. In these situations I came dangerously close to losing control.

Like Weinberg and Williams (1972), I found myself extremely alienated from informants during this stage. I came close to nearly believing that most gays *are* "paranoid" and "vicious." After finding myself on a number of occasions close to the brink of arguing with an informant, I turned to my gay friend (a trained researcher) for advice. After hearing how upset I became when informants challenged my credibility, my friend responded in roughly the following manner:

We've been friends for years. You helped me get my head together about my gayness. That's why I'm helping you. Your project is almost as important to me as to you. But man, there are a few things you better get straight. Who the hell do you think you are that your word should be taken at face value? You are, to most of these men, just another guy who has turned up with a safe story to justify his presence on the gay scene. True, you have people willing to vouch for you, but that helps only so far. Why should anyone not suspect your motives? Why should anyone not challenge you? By your very presence you are violating their privacy, intruding on their lives.

More important, you are trying to get them to consent to an interview during which they will be asked to tell you—a relative stranger—about aspects of their lives they may never have shared even with persons they love. In the course of the interview session—remember, I know the kinds of questions you plan to ask—you will ask these men to explain why they want a lover or why they lost one, how they came to recognize their gayness and how this affected them. You are bound to open up old emotional wounds, force people to confront painful memories. Most of the guys suspect this will happen. Would you readily agree to such a session with a relative stranger? Wouldn't you challenge his motives? Sound him out to see whether he is genuinely tolerant of your lifestyle? Try to determine whether the person is interested in you as a person or as a casual fling? Given your training, if you were in this situation you'd probably give the researcher more shit than you'll receive from all of the persons you contact combined.

At best, when you observe, you are a spy. At best, when you interview, you are an interrogator. You can't afford to think otherwise. You must always keep this in mind. The way I see it, the spy and the interrogator have no right to decent treatment let alone the right to expect it—let alone assume it.

As for your using the interview sessions as a means of getting tricks, ask your contacts if they would spend two hours talking someone into an interview and another three to four hours interviewing them simply for the sake of a night in the rack. Most wouldn't, so they should be able to relate to the argument.

Extremely grateful for the priceless advice, I returned to the field with what I felt to be a firmer sense of self and situation.

My tolerance and sincerity were inadvertently put to test during a lavish Sunday brunch attended by over a hundred homosexuals. The host, an independently wealthy professional, had invited me out of curiosity. He wanted to know about my project and informed me he might consent to an interview if he could be convinced it was worthwhile. Two hours after I had launched into my sales pitch and still pressing for the host's consent, an incredibly outgoing and likable guy whom I had interviewed the week before arrived. Seeing the host and me speaking together he rapidly crossed the room, greeted the host and then turned to me and said, "I really want you to know how much I liked being interviewed. If I can help you in any way, please let me know." With that, he threw his arms around me and kissed me on the lips.

I was never able to determine whether this situation was a deliberately engineered test of poise or tolerance, or simply a spontaneous burst of genuine affection. Having interviewed "Al," I suspect it was the latter. Either way, my initial reaction can most accurately be described as paralysis. I did not experience either distaste or delight. Rather, I felt numb and simply stood there, immobile, frozen. My face—openly scrutinized by those assembled— was later described as an expressionless waxen mask. Unable to speak or act and acutely aware of the sudden silence and almost tangible atmosphere of tension that had descended on the party, I frantically wracked my brain for a solution to my predicament. As soon as I was able to assemble a string of coherent thoughts, I said the first thing that came to mind. I turned to the host and remarked, "Well, I guess my interview sessions can't be all that intimidating." He smilingly replied, "That would certainly appear to be the case. Why don't we get together for an interview?" The element of tension left the room as rapidly as it had accumulated and within seconds the party mood again materialized. I excused myself and retired to the bar to make myself a very potent drink, amazed I had been able to handle such a potentially explosive situation. I was certain that a negative reaction of any sort to "Al's" behavior would have jeopardized the research.

My relationships with more conventional persons among acquaintances, friends, family, and colleagues also posed some problems. I was often asked to "tell the truth" and give the "real" reason for doing a study of male homosexuals. The explanation that the research had initially grown out of a sociology of deviance term paper did not ring true to people who felt they had a right to challenge my motives. I was sometimes asked whether I was engaging in a form of academic voyeurism in hopes of resolving sexual identity conflicts of my own; a polite way of asking whether I was gay and having difficulty accepting it. My unmarried status and apparent lack of current female involvements also provided fuel to fire the imaginations of the curious. A conservative, "establishment-type" banker acquaintance informed me that in the interests of protecting his professional "image" he could no longer risk socializing with me if I continued the research.

As Weinberg and Williams (1972) point out, these types of pressures are not without their effects. I found myself becoming wary of broadcasting the topic of my study. On the other hand, like Humphreys (1975), I felt that as a researcher I should not allow the dictates of conventional morality (or the opinions of family and colleagues) to determine what I should or should not investigate. Even so, as the investigation continued, like Weinberg and Williams (1972), I found myself more and more often employing justifications for the study far removed from the "original scholarly motivation," especially with members of my family of socialization. Ultimately, I found myself justifying the study to my family in humanitarian terms ("It will help them").

MAKING SENSE OF THE DATA

Making sense of the data was relatively easy because I conducted my observations mainly to obtain questions for a formal interview schedule and to meet potential interviewees.

During the prefieldwork phase, I asked my friend and his friends, whenever a suitable opportunity arose, to indicate what questions they would like to see included in the interview schedule. In this manner, over two hundred questions were generated and included in the formal interview schedule.

I would have utilized an approach to qualitative data analysis suggested by John Lofland (1971) had my research been mainly observational. Lofland argues that an observer may find it useful to make sense of his or her data by breaking the data down into types or categories of social phenomena to describe the forms and variations each type assumes. Categories of social phenomena that a researcher may choose to focus on are acts, activities, meanings, relationships, participation, and setting. (For an elaboration on what is entailed in using this type of analysis, see Babbie, 1979:206–207.)

ETHICAL CONSIDERATIONS

The ethical considerations I faced during the observational phase of this investigation included the issues of honesty, involvement, exploitation, and reciprocity.

Following my gay friend's advice, when I was only observing men in a gay setting I did not announce my presence as a researcher. When I overheard something that interested me, however, I would then introduce myself to the person, explain my presence, and try to draw the individual into conversation. (See Converse and Schuman's analysis of interviewing as conversation in Section 3.5.) The dilemmas I experienced regarding when I should or should not disclose my presence as a social researcher led me to conclude that the morality (or immorality) of disguised observation cannot be so easily determined as Erickson (1967) would lead one to believe. Similar conclusions have also been drawn by Horowitz and Rainwater (1970), Humphreys (1975), and Weinberg and Williams (1972).

There exists no generally accepted set of ethical standards or rules that can easily apply to all situations. What is right or wrong, proper or improper conduct in the abstract must almost always be modified to some extent when enacted in concrete human contexts. I would assert that most—if not all—social researchers need not lie to their informants. I would also assert that a researcher need not "tell all." Perhaps the most workable line of action might be to volunteer information only on a need-to-know basis or when directly asked. In short, one need not tell all, but what one tells should be accurate and honest.

A second ethical problem I faced was that of involvement. How involved should a researcher become in the behavior he or she is investigating? In part this question is academic, and in part the accuracy and/or success of the research may demand involvement or noninvolvement, depending on the behavior in question.

Involvement is partially an academic question, for from the outset of an investigation the researcher is directly involved because he or she is a human being, as are the individuals studied. In a sense, then, for a human being to study other hu-

man beings is like trying to push the bus in which one is riding. The study of how a social researcher's "humanity" colors the ways in which he or she views the objects of investigation is a topic that has received widespread attention by sociologists of knowledge and for this reason will not be elaborated on here (see Berger and Luckmann, 1967).

An equally thorny problem, however, is the issue of *physical* involvement or noninvolvement in the behavior one is investigating. Social scientists traditionally have argued that one must remove rather than immerse oneself in the behavior under investigation in order to preserve objectivity. As Merton (1972) has reported, the claim is now made that only a black can understand what it means to be a black, a woman what it means to be a woman; thus only those directly *involved* in the behavior under investigation can validly study it. The same could be said for the study of homosexuals. I agree with Merton, however, that being what one is studying does not necessarily guarantee that the information so gathered is any more or less valid than the data gathered by "outsiders," that is, nonparticipants. "Insider" information is not necessarily more valid. In addition to occupying a minority group status, most insiders occupy many other "conventional" statuses—occupational, marital, religious, and sexual—that can color the way in which they view their less conventional status(es). An insider status, however, could possibly sensitize a researcher to questions regarding his or her behavior that outsiders had previously overlooked, and engaging in the behavior he or she is investigating might possibly give an outsider a glimpse of what it would be like to be the kind of person being studied.

A colleague who has studied marijuana smokers, for example, would smoke marijuana with informants after interviewing them to indicate that he was "all right" and that he would not—since he was now implicated too—report them to the authorities. As a consequence, many informants gave this person the names of others they felt would participate in the study.

Noninvolvement in the behavior one is investigating, however, is mandatory in certain instances. For example, I refrained from engaging in homosexual acts not for moral or legal reasons or for fear that it would impair my "objectivity" or because it "turned me off." Rather, I avoided any type of sexual conduct whatsoever with any informants because it would have totally damaged my credibility as a professional researcher.

The extent to which a researcher becomes physically involved (if at all) with the behavior he or she is investigating is dictated by the goal of the study, the researcher's perception of the professional role, and situational demands encountered. For this reason, I would suggest that researchers spell out in detail—that is, "tell all"—in their research appendices, indicating exactly what transpired during the data collection process, the stance adopted toward the phenomenon under observation, the degree of involvement, and the goal of the research so that the reader will have some basis for assessing the validity and reliability of results so gathered.

Emotional involvement was another ethical consideration that I confronted. When I started this study, I assumed I would have no trouble remaining emotionally distant from my informants. At that time I thought that as long as I remained in a professional role I would be able to maintain my objectivity and avoid painful emotional feelings.

Following the advice of Lofland (1976), I employed the tactics of rationalization and escape through work as a means of remaining emotionally detached from my informants. Ironically, it was my very success at maintaining emotional detachment that almost led me to abandon the study. Although I was able to empathize with informants as they presented the following accounts, my inability to openly *express* my compassion in a situation where I felt some display of human warmth was mandated led me to seriously entertain the possibility that I had forsaken a fundamental element of my humanity in my quest for professional competence:

A salesperson: When it had been established that my lover was definitely dying of cancer, I contacted his mother. We were both in his room when he died. She didn't know about us. She thought I was just a concerned friend from work. I didn't dare cry, so I expressed my sympathy. She told me I had no conception of how the death of her son would affect her. Somehow I kept from crying. (Informant started crying.)

A hairdresser: Mother (a psychiatrist) decided I was homosexual when I was about ten years old. She pulled strings and had me declared incurably mentally ill and placed me in an institution. I ran away when I was 16.

A student: Because I wouldn't go to bed with him, a "queen" called my parents and told them I was gay. They asked me if it was true and I told them it was. My parents lost it and started calling me a creep, pervert, degenerate and demanded I leave home. I attempted suicide about a week later. My parents relented and allowed me to come home if and only if I agreed to undergo long-term, in-depth psychotherapy. (Informant started crying.)

Being privy to revelations of this sort was extremely painful. I found myself dangerously close to developing anti*heterosexual* prejudices, to believing that heterosexuals, especially males, were insensitive, unfeeling, lacking in compassion. On further reflection, however, my incipient heterophobia was for the most part dispelled. Despite my outrage, horror, and empathy for the problems these informants encountered, I was nevertheless able to remain expressionless and controlled as I recorded these incidents. Although I wanted very much to do or say something of a consoling nature, I did not. I would like to say I held back because I felt my gestures would be misinterpreted as sexual overtures, but that was not the only reason. I am forced to confront the ugly reality that I did not abandon the research role in a situation when at least some display of compassion would have been appropriate out of fear of compromising the study. Such an insight did little to improve my self-image. When Weber was once asked to explain why he undertook his wide-ranging studies, he replied, "I wish to know how much I can take" (Coser, 1971:222). Regarding my own study, I would have to say that, unlike Weber, I learned that I have absolutely no desire to "know how much I can take."

A third ethical dilemma I encountered was the issue of exploitation of subjects. This line of attack, not easily dismissed, was adopted by self-proclaimed members of the "New Left." Their objections focused on the moral and political issues involved in deviance research. How could I, for instance, "morally justify studying a group so vulnerable and anxious to gain acceptance that its members would talk to virtually anyone they felt might assist them in gaining their liberation"? "Didn't I feel I was exploiting gays, especially since the data they provided would almost certainly benefit me but do little to help them?" Although there are certainly elements of truth to both of these accusations, the first issue—exploitation of a vulnerable group—is essentially an empirical one that remains to be verified. As for the second accusation—exploitation out of self-interest—I cannot conceive of a way in which the potential benefits of this research for homosexuals as a group could be assessed. Taken alone, the results of my work will probably have little—if any—impact on altering the status of gays in American society. But the combined effects of this and many other recent investigations may somewhat improve the life situations of homosexuals.

Regarding the fourth ethical consideration—reciprocity—Glazer (1972) notes that a researcher's job does not end simply because he or she has finished collecting the data. In addition to evaluating and analyzing the data, the investigator may experience a sense of indebtedness to informants. Indebtedness can pose a problem, as Glazer notes:

Will his interpretation of the material be unduly influenced by the sponsors' interests, the informants' needs, or the respondents' sensitivities? How can the social scientist prevent such considerations from biasing his report? What kinds of compromise have occurred because the investigator gave in to illegitimate demands for reciprocity (1972:125)?

Glazer discusses three types of reciprocity: personal, group, and bureaucratic. Personal and group reciprocity are of interest here because these were issues in my research.

Personal reciprocity involves the right of informants to expect anonymity and confidentiality in return for their information; this claim I honored.

Beyond the issue of personal reciprocity is the issue of reciprocity to the entire group under investigation. What obligations—if any—are owed the group as a whole because of the participation of some of its members in a research project? As Glazer (1972:126) points out, social scientists are beginning to realize that their research and writings "can particularly influence the nature of public opinion and public policy toward disadvantaged groups." Given this awareness, then, should a researcher publish results that he or she strongly

suspects can and will be used to justify the continued oppression of more marginal groups in society? Or does fidelity to fact transcend all other considerations, including those of a humane and compassionate nature?

The academic nature of my own work spared me from having to confront the issue of whether to publish my results. But what if my study had been on the patterns of drug use among adult male homosexuals, and what if I had found that a majority were heavy drug users? Would I submit the results for publication knowing that this information could be used to justify discrimination against gays? At this point I would have to say I do not know what I would do. Speculation is pointless. About all I can say is that this is a decision I will make only when forced to, when I am in a situation that demands it.

When I had completed each interview I gave the interviewee the opportunity to ask me questions regarding my own life experiences and work. Since I had no way of contacting any of these men after the interview sessions, I also told them how they could contact me should they wish to obtain the results of the study once the data had been analyzed. I viewed this strategy as both a courtesy and a means of subject repayment. But I was still dissatisfied. I felt even more was owed my informants, so I cast about until I hit on a way I could do at least some of the men a favor without compromising either professional ethics or the research itself.

One of the first impressions I formed during my early days in the field was of the demand for gay professionals. A number of men told me they lived in constant fear of contracting a venereal disease and finding themselves forced to explain its sources to a heterosexual doctor. Other subjects expressed a need for spiritual advice from gay clergy who they felt would better understand their religious conflicts. Lovers owning joint properties were often fearful that if one partner should die, the other might find himself dispossessed by greedy relatives. Thus they sought to make arrangements through a gay lawyer—with whom they could be perfectly open—to devise an iron-clad will to protect the living partner's interests. A few younger males wished to contact a psychiatrist who could help them become better adjusted to—rather than cured of—their homosexuality.

An awareness of these demands prompted me to contact a number of gay professionals to learn if

I might refer potential clients to them. They were delighted and encouraged me to do so. I imparted this information to men concerned about any of these issues after we completed the formal interview session. Thus reciprocity may include the provision of services, mutual self-disclosure, and access to results as well as the guarantee of anonymity and confidentiality.

RESULTS

Data analysis revealed that age cohort, high school heterosexual activity, and high school homosexual activity involving more than kissing are variables that relate to the mean ages at which interviewees suspected their own homosexuality, labeled their feelings as homosexual, defined themselves as homosexual, began socializing with members of the gay community, and initiated their first homosexual love relationships.

Several findings emerged regarding age. In comparison to older respondents (ages 35–40), younger respondents (ages 20–25) were more likely to

> think they might be gay at an earlier age (16.3 vs. 17.3)
> label their feelings as homosexual at an earlier age (17.9 vs. 20.6)
> label themselves as gay at an earlier age (18.9 vs. 23.0)
> socialize with members of the homosexual subculture at an earlier age (19.4 vs. 23.9)
> enter their first same-sex love relationship at an earlier age (20.0 vs. 27.3)

High school *heterosexual* activity involving more than kissing is another salient variable for gay identity acquisition. In comparison with men with no such activity, those who experienced such heterosexual activity more than four times a month

> were older when they suspected that they might be gay (17.2 vs. 16.5)
> were older when they labeled their feelings as gay (20.6 vs. 18.7)
> were older when they defined themselves as gay (22.8 vs. 19.8)
> were older when they started associating with committed homosexuals (23.0 vs. 20.8)
> were older when they entered their first homosexual love affair (24.9 vs. 22.1)

The third variable related to the rate of gay identity acquisition is high school *homosexual* experience involving more than kissing. In comparison with men with no such homosexual activity, those who experienced such activity more than four times a month

> were younger when they suspected that they might be gay (15.5 vs. 18.1)
> were younger when they labeled their feelings as homosexual (17.2 vs. 21.1)
> were younger when they defined themselves as homosexual (18.1 vs. 21.1)
> were younger when they started associating with committed homosexuals (19.1 vs. 23.3)
> were younger when they entered their first homosexual love relationship (21.0 vs. 26.4)

In sum, we find that all three variables are significantly related to gay identity acquisition. The age results suggest cohort socialization differences, with the younger cohort living through adolescence in a time of increasing acceptance of homosexuality. The results for high school homosexual and heterosexual activity reveal opposite effects in that heterosexual activity is related to older gay identity acquisition, while homosexual activity is related to younger gay identity acquisition.

IMPACT OF THE STUDY ON MY PERSONAL LIFE

I lost a sense of uniqueness as the interview sessions and my observations disclosed striking parallels between my own life experiences and those of a number of men I interviewed. I came to see the differences between heterosexuals and homosexuals as matters of degree rather than kind. I realized how flimsy, contrived, and artificial the distinctions are between what our society considers to be gender-appropriate behaviors. I also gained tremendous insight into what it may be like to be a woman in a sexist society. As I became familiar with gay cruising techniques, I was able to determine when another man found me sexually appealing. As a consequence I found myself able to comprehend the double bind in which I suspect women so often find themselves. On the one hand, I was flattered to see that someone found me sexually attractive. On the other hand, I felt degraded, dehumanized for being assessed as if I were a piece of meat. I was unable to devise a means of reconciling these conflicting responses.

Like Weinberg and Williams (1972), I had always supported the position of polymorphous sexuality. Even so, I also was surprised to realize it is perhaps as easy to be socialized to homosexuality as heterosexuality, that same-sex relations may be as easily accomplished as opposite sex relations if the situation is conducive. Accordingly, many assumptions I had previously held regarding sex roles, gender behaviors, and sexual orientations were shattered. Since these assumptions stemmed from experiences in the straight world, I came to view the conventional world as alien, deceptive, and unpredictable. At this time, I saw the gay world as the more familiar, predictable, understandable, and worthy of belief. In short, I viewed myself as having been *betrayed* by conventional wisdom.

Since completing the actual research itself, I have on numerous occasions been presented with evidence suggesting that although I am viewed by more conventional persons as an "expert" in the area of social deviance, particularly the realm of homosexuality, my social identity is now tarnished. In short, because of my research interests I have come to bear the brand of social stigma; I am seen by many conventional persons as *sexually suspect*.

As one who possesses, in effect, the socially stigmatizing identity of the sexually suspect, I have learned that social stigma can be both a burden and a blessing. Since conducting this research I have come to feel trapped in a netherworld between the heterosexual and homosexual communities. I am not fully at ease in either world. I feel *alienated*, like an outsider looking in. Neither lifestyle seems the more valid, rewarding, or meaningful. Although this limbo existence is at times unsettling, even depressing, the overall effect has been positive. As a result of this research I have been able to establish warm and meaningful relationships with a number of persons in both the gay and straight worlds. As important, I have become more inner directed, less dependent on the judgments and opinions of others for sense of self-worth. And that has made all of the difference. Would I do it again? Without a doubt!

CONCLUSION

Jack Douglas has suggested that fieldworkers

. . . should begin with as little control in our methods and with as much natural interaction as possible in the setting; we should go from the relatively uncontrolled

methods to the more controlled, from those forms most likely to have uncertainty effects to those less likely (1976:32).

Accordingly, my first contacts with members of the gay community were quite natural and relatively uncontrolled; once in the field I simply observed. Next, I openly disclosed my research role to the men I initially contacted and asked if they could indicate to me what questions they as "insiders" felt should be included in any study of male homosexuality. Finally, I adopted a more formal and structured method of interaction with my informants when they took part in formal interview sessions. On balance, however, my formal interviewing methods were made possible and more profitable only through this extended period of observation. My research experience thus reinforces the principle of multiple strategies for analyzing social phenomena.

REFERENCES

Babbie, Earl R.
  1979 The Practice of Social Research, 2nd ed. Belmont, Calif.: Wadsworth.
Berger, Peter L. and Thomas Luckmann
  1967 The Social Construction of Reality. Garden City, N.Y.: Doubleday Anchor.
Carey, James T.
  1972 "Problems of access and risk in observing drug scenes." Pp. 71–92 in Jack D. Douglas (ed.), Research on Deviance. New York: Random House.
Coleman, Kate
  1971 "Carnal knowledge: a portrait of four hookers." Ramparts 10(December): 17–28.
Coser, Lewis A.
  1971 Masters of Sociological Thought. New York: Basic Books.
Dank, Barry M.
  1973 The Development of a Homosexual Identity: Antecedents and Consequents. Unpublished doctoral dissertation, University of Wisconsin.
  1971 "Coming out in the gay world." Psychiatry 34(May):180–97.
Denzin, Norman K.
  1978 The Research Act: A Theoretical Introduction to Sociological Methods, 2nd ed. New York: McGraw-Hill.

Douglas, Jack D.
1976   Investigative Social Research. Beverly Hills, Calif.: Sage.

Erikson, Kai T.
1967   "A comment on disguised observation in sociology." Social Problems 14 (Spring):366–73.

Gans, Herbert J.
1968   "The participant observer as a human being: observations on the personal aspects of fieldwork." Pp. 300–17 in Howard S. Becker et al. (eds.), Institutions and the Person. Chicago: Aldine.

Glazer, Myron
1972   The Research Adventure: Promise and Problems of Fieldwork. New York: Random House.

Gold, Raymond L.
1958   "Roles in sociological field observations." Social Forces 36(March):217–23.

Goode, Erich
1970   The Marijuana Smokers. New York: Basic Books.

Horowitz, Erving L. and Lee Rainwater
1970   "On journalistic moralizers." Transaction 7(May):4–9.

Humphreys, Laud
1975   Tearoom Trade: Impersonal Sex in Public Places. Chicago: Aldine.

Johnson, John M.
1975   Doing Field Research. New York: Free Press.

Kinsey, Alfred C. et al.
1948   Sexual Behavior in the Human Male. Philadelphia: Saunders.

Lofland, John
1976   Doing Social Life. New York: John Wiley.

1971   Analyzing Social Settings. Belmont, Calif.: Wadsworth.

Merton, Robert K.
1972   "Insiders and outsiders: a chapter in the sociology of knowledge." American Journal of Sociology 78(July):9–47.

Plummer, Kenneth
1975   Sexual Stigma. London: Routledge and Kegan Paul.

Polsky, Ned
1967   Hustlers, Beats, and Others. Chicago: Aldine.

Troiden, Richard R.
1977   Becoming Homosexual: Research on Acquiring a Gay Identity. Unpublished doctoral dissertation, State University of New York–Stony Brook.

Warren, Carol A. B.
1974   Identity and Community in the Gay World. New York: Wiley Interscience.

Wax, Rosalie Hankey
1957   "Twelve years later: an analysis of field experience." American Journal of Sociology 63(July):133–42.

Weinberg, Martin S. and Colin J. Williams
1972   "Fieldwork among deviants: social relations with subjects and others." Pp. 165–86 in Jack D. Douglas (ed.), Research on Deviance. New York: Random House.

Weinberg, Thomas S.
1977   "Becoming homosexual: self-discovery, self-identity, and self-maintenance." Unpublished doctoral dissertation, University of Connecticut.

Whyte, William Foote
1955   Street Corner Society, 2nd ed. Chicago: University of Chicago Press.

REFLECTIONS ON BEING A COMPLETE PARTICIPANT

John S. Fitzpatrick

PARTICIPANT OBSERVATION AND PROBLEMS IN THE FIELD

Participant observation is a method by which an observer maintains a presence in a social situation for the purpose of scientific investigation. The observer "participates in the daily life of the people under study, either openly in the role of researcher or covertly in some disguised role, observing

This article was especially prepared for this volume. Copyright © 1981 by John S. Fitzpatrick.

things that happen, listening to what is said, and questioning people, over some length of time" (Becker and Geer, 1957:28). The term *field* refers to the natural settings where subjects spend their lives. If the laboratory is thought of as the prototypical controlled (programmable) research environment, then the field can be thought to lie at the other end of the spectrum—a research environment the investigator cannot unilaterally control (Douglas, 1976:11–37). The participant observer in the field is not there to experiment on the subject population. Rather, the observer sees firsthand the aspects of society under study and does so by examining and reflecting on the character of everyday, commonplace events. The observer intervenes in the social life of the subject population and uses personal skills as well as the conceptual apparatus of a scientific discipline to generate data. The observer becomes part of the data in ways that can (within limits) be taken into account. Being "field involved," that is, taking part in (and occasionally being part of) the observed situation, is the observer's approach to obtaining data (Gold, 1977:2).

Participant observation is a commonplace activity; most people do it every day. A child telling his or her mother what happened at school is reflecting on the events of the day from the perspective of a participant observer, as does the eyewitness to an automobile accident or the junior executive summarizing the content of a sales conference in a memo to the boss. The difference between everyday participant observation and that practiced by the scientific social investigator is primarily attitude and precision. The scientific observer strives to maintain an attitude of detachment, objectivity, and skepticism; the everyday observer usually does not. Furthermore, the scientific observer seeks detailed precision in observing and wishes to understand the subtle differences between things and events. Conversely, the everyday observer acquires rough approximations, the essence but not necessarily the detail, of what is transpiring.

Although everyday participant observation is somewhat similar to the scientific variety, moving to the latter approach is a difficult process. It requires a substantial modification of perspective as well as acquiring new skills that allow the would-be investigator to collect and analyze data. The acquisition of a scientific attitude is not something that comes only from textbooks; it is achieved by a constant effort to obtain a neutral perspective through the identification and mastery of one's biases and predilections.

Research skills—the "how to" mechanics of designing and implementing a research project—are much easier to learn or teach. Good research requires a valid methodological strategy and a repertoire of tactics used to implement the methodology in the field. Strategy refers to "why" a particular methodology is chosen and includes consideration of error and bias, the replication potential of the research, and the function of the study to test or generate theory. Tactics include the "how to" procedures used to overcome common, practical problems such as access to informants, field mobility, language barriers, and record-taking that inevitably arise and must be solved if the research is to succeed (cf. Schatzman and Strauss, 1973:145; Douglas, 1976:167–87). Social investigators often assemble research designs that are strategically sound but tactically flawed, or vice versa; this dilemma applies to quantitative as well as qualitative research designs. Participant observation and other qualitative methods are relatively unstandardized (Dean et al., 1969a:20) and are usually selected to allow evolution as the research proceeds (Bogdan and Taylor, 1975:26). The lack of structure is part of the strength of the qualitative approach since it permits flexibility. But it is also an Achilles heel because it leaves the research to the mercy of, or at least susceptible to, the capriciousness of the research environment and the human actors within it. A social science investigator must be knowledgeable about the types of tactical problems he or she can expect to encounter and what can be done to mitigate their influence.

Discussing tactical problems is difficult. Many problems are tied to a specific environmental context and constitute a unique challenge. Other difficulties stem from the personal habits or idiosyncrasies of the investigator or subject population. Many of these situations require remedial measures on a case-by-case basis. Nevertheless, there are also tactical problems that are more general in scope and that stem from occupying the research role, from being physically in the field, and from having contact with subjects.

I will describe in this article some tactical problems faced by social science investigators and discuss some lessons learned, often painfully, by a researcher who occasionally underestimated their importance in the conduct of field research. As the reflections of a "complete participant" (Gold, 1958:219)[1] my experiences are probably more extreme than those usually encountered by sociologists using participant observation or other forms of qualitative methods. I spent several months working as a miner in an underground mine to study how miners adapt to occupational danger (Fitzpatrick, 1974). Examples from my field experience in the mine are used to illustrate the impact of tactical problems on the research process.

GETTING INTO THE SITUATION

The first major tactical problem for the field researcher is gaining entree into the research setting. Gaining entree is also an important problem that will set the tone of the remaining research experience. Skillfully handled, entree will be one of several turning points in the study, but if botched it can immediately terminate or seriously cripple the research.

Before making a formal attempt to enter the field, a careful reconnaissance of several research settings should take place. The investigator should seek to enter and study those settings in which he or she would be personally acceptable and psychologically comfortable. Certain personal characteristics such as age, sex, ethnicity, social class, technical skill, experience, strength, and stamina are typically required or associated with occupying a role in a research setting (McCall and Simmons, 1969:29). Furthermore, a researcher may be psychologically unprepared to accept research in certain settings. It is probably not wise for an individual with strong moral convictions to attempt a participant observation of brothel prostitutes. Likewise, females will find it difficult to study the social life in a steel mill, physically weak individuals will be unsuited for participant observation among longshoremen, and whites may be unacceptable for studies in many black organizations. Some things in life are not transcended and an observer may not be suited for research in a setting considered optimal.

Even if entree can be achieved, the investigator may find the research role too demanding to be personally comfortable and thereby inimical to the investigative process (cf. Schwartz and Schwartz, 1969:100–101). People do not like to be placed in uncomfortable circumstances. If a condition of dis-

comfort persists, the actors will move to modify the condition by removing themselves or rejecting the observer. Obviously, either action is detrimental to data collection. All participant observers and their subjects experience discomfort with the research process, especially during the initial phases of fieldwork. The discomfort, however, should disappear once the observer's identity and place have been established.

I did not experience any undue difficulty in assuming the role of a miner for the purposes of studying how miners adapt to occupational danger. My sex, age, race, and physical stature generally matched those of the subject population. Furthermore, when people meet they seek commonalities from which to build a relationship. Because I was born and reared in a mining area, was of working class parentage, and had previously held a number of blue collar jobs, I possessed a natural background of common experiences that I could share with miners. While it is important to be similar to the subject population, it can also be detrimental to be too familiar with them. In order to restrict the possibility of damaging bias, it is best to study strangers or settings where the investigator has no personal interest or emotional investment. Finally, as a covert observer at the mine, there was no need to explain the research process or to establish myself as a "good guy" who could be trusted with what was uncovered. Instead, I was defined as a novice miner, expected to fill that role, and treated accordingly.

A second consideration in the prefieldwork site selection process is to find a setting that offers the appropriate size, scale, and diversity to meet the substantive and theoretical needs of the research (cf. Schatzman and Strauss, 1973:19–23). I discovered the relevance of this point by accident. Because I was seeking to understand the totality of social life in a mine, I required a setting that contained a relatively large number of workers, extensive division of labor, bureaucratization, and great diversity in the physical structure of the underground environment; yet the setting had to be small enough to be viewed in its entirety. During my research, I learned from other miners that the original research site (to which I had been denied access) was probably too large and too specialized to meet the goals of the study. In this case, entree prohibited at one setting had the fortuitous outcome of pushing the study to another, apparently more favorable location.

Advance information about the "role structure" of the research setting and the probable assignment of the observer is extremely useful. The role occupied by the researcher is possibly the single most important determinant of what one will be able to observe:

Every role is an avenue to certain types of information but is also an automatic barrier to other types. The role assumed by the observer largely determines where he can go, what he can do, whom he can interact with, what he can inquire about, what he can see, and what he can be told (McCall and Simmons, 1969:29).

My playing the role of the complete participant by becoming a miner automatically closed off a number of potentially rich data sources. Gone was the chance to interview the mine's management personnel, examine organizational files, or review accident reports. As a miner I had to work a specific shift, be a member of a set production crew, and be at a particular location in the mine at specified times. These role requirements seriously constrained my opportunity to talk with and observe other workers, particularly those on the surface, such as clerical and maintenance personnel. These restrictions were not as deleterious as might be imagined since they focused data-gathering on mine production crews—the miners who routinely confronted occupational danger and who would therefore be the prime subjects of the study.

Once the prefieldwork reconnaissance has been completed and the observer is reasonably satisfied that an appropriate research role has been defined and a suitable research site located, he or she must seek formal entree into the setting. The specific steps necessary to gain entrance depend on the type of setting to be studied and the goals of the research. If the research goals are potentially controversial or harmful to the subject population, entree will be generally more difficult than if they are not. As a general rule, always frame research goals in a neutral context. If, for example, the intent of the research is to study alienation among assembly-line workers and you want the cooperation of some corporation, it probably will be more productive to define the project as "a study of employee satisfaction" rather than "an investigation of the effect of a dehumanizing work environment on manual laborers."

As research settings become larger, more formalized, and more complex, the entree process also becomes more involved. As an operating principle, seek the approval and cooperation of all relevant parties to the research. Relevant parties may be defined as those individuals and groups who have the power to hinder or stop the study. In studying complex organizations it is almost a necessity to seek entree through two or more channels simultaneously to ensure that decision-makers at all levels are knowledgeable about, and at least neutral to, the research. Various authors have designated these tactics as "working the hierarchy," "dual entry," or "double access" (Schatzman and Strauss, 1973:18–33; Kahn and Mann, 1969:45–52). Entree is also a continuous process. The researcher does not quit explaining or legitimizing the research just because permission was given to enter the situation. You must continually earn your legitimacy with subjects by demonstrating trustworthiness and credibility.

When I first sought formal entree into a mine, the research design included the role of "participant as observer" (Gold, 1958). I was to be a known observer conducting research through the cooperation of the host firm. But I did not satisfactorily convince the company of my intentions and the firm denied permission to conduct the study in their mines. Company officials were concerned about how the research would be conducted, why it was being done, what the results would be used for, what costs the firm would incur, and what benefits it would receive for cooperation. Organizations have many good reasons for not cooperating with "outsider" research; such reasons range from bad publicity and theft and sabotage to the researcher's becoming or fostering a morale problem. Furthermore, such altruistic causes as the advancement of science and knowledge are not always supported in business or industry with the same fervor as in academic circles.

Having been denied access, I found it necessary to modify the research design and adopt the role of the "complete participant" to achieve access at an alternate research site. As a covert observer I avoided entree hurdles but raised questions of research ethics. Some social scientists (Erickson, 1970; Warwick, 1975) have argued that undercover research jeopardizes the goodwill of research subjects and the general public on whom social investigators depend. Other authors (Glazer, 1972; Rainwater and Pittman, 1967) suggest that the knowledge and social benefits gained can justify covert research. There is merit to both opinions and researchers must seek to balance pragmatic needs with their responsibilities to the profession, society, the subjects, and themselves (Bogdan and Taylor, 1975:28–30).

Conducting research at the mine did not raise significant ethical concerns for me as a researcher. The study was conducted in order to understand how people who work in dangerous occupations adapt to the threats of their work environment, not to examine mine danger, safety, or working conditions. The research findings have been presented from a judgmentally neutral perspective and structured in a way to protect the identity and confidentiality of all participants in the field setting. Finally, I was hired to be a miner and fulfilled the obligations for that position (I was rated as an "above average" employee when I terminated my employment).

How a researcher relates to subjects on a day-to-day basis, the degree of participation in group activites (e.g., some activities are immoral or illegal), and how research findings are disseminated are also proper subjects for ethical scrutiny. As a general principle, don't attempt to deceive actors in a research setting. High moral principle aside, deception is risky. It is difficult to sustain a "con" or live a life of pretense for long periods of time. If you are caught, the penalties for deception can be severe, including having the research ruined, being arrested, seeing reputations destroyed, or being physically abused by irate subjects. Furthermore, the fear of being caught in a deceptive practice compounds the natural stress of the research role. In the mine I experienced considerable apprehension over the need to be and act like just another miner; this apprehension undoubtedly had some effect on data collection. My uneasiness did not abate until the fieldwork was complete.

BEING WHERE THE ACTION IS

For the social scientific investigator in the field, the action is where the people are. Some research settings are very fluid; the actors move from place to place without a definite pattern or time schedule. Other research settings are highly structured—at a specific place and moment the actors arrive and the action begins. The degree of structure to a research setting has broad implications for data collection tactics. Highly structured situations frequently inhibit movement and can thus close off the researcher from valuable data. Likewise, extremely fluid settings may be hard to follow and discern.

A mine is a highly structured work environment. The division of labor within the mine separates work crews by job type (e.g., trammers, stopers, slusher operators, drifters, etc.), each assigned to different locations within the mine. Large spatial distances separate work groups and, typically, a miner spends the entire work shift in the company of one or two persons. As a miner, separated from co-workers by work role (assignment) and spatial distance, I had to focus data collection on my work partners. Thus, my data largely consists of information gathered from a collectivity of dyads and triads. Observation of larger groups was limited to brief encounters during the day. These encounters occurred during certain daily routines—changing clothes, showering, and trips to and from the mine—and during special events—accidents, equipment breakdowns, safety drills, and ritualized horseplay on certain days of the year. Because I was forced to focus on one or two individuals at a time, my informants were quickly exhausted as data sources. It was also difficult to cross-check the reliability of the data when I could not corroborate data from one source with other sources. I needed to be able to move around and observe other miners, but that was impossible given the fact that I was assigned as a stope[2] miner. Furthermore, work assignments were rarely changed. Miners have a saying that the only way one got out of a stope was to bid (based on seniority), quit, or die. I was effectively blocked from contact with other miners during the greatest part of the work shift. This tactical problem was solved accidently when I missed a couple of shifts and returned to work to find myself with a new job assignment and a fresh opportunity for data collection.

In addition to the division of labor and physical structure of the mine, other role requirements affected data collection. The mine is dark, the machinery is loud, and the work tasks require full concentration. This is not an arrangement conducive to observation or conversation. In order to collect data I had to maximize available opportunities—and create others—for social interaction with work partners. When I designed my study, I did not anticipate the importance of structural and role barriers to data collection. I suggest to any researcher contemplating the observer role to carefully evaluate the potential impediments to field mobility and other limitations to being with the subjects you wish to study.

The development of rapport is another tactical problem associated with being where the action is. A new entrant to any social grouping must establish an identity, come to know the other actors in the unit, and earn their trust before acceptance is attained. When entering the field, it is best to "lie low" and, if necessary, sacrifice early data collection in order to earn acceptance (cf. Dean et al., 1969:68–70; Bogdan and Taylor, 1975:45–50).

Just as in life outside the research setting, it is impossible to establish good rapport with everyone you meet in the research setting. At least initially, seek to establish rapport with the more influential and insightful individuals in the setting. Rather than getting drawn into quarrels between individuals or factions, try to get along with people by maintaining a neutral stance. Getting along and staying neutral does not mean getting pushed around. Establish your role and ward off attempts by the subject population to define you differently if it is not conducive to the research. Don't worry about stepping on a few toes (it goes with being a newcomer to any situation) or making a few enemies (this is part of life). At the mine I earned the enmity of another novice miner because I routinely talked with the shift boss, an excellent informant. The novice miner interpreted this action as "kissing ass" and would have little to do with me thereafter. Situations of this type cannot be totally avoided, but do what you can to miminize them. If faced with the dilemma of having to make an enemy of one party versus another, go cautiously and pick the alternative that will hurt the research less.

GETTING THE GOODS

In participant observation the researcher must strike a balance between the overt, active process of collecting and eliciting information and simply letting it happen. The participant observer must participate in events as they occur but must also ask about things, seek explanations, and lead the subject population into providing information.

Participant observation takes time. The data just do not emerge overnight. It also takes time to see interconnections in a social situation. Two actions that do not appear related during the opening phases of research may come to be seen later as part of a larger system. Subjects also compartmentalize their lives. Topics of conversation and thought move in constellations. If an observer wishes to know what a subject population does for winter recreation, such an inquiry will appear more logical and probably be more fruitful if the subjects are talking about or participating in something related to recreation.

Soon after my entry into the mine, I noticed that the miners did not talk much about mine accidents or danger, a distressing discovery given my research goal of studying adaptation to occupational danger. Then two men required rescue after being trapped in a dragway.[3] The event acted as a trigger, the miner's thoughts focused on the perils of the job and the data came rushing out in the form of recollections and tales of past accidents, safety tips, narrations of what went on during the rescue, personal fears, and the like. I used this opportunity to question miners extensively about their reactions to danger. After a few days, things settled back to the normal work routine and it was again not possible to probe the topic of danger. This example also suggests another tactical consideration in fieldwork—once established in the field, make use of every opportunity to collect data. Pay particular attention to unique events, for they often explain or help interpret everyday happenings.

"Field-involved" participant observers use both observation and verbal exchanges with subjects to collect data. These approaches are complementary. One method can be used to validate data collected by the other. Social scientists have long noted the lack of correspondence between words and actions. One miner, for example, professed great fear of explosives and yet, after being socialized into the mine subculture, repeatedly smoked in the presence of explosives and on one occasion was seen doing so while standing on 150 pounds of dynamite. He had learned what all miners learn—"powder ain't all that dangerous"—but nevertheless continued to hold and express his premine conception of explosives in conversation. The participant observer must continually seek to test the correlation between words and actions, thought and deed.

The researcher must also guard against using one approach to data collection (usually verbal exchanges) to the exclusion of other forms of information. Once a rapport is established with a subject population it becomes easy, perhaps too easy, to discuss actions rather than observe them firsthand. Field observers generally collect most of their data through verbal means—talking with subjects, questioning them, having them react to the researcher's ideas, and by examining documents. But observation cannot be neglected. Frequently, one has to see something before it can be understood. I experienced this on many occasions in the mine. In fact, the socialization process for novice miners was based on demonstrations where experienced miners showed the new miners what had to be done and how to do it rather than simply telling them what to do.

When collecting data by verbal means, the researcher uses both informants and respondents. Respondents provide the investigator with personal accounts—what they thought, saw, and did during some event or about some issue. Informants provide descriptions of the group or research setting as a whole. In many ways the informant can be thought of as a narrator, knowledgeable about the setting and its actors, who provides the researcher with insight into what is going on. A respondent tells about personal experiences, while an informant tells about other people. One individual frequently serves in both roles.

Practically speaking, there is rarely a sharp distinction between respondents and informants. Instead, the researcher encounters a range of personalities, some of whom are good sources of information and others who are not. Four common types of subjects seem to appear in most fieldwork. The *helpful informant* is an individual who knows the research setting and who can and will help the investigator understand it. The *"I don't know" informant* is a person who also knows the research setting but who doesn't wish to divulge that knowledge. Feigned ignorance ("I don't know") is a typical modus operandi. This individual's reluctance to cooperate can be motivated by suspicion, fear of the researcher, or simply not wanting to get involved with other persons or projects. Many subjects go through an "I don't know" stage and then

warm up to and assist the researcher once credibility has been established.

The *tells-too-much informant* is an individual who is eager to help the researcher and feeds the observer information. The motivation for this type of person varies. Some simply want to help the researcher, others have self-serving interests in mind (such as fulfilling a need to tell all about oneself). The known observer meets this individual quite frequently but even the covert observer is not immune. It is often difficult to distinguish this type of informant from those who are merely helpful. The *pure respondent* is a person who cannot abstract or generalize beyond personal experiences. This individual seems oblivious to what happens in the setting as a whole and is useful only to the extent the researcher is interested in a personal life history.

Information received from subjects will be a mixture of fact and fiction. The researcher must take such information with the proverbial "grain of salt" and take steps to test and cross-check the consistency and reliability of the data. An observer should not go into the field with the intention of discovering the truth, as did one "investigative sociologist" (Douglas, 1976). Truth is not an absolute. A social investigator is in the field to understand a social situation and goes to the subjects to get their perspectives on phenomena being investigated. There is no great necessity to search for deep secrets or ulterior motives. When one adopts such a perspective, research becomes a form of conflict or a "con" game, with subjects viewed as the enemy or "marks" to be "taken."[4] Furthermore, a social investigator is not in the field to psychoanalyze subjects and discover what they "really" feel deep down. Psychology is best left to psychologists, exposés of wrongdoing and malfeasance to journalists, and discovery of truth to clerics and courts.

A final tactical concern in data collection is record-taking. From the beginning of prefieldwork reconnaissance through the completion of field activities, the observer should maintain a daily record of observations. Data will ebb and flow, some days being very productive, other days not. It is difficult to forecast when or where one will receive information, so the participant observer must be prepared for all contingencies.

Some research settings are amenable to the use of tape recorders and cameras or at least public note-taking. Other settings require the observer to remember what happened and later transpose the information to the field notes. Some material is inevitably forgotten in this process. The researcher can minimize this loss by entering data into the field notes as soon as practical after the observations were made. The mine was a setting where data had to be memorized and later recorded. Occasionally, I was able to scribble a few key words to aid my memory, but detailed record-taking on site was impossible.

The participant observer's field notes should contain at least seven different types of observations, although it is not necessary and probably impossible to record all seven observations for each field event. A record should be made of what the observer saw, what was heard or discussed, how the observer and other actors felt about the observer's presence in the field, the observer's interpretations of what happened in the field, and the physical structure and general environmental conditions of the research setting. The field notes should also contain notations relating the field investigation to the literature or theoretical constructs as well as questions for further study. When two miners were trapped in a dragway, my field log traced the developmental history of the event beginning with the first inquiry—"Where are Ned and Felix?"—through the rescue and subsequent discussion of what had transpired. Abbreviated entries from the field notes show some of the types of possible observations.

First Day

A. Ned and Felix failed to show up at the end of the shift. Hank went back in to see what was up.

B. "If the boys are in there asleep, they'll probably get canned" (miner's observation). Not likely to be asleep after the rounds went off (researcher's observation).

Second Day

C. The boys made it out OK. They were trapped behind a muck pile in the slot. They were in good spirits. Tried to dig themselves out but couldn't make it.

D. Some of the other miners razzed the lads about their episode. "Bring an alarm clock so you don't sleep late again."

E. The mood going off shift last night wasn't so merry. Hank and the old timer were very disturbed.

F. Hank gave the boys a few instructions: "From now on only one man at a time goes into the slot."

G. Questions: Are men compensated for their rescue work? How? What about the victims?

Data analysis begins with record-taking. By charting personal reactions, interpretations, and environmental conditions, the observer can detect his or her presence in the data and control potential bias. Continually examining the research record also facilitates the identification of substantive or theoretical categories that make sense out of the data and point the observer in new directions of inquiry.

MANAGING BIAS

The participant observer is part of the data. Subjects react to the presence of an observer and since the aim of participant observation is to study typical aspects of social life, there is always some uncertainty whether the observer's presence significantly affects the data-gathering process. The researcher must continually consider his or her effect on the actions of the observed.

All forms of social inquiry influence the observed. Human beings routinely modify their behavior to fit the circumstances in which they find themselves. An investigator cannot eliminate the potential bias inherent in reactions to symbolic (e.g., mailed questionnaire) or personal presence; he or she can only minimize that presence. The participant observer can minimize reactive effects by taking a neutral position in the research setting (i.e., avoiding conflict and leadership roles) and closely scrutinizing and recording personal actions, interpretations, and feelings while in the field in order to facilitate taking his or her presence into account in the subsequent analysis of the data (McCall, 1969:128–41; Schwartz and Schwartz, 1969:89–104). At the mine I noticed that fatigue and the sense of frustration experienced during the shift appeared to influence the character of my entries in the field log. Whenever I realized that scientific detachment was slipping away, I attempted to step back from the more bothersome aspects of mine work so as to get a fresh perspective. I also found it helpful to reread my field notes a few days after their initial recording and ask myself if their content appeared unduly influenced by some biasing factor.

A second tactical problem in managing bias is "going native"—accepting the values, norms, and opinions of the subject population as one's own. In doing so the researcher fails in the role of critical, unbiased observer and becomes one of the group. There is continual pressure, overt and subtle, on all observers to "go native," and to some extent all observers internalize a part of the research setting they seek to analyze. One evening, for example, someone dropped a coffee cup on the floor at a home I was visiting, creating a short burst of noise. A miner of several weeks experience, I immediately assumed a defensive, scramble position and directed my eyes toward the ceiling much as I would have done in the mine had I heard a similar sound. In the darkness of the mine, miners are sensitive to sound since it frequently cues danger. Cave-ins are often announced by the clatter of falling rocks. Unconsciously, I had internalized one of the miner's protective reactions. I also experienced direct pressure to go native. The shift boss routinely spoke of "making a miner" out of me and offered incentives to me. Other miners on the crew did likewise. Since neither party was aware of my research role, their actions were part of the standard socialization process for novice miners.

There is no way to avoid completely the pressure to go native. The researcher can sometimes conform behaviorally without adopting the group's attitudes. This feigned accommodation can often lessen overt pressure to conform to group expectations. Most of the time, you must simply bear the pressure. By periodically leaving the research setting (cooling off) and having contact with different sorts of people (especially colleagues), it is possible to change your perspective. It is also worthwhile for a researcher to chart changes in personal viewpoints vis-à-vis the subjects and reflect on the degree of attraction or repulsion to them. If these checks appear to indicate overidentification, the observer is "going native" and should endeavor to put more distance, at least mentally, between subject and him- or herself.

ANALYZING THE INFORMATION

The process of analysis begins soon after entering the field. As information is received, the fieldworker validates its reliability, identifies potential sources of bias, and probes new areas of inquiry. The need to test and cross-check data is neverending. One can always expect to receive some misinformation. Two ways of monitoring data quality are to make the same inquiry of several persons and to summarize tentative findings and have the subjects react to the ideas. Both methods seek to establish consistency in the data and ground the researcher's interpretations in a body of factually acceptable evidence.

The purposes of a participant observation study can be many. The goal may be to test or generate theory, collect descriptive background material, or formalize new concepts. Regardless of the goal, the data must be summarized to reduce the volume and given some structure to make the information comprehensible. These tasks require the researcher to build categories and link them together in a logical way. He or she has considerable flexibility in this operation and can develop categories and an explanatory framework from the ground up or borrow an existing framework and add data to it (Schatzman and Strauss, 1973:108–28; Glaser and Strauss, 1967; Barton and Lazarsfeld, 1969:163–96). Either method requires using the data to discover explanation rather than simply following a process of logical deduction from a set of "givens."

In order to analyze the data collected at the mine, I postulated that some form of occupational subculture would be present among miners. I sought to identify the nature and characteristics of the subculture (structure), the methods by which the subculture is transmitted (process), and the purposes served by the subculture (function). I then divided these categories into their constituent elements. The socialization of miners (process), for instance, occurs by two primary means: spoken instructions (verbal) and demonstrations (nonverbal). In turn, I divided each approach to socialization by content. Verbalizations oriented toward danger and safety were classified as "protective," discussions of other topics as "general." A portion of the classification scheme is diagrammed in Figure 1.

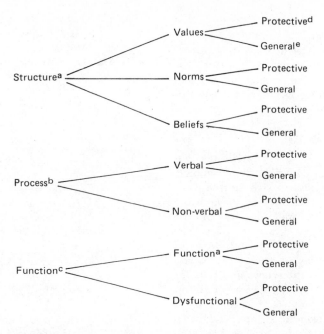

^aThe nature and characteristics of the social phenomenon under study (e.g., miner's occupational subculture)

^bActivities that are related to the occurrence of a social phenomenon and that sustain it over time (e.g., socialization of novice miners)

^cThe social consequences of the phenomenon under study (e.g., work safety)

^dEntities related to occupational danger or protection thereof (e.g., safety rules)

^eEntities unrelated to occupational danger (e.g., miners after work recreation preferences)

Figure 1 Classification scheme

I established links between classes by using the data to answer a series of questions. For example:

Classified Belief: Mine dangers are believed to be predictable and controllable.

Questions: 1. Are there exceptions to the belief?

2. Are there related beliefs that explain how danger is predicted and controlled?

3. What state (goal) are miners trying to achieve by believing mine danger is predictable and controllable?

4. What actions are required to achieve the goal?

Questions: 5. How are novice miners taught to believe in the predictability and controllability of mine danger?

From the answers received, I formulated new questions, deleted extraneous material from the classification scheme, and drew logical connections between the data elements. This process ultimately resulted in the identification of the "occupational subculture of danger" (cf. Fitzpatrick, 1974), a concept that explains how people who work in dangerous occupations adapt to the stresses, threats, losses, and injuries to which they are exposed in the course of their work.

The product of analytical research is explanation. The fieldworker seeks to capture a slice of reality through a research methodology and release it as a system of related accounts telling how and why actors in a situation behave as they do. There are many steps to the research process and countless ways of running aground, but the challenge is worth the effort.

NOTES

[1]Gold has identified four research roles for sociologists conducting fieldwork. The "complete participant" is a covert observer whose true identity and purpose are unknown to those being observed. The purpose and identity of the "participant-as-observer" is known to the subject population while the researcher shares in their social life. The "observer-as-participant" role is frequently used in one-visit interviews and calls for relatively more observation than does participation with the subjects. The "complete observer" role removes the fieldworker from social interaction with informants, such as by watching experimental subjects from behind one-way mirrors.

[2]Stope: any excavation underground to remove ore other than development work.

[3]Dragway: a location used to transfer ore or waste rock from one level to another by scrapping the material in a specially designed winch-powered bucket.

[4]Douglas's (1976) "investigative sociology" follows the research-as-conflict paradigm. This approach has also been condemned as "technically and morally unacceptable to social science" (Gold, 1977a:655).

REFERENCES

Barton, Allen H. and Paul F. Lazarsfeld
1969 "Qualitative data as sources of hypotheses." Pp. 163–96 in G. McCall and J. Simmons (eds.), Issues in Participant Observation. Reading, Mass.: Addison-Wesley.

Becker, Howard S. and Blanche Geer
1957 "Participant observation and interviewing: a comparison." Human Organization 16:28–32.

Bogdan, Robert and Steven J. Taylor
1975 Introduction to Qualitative Research Methods. New York: Wiley.

Dean, John P., Robert L. Eichhorn and Lois R. Dean
1969 "Establishing field relations." Pp. 68–70 in G. McCall and J. Simmons (eds.), Issues in Participant Observation. Reading, Mass.: Addison-Wesley.
1969a "Limitations and advantages of unstructured methods." Pp. 19–27 in G. McCall and J. Simmons (eds.), Issues in Participant Observation. Reading, Mass.: Addison-Wesley.

Douglas, Jack D.
1976 Investigative Social Research. Beverly Hills, Calif.: Sage.

Erickson, Kai
1970 "A comment on disguised observation in sociology." Pp. 252–60 in W. Filstead (ed.), Qualitative Methodology. Chicago: Markham.

Fitzpatrick, John S.
1974 Underground Mining: A Case Study of an Occupational Subculture of Danger. Unpublished Ph.D. dissertation, Ohio State University.

Glaser, Barney G. and Anselm L. Strauss
1967 The Discovery of Grounded Theory. Chicago: Aldine.

Glazer, Myron
1972 The Research Adventure: Promise and Problems in Field Work. New York: Random House.

Gold, Raymond L.
1958 "Roles in sociological field observations." Social Forces 36:217–23.
1977 "Combining ethnographic and survey research." Pp. 102–7 in K. Finsterbusch and C. T. Wolf (eds.), Methodology of Social Impact Assessment. Stroudsburg, Pa.: Dowden, Hutchinson, and Ross.
1977a Review of "Investigative Social Research" by Jack D. Douglas and "Doing Social Life" by John Lofland. Contemporary Sociology 6:654–56.

Kahn, Robert and Floyd Mann
1969 "Developing research partnerships." Pp. 45–52 in G. McCall and J. Simmons (eds.), Issues in Participant Observation. Reading, Mass.: Addison-Wesley.

McCall, George J.
1969 "Data quality control in participant observation." Pp. 128–41 in G. McCall and J. Simmons (eds.), Issues in Participant Observation. Reading, Mass.: Addison-Wesley.

McCall, George J. and J. L. Simmons
1969 "Field relations." Pp. 28–30 in G. McCall and J. Simmons (eds.), Issues in Participant Observation. Reading, Mass.: Addison-Wesley.

Rainwater, Lee and D. J. Pittman
1967 "Ethical problems in studying a politically sensitive deviant community." Social Problems 14:357–66.

Schatzman, Leonard and Anselm Strauss
1955 "Social class and modes of communication." American Journal of Sociology 60:329–38.

1973 Field Research: Strategies for a Natural Sociology. Englewood Cliffs, N. J.: Prentice-Hall.

Schwartz, Morris S. and Charlotte G. Schwartz
1969 "Problems in participant observation." Pp. 89–104 in G. McCall and J. Simmons (eds.), Issues in Participant Observation. Reading, Mass.: Addison-Wesley.

Warwick, Donald P.
1975 "Social scientists ought to stop lying." Psychology Today 8(February):38 ff.

SECTION 3.2

Content Analysis, Historical Analysis, Unobtrusive Measures, and Ethnomethodological Research

The vast majority of published social science research articles employ survey methods. This section considers some less frequently used strategies for analyzing social phenomena: content analysis, historical analysis, unobtrusive analysis, and ethnomethodological analysis. With the exception of ethnomethodology, these strategies could all be labeled "less obtrusive methods" because they involve less researcher involvement in the data-gathering process than do survey or experimental methods. They often involve less researcher involvement than observation.

BASIC ADVANTAGES

Because of reduced researcher involvement, these less obtrusive methods share a unique advantage: reduced or nonexistent reactivity (although some ethnomethodological research strategies do involve reactivity). Most research employing the less obtrusive methods promotes less bias resulting from the presence of a researcher. Hence, the elements being examined are studied in a more "natural" setting and subjects are less likely to alter their behavior and verbalizations in response to the presence and actions of the researcher. The use of such methods also allows the examination of phenomena that would be difficult, if not impossible, to examine through survey and experimental methods. Grusky (1963), for example, used the published win/loss records of professional baseball organizations to examine the relationship between field manager turnover ("managerial succession") and team standing ("organizational effectiveness"). Cohen and Fiedler (1974) studied suicide notes to determine what underlying categories, if any, exist in such notes and to examine sex differences with regard to these categories. In addition to reduced reactivity and the opportunity to examine phenomena otherwise unavailable, less obtrusive methods have a third advantage: they may increase the validity of results obtained by other methods. The fourth advantage is that longitudinal analyses are possible with less obtrusive methods. And finally, such methods are often relatively inexpensive in comparison to survey and experimental methods.

TYPES

Less obtrusive methods include a variety of approaches. Unfortunately, various terms are used for similar approaches. Content analysis, for example, can be placed in a category by itself, in the available-data category, or in the documentary analysis category (and perhaps in historical analysis as well). I have chosen to organize less obtrusive methods into four categories. The first is available data, which primarily involves nondocumentary statistical data. Examples include official statistics, actuarial records, census data, and archives. The second is content analysis and principally includes non-statistical documentary sources such as letters, novels, newspapers, memos, and charts. Unobtrusive measures, comprising the third category, include such data sources as physical traces, hardware, and observation. The fourth category is ethnomethodology, primarily a linguistic analysis of the norms and assumptions governing everyday life. Each of these categories is briefly reviewed in the context of the readings.

THE READINGS

Content analysis, the method used in the first article in this section, answers the following questions: Who says what to whom with what effect? David Luckenbill's article is an excellent example of such a definition of content analysis. In a developing interaction situation culminating in murder, who said what to whom such that a murder did or did not take place? Luckenbill skillfully conducted a content analysis of the files of 71 murder cases in order to develop his six-stage analysis of interpersonal transactions resulting in murder. Files included several data sources: police, probation, psychiatric and witness reports, offender interview reports, victim statements, and various court records. As with other content analyses, Luckenbill developed content categories in an attempt to assess the frequency of such social phenomena as face-threatening events, conversation topics, and types of retaliation. Structured categories allowed him to calculate percentages for comparison purposes; generally, the more structured the categories, the more quantitative the analysis can be and the more reliable the results of the analysis. These categories assisted him in a paramount goal of content analysis: the establishment of a theme or underlying dimension(s) in the data sources that might help explain the phenomenon under investigation. For Luckenbill, this theme is the importance of the social setting and the "character contest," with its ensuing face-saving mechanisms, that emerge in a murder transaction.

Luckenbill's personal journal reports some of the difficulties he encountered. The data were originally collected for police and court purposes, not for the purpose of a social scientific investigation. As a result, the author experienced some conceptualization and operationalization difficulties. He could not take a random sample of all murder cases, but had to settle for one county in one decade, and had to redefine "murder" for his purposes. Some documentation was missing and discrepancies often existed in cases with complete documentation; "interparticipant consistency" was used to maximize reliability. Fortunately, Luckenbill could place a fairly high level of credibility in the data sources, which is not always possible when doing content analysis. In addition, fairly standardized reporting procedures were used by the police and other officials, again a fairly uncommon occurrence among those recording the documents.

Douglas Klegon's article on historical analysis stresses the social scientific utility in "looking back." Such retrospective analysis, as opposed to mere reflection, can provide new insights into events of the past (with the emphasis on social meanings and the relevance of the social context), can provide new data to develop and test theories and hypotheses, can aid in the development of generalized explanations of classes of events (as opposed to the historian's focus on the uniqueness of an event), and can aid in predicting the future. Klegon emphasizes that, and illustrates how, historical analysis involves a variety of methodologies and can take the form of available statistical data and/or content analysis of documentary data. Historical analysis shares the advantages of other less obtrusive methods: the opportunity for longitudinal analysis, the lack of reactivity, and the relative inexpensiveness. But historical analysis also shares the disadvantages: bias in data recording, selective perception, selective survival, analysis difficulties, and limited generalizability beyond the data.

Unobtrusive measures are the topic of the example-filled article by Thomas Bouchard. Unobtrusive measures permit the gathering of data on variables without the subject/respondent's being aware of the data-gathering process. Bouchard updates and adds many examples to the excellent book on unobtrusive measures by Webb et al. (1966) and uses the same basic categories as Webb et al.: physical traces, archives, observation, and hardware. Physical traces include changes in physical materials (e.g., garbage analysis); archives include available-data and content analysis of documentary sources; observations are included in the field methods section of this volume (although Bouchard emphasizes nonparticipant observation while that section emphasizes participant observation); and hardware involves the use of electronic devices (variations and extensions of sound-recording equipment; an example might be the voice-stress detector to determine truthfulness of responses).

Bouchard notes the strengths of unobtrusive measures as twofold: they complement other methods and thereby extend the validity of results obtained by such multimethod approaches and they force the researcher to think of alternative methods to measure conventional variables (and to think of new variables). Furthermore, Bouchard explains that unobtrusive measures are behaviorally oriented, which some researchers consider an improvement over the verbally oriented measures used in surveys. Unfortunately, unobtrusive measures are rarely used in social science research (with the exception of archive analysis and observation); in the approximately 150 journal issues I reviewed in preparation for this volume I found only a few studies using nonobservation and nonarchival unobtrusive measures (although several articles described the usefulness of such methods).

Several factors may explain the infrequent use of unobtrusive methods: the lack of training social scientists receive in their use, the small sample sizes required, the high level of time involved, the low level of control that can be applied, and the mismatch between concept and indicator. Many unobtrusive measures also preclude causal analysis since it is often difficult to acquire unobtrusive measures of several possibly causally related variables on the same unit of analysis. In sum, unobtrusive measures are often the only or best measures for a given concept, but they are quite limited in terms of generalizability and causal analysis.

Ethnomethodology is a term composed of a number of Greek words meaning the methodical study of peoples. This branch of study is a fairly recent attempt to develop a systematic approach to studying the underlying rules, norms, and assumptions governing everyday life. As such, ethnomethodology is a phenomenological approach to understanding reality. It challenges the emphasis in natural science on objectivity and standardized concepts and emphasizes the analysis of how people themselves construct and account for their experienced realities (as opposed to how outsiders, such as social scientists, explain these realities). Ethnomethodologists focus their analysis on the "taken for granteds" that underlie every individual's daily behavior. In short, they define as problematic and worthy of analysis what most social scientists take as givens. As Bailey notes in his article in this section, ethnomethodologists study the processes of social interaction themselves rather than the results of these processes. As a result, the situation is treated as an important explanatory mechanism since the use and meaning of various terms and gestures may have different meanings in different situations.

An example may be useful. Meehan (1973) describes a situation in a first-grade classroom in which the children were shown a picture of a medieval fortress, complete with moat, drawbridge, and parapets and asked to circle the letter D, C, or G as the correct initial consonant of the word describing the structure. When a child circled the D, the traditional analyst scored the answer incorrect because he or she took it for granted that the right answer was C (for "castle"). But as an ethnomethodologist, Meehan attempted to determine the child's definition of the situation—how the child made sense of his or her own reality. In questioning the student, Meehan discovered that the child defined the picture as representing Disneyland, hardly an unexpected answer for a child, and definitely one that fits the child's definition of reality. What is defined as correct then depends on whose definition of the situation you accept. For additional examples, see Bailey's descriptions of norm-violating exercises.

Ethnomethodologists use several methodologies. They observe (e.g., what happens when a norm is violated), they use film and tape to reconstruct definitions of the situation by actors, they make content analyses of letters and documents, and they study the use of language. They seldom use surveys because surveys impose the social scientist's definitions of the situations on the respondent. Conversational analysis is a particularly useful strategy because it reflects the norms governing actors' behaviors and verbalizations and is the best way to assess how the actors themselves account for what they do (see Bailey's interesting description of conversation-closing behaviors). One strategy employing the ethnomethodological approach involves direct researcher involvement in the action in a nonnormal way in order to study how the participants respond. Obviously, such a high level of researcher involvement increases reactivity.

Ethnomethodology is similar in some respects to documentary analysis in that both attempt to ascertain the actors' own perspectives on reality; ethnomethodology is also similar to observation with its emphasis on the importance of the context and its emphasis on grounded theory (letting the emergent data determine the explanatory concepts). Note Bailey's comparison of ethnomethodology with the widely used survey approach. Although ethnomethodology is characterized by such weaknesses as small samples, low control, analysis difficulties, and low generalizability, it is a very useful strategy for analyzing phenomena that would be virtually unanalyzable with more traditional strategies.

The phenomenon to be analyzed is always the key determinant of the methodology employed. I hope that you will be convinced of the utility of considering various alternative strategies to survey and experimental designs on completion of this section.

REFERENCES

Cohen, Stuart L. and Joanne E. Fiedler
    1974   "Content analysis of multiple messages in suicide notes." Life-threatening Behavior 4(Summer):75–95.

Grusky, Oscar
    1963   "Managerial succession and organizational effectiveness." American Journal of Sociology 69(July):21–31.

Meehan, Hugh
    1973   "Assessing children's language-using abilities." Pp. 309–43 in J. M. Armer and A. D. Grimshaw (eds.), Comparative Social Research: Methodological Problems and Strategies. New York: Wiley.

Webb, E. J., D. T. Campbell, R. D. Schwartz, and L. Sechrest
    1966   Unobtrusive Measures: Nonreactive Research in Social Sciences. Chicago: Rand McNally.

CRIMINAL HOMICIDE AS A SITUATED TRANSACTION

David F. Luckenbill

By definition, criminal homicide is a collective transaction. An offender, victim, and possibly an audience engage in an interchange which leaves the victim dead. Furthermore, these transactions are typically situated, for participants interact in a common physical territory (Wolfgang, 1958: 203–205; Wallace, 1965). As with other situated transactions, it is expected that the participants develop particular roles, each shaped by the others and instrumental in some way to the fatal outcome (cf. Shibutani, 1961: 32–37, 64–93; Blumer, 1969: 16–18). However, research, with few exceptions, has failed critically to examine the situated transaction eventuating in murder (Banitt *et al.*, 1970; Shoham *et al.*, 1973). At most, studies have shown that many victims either directly precipitate their destruction, by throwing the first punch or firing the first shot, or contribute to the escalation of some conflict which concludes in their demise (Wolfgang, 1958: 245–265; Schafer, 1968: 79–83; Goode, 1969: 965; Toch, 1969; Moran, 1971). But how transactions of murder are organized and how they develop remain puzzles. What are the typical roles developed by the offender, victim, and possible bystanders? In what ways do these roles intersect to produce the fatal outcome? Are there certain regularities of interaction which characterize all transactions of murder, or do patterns of interaction vary among transactions in a haphazard fashion? Making the situated transaction the unit of investigation, this paper will address these questions by examining the character of the transaction in full.

METHOD

Criminal homicide is presently defined as the unlawful taking of a person's life, with the expressed intention of killing or rendering bodily injury resulting in death, and not in the course of some other criminal activity. This conceptualization excludes such forms of unnatural death as negligent homicide and vehicular manslaughter. This investigation will examine all forms of criminal homicide but felony murder, where death occurs in the commission of other felony crimes, and contract murder, where the offender conspires with another to kill in his behalf for payment.

The present data were drawn from all cases of criminal homicide over a ten-year period, 1963–1972, in one medium sized (350,000) California county. Sampling was of a multistage nature. Because criminal homicide may be mitigated through charging or plea negotiation to various types of manslaughter, it was necessary to gather all cases, for the years 1963–1972, found in the four charge categories of first and second degree murder, voluntary and involuntary manslaughter. In this way, ninety-four cases were gathered. Taking all cases of unnatural death except suicide documented in coroner's reports, those twenty-three cases not fitting the present conception of criminal homicide were eliminated. These consisted of fourteen vehicular manslaughters, eight felony murders, and one negligent homicide. The remainder, seventy-one deaths or seventy transactions (one double murder), were examined.

All official documents pertaining to these cases were secured. The character of the larger occasion as well as the organization and development of the fateful transaction were reconstructed from the content analysis of police, probation, psychiatric, and witness reports, offender interviews, victim statements, and grand jury and court testi-

Author's note: I wish to thank Donald R. Cressey and Homero E. Yearwood for their instructive comments and suggestions on several drafts of this paper. I also wish to thank Rey Baca, Joel G. Best, Howard C. Daudistel, Glen Olmstead, William B. Sanders, and Michael Williams for their assistance at various stages of progress.

From *Social Problems*, December 1977, pp. 176–186. Reprinted by permission of the Society for the Study of Social Problems and the author.

mony. These materials included information on the major and minor participants; who said and did what to whom; the chronology of dialogue and action; and the physical comportment of the participants. Material relating to matters of law and legal processing were not examined.

In reconstructing the transaction, I first scrutinized each individual document for material relating only to the step-by-step development of the transaction. I then used the information to prepare separate accounts of the transaction. When all the individual documents for each case were exhausted, one summary account was constructed, using the individual accounts as resources. In the process of case reconstruction, I found that the various parties to the transaction often related somewhat different accounts of the event. Discrepancies centered, in large part, in their accounts of the specific dialogue of the participants. Their accounts were usually consistent with respect to the basic structure and development of the event.[1] In managing discrepancies, I relied on interparticipant consistency in accounts.

This methodological strategy should provide a fairly strong measure of reliability in case reconstruction. By using several independent resources bearing on the same focal point, particular biases could be reasonably controlled. In other words, possible biases in singular archival documents could be corrected by relying on a multitude of independently produced reports bearing on the transaction. For example, the offender's account could be compared with witnesses' accounts and with reports on physical evidence.

The Social Occasion of Criminal Homicide

Criminal homicide is the culmination of an intense interchange between an offender and victim. Transactions resulting in murder involved the joint contribution of the offender and victim to the escalation of a "character contest," a confrontation in which at least one, but usually both, attempt to establish or save face at the other's expense by standing steady in the face of adversity (Goffman, 1967: 218–219, 238–257). Such transactions additionally involved a consensus among participants that violence was a suitable if not required means for settling the contest.

Before examining the dynamics of these transactions, it is useful to consider the larger context in which they were imbedded. A "situated transac-

tion" refers to a chain of interaction between two or more individuals that lasts the time they find themselves in one another's immediate physical presence (Goffman, 1963: 167). A "social occasion," in contrast, refers to a wider social affair within which many situated transactions may form, dissolve, and re-form (Goffman, 1963: 18). And, as Goffman aptly demonstrates, social occasions carry boundaries of sorts which establish what kinds of transactions are appropriate and inappropriate.

Social occasions which encompassed transactions ending in murder shared several features. First, all such transactions occurred in occasions of non-work or leisure-time (cf. Bullock, 1955; Wolfgang, 1958: 121–128; Wallace, 1965). The majority of murders occurred between the leisure hours of six p.m. and two a.m. and especially on weekends. More important, they were always found in leisure settings: almost half the cases occurred while members engaged in leisure activities at home; fifteen percent occurred while members frequented a favorite tavern; another fifteen percent occurred while members habituated a streetcorner or "turf"; little over twelve percent occurred while the offender and victim drove or "cruised" about the city, highway, or country roads; the few remaining cases occurred while members engaged in activities in some other public place such as a hotel room.

Second, occasions of murder were "loose," informal affairs permitting a wide range of activities definable by members as appropriate (cf. Goffman, 1963: 198–215). In contrast to work and such tighter occasions of leisure as weddings and funerals, where members are bound by rather strict sets of expectations, occasions of murder were permissive environs allowing the performance of various respectable and non-respectable activities. An "evening at home," the most prominent occasion in the cases, finds people engaging in many activities deemed suitable under the aegis of the private residence yet judged inappropriate for more formal affairs (cf. Cavan, 1963). Similarly, "an evening at the corner tavern," "hanging on streetcorner," or "cruising about town" have long been recognized as permissive settings providing access and opportunity to drink, take drugs, sell and purchase sex, or gamble without fear of censure by colleagues.

In the sample, members engaged in a variety of activities within such loosely structured occasions. In about seventy-five percent of the cases, the offender and victim were engaged in pleasurable pursuits. They sought to drop serious or work roles and pursue such enjoyable activities as drinking alcoholic beverages, dancing, partying, watching television, or cruising main street. In the remainder of the cases, members were engaged in reasonably serious concerns. Here, conversations of marital or relational futures, sexual prowess, beauty, trustworthiness, and integrity were central themes about which members organized.

A third feature of such occasions was their population by intimates. In over sixty percent of the cases, the offender and victim were related by marriage, kinship, or friendship. In the remaining cases, while the offender and victim were enemies, mere acquaintances, or complete strangers, at least one, but often both, were in the company of their family, friends, lovers, or co-workers.

Dynamics of the Situated Performance

These are the occasions in which situated transactions resulted in violent death. But examination of the development of these situated interchanges is not to argue that such transactions have no historical roots. In almost half the cases there had previously occurred what might be termed rehearsals between the offender and victim. These involved transactions which included the escalation of hostilities and, sometimes, physical violence. In twenty-six percent of these cases, the offender and, sometimes, victim entered the present occasion on the assumption that another hostile confrontation would transpire.

Whether or not murderous episodes had such rehearsals, an examination of all cases brings to light a conception of the transactions resembling what Lyman and Scott (1970: 37–43) term a "face game." The offender and victim, at times with the assistance of bystanders, make "moves" on the basis of the other's moves and the position of their audience (cf. Goffman, 1967: 239–258; 1969: 107–112). While these moves are not always of the same precise content or degree, it was possible to derive a set of time-ordered stages of which each shares certain basic properties. Let me first say that the "offender" and "victim" are heuristic labels for the statuses that either emerge in the transaction or are an artifact of the battle. In seventy-one percent of the cases, the statuses of offender and victim are determined by one's statement of intent to kill or injure the other. Hence, in sixty-three percent of the cases, the victim initiates the transaction, the

offender states his intention to kill or injure the victim, and the offender follows through by killing him. In eight percent of the cases, the offender initiates the transaction, later states his intention to kill or injure the victim, and follows through by killing him. But in twenty-nine percent of the cases, the statuses of offender and victim are determined by the results of the battle. Here, the initially cast victim initiates the transaction while the initially cast offender states his intention to kill or injure the victim. Due to strength or resources, the initially cast victim kills the initially cast offender in the course of battle. In discussing the first five stages, the labels of offender and victim will be used to refer to the statuses that emerge in the course of interaction and not the statuses resulting from the battle. Furthermore, the labels will be employed in a manner consistent with the pattern characteristic of the majority of the cases. Consequently, in thirty-six percent of the cases (those where the initially cast victim kills the initially cast offender and those where the offender initiates the transaction, later states his intention to kill or injure, and follows through), the adversary labeled "victim" kills while the adversary labeled "offender" is killed. In the discussion of the sixth stage the labels of offender and victim will be used to refer to the statuses resulting from the battle.

Stage I. The opening move in the transaction was an event performed by the victim and subsequently defined by the offender as an offense to "face," that image of self a person claims during a particular occasion or social contact (Goffman, 1967: 5). What constitutes the real or actual beginning of this or any other type of transaction is often quite problematic for the researcher.[2] The victim's activity, however, appeared as a pivotal event which separated the previous occasioned activity of the offender and victim from their subsequent violent confrontation. Such a disparaging and interactionally disrupting event constitutes the initial move.

While the form and content of the victim's move varied, three basic types of events cover all cases. In the first, found in over forty-one percent of the cases, the victim made some direct, verbal expression which the offender subsequently interpreted as offensive. This class of events was obviously quite broad. Included were everything from insults levied at some particular attribute of the offender's self, family, or friends to verbal tirades which disparaged the overall character of the offender:

Case 34 *The offender, victim, and two friends were driving toward the country where they could consume their wine. En route, the victim turned to the offender, both of whom were located in the back seat, and stated: "You know, you really got some good parents. You know, you're really a son-of-a-bitch. You're a leech. The whole time you were out of a job, you were living with them, and weren't even paying. The car you have should be your father's. He's the one who made the payments. Any time your dad goes to the store, you're the first in line to sponge off him. Why don't you grow up and stop being a leech?" The offender swore at him, and told him to shut up. But the victim continued, "Someone ought to come along and really fuck you up."*

A second type, found in thirty-four percent of the cases, involved the victim's refusal to cooperate or comply with the requests of the offender. The offender subsequently interpreted the victim's action as a denial of his ability or right to command obedience. This was illustrated in transactions where parents murdered their children. When the parent's requests that the child eat dinner, stop screaming, or take a bath went unheeded, the parent subsequently interpreted the child's activity as a challenge to rightful authority. In other cases, the violent escalation came about after the victim refused to conciliate a failing or dead relationship. In yet other cases, the victim failed to heed the offender's demand that he not enter some "off limits" territory, such as the "turf" of a juvenile gang.

The third type of event, found in twenty-five percent of the cases, involved some physical or nonverbal gesture which the offender subsequently defined as personally offensive. Often this gesture entailed an insult to the offender's sexual prowess, and took the form of affairs or flirtation:

Case 10 *When the victim finally came home, the offender told her to sit down; they had to talk. He asked her if she was "fooling around" with other men. She stated that she had, and her boyfriends pleased her more than the offender. The offender later stated that "this was like a hot iron in my gut." He ripped her clothes off and examined her body, finding scars and bruises. She said that her boyfriends liked to beat her. His anger magnified.*

Of course, the victim's activity was not always performed on the murderous occasion. In fifteen percent of the cases, the event was performed on some previous occasion when the offender was not present. Nevertheless, it was on the murderous occasion that the event was made known to the offender by the victim or bystanders and so was symbolically re-enacted.

Although the content and the initial production of these events varied, each served to disrupt the social order of the occasion. Each marked the opening of a transformation process in which pre-homicide transactions of pleasurable, or serious yet tranquil, order came to be transactions involving an argumentative "character contest."

Stage II. In all cases ending in murder the offender interpreted the victim's previous move as personally offensive. In some cases the victim was intentionally offensive. But it is plausible that in other cases the victim was unwitting. In Case forty-three, for instance, the victim, a five-week-old boy, started crying early in the morning. The offender, the boy's father, ordered the victim to stop crying. The victim's crying, however, only heightened in intensity. The victim was too young to understand the offender's verbal order, and persistent crying may have been oriented not toward challenging his father's authority, but toward acquiring food or a change of diapers. Whatever the motive for crying, the child's father defined it as purposive and offensive. What the victim intends may be inconsequential. What the offender interprets as intentional, however, may have consequences for the organization of subsequent activity.

In sixty percent of the cases, the offender learned the meaning of the victim's move from inquiries made of victim or audience. In reply, the offender received statements suggesting the victim's action was insulting and intentional. In thirty-nine percent of the cases, the offender ascertained the meaning of the impropriety directly from the victim:

Case 28 *As the offender entered the back door of the house his wife said to her lover, the victim, "There's _____." The victim jumped to his feet and started dressing hurriedly. The offender, having called to his wife without avail, entered the bedroom. He found his wife nude and the victim clad in underwear. The startled offender asked the victim, "Why?" The victim replied, "Haven't you ever been in love? We love each other."*

The offender later stated, "If they were drunk or something, I could see it. I mean, I've done it myself. But when he said they loved each other, well that did it."

In another twenty-one percent of the cases, however, the offender made his assessment from statements of interested bystanders:

Case 20 *The offender and his friend were sitting in a booth at a tavern drinking beer. The offender's friend told him that the offender's girlfriend was "playing" with another man (victim) at the other end of the bar. The offender looked at them and asked his friend if he thought something was going on. The friend responded, "I wouldn't let that guy fool around with [her] if she was mine." The offender agreed, and suggested to his friend that his girlfriend and the victim be shot for their actions. His friend said that only the victim should be shot, not the girlfriend.*

In the remaining forty percent of the cases the offender imputed meaning to the event on the basis of rehearsals in which the victim had engaged a similar role. The incessant screaming of the infant, the unremitting aggressions of a drunken spouse, and the never-ending flirtation by the lover or spouse were activities which offenders had previously encountered and assessed as pointed and deliberate aspersions:

Case 35 *During a family quarrel the victim had broken the stereo and several other household goods. At one point, the victim cut her husband, the offender, on the arm. He demanded that she sit down and watch television so that he could attend to his wound in peace. On returning from the bathroom he sat down and watched television. Shortly after, the victim rose from her chair, grabbed an ashtray, and shouted, "You bastard, I'm going to kill you." As she came toward him, the offender reached into the drawer of the end table, secured a pistol, and shot her. On arrest, the offender told police officers, "You know how she gets when she's drunk? I had to stop her, or she would have killed me. She's tried it before, that's how I got all these scars," pointing to several areas on his back.*

Such previous activities and their consequences served the offender as an interpretive scheme for immediately making sense of the present event.

Stage III. The apparent affront could have evoked different responses. The offender could have excused the violation because the victim was judged to be drunk, crazy, or joking. He could have fled the scene and avoided further interaction with the victim by moving into interaction with other occasioned participants or dealt with the impropriety through a retaliatory move aimed at restoring face and demonstrating strong character. The latter move was utilized in all cases.

In countering the impropriety, the offender attempted to restore the occasioned order and reaffirm face by standing his or her ground. To have used another alternative was to confirm questions of face and self raised by the victim. The offender's plight, then, was "problematic" and "consequential" (Goffman, 1967: 214–239). He could have chosen from several options, each of which had important consequences both to the face he situationally claimed and to his general reputation. Thus, the offender was faced with a dilemma: either deal with the impropriety by demonstrating strength of character, or verify questions of face by demonstrating weakness (Goffman, 1969: 168–169).

In retaliating, the offender issued an expression of anger and contempt which signified his opinion of the victim as an unworthy person. Two basic patterns of retaliation were found. In eighty-six percent of the cases, the offender issued a verbal or physical challenge to the victim. In the remaining cases, the offender physically retaliated, killing the victim.

For the latter pattern, this third move marked the battle ending the victim's life:

Case 12 *The offender, victim, and group of bystanders were observing a fight between a barroom bouncer and a drunk patron on the street outside the tavern. The offender was cheering for the bouncer, and the victim was cheering for the patron, who was losing the battle. The victim, angered by the offender's disposition toward the fight, turned to the offender and said, "You'd really like to see the little guy have the shit kicked out of him, wouldn't you, big man?" The offender turned toward the victim and asked, "What did you say? You want the same thing, punk?" The victim moved toward the offender and reared back. The offender responded, "OK, buddy." He struck the victim with a single right cross. The victim crashed to the pavement, and died a week later.*

Such cases seem to suggest that the event is a one-sided affair, with the unwitting victim engaging a passive, non-contributory role. But in these cases the third stage was preceded by the victim's impropriety, the offender's inquiry of the victim or audience, and a response affirming the victim's intent to be censorious. On assessing the event as one of insult and challenge, the offender elicited a statement indicating to participants, including himself, his intended line of action, secured a weapon, positioned it, and dropped the victim in a single motion.

While ten cases witness the victim's demise during this stage, the typical case consists of various verbal and physically non-lethal moves. The most common type of retaliation was a verbal challenge, occurring in forty-three percent of the cases. These took the form of an ultimatum: either apologize, flee the situation, or discontinue the inappropriate conduct, or face physical harm or death:

Case 54 *The offender, victim, and two neighbors were sitting in the living room drinking wine. The victim started calling the offender, his wife, abusive names. The offender told him to "shut up." Nevertheless, he continued. Finally, she shouted, "I said shut up. If you don't shut up and stop it, I'm going to kill you and I mean it."*

In about twenty-two percent of the cases, the offender's retaliation took the form of physical violence short of real damage or incapacitation:

Case 4 *The offender, victim, and three friends were driving in the country drinking beer and wine. At one point, the victim started laughing at the offender's car which he, the victim, scratched a week earlier. The offender asked the victim why he was laughing. The victim responded that the offender's car looked like junk. The offender stopped the car and all got out. The offender asked the victim to repeat his statement. When the victim reiterated his characterization of the car, the offender struck the victim, knocking him to the ground.*

In another ten percent, retaliation came by way of countering the victim's impropriety with similar insults or degrading gestures. This response entailed a name-calling, action-matching set of expressions resembling that which would be found between boys in the midst of a playground argument or "playing the dozens" (cf. Berdie, 1947).

The remaining cases, some eleven percent of the sample, were evenly divided. On the one hand, offenders issued specific commands, tinged with

hostility and backed with an aggressive posture, calling for their victims to back down. On the other hand, offenders "called out" or invited their victims to fight physically.

This third stage is the offender's opening move in salvaging face and honor. In retaliating by verbal and physically non-lethal means, the offender appeared to suggest to the victim a definition of the situation as one in which violence was suitable in settling questions of face and reputation.

Stage IV. Except for cases in which the victim has been eliminated, the offender's preceding move placed the victim in a problematic and consequential position: either stand up to the challenge and demonstrate strength of character, or apologize, discontinue the inappropriate conduct, or flee the situation and thus withdraw questions of the offender's face while placing one's own in jeopardy. Just as the offender could have dismissed the impropriety, fled the scene, or avoided further contact with the victim, so too did the victim have similar alternatives. Rather than break the escalation in a manner demonstrating weakness, all victims in the remaining sample came into a "working" agreement with the proffered definition of the situation as one suited for violence. In the majority of cases, the victim's move appeared as an agreement that violence was suitable to the transaction. In some cases, though, the offender interpreted, sometimes incorrectly, the victim's move as implicit agreement to violence. A working agreement was struck in several ways.

The most prominent response, found in forty-one percent of the cases, involved non-compliance with the offender's challenge or command, and the continued performance of activities deemed offensive:

Case 54 *The victim continued ridiculing the offender before friends. The offender finally shouted, "I said shut up. If you don't shut up and stop it, I'm going to kill you and I mean it." The victim continued his abusive line of conduct. The offender proceeded to the kitchen, secured a knife, and returned to the living room. She repeated her warning. The victim rose from his chair, swore at the offender's stupidity, and continued laughing at her. She thrust the knife deep into his chest.*

Similarly, a spouse or lover's refusal, under threat of violence, to conciliate a failing marriage or relationship served as tacit acceptance that violence was suitable to the present transaction.

Whether the victim's non-compliance was intentional or not, the offender *interpreted* the move as intentional. Take, for example, the killing of children at the hands of parents. In an earlier illustration, the first move found the parent demanding obedience and backed by a hostile, combative stance. In several of these cases, the child was too young to understand what the parent demanded and the specific consequences for non-compliance. Nevertheless, the child's failure to eat dinner or stop screaming was interpreted by the parent as a voluntary protest, an intentional challenge to authority. Consequently, the unwitting activities of victims may contribute to what offenders define as very real character contests demanding very real lines of opposition.

A second response, occurring in thirty percent of the cases, found victims physically retaliating against their offenders by hitting, kicking, and pushing—responses short of mortal injury:

Case 42 *The offender and a friend were passing by a local tavern and noticed the victim, a co-worker at a food-processing plant, sitting at the bar. The offender entered the tavern and asked the victim to repay a loan. The victim was angered by the request and refused to pay. The offender then pushed the victim from his stool. Before the victim could react, the bartender asked them to take their fight outside. The victim followed the offender out the door and, from behind, hit the offender with a brick he grabbed from a trash can immediately outside the door. The offender turned and warned the victim that he would beat the victim if he wouldn't pay up and continued his aggressions. The victim then struck the offender in the mouth, knocking out a tooth.*

In the remaining cases, victims issued counterchallenges, moves made when offenders' previous moves involved threats and challenges. In some cases, this move came in the form of calling the offender's bluff. In other cases, the counter came in the form of a direct challenge or threat to the offender, a move no different from the ultimatum given victims by offenders.

Unlike simple non-compliance, physical retaliation against offenders and issuance of counterchallenges signify an explicit acceptance of violence as a suitable means for demonstrating character and maintaining or salvaging face.

Just as the victim contributed to the escalation toward violence, so too did the audience to the transaction. Seventy percent of all cases were performed before an audience. In these cases, onlookers generally engaged one or two roles. In fifty-seven percent of these cases, interested members of the audience intervened in the transaction, and actively encouraged the use of violence by means of indicating to opponents the initial improprieties, cheering them toward violent action, blocking the encounter from outside interference, or providing lethal weapons:

Case 23 *The offender's wife moved toward the victim, and hit him in the back of the head with an empty beer bottle stating, "That'll teach you to [molest] my boy. I ought to cut your balls off, you motherfucker." She went over to the bar to get another bottle. The victim pushed himself from the table and rose. He then reached into his pocket to secure something which some bystanders thought was a weapon. One of the bystanders gave the offender an axe handle and suggested that he stop the victim before the victim attacked his wife. The offender moved toward the victim.*

In the remaining cases, onlookers were neutral. They were neither encouraging nor discouraging. While neutrality may have been due to fear, civil inattention, or whatever reason, the point is that inaction within a strategic interchange can be interpreted by the opponents as a move favoring the use of violence (cf. Goffman, 1967: 115).[3] Consider the statement of the offender in the following case:

Case 48 *Police officer: Don't you think it was wrong to beat [your daughter] when her hands were tied behind her back? [Her hands and feet were bound to keep her from scratching.]*
Offender: Well, I guess so. But I really didn't think so then, or [my wife] would have said something to stop me.

Stage V. On forging a working agreement, the offender and, in many cases, victim appeared committed to battle. They contributed to and invested in the development of a fateful transaction, one which was problematic and consequential to their face and wider reputation. They placed their character on the line, and alternative methods for assessing character focused on a working agreement that violence was appropriate. Because opponents appeared to fear displaying weakness in character and consequent loss of face, and because resolution of the contest was situationally bound, demanding an immediacy of response, they appeared committed to following through with expressed or implied intentions.

Commitment to battle was additionally enhanced by the availability of weapons to support verbal threats and challenges. Prior to victory, the offender often sought out and secured weapons capable of overcoming the victim. In about thirty-six percent of the cases, offenders carried hand guns or knives into the setting. In only thirteen percent of these cases did offenders bring hand guns or knives into the situation on the assumption that they might be needed if the victims were confronted. In the remainder of these cases such weapons were brought in as a matter of everyday routine. In either event, to inflict the fatal blow required the mere mobilization of the weapon for action. In sixty-four percent of the cases, the offender either left the situation temporarily to secure a hand gun, rifle, or knife, or transformed the status of some existing situational prop, such as a pillow, telephone cord, kitchen knife, beer mug, or baseball bat, into a lethal weapon. The possession of weapons makes battle possible, and, in situations defined as calling for violence, probable.

The particular dynamics of the physical interchange are quite varied. In many cases, the battle was brief and precise. In approximately fifty-four percent of the cases, the offender secured the weapon and dropped the victim in a single shot, stab, or rally of blows. In the remaining cases, the battle was two-sided. One or both secured a weapon and exchanged a series of blows, with one falling in defeat.

Stage VI. Once the victim had fallen, the offender made one of three moves which marked the termination of the transaction. In over fifty-eight percent of the cases, the offender fled the scene. In about thirty-two percent of the cases, the offender voluntarily remained on the scene for the police. In the remaining cases, the offender was involuntarily held for the police by members of the audience.

These alternatives seemed prompted by two lines of influence: the relationship of the offender and victim and the position of the audience vis-á-vis the offense. When there is no audience, the offender appeared to act on the basis of his relationship to the victim. When the offender and victim were intimately related, the offender typically remained on the scene and notified the police. Sometimes these offenders waited for minutes or hours before reporting the event, stating they needed time to think, check the victim's condition, and make arrangements on financial matters, the children, and work before arrest. In contrast, when victims were acquaintances or enemies, offenders typically fled the scene. Moreover, these offenders often attempted to dispose of their victims and incriminating evidence.

Seventy percent of the cases, however, occurred before an audience, and offenders' moves seemed related to audience reactions to the offense. Bystanders seemed to replace the victim as the primary interactant, serving the offender as the pivotal reference for his exiting orientations. The audience assumed one of three roles: hostile, neutral, or supportive. In the hostile role, accounting for nearly thirty-five percent of the cases, bystanders moved to apprehend the offender, assist the victim, and immediately notify police. Such audiences were generally comprised of persons who either supported the victim or were neutral during the pre-battle escalation. In several of these cases, bystanders suggested, without use of force, that the offender assist the victim, call the police, and so forth. These audiences were comprised of the offender's intimates, and he followed their advice without question. In either case, hostile bystanders forced or suggested the offender's compliance in remaining at the scene for police.

In almost seventeen percent of the cases, the audience was neutral. These people appeared as shocked bystanders. Having witnessed the killing, they stood numb as the offender escaped and the victim expired.

In the remainder of the cases, the audience was supportive of the offender. These audiences were usually comprised of persons who encouraged the offender during the pre-battle stages. Supportive bystanders rendered assistance to the offender in his escape, destroyed incriminating evidence, and maintained ignorance of the event when questioned by the police, breaking down only in later stages of interrogation. Thus, while a hostile audience directs the offender to remain at the scene, the supportive audience permits or directs his flight.

CONCLUSION

On the basis of this research, criminal homicide does not appear as a one-sided event with an unwitting victim assuming a passive, noncontributory role. Rather, murder is the outcome of a dynamic interchange between an offender, victim, and, in many cases, bystanders. The offender and victim develop lines of action shaped in part by the actions of the other and focused toward saving or maintaining face and reputation and demonstrating character. Participants develop a working agreement, sometimes implicit, often explicit, that violence is a useful tool for resolving questions of face and character. In some settings, where very small children are murdered, the extent of their participation cannot be great. But generally these patterns characterized all cases irrespective of such variables as age, sex, race, time and place, use of alcohol, and proffered motive.

NOTES

[1]Whenever detectives encountered discrepancies in accounts of the structure and development of the transaction, they would routinely attend to such discrepancies and repair them through their subsequent investigation.

[2]The offender's location of the pivotal event may be self-serving. That is, the offender may select as an event leading to his violence one which places the brunt of responsibility for the murder on the victim. Whether or not the offender's location of the pivotal event is accurate is moot, for the victim may not be able to report his opinion. In this discussion I accept the offender's contention that a particular activity performed by the victim was pivotal to the organization of his action.

[3]When the audience voices its dissatisfaction over the escalation of a character contest, it typically deteriorates. Of the thirty-two rehearsals found in the histories of the cases, about half did not result in death because of the intervention of a dissenting bystander. Discouragement usually took the form of redefining the victim's impropriety as unintentional, or suggesting that backing down at the outset of the escalation is appropriate given the occasion as one for fun and pleasure. While bystanders can be either encouraging or neutral in situations of murder, Wallace (1965) found that in twenty percent of the cases with an audience, some bystanders sought to discourage a violent confrontation, and would themselves often end in the hospital or city morgue. It cannot be determined if my findings are inconsistent with Wallace. He does not specify at what point in the development of the transaction discouraging bystanders intervene. While I found that bystanders were not discouraging in the escalation toward battle, I did find that several cases involved bystanders trying to discourage violence once opponents were committed to or initiated it. It was common in these cases for the bystander to suffer physical injury.

REFERENCES

Banitt, Rivka, Shoshana Katznelson, and Shlomit Streit
1970 "The situational aspects of violence: a research model." Pp. 241–258 in Shlomo Shoham (ed.), Israel Studies in Criminology. Tel-Aviv: Gomeh.

Berdie, Ralph
1947 "Playing the dozens." Journal of Abnormal and Social Psychology 42 (January): 102–121.

Blumer, Herbert
1969 Symbolic Interactionism: Perspective and Method. Englewood Cliffs, N.J.: Prentice-Hall.

Bullock, Henry A.
1955 "Urban homicide in theory and fact." Journal of Criminal Law, Criminology and Police Science 45 (January-February): 565–575.

Cavan, Sherri
1963 "Interaction in home territories." Berkeley Journal of Sociology 8: 17–32.

Goffman, Erving
1963 Behavior in Public Places: Notes on the Social Organization of Gatherings. Glencoe: Free Press.
1967 Interaction Ritual: Essays on Face-to-Face Behavior. Garden City, N.Y.: Doubleday.
1969 Strategic Interaction. New York: Ballantine.

Goode, William J.
1969 "Violence among intimates." Pp. 941–977 in Crimes of Violence, prepared by Donald J. Mulvihill and Melvin M. Tumin. Washington, D.C.: U.S. Government Printing Office.

Lyman, Sanford M. and Marvin B. Scott
1970 A Sociology of the Absurd. New York: Meredith.

Moran, Alvin
  1971   "Criminal homicide: external restraint and subculture of violence." Criminology 8 (February): 357–374.

Schafer, Stephan
  1968   The Victim and His Criminal. New York: Random House.

Shibutani, Tamotsu
  1961   Society and Personality: An Interactionist Approach to Social Psychology. Englewood Cliffs, N.J.: Prentice-Hall.

Shoham, Shlomo, Sara Ben-David, Rivka Vadmani, Joseph Atar, and Suzanne Fleming
  1973   "The cycles of interaction in violence." Pp. 69–87 in Shlomo Shoham (ed.), Israel Studies in Criminology. Jerusalem: Jerusalem Academic Press.

Toch, Hans
  1969   Violent Men: An Inquiry into the Psychology of Violence. Chicago: Aldine.

Wallace, Samuel E.
  1965   "Patterns of violence in San Juan." Pp. 43–48 in Walter C. Reckless and Charles L. Newman (eds.), Interdisciplinary Problems in Criminology: Papers of the American Society of Criminology, 1964. Columbus: Ohio State University Press.

Wolfgang, Marvin E.
  1958   Patterns of Criminal Homicide. Philadelphia: University of Pennsylvania Press.

RESEARCHING MURDER TRANSACTIONS

David F. Luckenbill

The investigation culminating in "Criminal Homicide as a Situated Transaction" was my first experience with field research. It was unlike the many projects I had previously undertaken as an undergraduate and graduate student involving the use of library materials to describe or assess some theoretical principle, research report, or debate. Field research was a more complex, time-consuming operation. I had to formulate a theoretically germane problem, enter a mysterious field, gather data relevant to the problem, analyze that data, and advance generalizations resolving the problem.

I found myself in a bewildering position once I had stepped beyond the confines of the library. A number of practical problems arose: How was I to gain access to a field housing suitable data, what technique would be useful in acquiring such data, and precisely how could I use that technique in

Author's note: I wish to thank Rey Baca, Joel Best, and Douglas W. Maynard for their instructive comments on this paper.

acquiring data? Many of the problems I confronted were not discussed in the methods books I had read nor were they addressed in the methods courses I had taken. There were, in short, no recipes for managing the many exigencies of research. As a consequence I repeatedly withdrew from the research operation, assessed the particular problem I confronted, tentatively worked out a possible solution to the problem, and adjusted the operation accordingly. The research enterprise, then, is like any other problem-solving action. It is a groping process in which the researcher adjusts to a multitude of exigencies posed by an ever-changing field (cf. Blumer, 1969:20–61).

FORMULATING THE PROBLEM

The seed for this investigation was sown in a graduate independent study course. While I intended to study deterrence, I quickly found myself negotiating with the professor on what would be a more interesting issue to explore. The topic of criminal homicide arose. But this topic, like any topic, is broad. One can study a number of concrete problems pertaining to murder. My first central task, then, was to formulate a specific problem to investigate. This was not simple.

In the first few months of the undertaking, I examined the literature on criminal homicide, reviewing dozens of books and articles on the subject. These reports discussed everything from the personality defects of murderers to the influence of alcohol on murder, from comparisons of murder and suicide to legal definitions of murder and malice aforethought.

Awed by the diversity of these reports, I tried to sort through and categorize the literature in terms of the central problems examined. I found that investigations of criminal homicide for the most part took one of two basic directions.[1] One direction focused on the distribution of murder over time and space and the characteristics of offenders, victims, and offense settings (cf. Brearley, 1932; Bullock, 1955; Wolfgang, 1958; Hepburn and Voss, 1970). A second direction focused on the explanation of murder, on why a person would kill another person. In some cases, this work attempted to locate within the offender a set of conditions explaining violence, such as unconscious fixations on death and punishment or defective personality structures (cf. Menninger, 1942; Bromberg, 1951; MacDonald, 1968). In other cases, this approach concentrated on locating outside the offender a set of conditions explaining violence, such as the frustration caused by an imperfect social system or the breakdown of the familial institution governing male aggression (cf. Parsons, 1947; Henry and Short, 1954).

While these lines of investigation provide information useful in understanding murder, it seemed that such research reflected an incomplete analysis of the activity. Some researchers studied murder in terms of the individual offender and other researchers studied murder in terms of the social structure in which the offender is imbedded. But I was convinced that murder is a socially situated transaction, something that two or more people do together in one another's immediate physical presence. And, as Mead (1934) argued long ago, the participants in a collective transaction orient their respective activities to one another. They interpret one another's gestures, using them as cues signifying intended lines of action, and adjust their performances in light of their interpreta-

tions. The transaction, then, is constructed by members in a succession of adjustments to a developing situation.

If Mead (1934) was correct, then it would be expected that murder is the outcome of a joint undertaking by the offender, victim, and possible audience. It would be expected that participants would develop certain roles that combined to produce the fatal outcome. Several reports were found lending credence to this expectation. Some studies showed that in many cases the victim directly precipitates his or her destruction (Von Hentig, 1948:383–450; Wolfgang, 1958:245–65; Schafer, 1968:79–83). Here the victim throws the first punch, pulls the knife, or fires the first shot. In the course of the interchange, however, the roles reverse with the originally intended victim becoming the offender. The pivotal role of the audience to the confrontation has also been demonstrated in the literature. Von Hentig (1948:216–18), for instance, found that a lynch mob's actions are facilitated by an encouraging group of bystanders.

What was missing in the literature on murder was a fairly detailed examination of the manner in which the participants interact in the situation as it progresses toward the fatal outcome. What are the typical roles developed by the offender, victim, and possible audience? How do those roles intersect? In short, how is criminal homicide performed as a situated transaction? This was the central problem to which my attention turned, and this problem called for data regarding the transactional process.

SELECTING A
METHODOLOGICAL STRATEGY

Once a problem is formulated, the researcher must consider the matter of research design, selecting a methodological strategy that provides him or her with a body of data with which to manage the problem. This was a fairly difficult task in my research. Because students of criminal homicide had not seriously examined how murder is performed, they could not provide me with a polished strategy for studying the process of interaction eventuating in murder. Consequently, I spent some time considering which of several different strategies would be most useful in gathering suitable data.

I first considered what I knew was a handy strategy for gathering information: library research, the secondary analysis of data gathered and published by others (cf. Glaser and Strauss, 1967: 161–83). I looked through stacks of books and rows of journals for cases of murder, detailed accounts of transactions ending in death. I found two principal types of documents that included murder cases. First, I located a number of biographies of murderers that sketched the details of their crimes. These documents for the most part were oriented toward lay audiences and focused on notorious cases (cf. Jesse, 1924; Shew, 1960). Second, I found several casebooks that provided rather brief descriptions of murder transactions (cf. McDade, 1961).

The data gleaned from these documents seemed to me unacceptable for purposes of examining the transaction. Precisely how such cases were compiled by the reporter was usually uncertain. Reporters often did not provide the reader with a description of the sources of information used in reconstructing murder transactions or the manner in which such transactions were reconstructed. On the other hand, there appeared to be gaping holes in the accounts. Many concrete questions I wished to explore were often unanswerable in terms of the published accounts. Take, for instance, the following two accounts:

Goodwin, Solomon: The two men had been drinking and getting along fine. Paddling in a canoe on a river, they fell to words, then blows. Goodwin hit Wilson with an oar; he fell out and was drowned (McDade, 1961:109).

M'Donnough, William: M'Donnough became intoxicated on punch at his daughter's house. When his wife returned home, he abused her; one word led to another and he finally cut her throat with a blunt knife. His actions sound mad, but he was condemned nonetheless (McDade, 1961:192).

With respect to the Goodwin case, was there an audience to the confrontation? If so, what did bystanders do as Goodwin and Wilson escalated their conflict? Under what conditions did the two men come to exchange words? Precisely what did they say to one another? Who initiated the first blow? With respect to the M'Donnough case, how did M'Donnough abuse his wife? How did the wife respond to his abuse? What words were exchanged? Was there an audience to the confrontation? If so, how did bystanders respond to the confrontation? These and many other questions can be raised with

respect to these cases. The point is that such accounts lack the specificity necessary to examine the process of interaction culminating in murder.[2]

Given the drawbacks of library research for my purposes, I considered the strategies of survey and observation. Although these strategies could have provided primary data on murder transactions, there were some problems in using them. Because I did not have funds with which to conduct research, I could not afford to survey a sample of participants. It was not feasible to track down and interview or administer a questionnaire to offenders and witnesses about the crimes of which they were party. But even if funding were not crucial, problems remained. To gather information from people about an event remote in time and space is difficult since memory is fragmented and subject to distortion, particularly when the event about which people are questioned was unpleasant.

Observational strategies also had their drawbacks. First, to have situated myself in settings that typically house murders would have been impossible. As Wolfgang (1958), Hepburn and Voss (1970), and others have found, one prominent setting of murder is the private residence, and this setting is inaccessible to the researcher. Second, assuming that I could have spent some time observing, it seemed likely that I would observe few, if any, murders while situated in an accessible setting. Consequently, the number of cases I could conceivably gather would have been very small. Finally, there were ethical problems in using observational strategies to investigate murder. To have placed my life and limb in jeopardy and to have sacrificed the victim's life by my nonintervention would have been unethical.

Given the shortcomings of survey and observational strategies for my purposes, I took my search to several fellow graduate students who had at that time been studying police operations. They suggested that I reconstruct a set of murder transactions using police reports on murder as a secondary source of data, a strategy similar to that employed by some historians in reconstructing notable events. Certainly, this strategy was not without its drawbacks, for the information used in reconstructing transactions may have been distorted. Offenders and witnesses may have provided police officers with self-serving accounts justifying their particular lines of action in the event. Furthermore, what the participants reported to the police officers may have been constrained by the manner in which the officers questioned them and the specific questions put to them.

Yet this methodological strategy had practical and theoretical advantages over the other strategies I had considered. First, it seemed to promise greater accuracy in understanding the process of interaction eventuating in murder. Police reports contained the observations of the offender, the witnesses, and in some cases the victim, and these observations were written in the words of the participants. Police reports, including the statements of the participants, were generally written only hours after the crime was committed. Consequently, the problem of fragmentary information owing to forgetfulness would be largely circumvented. Police reports, especially those pertaining to such serious crimes as murder, are usually detailed. Lengthy narratives on the event and photographs of the setting are generally included in the reports. Second, this strategy seemed less expensive than survey and observational strategies, for a complete set of data could be easily obtained from one central location. Third, I would be able to gather information on transactions occurring in a diverse number of settings. I was not likely to be constrained by what was accessible to an observer. Given these advantages, I decided to study murder by reconstructing the transaction through the use of police reports as a secondary source of data.

SECURING A SAMPLE

After I selected a methodological strategy, my attention turned to sampling, the process of acquiring cases to examine.[3] This was a formidable task and it was exacerbated by a number of unforeseen problems.

The first problem I encountered was how to gain access to police records on murder. Sampling is constrained by what is available to the researcher, and what is available is often constrained by the source of data. For this investigation I wanted to examine government documents that, because of their confidential nature, are often closed to the public. This meant that I had to gain special authorization to enter a police agency and examine its reports on specific murders. Such authorization was difficult to obtain. Police agencies are reluctant to let "outsiders" poke around, read confidential reports, and generally crack the protective shell covering its operations for fear of publicity and political backlash.[4]

In order to obtain authorization to enter a restricted field, the researcher must develop a relationship of trust with the source of data. The researcher must not only promise but also convince the source of data that he or she will act according to mutually acceptable rules of research conduct. The researcher must convince the source of data that he or she will be discreet and maintain the anonymity of the research site and the people involved. This development of trust is difficult to accomplish. One method is to proffer one's track record. Here, the researcher demonstrates that he or she has engaged in comparable research before and fateful consequences for the agencies or people involved did not materialize. Another way to develop trust and gain admittance is to use a sponsor, some person or agency of known integrity who will introduce and vouch for the researcher. I used this latter tactic in my investigation.

While searching for an accessible research site, I contacted a friend who worked for a criminal justice research organization in a neighboring city and requested his assistance. He asked me to send him a short proposal outlining the research. Once he received my proposal, he called the police chief of that city. The chief flatly refused to admit a student to carry out any sort of research within his department. When this fact was relayed to me, I visualized my research biting the dust. In desperation I asked if any other government agency in which he had influence housed documents pertaining to cases of murder. My sponsor said that the district attorney's office probably had fairly complete files and that he was a close friend of the district attorney. I then asked him to contact the D. A. and plead my case. He called the D. A. and assured him that my intentions were those of scholarship and not muckraking. While the D. A. was amenable to my research, he wanted to meet me personally. I met with the D. A. several days later. I described my research objectives as well as my plans of action and I promised him that I would not reveal the research site, social control personnel, or participants involved in the murders studied. After an hour the D. A. agreed to allow me to use the resources of his office to conduct my research. Thus, after several weeks of searching about and developing contacts, I managed to gain access to government reports on criminal homicide.

DEFINING MURDER

I entered the research site with the intention of studying criminal homicide. After I had examined several cases, however, I found that the legal definition of criminal homicide was not useful for my purposes. Included within the rubric of the legal definition are different kinds of events—events in which the offender kills for material gain and those in which the offender kills for nonmaterial gain, events in which the offender intends to kill another and those in which the offender does not intend to kill another. Because of this diversity, the dynamics involved in murder may differ from one situation to another. The dynamics of an event in which a third party hires the offender to kill on his or her behalf, for instance, may be different from those in which the offender kills in defense of his or her honor. The dynamics of an event in which the offender purposely kills another may be different from those in which a person dies from the offender's negligence. The researcher often must construct definitions suited to the theoretical and methodological purposes of the study in order to avoid the problems posed by strict adherence to penal code definitions (cf. Cressey, 1951).

I constructed a definition of criminal homicide for the most part consistent with the form of criminal homicide examined in other sociological reports. My definition included these three properties: (1) criminal homicide involves the unlawful taking of another person's life; (2) it involves the expressed intention of killing or rendering bodily injury resulting in death (i.e., the offender's action must be purposive); and (3) the activity does not occur in the course of some other criminal activity.

SELECTING CASES

The task was to select transactions that fit this definition of criminal homicide. One problem I encountered in the selection process was deciding how many cases were sufficient for understanding the transaction. Because researchers had not carefully considered how murder is performed, I focused on developing generalizations about this social act. This required that I examine enough cases to make it unlikely that generalizations

rested on freak incidents. The definition of a sufficient number of cases was bound by two practical matters. First, because I was working alone without benefit of funds to hire research assistants, I had to examine a manageable number of cases. This, I decided, was something like 50 to 75 cases. Second, I was limited to those cases available. The criminal justice system of the area to which I had access had reorganized its record-keeping system in 1962. All cases that had occurred in 1973 were unavailable because they were still in the midst of legal processing. Thus, I was limited to cases of murder occurring between 1963 and 1972.

In order to select a manageable, yet sufficient number of cases, I had to know the total number of available cases fitting my definition of murder, which proved to be an arduous undertaking. Initially, I constructed a roster of all cases of criminal homicide from the master calendar of cases kept in the district attorney's office. The master calendar was a ledger containing all felony cases that had been considered for court processing (including defendant appearances and grand jury proceedings). I assumed that all cases of murder for which records were available would be listed in the master calendar. But in the course of constructing the roster of murder cases, I discovered that all the cases that might suit my definition of murder were not included in the master calendar label, "187 P.C.," the California Penal Code designation for criminal homicide that I had been searching. I found only 57 cases between 1963 and 1972 and because some of these cases would be eliminated from examination as not fitting my definition, I began to worry that I would not secure a large enough sample of cases. To ensure that I had in fact acquired all cases of criminal homicide, I turned to the coroner's records for verification of the total number of cases of unnatural death in that ten-year period. Excluding cases of suicide, accidental homicide, and justifiable homicide, all of which are noncriminal events, the coroner's records showed that 94 unnatural deaths had occurred. Where, I wondered, were the missing 37 cases? After speaking with several assistant district attorneys, I realized that some cases had initially been labeled manslaughter and other cases had been reduced from murder to manslaughter. I adjusted my operation in light of this information and reexamined the master calendar, including in my roster all cases labeled "192 P.C.," the California Penal Code designation for manslaughter. Adding these cases to the first roster, I found 94 cases.

Satisfied that I had constructed a roster of all cases of criminal homicide, I turned my attention to eliminating cases that did not fit my definition of murder. Some 23 cases were eliminated. Fourteen cases were vehicular manslaughters in which a person died in the course of a traffic accident. These were eliminated because the offender, although held responsible because of negligence, had unintentionally killed the victim. Eight cases involved felony homicides in which a person was killed in the course of a robbery, burglary, or abortion. One case involved a negligent homicide in which a youngster died after touching an illegally constructed electrified fence.

This screening process left 71 deaths or 70 transactions (one double murder) fitting my definition of criminal homicide. I considered this a sufficient number of cases and all were subsequently examined.

DEVELOPING THE METHODOLOGICAL STRATEGY

It often seems from reading a research report that once a methodological strategy has been selected the researcher merely implements that strategy. This was not true of my investigation and I suspect that it is not true of many other investigations (cf. Cicourel, 1964). The technique of reconstructing events using secondary data was not plucked from a textbook or research report or from a course lecture and simply employed in the field. Rather, the strategy was a *plan of action*, a way to approach the data acquisition process. Indeed, the strategy developed over the course of the research. It took concrete shape as particular exigencies were confronted, assessed, and taken into account. This characterization gains support by noting several features of the research process.

Selecting Useful Documents

My first day in the district attorney's office was an orientation period. A secretary showed me where the case files were located, how particular files could be located, and where I could work without interruption. I was then handed two bulky folders containing all of the documents pertaining to two of the cases in my potential sample and sent on my way. As I examined each case I realized that the data acquisition process would be time-consuming, for it took some four hours to wade through each case. I also realized that many of the documents had nothing to do with my research problem. These documents dealt with issues of criminal justice processing, such as orders for court appearance, summaries of appellate court decisions relevant to the case, and interoffice memos regarding the legal status of personal effects. But several types of documents were relevant. Police reports, psychiatric reports, presentence reports prepared by probation officers, and grand jury court testimony included information on the murder transaction.

I had originally decided to use police reports as the basic resource for reconstructing the transaction. I had planned to write a complete description of the chain of activities in each case from the moment the participants entered one another's physical presence to the moment the offender fled the scene. After I had examined eight cases, however, I realized that reliance on police reports alone would bias the reconstruction process since the police reports might have missed certain crucial items that other reports contained. Consequently, I decided to examine all psychiatric reports, presentence reports, and grand jury and court testimony for each case in addition to police reports. Inclusion of these documents was useful for two reasons. First, these documents offered additional information on the event. They contained rather lengthy sections regarding the offender's orientation to the transaction. The presentence report and grand jury and court testimony also contained data regarding witnesses' orientation to the transaction. These documents, then, could serve as resources for adding specificity to and filling gaps in accounts constructed from police reports. Second, the documents offered a check on the reliability of the police reports. Because these documents were produced by officials operating in different government agencies and because these agencies had few informational links, I assumed that they could serve as relatively independent resources bearing on one focal point (cf. Webb et al., 1966). Thus, the methodological strategy was elaborated in the course of research by systematically including documents produced by other agencies.

Gathering Useful Information

At the outset of the study I considered two types of information necessary for understanding how murder is performed. I needed information regarding the manner in which the participants interacted in the course of the transaction. Specifically, I needed information on who said and did what to whom, the chronology of dialogue and action, and the physical comportment of the participants. I was also convinced that information on the personal attributes of the participants was vital. Several reports had argued that lower and working class people manage troublesome situations in a manner quite different from the way in which middle and upper class people manage them (Goode, 1969). If this is so, I figured, then differences in the way in which murder is performed may be explained in terms of the particular attributes of the participants. Consequently, I decided to seek information for each case on such attributes as age, ethnicity, gender, socioeconomic class, marital status, prior police record, and social relationships between participants.

After I had examined 28 cases, I developed a tentative sequential model of the murder transaction. This first model resembled that reported in the reprinted article. I found that murder was the outcome of an intense interchange between the offender and victim, who developed lines of action oriented toward saving or maintaining face and demonstrating strong character. In a succession of moves the participants developed a working consensus that violence was a useful tool for resolving questions of face and character. And this was so independent of the particular attributes of the offender and victim. Thus, while I continued to gather information on the attributes of the participants, I did not seriously attend to the problem of relating differences in personal attributes to differences in the transactional process.

While information on the attributes of the participants was ultimately disregarded, another type of information assumed importance. After 15 cases had been examined, I discovered a case in which the offender and victim had engaged in what I termed a rehearsal: they had involved themselves in an event in which hostilities escalated and violence ensued. But this episode ended in a bloodied nose, nothing more. While I was concerned with transactions eventuating in death, this rehearsal

was interesting because it offered me a source of comparative data. Understanding the conditions necessary for transactions ending in murder could be facilitated by studying basic differences between rehearsals and murders. Consequently, I carefully attended to incidents in which the offender and victim had engaged in a rehearsal prior to the murder.

Reconstructing Murder

Although I had decided to augment police reports with psychiatric reports, presentence reports, and grand jury and court testimony, this procedure produced its own problem: systematic irregularities between documents. Presentence reports, for example, were sometimes inconsistent with information drawn from psychiatric reports. In addition, I could not keep track of the ways in which specific documents were used in reconstructing the transaction.

Given these problems, I decided to alter the procedure. Instead of writing one account and then supplementing it with information drawn from other documents, I decided to prepare separate accounts of the transaction from each document. Once this was accomplished, I compared the accounts, noting points of similarity and contrast as well as areas in which some were more detailed than others. I then constructed one summary account of the transaction using the separate accounts as resources.

Developing a Coding Scheme

The investigation did not begin with a predesigned scheme for coding the actions of the participants.[5] Because I did not know what to expect of the participants, I did not want to constrain myself by designing a set of finely polished categories and then selectively attending only to items that fit those categories. Instead, the actions of participants were coded in the course of data acquisition. I used the summary accounts for 28 cases to outline the basic moves of the participants. Focusing on one move at a time, I examined all of the concrete actions of the participant involved and tried to find the pivotal feature these actions shared. Once this was accomplished, I sought to group together those actions sharing more specific properties. As additional cases were examined, the tentative coding scheme was assessed and changed accordingly.

In Stage 1, for instance, it appeared that the victim had performed some action the offender subsequently defined as personally offensive. Of course, the concrete actions of each victim varied considerably, as illustrated in the moves of the victims in the following cases:

Case 1:   The victim informed the offender, "You're a prick. You want to try something, then come on."

Case 2:   As the offender moved to the tavern door, he accidentally bumped into the victim. The victim shouted, "Watch where you're walking, asshole."

Case 4:   The victim started laughing at the offender's car, which he, the victim, had scratched a week earlier. The offender asked the victim why he was laughing. The victim responded that the offender's car looked like junk.

Case 5:   The offender asked the victim's girlfriend to dance. The victim, sitting next to his girlfriend, stated, "Stay away from her or I'll beat the shit out of you."

Case 8:   The victim suggested to the offender's wife that they leave the offender behind and travel to the country in order to have sexual relations. The wife, angered by the suggestion, told the offender what the victim had said.

Although the concrete activities of the victim varied, each action involved in some way an event the offender subsequently interpreted as offensive. These activities, moreover, could be differentiated in terms of the manner in which they were deemed offensive. In the first four cases described above, for instance, the victim issued a verbal statement to the offender disparaging some aspect of self or family or friends. In the fifth case, however, the victim did not issue an offensive statement to the offender but engaged in an inappropriate action toward the offender's loved one. As the research continued, I found a number of other cases that did not fit either of these two categories. I then developed a third category, one involving the victim's refusal to comply with the offender's commands.

CONCLUSION

The research process culminating in my article "Criminal Homicide as a Situated Transaction" involved a succession of adjustments to unforeseen exigencies. I entered the field with only a plan of action, a general method for attending to and manipulating information regarding the murder transaction. The particular kind of information I attended to and the particular way in which I manipulated that information took shape as I adjusted my strategy to several kinds of conditions. Financial and ethical considerations affected the feasibility of survey and observational techniques. The actions and relationships of my sponsor affected my access to different sources of information. The record-keeping procedures of the criminal justice system affected the scope of sampling. The quality of the records and the process of reconstruction affected the specific reports used and the manner in which they were used. The point is that I could not follow a recipe for research. Recipes for research, like rules, are abstract and categorical—they take concrete shape in the course of their use.

NOTES

[1]For a review of the theoretical as well as empirical literature on murder and other forms of criminal violence, see Luckenbill and Sanders (1977).

[2]The accounts found in some of these sources may be biased as well. The author's description of murder transactions may reflect his or her conceptions of murder, murderers, and murder victims. For example, Major Griffiths, a one-time superintendent of corrections in Great Britain, describes a number of particularly heinous murders. His descriptions are prefaced by the following:

I propose to deal next with the murderer on a large scale. I mean the miscreant who "takes life as coolly as he drinks a glass of water," and is no better than the unreasoning wild beast that by mere instinct springs upon his prey. This is the blackest specimen of the born criminal, the "throwback" to the savage, the brainless brute who is impelled to destroy life as a matter of course if the fancy takes him, or to satisfy the smallest needs, to secure the pettiest gains (Griffiths, 1902:30).

[3]The sampling process generally took the form of "theoretical" sampling, not "statistical" sampling. See Glaser and Strauss (1967:45–77) for a discussion of theoretical and statistical sampling techniques.

[4]This observation is equally applicable to other social control agencies as well as to criminals and deviants. For an interesting discussion of this, see Polsky (1967:109–43).

[5]I did, however, approach the process with a game framework, one that attempts to frame the actions of the opponents in terms of "moves." I also approached the process with a scheme for coding the participants. This scheme included the categories of "offender," "victim," and "bystander."

REFERENCES

Blumer, Herbert
 1969 Symbolic Interactionism: Perspective and Method. Englewood Cliffs: Prentice-Hall.
Brearley, H. C.
 1932 Homicide in the United States. Montclair: Patterson Smith.
Bromberg, Walter
 1951 "A psychological study of murder." International Journal of Psycho-Analysis 32:117–27.
Bullock, Henry A.
 1955 "Urban homicide in theory and fact." Journal of Criminal Law, Criminology, and Police Science 45(January-February):565–75.
Cicourel, Aaron
 1964 Method and Measurement in Sociology. New York: Free Press.
Cressey, Donald R.
 1951 "Criminological research and the definition of crimes." American Journal of Sociology 56(May):546–51.
Glaser, Barney G. and Anselm L. Strauss
 1967 The Discovery of Grounded Theory: Strategies for Qualitative Research. Chicago: Aldine.
Goode, William J.
 1969 "Violence between intimates." Appendix 19 in Donald J. Mulvihill and Melvin M. Tumin, with Lynn A. Curtis, Crimes of Violence. A staff report to the National Commission on the Causes and Prevention of Violence. Washington, D.C.: U.S. Government Printing Office.
Griffiths, Arthur
 1902 Mysteries of Police and Crime. Volume 2. London: Cassell.
Henry, Andrew F. and James F. Short, Jr.
 1954 Suicide and Homicide. New York: Free Press.
Hepburn, John and Harwin L. Voss
 1970 "Patterns of criminal homicide: a comparison of Chicago and Philadelphia." Criminology 8(May):21–45.
Jesse, F. Tennyson
 1924 Murder and Its Motives. New York: Alfred A. Knopf.
Luckenbill, David F. and William B. Sanders
 1977 "Criminal violence." Pp. 88–156 in Edward Sagarin and Fred Montanino (eds.), Deviants: Voluntary Actors in a Hostile World. Morristown: General Learning Press.
MacDonald, John
 1968 Homicidal Threats. Springfield: Charles C Thomas.
McDade, Thomas M.
 1961 The Annals of Murder. Norman: University of Oklahoma Press.
Mead, George H.
 1934 Mind, Self and Society. Edited by Charles W. Morris. Chicago: University of Chicago Press.
Menninger, Karl
 1942 Love against Hate. New York: Harcourt, Brace and World.
Parsons, Talcott
 1947 "Certain primary sources and patterns of aggression in the social structure of the western world." Psychiatry 10(May):167–81.
Polsky, Ned
 1967 Hustlers, Beats, and Others. Garden City, N.Y.: Anchor.
Schafer, Stephan
 1968 The Victim and His Criminal: A Study in Functional Responsibility. New York: Random House.
Shew, E. Spencer
 1960 A Companion to Murder. New York: Alfred A. Knopf.

Von Hentig, Hans
   1948   The Criminal and His Victim. New Haven: Yale University Press.

Webb, Eugene J., Donald T. Campbell, Richard D. Schwartz, and Lee Sechrest
   1966   Unobtrusive Measures. Chicago: Rand McNally.

Wolfgang, Marvin E.
   1958   Patterns of Criminal Homicide. Philadelphia: University of Pennsylvania Press.

THE SOCIAL SCIENTIST AS HISTORIAN: HOW IMPORTANT IS IT TO LOOK BACK?

Douglas Klegon

The cowboy rides into an isolated settlement. In an earlier period, before the town existed, there had been only hunters and fur traders. Now the cowboy reflects on the changing countryside, altered by a new wave of frontiersman—the farmer. The rider sits on his horse, a picture of individualism, used to periods of solitude. He lives in an environment where lawlessness is commonplace; the frontiersmen enforce their own laws and choose which laws to enforce. If the cowboy recognizes you as a friend, a fellow pioneer, then he will be eager to be helpful. But if he perceives you as an outsider, then you should be wary of this potential foe.

Can this picture of the West during the middle of the nineteenth century possibly be relevant for the social scientist of today? Can looking back at the western frontier help us understand processes within our urbanized society? Yes, says Murray Melbin (1978). He argues that the concept of "frontier" can be used to examine either the occupation of land or of *time*. Both are part of the "ecological niche" we occupy. Whereas the land west of the Mississippi constituted our frontier in the middle of the nineteenth century, today our frontier involves the rapid expansion of after-dark activity in urban areas. If Melbin's hypothesis of night as our new frontier is correct, then, as he points out, "the culture of the contemporary urban nighttime should reveal the same patterns and moods found in former land frontiers" (Melbin, 1978:6). Just as there were waves of land frontiersmen, so too there is a succession of users of nighttime: from isolated wanderers to production workers working the graveyard shift to those engaged in consumption activities. In both types of frontier there is a sparse and more homogeneous population. Settlements in both space and time are more isolated. There are fewer social constraints. New behavioral styles and deviant subcultures arise. There is more lawlessness, whether in a western "cow town" or an urban "combat zone." But there also is more helpfulness for in-group members, either fellow cowboys or night people. And as the frontier becomes more settled, exploitation of the basic resource becomes national policy, such as with the Homestead Act of 1862 or the expansion of multiple shift work in the 1970s. Finally, interest groups begin to emerge, such as the Greenback Party, the National Grange and Populists on the western frontier and the prostitutes (Coyote) and pro night-work business lobbies of today (Melbin, 1978). By looking back in this way, Melbin is able to understand a current social process: the expansion of nighttime activities. A historical perspective allows us to recognize that the process is not unique. As Melbin states, treating the expansion into nighttime "as a sequel to the geographic spread of the past centuries is to summarize the move within familiar ecological concepts of migration, settlement, and frontier" (1978:20).

Author's note: I wish to thank the editor, Theodore Wagenaar, for his helpful comments and suggestions.

THE IMPORTANCE OF LOOKING BACK

Unfortunately, some social scientists less readily recognize the potential utility of "looking back." In fact, social scientists are often hesitant to undertake historical analyses and utilize historical data. This reluctance probably has two sources. First, there is a feeling that historical events and processes may be of declining relevance in our complex, industrial, urbanized society. Given the pace of change, the past is often seen as having little power to explain our present social situation. Second, there is a methodological concern. Social scientists are apt to be suspicious of the reliability and validity of the historical record. For example, Lin (1976) suggests that documentary and historical methods suffer from limited accuracy and thoroughness of available materials. Researchers have no control over the original compilation of data and therefore are at the mercy of those who record information. Lin notes that the recorders of historical events and data can "use their own definitions of situations, define and select events as important for recording, and introduce subjective perceptions, interpretations, and hindsights into their recordings" (1976:216). Furthermore, even relatively unbiased recorders have not necessarily framed the data in a way amenable to manipulation within present-day social scientific perspectives. Thus, concerns of substantive relevance as well as of method exist when dealing with historical analyses.

Despite the factors that have made social scientists hesitant to look back, I will argue that there is much we *should* learn and much we *can* learn by examining the historical record. Before I attempt to convince you of that, however, let me first state what I will not address in this essay. First, this is only indirectly a "how to" essay. I will not be explicitly presenting general techniques for doing historical research. Instead, I will be presenting examples that use a variety of data and consider a variety of questions. To do otherwise would be beyond the scope of this essay, since social scientists utilizing historical data are really using many methodologies. Using documents as data, for example, may involve content analysis; historical actors, through their records, are in some ways similar to interview respondents; and, in some studies the researcher examining the historical record can be compared to a contemporary field researcher. All

researchers undertaking historical analyses do use some similar techniques and encounter common problems. In order to conduct a thorough search of relevant archives you need a good library, and, as I have learned, there is the problem of developing strategies for staying alert in the musty stacks of a State Historical Society Library. Since historical social scientific research really involves a type of datum rather than a distinct methodological technique, the "how to" is less important than demonstrating the benefits of adopting a historical perspective in the first place.

Second, in my choice of examples I do not stress the analysis of quantitative historical data and the use of complex mathematical and statistical techniques. The student should note that there is a growing debate among historians about quantification. The debate was intensified in 1974 with the publication of two books dealing with slavery in the antebellum South: *Time on the Cross* by Robert Fogel and Stanley Engerman and *Roll, Jordan, Roll* by Eugene Genovese. Despite areas of disagreement, the two books contain several parallel findings suggesting that slavery was economically viable and that slave owners were concerned with the well-being of their slaves. Fogel and Engerman, however, utilized elaborate quantitative techniques and mathematical modeling (cliometrics), whereas Genovese utilized traditional qualitative historical techniques. The controversy surrounding these two studies exists on many levels (see, for example, the *American Journal of Sociology* "Review Symposium" containing articles by William Wilson [1976] and by Immanuel Wallerstein [1976]). As summarized by Wilson, basic to the controversy is whether

quantitative techniques ultimately destroy the very essence of historical data, trivialize the findings, and force historians to ignore factors that are not amenable to quantification. . . . Is history to remain a humanistic discipline whereby the analysis of data depends upon the historian's sensitivity to subjective experience and his interpretative understandings, or is it to move in the "scientific" direction, relying on data that are quantified, controlled, and manipulated by mathematical techniques (1976:1190–1191)?

But to frame the quantification issue in the above manner seems somewhat misdirected. Anyone accumulating data to subject to mathematical manipulation must still utilize interpretative understanding and, as a participant observer might argue, the ideals of "science" and of "control" are not limited to interpreting quantitative data.

It seems more reasonable to note that depending on the issue both quantitative and qualitative data may be useful in achieving understanding or even prediction. In fact, Wallerstein (1976) suggests that the difference in Fogel and Engerman's methodology as opposed to Genovese's is partially a result of looking at different issues. Fogel and Engerman are trying

to figure out primarily why the firm acts as it does in terms of maximizing profit and only secondarily how the worker operates within these parameters to extract advantage. ... For [Genovese], the primary question is how the slave coped with an oppressive system, and only second how the slaveowner responded to the political action of the slaves (Wallerstein, 1976:1205).

Econometric models may make sense for investigating profit maximization behavior; qualitative studies of slave life make sense for examining the response of a legally repressed group of workers. In essence, the focus of inquiry partially determines the methodology utilized. The choice of quantitative versus qualitative data should not be viewed as an either/or situation.

Whereas social scientists would probably agree that the historian can profit by using quantitative techniques, they are less apt to recognize that social scientists can profit by looking back and using qualitative techniques. In this essay I will be trying to convince you of the truth of my statement that there is much we should and can learn by using historical data, particularly often overlooked qualitative data. I will therefore concentrate on presenting the results of several studies that utilize a variety of data and demonstrate the variety of hypotheses waiting to be investigated if only we look back.

SOCIAL SCIENCE AND HISTORY

There are several reasons why social scientists should be more cognizant of history. One is that social scientific categories and modes of analysis often can provide new insights into historical events. Analyses by historians have traditionally involved a concentration on a narrative of specific sequences and actions of individuals. When re-

searchers (whether trained as historians or social scientists) adopt a social scientific perspective, however, the focus shifts to the social meanings of events. The use of social scientific analytical categories can then lead to the formulation of new explanatory hypotheses about events.

An early effort by a historian to interpret an event by undertaking a systematic analysis of social categories was Charles A. Beard's (1913) classic study, *An Economic Interpretation of the Constitution of the United States.* The adoption of a social scientific framework is evident in Beard's statement that his goal was to examine the "hypothesis that economic elements are the chief factors in the development of political institutions" (1913:6). In order to investigate the interrelationships between major institutions, Beard included use of a methodology similar to the more recent "positional" methodology used in the analysis of the distribution of power. He systematically analyzed the participants at the Constitutional Convention in terms of their positional linkages to elite interests. As might be expected, Beard found a disproportionate representation of such groups as land speculators, merchants, manufacturers, and holders of public securities. The small farmer and debtor segments of society were practically without representation. Unfortunately, as Hofstadter (1968) points out, interest in Beard's findings overshadowed his techniques, and for quite some time little interest was shown in the methodology he used.

The use of the social scientific perspective to explicate events of the past is also evident in the work of the noted historian Herbert Gutman (see, for example, *Work, Culture and Society in Industrializing America,* 1976). Gutman is concerned with understanding the transition to an industrial society in terms of changes in work, social class, power, and mobility patterns. He does not just provide a narrative of events but uses original documents and other primary sources to analyze relevant social forces. Gutman's work, for example, throws doubt on the existence of a strong work ethic during the initial stages of industrialization. An artisan's workday in the New York shipyards during the second half of the nineteenth century included before-noon work stoppages when a peddler of cakes came by, then when the candyman came, and finally, by eleven o'clock, "a general sailing out of the yard into convenient grog-shops after wiskey [sic]" (quoted in Gutman, 1976:35). In the afternoon, about half-past three, there would be a cake-lunch, and then at about five, the candyman would return. The men then would work until sundown when they went home for supper. As other examples, Gutman provides descriptive evidence of a pattern of four-day work weeks and three-day weekends (including "Blue Monday") among barrel makers and notes that a major issue in a strike of Milwaukee cigarmakers in 1882 was the right to leave the shop without the foreman's permission. This type of information suggests that a strong work ethic and an orientation to the clock were not brought to the workplace by workers but rather constituted a new set of cultural expectations to which workers needed to be socialized.

THE ROLE OF REINTERPRETATION

The purpose of utilizing social scientific modes of analysis to examine historical events has often been to reinterpret those events. This was somewhat true of Beard's (1913) economic interpretation of the Constitution. In addition, this has been true of several works about the Progressive era, such as *The Corporate Ideal in the Liberal State* by James Weinstein (1968), *The Triumph of Conservatism* by Gabriel Kolko (1963), and *Education and the Rise of the Corporate State* by Joel Spring (1972). Much of the reinterpretation of the Progressive era is based on the analysis of elites and the distribution of power. Crucial to this literature is the distinction made explicit by Kolko: regulation *for* business versus regulation *of* business. Based on an examination of profitability figures, shares of market controlled, dividends, and case histories of several industries, Kolko (1963) argued that the merger movement at the turn of the century was a "failure"; that is, the manufacturing sector of the economy grew increasingly competitive and private efforts at establishing stability and control were insufficient. In response, Kolko finds large-scale manufacturers eager for governmental regulation designed to create greater market predictability. Thus, the data indicate that the regulatory agencies of the Progressive era were really creating regulations *for* business. Such historical analyses contribute to our understanding of strategies used by elite groups to help maintain their position in the class structure.

Similarly, Weinstein (1968) examines the historical record, finding that representatives of large-scale business enterprises favored workmen's compensation. It was seen as a means of increasing morale (and thereby production) as well as a way of preempting the need to create employer liability laws. Business owners found such liability laws undesirable since the costs would be unpredictable and borne directly by the employer. In the area of education Spring's (1972) analysis includes an examination of documents of the National Association of Manufacturers. Those documents indicate that the NAM supported the creation of trade schools as a way of limiting the power of labor unions. The creation of trade schools would allow the circumvention of the apprenticeship system, thereby affecting the occupational socialization of skilled workers. These examinations of the historical record, when organized from the perspective of social scientific analysis of elites and the distribution of power, called into question common assumptions about the meaning of events during the Progressive era.

So far I have presented examples of analyses by historians in which social scientific perspectives were used to explain historical events. For historians this is apt to be an end in itself. As Landes and Tilly argue, "Because we are all prisoners of our past, in the sense that our options are limited by what has gone before and our preferences are shaped by our image of who we are and have been, it is of the utmost importance that we try to free our history from myth and error" (1971:5). Social scientists, however, often want to do more than explain an event. We are apt to want to transcend the specificity of any concrete historical event and develop explanations about classes of events. Rather than using social science to explain historical data, the data of history can be used to explicate social scientific processes. Such a distinction, of course, is somewhat artificial. An analysis primarily focusing on a specific historical event can still tell us something about the emergence of institutional patterns or the range of applicability of social scientific concepts. The advantages of a social scientist's adopting a historical perspective are particularly evident when there is an explicit effort to explain social scientific processes. Used in this way, the historical record takes on direct relevance for supporting or challenging existing hypotheses and theories. The power of our theories needs to be tested across a range of sociotemporal contexts.

In a study that won the 1975 North Central Sociological Association Graduate Student Competition, T. D. Schuby (1975) used historical data to investigate the hypothesis of elite theorists that a castelike upper class arises in capitalist societies. Schuby concentrated on Detroit, first identifying twelve upper class families of 1860. He then followed the descendants of those upper class families through 1970, paying particular attention to indicators of social cohesion (incidence of intermarriage, common economic interests, and joint social club memberships) and social power (occupancy of key economic positions). On the basis of his data, Schuby concluded that families in the upper socioeconomic class were able to transmit positional power to their descendants. Those families consequently were able to maintain their influence over major economic units. Schuby's Detroit example thus adds historical support for the hypothesis of the perpetuation of a castelike upper class.

Historical data generally have been very useful in studying the process of social mobility. Gutman (1976:211–33), for example, by looking at the social origins and career patterns of the most successful iron, locomotive, and machinery manufacturers of 1830–1880, analyzes social mobility patterns in the industrializing city of Paterson, New Jersey. In a review of an anthology of studies of social mobility in the United States, Miller (1977) suggests that "the field of history is today the most interesting and innovating of the social sciences" (and not, he adds, because of the application of advanced mathematical modeling and statistical techniques to historical material). Miller notes that the historical record indicates that the question of a decline of mobility rates cannot be answered simply. Instead, he explains, "One has to specify time and place, what specific groups of people, what kind of mobility" (Miller, 1977:41). The historical record used in such fashion can provide data crucial for understanding and testing hypotheses about the process of social mobility.

HISTORY AND SOCIAL INSTITUTIONS

Historical research can also help us test hypotheses about the nature and extent of institutional change. In the case of at least one major institution—the family—historical data often fail to support popular notions about the extent of change and the "social disintegration" assumed to be associated with change. Bane (1976), for example, presents evidence indicating that despite recent increases in the likelihood of divorce, marital disruption rates have not increased (see Table 1). Instead, changes in death rates balanced changes in divorce rates. The falling overall death rate, partially offset by the increasing differential between male and female death rates, resulted in a slow decline in the proportion of widowed women at given ages. The rate of that decline in widowhood apparently matched changes in marital disruption as a result of divorce. The high divorce rate of the 1970s, however, is not likely to be balanced by continuing changes in death rates. Bane (1976) predicts that by the 1990 census perhaps only half of the women between 45 and 49 years old will be living in intact first marriages.

Table 1. Percentages
of Ever-married Women
Living with Their First Husbands

Census Year	Age of Women		
	45–49	50–54	55–64
1910	70.2	64.7	55.0
1940	68.4	64.0	54.9
1970	69.9	65.7	56.6

Source: Bane, 1976:30. Used by permission.

Even if marital disruption will become more prevalent, the data still do not indicate a decrease in the marriage rate itself. Bane (1976) points out that well over 90 percent of the people in the United States marry, and it is unlikely that the proportion will fall to the 90 percent level recorded earlier in the century. The proportion of women who remarry after divorce or widowhood has in fact actually increased (see Table 2), generally keeping pace with the divorce rate. As Bane points out, the extent of remarrying indicates that "it is not marriage itself but the specific marital partner that is rejected" (1976:34).

Historical data therefore suggest that the family has not undergone as much change and is not in such bad shape as many assume. In fact, Bane's book, from which the data presented here has been abstracted, is entitled *Here to Stay*. Although the divorce rate has recently been increasing, the historical data also tell us that experiencing the loss of

Table 2. Percentages
Remarried of Women
Divorced or Widowed

Census Year	Age of Women		
	45–49	50–54	55–64
1910	35.4	28.7	19.2
1940	38.6	31.3	20.8
1970	52.5	45.2	31.7

Source: Bane, 1976:34. Used by permission.

a marital partner is not new. And the data tell us that marriage is not dying out or being replaced by a series of short-term liaisons (Bane, 1976).

A PERSONAL EXAMPLE

An area in which I am particularly interested and in which historical data have proved particularly useful is the study of professionalization. Traditional approaches to the study of professions have often assumed that professionalization is the result of a set of basic traits characterizing certain occupations. Those traits, which are used to define the profession, include an abstract knowledge base, commitment to a calling, peer identification, service orientation, and ethical codes. As illustrated by the proliferation and variation of lists of such traits, however, there is great difficulty in applying traits to concrete occupations. This has led to a search for alternative explanations of professionalization. In calling for a historical approach, Roth has suggested:

Perhaps a historical approach to the development of occupations is the best antidote for the attribute rut. If we can see in some detail how present-day professions developed, we would be less inclined to conjure up a vision of a list of characteristics toward which certain lines of work are moving and see it rather as a long-term process of negotiation (1974:18).

Essentially Roth and other critics of the list-making approach are suggesting that new questions be asked. For example: How have certain occupations been able to obtain and maintain the special status and autonomy associated with professionalism? This is a historical question, and it has led to some new insights about the social origins and role of

the professional form of occupational organization (Klegon, 1978).

The adoption of a historical approach allows the researcher to examine the interplay of various social forces associated with the development of the modern professional form of occupational control. One generally accepted hypothesis, for instance, is that the prestige of professionals stems from the nature of their knowledge. That hypothesis could only be true if practitioners possessed specialized expertise prior to achieving a prestigious social position. Elliott (1972), however, has demonstrated that just the opposite may be true. By "looking back," Elliott found that "status professionalism" initially existed; that is, the practitioner's position as a professional was based primarily on his or her place in the social stratification system. It was only with industrialization that there was a shift to "occupational professionalism" based on the development of specialized knowledge and tasks. In essence, social position *preceded* the development of other aspects of professionalism. Not only does this historical analysis force us to rethink hypotheses about the origins of the present social position of professionals, but it also indicates that institutional forms (e.g., "occupational professionalism") may be specific to a particular time period.

In addition to aiding in the analysis of the development of professionalism in general, the historical record can tell us something about how specific occupations were able to professionalize. In so doing, historical data becomes useful for theory building. My examination of the historical development of professions has led me to conclude that resources (sources of power) are crucial: what is done, for whom, and by whom. Among physicians the resource of "what is done" seems to have been of major significance as a source of power. Kronus (1976) discusses the relationship between the development of an effective technology in the late nineteenth century and the ability of the medical profession in the United States to establish legal barriers against encroachment by pharmacists and druggists. But there is more to it than just the existence of knowledge to do a task, for other occupations seem to have relied on other resources.

Lawyers, another traditional profession, seemed to rely less on abstract theoretical knowledge. Instead, their professionalization resulted more from who they were and the social meanings of their knowledge. Specifically, the professionalization of lawyers in the United States, occurring in the late nineteenth and early twentieth centuries, stemmed from a group of relatively high status individuals who were beginning to perform important functions for powerful economic interests. The appearance of professionalism, and the neutrality associated with professional knowledge, allowed lawyers to raise their own status as well as to legitimate relationships of power within the emerging corporate economy (Klegon, 1975). The historical record suggests that the professionalization of lawyers was not a result of any characteristics inherent in their occupation but rather a result of interaction with wider social forces. In this instance, the use of historical data permits a macroanalysis of institutional interrelationships.

If an analysis of the historical development of professions indicates that resources are more important than characteristics of occupations per se, then what are the meanings of professional traits? One plausible hypothesis consistent with the resource perspective is that the traits often used to *define* professions really develop in response to the needs of practitioners. Traits therefore are adopted as part of a *strategy* for maintaining the social position of the profession. An example focusing on the early history of the American Bar Association (ABA) will illustrate how historical data can provide evidence in support of this hypothesis (for a further elaboration, see Klegon, 1975).

The creation of a professional association traditionally has been regarded as a key aspect of the professionalization process. Such associations are seen as facilitating a sense of professional community or professional culture. They are therefore regarded as beneficial, reflecting an occupation's commitment to high standards and ethical codes. But is this traditional picture accurate? What in fact are the social origins of professional associations, and what role have they played? Again, the question is framed historically.

The ABA, founded in 1878, initially served as a mechanism for social interaction. Members were not concerned with what we would today recognize as professional issues. Meetings were held in the resort city of Saratoga Springs and members praised the grand hotels and the presence of a famous race meet. Membership was small, even by 1900 consisting of barely over 1 percent of all lawyers. It was not until the start of the twentieth century that the ABA began to be more active. As with

other nonexperimental methodologies, historical research cannot establish the *cause* of such a change. The use of a historical methodology does, however, make possible an examination of associations with wider social changes.

From the perspective of factors affecting the internal composition of the legal profession, the increased activity of the ABA was associated with an increasing number of practitioners. Those claiming the status "lawyer" were also becoming more heterogeneous in terms of social background. In addition, the utility of a more active association was heightened by the increasing division of labor among lawyers. Along with the new complexity of legal business came the early subspecialists, the patent and trademark lawyers, as well as the growth of the big law firms. Hence, after the turn of the century, there was more reason for an active association: to help regulate the larger, more diversified group of lawyers that existed in the United States.

From the perspective of external factors affecting professionalization, the period of increased activity of the ABA was associated with changes in the economy that altered the tasks of lawyers. Advocacy became less important and the new role of corporate counselor gained prominence. As the corporation emerged as the basic business unit in American industry, lawyers became increasingly important for creating and legitimating orderly relations of power. This was particularly true given the failure of private efforts to establish stability and rational control over the market during the merger movement of 1897–1903. Thus, the timing of the period of increased activity by the ABA correlates with wider social changes: the changes in scope and organization of the economy, the subsequent role of lawyers as business counselors, and the need for the legitimation of the law by large-scale business enterprises.

The early history of the ABA demonstrates how the historical record can be used as data relevant to an examination of the functions of professional associations. The historical perspective shifts the focus to the dynamics behind the development of institutional forms and to the consequences of those forms. In particular, the data challenge the notion that professional associations exist in order to assure high levels of performance and service. Instead, the development of the ABA seemed to represent a response to wider social changes and the resulting problems faced by practitioners. This finding suggests that in formulating hypotheses about the present and future nature of professions, we must avoid looking at professions in isolation from wider social forces.

An examination of historical antecedents should prove equally important for explaining the current social position of particular occupations. Rueschemeyer (1973), for example, finds that differences between the legal professions in Germany and the United States are a result of historical differences in the relative timing of bureaucratic rationalization of government versus economic development and industrialization. In Germany, where bureaucratization of the state *preceded* economic development, lawyers are less apt to be autonomous professionals and more apt to be subsumed under civil service. Similarly, Parry and Parry (1974), in their discussion of the unsuccessful use of the professional strategy by teachers in Great Britain, found that teachers (unlike doctors) were not organized as professionals prior to the entry of the state into the educational field. Consequently, the state has been able to continue to block teachers' efforts at professionalization. Difficulties in teachers' achievement of professional status are therefore related to historical factors affecting the occupation vis-á-vis the state. The historical perspective demonstrates that differences between occupations are not just the result of their present position on the "road" to professionalization. Instead, such differences reflect historical patterns of institutional emergence and interaction that can be crucial for understanding present aspects of society.

If "looking back" leads to developing theories and confirming hypotheses, then not only should it help us understand the past and present but it also should help us predict the future. If the data indicate that the ability to successfully achieve professional status is related to a specific set of historical circumstances, then we can hypothesize that attempts at professionalization will be unsuccessful in the future under another set of circumstances. Many occupations are attempting to follow in the footsteps of traditional professions so as to gain greater autonomy and prestige. They are doing so, however, under an altered set of social conditions. Haug (1975) suggests that social changes such as the expansion of education, technological development (including computerization), and an altered division of labor within occupations have led to a weakening of the knowledge monopoly traditionally held by professionals. In addition, she suggests that the rise of consumerism has resulted in a decline in the public belief in professional goodwill. Haug (1975) sees these developments as subsequently leading to a decline in professional autonomy. Under this emerging set of social conditions, not only will it be difficult for new occupations to obtain professional status but existing professions may even have trouble maintaining their social position. One might predict in fact the expansion of alternative, nonprofessional strategies (i.e., unionization) in efforts to obtain an elite position within the occupational structure. Such a hypothesis is a logical extension of the analysis of historical data, which suggested conditions associated with successful professionalization.

CONCLUSION

I have stressed in this discussion the substantive findings of several studies rather than specific techniques and methodological problems. I should warn the reader that in the process I have presented some conclusions that are far from universally accepted. But I have done so deliberately in order to emphasize the fertile ground that exists when the social scientist looks into the past. In addition, I have not focused on specific methodological problems because I feel they are really similar to problems encountered in other types of research represented in this book. Whether you are examining the representations of historical actors or of contemporary respondents to an interview, you must be cautious of naively accepting statements made by "subjects." Whether the data are historical or contemporary, researchers need to be aware of possible discrepancies between overt recorded activities and behind-the-scenes activities and manipulations. Whether the researcher uses historical data or other nonexperimental data, problems of achieving control remain. And whether the researcher is using historical data or gathering data through observation techniques, the reader must trust the researcher to have appropriately sampled, reported, and interpreted events.

One of the major problems faced by social scientists who use historical data is that they find themselves in a "crack" between disciplines. Historians are apt to stress extensive use of primary sources and a detailed description of specific events. Social scientists, on the other hand, are apt to be more concerned with generalizability. When doing a historical study, the social scientist thus has a tendency to use more secondary, aggregated data and to emphasize interpretation and organization of the observations of others. The problem then is that both historians and social scientists are apt to claim that something is missing from the analysis. It may be difficult to convince social scientists of the methodological rigor of a study, for quantitative data are often not available or not appropriate. And it may be difficult to satisfy historians, since the researcher must avoid too much emphasis on historical techniques involving detailed investigation of primary sources and a specific narrative that could obscure the overall conceptual framework and generalizability the researcher is trying to achieve. I have no easy solution to this dilemma, except, perhaps, to repeat a sentence I wrote in the introduction to my dissertation: "I am asking for a bit of tolerance from both sociologists—who may find the study less quantitative than they prefer—and from historians—who may find less use of primary data and narrative than they are used to" (Klegon, 1975:7).

If the social scientist looking into the past is worthy of a bit of methodological tolerance, it is because there is so much worth looking back for. I hope this brief essay has led you, as a student of social scientific methodologies, to agree with me. For the use of social scientific categories and modes of analysis can provide new insights into historical events. The data of history can be used as examples of sociological processes. Historical analysis facilitates the examination of sociotemporal variability in institutional forms. And the historical pattern of institutional emergence and interaction can be crucial for understanding present and future aspects of society. Historical phenomena thus can provide examples to clarify and apply accepted sociological concepts as well as data to help formulate and test sociological hypotheses. The concept "empirical" should therefore include research based on an examination of the historical record. Social scientists, emphasizing social forces rather than a narrative of sequences of events and actions of individuals, can both contribute to and profit from an examination of the historical record.

REFERENCES

Bane, Mary Jo
1976   Here to Stay: American Families in the Twentieth Century. New York: Basic Books.

Beard, Charles A.
1913   An Economic Interpretation of the Constitution of the United States. New York: Free Press.

Elliott, Philip
1972   The Sociology of Professions. New York: Herder and Herder.

Fogel, Robert and Stanley Engerman
1974   Time on the Cross: The Economics of American Negro Slavery. Boston: Little, Brown.

Genovese, Eugene
1974   Roll, Jordan, Roll: The World the Slaves Made. New York: Pantheon.

Gutman, Herbert
1976   Work, Culture and Society in Industrializing America. New York: Knopf.

Haug, Marie
1975   "The deprofessionalization of everyone?" Sociological Focus 8(August): 197–213.

Hofstadter, Richard
1968   "History and sociology in the United States." Pp. 3–19 in S. Lipset and R. Hofstadter (eds.), Sociology and History: Methods. New York: Basic Books.

Klegon, Douglas
1978   "The sociology of professions: an emerging perspective." Sociology of Work and Occupations 5(August): 259–83.
1975   "Lawyers and the social structure: an historical analysis of the role of professionalization among lawyers in the United States." Unpublished Ph.D. dissertation, University of Wisconsin–Madison.

Kolko, Gabriel
1963   The Triumph of Conservatism: A Reinterpretation of American History, 1900–1916. Chicago: Quadrangle.

Kronus, Carol
1976   "The evolution of occupational power: an historical study of task boundaries between physicians and pharmacists." Sociology of Work and Occupations 3(February):3–37.

Landes, David and Charles Tilly (eds.)
1971 History as Social Science. Englewood Cliffs: Prentice-Hall.

Lin, Nan
1976 Foundation of Social Research. New York: McGraw-Hill.

Melbin, Murray
1978 "Night as frontier." American Sociological Review 43(February):3–22.

Miller, S. M.
1977 Review of "Three Centuries of Social Mobility in America," edited by Edward Pessen. Contemporary Sociology 6(January):40–42.

Parry, Noel and José Parry
1974 "The teachers and professionalism: the failure of an occupational strategy." Pp. 160–85 in M. Flude and J. Ahier (eds.), Educability, Schools and Ideology. London: Croom Helm.

Roth, Julius
1974 "Professionalism: the sociologist's decoy." Sociology of Work and Occupations 1(February):6–23.

Rueschemeyer, Dietrich
1973 Lawyers and Their Society: A Comparative Study of the Legal Profession in Germany and the United States. Cambridge: Harvard University Press.

Schuby, T. D.
1975 "Class, power, kinship and social cohesion: a case study of a local elite." Sociological Focus 8(August):243–55.

Spring, Joel
1972 Education and the Rise of the Corporate State. Boston: Beacon Press.

Wallerstein, Immanuel
1976 "American slavery and the capitalist world-economy." American Journal of Sociology 81(March):1199–1213.

Weinstein, James
1968 The Corporate Ideal in the Liberal State, 1900–1918. Boston: Beacon Press.

Wilson, William
1976 "Slavery, paternalism, and white hegemony." American Journal of Sociology 81(March):1190–98.

UNOBTRUSIVE MEASURES: AN INVENTORY OF USES

Thomas J. Bouchard, Jr.

The purpose of this paper is not to tout the merits of unobtrusive measures; they are as a rule inferentially weak. The intent is to illustrate a wide variety of them and, by example, to persuade the reader to consider seriously supplementing more traditional procedures with them. Neither will we discuss in any detail the problems entailed by their use. Every user should read the superb methodological discussion in Webb et al. (1966). Other excellent methodological discussions can be found in Brandt (1972, ch. 5) and Denzin (1970, chs. 11 and 12).

Author's note: This paper was written while the author was at the Oregon Research Institute supported by General Research Support Grant RR–05612 from the National Institutes of Health and Grant MH–12972 from the National Institutes of Mental Health Service. The author would appreciate being informed of any methods of references missed by this review so they can be included in a future article.

The Logic of Multiple Methods

If unobtrusive methods yield measures which are as a rule inferentially weak, why use them? Two reasons. First, because all methods are fallible and methods that are fallible in different ways complement each other even if one is absolutely weaker than the other. Convergence of findings by two methods with different weaknesses enhances our belief that the results are valid and not a methodological artifact. Second, researchers tend to

From *Sociological Methods and Research*, Vol. 4, No. 3 (February 1976), pp. 267–300. Reprinted by permission of Sage Publications, Inc. and the author. References updated.

develop preferences for single methods (e.g., the interview, the questionnaire, participant observation) and skills in their use. While this may increase the resolving power of the measures generated in specific instances, it also blinds the researchers to a myriad of other "events" and distorts those they record. It is important to keep in mind the distinction between observations (records) and data (Runkel and McGrath, 1972). A method generates observations, the researcher turns those observations into data and the data into measures of constructs. Methods are in a sense "event recorders." An example is useful here. Consider the movie camera or video camera as a data-gathering method (event recorder). The field of view of the camera only encompasses a limited perspective on an event. It is blind to everything that goes on outside the field of view. It distorts because it has a fixed locus, is two-dimensional in its recording, foreshortens, and often requires unusual lighting conditions. If we consider the camera operator as part of the method, these problems are all confounded by his skill and his biases. He may focus on what looks good at the expense of what is important. Close-ups may reveal what appear to be important considerations, but all opportunities to test rival interpretations are lost because close-ups are taken only of a selected subsample.

Similar considerations apply to any method. It is well known that substantial correlations between variables can occur simply because a common method was used to measure each of them (Campbell and Fiske, 1959). Given the modest predictive power of most social science research, it behooves a researcher to check and see if all his "predicted variance" might not be due to this fact.

Since every investigator is interested in generalizing his findings beyond the circumstances which characterize his method of measurement it behooves him to multiply his methods. A researcher who uses multiple methods in order to generate multiple measures is engaged in triangulation, and when the measures converge on a common finding, he is said to have generated convergent validity. High convergent validity enhances the researcher's confidence that all his measures are tapping a common construct. Confirmation of theoretical expectations with various measures generated by divergent methods contributes heavily to the validity of the construct.

The Problem of Reactivity

A special problem faced by many social science research methods is that of reactivity. The respondent (subject) knows he is being observed (tested), and so forth, and his behavior is affected thereby. Unobtrusive measures can often, but not always, eliminate the rival hypothesis "reactive measurement effects" (Webb et al., 1966: 173). When "a reactive measure effect" is a plausible rival hypothesis its elimination via the use of an unobtrusive measure greatly enhances the generalizability of a set of findings.

Great care must be taken in the choice of a measure when the intent is to exclude reactive measurement effects. There is a tendency to think that reactivity is restricted to verbal (interview) and test (questionnaire) behavior. This is shortsighted. People can and do dissimulate with their behavior. Furthermore, reactivity is not always a response to the experimenter. Routine records and documents which on their face might appear to be unbiased are often reactive to political considerations (Dalton, 1959). An individual or a group may be maintaining a facade with respect to everyone else in the environment. If this is true much of the data that one would normally consider to be unobtrusive or nonreactive is contaminated prior to the investigator's arrival.

Focus on Behavior

An underplayed advantage of unobtrusive measures is that they tend to focus the researcher on behavior and the results of behavior rather than on verbal expressions of behavior. This is no small gain in light of the consistent finding that test-taking behavior, especially in the form of attitude measures, is often unrelated to the behavior of real interest to investigators (Brayfield and Crockett, 1955; Wicker, 1969). In our opinion the goal of the behavioral sciences is the prediction and control of behavior in its broadest sense and we find it difficult to understand why researchers have held so tenaciously to paper-and-pencil methods rather than turning to a systematic examination of the structure of the behavior of interest (see Brandt, 1972; Wernimont and Campbell, 1968).

Webb et al. (1966) have suggested four large classes of unobtrusive measures: physical traces, archives, simple observations, and measures gathered with hardware. The following discussion is organized around this classification system.

PHYSICAL TRACES

Physical traces are generally very indirect indicators of psychological and social processes. They are, therefore, prone to misinterpretation and should be used with caution. An example of this error is the use of indices of floor wear to assess frequency of use, and indirectly, popularity. Alternative interpretations might be: A bathroom or water fountain was located in the area, the arrangement of furniture allowed no degrees of freedom, the floor material in that area had different characteristics and simply wore faster (poorly calibrated instrument). Contaminating factors such as these should be looked for when physical traces are used.

A logical scheme for classifying physical traces is shown in Table 1.

Table 1. Six
Categories of Physical Traces

	Accretion	Erosion	Traces
Uncontrolled	I	III	V
Controlled	II	IV	VI

As a result of human activities, physical material can accumulate (accretion, e.g., litter); it also may be used up (erosion, e.g., wear spots on the floor in front of popular museum exhibits). When changes in physical material wrought by people are minor, people are said to have left traces, e.g., fingerprints. It is often possible to manipulate physical material in such a way that its use in assessing accretion, erosion, and traces is enhanced. The size of the material units may be fixed or randomized, the texture (wear qualities) may be standardized, its frequency of exposure regulated, or its capacity to retain traces enhanced. We have been unable to find any examples for cells II (Controlled accretion) or IV (Controlled erosion). This means that no one (as far as we know) has manipulated physical material, except in a trace manner, in order to generate measures of human behavior. There are on the other hand a number of uses of uncontrolled accretion and erosion. It is of interest to note that a parallel situation exists with respect to systematic observation methods (see Bouchard, 1976). Investigators collect data in either contrived situations (e.g., experimental groups) or in a natu-

ralistic context. Natural settings are seldom purposefully manipulated in order to test hypotheses or facilitate the collection of data. This method is clearly underutilized by social scientists. Weick (1968) has called this method "tempered naturalness." It is another name for the "naturalist's alternative." "Manipulate only as much as necessary to answer your questions clearly and otherwise leave things alone, for there is order even in what seems to you to be the worst confusion" (Menzel, 1969: 91). Below we list examples by category when examples exist. Many of the examples are from Webb et al. (1966) and the page number where the material is discussed in that source is given. The remaining examples are also referenced. Unreferenced material is original.

Measure	Variable and/or Reference
Uncontrolled – Accretion	
Bent corners on library books	Usage rate (Webb et al., 1966: 37)
Dirt on sections of books and encyclopedias	Usage, interest patterns (Mosteller, cited in Webb et al., 1966: 38)
Dust on library books	Recency and amount of usage (Webb et al., 1966: 38)
Inventories	Before and after size of inventory can be used as a crude indicator of success of a sales campaign; absolute size of a shipment can index sales expectations
Litter	Used to assess effectiveness of anti-litter campaigns (Webb et al., 1966: 42)
Trash analysis	Empty liquor and beer bottles can index amount of drinking (Webb et al., 1966: 4)
	Waste baskets and garbage cans have been used as sources of information (Gold, 1964; Hughes, 1958; Shadegg, 1964)
	Empty boxes thrown out of a store indicate volume and rate of sales
Water volume usages (generalizable to all	Can indicate roughly the number of people who

Measure	Variable and/or Reference	Measure	Variable and/or Reference
utility usage)	use a facility (may be obtained from records or by monitoring the meter)	Bumper stickers on cars	Used to assess police prejudice (Heussenstamm, 1971) Check on ideological consistency (Wrightsman, 1969)
Controlled — Accretion No examples			
Controlled — Traces Glue spots between pages of magazines broken	Indicates pages read (Plitz cited in Webb et al., 1966: 44)	Cars in parking lot. Age, condition, value, and so on	Affluence of group (Brandt, 1972)
Lost key technique (keys with name and address on attached page in various cities)	Regional differences in willingness to help strangers (Forbes et al., 1972)	Chemical traces. Soil on shoes (location of individual); arsenic level in hair (poisoning); other chemical levels may reveal occupation. Police lab procedures	(Webb et al., 1966: 39)
Lost letter technique	Measure honesty (Merritt and Fowler, 1948) Political orientation of an area (Milgram et al., 1965; Milgram, 1969; Wicker, 1969; Bouchard and Stuster, 1969; Shotland et al., 1970; Weiner and Lurey, 1973; Luck and Manz, 1973; Cairns and Bochner, 1974) Willingness to help strangers (Forbes et al., 1971; Forbes and Gromoll, 1971) Attitude toward Negroes (Montayne et al., 1971)	Dress	Index of activity to be engaged in (women attending a meeting in levis was indicative of a sit-in in the South in the 1960s) Response to psycho-therapy (Kane, 1958, 1959, 1962; see also Roach and Eicher, 1965)
Plant materials systematically in the environment and watch responses. (Removal of already available items is also possible)	Probably very useful with children; see Holmberg (1954) for a fascinating anthropological example; removal of material may prompt conflict (see Menzel, 1969 for examples with primates)	Fingerprints on various documents	Diversity of prints indicates readership level (Webb et al., 1966: 40) Note: special paper may be used to increase detectability—now used on some checks
Tear a phone number (subject of interest described on a standard sheet of paper. Respondents asked to call if interested. Bottom of sheet is fringed with phone number to be called written on each fringe)	General measure of interest in a subject matter (count number of fringes torn off or number of phone calls)	Inscription on restroom walls	Level of sexual preoccupation. Cross-cultural and subgroup analysis possible (men vs. women; Philippines vs. U.S.; engineers vs. art students; and so on; Webb et al., 1966: 42)
		Intensity of writing measured by multiple carbons under sheets of paper	Intensity or forcefulness of feeling regarding an issue (Allport and Vernon, 1933: 52)
		Locked vs. unlocked cars Marginal notes on documents	Contrast males vs. females (Webb et al., 1966) proof that a particular individual saw a document, also attitudes (Dalton, 1967)
Uncontrolled — Traces Body marks—tattoos, scars, and so on	Indexes subcultural group membership, and so forth (Roach and Eicher, 1965)	Markings on buildings	Level of prejudice (swastikas; Ehrlich, 1963)

Measure	Variable and/or Reference
Nose prints on glass in front of exhibits	Visitor rate, age of visitors (Webb et al., 1966: 46)
Radio station setting in cars left at garages for repairs	Help garage choose which stations to advertise on (popularity of stations; Webb et al., 1966: 39)
Smells	Alcohol on breath indicates drinking behavior (cross-validated if respondent staggers). Cleanliness?
Tax stickers on cars	Economic level of shoppers, area from which shoppers come (Webb et al., 1966: 39–40)
Uncontrolled — Erosion	
Broken windows in school buildings, furniture scratches, wall markings	Community pride in school and student morale (Brandt, 1972; Wallace, 1965)
Level of liquor in bottles before and after an event	alcoholic consumption rate (Brandt, 1972)
Site analysis	General anthropological method to assess number of occupants, type of activities, and so forth (Rowe, 1953; Webb et al., 1966: 40)
Scratches and needed touch-up spots on cars, state of home, and so on	Pride in automobile and home ownership (Brandt, 1972)
State of rented equipment after camping trip	Responsibility of group or individual (Brandt, 1972)
Theft pattern in hotels-motels	Measures of motivations and self-conceptions of the various groups that frequent the hotels (Hayner, 1964); one could compare the relative honesty of various convention groups (e.g., Republicans vs. Democrats)
Wear level of floor material, and so on	Public interest in exhibits (Webb et al., 1969: 36)
Controlled — Erosion	
No examples	

ARCHIVES

Documents and records can be very useful to a field researcher but their use has been very circumspect because they can never be taken at face value. Even elementary statistics such as operating costs are juggled for political reasons (Dalton, 1959).

Angell and Freedman (1953), Madge (1965), Mann (1968), and Webb et al. (1966) all have excellent discussions of the serious limitations of various kinds of documents.

In some cases researchers are given access to and make extensive use of confidential records (Selznick, 1949). The researcher who does this should have a clear understanding, preferably in writing, of what he can and cannot publish (see Whyte, 1959).

A unique source of archival data in the communications industry is "out-takes," field interviews and other material gathered by TV and radio networks but never shown or published. An analysis of what is shown vs. what is gathered would make an interesting study. The fact that there are attempts to subpoena this material testifies to its potential importance. According to Emile de Antonio (Westerbeck, 1970) contacts in the network bureaucracies are always ready to help dig up interesting material. Some organizations may have film material available, gathered for different purposes, but useful to a researcher for establishing baselines or determining past practices.

Udy (1964) has made use of the Human Relations Area Files for cross-cultural comparative studies of organizations. A list of the institutions at which these files are located is given in Whiting (1968). Schoenfeldt (1970) gives a list of the major data archives in the western world readily available to researchers.

Many documents can be subjected to content analysis, a technique that has undergone extensive growth and sophistication with the advent of high-speed computers.

If a document can be shown to be free of the reactive measurement effects discussed earlier the application of the method of content analysis will yield data and measures that may appropriately be called unobtrusive. Some of the more recent treatments of this technique can be found in Holsti (1968), and in Gerbner et al. (1969). Most computer coding systems are variations of the General Inquirer (Stone et al., 1966). The General Inquirer is a set of computer programs designed to manipulate textual material. It will: "(a) identify systematically, within text, instances of words and phrases that belong to categories specified by the investigator; (b) count occurrences and specified co-occurrences of these categories; (c) print and graph tabulations; (d) perform statistical tests; and (e) sort and regroup sentences according to whether they contain instances of a particular category or combination of categories" (Stone et al., 1966: 68).

The categories specified by the user constitute a dictionary (see Stone et al., 1966; Holsti, 1968). Examples of available dictionaries are: (a) the Harvard III Psychosociological dictionary which assesses roles, objects, settings and psychological processes; (b) the Simulmatics dictionary developed to analyze products and corporate images; (c) the Lasswell Value dictionary; (d) the Kranz (1970) activities dictionary. See also Hartsough & Laffal (1970); Katz (1966).

Brant (1972: 203–206), has distinguished between routine records and documents and suggests a variety of uses for them. His two lists are given below. Those lists are followed by additional items from various sources.

Routine Records

Kind of Record	Variable Being Measured
Absentee and tardiness records	Work habits or motivation
List of unsolicited complaints or of commendations about various salesmen	Customer reaction
Military reenlistment and longevity figures	Morale indicator
Pay increase and promotion lists	Perceived value of individuals to an organization
Number of people one supervises	Measure of management responsibility
Production and other output figures	Performance of individuals, departments, and so on
Sales contest records	Selling effectiveness, effectiveness of incentive plans
Sales slips, at Delegates' Lounge bar in United Nations	Tensions indicator (Webb, 1966: 89)
Peanut sales at ball game	Excitement indicator (greater after than before

Kind of Record	Variable Being Measured
	seventh inning; Webb, 1966: 92)
Sales level of consumer goods	Effectiveness of display location advertisement, or style of packaging
Air trip insurance figures	Public concern before and after air crashes
Sales of layettes by colors (blue or pink)	Sex preference in different social classes
Sale price of autographs	Popularity indicator
Soap usage rate (surface level in liquid containers, amount of water displaced by bar of soap)	Value of cleanliness to personnel (Webb, 1966: 89)
Admission rate in psychiatric hospitals	General overall anxiety in culture
Club membership list	Indicator of segment of society involved
Committee reports	Institutional modification attempts
Board minutes	Official institutional policies
Actuarial records: birth, baptismal, death records, marriage licenses	Comparative demographic data (occupation, religion, time of day, cause of death, and so on)
Cemetery documents, burial lot records	Family membership

Documents

Source	Illustrative Data
Congressional Record	Statements of position on particular issues
Reader's Digest	Mathematics vocabulary in common usage
Society section of metropolitan newspaper	Upper-middle and lower-upper class activities
Telephone directories	Community ethnic group membership
Salaries of teachers or government employees	Community support
Government agency records (labor,	Living trends

Source	Illustrative Data
commerce, agriculture departments)	
Judicial records	Uniformity in sentencing antisocial behavior
Moody's Handbook	Corporate financial structure
Who's Who in America	Nature of cited accomplishments of successful men
Associated Press releases (available in complete form at the National Press Club and other places)	Details of news events of various sorts
Children's books on sale	Qualities of models (heroes and heroines)
Movie announcements in newspapers	Changing taboos and enticements
Want ads	Employer inducements
Federal and state laws	Official societal restrictions
Tax records	Regional differences in patterns of living
Obituary columns	Charity preferences
Picture displays on front of movie houses	Changing taboos and enticements
Mail-order catalogs	Apparel vogues, merchandise as reflection of living patterns
Property-transfer listings	Commercial activity of individuals
Legislative roll calls	Actions taken by individual legislators
Published speeches	Political, social, economic attitudes
Newspaper headlines	Press bias
City budgets	Perceived value or extent of support of various activities
Change of address forms in post office	Mobility data

Miscellaneous—Archival

Record	Variable and/or References
Analysis of letters exchanged between communist powers	Friendship-hostility dimension (Inoguchi, 1972)

Record	Variable and/or References
Content analysis of speeches	nAch and nPower (Donley and Winter, 1970)
Desk calendars	Establish time frames and sequences of events, and so on; used to construct time budgets
Diaries	Establish sequence of events, first contact, and so on
Grievance board records	Index conflict among minorities (Stuart, 1963)
Library files	Used to check on who read assignments— motivation?—level of interest?—impact of teaching method? (Robinson et al., 1966) May be useful in organizational contexts. Who is interested in what?
Literacy index for letters	Level of literacy of senders (Plog, 1966; Routh and Rettig, 1969)
Notebooks	Often contain useful observation relevant to matter other than what the notebook was primarily used for: notes in margins, and so on)
Number of patents	Industrial creativity (Taylor et al., 1963)
Out-takes (unused film held by TV stations)	May be used for documentary construction; contrast with the film that was used to establish bias. May be used to test hypotheses based on film used in broadcasts. May be used to establish base rates for certain behaviors of groups or individuals in the past. (Also see Matarazzo et al., 1964; Westerbeck, 1970)
Personal documents— letters, and so on	Attitudes of people away from home, immigrants, and so on (Thomas and Znaniecki, 1918)
Phone bills	Contact networks: who was contacted and when, how long they talked

Record	Variable and/or References
Promptness and frequency of use of new drugs by hospitals	Innovativeness of hospital (Rosner, 1968)
Sick call rates	Morale
Voting records	Measures of liberalism-conservatism, and so on (Sechrest, 1969)

SIMPLE OBSERVATION

"We all observe, but we rarely observe systematically" (Mann, 1968: 15). While observation is never "simple," careful systematic observation of events can yield reliable data, particularly if the observed behavior is not exceedingly complex. Virtually all systematic observation schemes contain lists of behaviors that could become the content of a simple observation scheme. The potential user of this method should, however, carefully appraise himself of the sources of bias it is heir to (Bouchard, 1976; Weick, 1968).

Below we list only a few examples of the wide diversity of behaviors that may be observed. They are arranged by type of behavior recorded in order to facilitate the generation of additional measures by the reader. Guest (1969) has reviewed a large number of category systems for use in field settings and is the best single source on the subject.

Interactions

Record	Variable and/or Reference
Action-interaction chart	Makes use of a map of the physical location for locating interactions (Melbin, 1953)
Activities	(Burns, 1954; Hinrichs, 1964; Kranz, 1970; Palmer and McGuire, 1973; Stewart, 1967)
Compliance with rules (wearing specified clothing, driving violations, and so on)	Measure of status in hospitals (Roth, 1957); who violates the law most? (Barch et al., 1957)

Record	Variable and/or Reference
Interaction initiated by supervisors with observers who discouraged such interaction	Measures degree of integration of supervisor into the organization (Schwartzbaum and Gruenfeld, 1969)
Social contacts (e.g., who eats with whom?)	Classifies individuals into nonjob competitive individuals; Gross (1961) and Blau (1963: 151) found large discrepancies between reported and actual lunch contacts (see Dean, 1958)
Who does what, with whom, when, where, for how long, and under what conditions?	3 x 5 card used for recording (Melbin, 1954; see also Atteslander, 1954)

Spatial and Territorial Behavior

There has been very little use of measures of spatial and territorial behavior to index psychological or social variables. The interested reader should consult Altman (1970), Cook (1970), Esser (1971), Hall (1959, 1966), Lyman and Scott (1967), Sommer (1969).

The main reason for the lag in development in this area is the lack of useful taxonomies of situation (see Bouchard, 1976).

Record	Variable and/or Reference
Distance of speakers from each other	Measure degree of psychological closeness (affiliation?; Hall, 1959; Willis, 1966)
Free browsing activity	Intellectual curiosity (Chapanis, 1971)
Seating arrangements of whites and Negroes	Index of attitude, measure of integration (Campbell et al., 1966; Davis et al., 1966)
Time spent in various types of territories or spaces	Interest in, avoidance of [home, work, colleagues, and so on]; (Altman, 1970; Baxter, 1970; Felipe and Sommer, 1966; Lyman and Scott, 1967)

Record	Variable and/or Reference
Milieu patient frequents (16 measures)	Rate of readmission, rate of discharge, median days of hospitalization (Palmer and McGuire, 1973)

Postural and Facial Cues

There is highly suggestive experimental literature in this area, but little of real use for field work at this time.

Record	Variable and/or Reference
Body position and movement	Use of body positions to present or project attitudes (Mahigel and Stone, 1971; Meharabian, 1969; 1971; reviews: Duncan, 1969; Wiener et al., 1972; Weick, 1968)
Eye blink rate	Emotionality (Harris et al., 1966; Kanfer, 1960)
Facial expressions— exchanged glances	Can be scored to reflect pleasantness, unpleasantness, discomfort, concern, comprehension of material, conflict, attentiveness, and so on (see Weick, 1968: 382–385; Ekman et al., 1971; Ekman and Friesen, 1971; Exline and Winters, 1965; Mordkoff, 1971)
Pupil size	Level of interest (Hess, 1965)

Verbal Behavior

Record	Variable and/or Reference
Analysis of voice frequencies for emotional responses	It has been reported that voice frequencies below 500 cps reflecting emotion are difficult to hide (Mahl, 1965; see Friedhoff et al., 1964)
Eavesdropping on conversations in public places (Overheards)	(Carlson et al., 1936; Cavan, 1966; Watson et al., 1948; see Madge, 1965: 138; Wolcott, 1970)

Record	Variable and/or Reference
Linguistic analysis of terms used in work context	(Becker et al., 1961; Psathas and Heslin, 1967; Strauss, 1968)
Perturbations in normal speech	Concern, anxiety (Panek and Martin, 1959)
Use of Mr. vs. first name	Measure of deference in an organization (Status?)
Voice quality/ hesitation phenomena/slips of the tongue	Anxiety, level of stress, and so on (Diehl et al., 1959; Krause and Pilisuk, 1961; Freud, 1914; Goldman-Eisler, 1961; Kasl and Mahl, 1965; Kramer, 1963)

HARDWARE

Most hardware is somewhat less than totally unobtrusive unless it is hidden. Nevertheless, even when it is not hidden, subjects tend to adapt to it particularly when it takes the form of miniaturized equipment. Such equipment can be considered relatively unobtrusive. In a brief article like this we can only touch the surface of this vast domain. We will discuss two major areas—electronic equipment in general, and photographic methods (still, movie, and video).

Electronic Equipment

Social scientists have barely begun to exploit the advantages available to them as a result of the micro-miniaturization of electronic devices. More of them should become familiar with the potentials of these devices (Baker, 1968; Schwitzgebel, 1968, 1970; Schwitzgebel and Bird, 1970). The journal *Behavior Research Methods and Instrumentation* regularly publishes useful articles about equipment.

Below we list a sample of devices that have been used and the records they accumulate.

Device	Records and References
Photoelectric cells	Movement of people
Actometer/pedometer	Specially adapted watch to record amount of child's activity (Schulman and Reisman, 1959; Lindsley, 1968)

Device	Records and References
Bone-conducting microphones	Frequency and duration of talk (Hayes and Meltzer, 1967)
Bugs in books	Trace in location of books (Mueller, 1970)
Face masks with microphones installed	Used to mask sounds when recording descriptions of behavior (Schoggen, 1964)
Hodometer	Electronic recording device placed on the floor to measure use of given areas and pathways (Bechtel and Srivastava, 1966)
Radiocardiogram transmitter	Stress in blind pedestrians (Peake and Leonard, 1971)
Sitting-sensed chairs	To measure duration and frequency of sitting and leaving the seat (Haring, 1968)
Transducers to measure mastication	(Rugh, 1970, 1971)
Transducer to measure penile erection	To indicate sexual arousal (Bancroft, 1966)
Ultrasonic device	Used to measure group activity level (Crawford and Nicora, 1964; Peacock and Williams, 1962)
Ultrasonic sound speakers	To measure body movement (Goldman, 1961)

A special class of electronic equipment that has wide applicability in the social sciences is telemetry equipment (Caceres, 1965; Mackay, 1969, 1970). The applications in this area are limited only by the researcher's imagination and money. Transmitters are now so small that it is possible to observe "alterations in the pattern of activity in the gut of human subjects subjected to the stress of public speaking" (Mackay, 1969: 244). Rugh (1970) developed a self-contained detection and telemetry system for studying mastication in the rat. He later modified the equipment for human use with the transmitter mounted in an eyeglass frame (Rugh, 1971; see Jackman and Cowgill, 1970). We note that mastication behavior in humans is of clinical inter-

est and can be used as an index of stress. While widely used with animals we know of no studies that have used telemetry to study territory usage in humans. It would seem to be particularly applicable with children. Suggestive model research with animals has been carried out by Kavanau (1969) who has also developed a great deal of sophisticated equipment.

Transponders which transmit only on receipt of a signal can be used to sample responses and thereby decrease the dross rate. The 3M Company has a tape cassette which can record up to 35 days and play back to a computer in two minutes. A great deal of versatile equipment is now available for recording multiple events (Krausman, 1970; Mostofsky, 1970; Sidowski and Spears, 1970).

An extensive study of spontaneous talk by Soskin and John (1963) made use of a voice transmitter carried daily by a husband and wife team. The conversations were recorded by a central receiving station. Purcell and Brady (1966) conducted a similar study with children.

It is also possible to send information to subjects as well as to receive it. This information need not be verbal. The feasibility of transmitting Morse Code through an electrocutaneous reception apparatus has already been demonstrated (Applied Psychological Services, 1966a, 1966b, 1966c). Intelligible signals may also be mediated through other modalities (Schwitzgebel and Bird, 1970).

Researchers who contemplate the use of behavioral instrumentation should examine the recent instrumentation issue of the *American Psychologist* (1975, No. 3) and the Annual Guide to Scientific Instruments published each September by *Science*.

Photography — Movies — Video Tape

"The camera has become an important part of the anthropologist's instrumentation, but there is, as yet, almost no photographic equivalent of a literacy with which to handle photographic observational materials systematically and communicatively" (Byers, 1964: 78).

Unlike the anthropologist, other behavior scientists have not discovered the camera yet, never mind learned how to deal with the records it generates. Thus, there is virtually no literature on the use of still photography as a source of data.

Menzel (1969) has used still photographs to analyze the space-using behavior of primates. His photographs are outstanding and illustrate how this record-collection method can be used to illustrate important concepts. Gump (1969) used time-lapse photography to sample the behavior of children in a classroom. Pictures were scored for posture, expression, orientation toward significant objects and persons, and the involvement or non-involvement of pupils in activities. Bullen et al. (1964) studied the activity of obese and nonobese adolescent girls with film. Greenhill (1955) studied audience reactions using infra-red photography.

Home movies can be used as a source of data about the behavior of children (Allen and Goodman, 1966). For example, it may be possible to determine at about which age certain behaviors (neurological? psychological?) began to be expressed. This might be cross-validated against school records, school work saved by the mother, and so on. These are archival records.

Another use of films is to have the groups being studied make documentaries of their activities. What they focus on may reveal what is important to them (source of this idea cannot be found).

Photographs can be used as stimulus material also (see Collier, 1957), but this takes us out of the domain of unobtrusive methods. The potential user of this method should examine Byer's (1964) excellent paper before setting to work.

The use of motion picture film and video tape is much more common among behavior scientists than still photography. This is perhaps because these media capture more of the dynamic properties of behavior, which most researchers are interested in. Most researchers, however, use film as a stimulus device rather than a source of records. Film and video tapes can be scored using virtually all of the systematic observation coding schemes available (Bouchard, 1976; Weick, 1968). These schemes will not be discussed here. We do wish to emphasize that film and video tape do distort and lie. Transcripts from these media compound the distortion. Machines are "event recorders" with different operating characteristics than the human sensorium. The camera zooms, foreshortens, does not scan as much, works from a relatively fixed focus, sometimes focuses from an unusual angle and often requires lights which influence the respondent's behavior in subtle ways (Michaelis, 1955). Films differ from video tapes which differ from still photographs and all three differ from audio tapes and transcripts in obvious and not so obvious

ways (McLuhan, 1964). Variance due to instrumentation effects is unexplored territory and casual generalizations from media-specific studies should be avoided.

Useful methodological discussions on the use of film can be found in Condon (1970), Ekman and Friesen (1969), Ekman, Friesen and Taussig (1969), Polunin (1970), Putz (1970), Radloff and Helmreich (1969), and Van Vlack (1966).

MISCELLANEOUS UNOBTRUSIVE MEASURES

A number of unobtrusive measures do not fit into the classification scheme we have chosen to organize this paper around. We have therefore grouped them under miscellaneous. The existence of this miscellaneous group indicates that the taxonomy we have used is not sufficiently comprehensive. It may be that as this list grows over time a better taxonomy will suggest itself. It may on the other hand eventually prove to be more useful to group the measures according to the class of variables they attempt to measure. With such a scheme an investigator could then ask "What unobtrusive measures are available for measuring socio-economic status, conflict, abilities, and so on?"

Record	Variable and/or References
Amplifying an incipient response	In an interview situation, failure to respond to an interviewee is stressful and forces him to respond more forcefully. This manipulation is difficult to detect (Chapple, 1953; Matarazzo and Saslow, 1961; see Weick, 1969: 378–379 for other examples)
Analysis of peer nomination data in small isolated groups	Group conflict (Seymour, 1971)
Embedding a measure in ongoing behavior	Using games structured in appropriate ways to test hypotheses (see Weick, 1968: 376)
Evoking behavior using individuals in context	Have members of a group who are informants ask predetermined questions for you (Dalton, 1967)

Record	Variable and/or References
Informant ratings	Shore personnel could rate the morale of ships they were not on very well (Campbell, 1955)
Materials survey of a home	Socioeconomic status (Chapin, 1947)
Political leanings of newspapers carried to office	Sociopolitical orientation (Dalton, 1967)
Posing as radio interviewers	(Miller and Levy, 1967)
Questionnaire items can be planted in standard forms (indeed, these forms often contain appropriate items to answer some questions)	
Simple presence of certain objects	The presence of a file cabinet which meets particular government specifications (U.S. Department of Defense, 1970) indicates the storage of classified information and may indicate that secret research is in progress. Status rankings can be made by noting the presence of a rug, location (corner, central, peripheral) of an office
Spatial arrangement of furniture	Reflects control on movement desired by organization [does it create certain interaction patterns?]; (Osmond, 1957; Sommer, 1967)
Use of lay observers in context to gather observations unobtrusively	(Back et al., 1950)
Watching someone when you have told that someone that you are watching someone else	Observation of mother-child interaction when mother thinks only the child is being watched (Bishop, 1951)

CONCLUSION

In this paper we have inventoried a large number of unobtrusive measures. None of the mea-

sures, however, was evaluated because the goal of this paper is not to criticize some measures at the expense of others. Rather we take the view that no measure is perfect and therefore all measures can be supplemented. The primary value of unobtrusive measures is as supplemental measures used in the context of converging data collection methods that exclude plausible rival hypotheses in an efficient and convincing manner. Unobtrusive measures are not a panacea for measurement problems in the social sciences; they are not even the measure of choice in most research contexts. Nevertheless, we strongly believe that their judicious and flexible use can result in an improvement in the overall quality of much social science research and we urge all investigators to incorporate them into their research designs when the situation warrants it.

A FINAL NOTE

This paper contains no discussion of the ethical questions that may arise when many of the measures depicted are put to use. Unobtrusive measures raise a wide variety of ethical problems and we strongly recommend to the potential users of such measures that they scrutinize carefully their measures' ethical implications prior to putting them to use.

REFERENCES

Allen, T. E. and J. D. Goodman (1966) "Home movies in child psychodiagnostics: the unobserved observer." Archives of General Psychiatry 15: 649–653.

Allport, G. W. and P. E. Vernon (1933) Studies in Expressive Movement. New York: Macmillan.

Altman, I. (1970) "Territorial behavior in humans: an analysis of the concept," in L. Pastalan and D. E. Carsen (eds.) Spatial Behavior of Older People. Ann Arbor, Mich.: Wayne State Univ. Press.

Angell, R. C. and R. Freedman (1953) "The use of documents, records, census materials, and indices," in L. Festinger and D. Katz (eds.) Research Methods in the Behavioral Sciences. New York: Holt, Rinehart & Winston.

Applied Psychological Services (1966a) "Studies into information presented through novel methods: information transfer through electrocutaneous stimulation." Report prepared for U.S. Army Electronics Command, Fort

Monmouth, New Jersey (April). Contract No. DA28-043 AMC-00186(e) (Wayne, Pennsylvania).

—— (1966b) Studies into information presentation through novel methods. II. Design for a soldier carried electrocutaneous reception apparatus. Report prepared for U.S. Army Electronics Command, Fort Monmouth, New Jersey (May). Contract No. DA28-043 AMC-00186(e) (Wayne, Pennsylvania).

—— (1966c) Studies into information presentation through novel methods. III. Two-way transfer through electrocutaneous transduction. Report prepared for U.S. Army Electronics Command, Fort Monmouth, New Jersey (July). Contract No. DA28-043 AMC-00186(e) (Wayne, Pennsylvania).

Atteslander, P. M. (1954) "The interaction-gram: a method for measuring interaction and activities of supervisory personnel." Human Organization 13, (1): 28–33.

Back, K., L. Festinger, B. Hymovitch, H. Kelley, S. Schachter, and J. Thibaut (1950) "The methodology of studying rumor transmission." Human Relations 3: 307–312.

Baker, R. A. (1968) "The future of psychological instrumentation." Behavioral Science 13: 1–17.

Bancroft, J. H. (1966) "A simple transducer for measurement of penile erection." Behavior Research and Therapy 4: 239–241.

Barch, A. M., D. Trumbo, and J. Nagel (1957) "Social setting and conformity to a legal requirement." J. of Abnormal and Social Psychology 55: 396–398.

Baxter, C. (1970) "Interpersonal spacing in natural settings." Sociometry 33: 444–456.

Bechtel, R. B. (1967) "Hodometer research in architecture." Milieu 1: 1–9.

—— and R. Srivastava (1966) "Human movement and architectural environment." Milieu 2: 7–8.

Becker, H. S., B. Geer, E. C. Hughes, and A. L. Strauss (1961) Boys in White: Student Culture in Medical School. Chicago: Univ. of Chicago Press.

Bishop, B. M. (1951) "Mother-child interaction and the social behavior of children." Psychological Monographs 65: 11(Whole No. 328): 1–34.

Blau, P. M. (1963) The Dynamics of Bureaucracy. Chicago: Univ. of Chicago Press.

Bouchard, T. J., Jr. (1976) "Field research methods: interviewing, questionnaires, participant observation, systematic observation, unobtrusive measures," in M. D. Dunnette (ed.) Handbook of Industrial and Organizational Psychology. Chicago: Rand McNally.

—— and J. Stuster (1969) "The lost letter technique: predicting elections." Psychological Reports 25: 231–234.

Brandt, R. M. (1972) Studying Behavior in Natural Settings. New York: Holt, Rinehart & Winston.

Brayfield, A. H. and W. H. Crockett (1955) "Employee attitudes and employee performance." Psych. Bull. 52: 396–424.

Bullen, B. A., R. B. Reed, and J. Mayer (1964) "Physical activity of obese and nonobese adolescent girls appraised by motion picture sampling." Amer. J. of Clinical Nutrition 14: 211–223.

Bunney, W. E. and D. A. Hamburg (1963) "Methods for reliable longitudinal observation of behavior." Archives of General Psychiatry 9: 280–294.

Burns, T. (1954) "The directions of activity and communication in a departmental executive group." Human Relations 7: 73–97.

Byers, P. (1964) "Still photography in the systematic recording and analysis of behavioral data." Human Organization 23, (1): 78–84.

Caceres, C. A. [ed.] (1965) Biomedical Telemetry. New York: Academic Press.

Cairns, L. G. and S. Bochner (1974) "Measuring sympathy toward handicapped children with the 'lost letter' technique." Australian J. of Psychology 26: 88–91.

Campbell, D. T. (1955) "The informant in quantitative research." Amer. J. of Sociology 60: 339–342.

—— and D. W. Fiske (1959) "Convergent and discriminant validation by the multitrait-multimethod matrix." Psych. Bull. 56: 81–105.

Campbell, D. T., W. H. Kruskal, and W. P. Wallace (1966) "Seating aggregation as an index of attitude." Sociometry 29: 1–15.

Carlson, J., S. W. Cook, and E. L. Stomberg (1936) "Sex differences in conversation." J. of Applied Psychology 20: 727–735.

Cavan, S. (1966) Liquor License. Chicago: Aldine.

Chapanis, A. (1971) "Prelude to 2001: explorations in human communication." Amer. Psychologist 26: 949–961.

Chapin, F. S. (1947) Experimental Designs in Sociological Research. New York: Harper & Row.

Chapple, E. D. (1953) "The standard experimental (stress) interview as used in interaction chronograph investigations." Human Organization 12, (2): 23–33.

Collier, J. (1957) "Photography in anthropology: a report on two experiments." Amer. Anthropologist 59: 843–859.

Condon, W. S. (1970) "Methods of micro-analysis of sound film behavior." Behavior Research Methods and Instrumentation 2: 51–54.

Cook, M. (1970) "Experiments on orientation and proxemics." Human Relations 23: 61–76.

Craik, K. H. (1973) "Environmental psychology," in P. H. Mussen and M. R. Rosenzweig (eds.) Annual Review of Psychology 24: 402–403.

—— (1971) "The assessment of places," in P. McReynold (ed.) Advances in Psychological Assessment. Vol. II. Palo Alto: Science & Behavior Books.

Crawford, M.L.J. and B. D. Nicora (1964) "Measurement of human group activity." Psych. Reports 15: 227–231.

Dalton, M. (1967) "Preconceptions and methods in men who manage," in P. E. Hammond (ed.) Sociologists at Work. New York: Anchor Books.

—— (1959) Men Who Manage. New York: Wiley.

Davis, M., R. Seibert, and W. Breed (1966) "Interracial seating patterns on New Orleans Public Transit." Social Problems 13: 298–306.

Dean, L. R. (1958) "Interaction, reported and observed: the case of one local union." Human Organization 17, (3): 36–44.

Denzin, N. K. (1970) The Research Act. Chicago: Aldine.

Diehl, C. F., R. White, and K. W. Burk (1959) "Voice quality and anxiety." J. of Speech and Hearing Research 21: 282–285.

Donley, E. and G. Winter (1970) "Measuring the motives of public officials at a distance: an exploratory study of American presidents." Behavioral Science 15: 222–236.

Duncan, S. (1969) "Nonverbal communication." Psych. Bull. 72: 118–137.

Ehrlich, H. J. (1963) "The swastika epidemic of 1959–1960: anti-Semitism and community characteristics." Social Problems 9: 264–272.

Ekman, P. and W. V. Friesen (1971) "Constants across cultures in the face and emotion." J. of Personality and Social Psychology 17: 124–129.

—— (1969) "A tool for the analysis of motion picture film or video tape." Amer. Psychologist 24: 240–243.

—— and P. Ellsworth (1971) Emotion in the Human Face: Guidelines for Research and a Review of Findings. Oxford: Pergamon.

Ekman, P., W. V. Friesen, and T. Taussig (1969) "VID-R and SCAN: tools and methods in the analysis of facial expression and body movement," in G. Gerbner, O. Holsti, K. Krippendorff, W. Paisley, and P. Stone (eds.) Content Analysis. New York: Wiley.

Esser, A. H. (1971) Behavior and Environment: The Use of Space by Animals and Man. New York: Plenum.

Exline, R. V. and L. C. Winters (1965) "Affective relations and mutual glances in dyads," in S. Tomkins and C. Izard (eds.) Affect, Cognition and Personality. New York: Springer.

Felipe, N. and R. Sommer (1966) "Invasion of personal space." Social Problems 14, 206–214.

Forbes, G. B. and H. F. Gromoll (1971) "The lost letter technique as a measure of social variables: some exploratory findings." Social Forces 50: 113–115.

Forbes, G. B., R. K. TeVault, and H. F. Gromoll (1972) "Regional differences in willingness to help strangers: a field experiment with a new unobtrusive measure." Social Sci. Research 1: 415–419.

—— (1971) "Willingness to help strangers as a function of liberal, conservative or Catholic church membership: a field study with the lost-letter technique." Psych. Reports 28: 947–949.

Freud, S. (1914) The Psychopathology of Everyday Life. New York: Macmillan.

Friedhoff, A. J., M. Alpert, and R. L. Kurtzberg (1964) "An electroacoustic analysis of the effects of stress on voice." J. of Neuropsychiatry 5: 266–272.

Gerbner, G., O. R. Holsti, K. Krippendorff, W. J. Paisley, and P. J. Stone [eds.] (1969) The Analysis of Communication Content: Development in Scientific Theories and Computer Techniques. New York: Wiley.

Gold, R. L. (1964) "In the basement—The apartment building janitor," in P. L. Berger (ed.) The Human Shape of Work: Studies in the Sociology of Work. New York: Macmillan.

Goldman, J. (1961) "A look at human measurement in industry," in L. E. Slater (ed.) Interdisciplinary Clinic on the Instrumentation Requirements for Psychophysiological Research. New York: Fier.

Goldman-Eisler, F. (1961) "The significance of changes in the rate of articulation." Language and Speech 4: 171–174.

Greenhill, L. P. (1955) "The recording of audience reactions by infra-red photography." Technical

Report SOECDEVCEN, 269-7-56. Instructional Film Research Program. Pennsylvania State University.

Gross, E. (1961) "Social integration and the control of competition." Amer. J. of Sociology 67: 270-277.

Guest, R. N. (1960) "Categories of events in field observations," in R. N. Adams and J. J. Preiss (eds.) Human Organization Research. Homewood, Ill.: Dorsey.

Gump, P. V. (1969) "Intra-setting analysis: the third grade classroom as a special but instructive case," in E. P. Willems and H. L. Raush (eds.) Naturalistic Viewpoints in Psychological Research. New York: Holt, Rinehart & Winston.

Hall, E. T. (1966) The Hidden Dimension. New York: Doubleday.

―――― (1959) The Silent Language. New York: Doubleday.

Hammond, P. E. (1964) Sociologists at Work. New York: Basic Books.

Haring, N. G. (1968) "Equipment listing with examples of application." Unpublished manuscript, University of Washington, Experimental Educational Unit.

Harris, C. S., R. I. Thackray, and R. W. Shoenberger (1966) "Blink rate as a function of induced muscular tension and manifest anxiety." Perceptual and Motor Skills 22: 155-160.

Hartsough, R. and J. Laffal (1970) "Content analysis of scientific writings." J. of General Psychology 83: 193.

Hayes, D. P. and L. Meltzer (1967) "Bone-conducting microphones." Amer. J. of Psychology 80: 619-624.

Hayner, N. S. (1964) "Hotel life: proximity and social distance," in E. S. Burgess and D. J. Bogue (eds.) Contributions to Urban Sociology. Chicago: Univ. of Chicago Press.

Hess, E. H. (1965) "Attitude and pupil size." Scientific Amer. 212: 46-54.

Heussenstamm, F. K. (1971) "Bumper stickers and the cops." Trans-Action 8: 32-33.

Hinrichs, J. R. (1964) "Communications activity of industrial research personnel." Personnel Psychology 17: 193-204.

Holmberg, A. R. (1954) "Adventures in culture change," in R. F. Spencer (ed.) Method and Perspective in Anthropology. Minneapolis: Univ. of Minnesota Press.

Holsti, O. R. (1968) "Content analysis," in G. Lindzey and E. Aronson (eds.) The Handbook of Social Psychology. Vol. II. Reading, Mass.: Addison-Wesley.

Hughes, E. C. (1958) Men and Their Work. Glencoe, Ill.: Free Press.

Inoguchi, T. (1972) "Measuring friendship and hostility among communist powers: some unobtrusive measures of esoteric communication." Social Sci. Research 1: 79-105.

Jackman, K. L. and R. C. Cowgill (1970) "Design and laboratory tests for a long-life FM transmitter for tagging small mammals." Behavior Research Methods and Instrumentation, 2: 230.

Kane, F. (1962) "The meaning of the form of clothing." Psychiatric Communications 5: No. 1.

―――― (1959) "Clothing worn by an outpatient: a case study." Psychiatric Communications 2: No. 2.

―――― (1958) "Clothing worn by outpatients to interviews." Psychiatric Communications 1: No. 2.

Kanfer, F. H. (1960) "Verbal rate, eyeblink, and content in structured psychiatric interviews." J. of Abnormal and Social Psychology 61: 341-347.

Kasl, S. V. and G. F. Mahl (1965) "The relationship of disturbances and hesitations in spontaneous speech to anxiety." J. of Personality and Social Psychology 1: 425-433.

Kavanau, J. L. (1969) "Behavior of captive white-footed mice," in E. P. Willems and H. L. Raush (eds.) Naturalistic Viewpoints in Psychological Research. New York: Holt, Rinehart & Winston.

Katz, E. W. (1966) "A content-analytic method for studying themes of interpersonal behavior." Psych. Bull. 66: 419-422.

Kramer, E. (1963) "Judgment of personal characteristics and emotions from nonverbal properties of speech." Psych. Bull. 60: 408-420.

Kranz, P. (1970) "What do people do all day." Behavior Science 15: 286-291.

Krause, M. S. and M. Pilisuk (1961) "Anxiety in verbal behavior: a validation study." J. of Consulting Psychology 25: 414-419.

Krausman, D. T. (1970) "A solid-state cumulative recorder for an analog registry of accumulative events." Behavior Research Methods and Instrumentation 2: (5), 228.

Lindsley, O. R. (1968) "A reliable wrist-counter for recording behavior rates." J. of Applied Behavior Analysis 1: 77-78.

Luck, H. E. and W. Manz (1973) "Lost-letter technique—a new instrument of measuring attitudes towards behavior." Zeitschrift für Soziologie. Jq2, Heft 4 (October): 352-365.

Lyman, S. M. and M. B. Scott (1967) "Territoriality: a neglected sociological dimension." Social Problems 15: 236–249.

Mackay, S. R. (1970) Biomedical Telemetry. 2nd ed. New York: Wiley.

—— (1969) "Biomedical telemetry: applications to psychology." Amer. Psychologist 24: 244–248.

McLuhan, M. (1964) Understanding Media: The Extensions of Man. New York: McGraw-Hill.

Madge, J. (1965) The Tools of Social Science. New York: Anchor.

Mahigel, E. L. and G. P. Stone (1971) "How card hustlers make the game." Trans-Action 8: 40–45.

Mahl, G. F. (1965) "Some observations about research on vocal behavior." Disorders of Communication 42: 466–483.

Mann, P. H. (1968) Methods of Sociological Inquiry. Oxford: Basil Blackwell.

Matarazzo, J. D. and G. Saslow (1961) "Differences in interview interaction behavior among normal and deviant groups," in I. A. Berg and B. M. Bass (eds.) Conformity and Deviation. New York: Harper & Row.

Matarazzo, J. D., A. N. Wiens, G. Saslow, R. M. Dunham, and R. B. Voas (1964) "Speech duration of astronaut and ground communicator." Science 143: 148–150.

Meharabian, A. (1971) "Nonverbal betrayal of feeling." J. of Experimental Research in Personality 5: 64–73.

—— (1969) "Significance of posture and position in the communication of attitude and status relationships." Psych. Bull. 71: 359–372.

Melbin, M. (1954) "An interaction recording device for participant observers. Human Organization 13: 29–33.

—— (1953) "The action-interaction chart as a research tool." Human Organization 12: 3–35.

Menzel, E. W., Jr. (1969) "Naturalistic and experimental approaches to primate behavior," in E. P. Willems and H. L. Raush (eds.) Naturalistic Viewpoints in Psychological Research. New York: Holt, Rinehart & Winston.

Merritt, C. B. and R. G. Fowler (1948) "The pecuniary honesty of the public at large." J. of Abnormal Social Psychology 43: 90–93.

Michaelis, A. R. (1955) Research Films in Biology, Anthropology, Psychology and Medicine. New York: Academic Press.

Milgram, S. (1969) "Comment on 'A failure to validate the lost letter technique'." Public Opinion Q. 33: 263–264.

——, L. Mann, and S. Harter (1965) "The lost-letter technique: a tool of social research." Public Opinion Q. 29: 437–438.

Miller, N. and B. H. Levy (1967) "Defaming and agreeing with the communicator as a function of communication extremity, emotional arousal, and evaluative set." Sociometry 30: 158–175.

Montanye, T., II, R. F. Mulberry, and K. R. Hardy (1971) "Assessing prejudice toward Negroes at three universities using the lost-letter technique." Psych. Reports 29: 531.

Mordkoff, A. M. (1971) "The judgment of emotion from facial expression." J. of Experimental Research in Personality 5: 74–78.

Mostofsky, D. I. (1970) "Multiplexed recording of multiple events." Perceptual and Motor Skills 31: 349–350.

Mueller, M. (1970) "Multiplexed recording of multiple events." Perceptual and Motor Skills 31: 349–350.

Osmond, H. (1957) "Function as a basis of psychiatric ward design." Mental Hospitals 8: 23–29.

Palmer, J. and F. L. McGuire (1973) "The use of unobtrusive measures in mental health research." J. Consulting and Clinical Psychology 40: 431–436.

Panek, D. M. and B. Martin (1959) "The relation between GSR and speed disturbance in psychotherapy." J. of Abnormal and Social Psychology 58: 402–405.

Peacock, L. J. and M. Williams (1962) "An ultrasonic device of recording activity." Amer. J. of Psychology 75: 648–652.

Peake, P. and J. A. Leonard (1971) "The use of heart rate as an index of stress in blind pedestrians." Ergonomics 14: 189–204.

Polunin, I. (1970) "Visual and sound recording apparatus." Current Anthropology 11: 3.

Plog, S. C. (1966) "Literary index for the mailbag." J. of Applied Psychology 50: 86–91.

Psathas, G. and J. J. Heslin (1967) "Dispatched orders and the cab driver: a study of locating activities." Social Problems 14: 424–443.

Purcell, K. and K. Brady (1966) "Adaptation to the invasion of privacy: monitoring behavior with a miniature radio transmitter." Merrill-Palmer Q. 12: 242–254.

Putz, V. R. (1970) "Dynamic visuometric techniques." Behavior Research Methods and Instrumentation 2: 240.

Radloff, R. and R. Helmreich (1969) "Electronic data collection in field research." Amer. Psychologist 24: 300–303.

Roach, M. E. and J. B. Eicher [eds.] (1965) Dress, Adornment, and the Social Order. New York: Wiley.

Robinson, J. A., L. F. Anderson, M. G. Hermann, and R. C. Snyder (1966) "Teaching with internation simulation and case studies." Amer. Pol. Sci. Rev. 60: 53–65.

Rosner, M. M. (1968) "Administrative controls and innovation." Behavior Science 13: 36–43.

Roth, J. A. (1957) "Ritual and magic in the control of contagion." Amer. Soc. Rev. 22: 310–314.

Routh, D. K. and K. Rettig (1969) "The mailbag literacy index in a clinical population: relation to education, income, occupation, and social class." Educ. and Psych. Measurement 29: 485–488.

Rowe, J. H. (1953) "Technical aids in anthropology: a historical survey," in A. L. Kroeber (ed.) Anthropology Today. Chicago: Univ. of Chicago Press.

Rugh, J. D. (1971) "A telemetry system for measuring chewing behavior in humans." Behavior Research Methods and Instrumentation 3: 73–77.

——— (1970) "A telemetry system for recording mastication in small animals." Medical and Biological Engineering 8: 497–500.

Runkel, P. J. and J. E. McGrath (1972) Research on Human Behavior: A Systematic Guide to Method. New York: Holt, Rinehart & Winston.

Schoenfeldt, L. F. (1970) "Data archives as resources for research instruction, and policy planning." Amer. Psychologist 25: 609–616.

Schoggen, P. (1964) "Mechanical aids for making specimen records of behavior." Child Development 35: 985–988.

Schulman, J. L. and J. M. Reisman (1959) "An objective measure of hyperactivity." Amer. J. of Mental Deficiency 64: 455–456.

Schwartzbaum, A. and L. Gruenfeld (1969) "Factors influencing subject-observer interaction in an organization study." Admin. Science Q. 14: 443–449.

Schwitzgebel, R. L. (1968) "Survey of electromechanical devices for behavior modification." Psych. Bull. 70: 444–459.

——— (1970) "Behavior instrumentation and social technology." Amer. Psychologist 25: 491–499.

——— and R. M. Bird (1970) "Sociotechnical design factors in remote instrumentation with humans in natural environments." Behavior Research Methods and Instrumentation 2: 99–105.

Sechrest, L. (1969) "Nonreactive assessment of attitudes," in E. P. Willems and H. L. Raush (eds.) Naturalistic Viewpoints in Psychological Research. New York: Holt, Rinehart & Winston.

Selznick, P. (1949) TVA and the Grass Roots. Berkeley: Univ. of California Press.

Seymour, G. E. (1971) "The concurrent validity of unobtrusive measures of conflict in small isolated groups." J. of Clinical Psychology 27: 431.

Shadegg, S. C. (1964) How to Win an Election. New York: Toplinger.

Shotland, R. L., W. G. Berger, and R. A. Forsythe (1970) "A validation of the lost-letter technique." Public Opinion Q. 34: 278–281.

Sidowski, J. B. and C. Spears (1970) "A versatile apparatus for measuring the frequencies and durations of animal and human responses." Behavior Research Methods and Instrumentation 2: 235–238.

Sommer, R. (1969) Personal Space: The Behavioral Basis for Design. Englewood Cliffs, N.J.: Prentice-Hall.

——— (1967) "Small group ecology." Psych. Bull. 67: 145–152.

Soskin, W. F. and V. P. John (1963) "The study of spontaneous talk," in R. G. Barker (ed.) The Stream of Behavior. New York: Appleton-Century-Crofts.

Stewart, R. (1967) "How managers spend their time." Management Today 92–160.

Stone, P. J., D. C. Dunphy, M. S. Smith, D. M. Ogilvie, and Associates [eds.] (1966) The General Inquirer: A Computer Approach to Content Analysis. Cambridge: MIT Press.

Strauss, A. L. (1968) "Strategies for discovering urban theory," in A. L. Strauss (ed.) The American City: A Sourcebook for Urban Imagery. Chicago: Aldine.

Stuart, I. R. (1963) "Minorities vs. minorities: cognitive, affective, and conative components of Puerto Rican and Negro acceptance and rejection." J. of Social Psychology 59: 93–99.

Taylor, C. W., W. R. Smith, and B. Ghiselin (1963) "The creative and other contributions of one sample of research scientists," in C. W. Taylor and F. Barron (eds.) Scientific Creativity: Its Recognition and Development. New York: Wiley.

Thomas, W. I. and F. Znaniecki (1918) The Polish Peasant in Europe and America. Chicago: Univ. of Chicago Press.

Udy, S. H., Jr. (1965) "The comparative analysis of organizations," in J. G. March (ed.) Handbook of Organizations. Chicago: Rand McNally.

—— (1964) "Administrative rationality, social setting and organizational development," in W. W. Cooper, H. J. Leavitt, and M. W. Shelly, II (eds.) New Perspectives in Organizational Research. New York: Wiley.

U.S. Department of Defense (1970) Industrial Security Manual for Safeguarding Classified Information. DOD 5220–22–M. 15 April.

Van Vlack, J. (1966) "Filming psychotherapy from the viewpoint of a research cinematographer," in L. A. Gottschalk and A. H. Auerbach (eds.) Methods of Research in Psychotherapy. New York: Appleton-Century-Crofts.

Wallace, S. E. (1965) Skid Row as a Way of Life. Totawa, N.J.: Bedminister.

Watson, J., W. Breed, and L. Postman (1948) "A study in urban conversation: sample of 1001 remarks overheard in Manhattan." J. of Psychology 28: 121–123.

Webb, E. J., D. T. Campbell, R. D. Schwartz, and L. Sechrest (1966) Unobtrusive Measures: Nonreactive Research in the Social Sciences. Chicago: Rand McNally.

Weick, K. E. (1968) "Systematic observational methods," in G. Lindzey and E. Aronson (eds.) Handbook of Social Psychology, Vol. IV. (2nd ed.) Cambridge, Mass.: Addison-Wesley.

Weiner, M. J. and E. Lurey (1973) "The 'lost-letter technique' as a predictor of the 1972 presidential election." J. of Psychology 84: 195–197.

Wernimont, P. F. and J. P. Campbell (1968) "Signs, samples, and criteria." J. of Applied Psychology 52: 372–376.

Westerbeck, C. J., Jr. (1970) "Some out-takes from radical film making: Emile de Antonio." Sight and Sound, summer.

Whiting, J.W.M. (1968) "Methods and problems in cross-cultural research," in G. Lindzey and E. Aronson (eds.) Handbook of Social Psychology, Vol. II. (2nd ed.) Reading, Mass.: Addison-Wesley.

Whyte, W. F. (1959) Man and Organization. Homewood, Ill.: Irwin.

Wicker, A. W. (1969a) "Attitude versus action: the relationship of verbal and overt behavioral responses to attitude objects." J. of Social Issues 25: 41–78.

—— (1969b) "A failure to validate the lost-letter technique." Public Opinion Q. 33: 260–262.

Wiener, M., S. Devoe, S. Rubinow, and J. Geller (1972) "Nonverbal behavior and nonverbal communication." Psych. Rev. 79: 185–214.

Willis, F. N., Jr. (1966) "Initial speaking distance as a function of the speaker relationship." Psychonomic Sci. 5: 221–222.

Wolcott, H. F. (1970) "An ethnographic approach to the study of school administrators." Human Organization 29 (2): 115–122.

Wrightsman, L. S. (1969) "Wallace supporters and adherence to 'Law and Order.'" J. of Personality and Social Psychology 13: 17–22.

ETHNOMETHODOLOGY

Kenneth D. Bailey

Ethnomethodology is based on the notion that everyday, commonplace, or routine social activities and interactions are made possible through the use of a variety of skills, practices, and assumptions. These skills, practices, and assumptions are what ethnomethodology calls "methods." A chief goal of ethnomethodology is to study how members of society, in the course of ongoing social interaction, make sense of "indexical" expressions. Indexicals are terms whose meaning is not universal but is dependent upon the context (e.g., "he," "she," "they"). Ethnomethodology, which has received greatly increased interest in recent years, is largely the creation of Harold Garfinkel (e.g., Garfinkel 1967; Garfinkel and Sacks 1970), who was inspired by the phenomenological sociology of Schutz

(1962; 1964; 1966). Goffman has also had an impact on this school of thought in his many writings (see Goffman 1959; 1962; 1963a; 1963b; 1967; 1969; 1971). Among recent ethnomethodological publications are the work of Bittner (1967a; 1967b), Churchill (1963), Moerman (1972; Moerman and Sacks 1974), Zimmerman and Pollner (1970), Sudnow (1972), Sacks (1972; 1974; Sacks and Schegloff 1974; Sacks, Schegloff, and Jefferson, 1974), and Schegloff (1968; 1972).

Ethnomethodology is primarily concerned with studying the commonsense features of everyday life, with emphasis on those things that "everyone knows." As Zimmerman and Pollner put it:

In contrast to the perennial argument that sociology belabors the obvious, we propose that sociology has yet to treat the obvious as a phenomenon. We argue that the world of everyday life, while furnishing sociology with its favored topics of inquiry, is seldom a topic in its own right (Zimmerman and Pollner 1970, p. 33).

Ethnomethodologists generally study social interaction as an ongoing process. Many of the studies involve conversational analysis (see especially the work of Sacks, Schegloff, and Jefferson 1974). Other studies involve nonverbal interaction (e.g., Garfinkel 1967) or interaction within a particular organizational system or setting (in Turner 1974 see, for example, the study of juvenile police officers by Cicourel and the study of the convict code in a halfway house by Wieder).

One major data-gathering technique of ethnomethodology is observation. Conversational researchers often study documents in the form of transcripts of recorded conversations. Much work, particularly that of Garfinkel, is often quasi-experimental. Because of character of the inquiry and the intensive observation required, most ethnomethodological studies are necessarily micro in nature. It would be possible, but probably not practical, to conduct a large-scale ethnomethodological study.

Some ethnomethodologists (for example, Garfinkel) are concerned with the shared meanings that words ("natural language") have for members of a group. The word "member" has special significance inasmuch as it implies a body of knowledge shared by all who are members. One result of ethnomethodological research is the demonstra-

tion that much information that is transmitted in a conversation "goes without saying," and is understood but never directly verbalized. Garfinkel (1967, p. 26) reports the following conversation by a student and his wife, with the left-hand column reporting what was actually said and the right-hand column reporting what the two conversants actually understood:

HUSBAND: I got some new shoelaces for my shoes.	As you will remember I broke a shoelace on one of my brown oxfords the other day so I stopped to get some new laces.
WIFE: Your loafers need new heels badly.	Something else you could have gotten that I was thinking of. You could have taken in your black loafers which need heels badly. You'd better get them taken care of pretty soon.

The purpose of Garfinkel's illustration is not simply to demonstrate that some things are understood without being said, but to explore the nature of what we mean by common understanding or "shared agreement" among the parties.

What Garfinkel seems to be saying is that to understand and make sense of what is said, one needs to know how it is said, or the rules that participants follow in the course of social interaction. Further, Garfinkel (1967, p. 29) says, "Then the recognized sense of what a person said consists only and entirely in recognizing the method of his speaking, of *seeing how he spoke.*" A good example concerns the type of speaking or writing that we refer to as sarcasm. We often cannot be sure of a speaker's meaning just by knowing the words that are spoken. Even if all words used are familiar to us and are not ambiguous, we attach a different meaning to them depending on how the person is acting. If he or she is acting a certain way (being sarcastic), the meaning of the words is different than if he or she is acting a different way (not being sarcastic). If we observe the speaker, we may be able to tell from his or her tone of voice, inflections, gestures and mannerisms, or other forms of nonverbal communication whether or not he or she is sarcastic. If the statement is written, determination of exact meaning can be exceedingly difficult, because we can tell what the author says but not how he or she says it.

ETHNOMETHODOLOGY VERSUS SURVEY RESEARCH

I picked survey research as a comparison with ethnomethodology for heuristic purposes, since the two are viewed by ethnomethodologists as having different, and perhaps incompatible, objectives. The experimental method, observation, and document analysis are perhaps more palatable to ethnomethodologists, because these methods are better able to deal with temporal processes and temporal ordering, which are very important concerns for ethnomethodologists.

Process versus Product

Ethnomethodologists feel that traditional sociological researchers such as survey researchers tend to take for granted the very things that they should treat as phenomena worthy of sociological study. That is, survey researchers (according to ethnomethodologists) take phenomena resulting from social processes as given, or as points for the study to begin. They attempt to find causes or correlates of these phenomena without attempting to explain how these phenomena arose or came to be of interest. According to ethnomethodologists, the problem arises largely because professional sociologists share everyday commonsense practices with laypersons, use the same natural language that laypersons use, and agree with laypersons about which are the proper problems to be studied. These professional sociologists, according to ethnomethodologists, study problems the same way laypersons do, though with more care and with more emphasis on reliability, validity, and so on. The professionals tend to consider lay accounts as faulty and their own as superior, while to ethnomethodologists the two are really quite similar and are both processes that are of interest as phenomena to be studied in their own right.

As Zimmerman and Pollner put it:

In terms of both the substantive themes brought under examination and the formal properties of the structures examined, professional and lay sociologists are in tacit agreement. For example, the sociologist and the policeman may entertain deeply different theories of how a person comes to be a juvenile delinquent, and they may appeal to disparate criteria and evidence for support of their respective versions. Yet they have no trouble in agreeing that there are persons recognizable as juvenile delinquents and that there are structured ways in which these persons come to be juvenile delinquents. It is in this sense of agreement—agreement as to the fundamental and ordered existence of a phenomenon independent of its having been addressed by some method of inquiry— that professional and lay sociologists are mutually oriented to a common factual domain.

The agreement indicates sociology's profound embeddedness in and dependence upon the world of everyday life. Not only does the attitude of everyday life furnish the context of sociological investigation, it also seems to furnish social scientific inquiry with a leading conception of its order of fact and program of research. The factual domain to which sociological investigation is directed is coterminous, with but mild variation, to the factual domain attended by lay inquirees (Zimmerman and Pollner 1970, p. 34).

Zimmerman and Pollner feel that by accepting the layperson's formulation of the topics to be investigated, sociology becomes part of the very thing it is trying to explain. Thus it is put in the position of the person trying to explain his or her dreams while still asleep and dreaming—it cannot be done. Only by awakening can he or she analyze the dream.

In order to see more clearly the ethnomethodologists' point that sociologists are taking the end result of a process as a given and proceeding from there when they should be studying the prior process, consider the concept of deviancy. The layperson and the professional sociologist may agree or disagree that a certain form of behavior is deviant (some persons today, both lay and professional, consider homosexuals deviant while others do not). The point is that generally sociologists do not take as their topic of study the process whereby a phenomenon such as homosexuality comes to be labeled by the society as deviant. Rather they take the deviancy as a fact or a given and then seek explanations of it, such as early childhood socialization, relations with mother and father, or parents' social class.

The ethnomethodological position does not treat a social phenomenon (for example, the labeling of a particular behavior such as homosexuality) as a given fact with which to begin the investigation, but rather as a topic of investigation in its own right. Although ethnomethodologists study many topics besides deviance (and researchers who are not ethnomethodologists study the labeling of deviants), those studying deviance are interested in the process whereby a particular form of behavior comes to be labeled as deviant by members of society, and the way that behavior is reacted to by the members once it is so labeled. At the risk of oversimplification, the labeling-theory position contends that deviants are created by being labeled as deviant and then reacted to as if they were deviant, until at last they really become deviant and act deviant. This is more or less the self-fulfilling prophecy at work. If the whole society labels you as "crazy" and treats you accordingly, it will encourage you to believe it yourself and to change your behavior to conform to a deviant role. For a discussion of the ethnomethodological approach to labeling theory see Pollner (1974).

Berger and Luckmann (1967) discuss the "social construction of reality," or the idea that some social phenomena are actually mental constructs. Numerous examples can be given of the construction of social reality through labeling. For example, when a murder case goes to a jury trial, there may be some question of whether the defendant is "legally sane" (knows right from wrong) and thus competent to stand trial for murder, or whether he or she is insane and should be committed to an institution for the criminally insane. Who can determine whether he or she is insane? The obvious answer is that "expert," "professional" psychiatrists will do it. However, the defense is often able to produce professional psychiatrists and psychologists to testify that the defendant is insane, while the prosecutor is able to produce psychiatrists and psychologists to swear that he or she is sane and should stand trial. Ultimately it is up to the jury of laypersons (the defendant's peers) to label him or her as either insane or sane. Regardless of whether he or she is "really and objectively" insane, what subsequently happens to him or her—whether he or she is sent to an institution for the criminally insane or tried for murder and sentenced to prison or executed—depends solely upon the label placed upon him or her by the jury.

Another example of labeling in an attempt to provide the "true meaning" to the situation occurs in evaluation letters of recommendation for faculty positions in universities. The letter is many times not taken at face value. Instead, the reader's personal knowledge of the letter's author is invoked. Many times the author is labeled as either a "strong letter writer" who will write glowing letters for almost anyone, or a "weak letter writer" who has very high standards and is not afraid to criticize the person being evaluated. After the writer is labeled, the letter itself can be labeled as either a "weak letter for that writer" or a "strong letter for that writer." Thus it is entirely possible for job candidate 1 to receive a letter of recommendation from writer 1 that is full of praise, while a somewhat critical letter for candidate 2 from writer 2 can be judged to be a "stronger" letter than that of candidate 1, simply because writer 1 is labeled as always praising persons and writer 2 is labeled as being critical and having higher standards.

To make the point that sociologists should study process rather than accept its effects as givens and proceed from there, Garfinkel and Sacks use an analogy:

If, whenever housewives were let into a room, each one on her own went to some same spot and started to clean it, one might conclude that the spot surely needed cleaning. On the other hand, one might conclude that there is something about the spot and about the housewives that makes the encounter of one by the other an occasion for cleaning, in which case the fact of the cleaning, instead of being evidence of dirt, would be itself a phenomenon (Garfinkel and Sacks 1970, p. 347).

Indexical Expressions

Another way in which the goals of ethnomethodologists differ from the goals of conventional social researchers is in their views toward the study of indexical expressions. Calling traditional researchers' activities "constructive analysis," Garfinkel and Sacks (1970, p. 345) say: "Ethnomethodology's interests, like those of constructive analysis, insistently focus on the formal structures of everyday activities. However, the two understand formal structures differently and in incompatible ways."

Indexicals are situation-specific words and phrases whose meaning may change from situation to situation and may depend on who is uttering the word or to whom the remarks are directed. Among the indexical words listed by Garfinkel and Sacks (1970, p. 347) are: "she, we, he, you, here, there, now, this, that, it, I, then, soon, today, tomorrow."

These words are not specific and require clarification or a context. When the Army recruiting poster shows Uncle Sam and says, "Uncle Sam Wants You," obviously "you" varies from situation to situation, depending on who is standing in front of the poster.

In addition to such terms whose referent can change from time to time, other expressions can be formed entirely from objective words but can be indexical in the sense that the meaning of the expression is different depending on who is uttering it. For example, in Wieder's (1974) study of the convict code in a halfway house, he reports that a convict was asked by the program director to organize a baseball team, and replied, "You know I can't organize a baseball team" (Wieder 1974, p. 161). The basic question in ethnomethodological research (or any social research) regarding this statement is, "What did he mean when he said he could not organize a team?" In this case it was understood to mean that such organization was precluded since it violated the convict code provision that states that prisoners cannot cooperate with officials. Wieder notes that if the same statement had been made by a staff member the meaning would have been different, but would have varied according to which staff member made it, the occasion on which it was made, who heard it, and so on. The remark could have meant that "You know that it is your job, since you are on the recreation committee and I am not." Or, if the speaker was a case-carrying parole agent and the program director was listening, it could have meant, "You know that I am already putting more time into the program that I can afford as it is; I couldn't possibly do more" (Wieder 1974, p. 162).

According to ethnomethodologists, conventional researchers are more concerned with converting indexical expressions into objective non-indexical expressions, or in substituting objective expressions for indexical ones, than they are in studying the rules by which sense is made of indexicals in ongoing everyday conversation. Ethnomethodologists, on the other hand, do not look at indexicals as problems to be remedied by conversion to objective expressions, but rather as phenomena of interest in their own right. As Garfinkel and Sacks put it:

Their [ethnomethodological] studies have shown in demonstrable specifics (1) that the properties of indexical expressions are ordered properties, and (2) that they are ordered properties is an ongoing, practical accomplishment of every actual occasion of commonplace speech and conduct. The results of their studies furnish an alternative to the repair of indexical expressions as a central task of general theory building in professional sociology (Garfinkel and Sacks 1970, p. 341).

The distinction between the two approaches should be clear. Both approaches seek order and the ability to generalize their findings, but they seek them in different ways, or perhaps in different places. The traditional approach takes an ambiguous, situationally or temporally specific indexical expression that is obviously not applicable to all times and all places (and is in this sense not universal or generalizable) and attempts to repair or clarify its meaning until it is generalizable. Ethnomethodology, on the other hand, allows the indexical to remain situationally specific and ungeneralizable and does not attempt to clarify or repair it. That is, ethnomethodology does not seek order in the meaning of the indexical expression. Instead, it seeks order in the way indexicals are handled in everyday ongoing discourse to ensure that the participants in the interaction are able to grasp the meaning of these expressions. While the particular contents of the indexicals do not have order irrespective of the time or place they occur, the rules by which conversationalists deal with indexicals do exhibit a generalizable order that is independent of, or transcends, the particular time, place, or characteristics of the conversationalists.

CONVERSATIONAL STRUCTURES

The work of the ethnomethodologists offers ample proof that conversations are not random occurrences, but are quite structured, with members of a society following numerous interactional rules. We may characterize these rules as "norms" that specify which behavior is appropriate for a person of a particular status, in a particular situation or context, and at a particular time. Many times persons adhere quite strictly to these norms without realizing that they are doing so, or indeed without even realizing that the norm exists. An example is the norm regulating the distance one person stands from another person in ordinary conversation. The allowable distance varies among cultures (see Hall 1966), but within a culture the distance is generally quite consistent and adhered to quite rigidly. You can conduct an "ethnomethodological experiment" by standing very close to or unusually far away from a person (even though you raise your voice so he or she can hear) and noting the result. I predict that the person to whom you are standing very close will move back as you move forward in order to maintain the usual distance, if you move unobtrusively and cautiously, he or she may not even realize that he or she is moving away from you (at least the first time). Conversely, the person standing at a distance will move closer to you in order to maintain the correct spatial relationship. There are other norms that one may follow without realizing it, such as raising the voice toward the end of a conversation. The status of the person is also important, as norms dictate different roles depending on such characteristics as one's sex, age, or whether one holds a particular office. Most persons use a higher voice pitch when talking to young children, perhaps without even realizing it.

There are a number of these norms that we take for granted and follow every day without realizing it. Nonverbal examples are presented by the norms governing choice of seat: (1) in a bus or subway train; (2) on a bus stop bench; (3) at a table in the school cafeteria if no empty tables are available; and (4) at a table in a seminar classroom. Sommer (1969) has done a number of experiments with seating arrangements at tables, and has found seating patterns to be quite predictable.

Any time we do something that others regard as strange behavior in our usual routine of everyday affairs, we are probably violating some norm. The person who laughs and talks to herself or himself is violating a well-understood and widely recognized norm, and the stares, scowls, and finger pointing of other persons serve as punishment or negative sanctions to bring his or her behavior back in line. Once when I was a graduate student I experienced an incident that I am still unsure how to label. I was having lunch at a table in the cafeteria of the student union. I was alone, and had a partially filled glass of water on the table. A young man suddenly appeared through the door from the kitchen area of the cafeteria, grabbed my glass of water, and retreated into the kitchen with it. Since I was aware of ethnomethodological experiments of this sort that had the character of "happenings" but were designed to elicit a reaction on the part of

the victim and record how he reacted, I thought at the time that this was a project for an undergraduate sociology class. I never found out for certain, though, and I also thought it could be the work of a practical joker or of a "crazy" person, as some of the cafeteria workers were from the state mental hospital. It was certainly a puzzling occurrence, and the only way to ascertain what it meant, or to explain it so as to relieve the ambiguity and puzzlement in my mind, was to label it in some form, such as the work of a joker, crazy person, or social researcher.

Garfinkel (1967) reports a variety of experiments he has designed to demonstrate to students the existence of such norms, and to observe and record the behaviors of others when the student violates the norms. In one such experiment Garfinkel required undergraduate students to spend from 15 minutes to an hour viewing the interaction within their homes as if they were boarders or strangers in the household, rather than playing their usual role as familiar family members. Students were instructed only to observe, not actually to act as strangers. Their written reports of what they observed did not take into account any usual "insider's" commonsense knowledge of household history, and references to subjective elements such as imputed motive were omitted. From their vantage point as "boarders," the students were surprised to see the way family members treated one another. The whole atmosphere was one of private rather than public behavior, with little respect for table manners, apparent freedom to criticize others, and a general absence of impression management. The students generally felt that the boarder's account did not represent their "real" home environment (Garfinkel 1967, p. 46).

In the next experiment students spent from 15 minutes to an hour not only assuming they were boarders but actually acting out this assumption. In approximately 80 percent of the cases family members reacted strongly to restore the situation to normal. Family members (who did not know what was happening) were bewildered, anxious, and embarrassed. Students were told by family members that they were being inconsiderate, selfish, and impolite. Students were asked if they were sick, stupid, or mad, or questions such as "What has gotten into you?"

The point to be made by this discussion is that conversation and interaction are closely regulated by orderly rules. Although these rules are often taken for granted as commonplace and are adhered to routinely or even subconsciously, they provide an orderly and generalizable structure of interest to ethnomethodologists. By discovering and cataloging these rules that members take for granted, ethnomethodologists can discover how sense is made out of indexicals; that is, how the meaning of indexicals is made clear through a situationally specific process in which the context may be problematic and differ from place to place or time to time, but the rules by which meaning is explicated remain objective, constant, and nonproblematic.

One way of explicating indexicals in conversation is what Garfinkel and Sacks (1970, p. 350) call "formulating," the process by which one of the conversationalists interprets or explains one part of the conversation. This is done by attempting to state the gist of the conversation, or to translate or summarize it. Formulating often involves showing how the conversation either follows or is a departure from a rule. But essentially formulating is a description of behavior designed to tell what the conversationalists are actually *doing* when they say a certain thing. Garfinkel and Sacks (1970, p. 350) offer the following conversational fragment:

JH: Isn't it nice that there's such a crowd of you in the office?

SM: You're asking us to leave, not telling us to leave, right?

SM's statement is a formulation that explicates JH's statement by telling what JH is really doing when he utters that particular sentence (i.e., telling persons to leave).

In addition to the practice of formulating, ethnomethodologists have studied other ways in which rules are followed to make the conversation meaningful and clear to the participants. Among topics studied are the sequencing of conversations, the manner in which conversations are terminated, and the specification of general rules by which conversations are conducted. For example, Sacks, Schegloff, and Jefferson (1974) studied turn-taking in conversations. They found, among other rules, that turn-allocation techniques are used, and that repair mechanisms are available for dealing with turn-taking errors.

The findings most interesting to me resulted from Schegloff and Sacks's (1973) work on ways in which conversations are terminated. They note that conversations normally consist of a series of turn-taking operations in which first one person, then another, speaks. If a speaker wishes to terminate the conversation he or she must somehow break the sequence. That is, he or she must take a turn at speaking, but must not continue to improve on or add additional useful information to the topic being discussed. He or she must terminate discussion of the current topic without initiating a new topic. Thus one must in essence "pass" on one's opportunity to speak by indicating that one has nothing new to say, often by uttering some "preclosing" word or phrase. This phrase will pass the turn to the next speaker, who is not compelled to terminate, but it will provide a clue that the other speaker is ready to terminate. Preclosings noted by Schegloff and Sacks include "well" ("we-ell"), "OK," and "SO" ("so-oo"). Another common one is "anyway," which is often preceded by "well" ("well, anyway"), or drawn out with the emphasis on the first syllable ("ANYway"). There are numerous other preclosings, such as "I've got to go now" (but often this, too, may be preceded by "well" and responded to with "OK") or the familiar "We are costing you too much money" that is often heard on long-distance telephone calls. As with adherence to other rules we have noted in this chapter, the speaker is probably often not aware that he or she is even following a rule in closing.

Before I read the ethnomethodologists' research reports, I was aware that I closed conversations, but not that there was any consistency in the way I did it, or that I said any particular words to occasion such termination. After I read about preclosings I noted that I nearly always closed with "well" or "OK" without thinking about it, and that others did the same.

VALIDITY AND RELIABILITY

Validity

Ethnomethodological studies seem generally to be quite valid, although ethnomethodologists often eschew the process of computing measures of validity or reliability. Defining a valid measure as one that "really measures what we wish to measure," ethnomethodological observation is probably valid simply because ethnomethodologists tend not to follow the traditional practice of proposing an indirect measure for some concept such as alienation or anomia that cannot be seen directly. In a real sense, it can be argued that a person's score on an anomia scale is a causal effect of his or her level of anomia (score is caused by anomia), but is not a direct measure of the always directly unobservable anomie. In contrast to this practice of first mentally constructing a conceptual label such as "alienation" and then attempting to establish its validity by determining whether it corresponds to empirically observed reality, ethnomethodology takes an approach that is closer to the grounded-theory approach . . . . That is, ethnomethodology searches for observable regularities and then labels them. For example, consider the concept of formulating, which describes the way participants explicate a conversational fragment by telling what the speaker is doing when he or she says the fragment. Inasmuch as formulating as a practice is first observed to occur and then labeled after the fact, it has almost perfect face validity, since the practice is the operational definition of the concept. There is no abstract, theoretical, or conceptual definition; the definition of formulation is merely the description of behavior that has been directly observed to occur empirically. Since there is no nonempirical component of the concept, there is no question of error in the fit of the nonempirical to the empirical component, which is what we mean by validity. If all concepts in sociology were amenable to direct observation (if we could see an actual id or attitude) our measurement problems would be considerably less. As Churchill says of his ethnomethodological work:

The indicator variables do not arise in my research. The categories of immediate response to questions are all that there are. The lack of indicator variables eliminates the whole set of measurement problems involved in how well the indicator variables represent the theoretical variables (Churchill 1971, p. 188).

Perhaps we can best assess the validity (or at least the reasonableness) of ethnomethodology by contrasting it with a more familiar method—the survey. Ethnomethodologists sometimes doubt the validity of survey research, both interviews and self-reports. We have noted that ethnomethodologists are concerned primarily with the way members of a society communicate by making sense out of unclear, ambiguous, problematic, or indexical words and expressions. They believe that the meaning of these problematic expressions is not predetermined and is not agreed on before the conversation ensues. Rather, the shared agreement or consensus on what is meant arises out of the very interaction. Thus the content (meaning of the conversation) is dependent on the situation in which it is performed, such as the particular place and time, and cannot be generalized. The rules by which the content is made clear, however, are not unique to the situation and can be generalized (though not perfectly). Since survey research has the goal of standardizing content, it is doomed to failure in the view of the ethnomethodologist, who believes that content cannot be generalized. If the survey researcher attempted to use a standardized survey to study the rules that govern conversations, the ethnomethodologist might think this enterprise more valid, since he or she believes that there is regularity in these rules. The problem here is that, as we have pointed out, persons using these rules are often unaware that they are using them, and so would not be able to answer a survey question about them. Thus the rules can be discovered only by observing the regularity of the behavior as the rules are adhered to, and then inferring the existence of the rules.

Further, the person answering the questionnaire, be it respondent or interviewer, will be following rules, and it is these rules that constitute the very phenomena the ethnomethodologist thinks are the most important to study. . . . In mailed questionnaires these rules (generally labeled instructions rather than norms or rules) may be kept to a minimum. At the very least they will say "Circle the appropriate answer," "There are no right and wrong answers, only give your opinion," or "Please answer fully." In interview studies, particularly if the interview schedule is long and complicated (e.g., with a lot of skip questions), the separate book of instructions to the interviewer may be very lengthy. Most of these rules (instructions) deal with what to do with exceptional or ambiguous cases that do not fit the structure of the questionnaire.

Churchill (1971, p. 189) gives the example of a question that asks how many years of schooling a respondent's father completed. He asks what should be done if the respondent's father completed eight years of schooling in Sweden, but has been told that eight years in Sweden is the equivalent of twelve years in the United States. In this case it is difficult for the respondent and the coder to know whether eight or twelve is the "correct" answer. The question of father's schooling is an indexical expression whose "correct" answer depends on the context. In the absence of a clarifying instruction to tell him or her the way to answer, the respondent must decide "what the researcher *really* means" (i.e., years of schooling regardless of country, or the United States equivalent?). In addition to the formal rules provided by the researcher and printed in the instructions, the respondent and the coder, as members of the system, know (although they may not realize it) the commonsense rules by which they answer questions in everyday life, and they will also rely upon these rules. Thus the phenomenon interesting to the ethnomethodologist is not the answer to the question but the doing of the answering, or the actual search procedure through which the respondent attempts to determine, from studying the questionnaire rules and from his or her own knowledge of everyday life and its rules, "what the researcher really wants."

The concern of the ethnomethodologist is that the answers to survey questions will not be an objective measure of independent social reality, but will be more an artifact of the particular set of rules given for completion of the questions and the setting in which the questionnaire is completed. That is, the rules will generate the data artificially, with the survey being a game that the respondent plays according to its printed rules in order to please and to give the researcher what he or she really wants, rather than what the respondent really thinks. As Garfinkel puts it when discussing standard reporting forms:

> If the researcher insists that the reporter furnish the information in the way the form provides, he runs the risk of imposing upon the actual events for study a structure that is derived from the features of the reporting rather than from the events themselves (Garfinkel 1974, p. 117).

Reliability

The reader can guess that ethnomethodologists would also have their doubts about reliability as assessed by survey researchers. If a survey researcher finds a high intercoder reliability coefficient, showing that all coders give consistently identical interpretations to ambiguous cases, an ethnomethodologist may be very impressed. However, he or she will not be impressed with how consistently the objective reality is being measured, but rather with how consistently all coders are able to follow the rules for "doing coding." If all coders interpret an ambiguous situation (such as the father educated in Sweden) incorrectly but consistently, reliability coefficient values will be high but misleading. Such consistency would indicate that some rule was being followed very rigidly, and this would be of interest to the ethnomethodologist.

Another factor damaging reliability in coding is that when coders face ambiguous cases that are not adequately resolved by coding rules, they often resolve them by invoking their own assumptions about and knowledge of the phenomenon being studied. Thus the data ultimately collected are not a pure, objectively collected measure of social reality, but more a reinforcement of, and product of, the researcher's assumptions. However, traditional researchers seem to be damned if they do and damned if they don't on this point. If an outside researcher surveys an organization with which he or she is not familiar, he or she can be accused of not asking the right questions and of imposing an artificial, irrelevant structure on the data through the questionnaire. On the other hand, if the researcher is a member of the organizational system with intimate knowledge of its rules and everyday operations, he or she can be accused of bias and of bending the data to meet his or her own assumptions and prejudices.

COMPARISON OF POSITIONS

In comparing the positions of ethnomethodology and traditional quantitative social researchers with regard to validity, reliability, and measurement in general, several points can be made.

Survey research . . . is defined primarily as a cross-sectional technique that collects data at a single point in time rather than over time. It is thus efficient for gathering data on the products of social activities but not on the activities themselves. Survey research is efficient for measuring an individual's present income and present level of occupation, but not for measuring the social processes by which he or she attained these products. However, it can be effective in prediction. Polls can predict the vote in a presidential election without explaining the rules by which voters decide for whom to vote. Since study of process by definition requires study over time, a procedure for which survey research is not well suited, for this reason alone survey research is not an efficient method for ethnomethodology. It is, however, an efficient method for those researchers who wish to study product rather than process (we should not forget that ethnomethodologists study documents, such as transcripts of conversations, that are themselves products). Survey research does a good job as long as the questionnaire can be answered routinely, does not have exceptions, and is not ambiguous. Even where ambiguity occurs (as in the Swedish education example), error is often negligible, since only a few respondents have unusual circumstances that render interpretation difficult.

However, when respondents find the question ambiguous and cannot ascertain "what the researcher really wants," then ethnomethodology becomes important, since it helps us understand why the respondent answers the way he or she does. A questionnaire can be successful only if it has few or no indexicals requiring repair through instructions. This is why we [have] emphasized ... that questions should not contain ambiguous words. The problem is that while researchers do not include words that are obviously indexicals in a questionnaire, it is difficult to consider all possible situations that might turn a straightforward question into an indexical. A researcher asking how many pregnancies a woman has had, for example, would consider this question to be "clear" and would probably not anticipate that women in certain situations would find the exact meaning of "pregnancy" ambiguous, and thus be uncertain about the correct answer to the question. If the respondents' situations do not vary (e.g., if all who become pregnant have full-term pregnancies resulting in live births), then the term "pregnancy" is not an indexical for this sample. However, how is a woman to answer who has twins or triplets? Are twins the result of one pregnancy or two? What about the woman who is pregnant only a short time and then has either a miscarriage or an abortion? Is such a partial pregnancy to be counted as a fraction of a pregnancy, no pregnancy, or a full pregnancy? If any of these ambiguous situations occur, then the term "pregnancy" becomes an indexical.

Even though Churchill (1971) says that ethnomethodologists use direct rather than indirect measurement, it seems to me that they are interested not only in observing and categorizing behavior that can be directly observed, such as behavior in conversations, but also in inferring the existence of rules that are the cause of these behavioral regularities. Ethnomethodologists certainly seem to be interested in discovering the existence of rules governing behavior. In his definition of shared agreement, Garfinkel (1967) talks of participants recognizing that something was said according to a rule. This definition implies that the existence of rules can be demonstrated. In the view of ethnomethodologists norms are vague and have to be adapted and made clear in each specific situation, but are nevertheless real. Further, Sacks's chain rule (as presented by Churchill 1971) says that "An American to whom a question is addressed should respond with a direct answer and then return the 'floor' to the questioner." It is obvious to me that Sacks never actually saw this "rule" any more than I can see "alienation"; all he saw were its effects (one might say aftereffects). He saw regularized behavior and inferred the existence of a rule that regulates this behavior. Thus the behavior (persons answering a question and then returning the floor to the questioner) is the operational definition, or indirect measure, of the unobservable rule.

Regularity of the observed behavior provides no guarantee that such a rule actually exists. Other explanations for the regularity of the behavior are possible, though they may be unlikely. It is possible that some chemicals affect the central nervous system in such a way that the regularity of behavior results. Perhaps hormonal differences cause differences in male and female behavior. I do not believe this to be true; I believe that a norm probably exists. The point is that there is certainly a possibility that the norm does not exist, and thus the possibility of measurement error, which suggests that ethnomethodologists should join other social researchers in assessing the validity of their measure (the observed behavior) for the concept in question (the rule that cannot be observed).

One might get the impression from reading ethnomethodology that "professional" or "traditional" social researchers deal entirely with effect rather than process. This is not true in regard to measurement, especially so-called operationalism. Bridgman's original definition of the term states:

In general we mean by any concept nothing more than a set of operations; the concept is synonymous with the corresponding set of operations. *If the concept is physical, as of length, the operations are actual physical operations, namely, those by which length is measured; or if the concept is mental, as of mathematical continuity, the operations are mental operations, namely those by which we determine whether a given aggregate of magnitudes is continuous (Bridgman 1948, pp. 5–6).*

What Bridgman seems to be saying is that a concept is not the result of a process but is defined by the process itself. He says that the meaning of the concept is found in operations or behavior, presumably behavior regulated by rules. This seems to me to be nearly identical to the ethnomethodologist's statement that the meaning of a concept is not independent of behavior but is explicated through ongoing behavior that is conducted according to rules.

We have saved the discussion of advantages and disadvantages until the end of the chapter because many readers are not well versed in ethnomethodology, and would not profit from such a discussion until the rudiments of the method had been explicated.

ADVANTAGES OF ETHNOMETHODOLOGY

1. *Longitudinal.* As a method of ongoing observation, ethnomethodology can record changes as they occur and does not have to rely on the memory of the participants as recorded in a cross-sectional survey.
2. Nonverbal as well as verbal behavior is studied.
3. Ethnomethodology provides an understanding of how respondents make sense of questionnaires, and why they answer the way they do. This approach should prove valuable in analyzing nonresponse in survey studies.
4. Ethnomethodology provides an understanding of how consistency rather than real reliability is sometimes achieved by coders following commonsense rules.

DISADVANTAGES OF ETHNOMETHODOLOGY

1. *Products.* Ethnomethodology is not the method of choice if one is interested in studying some social product, as opposed to the process by which that product was derived. That is, if you

wish to study attitudes that Americans have in common you would not use ethnomethodology, although you might use it to study the process by which those attitudes are derived.
2. *Large-scale studies.* Large-scale mass-attitude studies are more appropriate for survey research than for ethnomethodology, both because they study product rather than process and because they cannot be studied effectively with the observational and experimental methods preferred by ethnomethodologists.

Although ethnomethodology often has been omitted from discussions of traditional research methods, we hope the present [article] makes clear that ethnomethodology is not incompatible with traditional methods, but rather fills an important gap left by these methods. Not only does ethnomethodology concentrate on process and on the way that everyday matters are made sense of by participants in social interaction (thus covering a topic neglected by other methods), it also treats other methods themselves as phenomena to be studied, and in so doing provides us with important insights regarding such matters as the clarification of ambiguous survey questions and the reliability of coding survey data.

SUMMARY

. . . Ethnomethodology studies everyday, commonplace, routine social activities. A substantial portion of ethnomethodological research is directed toward the study of how participants in social interaction make sense of the proceedings. In conversations between two people a substantial part of the meaning is shared and understood in advance, rather than being stated literally. For example, if I ask "How was the party?", I am assuming shared knowledge between us of the party I referred to. This sort of shared and unspoken understanding is one thing that often makes interpretation of personal documents such as letters and diaries difficult. . . . Ethnomethodologists study how participants in social interaction clarify such shared understandings to ensure that they are communicating properly. They assume that communication begins with some things needing to be clarified, and clarification proceeds in identifiable stages according to distinct rules.

In addition to clarification of shared agreements, there are some words and phrases whose meaning depends partially or solely on the social context in which they are uttered. These are called indexicals. Examples are common terms such as "he," "she," "it," "you," and "they." Ethnomethodologists feel that even though the meaning of these terms can never be generalized to fit all situations, and can never be context free, the rules by which the meaning of such a term is made clear to participants in a conversation are general, and can be studied and learned. In general ethnomethodologists believe that emphasis in social research should be on the process of social interaction through which social reality is constructed and maintained, rather than on the end result or product of such interaction, which they feel is the major research focus of most social researchers. We concluded . . . with a discussion of validity and reliability.

REFERENCES

Berger, Peter L. and Thomas Luckmann
1967 The Social Construction of Reality. Garden City, N.Y.: Doubleday-Anchor Books.

Bittner, Egnon
1967a "Police discretion in emergency apprehension of mentally ill persons." Social Problems 14(Winter):278–92.
1967b "The police on skid-row: a study of peace keeping. American Sociological Review 32(October):699–715.

Churchill, Lindsey
1963 "Types of formalization in small-group research." Sociometry 26(September):373–90.
1971 "Ethnomethodology and measurement." Social Forces 50(December):182–91.

Garfinkel, Harold
1967 Studies in Ethnomethodology. Englewood Cliffs, N.J.: Prentice-Hall.
1974 " 'Good' organizational reasons for 'bad' clinic records." Pp. 109–27 in Roy Turner (ed.), Ethnomethodology. Harmondsworth, England: Penguin.

Garfinkel, Harold and Harvey Sacks
1970 "On formal structures of practical actions." Pp. 337–66 in John C. McKinney and Edward A. Tiryakian (eds.), Theoretical Sociology: Perspectives and Developments. New York: Appleton-Century-Crofts.

Goffman, Erving
1959 The Presentation of Self in Everyday Life. Garden City, N.Y.: Doubleday-Anchor Books.
1962 Asylums: Essays on the Social Situation of Mental Patients and Other Inmates. Chicago: Aldine.
1963a Behavior in Public Places: Notes on the Social Organization of Gatherings. New York: The Free Press.
1963b Stigma: Notes on the Management of Spoiled Identity. Englewood Cliffs, N.J.: Prentice-Hall.
1967 Interaction Ritual: Essays on Face-to-Face Behavior. Chicago: Aldine.
1969 Strategic Interaction. Philadelphia: University of Pennsylvania Press.
1971 Relations in Public: Microstudies of the Public Order. New York: Basic Books.

Hall, Edward T.
1966 The Hidden Dimension. Garden City, N.Y.: Doubleday.

Moerman, Michael
1972 "Analysis of conversation: providing accounts, finding breaches, and taking sides." Pp. 170–228 in David N. Sudnow (ed.), Studies in Social Interaction. New York: The Free Press.

Moerman, Michael and Harvey Sacks
1974 "On Understanding in Conversation." Pp. 145–71 in Festchrift for E. Vogelin. The Hague: Mouton.

Pollner, Melvin
1974 "Sociological and common-sense models of the labeling process." Pp. 27–40 in Roy Turner (ed.), Ethnomethodology. Harmondsworth, England: Penguin.

Sacks, Harvey
1972 "An initial investigation of the usability of conversational data for doing sociology." Pp. 31–74 in David N. Sudnow (ed.), Studies in Social Interaction. New York: The Free Press.
1974 "An analysis of the course of a joke's telling in conversation." Pp. 337–53 in J. Sherzer and D. Bauman (eds.), Explorations in the Ethnography of Speaking. Cambridge, England: Cambridge University Press.

Sacks, Harvey and Emanuel Schegloff
1974 "Two preferences in the organization of reference to persons in conversa-

tion and their interaction." Pp. 191–211 in N. H. Avison and R. J. Wilson (eds.), Ethnomethodology, Labeling Theory, and Deviant Behavior. London: Routledge and Kegan Paul.

Sacks, Harvey, Emanuel Schegloff, and Gail Jefferson
   1974 "A simplest systematics for the organization of turn-taking for conversation." Language (December): 696–735.

Schegloff, Emanuel
   1968 "Sequencing in conversational openings." American Anthropologist 70: 1075–95.
   1972 "Notes on a conversational practice: formulating place." Pp. 75–119 in David N. Sudnow (ed.), Studies in Social Interaction. New York: The Free Press.

Schutz, Alfred
   1962 Collected Papers I: The Problem of Social Reality. The Hague: Martinus Nijhoff.

   1964 Collected Papers II: Studies in Social Theory. The Hague: Martinus Nijhoff.
   1966 Collected Papers III: Studies in Phenomenological Philosophy. The Hague: Martinus Nijhoff.

Sommer, Robert
   1969 Personal Space: The Behavioral Basis of Design. Englewood Cliffs, N.J.: Prentice-Hall.

Sudnow, David N., ed.
   1972 Studies in Social Interaction. New York: The Free Press.

Turner, Roy, ed.
   1974 Ethnomethodology. Harmondsworth, England: Penguin.

Wieder, D. Lawrence
   1974 "Telling the code." Pp. 144–72 in Roy Turner (ed.), Ethnomethodology. Harmondsworth, England: Penguin.

Zimmerman, Don H. and Melvin Pollner
   1970 "The everyday world as a phenomenon." Pp. 80–103 in Jack Douglas (ed.), Understanding Everyday Life. Chicago: Aldine.

SECTION 3.3

Experiments

The experimental design is often considered the classic design. Developed by early scientists to ascertain causes and effects more clearly, experimental design has the longest history among research designs. Because the assessment of causality is a major goal among social scientists, this section focuses on experimental design, which, among the four basic research designs considered in this volume—observation, less obtrusive measures, experiments, and survey—allows the greatest level of causal inference.

THE BASIC DESIGNS

The basic, or "classic," design involves an experimental group and a control group, with the experimental group receiving the stimulus. Both groups are pretested and posttested on the outcome variable. For example, students in an introductory sociology class may be randomly assigned to a group receiving special computerized review sessions (the experimental group) or to a group not receiving such assistance (the control group). Students in both groups are tested on their understanding of sociology before the experiment begins (the pretest) and after the experiment ends (the posttest), and the differences between the pretest and posttest scores are calculated for each group. If the stimulus (the use of computerized review sessions) has an impact, then the difference between the pretest and posttest scores will be greater in the experimental group than in the control group.

A higher level of control, this time over possible effects of pretesting on the dependent variable, can be attained by adding two other groups much like the first two groups except that neither of the additional groups is pretested; this is known as the Solomon four-group design. For example, the students in the experiment described above could be assigned to one of four groups, one receiving both the pretest and the stimulus, one receiving only the stimulus, one receiving only the pretest, and one receiving neither the stimulus nor the pretest. Such a design would allow us to determine the effects of both taking the pretest and receiving the special computerized review sessions in terms of the posttest scores on sociological understanding.

A lesser amount of control could be obtained by simply using only two groups—the experimental and the control groups (randomly assigned)—and not pretesting either of them; this design is known as the posttest-only control group design. With this design, however, we would have to assume that the two groups were equal in terms of sociological understanding when the experiment began and we could only examine differences in posttest scores between the experimental and control groups to make conclusions about the effect of computerized review sessions.

Modifications of these true experimental designs abound. Some studies ignore the control group, yielding the one-group pretest-posttest design. Others ignore the random assignment in the determination of a control group; this is known as the static group comparison design. Still others repeat the observations or repeat the presentation of the stimulus at several points in time. Many of these modifications are necessary to employ the experimental design in a field setting; clearly lower levels of control exist in field applications of the design.

THE MAIN ADVANTAGE: CONTROL

The feature of experimental design that permits such a high level of causal analysis is control. Experimental design allows control in four aspects of the research process. First, experiments typically involve a high level of control over the research setting, particularly in the laboratory. Such is not the case for observation and surveys. Second, experiments generally involve a high level of control over the timing of the independent variable; experimenters can decide at what specific point to introduce the independent variable. Hence, one of the prerequisites for establishing causality—time order—is easily attained. In survey research it is often difficult to determine which variable(s) occurred first.

Third, experimenters can assign subjects randomly to the experimental or the control group, further eliminating the effects of extraneous variables and thereby strengthening the causal argument. Survey researchers find it difficult to assign subjects randomly to a group experiencing extramarital sexual relations or to a group not experiencing extramarital sexual relations. Parenthetically, note again that random assignment of subjects to experimental and control groups differs from random sampling procedures frequently employed in survey research. The random assignment principle enhances internal validity (control over extraneous variables), while random sampling enhances external validity (generalizability).

The fourth dimension of control is that the experimental researcher can generally measure the dependent variable both before and after the introduction of the independent variable. Such a before-and-after strategy allows a rather conclusive estimate of the effects of the examined independent variable. Since survey researchers generally only gather data at one point in time, they cannot measure the unique impact of a specific independent variable.

DESIGN WEAKNESSES

The major drawback of experimental design is the comparatively low level of generalizability (external validity), particularly for laboratory experiments. The main reason for the low level of generalizability is the artificial setting. How reasonable is it to make inferences about what goes on in the real world on the basis of a brief encounter in the lab? Furthermore, experiments typically rely on the use of volunteers. But as Jung (1971:28) indicates, volunteers are higher in the need for social approval

tend to have more unconventional personalities

more often tend to be first-born

are less well adjusted (in certain experiments)

tend to have higher need for achievement

Generalizability is reduced under such circumstances. Still another factor limiting generalizability is sample size. Laboratory experiments typically involve fewer than a couple dozen subjects. Few would accept as generalizable the results of a survey employing only twenty respondents.

Experimental designs exhibit several other weaknesses as well. For one, the presence of the experimenter may influence subject responses (this is known as reactivity). Experimenters may unwittingly influence subject responses to be in line with the expected results; recall the famous Rosenthal study (1966) demonstrating that teachers who were told they could expect their students to improve dramatically actually saw such improvement, even though the students were no different from students whose teachers were not told they could expect such results. The reactivity effect can be reduced with the double-blind design, in which neither the experimenter nor subjects know which group is the experimental group. Similarly, a subject's behavior may be altered simply because the subject knows he or she is being studied; recall the famous Hawthorne studies demonstrating that no matter how several factors affecting worker productivity were manipulated, production increased simply because workers responded to the attention paid them (Roethlisberger and Dickson, 1939).

Still another problem with experimental design is the length of time the independent variable is allowed to occur. For experiments lasting about an hour or so, it is questionable if the independent variable has time to take effect. In an experiment testing the effect of anxiety on performance, for instance, the effect may be more pronounced over a long period of time rather than in a period of about an hour.

Another problematic issue in experimental research is ethics. Many experiments involve lying to subjects and some involve questionable manipulations of causal variables. Consider, for example, the possible effects on subjects of a procedure designed to produce a low self-concept.

An additional shortcoming in experimental design is the limited number of variables that can be manipulated. Social phenomena can generally be attributed to a number of factors, and occasionally several independent variables may work together in influencing the dependent variable. But the typical experiment allows the testing of only a few (most often only one) of the possible causal variables. Multivariate analyses are therefore not as frequently reported in experimental research reports as they are in survey research reports.

THE READINGS

The first two readings illustrate the two settings for experimental studies—the field and the laboratory. In the first article, Eric Knowles describes a field experimental study of the boundaries around group interaction in order to examine the effect of two stimuli, group size and group status. Status was measured by manipulating age and dress of the interactors. The dependent variable—boundary penetration—was measured by simply observing the number of passersby who penetrated the group. For control purposes, Knowles employed two wastebarrels.

The second study, by William Griffitt and Russell Veitch, presents a laboratory study of the effects of population density and temperature on interpersonal behavior. This study was in part a response to previous research and speculation on the causes of urban riots. The authors decided to use the laboratory setting to reduce the effects of extraneous variables that might confound the effects of density and temperature in a field (i.e., urban) setting. Note how the use of the lab gave them more control over the stimuli and participants than experienced by Knowles in his field study (Griffitt and Veitch even specified the dress of the participants).

The third article, by Edward Borgatta and George Bohrnstedt, is an excellent discussion of the limitations on generalizability from experimental designs. The authors' concern is the extensive discussion in the literature of threats to internal validity (the adequacy of the design) but the limited discussion of external validity (generalizability). Borgatta and Bohrnstedt highlight several basic concerns regarding external validity, including the nature of the sample, the conceptualization and measurement of the variables being manipulated, the contaminating effects of the situation itself (especially the lab), and the strength of the stimulus. Their point is that both experimenters and readers of research reports should pay more attention to the generalizability of the results. Apply this point to the previous two articles: To what extent can the results of each be generalized to other people in other settings? Can the results of the laboratory study of density and temperature be generalized to explain urban riots? Note, too, how the principles of control over the subjects and stimuli and generalizability are often at odds; as control increases, generalizability often decreases. Once again we see that the design selected is contingent on the topic and the study goals and that the design selected has implications for both internal and external validity.

REFERENCES

Jung, John (ed.)
   1971   The Experimenter's Dilemma. New York: Harper & Row.
Rosenthal, Robert
   1966   Experimenter Effects in Behavioral Research. New York: Appleton-Century-Crofts.
Roethlisberger, F. J. and W. J. Dickson
   1939   Management and the Worker. Cambridge: Harvard University Press.

BOUNDARIES AROUND GROUP INTERACTION: THE EFFECT OF GROUP SIZE AND MEMBER STATUS ON BOUNDARY PERMEABILITY

Eric S. Knowles

While human groupings are usually studied to identify some of the intragroup processes, they are also social units that have stimulus value for others. Groups can be seen as social stimuli that elicit certain kinds of social responses. Milgram, Bickman, and Berkowitz (1969), for instance, reported that experimental crowds on a busy New York City street attracted people to join in the crowd activity (looking up across the street at a sixth story window) and that the effect of the crowd increased with its size. While most of the passersby were only momentarily affected (they glanced up as they strolled by), some stopped and joined the crowd, thereby extending the limit or boundary around the unit.

In their discussion of collective behavior, Milgram and Toch (1969) identify two characteristics of unit boundaries: (a) the sharpness of a boundary, denoting the ease with which members of a unit can be distinguished from nonmembers, and (b) the permeability of a boundary, referring to the openness of the unit to penetration or extension. It is likely that in the Milgram et al. (1969) study, the size of the crowd affected both the sharpness and the permeability of the boundary around it.

The smallest social unit, a single person, appears to have boundaries that, in most social interactions, are fairly impermeable. Sommer (1969) has

A report of this research was presented at the meeting of the Eastern Psychological Association, New York City, April 1971.

The author is grateful to Thomas Schleitwiler, Ken La Tour, Florence Peloquin, Ed Sdano, Elizabeth Vanden Heuvel, David Wolske, and Ann Wonderly for aiding in the development of this research, serving as observers and confederates, and commenting on an earlier presentation of this study. Appreciation also goes to Robert Jiobu for comments on an earlier draft of this article.

defined this bounded area as "personal space," the "area with invisible boundaries surrounding a person's body into which intruders may not come [p. 26]." Defined this way, personal space is a subjective concept, defined by the person, and, consonant with this view, Sommer has found that people would rather move then suffer penetration of the boundary around their personal space.

The space that individuals or interactions occupy, however, has stimulus value for others as well. The point at which an approach to another person is stopped has been studied as a function of the other person. Horowitz, Duff, and Stratton (1964), using this approach procedure with mental patients and normal subjects, found that a greater distance was left when the stimulus object was a person than when it was a hat rack. Argyle and Dean (1965) observed that people stood closer to a life-size photograph of a person with his eyes closed than to a photograph where the eyes were open. These studies suggest that, for a social unit of one, there are boundaries defining the limits of personal space and that these boundaries (a) can resist penetration, (b) are observed by others, and (c) can be strengthened and extended in several ways.

The present study investigated whether these generalizations from the study of personal space can be applied to the bounded interaction space of somewhat larger social units. An interacting pair, for instance, forms a single unit with a boundary around the interaction space. Lyman and Scott (1967) defined such a space as an interaction territory and hypothesized that "every interactional territory implicitly makes the claim of boundary maintenace for the duration of the interaction [p. 240]." Thus, an interaction between members of a small group should be relatively impermeable, resisting penetration from passersby.

In addition, if boundaries around interacting units have social stimulus value for passersby, the resistance of a boundary to penetration should be affected by qualities of the interaction and interactors. Specifically, for small interacting groups, the number of participants should increase the sharpness and the impermeability of the unit boundary. The larger the group (up to a limit) the clearer it should be that an interaction is occurring and the more potent should be the demand for a specific interaction territory. The status of the interactors should have little effect on the clarity of the unit boundary, but with high-status interactors the implicit control over the interaction territory should be increased. Thus, both of these variables, size and status, should affect the permeability of group interaction boundaries.

From these considerations, the following hypotheses were derived: (*a*) Passersby resist penetrating the boundaries of an interacting social unit; (*b*) the more members the interacting unit has, the more impenetrable the boundary is; and (*c*) the higher the status of the interactors, the more the unit boundary resists penetration.

METHOD

Interacting social units varying in size and status or a pair of wastebarrels were placed in the main traffic path of a hallway connecting two university buildings. The wastebarrels, approximately 38 centimeters in diameter and 75 centimeters high, occupied about the same floor area as an interactor and were used in a noninteraction control condition. The stimulus objects (people or wastebarrels) were placed in a hallway 295 centimeters wide so that a person's center of gravity or the center of the barrels was aligned over a mark 75 centimeters away from the wall, leaving a space of 145 centimeters between the marks (see Figure 1). The marks were placed in the hallway so that a line between them ran perpendicular to the flow of passersby.

An observer sitting six meters away in a widened portion of the hallway and thus out of the traffic flow recorded the number and sex of passersby walking through the stimuli (i.e., down the center of the corridor) or walking around the stimuli (i.e., next to one of the walls). Recordings of passersby behavior were made for 2-minute observation periods with the period beginning about 1 minute after the stimuli were in place. The five experimental conditions (wastebarrels, low status-low size, low status-high size, high status-low size, and high status-high size) were randomly assigned within each of five replications for a total of 25 observational periods. Because this was a field experiment where numerous factors could influence passerby behavior, short observational periods randomized within replications were selected to reduce any systematic bias from variables correlated with time such as traffic density, population variations, or previous sightings of the experimental setting.

Size

The stimulus interactions had either two (low size) or four (high size) persons. Pairs were composed of a male and a female; foursomes were composed of a male and a female on each side of the hallway, across from an interactor of the opposite sex. The spaces down the center of the corridor and next to the walls were the same for both interac-

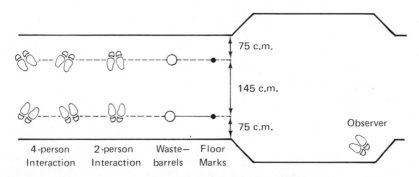

Figure 1 Hallway setting for the stimulus situations

tion sizes. With foursomes, the two people on the same side of the hallway stood on a line parallel to the wall. They did turn slightly away from this parallel line to face both of the opposite people. Interactors were instructed to face the people opposite them, maintain eye contact across the traffic flow, and carry on a discussion in a low voice.

Status

Status differences in the interactors were produced by jointly varying two dimensions: age and dress. These two signs of a person's position in the social structure were considered germane to a university setting. Two status conditions were developed. From an undergraduate group dynamics seminar, the instructor and the three oldest students (both males were 28 years old; the females were 34 and 38 years old), dressed in formal business clothes, formed the stimulus persons for the high-status conditions. Four younger students (the males were 19 and 21 years old; the females were 19 and 20 years old), dressed casually in informal school wear, comprised the low-status stimulus persons. The four-person interactions were composed of all the people available for each status condition. The four people in each status condition rotated membership in the two-person interactions.

Subjects

This experiment was conducted between the hours of 9:30 and 11:00 A.M. on Earth Day, April 22, 1970, at a university that emphasizes ecology. In addition to regularly scheduled classes, many special events were occurring: public lectures, displays, discussions, and symposia. The effects of this special day were threefold: (a) The amount of traffic in the hallway studied was somewhat greater than usual and averaged 8.6 persons per minute for the observational periods; (b) the traffic flow was somewhat more even than would occur on a day when class changes provided the major impetus for movement; and (c) the sample of passersby was more heterogeneous than the usual student-faculty population, including many parents and adult community members. During the scheduled observations, 429 people passed by the stimulus situations; 339 of these encountered the interactors, 90 encountered the wastebarrels. The number of people observed in each experimental condition did not differ significantly from the numbers expected

by chance ($\chi^2 = 5.66$, $df = 4$, $p > .2$). Since control of the comings and goings of passersby was not possible, some of the travelers may have participated in more than one encounter. However, since conditions were assigned randomly within replications, multiple encounters should not contribute any systematic bias.

RESULTS

It was hypothesized that interacting people would establish boundaries around the group that would divert passersby from walking through the interaction. To test this hypothesis, the four conditions involving interactors were compared to the control condition where wastebarrels were placed in the same position. Sex of the passerby did not affect responses to any of the variables in this study (all χ^2s less than 1), so the data are grouped for all passersby. With the wastebarrels, 75.6% of the passersby penetrated the space between the objects, that is, walked down the center of the corridor; with interacting groups, only 25.1% of the passersby penetrated the interaction (see Table 1). This difference was significant ($\chi^2 = 78.99$, $df = 1$, $p < .001$) and supported the hypothesis that interacting social units create boundaries that resist penetration from passersby.

Table 1. Number and Percentage of Passersby Who Walked through and around the Stimuli in Each Condition

| Condition | Passerby behavior | | | | | |
| | Through | | Around | | Total | |
	n	%	n	%	n^a	%
Four persons						
High status	15	17.2	72	82.8	87	100.0
Low status	18	22.8	61	77.2	79	100.0
Two persons						
High status	16	22.2	56	77.8	72	100.0
Low status	36	35.6	65	64.4	101	100.0
All interactions	85	25.1	254	74.9	339	100.0
Wastebarrels	68	75.6	22	24.4	90	100.0

[a]Differences in the total traffic for each of the five experimental conditions were not significantly different ($\chi^2 = 5.66$, $df = 4$, $p > .2$).

The additional hypotheses dealt with the social nature of group boundaries and proposed that characteristics of the interacting social unit affect the sharpness and permeability of group boundaries, both of which affect the rate of penetration by passersby. The size of the interacting group decreased the penetration of the interaction boundary. More traffic walked through the two-person group (30.0%) than walked through the four-person group (19.9%). This difference was significant ($\chi^2 = 4.67$, $df = 1$, $p < .05$) and supported the hypothesis that groups of larger size establish a group boundary that has greater clarity and/or impermeability for passersby. The status of the interactors also affected the behavior of passersby; more traffic walked through the low-status groups (30.0%) than walked through the high-status groups (18.3%). This significant difference ($\chi^2 = 4.96$, $df = 1$, $p < .05$) supported the hypothesis that higher status of the group members decreases the permeability of the group boundary.

Both the size and status of the group interactions affected the penetration rates from passersby. Subsequent multidimensional analysis of the data[1] (Feinberg, 1970) indicated that these variables did not interact, but operated additively on passerby penetration. Thus, it appears from the present study that the size of the group and the status of the group members have independent effects on the stimulus value of group boundaries.

DISCUSSION

The large differences between the penetration of wastebarrels and the penetration of interacting groups provide direct support for Lyman and Scott's (1967) hypothesis that an "interactional territory implicitly makes the claim of boundary maintenance . . . [p. 240]." An ongoing interaction has stimulus value for others; passersby avoid walking through an informal interaction even when it blocks a major portion of a well-traveled hallway. Many of the passersby in this study had to change their direction, turn sideways to "ease by," and even stop to wait for oncoming traffic in order to walk around rather than through the interaction.

While a majority of the traffic did avoid penetrating the interactions, still 25% of the passersby violated the interactional territory. While not concerning the hypotheses under consideration, it

would be interesting to know who these people were and what their response to the situation was. For instance, it seems likely that interactional boundaries are more permeable for high-status persons than for low-status persons. In the present study, the observers had the impression that faculty and administrators (high-status passersby) did have a higher penetration rate than students. It is also possible that a person's behavior is influenced to some extent by the actions of earlier pedestrians. Seeing someone else walk through an interacting group may alter a person's assessment of the permeability of the group boundary. Future studies of passerby behavior would profit from taking greater notice of passerby characteristics and sequences.

Many of the penetrators in the present study did respond to the interactors. While apologies such as "excuse me" and "sorry" were frequent, penetrators responded nonverbally as well. A common response was to duck the head and hurry through the interaction. This pattern allowed people to penetrate the interaction without interrupting the interactors' eye contact. Also, in contrast to people who walked around the interaction, penetrators almost never looked at the interactors once they approached within 2 or 3 feet. These impressions support the conclusion that an interaction does have stimulus value for others, even those who penetrate an interaction.

When compared to the Milgram et al. (1969) findings that crowds looking across the street at a sixth floor window tended to attract passersby, the finding in this study that conversations repelled passersby suggests that the nature of the group activity has a major effect on the permeability of the unit boundary. Some group activities appear to be inclusive, others exclusive of passersby. A more complete model of the effect of group boundaries on nongroup members will have to include statements about the group activity. When this is done, the finding in the present study that size and status were independent may take on added importance. The implication from this study and the Milgram et al. (1969) study is that size interacts with the group activity to make group boundaries more permeable when the group activity is inclusive (looking up at a sixth floor window) and more impermeable when the group activity is exclusive (carrying on a conversation). Status, however, may have a unitary effect on boundary permeability; the higher the status of the group members, the more impermeable the boundary, no matter what the activity.

The finding that penetration of a group was affected by the size and status of the group suggests that the boundary concept can be applied to collective behavior not only as an analytic tool (Milgram & Toch, 1969) but as an operationalizable concept to which other variables may be related empirically. While two qualities of group boundaries—their sharpness and their permeability—may affect the behavior of passersby, it is most likely that, in the present study, the size of the group and especially the status of the members had their primary effect on the permeability of the group boundary. While it would be useful in future research to distinguish boundary sharpness from boundary permeability, this study demonstrated that there is a relationship between group characteristics and passerby behavior, and that a concept of group boundaries appears to be a useful mediating link.

NOTE

[1]The suggestion of Feinberg's procedure and assistance provided by David Jowett are greatly appreciated.

REFERENCES

Argyle, M., & Dean, J. Eye contact, distance, and affiliation. *Sociometry*, 1965, 28, 289–304.

Feinberg, S. E. The analysis of multidimensional contingency tables. *Ecology*, 1970, 51, 419–433.

Horowitz, M. H., Duff, D. F., & Stratton, L. O. Body-buffer zone. *Archives of General Psychiatry*, 1964, 11, 651–656.

Lyman, S. M., & Scott, M. B. Territoriality: A neglected sociological dimension. *Social Problems*, 1967, 15, 236–249.

Milgram, S., Bickman, L., & Berkowitz, L. Note on the drawing power of crowds of different size. *Journal of Personality and Social Psychology*, 1969, 13, 79–82.

Milgram, S., & Toch, H. Collective behavior: Crowds and social movements. In G. Lindzey & E. Aronson (Eds.), *Handbook of social psychology*. (2nd ed.) Vol. 4. Reading, Mass.: Addison-Wesley, 1969.

Sommer, R. *Personal space: The behavioral basis of design*. Englewood Cliffs, N. J.: Prentice-Hall, 1969.

HOT AND CROWDED: INFLUENCES OF POPULATION DENSITY AND TEMPERATURE ON INTERPERSONAL AFFECTIVE BEHAVIOR

William Griffitt
Russell Veitch

Environmental conditions (usually referred to as "stressors" when abnormal or extreme) are known to influence a wide variety of performance,

This research was supported in part by Grant MH 16351-02 from the National Institute of Mental Health. The authors would like to thank Frederick H. Rohles and Nancy Calentine for their assistance in conducting the experiment. Gratitude is also expressed to Kenneth Kemp for his assistance in analyzing the data.

intellectual, and physiological behaviors (Glass, Singer, & Friedman, 1969; Terris & Rahhal, 1969; Wilkinson, 1969). Investigations of the influence of environmental conditions such as temperature, noise, lack of sleep, vibration, etc., have typically involved such response variables as vigilance, pursuit tracking, and serial learning (Wilkinson, 1969). The importance of determining the nature of environmental influences on intellectual and performance behaviors such as those mentioned is,

From the *Journal of Personality and Social Psychology*, February 1971, pp. 92–98. Copyright 1971 by the American Psychological Association. Reprinted by permission. References updated.

of course, obvious. The design of optimal man-machine systems and work environments is greatly facilitated through systematic investigations of the interactions among environmental factors and task variables.

In light of growing concern over environmental influences on nonperformance and nonintellectual behaviors (United States Riot Commission, 1968), systematic knowledge concerning the role of environmental conditions with respect to social behavior will assume crucial importance as variables such as noise level and population density reach the status of stressors in years to come. Examination of current and recent literature (Griffitt, 1970), however, reveals an apparent dearth of systematic studies of environmental influences on human social, affective, and emotional behaviors.

The ambient temperature of the environment is one such variable which has received limited examination with respect to its influence on human social behavior. Anecdotally, it is commonly observed that social behaviors in very hot and humid situations are quite different in affective tone from those behaviors in "comfortable" and even cold environments. Interpersonal responses are detectably more negative when one is "hot and uncomfortable" than when one is located in a more comfortable situation. Such observations have been sufficiently compelling to lead some investigators to examine experimentally the effects of ambient temperature on "social behaviors" in nonhuman species. For example, utilizing mice, Greenberg (1969) examined the incidence of aggressive assaults as influenced by genetic strain, population density, and ambient temperature. The frequency of aggressive incidents was found to increase with temperature until at very high temperatures (approximately 95 degrees Fahrenheit) all motor activity (including assaults) declined sharply. Others (Guhl, 1962) have examined similar behaviors in chickens and other nonhuman animals.

With few exceptions, information concerning human social responses under conditions of high temperature has been obtained primarily through nonsystematic observations and correlations. For example, in studies concerned with the effects of exposure to high temperatures on physiological, intellectual, and physical functioning, Rohles (1967) observed "continual arguing, needling, agitating, jibing, fist-fighting, threatening, and even

an attempted knifing [p. 59]." Further, an analysis of ghetto riots by the United States Riot Commission (1968) revealed that "In most instances, the temperature during the day on which the violence first erupted was quite high [p. 123]." It was reported that in 9 of 18 disorders, the temperature had reached 90 degrees or more during the day, while in 8 cases the temperature preceding the violence had been in the 80s. The above observations are sufficiently in accord with everyday experience to suggest that many interpersonal and social-affective behaviors are negatively influenced by conditions of high temperature.

The results of a recent investigation (Griffitt, 1970) lend support to the later proposition. Subjects were exposed to one of two conditions of ambient effective temperature and asked to respond with respect to attraction to strangers who either expressed agreement or disagreement on various attitudinal issues with the subjects' own views. Attraction responses were found to be significantly more negative under the "hot" condition (effective temperature = 90.6 degrees Fahrenheit) than under the "normal" condition (effective temperature = 67.5 degrees Fahrenheit). Further, subjective reports of the positiveness of affective feelings were positively related to attraction responses but negatively related to effective temperature. It was suggested that a broad class of social-affective behaviors (e.g., attraction, aggression, evaluative activities, etc.) would be negatively influenced by environmental conditions to the extent that such conditions elicit negative affective feelings.

The spatial relationships among people have been cited by many individuals (e.g., Hall, 1966; Little, 1965; Sommer, 1967) as potential sources of positive or negative affective experience. In light of recent and predicted population increase trends, the effects of "crowding" or high population density on social behaviors are of particular interest. Indeed, the United States Riot Commission (1968) referred to the "crowded ghetto living conditions, worsened by summer heat [p. 325]" as a basic factor involved in civil disorders. The physiological and behavioral effects of overcrowding in animals have been described by Christian (1963) and Calhoun (1962), who coined the term "behavioral sink" to describe the gross distortions of behavior which take place when animals are reared in extremely crowded situations. Seriously disrupted functions included courting, nest building, sex behaviors, social organization, and physiological functions.

If, as everyday experience frequently suggests, conditions of overcrowding tend to elicit feelings of discomfort or other negative affective responses, one would expect that interpersonal affective responses would tend to be generally more negative under conditions of high "population density" than under less crowded conditions. As part of the study mentioned earlier, Greenberg (1969) varied the density of mice in enclosed areas and observed the frequency of aggressive assaults. Within at least one genetic strain, frequency of assaults was found to be positively related to population density. These findings are similar to those reported earlier by Thiessen (1966).

The present experiment was designed to examine the effects of effective temperature and population density on social-affective behaviors in humans. It was hypothesized that interpersonal attraction responses and subjective evaluations of affective feelings are more negative under conditions of high effective temperature than under conditions of normal effective temperature, and more negative under conditions of high population density than in low-density conditions. The predictions were derived from an affective model of interpersonal evaluative behavior (Clore & Byrne, 1977) and from findings of an earlier investigation (Griffitt, 1970). The use of attitudinal agreement and disagreement in the present investigation as a reliable technique of eliciting differential attraction responses has as its foundation the extensive work of Byrne (1969) and his associates, demonstrating the positive relationship between the proportion of attitudes expressed by a stranger which are similar to those of a subject and the subject's attraction toward the stranger.

METHOD

Design

As in a previous study (Griffitt, 1970), subjects responded with respect to attraction to an anonymous same-sex stranger on the basis of inspection of the stranger's responses to a 24-item attitude scale. The stranger's attitudes were in agreement with those of the subjects on either .25 or .75 of the issues. The two levels of proportion of similarity

were combined factorially with two levels of effective temperature (normal and hot) and two levels of population density (low and high).

Subjects

Subjects were 121 male and female students in introductory psychology at Kansas State University who had been pretested on the 24-item attitude questionnaire. Each was randomly assigned to one of the eight experimental conditions. Each subject reported to the Kansas State University Environmental Research Institute to take part in an experiment described as an investigation of "judgmental processes under altered environmental conditions." To reduce variability in response to the effective temperature conditions, each subject was dressed in cotton bermuda shorts and a cotton shirt or blouse. Males and females participated in separate groups.

Procedure

Upon reporting to the environmental laboratory, subjects entered and were seated in a Sherer-Gillet standard environmental chamber, which is 7 feet wide by 9 feet long with a ceiling height of 9 feet. For half of the subjects, the effective temperature of the room was maintained at an average of 73.4 degrees Fahrenheit (normal). The other half of the subjects participated with the effective temperature maintained at an average of 93.5 degrees Fahrenheit (hot). Effective temperature is an index which combines into a single value the effect of dry-bulb temperature and relative humidity on the sensation of warmth or cold felt by the human body.[1] Subjects in the hot condition were exposed to an effective temperature which was well beyond that of 84.6 degrees Fahrenheit, which, according to previous work (Rohles, 1969), is the highest effective temperature rated as comfortable by test subjects. The effective temperature in the normal condition approximates the effective temperature most often rated comfortable by test subjects (Nevins, Rohles, Springer, & Feyerherm, 1966).

Across the two proportion conditions and two effective temperature conditions, two levels of population density were created by running subjects in either large or small groups. In the low-density condition, subjects were run in groups ranging in size from 3 to 5, while high-density subjects were run in groups ranging in size from 12 to

16. With the experimenter added in each case, the available space per person in the low-density group averaged 12.73 square feet, while in the high-density condition, the available space averaged 4.06 square feet per person. Subjects were seated in folding chairs arranged in rows such that face-to-face orientations were minimized, with only those subjects seated side by side able to achieve eye contact. In the low-density condition, excess chairs were removed from the chamber.

During the first 45 minutes of each experimental session, the subjects performed a series of paper-and-pencil tasks. Each subject responded to a 64-item Repression-Sensitization (R-S) scale (Byrne & Griffitt, 1969), a series of six semantic-differential rating scales designed to assess feelings on the dimensions comfortable-uncomfortable, bad-good, high-low, sad-happy, pleasant-unpleasant, and negative-positive. In addition, each subject responded on the dimension hot-cold to assess sensations of warmth. Following the ratings of feelings, subjects performed a symbol-cancellation task designed as a time filler, followed by responding to a short form of the Nowlis (1965) Mood Adjective Check List (MACL).

After completing the MACL, subjects were told that the next phase of the experiment involved making judgments about an anonymous stranger, based on inspection of the stranger's responses to the 24-item attitude questionnaire. Half of the subjects in each effective temperature condition examined the responses of a stranger who agreed with them on .25 of the issues, and the other half received a scale which agreed with them on .75 of the issues. The attitude scales were, of course, bogus ones prepared by the experimenter by the "unique stranger" method (Griffitt & Byrne, 1970) to agree with the subject on either .25 or .75 of the issues. After examining the attitude questionnaire, subjects were asked to rate the stranger on the Interpersonal Judgment Scale (IJS). The IJS is a six-item, 7-point rating scale dealing with the stranger's intelligence, knowledge of current events, morality, adjustment, subject's probable liking of the stranger, and his desirability as a work partner. Ratings on the latter two items are summed to yield the dependent measure of attraction ranging from 2 to 14, with a split-half reliability of .85 (Byrne & Nelson, 1965).

Following the attitude-attraction task, subjects again completed the ratings of feelings, the rating

of warmth, and responded to other semantic-differential questionnaires regarding the experimental room, instructions, and experimenter. The purpose of the experiment was then explained, and subjects were allowed to leave.

RESULTS

Temperature

The effects of the effective temperature manipulation on affective experience were examined by scoring the semantic-differential dimensions of feelings from 1 (negative) to 7 (positive) and summing (possible range = 6–42) to yield an overall measure of positiveness of feelings for the first (F_1) and the second (F_2) assessments. In addition, ratings on the hot-cold dimension were scored from 1 (cold) to 7 (hot) to yield two measures of temperature sensation (T_1 and T_2). The means of these

Table 1. Mean Ratings of Feelings (F_1 and F_2), Temperature Sensation (T_1 and T_2), Mood, and Other Stimuli across Effective Temperature Conditions

Variable	Effective temperature		
	Normal (73.4°)	Hot (93.5°)	$p <$
F_1	31.92	23.44	.001
F_2	29.46	19.42	.001
T_1	3.99	6.60	.001
T_2	4.25	6.78	.001
Mood			
Aggression	3.72	4.45	.05
Surgency	5.93	4.75	.01
Elation	5.69	4.16	.001
Concentration	9.12	6.66	.001
Fatigue	5.52	7.06	.01
Social affection	6.69	5.67	.01
Sadness	3.91	4.73	.05
Vigor	6.50	4.51	.001
Room			
Pleasant-unpleasant	4.06	2.84	.001
Comfortable-uncomfortable	3.97	1.90	.001
Experiment			
Pleasant-unpleasant	5.33	2.54	.001
Interesting-uninteresting	5.99	5.56	.07

Note: Ratings of the room and experiment were made on bipolar semantic-differential scales from 7 (positive) to 1 (negative).

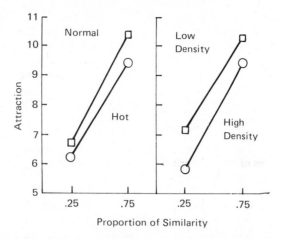

Figure 1 Mean attraction responses as a function of effective temperature (normal = 73.4 degrees, hot = 93.5 degrees), proportion of similar attitudes (left panel), population density (low = 12.73 square feet per person, high = 4.06 square feet per person), and proportion of similar attitudes (right panel)

scores, as well as the analysis of variance results across the two effective temperature conditions, are shown in Table 1. It is clear that the effective temperature manipulation was successful in achieving the desired effects. As in the previous investigation, the temperature sensation and feelings variables were substantially related, as indicated by the correlations between $F_1 - T_1$ ($r = -.55$, $p < .001$) and $F_2 - T_2$ ($r = -.63$, $p < .001$).

The influence of effective temperature on mean attraction responses to agreeing and disagreeing strangers is depicted in the left panel of Figure 1. Analysis of variance indicated that as predicted, attraction responses tended to be more negative under the hot than under the normal condition ($F = 3.17$, $df = 1/113$, $p < .07$). Mean values of the additional response variables which were significantly influenced by the effective temperature manipulation are shown in Table 1.

Population Density

Mean F_1, F_2, T_1, and T_2 values across the two density conditions are shown in Table 2. It is apparent that reports of affective experience are generally more negative in the high- than in the low-density condition. Additionally, even though the actual mean effective temperatures across density conditions were identical, subjects rated themselves as warmer in the high-density than in the low-density condition.

The right panel of Figure 1 illustrates the significantly negative ($F = 6.99$, $df = 1/113$, $p < .01$) influence of population density on attraction responses to agreeing and disagreeing strangers. Further evidence of the negative effect of population density on affective responses is shown in Table 2, which presents the mean values of those response variables significantly influenced by the density manipulation.

Attitude Similarity

Finally, as in numerous previous investigations (Byrne, 1969), attraction responses across all temperature and density conditions evoked by agreeing strangers were significantly more positive than those evoked by disagreers ($F = 62.14$, $df = 1/113$, $p < .001$). None of the interaction F ratios approached significance.

Interrelations among Response Variables

In previous writings (Clore & Byrne, 1977; Griffitt, 1970; Griffitt & Guay, 1969), it has been suggested that personal-affective experiences mediate the expression of *inter*personal or social-affective behaviors such as evaluations, approach-avoidance behaviors with respect to "nonsocial" objects are also mediated by personal-affective experiences. To the extent that these conceptualizations are accurate, it would be expected in the present investigation that evaluations of per-

Table 2. Mean Ratings of Feelings
(F_1 and F_2), Temperature Sensation
(T_1 and T_2), Mood, and Other Stimuli
across Density Conditions

Variable	Density Low	High	$p <$
F_1	28.67	26.68	.10
F_2	26.25	22.62	.01
T_1	5.04	5.55	.001
T_2	5.20	5.82	.001
Mood			
Surgency	5.82	4.86	.05
Elation	5.20	4.64	.07
Concentration	8.25	7.53	.10
Fatigue	5.79	6.79	.05
Social affection	6.54	5.82	.07
Vigor	6.15	4.86	.01
Room			
Good-bad	5.01	4.15	.01
Attractive-unattractive	3.32	2.75	.05
Adequate-inadequate	5.78	4.47	.001
Pleasant-unpleasant	3.83	3.06	.01
Well arranged-poorly arranged	5.24	4.21	.001
Comfortable-uncomfortable	3.65	2.22	.001
Experiment			
Pleasant-unpleasant	4.37	3.50	.002
Worthy-unworthy	5.82	5.04	.003
Interesting-uninteresting	6.02	5.53	.04

Note: Ratings of the room and experiment were made on bipolar semantic-differential scales from 7 (positive) to 1 (negative).

Table 3. Intercorrelations
among Response Variables

Variable	F_1	F_2	Attraction
Room			
Good-bad	.24**	.17*	.19*
Pleasant-unpleasant	.52***	.51***	.19*
Comfortable-uncomfortable	.58***	.63***	.22*
Experiment			
Pleasant-unpleasant	.70***	.70***	.21*
Attraction	.19*	.26**	

* $p < .05$.
** $p < .01$.
*** $p < .001$.

sonal feelings (F_1 and F_2), interpersonal attraction, and evaluations of nonsocial objects such as the experimental room and experiment would be positively related. Table 3 shows the correlations among semantic-differential ratings of the experimental room and experiment, F_1 and F_2, and attraction responses. It is apparent that ratings of personal affective experience (F_1 and F_2), social-affective responses (attraction), and nonsocial affective ratings (room and experiment) are positively related.

DISCUSSION

Under conditions of high temperature and high population density, personal-affective, social-affective, and non-social-affective responses were found to be significantly more negative than under conditions of comfortable temperature and low population density. The significant temperature effect provides a replication of a previous finding (Griffitt, 1970), while the "crowding" effect has not previously been demonstrated in humans.

With the absence of systematic data concerning human behavior, investigators have been forced to speculate concerning the influences of high population density or "overcrowding" on social behaviors (United States Riot Commission, 1968). The findings of the present experimental investigation, however, support the hypothesis that extremely crowded conditions do, in fact, influence social behaviors in a negative fashion. The parameters of overcrowding in humans are, if at all, only vaguely defined. The question of at what points on the density dimension do humans experience feelings of crowding which are initially unpleasant, then intolerable, is not answered by the present factorial investigation. Few would disagree, however, that human density conditions as they exist in the major American ghettos are subjectively evaluated as overcrowded and unpleasant. Hall (1966) has pointed out the difficulties in attempting to establish maximum, minimum, and optimum densities of human populations. It is clear, however, as pointed out by Carter (1969) that "the concentration of people in the larger urban areas, especially those of the Northeast, California, and the Great Lakes states, is making many Americans uneasy about the chamber of commerce belief that bigger means better [p. 722]."

The many factors potentially capable of altering the density-affect relationship have yet to be investigated. Using the present investigation as a model, for example, it might be expected that several factors would be effective in either intensifying or mitigating the relationship. The subjects of the present experiment were all run in same-sex groups, and it might be expected that heterosexual groups would have experienced the crowded situation as being somewhat more positive than did the present groups. It might be speculated that variations in the seating configuration such that face-to-face orientations are necessary would make the situation even more unpleasant. As a final example, the friendship relationships within a high-density group would be expected to influence the perceived pleasantness of the experience with "friendly" groups responding more positively than "unfriendly" groups.

NOTE

[1]The effective temperature of 93.5 degrees Fahrenheit represents a dry-bulb temperature of 109 degrees Fahrenheit and relative humidity of 46%. Effective temperatures in the hot condition ranged from a low of 91.4 degrees Fahrenheit (107 degrees Fahrenheit dry bulb—43% relative humidity) to 96.7 degrees Fahrenheit (114 degrees Fahrenheit dry bulb—46% relative humidity). The 73.4 degrees Fahrenheit effective temperature represents a dry bulb of 74 degrees Fahrenheit and relative humidity of 93%. The effective temperature range in the normal condition was 71.5 degrees Fahrenheit (72 degrees Fahrenheit dry bulb—93% relative humidity) to 76.5 degrees Fahrenheit (77 degrees Fahrenheit dry bulb—95% relative humidity).

REFERENCES

Byrne, D. Attitudes and attraction. In L. Berkowitz (Ed.), *Advances in experimental social psychology.* Vol. 4. New York: Academic Press, 1969.

Byrne, D., & Griffitt, W. Similarity and awareness of similarity of personality characteristics as determinants of attraction. *Journal of Experimental Research in Personality,* 1969, 3, 179–186.

Byrne, D., & Nelson, D. Attraction as a linear function of proportion of positive reinforcements. *Journal of Personality and Social Psychology,* 1965, 1, 659–663.

Calhoun, J. B. Population density and social pathology. *Scientific American,* 1962, 206, 139–148.

Carter, L. J. The population crisis: Rising concern at home. *Science,* 1969, 166, 722–726.

Christian, J. J. The pathology of overpopulation. *Military Medicine,* 1963, 128, 571–603.

Clore, G. L., & Byrne, D. The process of personality interaction. Pp. 66–82 in R. B. Cattel (Ed.), *Handbook of modern personality theory.* Chicago: Aldine, 1977.

Glass, D. C., Singer, J. E., & Friedman, L. N. Psychic cost of adaptation to an environmental stressor. *Journal of Personality and Social Psychology,* 1969, 12, 200–210.

Greenberg, G. The effects of ambient temperature and population density on aggression in two strains of mice. Unpublished doctoral dissertation, Kansas State University, 1969.

Griffitt, W. Environmental effects on interpersonal affective behavior: Ambient effective temperature and attraction. *Journal of Personality and Social Psychology,* 1970, 15, 240–244.

Griffitt, W., & Byrne, D. Procedures in the paradigmatic study of attitude similarity and attraction. *Representative Research in Social Psychology,* 1970, 1, 33–48.

Griffitt, W., & Guay, P. "Object" evaluation and conditioned affect. *Journal of Experimental Research in Personality,* 1969, 4, 1–8.

Guhl, A. M. The social environment and behavior. Pp. 97–112 in E. S. E. Hafez (Ed.), *The behavior of domestic animals.* Baltimore: Williams & Wilkins, 1962.

Hall, E. T. *The hidden dimension.* New York: Doubleday, 1966.

Little, K. B. Personal space. *Journal of Experimental Social Psychology,* 1965, 1, 237–247.

Nevins, R. G., Rohles, F. H., Springer, W. E., & Feyerherm, A. M. Temperature-humidity chart for thermal comfort of seated persons. Paper presented at the American Society of Heating, Refrigerating, and Air-Conditioning Engineers semiannual meetings, Houston, January 1966.

Nowlis, V. Research with the Mood Adjective Check List. Pp. 101–139 in S. Tomkins & C. Izard (Eds.), *Affect, cognition, and personality.* New York: Springer, 1965.

Rohles, F. H. Environmental psychology: A bucket of worms. *Psychology Today,* 1967, 1, 55–63.

Rohles, F. H. Psychological aspects of thermal comfort. Paper presented at the American Society of Heating, Refrigerating, and Air-Conditioning Engineers semiannual meetings, Denver, July 1969.

Sommer, R. Small group ecology. *Psychological Bulletin*, 1967, 67, 145–152.

Terris, W., & Rahhal, D. K. Generalized resistance to the effects of psychological stressors. *Journal of Personality and Social Psychology*, 1969, 13, 93–97.

Thiessen, D. D. Role of physical injury in the physiological effects of population density in mice.

Journal of Comparative and Physiological Psychology, 1966, 62, 322–324.

United States Riot Commission. *Report of the National Advisory Commission on civil disorders.* New York: Bantam Books, 1968.

Wilkinson, R. Some factors influencing the effect of environmental stressors upon performance. *Psychological Bulletin*, 1969, 72, 260–272.

SOME LIMITATIONS ON GENERALIZABILITY FROM SOCIAL PSYCHOLOGICAL EXPERIMENTS

Edgar F. Borgatta
George W. Bohrnstedt

Three major criticisms have been leveled at social psychological experiments in recent years. The first has raised questions about the ethics (APA, 1967) involved in: (a) the potential harm to human subjects and (b) deceiving subjects about the meaning of the experiment. The second is that experimental social psychologists too often have failed to realize that the experiment itself is a social occasion and that the results obtained may be due to subtle demand characteristics or to experimenter effects (Rosenthal, 1966; Rosenthal and Rosnow, 1969; Orne, 1962; Wuebben et al., 1974). Third, laboratory experiments have had little if any external validity.

Two kinds of charges have been made concerning external validity. The first is that many experiments have little practical relevance, especially for the policy maker trying to utilize social science findings (Chapanis, 1967; Cherns, 1969; Sanford, 1970; Silverman, 1971; Goodwin, 1971; Baron, 1971; Skellie et al., 1971). The second attacks the generalizability of findings because of publication procedures (Bakan, 1966; Walster and Cleary, 1970) and the conditions of and the subjects used in many laboratory experiments (Smart, 1966; Drabek and Haas, 1967; Neufeld, 1970; Holmes and Jorgensen, 1971; Oakes, 1972; Higbee and Wells, 1972). In this paper we emphasize some persisting questions about the generalizability of results from laboratory experiments, and we raise some additional questions as well.

This discussion utilizes the distinction between internal validity (the adequacy of the experiment itself) and external validity (the generalizability of the experimental results) made by Campbell and Stanley (1963). Needless to say, an experiment which does not have internal validity is limited in its external validity as well. While the Campbell and Stanley volume suggests ways for improving the internal validity of one's research, much less is said about ways for improving external validity.

Assuming that an experiment has been carried out that has a reasonable design from the point of view of internal validity, what factors may interfere with the generalizability of the experiment? The first issue that has to be considered is the one associated with the sample used in the experiment. While it may be true, for example, that experimental and control groups are assumed to be equivalent in the experiment because of randomization procedures, one can raise an additional question about the population from which both groups have been drawn. If one looks at the history of experimentation in social psychology, it is clear that most experiments have been carried out on college students, and most of them have relied heavily on students from lower-division psychology classes,

From *Sociological Methods and Research*, August 1974, pp. 111–120. Reprinted by permission of Sage Publications, Inc., and the author.

where participation in such experiments often is required. Indeed, recent studies by Schultz (1969) and Higbee and Wells (1972) indicate that over 70% of the studies published in the *Journal of Personality and Social Psychology* (JPSP) in the late 1960s utilized college student subjects. Higbee and Wells provide data that the use of college student subjects has increased dramatically in the past 20 years. In particular, only 20% of the studies in the *Journal of Abnormal and Social Psychology* (JASP) in 1949 utilized college student subjects. When the authors combined the research studies contained in both the 1969 volumes of *JPSP* and the *Journal of Abnormal Psychology* (JAbP), the two journals into which JASP split, they found that 53% of the articles utilized college student samples, suggesting that a real increase in the use of college student subjects has occurred and that the finding is not merely due to a splitting of the original JASP into JPSP and JAbP. Making the generalizability of many social psychology laboratory experiments even more questionable is recent evidence that the majority of these experiments have utilized only female subjects (Holmes and Jorgensen, 1971).

If one is building a theory of behavior, what kinds of limits are involved in such narrow selection of experimental/control groups? How representative with regard to such gross variables as age, economic background, and intelligence are these students, and would one expect findings based on them to generalize to the rest of the population? The answer must be, of course, in terms of whether these restricting factors in the selection indeed affect the variables that are being studied. If the answer is negative, then very little problem exists. Indeed, if the only effect of restricting one's sample to undergraduate psychology students is restricting variance in the variables under study, then the experimental results may actually *underestimate* true relationships, a favorable circumstance for generalizability (Horst, 1966: ch. 26). However, it is not possible to know the effects of this type of selection without knowledge about the causal structure of the variables in the population to which one wants to generalize. If being a 21-year-old male college student in a prestigious institution of higher education is unrelated to the independent and dependent variables of interest, the external validity of the experiment is not problematic. However, one suspects that the more social and the less psychological the social psychological experi-

ment, the less tenable this assumption is. We know that college student samples are likely to differ significantly from the general population on variables such as age, intelligence, values, and so forth—variables many social psychologists think important as mediating relationships. Experience levels and expectations of students, especially self-selected students in sociology and psychology courses, may differ markedly from what is found in the rest of the population, or in older age groups.

If one takes a broad view of what is meant by replication, then studies using college student subjects can serve as reasonable first studies. That is, if experiments are done not only on students, but also with old people, children, and members of various religious groups, in other contexts, in other cultures, and so on, and if findings are consistent across all of these experiments, then the relative imperviousness of the relationship to sample differences suggests external validity. The tradition for such replication in social and psychological science is extremely weak. Replications typically tend to be done in a way that guarantees the same set of selection factors will operate (i.e., with other psychology students required to participate in experiments for course credit), and when findings do replicate the experimenter may delude himself into thinking that the external validity of findings has been enhanced.

If interactions exist between the characteristics of one's sample and the independent variables under study, then the comments made above are even more critically important, whether one uncovers significant relations between variables with college students or not. If one unwittingly discovers relationships which hold only for college students (or any other highly idiosyncratic group) it is of obvious importance that it be shown that the relationship is not a general one. If a relationship does not hold for college students but does in a more heterogeneous population, the importance of replication with a non-college-student sample is obvious. Unfortunately, if one only uses college students in experiments, findings of the latter sort will never be discovered.

The issues associated with the problems of sampling are such that no simple solutions exist. In a sense, it is impossible to know, without testing, what the limitations of sampling are for extrapolation of findings. Indeed, it is just this circumstance that militates for carefully considered replication studies as a vital part of all research design. In addition, the problem of sampling is not easily divorced from additional problems of external validity discussed below.

Possibly the more serious problems which bear on the external validity of experiments are associated with limitations that are rarely given much attention. The first of these refers back to the problem of conceptualization of the variable and its empirical measurement. Many variables that are used in social and psychological studies may not be measured well, and in order to arrive at what is called manipulation of a condition, there may be no direct measurement at all. Consider a variable such as anxiety. Suppose an investigator wants to study the effect of anxiety on problem-solving, where anxiety is to be manipulated in the experiment. Usually this is done by exposing the subjects in the experimental groups to stimuli that are expected to create the anxiety. For example, events are staged or dupes are used to create circumstances that presumably will raise the subjects' anxiety levels. For example, the experimenter might create a situation where it appears there is a fire or a riot going on outside the laboratory, or one might suggest a person is inadequate for the task he is going to face. The question that then needs to be asked (aside from questions of ethics) is whether or not the anxiety of the experimental subjects was really raised. The experimenter might check on whether the manipulations "took" through paper-and-pencil measures presumed to measure anxiety but obviously not during the experiment. Possibly there could be access through more direct physiological measures, such as galvanic skin response. However, more direct measures of this sort may be difficult to use without arousing the subject's suspicion as to the true purpose of the experiment, in the same way that asking questions about one's anxiety may be suggestive to the subjects.

Assuming one can probe to determine whether or not the manipulation has caused something to occur, one still is faced with determining exactly what it was that was manipulated. For example, while the intention of the experimenter may be to alter the state of anxiety of the experimental subjects, instead of or in addition to this, he or she may alter their irritability, emotionality, fear, or alertness. As Ax (1953) has shown, physiological responses appear to be very similar for a whole gamut of emotions including excitement, anger, fear, joy, and elation, so that physiological arousal measures alone would seem inadequate for determining the emotional status of the subjects.

In addition to eliciting an emotional state different from the one posited, the manipulation may create demand characteristics or evaluation apprehension which in turn may affect the dependent variable(s) under study. While technically these are problems which affect internal validity, they represent a class of problems which also jeopardizes external validity, to a degree which is a function of the strength of the relation between other variables and the dependent variable, and whether or not there is an interaction between the true independent variable of interest and those unwittingly manipulated. If the dependent variable Y changes *only* when X is present along with some W, an unobserved, unwanted but unwittingly manipulated variable, external validity may be nil. Or, if X does not interact with W (but where W is due to X), and W has a strong effect on Y, one will necessarily (wrongly) attribute all the effect (or the lack of effect) on Y to the independent variable X. That is, if in Figure 1, the path from W to Y (labeled "d") is significant, external validity is jeopardized. On the other hand if the manipulation X' causes some unwanted W but the path from W to Y is zero, there is no problem with external validity.

One should try to assure that the manipulation of X' does indeed arouse the desired X by using multiple manipulation checks where possible (i.e., pencil-and-paper measures, physiological measures, and so on). Then assuming no unwanted W(s) were also manipulated along with X, one can use structural equation techniques to estimate the effect X has on Y (Costner, 1971). One also can try to measure whether other effects due to evaluation apprehension or other experimental arrangements exist *assuming* one knows and can measure all of them—an unlikely assumption. And as Wuebben et al. (1974: 253) point out, experiments designed to assess demand characteristics may themselves create additional demand characteristics.

Another problem associated with the experimental manipulation has to do with the magnitude or strength of the stimulus that is presented. One way of describing a finding of an experiment is to state something like the following: "Since the experimental group(s) differ significantly from the control group(s), it is inferred that the hypothesized relationships between problem-solving

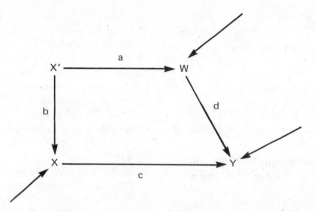

Figure 1 Causal structure indicating how the experimental manipulation X'
can have effects on some unwanted, unmeasured variable W, as well as on X itself

ability and anxiety is demonstrated." However, a competing interpretation of the same experiment might be: "An experimental manipulation was devised in which the level of anxiety was raised to a strength sufficient to interfere with problem-solving ability." Note that this second interpretation treats the experiment as a limiting case; that is, the relationship may be relatively unique to this experimental demonstration. Phrased more directly, the experimental manipulation of anxiety may be relatively extreme and indeed beyond the normal scope of experience in which the more general theory from which the hypothesis is drawn would be expected to operate. Extreme conditions of almost any type presumably can have "significant effects" on variables to which they may be only weakly related. Thus, have the experimenters shown that a relationship exists in the range of behavior and involving magnitudes of relationship which are meaningful for theory, or has the experimenter merely shown, as suggested in the criticism, that a stimulus can be raised to such an extreme level that it "makes a difference"? To the degree that one uses stimulus values which do not exist outside the laboratory, the results are of questionable utility in making generalizations. It should be mentioned that this kind of threat to external validity is especially prevalent in a science that uses statistical significance levels as a criterion for publication of research findings. Were experimental social psychologists encouraged by journal editors to report parametric estimates in addition to significant test results, the experimenter who gets significant results by manipulating extreme con-

ditions of the experimental variable would be exposed.

To get any estimate of magnitude of relationship, of course, would mean conceptualizing variables in what may be unfamiliar terms for many researchers. For example, an experimenter would possibly come to say something that approaches the following: "The experimental manipulation was pretested to determine the amount of anxiety change that occurred. In separate tests it was determined that the anxiety level was raised .84 standard deviations for a sample, using the population distribution on the anxiety score as the basis of standardization." People differ in anxiety, and presumably each person varies in his anxiety score. Relative to such notions of measurement, how much change was there in the variable?

Do the above criticisms when linked with all the others referenced earlier suggest that the experiment is worthless to social psychology? Per se, no. But those who would like to use the experiment exclusively need to pay much closer attention to problems of external validity than they have previously. And as McGuire (1967) has suggested, social psychology needs to shift to a theory-oriented science conducted in more natural settings. What we have pointed out are not problems with experimental design, but rather what Weick (1967) points out are limitations of the experimenters. Too often, they have been seduced by the niceties and "purity" of the laboratory experiment itself; not enough serious attention has been given to problems of external validity. Importantly, limitations on generalizability and the measurement of variables in experiments are no less serious than they are in other research designs used in social psychology and sociology.

REFERENCES

American Psychological Association (1967) Casebook on Ethical Standards for Psychologists. Washington, D.C.

Ax, A. F. (1953) "The physiological differentiation of emotional states." Psychosomatic Medicine 15: 433–442.

Bakan, D. (1966) "The test of significance in psychological research." Psych. Bull. 66: 423–437.

Baron, J. (1971) "Is experimental psychology relevant?" Amer. Psychologist 26: 713–716.

Campbell, D. T. and J. C. Stanley (1963) Experimental and Quasi-Experimental Designs for Research. Chicago: Rand McNally.

Chapanis, A. (1967) "The relevance of laboratory studies to practical situations." Ergonomics 10: 557–577.

Cherns, A. (1969) "Social research and its diffusion." Human Relations 12: 209–218.

Costner, H. L. (1971) "Utilizing causal models to discover flaws in experiments." Sociometry 34: 398–410.

Drabek, T. and E. Haas (1967) "Realism in laboratory simulation: myth or method?" Social Forces 45: 337–346.

Goodwin, L. (1971) "On making social research relevant to public policy and national problem solving." Amer. Psychologist 26: 431–442.

Higbee, K. and G. Wells (1972) "Some research trends in social psychology during the 1960's." Amer. Psychologist 27: 963–966.

Holmes, D. and B. Jorgensen (1971) "Do personality and social psychologists study men more than women?" Representative Research in Social Psychology 2: 71–76.

Horst, P. (1966) Psychological Measurement and Prediction. Belmont, Calif.: Wadsworth.

McGuire, W. J. (1967) "Some impending reorientations in social psychology: some thoughts provoked by Kenneth Ring." J. of Experimental Social Psychology 3: 113–123.

Neufeld, R. J. (1970) "Generalization of results beyond the experimental setting: statistical versus logical considerations." Perceptual and Motor Skills 31: 443–446.

Oakes, W. (1972) "External validity and the use of real people as subjects." Amer. Psychologist 27: 959–962.

Orne, M. T. (1962) "On the social psychology of the psychological experiment: with particular reference to demand characteristics and their implications." Amer. Psychologist 17: 776–783.

Rosenthal, R. (1966) Experimenter Effects in Behavioral Research. New York: Appleton-Century-Crofts.

——and R. L. Rosnow [eds.] (1969) Artifact in Behavioral Research. New York: Academic Press.

Sanford, N. (1970) "Whatever happened to action research?" J. of Social Issues 26: 3–23.

Schultz, D. P. (1969) "The human subject in psychological research." Psych. Bull. 72: 214–228.

Silverman, I. (1971) "Crisis in social psychology: the relevance of relevance." Amer. Psychologist 26: 583–584.

Skellie, A., M. Lipsey, and J. Gordon (1971) "Research and relevance: psychology's potential for concern." APA Proceedings 6: 405–406.

Smart, R. (1966) "Subject selection bias in psychological research." Canadian Psychologist 7: 115–121.

Walster, G. W. and T. A. Cleary (1970) "A proposal for a new editorial policy in the social sciences." Amer. Statistician 24: 16–19.

Weick, K. (1967) "Promise and limitations of laboratory experiments in the development of attitude change theory," pp. 51–75 in M. Sherif and C. W. Sherif (eds.) Attitude, Ego-Involvement and Change. New York: John Wiley.

Wuebben, P. L., B. C. Straits, and G. I. Schulman (1974) The Experiment as a Social Occasion. Berkeley: Glendessary.

SECTION 3.4

Evaluation Research

An increasingly popular form of investigation, evaluation research involves an assessment of how well a social program or intervention has worked. For example, a study may be done to assess the effect of school busing on the attitudes of both white and black children. As such, evaluation research is part of a larger branch of research known as applied research. Applied researchers generally focus on solving social problems and developing social policies. The increasing demand for applied research arises from the needs of the public and various governmental agencies for answers to such social problems as poverty and delinquency. Evaluation research emerges out of similar demands for assessments of how well various social interventions have worked.

WHAT IS EVALUATION RESEARCH?

Evaluation research can be defined most simply as research designed to assess program effectiveness. Two features are important: (1) the assessment requires the comparison of program effects with the goals set for the program and (2) the implications of the research are generally spelled out for decision-making purposes (Weiss, 1972:4). These additional definitions of evaluation research may be helpful:

Evaluative research asks about the kind *of change the program views as desirable, the* means *by which this change is to be brought about, and the* signs *according to which such change can be recognized (Suchman, 1967:15).*

Ideally [evaluation research] involves delineating: what exactly was done; with whom; under what circumstances; by whom; at what point in time; with what results; from whose perspective; and whether the benefits were worth the price paid (Weber and Polansky, 1975:183).

DeGeyndt (1970) notes that evaluation research typically involves several focuses: assessment of content (specific techniques and procedures), assessment of process (sequence and pattern of services rendered), assessment of structure (facilities and staffing), assessment of outcomes (changes in individual recipients of services), and assessment of impact (effect on larger target population, emphasizing availability, acceptability and accessibility of services). The most common focus is that on outcomes, particularly in relationship to goals. From these definitions of evaluation research, you can see that evaluation researchers generally presuppose the existence of social change in their efforts to determine the effects of social interventions.

EVALUATION RESEARCH AND BASIC RESEARCH

Although evaluation research is placed in a separate section because of its emphasis on policy, you should not assume that evaluation research differs radically from basic research. In fact, evaluation researchers use the same methodology and tools as do basic researchers; the major difference is the setting and the goal. Researchers in both fields face similar research difficulties, such as reliability, validity, and operationalization.

Analyses by Coleman (1972), Smith (1975), and Weiss (1972) note several differences between basic and evaluation research. First, and most important, basic researchers emphasize the development of a body of cumulative theoretical knowledge with little thought to how that knowledge might be used. Evaluation researchers emphasize the analysis of program effects so that results can aid decision-makers in improving the program. Second, the evaluation researcher answers client-provided questions while the basic researcher answers primarily self-generated questions. As a result, control over the research process is considerably reduced for the evaluation researcher, resulting in more modifications to the research design than is characteristic of basic research.

Third, evaluation researchers generally focus on "what effect" and "what ought to be," while basic researchers focus on "what is." Fourth, evaluation researchers more frequently encounter resistance and political pressure since they must execute their research in an agency that devotes its energy to services rather than research. And fifth, the evaluation researcher emphasizes specific policy answers, while the basic researcher emphasizes generalizability. These differences ultimately derive entirely from the first one: evaluation research and basic research have different goals.

BASIC PROCEDURES

Like other types of research, evaluation research follows a logical process. According to Weiss (1972), several basic steps can be outlined. When the research begins, the purposes of the evaluation must be carefully determined. These could include such reasons as improving the program, comparing the program with other programs, and assessing impact on recipients. Next, the researcher determines the groups to be served by the evaluation. The most likely candidates are the various client groups, but others might include funding agencies, governmental agencies at various levels, directors or project managers, and even scholars.

The evaluator then determines the goals of the program. It is crucial that the program goals be specified early so that the research design can be developed accordingly and so that later disagreements about program effects can be minimized. The goals must be clear, specific, and measurable; short-term goals must be differentiated from long-term goals. Appropriate and acceptable measures for the goals must be developed. This is a time-consuming stage since the researcher must formulate measurements and then determine what constitutes success on these measures. It is difficult, for example, to develop measures for such goals as "to help youth become better citizens."

Now an appropriate research design must be developed. Ideally, the classical experimental design should be employed: an experimental group and a control group, both of them pretested and posttested. Unfortunately, the realities of social service agencies often preclude the use of this design. Evaluators are frequently called in after the program has been instituted to determine its effectiveness. In addition, the use of a control group means withholding treatment from some clients; serious ethical concerns may make such a procedure untenable. Furthermore, the random assignment to experimental and control groups required by the classical experimental design may be both impractical and unethical, since professional ethics require that clients be placed in treatment groups according to their suitability for such treatment. Modifications to the classical experimental design are therefore frequently used. Instead of control groups receiving no treatment, a new treatment may be compared with an already used treatment or multiple groups may be used to examine separate aspects of the new treatment. Such designs as the one-group pretest-posttest or a design comparing two nonrandomly assigned groups are frequently used.

The evaluator should pay attention to utilization and dissemination of the evaluation findings. Many evaluation researchers write a brief report and quickly leave the scene instead of remaining in the agency to provide some concrete ideas about the implications of the results for agency decision-making. The organizations themselves also frequently resist following through on the implications of the study, particularly if negative effects have been uncovered. These difficulties in utilization and dissemination are unfortunate since the real test of evaluation research lies in its impact on social policy.

THE READINGS

The three articles in this section illustrate and expand on the general features of evaluation research. The first article, by Janet Moursund, is an excellent analysis of the importance of goals and goals analysis in getting started with evaluative research. She suggests that the evaluator distinguish research goals from program goals and recognize the correspondence between intended goals and actual goals. Note her use of the "goal triangle," an approach she developed to link long-term goals with short-term goals and the criteria for assessing goal attainment. Perhaps most useful is her analysis of the role of the researcher in determining, measuring, and assessing goals and their attainment. Moursund particularly urges evaluators to become familiar with the problem area and to be as specific as possible regarding goals. Somewhat unique to her contribution is her emphasis that evaluation researchers probe into *why* the results occurred the way they did. Such probing may contribute considerably to more complete understanding of the intended as well as the unintended consequences of the program.

The second article, an example of a published report of an actual evaluation study, reports on the effectiveness of using lawyer-volunteers to assist parolees in adjusting to their release and reintegration into society. John Berman used the classical experimental design, which involved pretesting and posttesting on the outcome measures and random assignment to the lawyer-volunteers and traditional parole supervision. Although he experienced some difficulties in executing the design (such as a high dropout rate), the use of the experimental design is by far superior to the common practice of relying only on administrative anecdotal records or on recipient evaluations of the treatment. Notice, too, that Berman employed triangulation (the use of multiple methods): he used participant observation in a halfway house and interviews with parolees before setting up the experiment. Such procedures increase the validity of the measures and the results. Validity was further enhanced because participants did not know they were part of an evaluation study and because Berman used multiple measures of outcomes.

There still remain a few problems in the parole study. First, the subjects were nominated by parole agents, which injected a selection bias. In addition, because we are not told how many agents were employed (each nominated five men), we do not know how many men Berman began the study with; we know only that "many men had to be dropped" and that in the end 16 men were in the experimental group and 16 were in the control group. A high dropout rate reduces the validity of the results. Third, you should be reminded that sample size influences the statistical significance of the results. With only 16 in each group (and frequently fewer as a result of missing data), differences must be very large to be statistically significant.

Berman notes in his discussion that one possible reason why few effects were discovered was that the parolees had been out of prison an average of about six months before the lawyer-volunteers began their services; perhaps the parolees had already "stabilized" in that time period in terms of the outcome measures and hence the lawyer volunteers were "too late" to do any good. This point illustrates that the evaluation researcher should take extraneous variables into account in both designing and interpreting a study.

The last article is an insightful analysis of the problems evaluation researchers encounter in carrying out their designs. H. Laurence Ross and Murray Blumenthal received a high level of cooperation from persons at high levels in the justice system and received federal backing to do their assessment of alternative sentences for driving while intoxicated and for moving violations. They carefully developed a design employing randomized assignment, but a number of problems occurred. Floods diverted officers from traffic duty, courts became overloaded, police officers used their own discretion instead of following the experimental design, judges exercised their agreed-on right to deviate from prescribed sentences far more often than was expected by the researchers, and defense lawyers heard of the study and obtained continuances into the less stringent sentencing months of the study for their clients.

Note carefully the authors' suggestions for other evaluation researchers, particularly the emphasis on obtaining support for the study at all levels of the organization (instead of just the highest) and the insistence that assignment to treatment groups remain in the hands of the researcher. In the discussion and resolution of ethical issues, Ross and Blumenthal address the principle of the punishment's fitting the crime and the punishment's fitting the criminal; random assignment would involve some violation of these two principles.

All three of the articles in this section illustrate a fundamental feature of evaluation research: the application of basic research methodology to an action setting. It is the action setting, generally inhospitable to research, that produces virtually all of the problems experienced by evaluation researchers. But the action setting is also where research can have policy relevance.

REFERENCES

Coleman, James S.
    1972   Policy Research in Social Science. Morristown: General Learning Press.
DeGeyndt, W.
    1970   "Five approaches for assessing quality of care." Hospital Administration
           15(Winter):21–41.
Smith, H. W.
    1975   Strategies of Social Research: The Methodological Imagination. Englewood
           Cliffs: Prentice-Hall.

Suchman, Edward A.
    1967   Evaluative Research: Principles and Practice in Public Service and Social
            Action Programs. New York: Russell Sage Foundation.
Weber, Ruth E. and Norman A. Polansky
    1975   "Evaluation." Pp. 182–201 in N. A. Polansky (ed.), Social Work Research:
            Methods for the Helping Professions. Chicago: University of Chicago
            Press.
Weiss, Carol H.
    1972   Evaluation Research: Methods for Assessing Program Effectiveness. Engle-
            wood Cliffs: Prentice-Hall.

GETTING STARTED WITH EVALUATIVE RESEARCH

Janet P. Moursund

"We have often been told," comments Robert Bierstedt (1960), "that sociology is a mean and petty science, pursued by people who delight in counting the privies in Pittsburgh and discovering, with the most versatile of techniques, that people with high incomes spend more money than people with low incomes" (p. 5). The same criticism has been made of most of the social sciences. Only a careful attending to and specifying of research goals can rescue social research from this kind of petty irrelevance. No research, whether it is the traditional, laboratory-based experimental study or an in-the-field action study, can realize its full potential unless its planners have carefully considered the goals of the research and the assumptions on which those goals are based. In traditional scientific research, the goal of a given study or project is usually made explicit in the form of a hypothesis or set of hypotheses and can be generally described as "adding to the store of scientific knowledge." However, such a hypothesis is only one small part of the total goal structure underlying the research; more fundamental assumptions about the appropriate scope and thrust of scientific endeavor are always involved.

Scientists make assumptions about the legitimacy of the techniques they will use, the proper relationship between subject and experimenter, or the relative importance of one area of inquiry as compared with another. Moreover, there are always more or less "hidden" goals operating within any research effort—for example, furthering one's career, proving some pet theory, getting significant results so that future projects will receive funding. The total array of individual and collective perceptions of the "why" of any research project is far more intricate and detailed than a simple reading of the research hypotheses would suggest.

PROGRAM EVALUATION

In program evaluation, goals and assumptions are often more complicated and difficult to uncover than they are in more traditional forms of research. The question "Why are we doing this?" may be met with astonishment that the questioner doesn't know such an "obvious" thing or with anger over anyone's daring to question the value or wisdom of an established set of practices. But the question must be asked—and answered—before evaluation can proceed. Lewis Dexter (1966) has commented that much research "is likely to be wasteful because basic questions are not formulated. Therefore, a good deal of research is undertaken which is not pertinent to answering the real source of concern" (p. 9). Formulation of these basic questions, however, is often more difficult than one might expect.

Determining Goals

One of the fundamental goals of program evaluation is to determine whether a project or program is doing what it is intended to do—that is, whether it is meeting its goals. In order to decide whether a goal is being met, one must know what that goal is. In other words, program evaluation actually has two sets of goals: the goals of the evaluation process itself (the research goals) and the goals of the program being evaluated (the program goals). These two sets of goals are inextricably tied together and sometimes overlap, but they are not identical. Indeed, in some instances, they may be antagonistic.

It is generally agreed that one fundamental goal of evaluation research is to determine whether the stated goals of a program are being met. Some researchers have argued that a second and equally valid function of evaluation is to determine whether the stated goals are the actual goals on which the program is operating and, if so, whether these goals are appropriate. That is, in looking at the ways in which program goals are and are not met and the reasons for failure to meet them, the evaluator is in a good position to look also at the goals themselves. Perhaps goal X of a particular program is not being met because it really isn't what the clients (that is, the people the program was intended to serve) want. Perhaps goal Y was specified at the insistence of a powerful client lobby but is seen by the professional staff as harmful in the long run. It may be the duty of the evaluator to point out such conflicts and to work for restating, adjusting, abandoning, or adding to the list of formal program goals.

What this means, of course, is that the process of evaluation is circular. We can't evaluate until we have something to work with, but ideally the "something" with which we work should have emerged from the evaluation process. Scriven's (1967) distinction between formative and summative research may be helpful in this context. Formative research goes on during the planning and developmental stages of a program and is an integral aspect of goal setting. Summative research, on the other hand, takes place after the program is over (or after it has been running some predetermined length of time) and is aimed at determining whether program goals have been met. Unfortunately for the neatness of such a distinction, most programs don't seem to function this

way. Evaluation is used at many points along the way, and may often serve simultaneously in a formative and a summative way. Indeed, it seems desirable that this should be so: if one is to go to the considerable trouble and expense involved in carrying out research, as much information as possible should be gained—and used—from the data gathered. It would seem unnecessarily wasteful to study what some program should aim at without looking also at how close it is coming to those desired goals. Similarly, summative research should not only indicate whether goals are or are not being met but also give some hints as to why or why not and suggest the relative appropriateness of various goals in the context of the program's success or failure in reaching them.

Where to Start?

Program planning and program evaluation, then, seem to be inextricably bound together. Each one feeds into the processes of the other; neither makes much sense by itself. Suchman's (1967) conceptualization of this process is shown in Figure 1. There is no "beginning" to the process characterized in this way. Wherever we cut into the circle, we are assuming a previous step. But we have to begin somewhere, and traditionally one starts with setting up, or ascertaining, the goals of the program one wishes to evaluate.

Having decided to do this, though, we run into other problems. First, whose goals are we going to use? Even if we limit our discussion at this point to openly held goals, there still may be differences of opinion among concerned individuals. The professional staff can probably tell us, more or less explicitly, what they are trying to do in the program. The clients can probably tell us what they want, and, surprisingly often, what they want is not quite what the staff is trying to give them. We can ask various people in the community at large (who support the program through taxes and/or good will or at least allow the program to survive) what they think the program is "for," and again we will find a variety of conflicting answers.

Let's say, for instance, that a team of researchers have obtained funds for an evaluation of the mental therapy program at Texyork State Hospital. They assume, with some justification, that the basic goal of the hospital's program is to cure as many mentally ill people as quickly and as permanently as possible. A goal of the research project is, there-

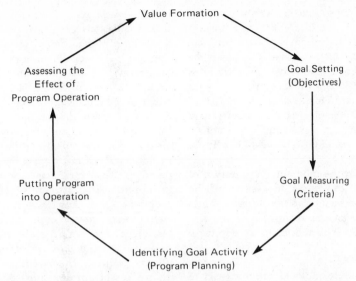

Figure 1   The circular process of program planning and program evaluation (Figure 1 in Chapter 3 of *Evaluative Research: Principles and Practice in Public Service and Social Action Programs,* by Edward A. Suchman, Ph.D. © 1967 by Russell Sage Foundation, New York; reprinted by permission)

fore, to determine whether such quick and permanent cures are happening. Probably underlying this research goal is an unstated assumption that the research findings will be used to further the hospital goals; that is, program evaluators usually assume that their research will be used to facilitate future progress toward the goals of the program being evaluated.

So far, it seems reasonable that the research goals and the goals of the program are both overlapping and compatible. But now let's jump several months into the future, when results are beginning to come in. The researchers interpret their data as showing that none of the therapeutic techniques currently in use at Texyork is working, that hospital staff could be cut back by 20 percent with no loss to patient well-being, and that patients could best be helped by major changes in ward routine. When these findings are communicated to hospital administrators, all feelings of cooperation and mutual concern disappear, and both researchers and hospital personnel become aware of some of their not-so-obvious goals. The researchers hope to make some "interesting" discoveries; they want publishable findings to further their careers. Hospital staff members want job security with the added comfort of some "scientific evidence" that they are doing all

they can to help their patients. It is unfortunate that human goals such as these are often regarded as "bad" or "self-serving" so that people are reluctant to admit to them. Such reluctance leads to defensiveness, which further disrupts communication and promotes conflict. The kinds of conflicts that can occur when these sorts of differences emerge midway or more in a research effort can be very damaging indeed—to the project and to the morale of everyone involved. It is far better to anticipate such differences at the outset and to bring them out in the open; the pain and difficulty of initial honesty is usually outweighed by the gains in communication and cooperation and the overall smoothness with which the research can then go forward.

PROBLEMS IN DESIGNING PROGRAM EVALUATION

Weiss (1972) has suggested four major problems in determining the real goals to be dealt with in evaluation research. First, the goals of the program being evaluated may be quite hazy and ambiguous. Second, even when goals are stated, the list may not be exhaustive; the program often aims toward objectives not included among its "official" goals. Third, most programs are fairly complex, with different parts doing different things. It is difficult to decide how the subgoals of each program part interact to accomplish the overall goals of the program. Finally, good evaluative research must be as concerned with *why* things happen as with *whether* they happen. This qualitative aspect of evaluation is usually neglected in proportion to the difficulty of carrying it out, but it is a crucial part of evaluation; its importance can hardly be overstated.

Putting aside for the moment the question of getting at the "why" as well as the "whether," the other goal problems seem to relate to two issues: differences in values and confusion over long- and short-term goals. Let's look at each of these in turn.

Differences in Values

Goals are always formulated on the basis of values, either implicit or explicit. Without values, there can be no goals and no programs. The values may be as diffuse as "I believe in a better world" or "My family must be taken care of" or as specific as "People who have been in prison have a right to equal employment opportunities." Specific values are "branches" of more general ones: "Exconvicts should have equal employment opportunities because they're people and all people have basic rights that shouldn't be violated."

Differences in goals often arise because of differences in values. Consider, for example, the problem of criminal rehabilitation. I may believe that exconvicts, being people, have a right to seek employment; my nextdoor neighbor may believe with equal fervor that felons abdicate their social rights when they choose to violate society's laws. The potential employer may value the satisfaction of his customers over everything else; the parole officer may be honestly convinced that the best thing for the paroled prisoner is a year or so of unskilled labor until "he gets his feet under him again." Each of these values may lead to a different idea of the appropriate goals for a prison rehabilitation program. Discussions about such goals will be profitless until the differences in underlying values are made explicit.

Confusion over Long- and Short-Term Goals

Closely related to some of these value differences is confusion over long- and short-term goals. I may agree with the parole officer that, in the long run, the ultimate goal in prison rehabilitation is that the exconvict return to society as a self-actualizing human being, but we may disagree on the short-term steps leading to that end. The parole officer and the businessman may agree that it is important to maintain a stable and trustworthy business community, but they may disagree over the means for reintegrating society's "losers" into that community. Other philosophies and value sets are quite incompatible in any time span: "Lock him up forever; he's not a man but an animal" as opposed to "Crime reflects sickness in society and in individuals, and sickness can be cured." Many programs—especially those in the area of social welfare—can never hope to operate within the framework of a set of goals and/or values that is pleasing or acceptable to everyone in the community. In planning the evaluation process, potential differences of opinion must be anticipated; if the particular goal or value framework of the program is made clear at the start, the program's success or failure can be understood in the context of this framework.

Overt and Covert Goals

Another major conflict that should be dealt with in specifying goals of both the program and the evaluation process is the conflict between overt and covert goals. All of us work on the basis of some covert goals, whether or not we are aware of them. As a teacher, I am concerned with keeping my job, being seen as a competent professional, and maintaining the respect and liking of my students and colleagues, as well as with furthering the stated goals of the university within which I work; but I may be unaware of the degree to which one or more of these concerns affects my perceptions. Fortunately, covert goals often mesh without conflict into the overt-goal structure with which a program is concerned. But sometimes this doesn't happen. Conflict between overt and covert goals may occur in the context of personal versus institutional needs or as a function of incompatible value systems held by various groups of people. Again using myself as an example, what if I get a call from the Athletic Director, requesting that I raise the grade I gave a star football player so he can remain eligible for the big game next week? Such a value conflict may make me sharply aware of goals and values that had been unclear to me before. Another common sort of value conflict occurs when a professional or professional group holds a value that is rejected by the community. The professionals may set up a number of overt program goals that the taxpayers will approve of, but tacitly work toward meeting private goals that might not gain such support. Some local Planned Parenthood Association groups, for example, have been accused of working more or less covertly for size limitation for all families, whereas the community's goal for the Association was simply assistance in family planning.

THE RESEARCHER

Where does the researcher fit into all of this? Clearly, his own goals and values and attitudes are a part of the overall picture. Here, again, it may be useful to emphasize one of the major differences between the older, more traditional view of research and the more recent approach. In the former, there is an intensive effort to maintain objectivity—to separate the researcher from his subject matter. Values, as such, have no place in the traditional research scheme—or, perhaps more accurately, the supreme value is the acquisition of knowledge to which all else is secondary. The declaration of objectivity, however, does not ensure its existence. In evaluation research, as in most applied social science, there is a growing recognition that value orientations are as inherent in research as in any other human activity. "We have realistically recognized, of course, that a complete objectivity, though a methodological desideratum, is nevertheless for any individual a psychological impossibility and that what we should hope for is not a total absence of bias but rather an overt awareness of it" (Bierstedt, 1960, p. 8). The researcher cannot hope to suppress his own attitudinal response as he looks at the array of attitudes, of feelings, and of specified and unspecified (but very real) goals that come from people around him. He must clarify his own thinking in order to be aware of the ways in which his values may bias his perception. His first—and continuing—job must be to ask himself "Where do I stand on this? What do I think this program is all about? What are the values I hold that cause me to feel this way?" As he gathers information (and opinions) throughout the circular course of the evaluation process, he should keep close tabs on his own internal reactions. He must be aware of changing assumptions within himself. Only if he has a clear access to his own internal value structure can he deal in a clean and uncluttered fashion with the values of others.

Understanding the Problem Area

In addition to the ability to understand and be aware of his own interpersonal processes, the competent researcher must have a broad understanding of the problem area with which his particular research project is to deal. He should know the major research and theory upon which the program is based. He should be aware of the variables that could affect outcomes for individuals and groups. If he is in a mental health setting, for instance, he should know some of the current thinking about the nature of mental illness, he should have a working understanding of the kinds of therapy being practiced, and he should be aware of the implications of mental health and mental illness (however defined) on both the client and those with whom the client interacts. Every bit of information is grist for his mill; each piece fits into his overall judgment; each fact or idea or opinion should be (at least potentially) assessed and accounted for. Understanding the problem area is especially important for a project planner or administrator, but it is also important for the "low-status" staff member. The more each member of the research team knows about the basic facts and theoretical framework of the problem area, the more thorough and sensitive will be the end product of the evaluation effort.

Andrew (1967) discusses the problems that often arise when a researcher unfamiliar with the problem area is called in to plan an evaluation project. Often the research is designed beautifully, with all kinds of contingencies anticipated and taken care of; but, because the design is so sophisticated, it calls for more subjects (or time, or research personnel) than are realistically available. However, the research specialist is so convincing in his arguments that the project is begun, and it breaks down in midstream. At this point, a bubble-gum-and-bailing-wire repair job is done: various experimental groups are reorganized and made smaller, some of the restrictions on who may and may not be included are lifted, and definitions are changed; the result is shoddy, ambiguous, and generally dissatisfying. It is far better, in the long run, that the research planner also be (or begin as) a specialist in some subject area in which he will later carry out his research. Even then, learning more about the sphere of activities in which he will be expected to function is an unfinished and unfinishable task for the researcher; it is part of the ongoing evaluation process, and it plays a crucial role in determining a project's success or failure.

Setting Up Evaluation Objectives

The researcher must be careful not to become so general and idealized in his approach that he avoids the specific and immediate evaluation demands: to set up objectives (however tentative or temporary) by means of which the assessment process can begin. To do this, he might use a checklist for gathering information from various sources. Suchman (1967) has provided one such list. He asks:

1. *What kinds of objectives is the program concerned with? That is, are we primarily interested in behaviors, in knowledge, or in attitudes? Is the program trying to maintain these objectives or to change them?*
2. *Who is the target of the program—individuals, small groups, the whole community? Does the program deal with the target directly or indirectly through an intermediate target group?*
3. *What is the time span with which we are concerned? Is the program primarily interested in immediate results, or in long-range change or maintenance?*
4. *Are program objectives unitary or multiple? In either*

long- or short-range terms, are we talking about a single goal or a cluster of goals?
5. *How great must the effect of the program be before we consider it a success? Must it reach all of its potential target or only some proportion of it? Must we be able to observe major changes, or will we be content with small ones?*
6. *Finally, what are the means to the program goals? Who is to carry out the program, what will they do, and how shall we measure their success? This latter question leads to the problem of setting up criteria, which must be clearly distinguished from setting up the goals themselves.*

As the checklist is used, an outline of the program begins to emerge, and the researcher can begin to think in terms of a consensus of opinion and values. If the evaluation process is going on during the planning of the program, the researcher may have the opportunity to interact with groups of individuals who represent conflicting points of view. The researcher can facilitate the formulation of specific program goals that are acceptable to all three major groups: the receivers of services, the deliverers of services, and the community as a whole. Ultimately, though, the researcher's own values and assumptions will be called into play, along with those of the people responsible for planning and directing the program itself. It is the joint responsibility of program planners and researchers to translate what is said by members

	Receivers		Deliverers		Community
	Client	Client Intimate	Program Staff	Other Professionals	
External, Observable Effects	fewer children fewer abortions more stable marriage	other children in family: higher school achievement		lower caseloads for emotionally disturbed children and for welfare mothers	lower overall birthrate lower percent of taxes going to welfare costs
Internal, Inferable Effects	happier increased ego-strength	other children in family: better emotional adjustment	feelings of satisfaction	less frustration due to having no referral agency for family-planning problems	

Figure 2 Possible effects of a family-planning clinic on various groups in the community

of the three major concerned groups—receivers, deliverers, and community—into a clear set of objectives with related criteria for meeting the objectives. One way of making the goals and values of the various groups explicit is to conceptualize which groups a project might affect and what kinds of effects (both desired and otherwise) might occur. While the number and type of such groups may be slightly different for different programs, the diagram in Figure 2 is probably general enough to fit most circumstances. Filling in all the cells of this diagram (as has been done in Figure 2 for a hypothetical family-planning clinic) will help both program administrators and research planners to be more actively aware of the scope of the project and the possible areas into which the evaluation process might extend. Too often, researchers restrict themselves to studying a program's effects on a designated client group, ignoring effects on others whose lives are touched by the program or by program-related activities. This can be a serious problem for two reasons: First, important program effects outside the client group may never be recognized; second, actual client behaviors may often be explained or understandable only in terms of related behaviors of nonclients.

THE "GOAL TRIANGLE"

We have discussed the many kinds of goals a program might have, the likelihood of inconsistent or conflicting goals, and the need for specifying a program's goals in order to proceed with program evaluation. Another way of looking at goals may facilitate a more concrete approach to this problem. The broad, general, and often long-term goals of a particular program may be seen as the apex of a triangle. Under this apex is a set of desired, often short-term program outcomes that are more specific, more closely tied to actual behaviors, and are seen as contributing to the program's ultimate goal(s). At the base of the triangle are criteria by which one can determine (theoretically) whether the objectives have been reached. The criteria are strictly tied to measurable behaviors and form the direct link in the research procedure between thinking and hypothesizing, on the one hand, and actual real-world happenings, on the other. (This approach is detailed more fully in CORD, the National Research Training Manual, published by the Teaching Research Division of the Oregon State System of Higher Education.)

Outcomes and Criteria

In evaluation planning, one moves from specifying the goals of a program to specifying the outcomes that are stepping stones to those goals or that may indicate in a concrete way whether goals are being met. When the outcomes have been specified, the next step is to choose criteria by means of which we can determine whether the desired outcomes are present. To interpret the results of the research, the chain works in the other direction: the criteria are looked at directly, and the presence or absence of the outcomes is inferred from the criteria. From this information, in turn, conclusions are drawn about the degree to which goals are being met (see Figure 3).

Consider, for example, an elementary school reading program. The ultimate goals might be (1) to develop enough reading ability to be able to move into intermediate school programs and (2) to begin to be able to enjoy some activities in and out of school that involve reading skills. The more specific outcome level might include such things as (1) to be able to recognize a basic 600-word vocabulary, (2) to be able to sound out new words according to the rules of phonics, (3) to be able to read and understand material at the third-grade level of difficulty, (4) to give evidence of enjoying the activity of reading, and (5) to show eagerness to improve reading skills. Each of these objectives is logically connected to one or both of the ultimate goals.

Setting up criteria, at the base of the triangle, is often more difficult. Good criteria have two primary characteristics: they must relate logically to the desired objectives, so that satisfying a criterion clearly implies that the objective has been attained, and they must be clear enough so that it is easy to tell whether they have been satisfied. It is usually easy to find criteria with one of these characteristics, but hard to find them with both.

Ideally, every criterion should be defined operationally—that is, in terms of the set of operations that must be performed if the criterion is to be met. Since these operations must be externally observable, a properly spelled-out operational definition leaves no room for ambiguity: either it is met or it isn't. But choosing a criterion that can be defined this clearly may mean loosening the link between criterion and outcome. In the reading-program example, one might choose as a criterion the passing of a standardized test of reading com-

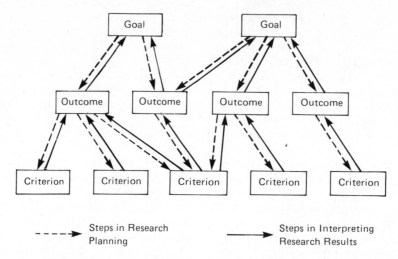

Figure 3   The triangle of inference in evaluation research

prehension. The outcome of the criterion is clear: either a student makes a certain numerical score or he doesn't. But the logical relationship to the objective (reading and understanding third-grade material) is not as well-founded. The student may not be motivated to do well on the test; he may be frightened and "clutch" in the testing situation; he may have been coached specifically for that test so that his performance exceeds his actual reading ability; the test may be scored on the basis of certain points not necessarily relevant to reading ability; and so on. If any of these factors are present, the satisfying of the criterion does not necessarily imply that the objective has been met.

On the other hand, the criterion may connect logically with the objective or even be the same as the objective, but it may be very difficult to determine whether the criterion has been satisfied. "Be able to read and demonstrate comprehension of new material at the third-grade level of difficulty" may be set up as a criterion as well as an objective. But what is meant by "demonstrating comprehension"? How complete must "comprehension" be? What is the "third-grade level of difficulty"? Does it refer to the length and/or number of words used, the complexity of the concepts dealt with, or what?

Setting up adequate criteria usually involves a compromise between the need for clearly defined terms and the need for unambiguous and indisputable relationships to objectives. To manage this task well calls for wide knowledge of the variables involved, a creative and innovative approach, and a great deal of self-discipline.

As you begin to consider specific evaluation problems, you will see that it is not always possible to separate goals, outcomes, and criteria. Often the dividing lines will be very fuzzy, and sometimes one category will drop out or collapse into another. For example, a goal of a school's hot-lunch program might be the elimination of poor nutrition as a cause of poor academic work. One of the desired outcomes of the program could be that all children whose family income falls below a certain figure receive a hot lunch every day. No additional criterion is needed for this outcome; it is in itself an observable event. Another sort of collapsing might occur in the case of a socio-medical aid station in a big-city ghetto. A goal of this program could be the detection and cure of venereal disease carriers. In this case, a desired outcome might be constructed by specifying some number of cases to be dealt with over a given period of time, but this is really very little different from the goal itself. Goals and outcomes may collapse into each other, as may criteria and outcomes. In fact, it is not impossible that all three, under some circumstances, might collapse into one observable event, which is in itself the raison d'etre of the program.

Hypothetical Constructs

We should not leave the matter of definitions, criteria, and so on without touching on the notion of hypothetical constructs. This term is discussed in some detail in an article by McCorquodale and Meehl (1948). A hypothetical construct is some nonobservable entity or process that we assume to be present. We tend to posit hypothetical constructs very often as interventions between criterion and outcome in research. In fact, many outcomes, as stated, are hypothetical constructs—for instance, "enjoying the activity of reading." We can observe behaviors such as smiling when it's time to read, or choosing a book over a puzzle during a free time, or discussing books with friends, and from these we infer the presence of the nonobservable construct "enjoyment of reading." There is nothing wrong with using hypothetical constructs. Our research would be dull and barren without them. Indeed, it is frequently, if not always, the hypothetical construct that leads our carefully controlled procedures back to the real world in which we are interested. But it is very important that we be aware of using them. One of the most common design errors involves confusing a hypothetical construct with the observable data from which it is inferred.

Negative Outcomes

We have been talking so far about the kinds of outcomes that we hope to see or to demonstrate as a result of our program's functioning. We will look, in later chapters, at how to determine whether these outcomes really do happen and whether they are a result of the program in which we are interested. But many things can happen as a consequence of the operation of a program, and not all of them need be desired. The good researcher should be aware of the possibility of negative outcomes and take them into consideration in his total evaluation of a program.

Negative outcomes may, for research purposes, be divided into two categories: (1) those that are directly related to the stated positive outcomes (and usually have the effect of masking or partially concealing positive results) and (2) those that are not directly related to stated outcomes (and may thus completely evade the evaluation effort unless they are specifically tracked down).

As an example of the first sort of negative effect, consider a tutorial program on a college campus. The goal of the program is to improve students' academic functioning, and the program seems to be succeeding in that students report they

are studying better, learning more, and so on as a result of the program. One of the specific desired outcomes of the program is that students' GPAs be improved, and here problems have cropped up; in spite of the encouraging feedback from people involved, students' GPAs are generally unchanged after one year of participation in the program. The researcher who both understands the area in which he is working and is on the lookout for negative outcomes may spot the cause of the discrepancy. Students in the program have told their advisers about it, and many of the advisers have then assumed that students were receiving academic advice as well as tutorial services from the program. The advisers stopped helping the students, and, as a result, the students frequently found themselves registered in courses that were too difficult, irrelevant, or otherwise inappropriate for them. Their grades in these classes were poor. Here we can see two kinds of outcomes, one positive and one negative. The students did improve their study skills, but (as an indirect result of the program) their advisers stopped helping them. This lack of advice produced course loads that resulted in poorer grades for the students, thus canceling out or masking the effects of the increased academic competence they had acquired.

As stated before, evaluation research should concern itself not just with what a program does or does not do but with why results occur. In this example, running a statistical test to see if the hypothesis "Student grades would improve as a result of participation in the program" was upheld would have led to the erroneous conclusion that the program was having no effect. A more thoughtful consideration of what was really going on would have two consequences: (1) more valid conclusions about the effectiveness of the program and (2) changes in the program (or external to the program) so that the negative results could be avoided in the future.

Consideration of negative outcomes should occur at every stage of evaluation, from the initial goal-defining period right through the analysis and interpretation of evaluation data. No other aspect of evaluation is more important in making the evaluation process truly circular—that is, making it lead to program improvement.

When a negative outcome masks or confuses data so that results of evaluation don't "come out" as expected, there is usually some surprise on the part of the researcher and some natural attempts to dig further, to find out "why." In this sense, such negative outcomes call attention to themselves. The other sort of negative result, the kind not directly related to stated objectives, is more subtle. Unless the researcher thinks of it himself and decides to check it out, it can go undiscovered almost indefinitely. And, since it is undiscovered, the program will not be changed so as to do away with it. For instance, consider a work-release program for inmates of a state prison. The objectives of the program have to do with rehabilitation of prisoners, prison morale, post-prison employment, and so on, and most of these objectives are being met in relatively satisfactory fashion. But let's say that nobody thought to ask about the effects of the program on those men not included. Let's further hypothesize that, if we looked at the records of men initially considered for the program but later rejected, we would find that they get into trouble more often, are less often given parole, do more poorly on work assignments, and so on than those men never considered for work release at all. We might conclude that a negative effect of the program is to embitter those men who had hoped to be in it but who hadn't made it. This negative outcome, which might affect a sizable number of men, would go completely undetected if someone didn't suspect it and actively seek it out. The extreme importance of being familiar with and competent in the setting in which evaluation takes place simply cannot be overemphasized.

Evaluation Backlash

Another negative effect that might be overlooked in setting up an evaluation scheme can be characterized as "evaluation backlash." Evaluation backlash usually falls into category one—a negative outcome that tends to mask or confuse program effects. However, evaluation backlash can also be a category-two effect. Evaluation backlash can interfere with the evaluation process or with the program itself so that stated goals and objectives are not met or are met to a lesser degree.

Evaluation backlash most often occurs when various groups—usually clients or staff—become annoyed, frightened, or confused by whatever data-gathering procedures have been chosen for the evaluation process. For example, I was involved in a project designed to test the effectiveness of psychotherapy with hospitalized schizophrenics. One criterion we used was scores on a battery of personality tests. To measure "progress" over a long period of time (the project ran for more than five years), the tests had to be administered and scored at regular intervals. Some were given every three months, and some every six months. After the second or third testing, evaluation backlash began to set in. Some of the tests were quite long (one had 566 questions!), and the patients were tired of them and didn't want to be bothered any more. The validity of the criterion (the relationship between the measured test scores and the hypothetical construct of "improvement" or "progress") could be seriously questioned.

Such repeated testing or interviewing of the same person has the potential for another kind of evaluation backlash: Will people remember the questions and the answers they gave from the last time they were tested or interviewed? To the extent that they do remember and that the remembering affects their response, the validity of the procedure is again brought into question. . . .

Sometimes the presence of evaluation can change the effects of the program. As a result of being interviewed, a client may think or feel or behave differently; the data gathering can become, in effect, part of the program. This is not so bad if the effects of the presence of evaluation are positive (though they can make the researcher's job more difficult, since such effects are often hard to isolate and evaluate), but the results may be negative as well as positive. An example might be a potential client who is given a lengthy initial interview and is so threatened by it that he doesn't come back again. The mechanics of the evaluation have effectively prevented him from benefiting from the program. Another possible adverse effect of the evaluation process is that staff members may have to use precious time to fill out forms for the evaluation, or they may be antagonized or frustrated by the research itself or by a member of the research staff and pass that anger on to the clients.

The point of this discussion is that the researcher must carefully consider the effects of his measurement procedures. The cook, directed to add a tablespoon of molasses to her recipe, must take into account that much of the ingredient will stick to the tablespoon and never get into the pudding unless she is careful to scrape it off—she must be aware of the effects of her technique of measurement. Similarly, the researcher must take care lest his measurement techniques interfere with or augment the actual program. A good rule of thumb is that the actual data gathering should be as simple, as nondemanding of clients, staff, or others, and as quickly accomplished as possible. Obviously, this will involve a compromise; the researcher would like to gather much more detailed information than is practical. Although the researcher should always consider what is ideal, in practice he must begin with a plan that he sees as a reasonable compromise between what he would like to know and what the data sources would like to give him. He must be sensitive to feedback about his data-gathering procedures and willing to change them if they turn out to be too difficult for clients or staff members to accept.

PILOT STUDIES

Pilot studies are often used in many areas of research, particularly when the area being investigated is relatively complex and/or large. The pilot study is used to gather information related to the main thrust of the research—information that is helpful (and sometimes even necessary) in planning or carrying out the research but that is not necessarily part of the main stream of goal-outcome-criterion that we have been considering so far. The pilot study is a sort of courier or herald; it precedes the major data-gathering and analysis efforts of the research and generally serves to facilitate those efforts. It is usually on a smaller scale than the main research. It can be carried out in less time by fewer people, involves fewer subjects directly, and costs substantially less than the main project. The pilot study can seldom stand alone; most pilot studies are useful primarily for their contribution to the main project of which they are a part. The pilot study, then, comes by its name appropriately; it does, in a sense, pilot the main research, going ahead to warn of snags and problems and to gather information about unknown or ambiguous areas.

A pilot study is a little research project in itself, in spite of its usual dependency on the parent project. It has goals and sets up criteria for meeting the goals. Unlike evaluation research, though, pilot-study goals often end when some characteristic of the group under consideration is discovered or some problem is identified.

Notice that in program evaluation the "goal" is to see whether the goal of the program is being reached. While the pilot study is helpful or necessary to the success of the overall research project, it does not usually relate directly to the goal of the program being evaluated. Also, there will nearly always be a collapsing of "goal" and "outcome" in a pilot study; the study is designed to handle a specific, short-term problem.

Pilot studies can be used in a variety of ways to improve the main research project. Most commonly, they are used to check out some specific factor or feature of the research. A pilot study can be set up to explore some initial conditions of the program being evaluated—some characteristic of the client population, or staff, or other group that might affect the design of the research. A pilot study can answer questions about whether a particular technique or instrument will work, given the structures of the evaluation setting. For example, "Is our questionnaire valid for this population?" "Are people in the community more responsive to telephone or door-to-door contacts?" "Will staff members remember to record their client ratings after each interview?" Most evaluation designs involve the use of a variety of procedures that can benefit from such check-outs.

Pilot studies are sometimes used to look for flaws or "bugs" in the evaluation scheme as a whole. Using a pilot study to check out one aspect of a design requires that the research team be able to identify the potential problem in advance. Occasionally, the research team may feel that their overall scheme is so complex that there are likely to be unexpected problems, "glitches," that they can't anticipate until they see how the whole thing fits together. They might then decide to run a smaller "model" of the design—in essence, to do the project in miniature—just to see where such glitches turn up.

Pilot studies can also be used to gather data of a more descriptive or anecdotal nature than would be desirable for the major part of the evaluation. Such data help the researcher gain insight into some research-related problems and add valuable "flavor" to the drier, more quantitative kinds of information that will be used in later, formalized parts of the research program. Pilot-study data may point the major program evaluation in useful directions that might otherwise be overlooked. "The embryonic state of the field [of program evaluation and "action research"] makes it exceedingly important to accumulate a body of knowledge through accurate observations and descriptions of the relevant social phenomena" (Fairweather, 1967, p. 41). Beginning this accumulation in a pilot study can steer the overall project into the most meaningful areas for formal, quantitative methods later on and can clarify the issue of which of a vast welter of descriptive details are most likely to be productive and relevant in terms of overall-program-goal evaluation.

At this point, you may be wondering why anyone would bother to set up a separate pilot study. If there are things one needs to know, why not just find them out as a part of the main research design? If problems come up, why can't they be solved then and there, rather than anticipating them in some sort of trial-run procedure? There are several advantages, as well as some disadvantages, to using pilot studies.

One of the major advantages in using a pilot study is the saving of time and/or money (for the researcher, they usually amount to the same thing) by finding flaws early in the research process. To have embarked on a whole range of data-gathering activities only to find that the data are of doubtful usefulness because of some error in reasoning—perhaps a failure to take some important point into consideration—can be very expensive indeed. In one study (one that I had a hand in messing up, by the way), the design was intended to explore differences between cohesive and noncohesive student discussion groups. Volunteers were asked to sign up and to indicate the names of preferred group comembers. Researchers constructed the two kinds of groups on the basis of this information. Afterward, the researchers realized that the most popular students had been assigned to "cohesive" groups and the more socially isolated students, not being chosen as preferred comembers, wound up in "noncohesive" groups. Since it was too late to change selection procedures or group membership, the research proceeded; however, all differences between these groups were quite confounded by the absence of differentiation between cohesiveness and members' social status. In other words, if differences between the groups did show up (and in fact they did), it would be impossible to tell whether they came about as a result of differences in group cohesiveness, differences in the social status of group members, or some combination of the two. In this design, it would have made much more sense to run a pilot study of just one or two groups.

The unanticipated error might have shown up and could have been corrected before the major research got under way.

Similarly, a pilot study can provide training ground for the research team. Just as flaws in the design can be worked out with minimal expense in a pilot study, flaws in procedures can be discovered and taken care of. Interviewing techniques can be made uniform to afford better comparability of data in the major study. Inefficiencies in the recording procedure can be discovered before it is too late to change them. Scheduling conflicts, equipment-using skills, and other small details that contribute to a smoothly operating team have a chance to be tried out and improved in the context of a small pilot study in which mistakes don't count quite so heavily as they will later on.

Another major advantage is that a pilot study allows a feasibility check on, or even the actual development of, some technique or instrument. The design of the major evaluation project might depend on the use of a questionnaire developed specifically for the project; it would be foolhardy to allow the success or failure of one's whole design to hang on an untested instrument. Collection of valid data might depend on counselors in the program filling out rating sheets at the end of each client interview. Again, it would seem highly desirable to find out whether the counselors can and will do this regularly before committing oneself to the procedure.

In short, there is seldom a research plan that could not benefit from the use of at least one pilot study to check out some feature or features of its design. Nevertheless, much valuable research has been carried out without pilot studies. How does one decide whether to use a pilot?

First, one can reasonably ask how big the major research is. If it is a small undertaking, to be done relatively quickly, then a pilot study would be rather silly; in a sense, the study serves as its own pilot. A good rule of thumb is that a pilot should be used only when it costs one-third (or less) the cost of the main project and when it will take one-half to one-third (or less) the time to complete as the main study. Otherwise, running a pilot would be rather like sending a destroyer out to escort a tugboat.

If you are setting up a relatively large project, look first at the instruments and techniques you plan to use in gathering and recording your data.

Have they been used before with this kind of population? Are you satisfied with their validity and reliability. . . ? Are the people who are to use them familiar with them and sufficiently competent in their use? If the answer to any of these questions is no, you may need a pilot study.

Finally, look at the overall scheme of the research. Just how complex a plan do you have in mind? At each stage in its execution, are there things you aren't sure of, things that may go wrong? Often we find ourselves so eager to plunge in, so enthusiastic over what we intend to do, that we are too impatient to sit back and engage in an overview. This very enthusiasm can lead to costly errors.

It is, of course, the cost in time and money that often makes us reluctant to bother with pilot studies. They do cost extra money, and they do often delay the main thrust of the research. Moreover, it may be difficult to set up a pilot study in such a way that it won't contaminate the population on whom you intend to carry out the main project. There is no set formula, no single way of deciding when the information potential of a pilot study is great enough to justify the extra time and effort; ultimately, it is a matter for the good judgment of the research planners themselves.

SUMMARY

In planning evaluation research, it is necessary to specify the goals of both the program being evaluated and the research project aimed at accomplishing that evaluation. A clear statement of goals is difficult to make for many reasons, most of which center around differences in value orientations or confusion over long- and short-term goals.

While recognizing the necessity of dealing with goals and values in a broad and long-range sense, the researcher must also think in terms of concrete program objectives. One procedure is to think specifically of the various groups of people who may be affected by the program, asking what the desired outcome(s) of the program might be for each of these groups.

Outcomes are short-range, concrete events that lead to the attainment of a goal or indicate that a goal is in the process of being attained. Whether a particular outcome has occurred is determined by examining the criteria for that outcome; criteria are specific, observable events or behaviors that are amenable to measurement and that are strictly tied to their respective outcomes. An outcome may not be directly observable; it may be a hypothetical construct such as an attitude change or increased employability. By definition, criteria are observable; by observing criterion variables, we determine or infer the occurrence of the outcome.

Outcomes may be negative as well as positive. Negative outcomes may occur in such a way as to interfere with some positive outcome, making it look as though the program is not moving toward its goals. Or, alternatively, negative outcomes may affect people touched by the program in ways not measured by the selected criteria. Evaluation backlash is a kind of negative effect that can work in either of these two ways.

A researcher can check his design, data-gathering techniques, and the overall "flow" of his project through the use of a pilot study. Pilot studies are also helpful in predicting cases of negative outcomes and in suggesting useful areas of inquiry that might otherwise be overlooked.

REFERENCES

Andrew, G.
1976 "Some observations on management problems in applied social research." American Sociologist 2(May): 84–89, 92.

Bierstedt, R.
1960 "Sociology and human learning." American Sociological Review 25(February): 3–9.

Dexter, L. A.
1966 "Impressions about utility and wastefulness in applied social science studies." American Behavioral Scientist 9(June): 9–10.

Fairweather, G. W.
1967 Methods for Experimental Social Innovation. New York: Wiley.

MacCorquodale, K. and P. H. Meehl
1948 "On a distinction between hypothetical constructs and interviewing variables." Psychological Review 55 (March): 95–107.

Scriven, M.
1967 "The methodology of evaluation." In R. W. Tyler, R. M. Gagné, and M. Scriven (eds.), Perspectives of Curriculum Evaluation. AERA Monograph Series on Curriculum Evaluation, #1. Chicago: Rand McNally.

Suchman, E. A.
    1967 Evaluative Research. New York: Russell Sage.

Weiss, C. H.
    1972 Evaluation   Research.   Englewood Cliffs: Prentice-Hall.

AN EXPERIMENT IN PAROLE SUPERVISION

John J. Berman

Since its introduction in the United States in the last quarter of the 19th century, the institution of parole has stimulated a great deal of discussion both pro and con (Caldwell, 1965). The major argument in favor of parole is that it provides a transition period between total institutionalization and total freedom during which an ex-offender can be very carefully counseled and supervised by a parole agent. The agent is supposed to guide the conditionally released person in his/her efforts to reenter society as a law-abiding citizen, while at the same time protecting society by keeping a close watch on this person to make sure he/she does not relapse into criminal behavior (Dressler, 1969). One major argument against parole is that it takes from the courts powers that belong there and places them in the hands of a parole board which is likely to be more susceptible than the courts to political influences. More specifically, it is argued that parole allows a person to avoid punishment which the courts had said he/she ought to receive, and it does not protect the community against the offender for as long a time as the courts had deemed necessary. Another more pragmatic argument against parole is that it simply has not proven to be effective in reducing recidivism (Sutherland and Cressey, 1974; Carney, 1977). If parole is indeed as ineffective as some authors claim, the reason might well lie in the untenable position given to the parole agent in the parole system.

An analysis of the difficulties a parole agent encounters must certainly include the following three. First and foremost is the usual size of the agent's caseload. It is not uncommon for an agent to have as many as 100 parolees under his jurisdiction (Sutherland and Cressey, 1974). In this kind of situation, an agent obviously cannot spend much time with any one person; the most he/she can offer an ex-offender is a few minutes of conversation a month—hardly time enough for the intensive counseling and supervision which is supposed to take place on parole. A second major difficulty parole agents face is that they wear two hats: that of the counselor and that of the law enforcer. Indeed, since the very purpose of parole is to both help ex-offenders and police them, the agent is necessarily placed in the awkward position of having to simultaneously perform two contradictory roles (Cressey, 1965). The President's Commission on Law Enforcement and Administration of Justice (1967) reported that in recent years agents have been encouraged to emphasize the role of the counselor. However, the fact that an agent can return a parolee to prison has the potential to greatly hinder the agent's activities in that role. For example, a parolee might, with good reason, be hesitant to discuss with his agent those aspects of his life that are causing him the most difficulty such as engaging in further crimes or the illegal use of drugs. A third difficulty faced by agents is that they usually are not high-status people in their community. This has always presented difficulties for parole agents in that it is important in a counseling relationship that the counselor have the respect of the person being counseled. However, the agent's relatively low status hinders him more in

Author's note: This research was supported by a Woodrow Wilson Dissertation Year Fellowship, a Russell Sage Foundation grant to Northwestern University, and by National Science Foundation Grant GS 30273x, D. T. Campbell principal investigator.

From *Evaluation Quarterly,* February 1978, pp. 71–90. Reprinted by permission of Sage Publications, Inc., and the author.

recent times because of the emphasis currently being placed on the agent as a mobilizer of community resources. According to Newman (1973), today's parole agent is expected to act on behalf of the parolee as a broker with various elements in the community (such as government bureaucracies, private employers, and the like), and in such encounters status can be crucial to effectiveness.

In an attempt to overcome these difficulties experienced by those who supervise parolees, the Young Lawyers Section of the American Bar Association initiated the Volunteer in Parole Program, in which lawyers volunteered to spend at least six hours a month with a parolee from the state penitentiary system. Six hours a month may not seem like a great deal of time; but compared to the usual amount of contact per month, six hours can be considered intensive supervision. It was felt that the caseload problem would be attenuated by not only this increase in amount of supervision but also by the fact that each lawyer would be matched to only one parolee. Thus, whatever abilities, energies, or contacts the laywer had would all be used for the benefit of just one person. It was felt that the two-hat dilemma would be mitigated because the lawyer would have no power to have the parolee arrested. Surely the lawyer could tell authorities about a parolee's infractions if he so chose. But it was made very clear to the lawyers in their training and presumably to the parolees when they were introduced to the lawyers that the lawyer's function was to counsel and/or befriend, and not to police. Finally, it was felt that the difficulties presented by the relatively low status of the parole agent would not be experienced by these volunteers because of their much higher status as lawyers. Thus, it was assumed that a lawyer would find it easier than an agent to gain the respect of a parolee and to deal effectively in the community on behalf of the parolee.

The program was instituted in several states. The purpose of this paper is to report the results of an evaluation of this Volunteer in Parole Program for the State of Illinois. The major question of interest was the effectiveness of this program compared to regular parole supervision. In December 1971, lawyers recruited through the Illinois Bar Association attended a two-day training session which attempted to familiarize them with the Illinois correctional system in general and parolees in particular. The lawyers were told that they would

be introduced to a parolee and the two of them would have to determine between themselves just how the lawyer could help the parolee. That is, the lawyers were not given any specific instructions about what the relationship should be or what they should do; the only rule they were given was that they could not represent the man in a court of law.

METHOD

Design

Many outcome evaluations consist of nothing more than anecdotes reported by officials holding key positions in the program that is being evaluated. Some evaluations are better in that they are based on the responses of the people for whom the program was developed. The problem in this latter case is that a control group is needed against which to compare the responses of those in the program. Those few evaluations that employ a control group are often deficient because the control group is not randomly selected.

The present evaluation employed random assignment of parolees to the program and a pretest-posttest design. Both treatment (those in the program) and control groups were interviewed before the program began and then again after the program had been in effect nine months. Two interviewers were used, each interviewing approximately half of each group at the time of the pretest and then the same respondents at the time of the posttest. One of the interviewers was a white graduate student in his mid-twenties; the other was a black in his mid-forties who had worked as a professional interviewer for a nationally known research group and who had participated previously in surveys of ghetto residents.

Interviews

The interview schedule was developed on the basis of two months' participant observation at a halfway house for parolees and was pilot tested on parolees whom the author knew well. Three types of questions were asked: those requiring the respondent to answer in his own words; those requiring a response on a 6-point scale ranging from completely disagree to completely agree; and those requiring a proportion or percentage response on an 11-point scale ranging from 0% to 100%. For the agree-disagree questions those interviewed were given a card containing six categories (three degrees of agreement and three degrees of disagreement) and, after each item was read to them, were asked to indicate which half of the scale best reflected their attitudes (i.e., "Do you in general agree or disagree with this statement?"); then they were asked which of the three categories within that half best fit them. The questions that required respondents to estimate a percentage were handled similarly; that is, respondents were first asked if they thought the percentage was high, low, or in the middle, and then were required to chose a specific centile within the larger category they had chosen. Most of the interviews were conducted in the parolee's place of residence, although a few took place in restaurants or bars and about ten took place over the phone. The average interview lasted 75 minutes. At neither the pretest nor the posttest did the researchers present themselves as evaluating the program but rather as conducting a survey of men on parole.

Parolee Selection

Parolees were nominated for the program by their agents, who were instructed to nominate five of their clients whom they felt could benefit most from the program. From the five each agent nominated, two were randomly chosen to be in the program and two in the control group. The fifth parolee nominated by each agent was not used, except in those instances where between the time of selection and the time of implementation a nominee had to be dropped from consideration for one reason or another. There were seven of these instances, and three of these "fifth" men were put into the program and four into the control group. During the nine-month interim between the pretest and the posttest, many men had to be dropped from the evaluation for various reasons. For the final analyses, there were 16 men in the treatment group and 16 in the control group.

Outcome Measures

Arrest Rates   Any evaluation of a parole program must look at the arrest rates of those involved. Therefore, the arrest records of both treatment and control groups were obtained from official FBI reports for the nine-month period that was being evaluated.

Employment   Most investigators agree that employment is the biggest problem faced by men returning from prison and that it is highly related to recidivism (Glaser, 1964; Irwin, 1970). It was expected that the volunteer lawyers would do better than agents at getting parolees jobs because of the lawyers' higher status. That is, lawyers were assumed to have more contacts with potential employers (through clients, clubs, and the like) and more influence with an employer who was creating problems for a parolee. Also, laywers were expected to be more effective because they had only one parolee job to consider, not over one hundred as does an agent. To get a measure of the participating parolees' employment performance, several indices were used: whether or not a man was working; if he was, how much money he was making a week; how much he liked his job; and the proportion of time he was working between the beginning of the program and the posttest.

The first two of these measures were obtained by asking the parolee himself and then checking his response against the records kept by the parole agent. Whenever there was a discrepancy, which was infrequent, the average was used in the analysis. An index of how much a parolee liked his job was obtained by summing the responses to two 6-point questions, one asking how satisfied a man was with his job, the other asking him how satisfied he was with his salary. The proportion of time a parolee was working was obtained by asking the respondents at the time of the posttest how long they had worked at each job they had had since the pretest interview. The time at each job was coded in terms of months, summed, and divided by nine, which was the number of months between the pretest and posttest.

Use of Community Facilities   It had appeared to the program developers that a small percentage of men on parole actually made use of the programs in the community for which they qualified. Welfare or public aid, Illinois State Employment Service, and a special employment service set up for parolees (Division of Correctional Employment Service) are examples of such programs. Both because of a lawyer's greater knowledge of the law and because of his higher status, it was expected that the volunteers would be better than agents at helping parolees make effective use of such services. To determine this, each parolee was asked whether or not he had been to any of these agencies and if he felt the agency had done all they could for him.

Attitudinal Dimensions It was decided that other criteria of the program's success would be changes in certain attitudes that might be related to a parolee's successful adjustment. Consequently, respondents were asked questions about each of several attitudinal dimensions. A principal components factor analysis with a varimax rotation was performed on all of these questions in order to see if the factors which had been anticipated would indeed emerge, and to see which items would load heavily on these factors. Questions that loaded above .5 on a factor and .25 more on that factor than on any other were considered to be part of an attitude scale, and these were standardized and summed to form an index. The six indices formed in this manner together with the questions that were included in each are presented in Table 1.

Table 1. The Questions
That Were Used to Form Each
of the Six Attitudinal Dimensions

1. General Happiness
   a. Compared to how hard you thought it was going to be when you were in the joint to make a living on the streets, how hard has it been? (open-ended)
   b. Taking everything together, how happy are you with the way things are going in your life now? Are you satisfied or dissatisfied?
   c. How do you feel about the progress you have made in getting everything together since you've been out of prison? Are you satisfied or dissatisfied?
   d. Compared to how happy you were before you were arrested, how happy are you now? Are you satisfied or dissatisfied compared to then?
   e. Think now of three men you know best and think of how happy they are with the way things are going in their lives now. Compared to them how happy are you? Are you satisfied or dissatisfied compared to them?
   f. You have found it a lot easier to make a living on the streets than you thought it would be when you were in prison. Do you agree or disagree?
   g. You're disappointed with the progress you have made since getting out of prison. Do you agree or disagree?

2. Stigma
   a. When people find out you've been to the joint, they give you less respect than they give to other men. Do you agree or disagree?
   b. When people find out you've been to prison, they seem to hold it against you a little bit. Do you agree or disagree?
   c. What percentage of people you meet shy away from you when they find out you've been to the joint?

3. Society's Concern
   a. The average citizen is now starting to become concerned about the parolee. Do you agree or disagree?
   b. The average citizen makes no effort to help out a parolee. Do you agree or disagree?

4. Difficulty in Keeping Parole Rules
   a. Parole rules do not interfere greatly with a man's life style. Do you agree or disagree?
   b. Being a parolee really puts a man at a disadvantage in this community because of parole rules. Do you agree or disagree?

5. Attitudes toward the Courts
   a. You got a bad deal from the justice system. Do you agree or disagree?
   b. What percentage of court decisions are fair?
   c. Considering all the problems the court system has to face, the courts do a pretty good job of administering justice. Do you agree or disagree?

6. Unrealistic Expectancies
   a. What are the chances that you will eventually be a vice-president, president, or executive of some company?
   b. No matter how hard you tried, you could not work your way up to be a president, vice-president, or executive of some company. Do you agree or disagree?

The first factor, general happiness, is an overall measure of satisfaction with life. It was felt that such a factor would be an interesting global index of the volunteers' effectiveness at intervening in the parolees' lives. The second dimension is a measure of stigma. Most parolees can get by in almost all social situations without their past becoming known. However, as Goffman (1963) has noted, when a person's stigma is not obvious, the task becomes one of managing information, that is, of continuously deciding whether to tell or not to tell, to lie or not to lie, to let on or not to let on. Irwin (1970) felt that an important negative effect of a sense of stigma among ex-offenders was that it encouraged them to remain in a criminal subculture where the cost of mismanaging the information about their past would be considerably less. Thus, even though the parolees' stigma is not immediately visible, it may very well create difficulties. It was thought that one effect of this program would be a lessening of the sense of stigma as a result of being befriended by a high-status person such as a lawyer. "If this person is accepting me, perhaps it is not so bad to be an ex-convict" was the hypothesized reaction of the parolees in the program.

The third dimension is the respondents' perceptions of the degree of concern society feels for the parolee. The author had observed while doing participant observation that parolees tended to feel that society had put them in prison and forgotten about them and now that they were out society was not at all concerned about any of their problems. It seemed that the experience of having someone important in that society—namely, a lawyer—show concern might change the attitudes of those in the program toward society as a whole. This was felt to be beneficial because it was assumed that it is easier for a person to conform to the rules of a group that he feels is concerned than of a group that he feels does not care.

The fourth factor is the difficulty parolees experienced in keeping parole rules. It was felt that a man who perceives parole rules as greatly interfering with his life and is overwhelmed by them tends to give up all attempts to keep them. Thus, one way the program could succeed would be to affect respondents' perceptions of how hard it is to do a good parole. This particular program was expected to accomplish this because the lawyers, unlike parole agents, did not have the power to return a parolee to prison for a parole violation. The ex-offender could, therefore, concentrate on keeping the more important rules without having to worry about being returned to prison for some minor technicality.

The fifth area investigated was the parolees' attitudes toward the justice system. Negative opinions on the part of parolees toward the courts have been frequently noted (Glaser, 1964; Berman, 1976). Furthermore, Sykes and Matza (1957) argued that these negative opinions contribute to a neu-

tralization of the moral bind of the law. That is, it is easier to break the law if one has little respect for the justice system. If this is true, a parolee program might well be considered beneficial if it produces a more positive attitude toward the courts. With regard to the present program, it was expected that such an effect would occur because an integral part of the court system, that is, a lawyer, was spending his time, showing concern, and so forth.

The sixth dimension is unrealistic job expectancies. Glaser (1964) among others has noted that parolees typically have unrealistic expectancies about what types of jobs they can get and the amount of money they can make. Furthermore, he felt this was harmful because it guaranteed that the ex-offender would experience frustration and disappointment when his expectancies were inevitably disconfirmed. The lowering of ex-offenders' expectancies was one of the topics stressed in the volunteer lawyer's orientation meeting. Thus, it seemed appropriate to include it as a measure of the program's success.

Process Measures

In addition to the outcome measures, that is, measures which could be used to compare the effectiveness of this program with regular parole supervision, several questions about the process of the program were also included in the posttest interviews. Specifically, those in the program were asked how frequently they talked to their volunteer, whether they talked mostly on the telephone or in person, what their attitudes toward the volunteer were, and what their volunteer had actually done for them. This last piece of information was obtained by reading to the participant a list of 15 behaviors and asking after each whether or not the volunteer had indeed done this (e.g., helped find a job, gave legal advice, helped find a place to live).

RESULTS

Outcome Measures

In order to assess the effects of the program, three types of analyses were employed: a one-way (treatment versus control) analysis of covariance was used for those continuous dependent variables for which pretest (covariate) measures were available; a similar analysis of variance was used on continuous variables for which pretest measures were not available; chi-squares were performed on discrete variables.

Arrest Rates During the nine-month period over which the program was evaluated, only 3 of the 32 men who were used in this research were arrested. None of these were from the group that was matched to the lawyers. However, from the time of the pretest to the time of the posttest, 2 people in the treatment group were lost because they were back in prison and 2 were lost because they had absconded from parole, while among the control group none were back in prison and only one had absconded. If absconding from parole, being back in prison, and being arrested are summed to form one index, the results are that 4 from each group were in trouble at the time of the posttest.

Employment The program did not affect any of the measures of employment. As can be seen in Table 2, the same percentage in the control group as in the treatment group were working at the time of the posttest. Among these employed, the mean difference between the groups with respect to weekly salary was not significant, nor was the mean difference in the measure of how much they liked their jobs. During the period of the program, both groups were employed on the average about 70% of the time. As a measure of how hard they thought it was for a parolee to get a job, respondents were asked to answer on a 6-point scale from completely agree to completely disagree the following question: "It is next to impossible for a parolee to get a job." Again there were no differences between the groups. Finally, on an open-ended question about what problems a parolee faces, the proportion of treatment ex-offenders who mentioned jobs were a problem was not significantly different from the proportion of control ex-offenders giving the same response.

Use of Community Agencies It had been decided that one way the program could be considered successful would be if a larger percentage of those in the program than in the control group would have made use of the welfare or public aid office, the state employment service, the Division of Correctional Employment Service, or any other city, state, federal, or church program. Table 3 shows the percentages of each group that had made use of these agencies. The differences between the proportions seems to indicate that those in the program did make more use of community agencies. However, these differences were not significant, and an inspection of the pretest proportions showed that the same degree of difference between treatment and control groups existed before the program started. The program, then, had no effect on use of community agencies.

Attitudinal Dimensions Other criteria of the program's effectiveness were several attitude

Table 2. Employment Indices[a]

	Treatment	Control	F	χ^2
1. Percentage working at the time of the posttest	69%	69%	—	.00
2. Weekly salary for those working	$109	$148	3.03	—
3. Extent to which respondents liked their job	.46	−.48	1.78	—
4. The proportion of time between pretest and posttest that respondents had a job	70%	73%	.05	—
5. Extent to which respondents agreed to the statement: It's almost impossible for a parolee to get a job	4.13	4.44	.29	—
6. Percentage of respondents who mentioned employment when asked what the biggest problems faced by parolees are	38%	31%	—	.00

[a]All figures are based on a sample size of 16 in each group except items 2 and 3 which are based on the 11 in each group who were working at the time of the posttest.

Table 3. Use of Community Agencies[a]

	Treatment	Control	χ^2
1. Proportion that had been to welfare or public aid	50%	44%	.00
2. Proportion that had been to Illinois State Employment Service	63%	38%	1.13
3. Proportion that had been to Division of Correctional Employment Service	50%	31%	.52
4. Proportion that had been to any other kind of program	50%	25%	1.20

[a]All proportions are based on a sample size of 16 in each group.

scales: general happiness, stigma, society's concern for the parolee, the difficulty in keeping the rules of parole, feelings about the courts, and unrealistic job expectancies. Table 4 displays the means of these scales for treatment and control groups.[1] As can be seen there, the program did not significantly affect a parolee's general happiness, his feelings of being stigmatized, the difficulty he experiences in keeping parole rules, or his attitudes toward the courts. However, those in the program did feel more positively about society's concern for them and showed a tendency to have less unrealistic expectancies than those in the control group.

Use of the Volunteer Lawyer In order to get a measure of how parolees were using the volunteers, each respondent was asked whom he would go to for help in getting a job, whom he would get in touch with if he got in trouble with the law, whom he would put down as a character reference if he needed one, and whom he talks with when he has troubles. It should be noted that those in the program were not asked whether or not they would go to their lawyer in these situations, but were asked *whom* they would go to, and the dependent variable of interest was how frequently those

in the program would name their volunteer lawyer.

In response to the question of who would be consulted for help in getting a job, only 1 of the 16 in the program mentioned the volunteer. In response to the question about who could be called if one got into trouble with the law, only 2 said the lawyer. However, 4 parolees (25%) said they would

Table 4. Means of the Six Attitudinal Dimensions Adjusted for the Corresponding Pretest Score as a Covariate[a]

	Treatment	Control	Covariance F
1. General happiness	−.46[b]	.45	.32
2. Extent to which stigma was felt	−.22	.22	.36
3. Respondents' perceptions of how concerned society is about the parolee	.52	−.52	4.74*
4. Extent to which respondents felt that keeping parole rules was difficult	−.40	.39	2.02
5. Positive attitudes about the court system	−.01	.00	.00
6. Amount of unrealistic job expectations	.04	.98	2.48

[a]All numbers are based on a sample size of 16 in each group. A score on each of these dimensions was obtained for each parolee by standardizing and summing the responses to two or more questions.

[b]The results for general happiness are not those of a covariance analysis but those of an analysis of variance on the posttest index only. See footnote 1.

*p .05

put down the lawyer as a character reference, and 6 (38%) named the volunteers as the one they could go to when they were troubled. Apparently the lawyers had in fact become "counselors" for a significant proportion of those in the program.

Process Measures

The questions asking respondents about various aspects of the volunteer lawyers' behavior were included in order to answer two questions about the process of the program. The first was what exactly the lawyers and parolees did during the nine months they knew each other. The second was whether there was any type of systematic relationship between specific lawyer behaviors and specific parolee outcome measures.

With regard to the first issue, one important question concerned how often they talked to their volunteer. Of the 16 respondents, 31% said one or two times a week, 56% said one or two times a month, and 12% said less than once a month. To check on the possibility that these contacts might have been rather superficial, respondents were asked whether they usually talked to their volunteer in person or on the telephone; 69% said in person. Thus, it appears that the vast majority of this group were in fact meeting their volunteer face-to-face at least monthly.

There were several questions that probed attitudes toward the volunteers and apparently indicate that in general the parolees and volunteers did establish more than a superficial relationship. For example, 94% of participants answered affirmatively when asked if they considered the volunteer a good friend, 81% answered affirmatively when asked if they felt free to talk to the volunteer even about very personal things, and 93% said that it was not the case that the volunteer could be helpful if he wanted to be but the volunteer did not want to take the trouble.

Also relevant to the question of what occurred between the parolees and the volunteers were the results obtained by having respondents indicate how many of 15 potential helping behaviors their volunteers had actually performed. These results are presented in Table 5, where it can be seen that according to the parolees the most frequent means by which they were helped were for the volunteer to give them advice about parole regulations, to give them help or advice on financial problems, to

give them legal advice, and to talk to them when they needed somebody for this purpose. These results parallel those reported above, which showed that a significant proportion of respondents saw the volunteer as one they would go to when they were troubled but not as one they would see for help in getting a job.

Table 5. Percentages of Parolees Who Indicated the Lawyers Helped Them in Various Ways

	Percentage Responding Affirmatively (N=16)
Helped Find a Place to Live	0
Gave Me Advice about Parole Regulations	31
Gave Me Help or Advice on Personal Problems	19
Gave Me Help or Advice on Financial Problems	25
Gave Me Help or Advice on Problems with Employers	6
Gave Me Help or Advice on Problems with Police	13
Gave Me Legal Advice	31
Helped Me Get Job Training	13
Helped Me Get a Job	19
Helped Me Get Into School	0
Helped Me with a Drug Treatment Program	0
Talked to Me When I Needed It	25
Made Sure I Stayed Out of Trouble	6
Has Not Done Anything for Me	19

In order to investigate the possibility of any linear relationships between these specific behaviors and outcome measures, correlation coefficients were computed between each behavior (including how often they talked to their volunteer and whether it was in person or on the telephone) and all the outcome measures. It was hoped that such an analysis would provide very useful information about what types of help by the volunteer produced what types of effects in the parolees. Unfortunately, the number of correlations significant at the .05 level was less than would be expected by chance alone given the number of tests; and those that were significant failed to display any meaningful pattern.

DISCUSSION

This evaluation showed that the program had no effect on arrest rates and no effect on parolees' employment. A piece of information which may help answer the question of why the lawyers did not influence these aspects of parolees' lives is the fact that at the time of the pretest the 32 men studied here had been out of prison an average time of six months. This suggests that they had been out long enough to "stabilize" before they had even met their lawyer.

Other researchers who have done work with parolees have felt that the first month after release is the most tumultuous and the most critical for the ex-offender (Glaser, 1964; Irwin, 1970). During this time, a person has to deal with several major difficulties all at once: figuring out a way to earn a living; finding a satisfactory place to live; making new friends; reestablishing old relationships with his family; dealing with the stigma of being an ex-convict; and in general adjusting to a new way of life. After a couple of months these issues are settled one way or the other: he finds a job, or he decides there is no suitable employment so he stops looking for work; he is taken back by his wife and family, or he accepts the fact that he must make a life without them; he finds a place to live that is at least tolerable; he makes new friends or finds his old ones; he gets used to the fast pace of the streets.

The idea that stabilization was a reason the lawyers did not affect the parolees' arrest rates is supported by the fact that 42% of the men who violate parole in Illinois do so in the first month they are out, and for the second through the sixth month out of prison the percentage of total violations drops to around 7% each month. The notion that those in the program had stabilized was also supported by some anecdotal evidence collected at luncheons which were held for the lawyers participating in the program. Many lawyers at these luncheons expressed the feeling that they were of no use to their parolees either because the man had a job, was staying out of trouble, and did not seem to need any help, or because the man's situation was very bad and every suggestion or offer of assistance made by the lawyer was rejected by the parolee.

What can be concluded is that if programs of this type are to have impact, they ought to concentrate on parolees who are just coming out of prison; and it may be preferable if the volunteer-parolee relationship begins shortly *before* the man is out of prison. This way their relationship would be established before that critical first month out, and the lawyer could help the ex-offender get a better job than he would be able to get on his own, make sure the parolee used the community agencies that are available to him, and provide the friendship that newly released men seem to need so badly.

This evaluation also showed that the program had no affect on parolees' use of community agencies such as welfare, state employment services, and so on. The results of the pretest showed that less than a third of the men interviewed had made any use of these agencies even though over two-thirds at some time since their release needed and qualified for such assistance. It had been hoped that the volunteers in this program would have helped this situation, but apparently they did not. It is possible that the first month out is the time during which ex-offenders need such services the most; and therefore, if only new releases had been used, effects would have emerged. However, another reason why these lawyers did not steer their parolees to community agencies in any significant numbers may have been that the lawyers were simply not aware what agencies existed nor how to go about making use of them. If this is true, a relatively simple remedy is to have the volunteer program in each city put together a list of all welfare or public aid agencies, employment services, job training programs, and so on. It may also be emphasized in the lawyer training sessions that getting a man into a job training program, or if necessary a drug program, or securing some cash from public aid during periods of unemployment can very well be the most important thing the volunteer can do.

With regard to the attitude measures, the evaluation showed that the program did not affect participants' general happiness. This is not surprising, since the program did not affect the parolees' work situation and the happiness scale was correlated .69 with whether or not a man was working—an interesting finding in its own right, because it means that for a parolee happiness is having a job. The results also showed that being in contact with a lawyer did not affect parolees' feelings of stigma, their perceptions of how hard it is to keep parole rules, or their opinions about the fairness of the courts.

On the positive side, the program did affect parolees' perceptions of how much society was concerned about them. That is, having someone of a lawyer's stature go out of his way to help an ex-offender was sufficient to change the participants' attitudes about society as a whole. It seems reasonable to assume that an increase in this kind of attitude is associated with a decrease in feeling of alienation and hostility toward society, which is certainly a desirable change.

Another effect of the program was to make the participants somewhat more realistic in their job expectations. Glaser (1964) and Irwin (1970) have commented on the totally unrealistic aspirations held by people coming out of correctional institutions; and the results of the pretest in this research showed that 80% of the respondents felt that they could legally make 15 or 20 thousand dollars a year, while 70% felt they could work their way up to be an executive of some company. Such high expectations can be dangerous for an ex-offender because they are almost certain to be disconfirmed, and this leaves the parolee frustrated and disappointed. Thus, the program's success in putting parolees more in touch with reality as far as employment possibilities is a point in its favor.

Another interesting aspect of the data is that a significant proportion of those in the program did not mention the volunteer lawyer as one they could go to if they needed a job or if they got in trouble with the law, but a significant proportion did mention the lawyer as one they could use as a character reference and as a person they could talk to when they had problems. The fact that lawyers were not mentioned as sources for jobs is consistent with the findings that lawyers had no effect on participants' employment. The fact that they were mentioned as someone with whom to talk is consistent with the results obtained by asking the ex-offenders what the volunteer had actually done for them.

The overall pattern that emerges from the data of this evaluation is that the program was not effective in changing concrete aspects of parolees' lives (e.g., jobs and arrests), but it was effective in providing parolees a relationship with a high-status person. Since it is usually assumed that having such a friend is helpful in coping with the more concrete problems, what needs to be explained is why more differences did not appear on such variables as arrest rates, general happiness, feelings of stigma, and so on. One explanation is that having such a friend is not as important as might be expected. The evidence here shows that having a friend who is a lawyer is not an important determinant of the major dependent variables investigated. General happiness, for example, seems to be influenced much more by employment than by whether or not a parolee has a lawyer to talk to. Another explanation is that the effects of having such a friend take longer to emerge than the nine-month period allowed here. In other words, it is possible that the program produced lawyer-parolee friendships which, if given a longer time to continue, will in turn produce more general happiness, lower arrest rates, better employment situations, and so on. However, determining the length of time in which a program "ought" to produce its effects is and probably always will be a very difficult problem in program evaluation.

NOTE

[1]For the results of the analysis of covariance to be interpretable, two assumptions must be met in addition to those required for the analysis of variance (Myers, 1966). First, the means of the covariate must not be significantly different for the cells that are compared; this was true for all the scales in Table 5. Second, the slopes of the regressions of the dependent variable on the covariate for each cell must not be significantly different. This was true for all the scales in Table 5 except the first; consequently, the means and F ratio reported in Table 5 for general happiness are not those of analysis of covariance but are the results of an analysis of variance on the posttest index only.

REFERENCES

Berman, J. J. (1976) "Parolees' perception of the justice system: black-white differences." Criminology 13, 4: 507–520.

Caldwell, R. G. (1965) Criminology. New York: Ronald Press.

Carney, L. P. (1977) Probation and Parole: Legal and Social Dimensions. New York: McGraw-Hill.

Cressey, D. (1965) "Prison Organizations," pp. 1023–1070 in J. March (ed.) Handbook of Organizations. Chicago: Rand McNally.

Dressler, D. (1969) Practices and Theory of Probation and Parole. New York: Columbia Univ. Press.

Glaser, D. (1964) The Effectiveness of a Prison and Parole System. Indianapolis, IN: Bobbs-Merrill.

Goffman, I. (1963) Stigma. Englewood Cliffs, NJ: Prentice-Hall.

Irwin, J. (1970) The Felon. Englewood Cliffs, NJ: Prentice-Hall.

Myers, J. (1966) Fundamentals of Experimental Design. Boston: Allyn & Bacon.

Newman, D. (1973) "Legal model for parole: future developments," in B. Frank (ed.) Contemporary Corrections. Reston, VA: Reston Press.

President's Commission on Law Enforcement and Administration of Justice (1967) Task Force Report: Corrections. Washington, DC: U.S. Government Printing Office.

Sutherland, E. and D. Cressey (1974) Criminology. Philadelphia, PA: J. P. Lippincott.

Sykes, G. and D. Matza (1957) "Techniques of neutralization: a theory of delinquency." Amer. Sociological Rev. 22: 664–670.

SOME PROBLEMS IN EXPERIMENTATION IN A LEGAL SETTING

H. Laurence Ross
Murray Blumenthal

As politics and law become more receptive to social scientists' testimony concerning "extra-legal" facts, sociologists are increasingly becoming involved in applied research concerning political and legal topics (D. T. Campbell, 1969; Rosen, 1972). A significant and, in our opinion, highly beneficial form of involvement is research designed to determine whether legal endeavors are effective in achieving the governmental purposes for which they are enacted. The brief career of evaluative research in law has turned up many instances of costly programs which seem to be accomplishing little in return for the efforts and sacrifices being devoted to them (B. J. Campbell, 1970), along with a smaller number where results can be shown (e.g., Glass, Tiao and Maguire, 1971; Baldus, 1973; Ross, 1973). In addition, several studies reveal the existence of unintended and undesired consequences, suggesting the need or opportunity for program revisions to coordinate goals and results (Ross, 1974). This paper describes some problems of practice and ethics experienced in designing and carrying out an experimental study of traffic law. They are reported in the belief that they are likely to be experienced by others working in the growing field of evaluative research in law, who will be better prepared to meet them with the benefit of our hindsight.

The study was undertaken in what appeared to be unusually favorable circumstances. The United States Department of Transportation was considering issuing standards for state legislation involving mandatory court appearance by drivers accused of moving traffic violations, but no firm requirements had been set. Furthermore, the D.O.T. was interested in formulating recommendations to judges concerning the use of fines, probation, clinics, and other alternatives for the disposition of drinking-and-driving cases. Strong opinions on both topics were circulating among "safety specialists," but there was little scientifically grounded knowledge available. The D.O.T. requested a study to obtain higher quality information on which its policy recommendations could be founded. The lack of governmental commitment to a particular policy at the time the research was undertaken supported the

From The American Sociologist, August 1975, pp. 150–155. Reprinted by permission.

independence of the research and also promised that competent research could have a significant practical effect upon the formation of policy.

An additional favorable circumstance was the great interest of the presiding judge of the lower court system of a large city in obtaining information on the effectiveness of his enterprise in the traffic-control field. Although the court system in question had a most favorable reputation among the safety establishment, the judge was skeptical, interested in improving his organization, and very receptive to social science. He requested that his city's court system be the site for the research proposed by the D.O.T., and promised all needed cooperation.

The D.O.T. posed two specific questions for research:

1. For the violator of ordinary traffic rules, such as lane laws or stop sign laws, does appearance in court before a judge produce a better subsequent driving record, in terms of accidents and violations, than appearance at a violations bureau where a plea of guilty is routinely made and a scheduled fine paid?
2. For the driver convicted for the first time of driving while intoxicated, does traditional probation (or probation combined with educational or clinical programs) produce a superior subsequent driving record than a monetary fine?

ETHICAL PROBLEMS IN RESEARCH DESIGN

The treatments in question were all in use in the cooperating court system, though appearance before the judge was voluntary rather than mandatory for the ordinary traffic-law violator, and the penalties for driving while intoxicated were assigned at the discretion of the sentencing judges. A preliminary study was done to review the driving histories, prior and subsequent to the finding of guilt, of drivers experiencing the specified conditions during a given year. The preliminary study found few differences in subsequent accidents and violations corresponding to the penalties received, but it did find numerous differences in prior records, testifying to the fact that there is strong selection on prior grounds concerning who experiences which condition. For example, drivers go to trial rather than plead guilty to a violations bureau

when charged with a minor traffic-law violation if the record of a conviction (with consequent "points") is likely to jeopardize their driving licenses. Thus, drivers normally appearing in court have worse prior records than those appearing before the violations bureau. Likewise, judges tend to apply the more elaborate programs available for drinking drivers to those who have worse prior traffic records. The results of the preliminary study suggested that trustworthy conclusions concerning the effects of the specified conditions would require the use of an experimental design wherein drivers would be selected to experience the conditions in a manner as close as possible to random assignment.

We were concerned that the assignment of individuals to legal punishments on a non-legal basis not run afoul of ethical sentencing practices. There are two somewhat opposed principles in law concerning the proper basis for sentencing. One such principle is that the punishment should fit the crime, and that there should be equal treatment for equal offenses. The second is that the punishment should fit the criminal, this fit to be achieved through the exercise of judicial discretion in the specific case. Neither principle is on its face compatible with arbitrary assignment of punishments. Although we saw these principles as posing problems for the development of a valid research design, we believe we were able to come to a compatible resolution.

To study the moving-violation issue, we provided the traffic division of the municipal police department with alternative tickets. The standard ticket used in the city directs the motorist to appear at a violations bureau, where he may choose to plead guilty and pay a scheduled fine or request a court appearance (to plead not guilty or to offer extenuating circumstances with a plea of guilty). We arranged that during the study period the police would use the standard ticket or the alternative tickets depending upon the week in which the ticket was written. During one week, the motorist was directed to appear in court rather than at the bureau. In another week, the motorist was given the option of mailing his guilty plea, with a standard $20.00 fine, avoiding the need to appear in person at the bureau. In yet another week, a warning ticket was issued, with no further consequences for the offender. In order to meet our own ethical and practical criteria, the alternative tickets were to be issued only for a narrow range of ordinary traffic offenses, eliminating the trivial (brake light out) and serious (reckless driving).

A similar design was used for the drinking drivers. The study was limited to first offenders. Depending on the month in question, the trial judges agreed to sentence the offender to a fine of some amount, to probation of some duration, or to some educational or clinical program available to the court and deemed appropriate to the defendant, such as a course in alcohol problems or outpatient treatment for alcoholism at the city hospital. No limits were set on the amount of the penalty, but just on its general nature, and it was agreed that if the judges thought the penalty of the month was grossly inappropriate to the case at hand they could depart from the schedule in the interests of the individual defendant. We expected such departures to be rare, and planned to eliminate the cases from the final analysis.

For several reasons, we believe that the study design, which approaches the experimental (except that for practical reasons assignment was made by week or month rather than at random), stands up sufficiently when measured by the aforementioned principles.

1. All the prescribed treatments were commonly used in this court system for the types of cases to which they were applied in the experiment. We did not consider, for example, a jail penalty for the drinking drivers, even though this penalty was statutorily available, since it had very rarely been applied to first offenders in the past.

2. In the drinking and driving study, the experimental prescription went only to the quality or type of sanction, not to its quantity or amount. This was done to permit the judge to offset a type of sanction he felt to be more punitive by using less of it. The judges were furthermore free to depart entirely from the experimental prescription in cases where it seemed grossly inappropriate.

3. In the moving-violation study, the inconvenience involved in the most formal procedure (mandatory court) was not very much greater than that involved in the standard procedure (violations bureau).

4. The value of the possible results of the study—preventing the enactment of useless or harmful legislation on a national scale, and permitting official recommendation of empirically valid forms of treatment—seemed sufficient to

outweigh any marginal costs to the citizens involved in the research process.

In fairness it must be admitted that some colleagues did not agree that our design met all reasonable ethical objections, but we were supported in our belief by the officials of the D.O.T. and the municipal court and therefore proceeded to use the design. In retrospect we still believe that this research design was ethical in context, but might have reservations concerning similar designs in different factual situations.

PRACTICAL
DIFFICULTIES IN IMPLEMENTATION

Having surmounted, to our satisfaction, the ethical problems raised by the research design, our study encountered a series of practical difficulties worth recounting for the guidance of future researchers. A first problem was floods in the locality (an unconvinced colleague suggests the wrath of the Deity at our ethical violations), diverting police attention from traffic duty, throwing the project off schedule. This destroyed plans to have the anticipated extra load on the court from the mandatory appearance tickets compensated by the lessening due to the warning tickets. The court was overwhelmed by the case load, and some employees refused to be party to a second week of mandatory appearance tickets. The balance of mandatory court appearances was obtained by issuing standard tickets, with the clerk of the violations bureau being directed to send a certain proportion to court on the basis of the last digit of the citation number.

A further disparity in the realization of the plan was discovered when we compared the backgrounds of drivers receiving mandatory court appearance tickets from the police with those receiving standard tickets. These groups should have been equivalent but for random error and for factors associated with the weeks during which they were apprehended for violations. Comparing them on eight background measures, we found four differences significant at the $p < .05$ level, differences in age, minority status, previous accidents, and whether an accident was associated with the citation being issued. The mandatory court appearance group contained more young people, more drivers experiencing an accident, fewer minority-group members, and more drivers with prior accident records than did the group receiving the standard citation. Some of the differences were large enough to be of concern to us. For example, of those receiving the standard citation, 18 percent had had prior accidents, whereas 24 percent of those receiving the mandatory court appearance citations had had prior accidents.

We can only speculate concerning the origin of these differences. We hesitate to attribute them to time-linked differences in the type of violator, and the statistical significance of the differences makes implausible an interpretation of random error. We speculate that they represent decisions by police officers to spare some violators the mandatory court appearance tickets. The police always carried standard tickets with them to be used in cases of violations outside the range of offenses subject to the experiment. We think it likely that these forms were used to "give a break" to some drivers, or to avoid the antagonism of others, particularly members of minority groups. It is also likely that some drivers who would have received a standard citation were given a verbal warning during the mandatory court appearance weeks, as police discretion directed.

The difficulties presented by police deviations from the prescribed schedule were compounded by deviations introduced by the court personnel. One instance of departure from instructions is inferred from the comparison between drivers sent to court and those allowed to use the routine procedure, when this decision was to be made by the clerk of the violations bureau according to the last digit of the citation number. Had the clerk adhered to his promise, we would be surprised to find marked differences between the groups, but two of eight comparisons in background characteristics of the violators assigned to the two procedures yielded differences significant at the $p < .05$ level. Of those sent to the court, 23 percent were under age 20, compared with 17 percent of those allowed the standard procedure, and 57 percent of those sent to court had more serious violations (within the range studied), compared with 65 percent of those allowed the standard procedure. These differences are speculatively explained by a bias on the part of the clerk in favor of giving young drivers the courtroom experience, while sparing those accused of more serious violations.

The largest and most serious departures from promised cooperation with the study design were in the judges' handling of intoxicated driving offenses. The judges, like the police, had agreed to vary treatments according to the time the decision was to be made. In January, all offenders were to receive a fine of an amount judged appropriate for the offense and the offender. In February, all offenders would be placed on probation for a period deemed appropriate by the judge. In March, the judge would select as a condition of probation some educational or clinical program thought most suitable to the offender. These dispositions were to be repeated for five three-month cycles in order to reach a goal of 200 subjects in each condition. We agreed that in "exceptional cases," where the interests of justice seemed to demand a treatment other than the one prescribed, the judges could depart from the prescriptions. We expected these cases to be rare, and planned to eliminate them from further analysis.

Our expectations were sorely disappointed; in the months where the prescribed treatment was a fine the judges did keep their promises to us. However, in months when probation was to be applied, only 68 percent of the convicted motorists received the stipulated treatment, and only 48 percent received the stipulated treatment during the educational-clinical periods. This gap was noted early in the study, and considerable effort was devoted to reminding the judges of their promises and to pleading for greater cooperation. The judges responded to our figures and our pleading by insisting that they were in fact cooperating, that they supported the study in principle and in practice, and that if there was a departure from the agreed plan it must have been on the part of the other judges. When confronted with details of cases in which they had departed from stipulations, the judges had no difficulty in showing that these were the "exceptional" ones in which they had to depart from the stipulated treatments. Our meetings with the judges were held in a fine restaurant at government expense, but this factor did not appear to produce the sought-for feeling of obligation. Our influence with the judges declined considerably when the presiding judge who had requested the study was replaced, following a municipal election that changed the party in control of city government. The new presiding judge was not obstructionist, but he did not support the study by putting pressure on the trial judges to honor the court's agreement with the researchers.

Why did the judges cooperate so little with the study, despite the fact that it had been commissioned by the court and that a respected presiding judge had committed his staff to cooperate? One consideration is certainly that the need for the research and the commitment to it were acknowledged by the presiding judge rather than by the trial judges who made the sentencing decisions. Although considerable effort was made to explain the study to the trial judges, their commitment was never as profound as that of the presiding judge. When the latter was replaced, the research prescriptions were left with little support.

In contrast, there were strong pressures on the judges to utilize fines in all cases of driving while intoxicated. To a greater extent than we initially realized, the defendants disliked the restrictions contained in the probationary and educational-clinical conditions, and strongly preferred fines. This preference was naturally even greater for defendants of some means, who found the loss of one or two hundred dollars a much less burdensome penalty than the alternative prescribed by the research.

The defendants' desires to be fined rather than to be placed on any kind of probation were apparently most effective in obtaining a departure from prescriptions of the research when the defendants were represented by counsel. Whereas in the months when fines were scheduled more than 90 percent of both represented and unrepresented defendants were given fines, in probation months 48 percent of the represented were fined, as compared with only 10 percent of the unrepresented, and in educational-clinical treatment months 47 percent of the represented and 32 percent of the unrepresented were fined. Quite simply, it appears that the researchers, being only temporarily in the situation and lacking consistent strong support from the court authorities, were at a disadvantage when compared with defense lawyers,[1] permanent members of the legal community, whose professional and social ties with the judiciary made their demands imperative (Blumberg, 1967).

CONCLUSIONS

In sum, a study planned to yield equivalent treatment groups and highly interpretable results, based on promises of cooperation from enlightened judges and police officers, was greatly compromised by a variety of failures of the decision-makers involved to follow the experimental prescriptions. The reasons for these failures appear to be that the weight of promises by top-level representatives of bureaucracies is considerably attenuated at the bottom of the organizational structure, absent strong control procedures, and that the day-to-day pressures of bureaucratic "clients"—even when these are law violators—are more weighty than those which researchers can bring to bear.

The main lesson to be gleaned from this experience is that to assure the realization of random or arbitrary procedures in research designs, choice must be eliminated from nonscientific personnel, no matter how well motivated they may appear to be. We have learned that gross departures can take place from the simple stipulation that a given kind of sentence will be meted out in a given month. Even the clear and simple instruction that a clerk is to administer one procedure to forms bearing a certain last digit and a different procedure to those bearing a different digit could not be accomplished without bias. Our experience has led us to the following suggestions for other researchers planning experimental studies in the legal system and in other similar bureaucratic settings:

1. Promises of cooperation from leadership are not sufficient to obtain commitment from the front lines of a bureaucracy. At the risk of initial rejection of the study by the front-line personnel, these actors must be informed, consulted and actively involved in the study at its inception, as it is they who must resist pressures to deviate at a later date.

2. Where possible, decision-making resulting in assignment of subjects to treatment groups should be in the hands of the experimenter, and not delegated to bureaucratic personnel who perform analogous tasks in the course of their routine duties.

3. If it is not possible to avoid assignments by independent personnel, the project staff should constantly monitor the results and offer feedback to the personnel involved. (This procedure did not appear to help us much with the judges, but it might have been effective with the clerk, had we employed it, since client pressures on him were less intense than those on the judges.)

4. Where client pressure to deviate from research prescriptions is likely to be intense, this pressure should be allowed to have its effect before the decision affecting experimental validity is

made. Thus, we might have provided that the study of sentencing intoxicated drivers would apply only to those defendants whom the judges would be willing to sentence in any of the three modes. If the judge felt that a fine was the only appropriate sentence, he should have been free to administer it. Only if he felt that any of the treatments would have been appropriate could he have been directed to open a sealed envelope to determine the experimental prescription. Of course, this procedure would have compromised the external validity of the study, but internal validity would have been maintained. The results would have been interpretable for the group meeting the experimental criteria.

In our substantive report (Blumenthal and Ross, 1973), we developed techniques that we believe salvaged a good part of our originally intended analysis. In addition, when we realized that the judges could not be persuaded to comply fully with the research requirements concerning drinking-driving defendants, we utilized the opportunity to study this aspect of judicial behavior. Despite the value of the serendipitous investigation, we wish we had been able to have the benefits of our present hindsight. We offer the above suggestions for the benefit of others.

NOTE

[1]Additional evidence pointing to the effectiveness of lawyers in undermining the research commitments of the judges is provided by the fact that in the months when the fine was legitimated by the research design, represented cases bulked larger than in other months. Apparently, word of the research prescriptions was obtained by the criminal lawyers in the community, who managed to get continuances of their cases into months when the sentences would coincide with their clients' wishes.

REFERENCES

Baldus, D. C.
 1973 "Welfare as a loan: an empirical study of the recovery of public assistance payments in the United States." Stanford Law Review 25: 125–250.

Blumberg, Abraham S.
 1967 Criminal Justice. Chicago: Quadrangle Books.

Blumenthal, Murray and H. Laurence Ross
 1973 Two Experimental Studies of Traffic Law. Washington, D.C.: Department of Transportation Reports DOT HS–800 825 and DOT HS–800 826.

Campbell, B. J.
 1970 "Highway safety program evaluation and research." Traffic Digest and Review 18:6–11.

Campbell, D. T.
 1969 "Reforms as experiments." American Psychologist 24:409–429.

Glass, G. V., G. C. Tiao, and T. O. Maguire
 1971 "The 1900 revision of German divorce laws: analysis of data as a time-series quasi-experiment." Law and Society Review 6:539–562.

Rosen, Paul L.
 1972 The Supreme Court and Social Science. Urbana, IL: University of Illinois Press.

Ross, H. Laurence
 1973 "Law, science and accidents: the British Road Safety Act of 1967." Journal of Legal Studies 2:1–78.
 1974 "Interrupted Time-Series Methods for the Evaluation of Traffic Law Reforms." Proceedings of the North Carolina Symposium on Highway Safety 10:32–67.

SECTION 3.5

Survey Research

Survey research is by far the most popular research design in the social sciences. Approximately 90 percent of all articles in sociological journals involve survey research (Brown and Gilmartin, 1969: 288).

TYPES OF SURVEYS

Several criteria distinguish between types of surveys. They can be distinguished first in terms of the time period covered. Surveys done at only one point in time are labeled *cross-sectional* surveys, whereas those done at more than one point in time are labeled *longitudinal* surveys. Longitudinal studies are superior in terms of establishing the causal sequence of variables. There are three types of longitudinal surveys. One is the *trend analysis*, which involves two or more different samples of persons at different times but from the same general population. In 1954, for example, 40 percent of Detroit area respondents stated that two or fewer children constituted the ideal family size; in 1971 this value was expressed by 66 percent of respondents (Duncan, Schuman, and Duncan, 1973, whose entire study reports on such trend studies).

A *cohort study* is a survey of persons sharing some experience, such as post–World War II babies born during the "baby boom." Another example would be a study involving a random sample of freshmen followed by another random sample of those freshmen who were seniors four years later to assess the impact of college on students' social and political attitudes. Note that a cohort study does not involve identical persons in both studies; samples are again taken from the larger group sharing the common experience. *Panel studies* involve an examination of the *same* persons at multiple time intervals. Jacobson (1977:4) reports a study done by Heath on 68 male graduates of Haverford College; all were in their freshman year in the early sixties. He found, for example, that men with higher verbal aptitude while freshmen tended to be more self-centered as adults and that those with higher quantitative aptitude experienced more interpersonal immaturity as adults. Panel studies are ideally suited to assess changes in individuals over time.

Surveys can also be compared in terms of degree of structure. Unstructured questions allow the respondent to respond freely, while structured questions present fixed choices from which to choose the best response. The unstructured approach is more appropriate for intensive study of phenomena (particularly complex phenomena) and for the purpose of suggesting hypotheses, helps ensure that all possible answer categories are allowed, and allows more involvement and personal expression by the respondent. An example of an unstructured question is, "What impact has your college experience had on your social and political orientations?" But unfortunately analysis of unstructured responses is very difficult and costly and comparability is reduced. In addition, unstructured questions require a lot of the respondent's time and hence reduce both the number of variables the researcher can investigate and the response rate.

The structured approach is more standardized and permits easy comparability. The answer categories are all presented, yielding a frame of reference for the respondent. An example of a structured question is, "Which of the following categories best describes your political orientation?" Response categories of "strongly conservative," "somewhat conservative," "middle-of-the-road," "somewhat liberal," and "strongly liberal" would follow. Analysis of structured questions is far cheaper and easier, and more variables can be measured in the same time period. Also, structured questions involve less interviewer bias. On the other hand, they force the respondent to select a response, even though the respondent may not have an opinion. Possible answer categories other than those developed by the researcher may be overlooked. And respondents may interpret an item differently, an occurrence that would show up only with the unstructured approach.

A third dimension on which surveys can be compared is the extent of personal involvement. Interviews involve more personal contact whereas questionnaires involve less. Questionnaires thus offer more anonymity than interviews. But interviews produce a much higher response rate, primarily as a result of the personal involvement. They do not require literacy on the part of the respondent, they permit flexibility to revise items, and the interviewer can detect if the respondent misunderstands a question. Such advantages, however, come at great cost in personnel, time, and money. The questionnaire's strong points are its higher reliability, lack of interviewer bias, and accessibility. Ultimately, however, the selection of method is contingent on the researcher's goals.

ADVANTAGES AND DISADVANTAGES

One advantage of the survey design is that it permits study of a representative cross section of the population. The researcher can thus analyze many different types of persons instead of relying on, say, college students (as is more typical with experiments). Larger samples are also possible with survey research. Experiments typically involve fewer than fifty to one hundred persons, but surveys can involve thousands of people. Assuming that the sample is selected randomly, a survey generally results in increased generalizability because the data are more representative of the larger population.

Many social science topics are best analyzed through the survey method. Examples might include attitudinal research, a study on the impact of participation in high school extracurricular activities on educational aspirations, and correlates of voting behavior. In addition, survey research affords the use of a larger number of variables (experiments are usually limited to one or only a few variables). Studies of occupational status can therefore incorporate a host of variables reflecting family background, school characteristics, and social psychological variables. Inclusion of a larger number of relevant variables results in more complete explanatory studies, and allows multivariate analyses.

Surveys also allow the study of changes over longer periods of time (although field research also has this advantage). The Survey Research Center at the University of Michigan, for example, is currently following a sample of high school graduates over a number of years to assess the causal relationships of prior attitudinal and behavioral factors on subsequent similar factors. Surveys such as these have the advantage of being economical in terms of time and money. With adequate prior planning, a massive survey of college students can be executed in a reasonably brief period of time. Alexander Astin at UCLA conducts annual surveys of over 200,000 freshmen.

But the survey design also has weaknesses. A low level of control exists over the timing of the independent variable and the placement of respondents in the "experimental" and "control" groups. Hence, researchers cannot select subjects to receive the treatment of a broken home or a divorce and cannot control the injection of such "stimuli" into the lives of the respondents. As a result, other factors besides a broken home origin or divorce experience may influence the dependent variable apart from the hypothesized independent variable. Mailed questionnaire surveys are also often plagued with low response rates; response rates of 40–50 percent are typical for such surveys, and many mail surveys attain even lower response rates. Telephone surveys generally produce higher response rates and interview surveys involve still higher response rates; it is not uncommon to attain 80–90 percent response rates with interviews. Undoubtedly, survey respondents differ from nonrespondents in some respects. Ognibene (1970) found that when compared to respondents, nonrespondents have less education, do less reading, have lower status jobs, and differ on attitudes. Finally, there is the problem that people do not always behave in the way they say they do on surveys. To the extent that a discrepancy exists, the validity of survey results is reduced.

THE READINGS

The article by Zick Rubin and Stephen Shenker on self-disclosure is a good example of a structured, cross-sectional questionnaire survey design. As such, it illustrates the advantages of this design: a fairly large sample (63 pairs of friends) that is highly representative of Harvard and Radcliffe freshmen, standardized wording of questions, ease of studying attitude and behaviors, the use of several independent variables, ease of data analysis, and economy (the study was done in several weeks' time with the assistance of students and involved minimal cost).

Surveys typically involve individuals as the unit of analysis. Note that Rubin and Shenker gathered data from individuals but then used the pair (either roommates or hallmates) as the basis for their analysis of the effects of friendship, proximity, and sex on self-disclosure.

This article also illustrates issues raised in other sections of this volume. For example, the authors tie their hypotheses to the theoretical literature on self-disclosure. Note that the main reason for using dyads was to increase the reliability of the results. Note their use of a pretest to develop reliable and valid measures. Note the use of multivariate analysis to more clearly indicate the causal relationships. And note the statistics used; analysis of variance is used give the nominal level independent variable and interval level dependent variable (see Section 4.1).

The second article, by Jean Converse and Howard Schuman, deals with interviewing strategies and the third article, by Thomas Heberlein and Robert Baumgartner, deals with factors associated with response rates in mailed questionnaires. The Converse and Schuman article is based on the reflections of numerous student interviewers at the Survey Research Center at the University of Michigan. Many examples and quotes by these student interviewers are included in the article. The article provides both an insider's perspective and an analytical framework for the interviewing process; it is more a process than a highly refined technique.

As a process, interviewing involves constant negotiation of the social situation and a skilled interviewer to respond and adjust quickly to the demands of the situation. The establishment and maintenance of rapport is paramount; the authors discuss how interviewers must shed their self-consciousness and exercise self-restraint so that the interview is not biased. They also discuss the role of conversation in an interview and how some of these conversation effects can bias the interview. Throughout the analysis, Converse and Schuman deal with the balance between pushing for data and meeting the respondent's needs as a person—the conflict the interviewer faces between his or her role as technician and as human being. The authors also discuss some of the strategies involved in successful interviewing, particularly effective probing.

The article on response rates to mailed questionnaires by Heberlein and Baumgartner is in my opinion the best article to date on the topic. Since the statistics in the article are complicated, the version presented in this volume is my condensation of the original article.

A great deal of research exists on the topic of response rates to mailed questionnaires, undoubtedly because response rates are directly tied to generalizability of results. Most of these research studies report on manipulating a few variables, such as length of the questionnaire, number of follow-ups, personalization, and color of the questionnaire, within a restricted sample. Other articles are reviews of previous research done on response rates; you may wish to read Linsky (1975) for a good example of such an article. Heberlein and Baumgartner take a very different approach. They used 98 questionnaire studies as cases in their own study constructed to assess the effect of various research characteristics, sample characteristics, questionnaire characteristics, and research procedures on the initial and final response rates to mailed questionnaires. The importance and relevance of the topic and the total number of contacts were found to be the two most predictive factors.

Although Heberlein and Baumgartner note no significant changes in response rates over the years in the studies they examined, there is some evidence that the general population is less likely to respond to questionnaires in recent years (*Footnotes,* 1974:2). The lower the response rate, the less assurance that the sample acquired accurately reflects the sample originally selected on the larger population (see Section 2.3 on sampling). Two points, however, mitigate this conclusion. First, the research of Koenig et al. (1977) demonstrates that moderate response rates do not necessarily mean that the acquired sample incorrectly reflects the larger population; these researchers found that samples with 40–50 percent response rates quite accurately reflected the population. Second, the use of carefully designed surveys incorporating the research findings on response rates will generally result in response rates in excess of 75 percent. Dillman (1978) extensively describes and illustrates these strategies. In sum, the survey design remains the best design for studying a large number of variables for a large number of people.

REFERENCES

Brown, Julia and Brian G. Gilmarten
    1969   "Sociology today: lacunae, emphases, and surfeits." American Sociologist 4(November):283–91.

Dillman, Don A.
    1978   Mail and Telephone Surveys: The Total Design Method. New York: Wiley
        Interscience.
Duncan, Otis D., Howard Schuman, and Beverly Duncan.
    1973   Social Change in a Metropolitan Community. New York: Russell Sage.
Footnotes
    1974   "Survey research problems getting worse, study shows." Footnotes
        2(May):2.
Jacobson, Robert L.
    1977   "Does high academic achievement create problems later on?" Chronicle of
        Higher Education, May 23, p. 4.
Koenig, Daniel J., Gary R. Martin, and Lauren H. Seiler
    1977   "Response rates and quality of data: a re-examination of the mail question-
        naire." Review of Canadian Sociology and Anthropology 14(4):432–38.
Linsky, Arnold S.
    1975   "Stimulating response to mailed questionnaires: a review." Public Opinion
        Quarterly 39(Spring):82–101.
Ognibene, Peter
    1970   "Traits affecting questionnaire response." Journal of Advertising Research
        10(June):18–20.

FRIENDSHIP, PROXIMITY, AND SELF-DISCLOSURE

Zick Rubin
Stephen Shenker

"A friend," Emerson wrote, "is a person with whom I may be sincere. Before him I may think aloud." A large number of studies have documented the link between friendship and the disclosure of personal thoughts and feelings that Emerson's statement implies (see Chaikin & Derlega, 1974; and Cozby, 1973, for useful reviews). But little of this research takes us beyond the empirical generalization that friendship and self-disclosure tend to be related. Little is known about the conditions under which this link is stronger or weaker. The primary goal of this study was to explore in greater detail the links between friendship and self-disclosure in the context of real-life dyadic relationships. An additional goal was to explore the role of physical proximity in establishing patterns of self-disclosure—specifically, whether the two members of the dyad lived in the same or different dormitory rooms.

Predictions were made concerning the links between friendship, proximity, and self-disclosure in different topical areas. It was predicted that friendship would be positively related to self-disclosure in all areas, but that this relationship would be greatest with respect to intimate topics, such as one's self-concept and relationships with others. Whereas people's willingness to disclose superficial information about themselves may have relatively little to do with the closeness of their

This study was planned and conducted while the authors were at Harvard University, in collaboration with Christine Arkell, Richard Baron, David Felson, Edward Koh, Gary Greenberg, Nancy Shea, Peter Smith, and Karen Wilson. We are also grateful to Susan G. Willard and Christine Dunkel for their assistance with the data analysis and to Charles T. Hill and David Kenny for their comments on the manuscript.

friendship, disclosure of more intimate information seems to be more intrinsically related to friendship. It was expected that, as suggested by previous studies (e.g., Newcomb, 1961; Priest & Sawyer, 1967), assigned roommates would come to be closer friends than would non-roommates living on the same floor. It also seemed reasonable to expect greater self-disclosure among roommates than among non-roommates, even when their degree of friendship was held constant. A more specific prediction was that the greater self-disclosure among roommates would be most pronounced with respect to superficial topics and least pronounced with respect to more intimate topics. Whereas the fact that two people live in the same room may make it almost inevitable that they will discuss such matters as their political attitudes or musical tastes, the constraints to discuss more intimate matters should be less pressing. Thus we are predicting that whereas friendship will be most highly related to the extent of intimate disclosure, proximity will be most highly related to the extent of relatively superficial disclosure.

An additional purpose of this study was to investigate sex differences in patterns of self-disclosure. Previous studies have concluded that women tend to disclose themselves to their same-sex friends to a greater extent than men do (Jourard, 1971). It has also been suggested that friendship and self-disclosure are more highly related to one another among women than among men (e.g., Booth, 1972; Jourard, 1971). Both of these suggestions are in general accord with the notion that women are trained to be "social-emotional specialists," for whom the expression of feelings and the sharing of confidences play a more central role in friendship than they do for "task-oriented" men (Parsons & Bales, 1955). But although these suggestions have achieved some degree of popular acceptance, they are not well documented; very few studies have systematically compared male and female patterns of self-disclosure. The present study focused directly on such cross-sex comparisons.

A final purpose of this study was a methodological one. Whereas various theoretical frameworks refer to the role of self-disclosure in the development of relationships (e.g., Altman & Taylor, 1973; Rubin, 1974), methodological sophistication has lagged behind theoretical development in this area. For example, questionnaire studies of self-disclosure have usually been based on reports from only one member of a dyad, and the reliability of such reports is almost never assessed. Assessments of the reciprocity of self-disclosure derived from such reports from only one person are highly suspect. In the present report we will devote considerable space to the issue of reliability and to possible biases underlying people's reports of self-disclosure. Such biases deserve attention not only because they may lead to artifactual conclusions, but also because they may be of considerable theoretical interest in their own right.

METHOD

Developing the Self-disclosure Questionnaire

Although previous investigators have developed pools of "intimacy-scaled" items (e.g., Taylor & Altman, 1966; Worthy, Gary, & Kahn, 1969), none of the existing item pools seemed entirely appropriate for the present subject population. Therefore, a new pool of 60 items was developed, borrowing from those used by Jourard (1971) and Taylor and Altman (1966) and adding new items of our own. The items were categorized in four clusters, in what we thought would be ascending order of intimacy—tastes, attitudes, interpersonal relationships and self-concept (to be referred to as interpersonal), and sex. These items were administered to 22 female and 28 male freshmen at Harvard and Radcliffe (members of the same population to be sampled in the later study). The students were asked to rate each item on an 11-point scale of intimacy, with endpoints defined as follows:

1 = Not intimate at all; i.e., the sort of thing one would freely disclose to almost anyone, or which is extremely impersonal in nature.

11 = Extremely intimate; i.e., the sort of thing one would disclose only with great difficulty, or which is extremely personal in nature.

As expected, the mean intimacy ratings were greatest in the sex area, followed by interpersonal, attitudes, and tastes. Women's rating tended to be higher than men's, especially in the sex area. From this initial pool, 32 items were selected—eight in each of the four content areas—for inclusion in the questionnaire. The items were selected with a view toward preserving the intimacy ordering of the four topic areas, while at the same time including some range of intimacy within each area. The 32 items are presented in Table 1, together with the mean intimacy ratings of men and women. As on the total initial pool of items, women gave higher intimacy ratings than men. The sex difference was greatest on sex items, somewhat smaller on interpersonal items, still smaller on attitude items, and nonexistent on taste items. The substantial difference between men's and women's intimacy ratings of the sex items emphasizes the fact that "intimacy" is not a universally agreed upon attribute, but rather depends upon prevailing cultural norms. Nevertheless, our male and female raters produced the same rank-ordering of the four topic areas with respect to intimacy. Over all 32 items, the correlation between women's and men's rankings was .96.

On the questionnaire respondents were asked to report on a 3-point scale how much they had revealed about each topic (presented in random order) to a specified target person. The 3-point scale was defined as follows:

Circle 0 if you have told _____ nothing about this aspect of yourself.

Circle 1 if you have told something about this aspect of yourself to _____, but never fully or in great detail. I.e., _____ has a general idea of this aspect of you.

Circle 2 if you have talked to _____ fully or in great detail about this aspect of yourself. I.e., _____ has rather full information about this aspect of you.

Table 1. Mean rated intimacy of self-disclosure items

	Women (N = 22)		Men (N = 28)		Average
	M	SD	M	SD	M
I. Sex					
1. My first sexual experience.	9.05	2.80	7.96	2.85	8.51
2. Persons with whom I have had sexual activity.	8.73	2.86	7.89	3.07	8.31
3. Feelings I have had after engaging in sexual activity.	9.50	2.37	7.07	3.31	8.29
4. The kinds of sexual activity I prefer.	9.27	2.41	7.14	3.30	8.21
5. Feelings about my sexual adequacy.	9.50	2.44	6.75	3.43	8.13
6. My feelings about my own sexual attractiveness.	8.45	2.61	6.39	2.62	7.42
7. The extent of my sexual experience.	8.50	2.86	5.79	3.45	7.15
8. My feelings about having premarital sexual intercourse.	4.45	2.99	3.50	2.89	3.98
All sex items	8.43	2.67	6.56	3.12	7.50
II. Interpersonal Relations and Self-Concept					
1. Disappointments or bad experiences I have had in love affairs.	8.00	3.37	6.46	2.77	7.23
2. Times when I felt that I was in love.	7.09	3.32	6.04	3.53	6.57
3. The things that I worry about most.	6.68	3.15	6.46	3.04	6.57
4. My attitudes toward my closest friends.	7.36	2.97	5.32	2.82	6.34
5. The kinds of things that make me especially proud of myself.	6.09	2.96	5.50	2.75	5.80
6. My thoughts about how intelligent I am compared to the other people around me.	6.18	2.70	4.43	2.54	5.31

Table 1. Continued

	Women (N = 22)		Men (N = 28)		Average
	M	SD	M	SD	M
7. Why some people like or dislike me.	5.95	3.02	3.86	2.74	4.91
8. My feelings about my parents.	5.14	2.40	4.64	3.57	4.89
All interpersonal items	6.56	2.99	5.34	2.97	5.95
III. Attitudes					
1. My religious views.	4.91	2.54	2.00	1.68	3.46
2. How important school grades are to me.	3.27	2.66	2.32	1.87	2.80
3. My feelings about the Harvard student body.	2.59	1.89	2.14	2.30	2.37
4. The kind of work I would like to do in the future.	2.36	1.40	2.07	1.86	2.22
5. My feelings about my teachers at Harvard.	2.05	1.70	2.21	1.68	2.13
6. My feelings about the Vietnam War.	2.09	1.48	1.61	1.31	1.85
7. My opinion of the American political system.	1.82	1.33	1.71	1.46	1.77
8. My view of the Nixon administration.	1.59	1.37	1.50	0.94	1.55
All attitude items	2.59	1.80	1.95	1.64	2.27
IV. Tastes					
1. How I feel about smoking pot.	1.71	1.30	2.91	2.09	2.31
2. Hobbies that I have or would like to take up.	1.77	1.27	1.82	1.37	1.80
3. My tastes in clothing.	1.73	1.39	1.75	2.10	1.74
4. My likes and dislikes in music.	1.91	1.23	1.54	1.50	1.73
5. How I would like to spend my summers.	1.68	0.89	1.68	1.36	1.68
6. My likes and dislikes in fiction.	1.32	0.65	1.46	1.10	1.39
7. Types of newspapers and magazines that I enjoy.	1.27	0.70	1.32	0.77	1.30
8. My preferences in food.	1.18	0.59	1.39	0.69	1.29
All taste items	1.57	1.00	1.73	1.37	1.66

Note.—1 = Not intimate at all; 11 = Extremely intimate.

On the next page of the questionnaire, the respondent was asked to respond to each item on the same scale, with respect to the amount the target person had disclosed to him. Preceding the two self-disclosure scales, the questionnaire also included several questions about the dyad's degree of friendship.

Procedure

The questionnaire was administered to freshmen at Harvard and Radcliffe late in the fall term, when the pairs had been living in the same room or on the same dormitory floor for approximately four months. Roommate pairs had been assigned by university officials before the freshmen arrived on campus. Certain habits and preferences—e.g., smoking, hours, stated racial or religious preferences—are taken into account in making these assignments. There is no association between such characteristics and the particular dormitory or floor to which students are assigned. Pairs of students who knew one another before arriving on campus were excluded from the study.

Four types of pairs were included in the study, to be referred to as male roommates, male hallmates, female roommates, and female hallmates. All of the respondents lived in double rooms (i.e., two persons living in one room) in same-sex dormitories and used a bathroom shared by everyone on the floor. Although the men's rooms were on the average somewhat larger than the women's, the general type of rooming arrangement was similar. Specific dormitory floors were assigned in advance to the roommate and hallmate conditions. Because of the details involved in administering hallmate questionnaires (see below) it was convenient to assign to this condition floors with a fairly large number of eligible rooms on them. Therefore certain entire floors were used to recruit the hallmate pairs, while more scattered rooms were used in the roommate condition. There is no reason to believe that respondents in the two conditions differed on any preexisting characteristics. Almost every freshman double room at Harvard and Radcliffe that satisfied the geographical requirements was used in order to obtain the desired number of pairs. The questionnaires were administered by five male and three female researchers, themselves Harvard and Radcliffe freshmen. Researchers generally collected data from respondents of the opposite sex to minimize the likelihood that the researcher and respondent would know one another. Each researcher was assigned a list of rooms for the roommate condition and another list for the hallmate condition. Rooms could not subsequently be switched from one condition to another. The administration of the questionnaire proceeded as follows:

Roommate condition. If both roommates were present when the experimenter arrived at the room, each was asked to fill out a questionnaire concerning "friendship and acquaintanceship at Harvard." In this condition as in all others the students were first asked if they had known each other before arriving on campus, and if they had they were eliminated from the sample. The students were told that their responses would be kept confidential and were requested not to talk to each other while filling out the questionnaire. The experimenter then left and returned about 15 minutes later to pick up the completed questionnaires, which took about 10 minutes to fill out. If only one of the roommates was at home, he or she was given the questionnaire and designated member A of the

pair. The experimenter returned later that evening or, if necessary, on succeeding days, to administer the questionnaire to member B. Although A was asked not to discuss the questionnaire with B, we note the possibility for communication from A to B about the questionnaire in the intervening period.

Hallmate condition. In creating the hallmate pairs, we wanted to avoid creating pairs in which the two partners hardly knew one another, a situation which would have occurred frequently if random pairing had been employed. Inasmuch as roommates are not necessarily close friends, however, we did not want the hallmate pairs necessarily to be "best friends" either. The procedure adopted was to ask each eligible person on a hallmate floor to write on a slip of paper his or her name and the name of the same-sex person on the floor he or she knew best, excluding his or her roommate. It was stressed that this was not necessarily the person he or she liked best, but simply the person he or she knew best. The slips were arranged in the order in which they were completed (usually in order of room number), and pairings were subsequently made from these choices. The first person to choose a particular other received that person as his or her partner. Anyone else choosing either member of that pair was eliminated from the sample. Questionnaires were then administered separately to each member of the formed pairs. Each person was told who his or her target person would be, without any explanation of just how the pairings were made. For purposes of analysis the chooser in each pair is designated member A and the chosen person as member B.

It is to be noted that the procedure for selecting pairs of roommates and of hallmates is not comparable in all respects. Most notably, the hallmate pairs are asymmetrical—member A chose member B, and this choice was not necessarily reciprocated—whereas no such asymmetry was involved in the roommate pairs. Nevertheless, aspects of the results to be presented suggest that the method of selecting pairs was successful in achieving its basic aim: to create pairs of roommates and hallmates who were roughly comparable in their degree of friendship, but who differed with respect to their degree of physical proximity.

An attempt was made to obtain 20 pairs in each of the sex × proximity conditions. Well over half of the questionnaires were completed on the first evening of administration, and most of the remainder were collected within four days. Virtually none of the people asked to take part in the study refused to do so. However, a number of students could not be found in their rooms even after repeated visits. The actual number of pairs obtained in each condition were 14 male roommates, 14 male hallmates, 15 female roommates, and 20 female hallmates. Because the responses of individuals are not independent, all analyses are conducted on the pair level ($N = 63$ pairs).

RESULTS AND DISCUSSION
Disclosure Scores

Respondents' scores on the eight individual items within each of the four topic areas were summed to provide the basic indices of disclosure. Each respondent generated eight subscores: four indices of disclosure "given" to the partner, and four indices of disclosure "received" from the partner. On each index scores could range from 0 to 16. The actual grand mean was 6.49.

Reliability, Perceived Reciprocity, and Actual Reciprocity

The reliability of the self-disclosure reports was assessed by correlating across pairs the sender's reports of "disclosure given" and the receiver's reports of "disclosure received" in each of the four topic areas (see Table 2). Each of these correlations is computed by taking the average of two component correlations—that between A's given and B's received, and that between B's given and A's received. The obtained correlations suggest that the

self-disclosure reports are at least moderately reliable, with values ranging from .62 to .72 for men, and .51 to .78 for women. These values were also compared to the correlations between one partner's report of disclosure given in one area and the other partner's report of disclosure received in other areas. In almost all cases the reliability indices exceeded these inter-partner cross-area correlations, suggesting that self-disclosures in different topical areas were discriminated reasonably well in the two partners' reports.[1]

The perceived reciprocity indices given in Table 2 are the correlations between a person's reports of disclosure given to the partner and of disclosure received from the partner. Thus they represent intra-subjective perceptions of symmetry or reciprocity. As in the case of the reliability indices, each correlation is actually the average of two correlations—one obtained from A and the other from B. The actual reciprocity indices are the correlations between A's disclosure given and B's disclosure given in each area. Thus they represent inter-subjective perceptions of reciprocity. As Table 2 indicates, there is an extremely high level of perceived reciprocity in all topical areas, with values in almost all cases exceeding both the corresponding reliability index and the corresponding index of actual reciprocity. In other words, there is a very strong tendency for respondents of both sexes to report that they have disclosed amounts proportionate to the amounts they have been disclosed to. This tendency was found to an approximately equal degree among pairs of roommates and pairs of hallmates.

Table 2. Indices of reliability, perceived reciprocity, and actual reciprocity.

	Women			Men		
	Reliability[a]	Perceived reciprocity[b]	Actual reciprocity[c]	Reliability[a]	Perceived reciprocity[b]	Actual reciprocity[c]
Sex	.78	.76	.62	.68	.68	.48
Interpersonal	.58	.78	.48	.76	.88	.63
Attitudes	.56	.83	.60	.66	.87	.69
Tastes	.51	.78	.49	.62	.90	.69
All topics	.66	.88	.64	.76	.92	.71

[a]Average of correlations between A's given–B's received and B's given–A's received.
[b]Average of correlation between A's given–A's received and B's given–B's received.
[c]Correlation between A's given and B's given.

The high degree of perceived reciprocity of self-disclosure may be accounted for in terms of a pervasive tendency for people to view social relationships as symmetrical. The notion that self-disclosure should be symmetrical is implicit in Gouldner's (1960) discussion of the more general "norm of reciprocity" underlying social relationships. The specific tendency to view self-disclosure as symmetrical has been documented by DeSoto and Kuethe (1959), who found that if subjects are told only that "A confides in B," they tend to ascribe a very high probability to the fact that "B confides in A" as well. The present results suggest that such a perceptual tendency applies even to people's reports of self-disclosure in their own relationships. Since reports of disclosure given always preceded reports of disclosure received, respondents may have adjusted their reports of the latter in order to conform more closely to the former, thus paying tribute to the reciprocity norm. It is also possible that more general response biases, such as the tendency to respond in extreme rather than moderate terms, also contributed to the extremely high indices of perceived reciprocity. A similar tendency for perceived reciprocity greatly to exceed actual reciprocity was reported by Levinger and Senn (1967) in a study of self-disclosure in married couples.

The perceived reciprocity indices clearly overestimate the true degree of reciprocity of self-disclosure. These data make clear, therefore, that estimates of self-disclosure reciprocity which are obtained from only one person cannot be taken at face value. The actual reciprocity indices presented in Table 2 may also overestimate the true degree of reciprocity to some extent. This would be true to the extent that both partners' reports were biased by the same or similar factors, such as how much time they spent together. Nevertheless, the data suggest that there is a considerable degree of actual reciprocity, with correlations ranging from .48 to .69 for men and from .48 to .62 for women.[2] There is no evidence to indicate whether reports of disclosure given or of disclosure received are more reliable. In the present analysis of the self-disclosure data, both types of reports are given equal weight.

Reports of Friendship

In the analysis of variance of self-disclosure reports that follows, one of the factors is the reported level of closeness of the dyad's friendship. Before presenting the self-disclosure data, therefore, we will first present the data concerning reported friendship. Two "attraction" questions were included on the questionnaire. One question asked respondents to indicate on a 7-point scale "How close is your friendship with _____?" The other asked them to indicate on a 7-point scale "How much do you like_____?" There was considerable agreement between the two partners' "closeness" reports, with A–B correlations of .62 for men and .60 for women. There was less agreement on liking reports, with correlations of only .38 for men and .45 for women. The greater agreement on the friendship question seems reasonable, since it calls for the estimate of a shared dyadic characteristic (the closeness of their friendship), whereas the liking question refers to a unilateral attitude. In the subsequent analysis of self-disclosure reports the closeness estimates will be employed as a categorizing measure.

A 3-way analysis of variance of the closeness estimates was conducted. There were two between-dyad factors, Sex and Proximity (Roommate or Hallmate), and one within-dyad factor (Member A or Member B). The analysis of variance produced a significant main effect of Proximity, F (1,60) = 4.13, $p = < .05$, and a marginally significant Sex $\times$ Proximity interaction, F (1,60) = 2.80, $p = .10$. The mean scores presented in Table 3 indicate that both of these between-group effects are primarily attributable to the fact that male hallmates reported their friendships as being less close than did respondents in any of the other three groups. The differences among the other three groups were small and nonsignificant. One possible explanation for the obtained pattern is that women assigned to the hallmate condition were more likely than men to nominate a close friend as the person they "knew best" on their floor. Such a difference might be attributable to a general tendency—to be documented later—for friendship and self-disclosure (which would involve "knowing well") to be more highly linked among women than among men. It is also possible that the hallmate floors in the women's dormitories tended to be closer-knit than the hallmate floors in the men's dormitories. In any event, it is to be noted that pairs of female hallmates in our sample tended to be virtually as close as female roommates, and significantly closer than male hallmates.

Table 3. Mean reported closeness of friendship

| | Member of dyad | | | | Average[a] | |
| | Member A | | Member B | | | |
	Female	Male	Female	Male	Female	Male
Roommate	4.67	4.64	4.87	5.36	4.77 (15)	5.00 (14)
Hallmate	4.40	3.40	4.90	4.20	4.65 (20)	3.80 (15)
Average	4.28		4.83			

Note.—1 = Not close at all; 7 = Extremely close.
[a]Numbers in parentheses are the numbers of pairs in each of the four conditions.

Table 3 also reveals an unanticipated but highly significant main effect of the A–B factor, with member B across all conditions reporting that the pair had a closer friendship than member A did, $F(1,60) = 10.63$, $p < .002$. The interpretation of this finding is especially challenging because the A–B factor had a somewhat different meaning in the roommate and hallmate conditions. In the roommate condition, A was simply the first person to fill out the questionnaire (and when both roommates were contacted simultaneously the A–B assignment was arbitrary). In the hallmate condition, A was the person who nominated B as his partner (although in some instances the two may have nominated each other, in which case A was simply the first of the two to make the nomination). More often than not A also filled out the questionnaire first in the hallmate condition. To unravel "the case of the lopsided friendships" it seems necessary to postulate a combination of factors which center on the theme that when B filled out the questionnaire about A he was likely to know or to suspect either that A had already filled out a questionnaire about him or that A had nominated him as the person he knew best on the floor. Such knowledge or suspicion may have been sufficient to cause B to perceive his friendship with A as closer than he would have otherwise, thereby creating the obtained main effect. It may be that the knowledge that someone has either nominated you or devoted time to answering questions about you (presuming that he is not clearly perceived as a mortal enemy) is sometimes sufficient to foster an attribution of

closeness. Further research on such attributional processes would be of considerable interest.

The Analysis of Variance Design

The self-disclosure data were analyzed in an unweighted means analysis of variance design, using the pair as the basic unit of analysis. There were three between-group factors: two levels of Sex, two levels of Proximity (Roommate or Hallmate), and two levels of Friendship (Close or Not Close). To categorize the pairs on friendship we computed the geometric mean of the two partners' closeness reports. Use of the geometric mean rather than the arithmetic mean had the effect of lowering the friendship scores of pairs in which there was a disparity between the two partners' reports, an outcome that seemed desirable in light of the dyadic nature of friendship.[3] To equalize cell sizes, the dyads were divided into close friend and not close friend groups by dividing them at the median within their sex × proximity condition. These medians were 4.9 for female roommates, 4.5 for female hallmates, 4.9 for male roommates, and 3.9 for male hallmates. Thus it should be borne in mind that both "close friend" and "not close friend" pairs of male hallmates tend to be less close than corresponding pairs in any of the other three conditions.

In addition to these three between-group factors, there were three cross-cutting within-group factors: two Members of each dyad (A and B), two Directions of disclosure reports (Given and Received), and four Topics of disclosure (Sex, Interpersonal, Attitudes, and Tastes). The analysis is summarized in Table 4. There were no main effects or simple interactions involving the A–B factor, and those more complex interactions that were obtained were not of great magnitude. To simplify the table, therefore, effects involving this factor are not included.

Main Effects on Disclosure Reports

The analysis of variance revealed three main effects on self-disclosure reports. There was greater disclosure among roommates than among hallmates (7.39 vs. 5.59) and much greater disclosure among close friend than among not close friend dyads (8.40 vs. 4.58). Both of these effects are substantial ones, accounting for 4.5% and 20.3% of the total variance of self-disclosure reports respectively. The factors of Friendship and of Proximity cannot be regarded as totally independent of one another, since the friendships in the male roommate condition tended to be closer than those in the male hallmate condition. Nevertheless, there is evidence for the independent effect of proximity on disclosure patterns. Among each of the four Sex × Friendship subgroups there was a clear tendency for greater disclosure among roommates than among hallmates.

In addition to these between-group main effects, there was a significant main effect of the topic of disclosure, accounting for 8.1% of the total variance. Most disclosure was reported with respect to attitudes (7.68), followed by tastes (7.19), interpersonal (6.58), and sex (4.51). Except for the reversal of attitudes and tastes, this ordering is precisely the inverse of the ordering of the four topics on rated intimacy. Finally, there was a slight overall tendency for women to report greater self-disclosure than men (6.80 vs. 6.18), but the effect fell far short of significance ($p = .27$). In the present instance, then, the notion that women disclose more than men do proves to be an oversimplification. As we will see, there were indeed sex differences in patterns of self-disclosure, but they involved interactions with other factors.

Friendship and Topical Disclosure

The analysis of variance revealed significant or near-significant Friendship × Topic and Proximity × Topic interactions, which we will dicuss in turn. The Friendship × Topic interaction ($p = .001$) is depicted in Figure 1. The nature of this interaction is quite orderly: As the intimacy of the topic increases from low levels (tastes and attitudes) to higher levels (interpersonal and sex), the friendship level of the dyad becomes increasingly related to self-disclosure. (Friendship is somewhat more highly related to interpersonal disclosure than to sex disclosure, however, perhaps in part because of the fact that the amount of disclosure about sex in the not close friend dyads is near the bottom of the scale, thus limiting the potential close–not close difference.) This interaction was predicted. Whether or not one chooses to tell another person about one's views of the Carter administration or one's favorite magazines may have rather little to do with the closeness of their friendship. When it comes to telling another person about one's sexual experiences or self-concept, on the other hand, the closeness of their friendship will be much more important. Results conforming to this pattern have also been obtained in a role-playing simulation of the acquaintance process conducted by Frankfurt (summarized in Altman & Taylor, 1973, pp. 84–93). It should be stressed that no single causal link between friendship and self-disclosure is documented by the present data. It is likely that the link

Table 4. Summary of analysis of variance of self-disclosure reports

Source	df	F
Sex (male/female)	1	1.26
Proximity (roommate/hallmate)	1	10.33**
Friendship (close/not close)	1	46.43***
Dyads	55	
Direction of report (given/received)	1	1.36
Direction × dyads	55	
Topic of disclosure	3	32.38***
Sex × Topic	3	7.32***
Friendship × Topic	3	4.28*
Sex × Friendship × Topic	3	3.10*
Topic × dyads	165	
Direction × Topic	3	2.81*
Direction × Topic × dyads	55	

*$p < .05$.
**$p < .01$.
***$p < .001$.

Note.—Table includes all main effects and those interactions significant at the .05 level. Effects involving the A–B factor are not included.

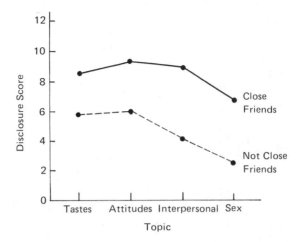

Figure 1 Average reported disclosure as a function of Friendship and Topic

is bi-directional. That is, people may be more likely to reveal intimate matters to their close friends than to less close friends, and they may come to be closer friends (or to attribute greater closeness to their relationship) as a result of intimate revelations. Finally, we shall see shortly that the Friendship × Topic interaction was not found to an equal degree among both men and women. In fact, it was primarily the female subjects who produced the pattern of results just discussed.

Proximity and Topical Disclosure

The general tendency for roommates to disclose themselves more than hallmates has already been discussed. It was predicted, in addition, that this proximity effect would be greatest with respect to relatively superficial topics of disclosure, and less striking with respect to more intimate topics. In intimate areas, it is reasoned, one does not disclose oneself merely because one happens to share a room with the other person. Whether or not one discloses oneself will depend to a much larger extent on one's feelings of friendship toward the other, as discussed above. In more superficial areas, however, spatial arrangements may exert a greater influence on disclosure. In the process of living in the same room with another person over a period of several months certain topics will almost inevitably come up, including many of those on our list of attitudes and tastes, whereas these topics are less likely to come up among dyads who do not live together. The obtained Proximity × Topic interaction was only marginally significant, F (3,165) =

2.34, $p = .076$. But it corresponded precisely to our prediction, as shown in Figure 2. The tendency for roommates to disclose more than hallmates was greatest in the taste area, smaller for attitudes and interpersonal, and virtually nonexistent for sex. This interaction was obtained in spite of the fact that male roommates tended to be closer friends than male hallmates, a difference which would tend to reverse the shape of the interaction. It is likely that if roommates and hallmates could have been equated on the closeness of their friendships, therefore, the obtained interaction would have been more striking.

Sex Differences

As reported earlier, there was no main effect of sex on self-disclosure reports. There were, however, several significant interaction effects involving the Sex factor. These effects point to some interesting and subtle sex differences in the patterning of self-disclosure. First, there was a significant Sex × Topic interaction ($p < .001$). As Figure 3 reveals, women tended to disclose much more than men in the interpersonal area ($p < .001$). There were no significant differences between the two sexes with respect to the other three topics, although with respect to attitudes there was a slight tendency for men to disclose more than women ($p = .33$). The tendency for women to reveal more than men about their interpersonal relationships is consistent with the image of women as "social-emotional specialists," while the slight tendency for men to reveal more about political and

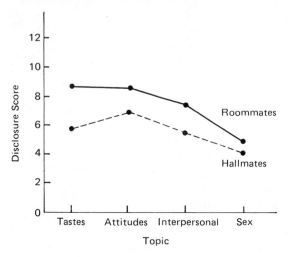

Figure 2   Average reported disclosure as a function of Proximity and Topic

social attitudes may be consistent with their image as "task specialists." An analogous tendency for women to reveal more in social-emotional but not task-related areas was found in a laboratory study by Rubin and Hill (cited in Rubin, 1974).

There was also a significant three-way interaction between the factors of Sex, Friendship, and Topic ($p = .029$). This interaction further specifies the Friendship $\times$ Topic and Sex $\times$ Topic interactions already discussed. Among women, the relationship between friendship and self-disclosure increases steadily as we move from less intimate to more intimate topics with the strongest relationship in the sex area. Among men, on the other hand, the relationship between friendship and self-disclosure is about equally strong in all four topic areas. The data suggest that women tend to link self-disclosure in intimate areas with close friendship to a greater extent than men do. On the basis of his earlier research, Jourard (1971, p. 25) concluded that "the strong association between liking and disclosure was peculiar to females." The present data point to a more subtle conclusion. The link between friendship and self-disclosure was clearly found among both sexes. (Note that the two-way interaction between Sex and Friendship

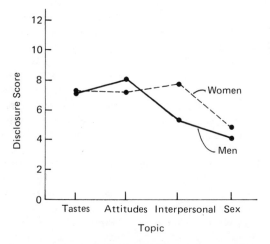

Figure 3   Average reported disclosure as a function of Sex and Topic

across all topic areas was not significant.) But whereas among men this link is about equally strong for disclosure in all topic areas, among women the strength of the link is directly related to the intimacy of the disclosure topic.

Why is self-disclosure in intimate topic areas more strongly related to friendship among women than among men? Once again, this finding seems to be in accord with prevailing notions of sex-role differentiation.

For "social-emotional" females, the expression of feelings and exchange of confidences about intimate matters, such as sex and interpersonal relationships, may play a more central role in friendship than they do for "task-oriented" males. Douvan and Adelson (1966) suggest such a sex difference in their discussion of adolescent friendships. They propose that girls' same-sexed friendships are closely tied to the desire to explore one's sexual nature and individuality, whereas boys' friendships are more closely related to the struggle for autonomy against the elder generation. They go on to suggest that dyadic friendships are more intense and intimate for adolescent girls than for boys. Some congruent evidence comes from a recent questionnaire study of adult friendships (Booth, 1972) which found that women reported considerably more sharing of confidences than men did. Similarly, Rubin (1970) reported that college women "loved" their same-sex friends more than men did, on a "love scale" which includes components of attachment, caring, and intimacy. It should be noted that none of these explanations resolve the question of the causal link between friendship and self-disclosure. It may be that both sexes define "closeness" of friendship in similar terms, and that there is a stronger link between such closeness and intimate self-disclosure among women than among men. Alternatively, as Booth (1972) has also suggested, the link may be due in part to attributional and/or linguistic factors— women may be more likely to label as "close friends" people whom they confide in. It seems likely that both of these mechanisms underlie the obtained relationship to some extent.

Disclosures Given and Received

There was no overall tendency for respondents to report giving more disclosure than they received or vice-versa. But there was a significant interaction between the Direction (Given vs. Re-

ceived) and Topic of disclosure ($p < .05$). There was a tendency for respondents to report giving more disclosure than they received with respect to the relatively superficial topics of attitudes and tastes. There was no such tendency, and if anything a slight trend in the opposite direction, with respect to the more intimate topics of sex and interpersonal. There are several possible interpretations of these trends, in terms of both memory effects and response biases. Unfortunately, the data do not provide any clear indication of which set of reports—those of disclosure given or of disclosure received—is a more accurate reflection of reality. In spite of the obtained trends, however, the general pattern of means indicates a close correspondence between reported levels of disclosure given and received.

Conclusions

A large number of findings have been reported concerning the links between friendship, proximity, and self-disclosure in the context of the freshman dormitory. As predicted, friendship was most highly related to self-disclosure in intimate topic areas, while proximity tended to be most highly related to self-disclosure in more superficial topic areas. It was also found that intimate self-disclosure and friendship were more highly related to one another among women than among men. These findings help to emphasize the interplay of factors—personal, role-related, and environmental—which underlie patterns of friendship and self-disclosure (cf. Altman & Taylor, 1973). They also emphasize the importance of viewing self-disclosure in differentiated terms, rather than as a single monolithic entity. It is suggested, for example, that the fact that two people have been assigned to be one another's roommates will have a major effect on their self-disclosure in certain areas associated with day-to-day living, but may have relatively little direct effect on their more intimate self-disclosure. It is also suggested that intimate self-disclosure may play a more prominent role in the friendships of women than of men. It is doubtful that this difference has much to do with innate characteristics of the two sexes; it seems more likely to stem from differential patterns of socialization. To the extent that some of these differences in socialization are now in the process of being reduced, we may expect intimate self-disclosure to come to play a similarly important role in the friendships of both sexes.

Finally, several methodological points may be offered, together with suggestions for further research. First, these findings were obtained from a very restricted population—freshmen at a particular New England university. The extent to which the findings may be generalizable to other populations remains a question for further research. Second, the questions involving the reliability and validity of self-disclosure reports are by no means resolved by the correlations reported in this paper. Indeed, several pieces of evidence converged on the conclusion that self-disclosure reports may be distorted in one or more ways. Further research concerning the systematic biases which may underlie self-disclosure reports, including the tendency to overestimate the degree of reciprocity between members of a dyad, would be of great value. Such research would not only be methodologically useful, but would also be of theoretical interest in its own right. Third, studies of self-disclosure conducted at one point in time, such as the present one, leave unanswered many important and fascinating questions concerning causal processes in the development of relationships. In order to shed light on these causal processes, methodologically sophisticated longitudinal studies are called for (e.g., Curry & Kenny, 1974).

NOTES

[1]These comparisons also indicated that there was a greater degree of discriminability among the four topic areas among women than among men.

[2]Collapsing across the four topic areas, the actual reciprocity indices were .59 for male roommates, .77 for male hallmates, .67 for female roommates, and .61 for female hallmates.

[3]For example, a hypothetical pair in which both partners responded to the friendship question at the midpoint of the scale would be given a pair friendship score of

$$\sqrt{(4)\,(4)} = 4,$$

whereas a hypothetical pair in which one partner responded "1" and the other responded "7" would obtain a friendship score of

$$\sqrt{(1)\,(7)} = 2.64.$$

In most cases, however, the two partners' friendship scores were fairly close to one another, as reflected by the A–B correlations of about .60.

REFERENCES

Altman, I., & Taylor, D. A. *Social penetration: The development of interpersonal relationships.* New York: Holt, Rinehart and Winston, 1973.

Booth, A. Sex and social participation. *American Sociological Review*, 1972, 37, 183–193.

Chaikin, A., & Derlega, V. *Self-disclosure.* Morristown, N.J.: General Learning Press, 1974.

Cozby, P. C. Self-disclosure: A literature review. *Psychological Bulletin*, 1973, 79, 73–91.

Curry, T. J., & Kenny, D. A. The effects of perceived and actual similarity in values and personality in the process of interpersonal attraction. *Quality and Quantity*, 1974, 8, 29–44.

DeSoto, C. B., & Kuethe, J. L. Subjective probabilities of interpersonal relationships. *Journal of Abnormal and Social Psychology*, 1959, 59, 290–294.

Douvan, E., & Adelson, J. *The adolescent experience.* New York: John Wiley, 1966.

Gouldner, A. W. The norm of reciprocity: A preliminary statement. *American Sociological Review*, 1960, 25, 161–169.

Jourard, S. M. *Self-disclosure: An experimental analysis of the transparent self.* New York: Wiley-Interscience, 1971.

Levinger, G., & Senn, D. J. Disclosure of feelings in marriage. *Merrill-Palmer Quarterly of Behavior and Development*, 1967, 13, 237–249.

Newcomb, T. M. *The acquaintance process.* New York: Holt, Rinehart and Winston, 1961.

Parsons, T., & Bales, R. F. *Family, socialization, and interaction process.* Glencoe, Ill.: Free Press, 1955.

Priest, R. F., & Sawyer, J. Proximity and peership: Bases of balance in interpersonal attraction. *American Journal of Sociology*, 1967, 72, 633–649.

Rubin, Z. Measurement of romantic love. *Journal of Personality and Social Psychology*, 1970, 16, 265–273.

Rubin, Z. Lovers and other strangers: The development of intimacy in encounters and relationships. *American Scientist*, 1974, 62, 182–190.

Taylor, D. A., & Altman, I. Intimacy-scaled stimuli for use in studies of interpersonal relations. *Psychological Reports*, 1966, 19, 729–730.

Worthy, M., Gary, A. L., & Kahn, G. M. Self-disclosure as an exchange process. *Journal of Personality and Social Psychology*, 1969, 13, 59–63.

THE ROLE OF THE INTERVIEWER

Jean M. Converse
Howard Schuman

LEARNING THE ROLE

The Ultimate Strategy

In a recent training session, a professional interviewer-and-supervisor of long experience and much personal warmth appeared as a guest lecturer. Students grilled her for what she would do *if:* What if the respondent refused to answer a whole batch of questions? What if another member of the family marched in and ordered her to leave? What if a party were going on? Liquor? Dope? They kept peppering her with questions, straining to conjure up still more unholy situations. The interviewer waited for a moment of quiet, and then smiled:

I am calling at another person's home. If I am not already a guest, I hope to become one. So I hope I behave as I try to on other such occasions—with graciousness, tact, friendliness, courtesy. . . .

I cannot really say what I would do exactly under the circumstances you mention because it would depend on the particular people at the particular moment. All that I can say is that when they happen, I will try to behave as I always try—with respect, with courtesy.

The barrage of questions subsided.

The professional interviewer counseling conventional tact and courtesy has already achieved a competence bred of experience, confidence, and poise. She has blended her own personal attributes and beliefs in a style of relating to respondents that poses no strain to her own sense of her total personality. The role of interviewer has become a real part of her, *one* of her ways of behaving "naturally." If her advice is excellent for almost any interaction, it nevertheless reveals little of how she *got* that way.

Shaking Off Self-consciousness

Most beginning interviewers feel a strain between the way they behave "naturally," and the way they are to behave in interviews. They observe themselves (often too minutely, of course) and feel false, awkward, and perhaps even manipulative because they cannot quite make the structured role of interviewer fit with the other styles of their own behavior. In fact, the beginner can be so intensely aware of himself and his own experience that he observes nothing so well as his own discomfort. The following interviewer is perhaps a bit more insightful than many; at least she looks up to notice that she is generating nervousness in *other* people:

In my early interviews, I began to notice that I was sending my reactions of nervousness almost by direct wire. When I felt my own manner becoming tense or unnatural, I noticed that some of my respondents actually began to behave in something of the same way— began to tap their foot, or move around the room.

Her recovery from self-absorption apparently proceeds apace, because she reports that successive respondents grew more relaxed and less twitchy.

Fearful that respondents will not accept them, some beginners fall prey to elaborate efforts to charm and please:

I found the temptation to handle situations in such a way that respondents would like me was overwhelming. In most cases it had nothing to do with the gluey term rapport. I just wanted people to like me—for my own ego. So I nodded like mad, murmured encouraging sounds, looked terribly interested, laughed at all jokes, patted all dogs, said hello to all children, etc., because those seemed to be good ways to get people to like me.

Abridged from Chapter 2 of *Conversations at Random: Survey Research as Interviewers See It* (New York: Wiley, 1974). Reprinted by permission of the Publishing Division of the Institute for Social Research and the authors. Footnotes renumbered.

(If anything, the behavior of this interviewer has doubtless become a good deal more "gluey" than some plain old *rapport* might have been.)[1]

Whether interviewers shrink "inward" in their discomfort or sally forth to charm all comers, the separation between one's usual self and the required interviewer personality is typical of the beginner's sense of strain....

Self-restraints of the Trade

Suppressing Opinions.   The fact that interviewers are not to express their own opinions is a cardinal tenet of interviewer training, and most interviewers are very conscientious about observing this rule. Only now and then does the pressure on the interviewer get too high. In the following account, an interviewer learns the hard way that neutrality is indeed the best policy:

When the respondent said, "Women shouldn't go past the first grade; then they couldn't take jobs away from men," I failed utterly to subdue my feminist spirit. I said, "What if she never marries or what if her husband dies or deserts her and she has children?"

I lapsed instantly into silence. I had biased the interview, in that I had revealed myself even more thoroughly to be the kind of female the respondent most objected to: not only was I working—I was in favor of women working!

Restraining Prejudice.   There is good evidence that blurting out opinions, however, is a less-serious problem than unconscious interviewer stereotyping of the respondent: anticipating his opinions, exaggerating a consistency in his views, or making assumptions on the basis of the respondent's group membership and social location.[2] This may lead the respondent to answer—unconsciously or not—the way the interviewer seems to expect; or it may lead the interviewer to make errors on the questionnaire, inadvertently checking the answer he anticipated hearing. This subtle form of interviewer influence doubtless deserves much more attention in training sessions than the direct impact of interviewer opinions. But it is a more difficult and complex matter: harder to "teach out" of interviewers, more difficult for interviewers to detect on their own.

In the following account, a self-critical interviewer analyzes her failure as one of professional neutrality, without fully understanding how she has anticipated her respondents' reaction on the basis of stereotyped expectations.

The study of black attitudes on which this interviewer worked was launched in the field a year after the Detroit riot of 1967, and a mere three weeks after the assassination of Dr. Martin Luther King. It was not an easy time for a white, liberal student to bottle up her own feelings; in fact, she becomes aware of how the interviewing situation actually focused and intensified her own guilt about racial conflict:

I had chosen to interview blacks, instead of whites, for very personal reasons that had not the remotest connection with furthering the cause of the social sciences, but I did not really understand my own motivation until I had done about half of my interviews. The assassination of Martin Luther King had shaken me to my bones. In some obscure way I shared the responsibility for it—I, the Do-Nothing Liberal, hiding in the graduate school library, laughing at the very idea of bigots and race prejudice.

After Dr. King was shot, I thought the only hope for racial peace in this country, apart from structural changes I felt powerless to effect, lay in whites and blacks getting together to talk. I didn't think it mattered much what they talked about, as long as they just started talking. My conviction of this was very irrational and very strong. Some primeval feeling.

Her attempt to put interviewing in the service of racial harmony does not work. The questionnaire is not a good instrument for the kind of "talking" that might have satisfied her soul; and her zeal for interviewing, high at the outset, collapses....

Expecting the Unexpected.   As David Riesman observes, the basic task of the interviewer is to "adapt the standardized questionnaire to the unstandardized respondents,"[3] but the marvelous intricacies of the unstandardized respondent are discoveries that interviewers usually make on their own: experience. Can more of this experience be brought into the initial training session? Such a process should offer two advantages: interviewers should be more comfortable and capable at the outset; the information they gather should be freer of their own stereotyping through expectations.

When an interviewer reports his own surprise at a respondent's reaction, we can be warned that he is working with somebody's overgeneralizations. He may have taken the general propositions of training for genuine predictors about people. But nothing always works—not even the tried-and-true idea that most people are reassured by the anonymity and confidentiality of polling:

Early in the week I stressed the anonymity angle, but after a while I merely gave it a mention. For most of my respondents, the questions were not touchy or threatening, and the respondents had no apparent need to be anonymous. In fact, a couple of men were really quite put off by the idea. One was actually quite incensed that we had not known his name and had sent a letter to the Head of Household. Another, who was quite resistant to the interview, began to relax and enjoy the whole thing only after I had duly noted his name on the questionnaire.

Discipline by Discovery.   The holding of strong convictions is not apparently the tragic flaw for interviewers. At least Stephen A. Richardson and his colleagues find that although field supervisors are prone to *assume* that the interviewer with strong value judgments may well "introduce bias and distortion into the research data he collects and . . . antagonize the people with whom he deals," the assumption is probably unwarranted.[4] . . .

Detroit Area Study interviewers certainly engage in a process of vexation and ventilation now and then, so we are well pleased to find that this may be associated with competence. There is another, perhaps stronger theme in our interviewers' reports, however, that we suspect incorporates something of the same self-discipline: the sense of learning and discovery. Interviewers often report with considerable exhilaration that their own personal and intellectual worlds have been widened by breaking out of the academy and walking in the cross-section. . . .

Interviewers who find this kind of discovery in the field apparently enjoy a certain personal advantage. They seem to *like interviewing more*—and more often come back "high" on the realities of people than bruised by the hard edges of the respondents' minds. We entertain what must be counted merely a faith that these more reflective interviewers also produce the necessary restraint and self-discipline as a by-product. At least their focus seems correct: the respondent himself is in the foreground, seen against the backdrop of his own life and situation, rather than veiled by ab-stractions of the interviewer's mind or blurred by agitations of the interviewer's own psyche. . . .

CONTINUING CROSS-PRESSURES

The interviewer is charged with the responsibility of conducting *inquiry* in something of the manner of a *conversation*. The product of the encounter is supposed to be good "hard" data—the stuff of codes and numbers and computer analysis. The process is supposed to be at least somewhat "soft"—the stuff of pleasant acquaintance. Beginners may have particular difficulty, but all interviewers continue to experience cross-pressures that would seem to be the very nature of the job.

The Pull of Conversation

The Respondent's Reach for Information. To many respondents, the interviewer is something of a curiosity. He is warm and friendly but he comes not in search of friendship—just answers. He carries on dialogue in a way that almost nobody does—just asking and asking, without talking about himself. Certain respondents try to test this interviewer-creature, sometimes in a search for relationship; more often in a quest for information about him and how he ticks—either because he finds the interviewer interesting and wishes to know more about him or because his own conversational ease requires more give-and-take than the interviewer's minimal responses provide.

In certain studies, the nonparticipating neutrality of the interviewer has proved utterly impossible. Daniel Lerner, for instance, reports that many of his highly educated Frenchmen simply would not talk to an ever-absorptive neutral.[5] He had to be willing to reciprocate—give his own ideas, even at times engage in spirited debate—or his respondents turned him out. This meant that along with his neutrality, Lerner had to give up his structured interview schedule as well.

When a respondent strains for information about the interviewer, delay is the recommended procedure: the interviewer explains that he is not to express his own opinions until after the questionnaire is over, and most respondents accept this rule of the game. . . .

The Respondent's Reach for Relationship. Respondents occasionally reach out to the interviewer for sheer company and warm personal contact. Lonely people may welcome the interview, not really to express their own public opinion or to determine the interviewer's, but simply to break their own isolation, as in this account:

She was a middle-aged woman whose children were grown and she lived alone with her husband, who was not at home. She was anxious to talk, but not really about the questionnaire. She gave answers only to placate my questions—and rapidly, as if to leave more time to talk about her family life. Every other word had something to do with her own childhood and the years in which her children were younger.

The Interviewer's Pull. Interviewers find that they, too, feel some strain toward relationship. One interviewer explains that she wished to be less fettered by strict question-and-answer, more free to take up the back-and-forth of conversation, especially in two kinds of situations. First, when she found the respondent especially appealing:

Although I tried to maintain the recommended stance with every respondent—not being so friendly as to lose my own objectivity or bias the respondent's views—it was much easier to do so with respondents with whom I had nothing in common. It was much harder with really congenial people. It seemed that the more I sensed similarity between myself and the other person, the harder it was to resist incorporating bits of social conversation.

This is an almost classic instance of the interaction that inspires distrust of rapport[6] and perhaps this interviewer is too responsive generally. It seems likely, however, that many interviewers occasionally feel this pull toward personalism (although in the best of all possible studies, the "error" thus produced would be small and random), and that it very probably cannot be sterilized out of survey research except at the cost of other, even more important values.

The second strain toward informal conversation reported by the same interviewer is probably also difficult to avoid entirely:

Mere chitchat of a cordial, friendly kind was sometimes just a breather. At certain times, especially after a few interviews, I would begin to feel that I was a machine that was wound up with questions. It seemed a pleasant break just to talk for a few minutes, to rest at the oasis before driving on.

Solving this kind of "problem" may be the task of researchers writing certain kinds of questionnaires—a matter to which we will return—or both problems may be largely insoluble. . . .

The Push of Inquiry

While the interviewing interaction creates pressures for warm, social conversation, the interview schedule counteracts with the pressure for cool, scientific inquiry. (The obvious solution, a marvelously conversational questionnaire that fits every situation is, just as obviously, impossible.) A typical survey schedule can be counted on to feature at least some question that will stop any conversation cold.

The Comedy of Questions. Even in the questionnaires that are decked out with a fair measure of conversational style and grace, a given question can be exquisitely inappropriate to a given respondent. "What remedy is there except biting humor," asks one interviewer, "when she's screaming at a house full of children and the noise makes your ear drums snap, and you have to ask her if she's having any problems with noisy neighbors!". . .

Other kinds of occasional "outrage" can be borne if the interviewer is able to grin as well as bear. Surely humor saved this situation, as the black respondent and his white wife were confronted by questions of racial attitude. Did he trust *most* white people, *some*, or *none* at all? They both laughed—and he judiciously answered *some*. When the interviewer asked how he would feel if a close relative married a white person, he and his wife both chimed in with hilarity: "Wouldn't mind at all, not a bit!" Very probably the only antidote to such ingenious inappropriateness is the very dose of the comic that the respondent helped the interviewer to apply.

Questions Close to the Tragic Bone. Should the interviewer ever protect the respondent from inquiry? The question is not often pursued by survey ethics: we assume that we insure the individual's anonymity; we guarantee the confidentiality of his answers; we generally do not deceive him—and this is enough. His candid answers are the very stuff of social science and should be of no harm to him.

For the great majority of respondents, that view is doubtless warranted. But what of the occasional respondent who should be protected from his own candor? The person whose very answering seems to jeopardize some of his own equanimity? The question is a fair one, for some unusual situations at least, and an interviewer brings it for thoughtful examination:[7]

How far should the interviewer pursue a series of questions which are obviously distressing to the respondent? Though it is true that most people know how to fend off the question which is sensitive and distressing, some people do not know how. They are so weak or so dependent or so honest that they will go right on answering the question that they don't want to answer, growing increasingly upset.

To take a real example that happened during our pretest: The man whose major "social problem" had been with the police, after he had committed a very serious crime. He kept saying that the interviewer should not be asking about it. The interviewer kept asking—and he kept responding. Should the interviewer have stopped? . . .

Clearly, sociology needs data to continue to develop as a social science, and perhaps to this end it is legitimate to ask questions which may be mildly distressing to the respondent? But we do need to draw the line somewhere. Where?

The problem is reminiscent of Stanley Milgram's experiment, in which subjects delivered what they thought were painful shocks to another person. Some subjects wanted to stop—and kept saying so, over and over again, without apparently being able to resist the authority of the experimenter. As Milgram observes,

Many subjects cannot find the specific verbal formula that would enable them to reject the role assigned to them by the experimenter. Perhaps our culture does not provide adequate models for disobedience.[8]

For some people, the role of the interviewer apparently conveys something of the same irresistible authority. . . .

There are certainly instances in which relentlessly pursuing a question against the respondent's wishes is totally inappropriate, and yet the interviewer may ultimately ask the question without upsetting the respondent. Sometimes it is simply a matter of giving the respondent a *choice*. If he is asked rather than pressured, the content of his answer may not really be so troubling to him. Leav-

ing the issue temporarily and coming back later can serve to allay the respondent's anxiety. If a respondent repeatedly tells an interviewer that he "doesn't want to talk about that," that it "shouldn't be asked," the interviewer is well-advised to listen to his own tone of voice. Is he sounding like a question machine? How has he responded to the reluctance that the respondent is expressing? Some respondents may indeed be too "weak or dependent or honest" to defend themselves against interviewers who are steamrolling rather than asking their questions. . . .

ROLE REQUIREMENTS IN CONFLICT

The Contradiction

The dual role involved in conducting inquiry through conversation is commonly set forth in texts on interviewing—without quite the emphasis on conflict that our interviewers report. The Survey Research Center, for instance, puts it this way in its interviewer's manual:

The interviewer plays two roles . . . that of a "technician" who applies standard techniques and uses the same instrument (the questionnaire) for each interview; and that of a human being who builds a permissive and warm relationship with each respondent. . . .[9]

Or take this much briefer treatment of interviewer training: "As an interviewer, you merely soak up information like a sponge, without giving any back." The instructions continue, "You should be adaptable to anyone and gracious to all. . . . Your attitude must be sympathetic and understanding."[10] Is it fair to summarize: be as adaptable and sympathetic as a sponge?

Such language smacks of conflict, and certain of our interviewers contend that the process requires a continuing compromise of styles on the job. In the following analysis, an interviewer crystallizes two kinds of behaviors that she sees as at once essential *and* antithetical, recommending that this form of absurdity be tackled head-on in interviewer training as a form of role "marginality."[11]

The interviewer is required to be two things to all people. First, he must be a diplomat: warm, sympathetic, sensitive to the respondent—just the sort of person who in ordinary social life does not go about asking embarrassing questions because, through sensitivity and tact, he knows how to avoid them. But at the same time, he must be something of a boor: *no sympathetic understanding of the respondent will prevent him from elbowing his way right in with questions that might embarrass or discomfort the other person.*

In her reflections on her own and other students' experiences, the interviewer speculates that it is perhaps more difficult to *blend* these contradictory styles than it is to select one or the other. . . .

In actual practice, the writer sees students devising modes of *compromise* when experiencing the counterpressures of diplomacy and boorishness. The favorite seems to be the role of "helpless subordinate."

When unpleasant or difficult questions came up, students adopted a posture of regret, as if to say, "I'm terribly sorry to ask you this but this is an assignment and I have to. It's not my fault—it's my professor's."

Some other interviewers take on the manner of "friendly obliviousness." Often more by gesture or tone of voice than by actual words, they try to give the lie to difficulty, as if to say, "Since I am a friendly person, asking this question in a friendly tone of voice, how could it possibly be embarrassing or impolite?"

Neither of these compromises is without strain. The "helpless subordinate" may serve the student better because there is some real truth to it—more truth perhaps than for the professional who is under no compulsion to earn a livelihood specifically in interviewing, after all—but the "friendly obliviousness" requires the strain of forcing an unconcerned manner.

The student-writer suggests two main ways of dealing with the problem. One is to make the wording of the questions themselves as diplomatic as possible. For instance, if the respondent's political preferences are at issue, the question should be framed in some way that makes the respondent feel that he has a choice, as in, "Would you mind telling me who you were for in the last election?" More interestingly, the writer suggests that field training of interviewers deal realistically with the contradictory requirements of the role—by helping interviewers work out effective compromises and by instituting procedures that recognize the interviewer as a "border individual" or "detached worker." Such training practices would insure that

interviewers kept in close contact with each other and with the research staff through frequent workshops, seminars, and discussions—not only at the outset of training but in the continuing course of the survey.

Maintaining the Marginality

If our beginning interviewers are representative, the role of the *diplomat* is probably the preferred one in the early stages of interviewing experiences. The "human being" probably prevails over the "technician." But is there, over time, a comparable exaggeration of the technician? . . . Interviewers may well get rather case-hardened by their arduous efforts under tough working conditions and come to treat their respondents with too much technical skill. Perhaps this is not a general problem; but if the rigors of the field and the "bias" of researchers do not ultimately bend interviewers into "technicians," traditional training and field practice suggests that they *deserve* to, through the tendency to reward and reinforce the technically correct product more than the demanding and dramatic human process. . . .

The human side of the interviewing enterprise requires that the interviewer maintain two human resources at substantial levels: sheer physical stamina necessary to find the selected respondent in the first place and psychological resilience that continues to take pleasure in meeting and interacting with all kinds of people, even after being buffeted by refusals. . . .

MANEUVERS IN THE FIELD

On Being Refused and Accepted

The training of the interviewer focuses on the actual conduct of the situation—adhering carefully to the question as worded; being sensitive to the respondent's thought and feeling; restraining one's own opinions and biases. But the beginning interviewer's overwhelming concern is that he will not even *be* an interviewer. What if nobody lets him in?

Most interviewers have a permanent memory of that first call. Preparing a face—pleasantness, surely. Harmlessness. Civic worth. Certainly the look that radiates the disclaimer, "No, I am not selling a thing!" No interviewer we know reports preparing a face that shines with the Joy of Interviewing—not the first time. One young man found that his car served as his psychological dressing room from which, after a self-administered pep talk, he could advance to the "onstage" doorstep with more bravado (as long as he parked his car out of view of the respondent's house). Another student confesses that he was so taken aback at finding his first respondent ready and willing that he missed the mesage:

> When I introduced myself at the door and the woman immediately said, "Come right in," I didn't really hear her. I just went on talking "persuasively," explaining the value of the study. She had to interrupt me and say it a second time: "I said, Come right in."

Another Interviewer or Another Try. Sometime or other, the interviewer will not be admitted. Some refusals are final and remain so despite the interviewer's best efforts to inspire interest or allay suspicion. Surely this note left on a front window was crisp enough:

> Dear Mr. Professor—Not interested in your study. Have better things to do. Sorry.
>
> James A. Auburn

There is always the supervisor's hope that her best interviewer will get through, but in this case we never did hear the views of "Mr. Auburn."[12]

Just as an interviewer may be welcomed because of a fluke—one respondent rejoiced to find that the interviewer looked just like an Army buddy who had saved his life—he may be rejected for some very particular and idiosyncratic reaction of the moment. Sometimes the "idiosyncratic" reaction is a matter of the interviewer's sex. A young woman recently crowed, in writing, "How *could* Dave have found her 'suspicious and hostile'? She invited me in immediately and gave a wonderful interview!" A young male stranger may indeed inspire fear but a young female may inspire jealousy, so no way is entirely without peril. . . .

There are two sources of public distrust for which there is probably no easy remedy.

Scientific survey research seems plagued by salesmen and others who have flagrantly misused the survey technique, such that householders have become extremely suspicious not necessarily of a survey itself but of the word survey. *One of my respondents told me of someone who had recently come to their door doing a "survey*

of children and family life for Sutter School," and of course he was the legendary encyclopedia salesman.

The most inventive charlatan of the "survey" known to us was selling cemetery plots; unfortunately we dismissed him in utter exasperation before hearing the full spiel.[13]

The second is a more pervasive distrust and caution. Some interviewers interpret it as a literal fear of crime; others see in it a more diffuse malaise—a desire to retreat into the relative "privacy and security of one's own home as one's place in the broader society becomes more and more uncertain."[14] . . .

Interviewers facing their individual refusals will have to make the judgment: another interviewer or another try. But if interviewers muster all their own courtesy and calm in those refusals, resolutely assuming that the refusal does not reflect on them personally or professionally, they can make it more likely that a respondent will ultimately prove willing. One student brings to refusals what may well be small solace—the remedy of experience—but the point is well taken:

> I started out with great anxiety about rejections or refusals. After a time I learned how to defend myself— but I think it's really quite true. A refusal is not really an adverse criticism of one's own personality or interviewing abilities. After all, the refusing person usually does not even see the interviewer to talk to. It is usually the result of some private feeling or lack of understanding on the part of the respondent.

Getting the Interview

Often it is not really clear why a given respondent seems unwilling. The reasons may be subtle, multiple, and the critical reservations may never really surface. It is really lack of time now? Inconvenience of the moment? Fear and suspicion? Feelings of personal inadequacy? Unfamiliarity with this survey business? Incurable disinterest in the whole thing? The interviewer's prime goal is to stay with the prospective respondent long enough to dope out what the trouble is. The lucky doorstep diagnostician, applying the insight of trial and error, usually locates the probable cause only by discovering that *something* has made for an apparent cure. The respondent finally says something on the order of, "Well, okay, come on in." What really happened to make this possible may not be clear to the interviewer or to the respondent; the interviewer did or said *something* right, and the following cures are most often reported:

1. *An appointment could be made—or a second, or a third.* Some respondents have no intention of *ever* finding the time, but other genuinely busy persons may be willing if the interviewer is clearly intent on accommodating to that busy schedule: he makes it clear that the respondent can choose the hour. Such an appointment is, of course, never a guarantee. When an interviewer arrives right on the dot to find an empty house, only the most trusting spirit will fail to suspect that the specific time was set for the nefarious purpose of nonmeeting. But even the most skeptical interviewer is well advised to suspend his disbelief, assume a genuine misunderstanding or forgetting, and set out in search again! A few respondents have even confessed—a bit rueful, no doubt, at their own deception—that they finally agreed to be interviewed because they came to be genuinely impressed at the time and trouble the interviewer took.

2. *The time-length was acceptable.* When the wavering respondent finally asks, "Well, how much time will it take?" the harrowing ethical moment has arrived. Few interviewers report telling the bald truth ("Well, the average seems to be an hour—some shorter and some a good deal longer"). And yet those who grossly minimize the expected time in some sort of mumbly deception may well get in trouble. The respondent may well feel deceived and angry; the last half of the interview may be hustled, garbled, or entirely broken off as the respondent rushes away to another appointment....

3. *Somebody else was interested.* A woman who had refused on the first visit came to the door on the second call with all cordiality: "Come right in! My neighbors would not say what it was all about but they said it was interesting. I was *hoping* you'd come back." The joyful greeting is hardly the word of the representative refusal, to be sure, but occasionally someone else in the family or neighborhood provides an unsolicited ally, and allies can be sought out, too. Interviewers have asked sympathetic respondents to provide an introduction to a reluctant neighbor or to leave a note that the study is legitimate. Interviewers rarely know just who their allies will be and, on their patient road to the real encounter, they may have to conduct several informal "pretests."...

4. *The interviewer stopped apologizing.* Many interviewers report that they must subdue their own guilty, defensive feelings before they can convey confidence and legitimacy to the respondent. One student realized that he was, himself, *feeling* as if he were a door-to-door salesman, intruding on the respondent. When he began to refashion himself in his own mind as something like a census taker, his outward manner changed. Without feeling that he had become brash or overly aggressive, he took on more purposefulness and poise. In his explanation at the door, he took to saying, "Hello, I'm the survey taker from the University of Michigan," rather than asking the defensive question, "Would you mind . . . ?" Beginners are well advised to scrutinize their own mental image. Can they almost see a demonstration vacuum-cleaner or an Avon kit in their hand? Put it down. Pick up a mental briefcase, a clipboard, or a census form. The shift into a feeling of legitimacy usually occurs in a process that is a good deal less conscious, to be sure. In fact, there is doubtless nothing quite like successfully completing a couple of good interviews for patching together a semblance of professional poise.

5. *The respondent-turned-person.* If the product of a survey is a mere statistical Thing (often seen to "dehumanize" individuals into faceless aggregates), the process of interviewing projects a kind of democracy of the individual. The blatant equality of the cross-section survey poses certain kinds of problems precisely because it flies in the face of our social practice and runs against the grain of our individual experience.

The practice of literal equality is, after all, something of a deviant in our cultural life. In all realms of our experience, it is as clear to all of us as it was to Orwell's animals that *some are more equal than others,* and we leave the Theory of Man as the unique, valuable, nonreplaceable individual to a Rousseau or a Whitman, without letting it much trouble the practice of our daily lives. Perhaps statistical-minded researchers would not own up to being die-hard defenders of the Romantic tradition, but they do indeed insist on a theory of even-handed equality for Man in the Sample (and Woman as well). Some critics of public opinion polling find this inattention to social and institutional hierarchy a perfectly wrong-headed disregard of the way in which the world works.[15]

Interviewers charged with putting this theory

into practice run into skeptics, too. Most of us have precious little experience with this "unrealistic" view. Some of us are simply *too important* to be reduced to mere respondent status. Our time is too valuable, our responsibilities too awesome, or our thoughts too elegant and grand to fit the grid of standardized questions. For the interviewer, there is rarely an effective method of bringing these hopelessly important folk down to the level of mere random equality. (At least we can report that no interviewer is on record as saying, "Listen, buddy, in *your* world you may be a millionaire, but in my world, you are just one of a random batch, see. . . .")

More people feel that they are *not important enough* to be respondents. Taciturn men will suggest their more garrulous wives; politically diffident women will offer their more knowledgeable husbands; somebody else will do—and probably much better. "Why don't you just go across the street to that brown house; those old folks would really welcome some company." Another resistant man finally put it straight to the young woman: "Listen, I know you're studying men's jobs, but I've been cutting meat my whole life and my job just couldn't be interesting to you." (There proved to be much new information and unsuspected complexities in the meat business.)

Faced with this kind of reluctance, the interviewer's first temptation is to press the respondent with the explanation of random sampling. Sometimes that explanation is, indeed, persuasive; but random sampling itself is complex and poorly understood. When the interviewer succeeds in such a case, it can be because he has made an intellectual conversion through his particularly lucid explanation, and the respondent is ready to give his all for social science. But it is more likely to be because the interviewer has made some sort of personal, behavioral demonstration that this particular respondent is valuable and important to him. Interviewers find that some of the most routine aspects of even finding a respondent in the first place—calling back, making appointments, and accommodating the respondent's busy life—give behavioral evidence that the interviewer really means it: he is genuinely interested in this particular person. The quality of the exchange on the spot must make the same point even more vividly, especially if the person doubts his adequacy. . . .

One young man unconsciously applied exactly

that identity between the worth of persons and the requirements of sampling, when he encountered a woman who was unwilling because she was "an uninformed housewife." She should *represent* all the people who were not terribly interested in politics or public affairs, he explained—and the interview was on.

Cutting the Conversation to Size

Some respondents give no-nonsense interviews: they answer questions briskly and directly, with superb comprehension, in record time. A 30-year-old schoolteacher, widowed with young children, dazzled an interviewer recently with just such a performance. During the interview, which was sandwiched in between two social engagements, the woman cooked dinner, ate the meal, supervised the children, washed the dishes, and snapped off beautifully lucid answers to all questions—in 40 minutes.

Other people use interview questions to spin off into private realms of experience and reminiscence. How to get the respondent to *stop* talking is rarely given as much attention in the literature or the training as how to prime the conversation and keep it flowing. Perhaps the emphasis on "opening up" communication is, as David Riesman suggests, a heritage from the psychoanalytic tradition, which inadvertently casts the interviewer in the role of analyst mining the psyche of the "closed" client for well-buried insights.[16] Interviewers know full well that some respondents require nothing so much as a little closing-up.

Knowing how is especially difficult for beginning interviewers. In their zeal to gain rapport, they often have to labor *not* to give sympathetic, wide-eyed listening to everything the respondent says, relevant and irrelevant alike. When the respondent lingers with his reverie or digression, experienced interviewers resort to methods ranging from soft gestures to straight talk. Some form of gentle inattention sometimes does it—putting down the pencil, looking away for a moment, even leafing through the questionnaire. If the respondent is too preoccupied with his own thought, such soft flutterings may go undetected, and the interviewer may have to escalate up to direct interruption. One interviewer reports this habitual style of intervention:

Ahh, let me stop you here—on your boy's experiences in high school—because there is a question, later on, that is right on the matter of education. The next question is not really connected, but I have to ask them in order....

There is another suggestion that interviewers offer for handling the respondent's digression. Once in a while, *let* him. *Listen.* The respondent may indeed just need a brief breather. He may be feeling some emotional strain from a particular question, or he may simply need to relax a bit, into the comfortable shapes of his own "unstandardized" thought, from the sheer concentration he has marshaled in order to answer so many questions in succession....

The Neutral Probe

In Pursuit of Specificity. The activity called *probing* sounds perhaps just a bit more surgical than befits the gentle art of asking questions. But the poetry of survey research is thin; the word has taken a prominent place in the lexicon of polling and quickly enters the habitual vocabulary of interviewers.

The interviewer is to probe for additional information or clarification when he hears something that he does not understand or, even better, something that a third person would not understand. The glittering generality will turn up somewhere in virtually any interview. In a matter of a few hours, one interviewer accumulated these laconic truths:

It's the parents.
Lack of communication.
Job concerns.
They're just too young.

The *question*—"What is the main reason teenagers drop out of school?"—was probably no less vague and general and, perhaps, was the main reason that the initial answers were so unsatisfactory. Even to better questions, however, many respondents will answer with their own shorthand: highly concentrated code-words that would be meaningful in an ordinary conversation, to which a friend-listener would bring knowledge of the speaker's preoccupations, response-sets, styles of thought and language, and so on. The interviewer does not bring enough information to decode what such answers mean, and he must realize that instantaneously enough to probe at once (even when he also

thinks, in *his* shorthand, that "they're too young" or "it's the parents"). Interviewers usually learn early in their experience to detect most of the uselessly general answers, first by understanding clearly the research intent of the question and then applying that knowledge to the relevance and completeness of each answer after another. There is no general procedure, other than the application of the usual virtues: sensitive listening and quick wit....

In Avoidance of Ignorance. How the interviewer is to probe a "don't know" answer is generally a more slippery matter. What does such an answer really mean? Only the dullest listener would fail to distinguish between these two extremes:

> I don't know...I have never given it a thought. Don't have the slightest idea. Just don't know about that one....

and this:

> I don't know...hmm...Let me see, I suppose I'd say...

But there are many other versions of the same words that are much more opaque to instant interpretation. To take just a few:

> I don't know (and I don't care and I don't give a damn and this is boring).
> I don't know (and I'm not saying and it's none of your business).
> I don't know (but I do know that what I might say would probably strike you as stupid).
> I don't know (and I don't want to know and the whole thing makes me uneasy to think about it and let's go on).

Only the interviewer can decide whether to probe for the "real" answer or to record the fact that she already has it.

If the interviewer presses the respondent for a substantive answer, how many times should he probe? Instructions are difficult to standardize not only because each situation has subtleties and ambiguities that the interviewer must interpret on the spot but also because researchers themselves are often not entirely clear how they feel about public *nonopinion*, and what use they will make of it, and their instructions are likely to reflect some of that uncertainty.[17] Researchers tend to favor the respondents who *do* know, often enough discarding the "don't knows" along with the "not-ascertaineds," letting the computer whir along with the cases in which the respondent said something or other, even if some uncertain portion of that group may well have invented an opinion for the occasion. Sometimes no doubt to please the nice interviewer.

Certain professionals in the survey field argue that nonopinions are the most important matter. As Leo Bogart puts it, "The question of *what* people think about public issues is really secondary to the question of whether they think about them at all."[18] It is nevertheless a rare piece of published analysis that shows much fascination for non-opinion. . . .

Styles of Probing. Generally suggested probe wordings are usually more helpful for crystallizing the meaning of the glittering generality than for penetrating the "real" meaning of professed ignorance. In either case, the interviewer is to select a probe wording that is neutral, supportive of the respondent, and productive of more information. Interviewer training usually provides some sort of probing glossary, from which the interviewer is to choose an appropriate sentence:

Could you tell me a little more about that?
How do you mean, exactly?
Why would you say you feel that way?

Interviewers report that they *try* to stick to the probe script, but their reported experience makes it clear that their way of interpreting that script varies rather considerably. Some interviewers hang as closely to the literal language as they possibly can; others confess that they adapt their own probe language to the respondent's general style.

One dutifully conservative interviewer, who adhered carefully to the script, found that she began to amuse her respondent:

About halfway through, in a good-natured and friendly way, the respondent began to mimic my probes, with an exaggerated emphasis: "I know, Why do I feel that way? Could I be a little more specific? Yes, How do I mean, exactly?"

The interviewer's language can become so neutral that it will formalize and chill the spontaneity of the relationship as it sends out signals that the interviewer is in better contact with the script (be it questionnaire or probing language) than with the respondent.

At the other liberal extreme, we find interviewers who, without deviating from the literal wording of the *question,* adapt their probing language and manner to the style of the respondent. . . .This freer probing style is presented in some detail by an inteviewer who had come to feel in his pretest experience that his probing manner heavily influenced rapport. In effect, he wrote his own probing script and tried to make selections to match the respondent. He reported great pleasure in using probes as a quick-change artist would use costume. To take three examples:

1. *For the respondent using argot, especially when the interviewer is not sure of its meaning:*

"The people at the University don't usually get the meaning of this language, so could you explain . . ."   *or*

"Man, I thought I was with it, but I'm not there either. What does . . . mean exactly? I see, now I'm getting it . . ."

2. *For the sensitive respondent feeling inadequate, needing reinforcement:*

"I sense that there's a bit more behind what you said. You're really onto something here. What do you mean by . . .?"   *or*

"I hope you don't feel that I'm pushing you on this, but we're not supposed to guess anything, because we might not get your feeling down exactly . . ."   *or*

"I'm pretty sure I know what you mean and what you're driving at here, but could you say a little more . . ."   *or*

"I've done three interviews today and I've found that people use the word in different ways. Could you tell me what you mean by 'more education'?"

3. *For the respondent with whom rapport is already high:*

"I'd like to pin you down a little more on what you just said . . ."   *or*

"I'm going to have to stop you here again, because I'm not really sure what you mean . . ."   *or*

"I don't really follow you. You've laid it out generally but what do you mean exactly by . . .?"

Do self-styled probe artists of this kind contaminate the data by adapting too readily to the respondent as they see him? Are such chameleon interviewers likely to take on too much of the respondent's local color, and bring back another small collection of "nonattitudes"? (One can also ask if the "conservative" interviewer who strikes her respondent as mechanical and impersonal brings back too little of that local color.) We are not prepared to answer such questions—except to add an inconclusive footnote that the candid interviewers just cited were rated by supervisors as excellent; and to speculate that such interviewers adapt quickly to their fundamental intuition that there is no single interviewer style that fits every occasion or all respondents. . . .

Editor's Postscript: *The authors conclude this chapter with a brief comparison of interviews with conversations and a summary of the chapter. Chapter 3 illustrates how interviewers contribute to question revision, discusses the role of the open-ended question, and suggests that interviews emphasize rationality at the expense of emotionality. Chapter 4 is a brief epilogue and Chapter 1 a brief prologue. An annotated bibliography follows Chapter 4.*

NOTES

[1]This is surely Herbert H. Hyman's "intrusive" interviewer. [See Note 2.]

[2]In his classic work, *Interviewing in Social Research*, Herbert H. Hyman distinguishes between "role expectations" and "attitude-structure expectations" and presents evidence that these two processes are more powerful determinants of interviewer's bias than the interviewer's own beliefs or ideology. Hyman's very valuable reexamination of the theory and practice of interviewing proceeds initially from the "phenomenology of the interview"—intensive accounts of their own experience by a small group of experienced interviewers as well as reports of reinterviewing of respondents. See Hyman, *Interviewing in Social Research*, Chicago, University of Chicago Press, 1954, especially Chapters II and III.

[3]David Riesman, in Paul F. Lazarsfeld and Wagner Thielens, Jr., *The Academic Mind*, Glencoe, Ill., Free Press, 1958, p. 305.

[4]Stephen A. Richardson, Barbara Dohrenwend, and David Klein, *Interviewing: Its Forms and Functions*, New York, Basic Books, 1965, p. 357.

[5]See Daniel Lerner, "Interviewing French-

men," *American Journal of Sociology*, 62(2), September, 1956, 187–194.

[6]See Barbara Snell Dohrenwend, John Colombotos, and Bruce P. Dohrenwend, "Social Distance and Interviewer Effects," *Public Opinion Quarterly*, 32(3), Fall 1968, 410–422; Hyman (see above), and Carol H. Weiss, "Interaction in the Research Interview: The Effects of Rapport on Response," *Proceedings of the Social Statistics Section*, American Statistical Association, 1970, pp. 17–20.

[7]This material is taken from a paper written for the Detroit Area Study in 1967 by Dawn Day Wachtel.

[8]Stanley Milgram, "Some Conditions of Obedience and Disobedience to Authority," *Human Relations*, 18(1), 1965, 67.

[9]*Interviewer's Manual*, Ann Arbor, Institute for Social Research, University of Michigan, 1969, p. 4–1, (25). Our italics. The forthcoming edition of the SRC Manual will reportedly place less stress on rapport building and more on an impersonal, professional approach—consonant with certain aspects of the experimental work of Charles F. Cannell and his associates at the Survey Research Center, and a shift in emphasis that Richardson has found operating more generally in the interviewing field.

[10]Charles H. Backstrom and Gerald Hursh, *Survey Research*, Evanston, Ill., Northwestern University Press, 1963, p. 135.

[11]This material is taken from a paper written for the Detroit Area Study in 1967 by Julianne Oktay, now at Goucher College.

[12]Once in a great while, a more charming and discursive letter makes its way to the office, designed to keep the interviewer informed about what's been happening in the family since the interview.

[13]W. Donald Rugg relays that over half of the interviewers of the Opinion Research Corporation report that they have at some time been refused an interview because the respondent thought it was a sales pitch. See "Interviewer Opinion on the 'Salesman as Interviewer' Problem," *Public Opinion Quarterly*, 35(4), Winter 1971–1972, 625–626.

[14]Stanley Milgram's concept of "overload" is less fearful but perhaps more general. Urbanites' heightened sense of physical and emotional vulnerability to excessive numbers of contacts with people and problems, as well as to urban crime, leads them to restrict communication with strang-

ers. See "The Experience of Living in Cities," *Science*, 167 (3924), March 13, 1970, 1461–1468.

[15]For a classic statement of this criticism, see Herbert Blumer, "The Mass, the Public, and Public Opinion," in *Reader in Public Opinion and Communication*, edited by Bernard Berelson and Morris Janowitz, 2nd ed., New York, Free Press, 1966, pp. 43–50.

[16]See David Riesman and Mark Benney, "The Sociology of the Interview" (1955), in Riesman,

Abundance For What? And Other Essays, Garden City, New York, Doubleday, 1964, pp. 517–539.

[17]See Michael J. Shapiro, "Discovering Interviewer Bias in Open-Ended Survey Responses," *Public Opinion Quarterly*, 34(3), Fall, 1970, 412–415, for an analysis of variation in open-ended answers.

[18]Leo Bogart, "No Opinion, Don't Know, and Maybe No Answer," *Public Opinion Quarterly*, 31(3), Fall 1967, 337.

FACTORS AFFECTING RESPONSE RATES TO MAILED QUESTIONNAIRES: A QUANTITATIVE ANALYSIS OF THE PUBLISHED LITERATURE

Thomas A. Heberlein
Robert Baumgartner

INTRODUCTION

Research on mail questionnaires response rates generally has studied the effect of a single factor (such as monetary incentives), or a group of related factors, on the response rate while attempting to hold all other potential factors constant. Unfortunately, any single study generally examines a few factors at most. What is needed is a single analysis of most of the potentially relevant factors. Such a study involving only one set of respondents (i.e., one survey) would of necessity be limited to an analysis of only a few factors. Hence, we decided to try a different mode of analysis, treating each study

as a respondent in a survey in an attempt to examine the effect of each of many factors on response rates.

METHODS

We coded 71 independent variables in 98 separate published studies on response rates. In many of the studies, the design used more than one treatment of a given independent variable and, in these cases, each treatment was coded separately. For the 98 studies coded, there were 214 treatments of the independent variables. Since the unit of analysis was the individual treatment, we used a total of 214 cases in the analysis.

Four categories of independent variables emerged. General research characteristics comprise the first, and include such variables as year of publication, discipline of resarcher, and type of research organization. The second, sampling and sample characteristics, includes such variables as sample size, source of sample, and type of population studied. The third category includes such questionnaire characteristics as subject of the questionnaire (self, family, etc.), length of questionnaire, type of data requested (attitudes, behavior,

Support for this research was provided by the College of Agricultural and Life Sciences, University of Wisconsin, Madison, under Hatch Grant Project No. 5117. The authors would like to thank J. Stanley Black, Richard Campbell, Don Dillman, Kenneth Green, and an anonymous reviewer for this journal for their helpful comments on earlier drafts. The authors, however, take sole responsibility for the interpretations and conclusions in the article. This is a revised version of a paper presented at the annual meeting of the Rural Sociological Society, 1977, Madison.

Condensed by Theodore C. Wagenaar from the *American Sociological Review*, August 1978, pp. 447–462. Used by permission.

demographic information), and salience of the topic to the respondent. The fourth category, research procedures, includes the total number of contacts, class of mail used, length of time between contacts, use of incentives, and respondent identification procedures.

The salience variable was operationalized by using a three-point scale of salient, possibly salient, or nonsalient; ratings were done by the second author. A salient topic was one that dealt with important behavior or interests that were also current (e.g., a Veterans' Administration survey of the educational plans and interests of veterans who had expressed interest in V.A. educational assistance programs). Topics judged possibly salient were important issues or behaviors that were not necessarily current or timely (e.g., a survey of occupational status and mobility of former students of a university). Topics judged to be nonsalient were those that neither concerned important issues or behaviors nor were current (e.g., a study of consumer purchasing behavior in a geographical sample of urban households).

Not all of the studies analyzed reported information for all of the independent variables. Where possible, we made assumptions about missing data (e.g., unless explicitly stated in the article, we assumed that a given procedure was not used). We also wrote to some of the authors for additional data on questionnaire length.

Both regression analysis and path analysis were employed. Regression analysis allows the development of prediction equations indicating the net contribution of each independent variable on response rates, and path analysis allows the development of a time-ordered causal model indicating the direct effect of each variable on response rates as well as the indirect effects of a given variable through variables coming after that variable in time sequence.

FINDINGS

On the average, 48 percent of those who received one mailing of a questionnaire returned it. The standard deviation is 20 percent, suggesting a wide range of response rates. It seems unlikely that such tremendous variation is simply random, and the goal of our analysis will be to identify those factors that can explain at least part of this variation.

Contacts

One additional follow-up mailing results in an additional 20 percent return (standard deviation = 7.7). A second follow-up yields an additional 12 percent (standard deviation = 6.2), and a third follow-up yields an additional 10 percent (standard deviation = 5.1). Note the substantial variability in the effectiveness of follow-ups, which makes simple generalizations difficult.

Interestingly, half of the studies had only one contact with the respondent. Also, follow-ups beyond the third do not significantly improve the final response rate.

Salience

Questionnaires were more likely to be returned if they were judged to be salient to the respondent. Surveys on topics not salient to the respondent averaged a 42 percent response, while those topics judged to be salient obtained a 77 percent return. Those judged possibly salient showed yields of 66 percent. Salience and the number of contacts together explain half of the variance in final response rates. Since these two variables are so important, in the discussion that follows we focus on those variables that affect final response rates independently of contacts and salience.

General Research Characteristics

Government-sponsored research got higher responses (about 12 percent) independent of contacts and salience. Recent surveys get no higher responses than questionnaire studies done in the 1940s and 1950s.

Sampling and Sample Characteristics

Students, employees, and military personnel are more likely to return questionnaires. Surveys of the general population are less likely to be returned than surveys of special subgroups.

Questionnaire Length and Topic

In our data the average questionnaire had 72 questions on seven pages and took less than one-half hour to complete, although a great amount of variation exists. In spite of this variation, however, no significant zero-order relationship exists between length and response rates. When we controlled for salience and contacts, we found that questionnaires with more items get slightly lower returns (each additional question reduces responses by .05 percent).

The variables tapping questionnaire content generally have little effect on response rates once saliency and contacts are controlled. One exception was that respondents were more likely to return questionnaires if the topic of the questionnaire involved other people.

Research Procedures

Contacting respondents prior to the first mailing of the questionnaire has no extra effect on response rates. Contacts before or after the first mailing are equally effective. Enclosing a new copy of the questionnaire with follow-up reminders does not seem to increase responses beyond the effect of the reminder itself. Even with controls for salience and contacts, the use of a special mailing procedure (certified or special delivery) or a personal or telephone contact does increase response rates. Also with the controls, metered or franked postage on the outer envelope did increase response rates (by about 9 percent).

Relatively few studies used incentives. Hence, no strong relationship with response rates could be demonstrated. However, these few studies do suggest that incentives may increase response rates if more widely used: the two studies paying $1.00 had 80 percent returns, the nine studies paying 50¢ had 66 percent returns, and the seven studies paying 25¢ had 45 percent returns (all using only one contact).

Initial Response Rates

The results discussed thus far involve final response rates, with salience and contacts controlled. But given the importance of the initial response rate for the final response rate, and given the fact that the initial response rate may influence the researcher's decision to use special procedures, it may be useful to analyze predictors of the initial response rate.

We entered the nine variables with a significant relationship with initial response rates (or responses with only one contact) in a regression equation to assess their relative importance. Perhaps the most interesting finding is that these nine variables explain only 40 percent of the variance in initial responses (recall that about 50 percent of the variance in *final* response rates was explained by salience and number of contacts). This low predictability of initial response, no doubt, is due to the lack of variables assessing the design and layout of the instrument, the respondent's knowledge and affiliation with the signer of the cover letter, and the construction of the cover letter itself. These could not be coded from the published record, but no doubt affect initial response.

Several of the nine variables resulted in decreased initial response rates. Studies done by marketing researchers result in a decrease of about 11 percent, studies focusing on attitude questions result in a decrease of about 11 percent, the use of a general population results in a decrease of about 12 percent, and a focus on voluntary organizations as a topic results in a decrease of about 14 percent. Others resulted in increased initial response rates. Each 25¢ increment in incentive results in an increase of about 6 percent. Each increment in the three-point salience scale results in an increase of 6 percent. A school or army sample results in an increase of 9 percent, an employee population results in an increase of 12 percent, and research done by government organizations results in an increase of about 7 percent.

Follow-up Contacts

We examined the effect of several variables on the number of follow-up contacts. Apparently, investigators do not react to low initial response rates by adding more follow-ups, since this variable shows no relationship. Studies on student populations tended to have one additional contact. Also, as questionnaires get longer, more follow-ups are used. Questionnaires that asked questions about other individuals also have more follow-ups. Furthermore, the use of special procedures such as telephone calls or special mailing on the second or third contact significantly increased the final response rate.

Final Response Rate Reconsidered

Our previous discussion of factors influencing final response rate reflected controls for salience and number of contacts. In this section we report on a reanalysis of factors influencing the final response rate, this time analyzing the effect of each variable with *all* the other significant variables controlled (not just salience and contacts).

As might be expected, the initial response rate is by far the most predictive of the final response rate. Undoubtedly, this is due to the fact that both reflect the same things (response rate) at different times. However, in order to use this regression equation including initial response rate to predict final response rate before a study begins, the initial response rate must be known. This is obviously not possible. Hence, we recalculated the regression equation for all significant variables excluding initial response rate. Starting with a base response level of 36 percent, the following variables increase or decrease this value:

> research done by market researchers *decreases* final response rate by 10 percent
>
> research done by government organizations *increases* final response rate by 10 percent
>
> use of a general population *decreases* final response rate by 7.5 percent
>
> use of an employee population *increases* final response rate by 12 percent
>
> use of a school or army population *increases* final response rate by 10 percent
>
> saliency of topic to respondents *increases* final response rate by 7 percent for each step on the three-point scale (not salient, possibly salient, salient)
>
> length of questionnaire (in number of pages) *decreases* the final response rate by about .5 percent for each page
>
> the total number of contacts *increases* the final response rate by 7.5 percent for each contact
>
> the use of special procedures on the third contact *increases* the final response rate for each increment (0 = no third contact, 1 = regular mail, 2 = special mail, 3 = telephone or personal)
>
> each 25¢ increment in incentive (up to $1.00) on the first contact *increases* the final response rate by 6 percent

A reminder: The effect of each variable noted above is a unique effect; that is, the effects of all other variables in the list have been held constant in calculating the effect of a given variable. All of these factors together explain 66 percent of the variance in the final response rate.

If one predicts a low final response, new procedures can be introduced. Responses can be increased most effectively by adding contacts, special contact procedures and incentives. Cutting the pages will help some but not as much as increases for the other variables. The predicted response of a market research sponsored, five-page survey of a general population would be 23.9 percent. By using three contacts, with a telephone call for the third contact, along with a $1.00 incentive on the first mailing, the predicted response could be increased to 89 percent.

DISCUSSION

In this study we examined 71 independent variables possibly related to response rates and found several of them to be related to initial and final response rates. We found the salience of the questionnaire topic to the respondent and the number of contacts to be the most significant factors. Obviously the more relevant the topic for the respondent, the higher the interest in completing the questionnaire. And additional contacts may further convince potential respondents of the importance of their input. The use of special procedures on the third contact may also have this effect.

The higher response rates for government-sponsored research may reflect a belief that information provided may have some impact on others through policy changes. Market research, on the other hand, may be of less importance to the respondent, particularly if he/she believes the information may be used to benefit a profit-making firm.

Lower responses from general populations may also be explained in this framework. Specific appeals to self-interest or specialized questionnaire content are more difficult when sampling from driver's licenses or voter registration lists. It is still possible to achieve high response rates from general populations, but there is an initial inertia that must be overcome. Employees may be more likely to respond because their responses are seen as important to their livelihood.

The length is usually considered a cost barrier to be avoided if at all possible. Given our finding of no zero-order effects, but an observed negative effect of length only when other factors are controlled, it is possible that questionnaire length affects perceived importance in a way that tends to offset costs. Longer questionnaires may impress the potential respondent with the importance of his/

her input. Tossing out a one-page instrument may be relatively easy to do, but discarding 30 pages of questions is depriving the investigator of a good deal of information. Also, if the researcher has taken the time to compose 30 pages of questions, it is clear that this research is a serious matter, not merely a passing curiosity. Length, then, may signal importance to the respondent, possibly even enough to overcome the costs associated with it.

The costs of returning a mailed questionnaire may be lower for some groups, which in part can account for the observed higher returns. Students, for example, may find it easier to read and respond to questionnaires since they have been trained to carry out such cognitive tests, and these skills probably lower the cost barrier. Alternatively, or as a complement, both students and individuals obtained from military records may find a request to complete a form more familiar and easier to comply with than other groups.

There are also certain costs in *not returning* a questionnaire which may offset the costs of filling it out. The finding that employees are more likely to return questionnaires may reflect a concern for consequences revolving around a failure to comply with a request. The respondent may feel that potential occupational retaliations for not returning a questionnaire represent a higher cost than the time and effort to complete it.

CONCLUSIONS

Further research, preferably of a large-scale experimental nature, is necessary to validate our results and examine other variables. We were unable to examine many variables reflecting such items as cover letters, questionnaire formats, situational effects, and social-psychological motivational factors.

We would also like to suggest that more attention be given to developing a theoretical basis for questionnaire response. For example, since the return of a questionnaire is itself a behavior, the work being done by attitude–behavior theorists is relevant. Those theories useful for the prediction of behavior also should apply to filling out questionnaires, just as they apply to voting and other behaviors.

Altruism is another area with the potential for generating propositions that could be tested with responses to mailed questionnaires. Sending a person a questionnaire is a request for help. The circumstances under which individuals come to the assistance or fail to help another should apply to returning a questionnaire.

It seems possible to reinterpret our speculations about costs and importance within both the attitude-behavior and the helping-behavior theoretical frameworks. To do this would, we feel, be the most fruitful grounding for future mailed questionnaire research.

PART FOUR

Analysis of Data

SECTION 4.1

Social Statistics and Data Analysis

Our society has become increasingly dependent on the use of statistical information for decision-making. Virtually every edition of a newspaper or magazine contains at least one article reporting statistics in support of an argument or conclusion. Thus it is becoming increasingly important for consumers of such research to have some knowledge of statistics and their applications. This basic knowledge is particularly important for those of you entering the service professions, for you will be constantly confronted with the need to read, interpret, and make policy recommendations on the basis of research reports involving statistics.

Recall the diagram of the overall research process that Wallace outlined in the first article in this volume. Note that data analysis is a significant component of that diagram, entering the process after the data collection and operationalization stages. The data that have been gathered to operationalize the concepts must now be analyzed in order to make decisions to accept or reject the hypotheses developed and to relate the results of those tests of the hypotheses to the theories on which they were based. Like the other stages of research, data analysis provides a crucial link in the process of social research; without both data acquisition and data analysis, social research remains largely theoretical and nonscientific.

Most statistics used in social research are fairly easy to calculate and comprehend. Yet many students are afraid of statistics; mere mention of the term evokes groans and, all too often, a flurry of drop requests. Undoubtedly this reaction is a result of the use of formulas and numbers, which are more foreign than the verbal accounts of other aspects of the research progress.

The article in this section tells how to read and interpret some of the more popular statistics used in social research. The goal is to provide you with some guidelines and illustrations for interpreting social statistics. In keeping with the emphasis in this volume on application, no formulas are used. Obviously, such an approach is somewhat oversimplified. I therefore encourage you to take a statistics course to become more knowledgeable about the origins, assumptions, calculations, and hence the limitations of statistics. For those of you interested in pursuing the topic on your own, I recommend any one of the following introductory level books: *Social Statistics without Tears* (Johnson, 1977), *Everything You Always Wanted to Know about Elementary Statistics (But Were Afraid to Ask)* (Schutte, 1977), *Winning with Statistics* (Runyon, 1977), or *How to Use (and Misuse) Statistics* (Kimble, 1978).

The article begins with a review of a few basic concepts. Univariate analysis (one variable) is then discussed, with emphasis on frequency distributions and dispersion measures. Subsequently, bivariate (two variables) and multivariate (more than two variables) analyses are covered, with the emphasis in both sections on assessing causal relationships. The article concludes with a consideration of statistical inference, with the emphasis on making inferences from the data gathered on a sample to the larger population from which the sample was taken.

REFERENCES

Johnson, Allan G.
    1977   Social Statistics without Tears. New York: McGraw-Hill.

Kimble, Gregory A.
    1978   How to Use (and Misuse) Statistics. Englewood Cliffs: Prentice-Hall.

Runyon, Richard P.
    1977   Winning with Statistics. Reading: Addison-Wesley.

Schutte, Jerald G.
    1977   Everything You Always Wanted to Know about Elementary Statistics (But Were Afraid to Ask). Englewood Cliffs: Prentice-Hall.

SOCIAL STATISTICS WITHOUT FORMULAS

Theodore C. Wagenaar

Statistics are a tool for understanding data. Thus far in this volume we have read about the nature of science and theory, sampling and measurement, and the various research designs for gathering data, all of which are important considerations in *gathering* data for your topic. Now the time has come to learn how to make some sense of the data you have gathered. Suppose you now have data on 100 variables for 700 people (or organizations, communities, etc.). You would have to find some way to order this information. The purpose of statistical analysis is to *reduce* data to some manageable form so that conclusions of various sorts can be drawn. As you progress through this article, continually note how each statistic helps you understand some aspect of your data or data reported by other researchers.

BASIC CONCEPTS

A few basic concepts should be noted first. Social scientists usually deal with variables. A *variable*, to put it plainly, is any event or phenomenon we choose to study. Love can be a variable or support for the ERA can be a variable. In order to study these variables, however, we try to define them as precisely as possible. When we have a clear definition of the variable, it becomes easier to develop ways of measuring it.

Social scientists typically deal with variables in terms of cause and effect. The variable that is caused by (i.e., dependent on) another variable is known as the *dependent variable*, while the variable that possibly causes such a dependent variable is known as the *independent variable*. The key is time order; the independent variable comes before the dependent variable. As an example, we may observe that religious affiliation influences attitude toward abortion; religious affiliation is the independent variable and attitude toward abortion is the dependent variable.

Three prerequisites must be met in order to establish the independent variable as probable cause of the dependent variable. First, the independent variable must precede the dependent variable in time sequence. Second, the two variables must be related. And third, other possible causes of the dependent variable must be ruled out.

A fundamental concept in applying statistics is the *level of measurement* of a variable. There are four levels of measurement, each of which uses numbers in different ways. At the *nominal* level, numbers have no intrinsic meaning. They are assigned purely for convenience. For the variable "sex" we could specify that 1 = male and 2 = female, although we could have said just as easily that 1 = female and 2 = male. We can make no comparisons on the basis of these numbers alone, because the numbers are in no way related to each other; 2 is not twice as female as one. Instead, numbers at the nominal level are simply labels for the different categories (attributes) of some variable. *Ordinal* level variables allow us to specify rank order among respondents or among responses. For example, in a Likert-type item (1 = strongly agree, 2 = agree, 3 = neutral, 4 = disagree, 5 = strongly disagree), each value indicates a higher or lower level of agreement than the other values. Here the numbers do have some intrinsic meaning: they specify order. The distances between values, however, are not equal; that is, the amount of agreement between scores of 2 and 3 may not equal the amount of agreement between scores of 3 and 4.

Interval level variables specify not only order but also that the distance between one value and the next is the same as that between any other adjacent values. In other words, the distances between values are equal. One example is I.Q. The numeric difference between 90 and 100 is the same as that between 100 and 110. But since there is no absolute agreed-on zero amount of intelligence (i.e., no real zero), we cannot say that a person with a score of 150 is twice as intelligent as a person with a score of 75. *Ratio* level variables, however, do have a real zero. We can say that a person 50 years old is twice as old as a person 25.

Why is it important to know the level of measurement of your variables? *Because the level of measurement determines which statistics are appropriate to analyze your data.* A computer will calculate any statistic for any variable, but an accurate interpretation of the results requires that you choose the proper statistics for the level of a given variable. The computer, for example, could calculate a mean of 1.66 for your sex variable (1 = male, 2 = female). Would that figure suggest that for each male there are .66 females? Or that all of your sample is bisexual but leaning toward the female? Obviously, such interpretations would be incorrect. The reason is because the mean is an inappropriate statistic for nominal level data.

Another relevant concept concerns the complexity of analysis. *Univariate* analysis involves only one variable and is used primarily for descriptive purposes, that is, to describe the frequency distribution of some variable. For example, how many men and women are there in the sample? How many people support abortion on demand?

When two variables are examined simultaneously, a *bivariate* analysis is made. You might wish to relate sex and support for the Equal Rights Amendment in order to establish the nature of the relationship between the two. *Multivariate* analysis involves the examination of three or more variables simultaneously, often to determine the effect of each independent variable on a dependent variable separately and in combination with the other independent variables. You might wish to examine the separate and combined effects of organizational size, rules emphasis, and amount of supervision of workers on factory worker productivity. The goals of both bivariate and multivariate analyses tend to be more explanatory than descriptive; they focus more on developing explanations for a dependent variable using the independent, causal variables than on simply examining the frequency distributions of each of the variables.

An additional basic concept involves the difference between descriptive and inferential statistics. The difference between these two types of statistics derives from their respective purposes: descriptive statistics organize and summarize data whereas inferential statistics make some types of inferences from a sample to a larger population. *Descriptive* statistics can be univariate, bivariate, or multivariate but generally produce a single value that tells us something about the data. A mean, for example, may describe the central tendency in a distribution of scores; a measure of association may describe the strength and direction of the relationship between two variables. *Inferential* statistics, on the other hand, are more concerned with the extent to which one can accurately generalize to a larger population or the level of confidence that can be placed in the data's being a "real" reflection of reality as opposed to a chance reflection due to sampling error and other problems. I will first review several descriptive statistics and then briefly review inferential statistics.

UNIVARIATE ANALYSIS

Frequency Distributions

There are three broad classes of univariate statistics: frequency distributions, measures of central tendency, and measures of dispersion. *Frequency distributions* allow the researcher to examine the range of scores on a variable and see how many cases fall into each possible category. Such a procedure is useful for examining the variation among the categories. If almost everyone in a sample is in favor of gun control, for example, there is not much point in proceeding to a bivariate analysis of sex related to support for gun control.

Table 1 provides an example of a frequency distribution on the issue of contraceptive use among college students at first intercourse. I have reported both the raw numbers and the percentage, although the common procedure is to report only the percentage figures and place the base number of cases at the bottom of each column in the table. Table 1 indicates that nearly 50 percent of the students surveyed used no contraception at first intercourse, while about 25 percent used condoms, about 20 percent used withdrawal, and only 9 percent used the pill. In many cases, such as this one, frequency distributions themselves may aid the researcher in answering questions relevant to theory. The example just cited may assist family researchers in developing explanations for the rather high nonuse rate of contraceptives among college students.

Frequency distributions may be quite brief, as in Table 1, or they may be quite lengthy (such as reporting all the GPAs among the students in Table 1). If many categories exist, a typical procedure is to collapse the distribution into smaller categories. In order to report student GPAs, for ex-

Table 1. Contraceptive Use at First Intercourse among Unmarried Sexually Active College Students, 1976*

Method	N	%
Nothing	91	47
Withdrawal	41	21
Condom	44	23
Pill	18	9
	194	100

*Rhythm, foam, IUD, and diaphragm were almost never mentioned by respondents; thus they are grouped here with methods of similar theoretical effectiveness.

Source: Adapted from "Correlates of contraceptive behavior among unmarried U.S. college students," K. G. Foreit and J. R. Foreit, *Studies in Family Planning* 9 (June 1978): 169–74. Used by permission.

ample, we might group them by half-point categories: 4.0–3.6, 3.5–3.1, 3.0–2.6, and so forth. Even this distribution could be further collapsed to 4.0–3.1, 3.0–2.1, and so forth. The point is that the researcher organizes data according to his or her needs. If the goal is to compare high-GPA students with low-GPA students on study habits, a simple grade-by-grade categorization is sufficient to answer the question. If, however, the goal is to find out which textbook most facilitates student learning, more refined measures would be necessary.

A few cautions: When reading frequency distributions remember to focus on the percentage figures instead of the raw numbers. Note also that frequency distributions are sometimes reported as bar graphs, known as *histograms*, or as lines going from the midpoint of one bar on the graph to another; these lines are called frequency *polygons*. Finally, notice that frequency distributions are not generally reported in research reports unless they deal directly with a hypothesis or research question.

Central Tendency

Measures of central tendency reflect the central value around which the values of a variable tend to group. Central tendency is what we are referring to when we talk about an "average" score. There are three types of measures of central tendency: the *mode*, which is the single value appearing most frequently; the *median*, which is the value that cuts a distribution into two halves; and the *mean*, which is the arithmetic average (add up the scores and divide by the number of scores to arrive at this figure). It is important to know the level of measurement of your variables in order to determine the appropriate measure of central tendency. The mode is most appropriate for nominal level variables, the median for ordinal level variables, and the mean for interval and ratio level variables. You can, however, legitimately calculate a mode for ordinal, interval, and ratio level variables or apply a median to interval and ratio level variables.

For an example of the mode, please look at Table 1 again. Among the categories of the variable "contraceptive use," the category with the largest number of cases is "nothing." To illustrate the median, let's examine the number of children of a randomly selected sample of 1,291 persons who are or have been married at some point in time (see Table 2; the data from the National Opinion Research Corporation, General Social Survey, 1978). The median for these data is 2.1; half the persons fall below this value and half above. You may wonder why this variable is not a ratio since a real zero exists and the intervals seem to be equal. Look at the last interval, "eight or more." This interval is not equal to the others. To calculate the mean, we would need to know exactly how many children each person has, and we have no way of knowing this number for the respondents in the "eight or more" category. Hence, the variable must be treated as an ordinal variable.

To illustrate the mean I will use the variable age for the entire NORC sample. The mean age is 44.7 (I'll spare you the frequency distribution). This value represents the division of the number of persons into the sum of all the ages. The mode for this variable is 26 and the median is 42.6; the differences among these three measures of central tendency reflect both calculation and interpretation differences.

A few comments on these measures of central tendency. The mean is the most accurate representation of the sample, but it also is the most seriously affected by extreme scores. In the example on age the mean was higher than the median because of the inclusion of a few very old persons. Be sure to inspect the frequency distributions of variables, if reported. If extreme scores exist, the median is the preferred measure. Remember that a mean can-

Table 2. Number of Children for a Random Sample of Americans Age 18 or Older Who Are or Have Been Married (1978)

Number of Children	N	%
Zero	210	16.3
One	224	17.4
Two	358	27.7
Three	219	17.0
Four	134	10.4
Five	62	4.8
Six	39	3.0
Seven	24	1.9
Eight or more	21	1.6
	1,291	100.1

Source: National Opinion Research Corporation, General Social Survey (1978).

not be calculated with an open-ended upper or lower value (e.g., eight or more children). In such cases the median is again preferred. Note that the data must be in rank-ordered format to calculate the median. And remember that the only measure of central tendency appropriate for nominal level variables is the mode.

In conclusion, three criteria exist for determining an appropriate measure of central tendency. The first is the level of measurement. The second is the shape of the distribution; if extreme scores exist, use the median. The third is the researcher's objectives. A fertility expert would probably prefer to use the median number of children as we calculated it above (2.1 children). A builder or home economist, however, might be more interested in the modal number of children, which is 2. Students generally prefer to compare their grade to a median rather than a mean because one or two students with very low grades may bias the mean downward. So be alert in reading research reports to make sure the author is using not only the correct measure of central tendency but also the measure that best reflects the goals of the research.

Dispersion

Measures of *dispersion* are single values reflecting the overall amount of variability in a set of data. They indicate how far outward the data spread around the central tendency measures.

Since nominal level variables employ numbers that have no intrinsic meaning, we do not calculate measures of dispersion for them. About the only measure of dispersion appropriate for ordinal level measures is the *range*, which is the distance between the highest and lowest values. The range is even more relevant for interval and ratio level measures. But the range is not very useful, especially when extreme scores are present. Some people use the *interquartile range*, which is the distance between the first and fourth quartiles, in order to eliminate the effect of extreme scores.

By far the most common measure of dispersion is the *standard deviation*, which is a single value representing the overall variation in a set of interval or ratio level data. The computation involves the calculation of the average difference between the mean and the individual scores. As an example, the first exam I gave this term yielded a mean of 22.7 and a standard deviation of 5.3, while the second exam yielded a mean of 27.4 and a standard deviation of 3.2 (both exams had 35 items). By comparing the standard deviations on the two exams, we see that the scores on the first exam displayed more variation among themselves, and hence from the mean, than did the scores on the second exam. The increase in the mean and the decrease in the standard deviation may have occurred because the lowest scoring students dropped the course between the two exams. It is entirely possible that two sets of similar data may have the same mean but quite different standard deviations as a result of different amounts of variation among the scores

in the data sets. So the main point thus far is this: the standard deviation represents the overall degree of deviation from the mean in a set of data.

How do you interpret the standard deviation? I will bypass a lot of history and statistical theory and go straight to the normal curve, which represents the data according to the frequency of each of the possible scores (see Figure 1). You can see from this illustration that scores near the mean have higher frequencies than those further from the mean; that is, most of the scores in the distribution tend to cluster around the mean. If we think of the area under the curve as representing 100 percent of all the scores, the proportion of the scores between one standard deviation and the next is that amount of area under the curve in that segment. This proportion decreases as we move away from the mean because fewer people have scores far from the mean. The approximate percentages of the area, and hence the number of cases, for each standard deviation are noted in the figure.

Let's look at a concrete example. The mean grade point average of our hypothetical class is 2.6, and the standard deviation is .4. Looking at Figure 2 (the first row), we can see that about 34 percent of the students have GPAs falling between the mean and +1 standard deviation (i.e., between 2.6 and 3.0) and another 34 percent fall between the mean and −1 standard deviation (i.e., between 2.6 and 2.2). Just short of 14 percent of the GPAs lie between +1 and +2 standard deviations (i.e., between 3.0 and 3.4), and the same proportion lie between −1 and −2 standard deviations (i.e., be-

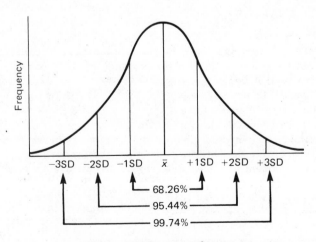

Figure 1   The normal curve

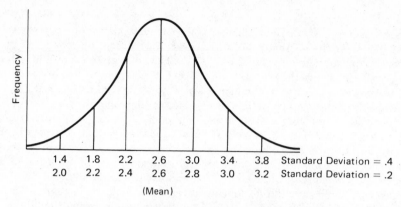

Figure 2 Distribution of GPAs in an introductory
research methods class of 100 students (hypothetical data)

tween 2.2 and 1.8). About 2 percent fall between
+2 and +3 standard deviations (i.e., between 3.4
and 3.8), and about 2 percent fall between −2 and
−3 standard deviations (i.e., between 1.8 and 1.4).
Very few GPAs lie beyond 3.8 or below 1.4.

Notice what the distribution would look like if
the standard deviation were .2 instead of .4 (see
Figure 2, second row). About two-thirds of the
GPAs would then lie between 2.4 and 2.8, instead
of between 2.2 and 3.0 as they do when the standard deviation is .4; the variability is more restricted with a lower standard deviation. In sum,
the standard deviation represents the degree of
variability in a set of scores. The higher the standard deviation, the further from the mean you
have to go to include two-thirds or any other proportion of the scores.

BIVARIATE ANALYSIS

Tables

Perhaps the simplest way to portray a bivariate
relationship is through the use of a table. Let's take
the table on contraceptive use that we used in univariate analysis (Table 1) and add an independent
variable, sex. These data are reported in Table 3.
Notice that we still have 194 people (82 men and
112 women); we have simply broken them down
into the separate categories on the variable "sex."
We can now analyze our dependent variable, contraceptive use, in terms of our independent variable, sex, and probe for any relationship between
them. Recall that one prerequisite for establishing
causality is the presence of an association between
two variables. Comparing men with women, we

see that more men than women report using nothing (a 12 percentage point difference), while
women report greater use of withdrawal (an 11
percentage point difference) and condoms (a 6 percentage point difference). Men report higher use of
the pill (by their partner, we hope) at their first
intercourse (a 5 percentage point difference).
Given the lower percentage of women who report
using nothing, we conclude that women are apparently more concerned about contraception at first
intercourse than are men, undoubtedly because
they stand to lose more should a pregnancy occur.

Table 3. Sex by Contraceptive Use at
First Intercourse among Unmarried
Sexually Active College Students, 1976*

Method	Sex			
	Men		Women	
	N	%	N	%
Nothing	44	54	47	42
Withdrawal	12	15	29	26
Condom	16	19	28	25
Pill	10	12	8	7
	82	100	112	100

*Rhythm, foam, IUD, and diaphragm were almost
never mentioned by respondents; thus they are
grouped here with methods of similar theoretical
effectiveness.

Source: Adapted from "Correlates of contraceptive
behavior among unmarried U.S. college students,"
K. G. Foreit and J. R. Foreit, *Studies in Family Planning* 9 (June 1978): 169–74. Used by permission.

With this illustration in mind, let me make a few points regarding table construction and interpretation. First, the independent variable is generally put on top and the dependent variable on the side of a table. Second, percentages should be figured within each category of the independent variable, separately for men and women in this case. We might wish to know the percentage of the men in the study who employed no contraception as compared to the percentage of women who employed no contraception. We could have done it differently, but incorrectly, by calculating the percentage of all those employing nothing who were men (48%) and who were women (52%). Notice how this method yields the opposite conclusion; it appears that women more frequently employed nothing. This conclusion is in error simply because there were more women in the study. To examine the relationship of the independent variable to the dependent variable we must compare the values of the dependent variable *across* the categories of the *independent* variable; this approach allows us to examine the values on the dependent variable in terms of the values on the independent variable.

Third, only percentage figures are normally presented in the body of the table. The total (or base) number of cases in each category of the independent variable is placed at the bottom of each category. Given the percentages and the base, you can easily reconstruct the raw data values by simply multiplying the base by the appropriate percentage figure.

Fourth, the content of a table should be clearly explained in its title. The title should note the two variables being related, briefly note the nature of the subjects sampled, and preferably include the date the data were collected. The categories of the two variables should be described well enough that the reader can interpret the table without reference to the text of the article.

Let's examine one more table for practice. Table 4 reports the relationship between participation in organizations and attitude-toward-self scores for a sample of 180 prison inmates. Sixty-eight percent of all inmates who participated in organizations had attitude-toward-self scores above the mean, while only 37 percent of the nonparticipants had scores above the mean, a 31-point difference. Apparently organizational involvement among prison inmates is positively associated with the attitudes they hold about themselves.

Table 4. Relationship between Participation of Inmates in Organizations and Attitude-toward-self Scores, 1977 (in Percent)

Attitude-toward-self Score	Participation in Organizations	
	No	Yes
Below mean	63	32
Above mean	37	68
	100	100
	(82)	(97)
No answer, 1		

Source: Adapted from "Measuring inmate morale," Mary W. Macht, Fredrick W. Seidl and D. Richard Greene, *Social Work* 22 (July 1977): 288. Copyright 1977 National Association of Social Workers, Inc. Used by permission.

Some tables may deviate from the format described above, although the general principles of interpreting such tables are very similar. Authors may report mean scores on the dependent variable for each category of the independent variable; as examples, see Table 4 in Brogan and Kutner (Section 2.2) relating religious affiliation to sex role orientation or Table 1 in Griffitt and Veitch (Section 3.3) relating temperature to feelings. Other authors may incorporate more than one dependent variable in a table; for an example, see Table 4 in Berman (Section 3.4) relating the presence of lawyer-volunteers to six attitudinal dimensions of parolees. Still other authors may report one-half of a dependent variable if it has only two categories; a researcher might choose to report only the percentage of voters in an election since the percentage of nonvoters could then be determined by subtracting the percentage voting from 100 percent.

Measures of Association

Bivariate tables allow us to determine if two variables are related. By comparing percentage figures across categories of the independent variable, we can also infer how strongly two variables are related. A more compact method for reporting the degree of a relationship would be the use of a measure of association, also known as a correlation. A *measure of association* is a single value representing the strength of association between two variables.

Most measures of association are based on a principle known as proportional reduction in error. Although a complete explanation of this principle is beyond the scope of this article, the basic procedure is to predict scores on the dependent variable knowing only the distribution on that variable and then to predict scores on the dependent variable given the distributions of *both* the independent and the dependent variables. The net improvement in shifting from the use of one variable (the dependent variable) to the use of both variables is the measure of association. In short, this principle reflects the degree to which variation in the dependent variable is accounted for by the variation in the independent variable.

The crucial point to remember about measures of association is that the choice of which one to use depends on the levels of measurement of the variables involved. Here is a list of the most common measures of association for the various levels of measurement:

Nominal	Ordinal	Interval	Ratio
phi	gamma	Pearson's r	Pearson's r
Yule's Q			
Cramer's V	Yule's Q		
contingency coefficient	Kendall's Tau		
lambda	Somer's d		
Goodman and Kruskal's tau	Spearman's rho		

In reading research reports, make sure the author is using the appropriate measure of association for his or her level of measurement.

How are measures of association interpreted? Many different rules of thumb are available. My own follows (adapted from Davis, 1971:49):

.50 or higher, a strong association

.25 through .49, a moderate association

.10 through .24, a weak association

.01 through .09, a negligible association

.00, no association

If the variables are ordinal, interval, or ratio, a plus or minus sign will also be attached, indicating a positive or negative relationship. A positive sign means that as the independent variable increases the dependent variable also increases. A negative sign indicates that as either value increases the other decreases.

As an example, the Yule's Q for the data in Table 4 was +.56, indicating a strongly positive association. Participation in organizations by inmates was strongly positively related to attitude-toward-self scores. In the article on father absence among daughters (Section 4.2), the Hunts reported a gamma of +.33 between esteem and school grades for whites and a gamma of +.06 between the same two variables for blacks. Thus for whites school grades are moderately positively associated with self-esteem, while for blacks the relationship is negligible. These values indicate both the direction and strength of the relationships examined and hence yield an indication of the extent to which the variation in the dependent variable is accounted for by the variation in the independent variable. Note, however, that nominal level measures do not include an indicator of direction since such an indicator would be meaningless for these variables.

Comparing dependent variable means across categories of nominal level independent variables is another technique for assessing bivariate associations. But since these statistics are more inferential, they are reviewed in the section on statistical inference.

MULTIVARIATE ANALYSIS

Recall that the third prerequisite for establishing causality is to rule out the effects of other variables. In order to be more certain of a possibly causal relationship between sex and attitudes toward abortion, for example, we might control for religion and marital status. If the relationship between sex and abortion support persists despite these controls, we are more certain that a valid relationship exists. But we can never be completely certain since we cannot control for all possible variables. Multivariate analysis is generally performed for two reasons. First, a researcher may wish to increase the confidence in a particular independent-dependent relationship by ruling out the causal effects of other variables. Second, a researcher may wish to examine the effect of each of *several* independent variables on a given dependent variable, with the effects of other independent variables held constant. Let's now consider several possible approaches to multivariate analysis.

Tables

The principles regarding table use in multivariate analysis are the same as those noted previously for bivariate analysis, except that now an independent-dependent variable table is calculated *for each category of the control variable.* As a rule, tables are used primarily for nominal level variables. They may also be used for ordinal, interval, or ratio level variables if their values are collapsed into discrete categories. Let's look at an example.

In a study of 1,025 suicides (see Table 5, upper right) Cohen and Fiedler (1974) examined the relationship between marital status and the leaving of a note. As you can see from the table, divorced or separated persons who commit suicide are slightly more likely to leave a note, but the measure of association indicates a negligible relationship (Cramer's V = .08). They also found that women are slightly more likely to leave a note, but again the measure of association indicates a negligible relationship (phi = .08). They then decided to examine the bivariate relationship between marital status and note-leaving while controlling for sex, making it a multivariate analysis. We can now look at the relationship between marital status and note-leaving for men and women separately (see bottom

Table 5. Suicide Notes by Marital Status and Sex,
Zero-order and Partial Tables (in Percent)

Zero-order Tables

| | Sex | | | | Marital Status | | |
	Male	Female		Single	Married	Widowed	Div-Sep
Left a note	19	26	Left a note	20	20	21	30
No note	81	74	No note	80	80	79	70
	100	100		100	100	100	100
	(698)	(325)		(216)	(515)	(156)	(138)

Chi Square = 6.46, p ≤ .05
Phi = .08

Chi Square = 6.87, not significant
Cramer's V = .08

Partial Tables

| | Sex | | | | | | |
| | Male | | | | Female | | |
	Single	Married	Widowed	Div-Sep	Single	Married	Widowed	Div-Sep
Left a note	17	17	24	25	31	25	16	40
No note	83	83	76	75	69	75	84	60
	100	100	100	100	100	100	100	100
	(164)	(345)	(89)	(93)	(52)	(170)	(67)	(45)

Chi Square = 4.42, not significant
Cramer's V = .08

Chi Square = 8.53, p ≤ .05
Cramer's V = .16

Source: Adapted from "Content analysis of multiple messages in suicide notes," Stuart L. Cohen and Joanne E. Fiedler, *Life-threatening Behavior* 4 (Summer, 1974): 81. Used by permission of Human Sciences Press, New York. The measures of association are not in original; they were calculated by the author.

half of Table 5). We observe a negligible association between marital status and note-leaving for men ($V = .08$) and a weak association for women ($V = .16$). Since the original bivariate relationship between marital status and note-leaving was negligible ($V = .08$), we conclude that a difference exists between the two partials. *Partials* are bivariate tables calculated for the different categories of the control variable, in this case, one for men and one for women. The relationship between marital status and note-leaving is stronger for women than for men.

As with all nominal level measures of association, we must examine the within-category percentages to clarify and understand what the relationship means. We see that not many differences exist between the marital status categories for men but that for women considerable differences exist. Widowed women were the least likely to leave suicide notes, while divorced or separated women were by far the most likely to leave notes (compare these data for men). So far we have determined that the data for men are quite similar to the original table relating marital status to note-leaving, while the data for women are quite different from the original table. Remember, our interest is still in relating marital status to note-leaving, not so much in comparing men with women; we control for sex primarily to clarify our understanding of this original relationship. The authors could have started with the relationship of sex to note-leaving and then controlled for marital status, but that was not in keeping with their theoretical focus.

This process of multivariate analysis with tables is often referred to as *elaboration*. Let's briefly review the possible results of the elaboration process. Starting with a moderately strong bivariate relationship and then controlling for another variable, the following results may occur:

1. The partials may be virtually identical to the original table, i.e., the original relationship still exists for each partial. This is called *replication*.
2. All of the separate partials may reflect no association at all between the independent and dependent variables, while the original table revealed a moderate association. This is called *explanation* if the control variable occurs before both the independent and dependent variables in the time order and *interpretation* if the control variable occurs between the independent and dependent variables in the time order.
3. Each partial may reflect a different degree of association. This is known as *specification* because the control variable specifies the conditions under which the original relationship holds true.

In the first two possibilities, the partials display similar relationships between the independent and dependent variables for each category of the control variable. In the case of specification, however, the partials display different relationships between the independent and dependent variables for each category of the control variable.

For an example of explanation, consider the often cited relationship between the amount of ice cream consumed and the number of rapes occurring in an area—as ice cream consumption increases, the number of rapes increase. The appropriate control variable, of course, is temperature. Both the number of rapes and the amount of ice cream consumed are a function of temperature: both occur more frequently in the summer. Since the control variable comes before both the independent and dependent variables, this is an example of explanation.

In the suicide note study we saw an instance of specification. The partials were quite different from each other; they helped specify the original independent variable–dependent variable relationship. Marital status is associated with suicide note-leaving, but only among women. It is not so important to remember these terms; what is important is to carefully review partial tables you see in research reports and see how they help you to understand the original relationship. For an excellent example of this process, see the Hunts' article in Section 4.2 on father absence effects on daughters.

Correlations

Although the preceding discussion involved primarily nominal variables, similar interpretation procedures are used when we have ordinal, interval, or ratio level variables and are using correlations to perform multivariate analysis. These procedures are called *partial correlation* analysis. Again, our goal is to examine the partials in comparison with the original relationship.

Let's use the NORC data to illustrate. The original correlation between education level and abortion support was .25, a moderately positive relationship. The higher one's education, the higher one's support for abortion. When I controlled for age, on the assumption that older people may have less education and may display lower levels of support for abortion, the resulting correlation was again .25. We see here a clear instance of replication. In a study I did recently I found a correlation of −.50 between the population turnover in a community and the achievement level in that community's elementary schools (see Wagenaar, 1978). Communities with higher population turnover rates had lower achievement levels. Reasoning that population turnover might be a function of neighborhood socioeconomic status and that neighborhood socioeconomic status is correlated with achievement, I controlled for neighborhood socioeconomic status. The resulting correlation was −.16, a clear instance of explanation because the original relationship virtually disappeared and the control variable came before population turnover and achievement in time.

Multiple Regression

These last three sections of the review of multivariate analytical techniques briefly summarize three additional techniques you may see in your reading of social science research articles: multiple regression, path analysis, and factor analysis. The first two are frequently used to develop causal models, while the third is used to determine the existence of underlying dimensions among a number of items. All three are intended for use with interval or ratio level variables, but nominal variables can be used if they are dichotomous (have only two categories) and not too many are included. As for ordinal variables, several statisticians have argued that ordinal level variables can be used without necessarily biasing the resulting statistics. As a rule, however, these techniques should be employed only for interval or ratio level measures.

Multiple regression analysis allows us to examine the variation in a dependent variable as accounted for by several independent variables. Hence, equations can be calculated that predict a person's score on a dependent variable given certain scores on the independent variables. Multiple regression also allows the determination of the relative importance of each of the variables in the equation.

Multiple regression, then, seeks to explain the variation in a dependent variable. It searches first for the variable that explains the most variation in the dependent variable and enters that variable into the equation. Then it goes back to the remaining list of variables and searches for the next most important variable and enters that second variable into the equation, continuing until all the independent variables have been considered. This is one statistic regression analysis provides: contribution to *variance explained* in the dependent variable. Social science variables seldom account for greater than 20–30 percent of the variance in a given dependent variable.

Another statistic provided is the *beta*, which is also known as the standardized regression coefficient and which standardizes the variables to a common scoring system so that we can compare across different types of variables. The beta actually reflects the change in standard deviations of the dependent variable with each increase of one standard deviation of an independent variable, holding constant for the other variables in the equation. The beta yields the unique effect of each of the independent variables on the dependent variable. The interpretation of betas follows the guidelines suggested for measures of association.

Table 6 reports on a multiple regression analysis of time spent watching television, with education, age, job satisfaction, and frequency of newspaper readership as independent variables. The simple r (Pearson's r) is a bivariate measure of association. The multiple r indicates the combined correlation between the dependent variable and the variables thus far. Looking at row 2, age and education have a combined correlation of .21 with television watching. The total R square simply indicates how much of the total (100%) variance in the dependent variable has been accounted for by the variables thus far in the equation. Looking at row 3, a total of 5 percent of the variance in television watching is accounted for by education, age, and job satisfaction. The next column, R square change, indicates how much a given variable contributes to the variance explained; job satisfaction explains an additional .7 percent over that explained by education and age. And the beta, perhaps the most im-

Table 6. Regression Analysis of Amount of Time Spent
Watching Television with Education, Age, Job Satisfaction,
and Frequency of Newspaper Readership, NORC data, 1975, N = 1500

Variable	Simple r	Multiple r	Total R square	R square change	Beta
Education	−.17	.17	.029	.029	−.20*
Age	−.06	.21	.043	.014	−.11*
Job satisfaction	.10	.23	.050	.007	.08
Freq. newspaper reading	.09	.23	.051	.001	.02

*Indicates statistical significance level ≤ .05

portant statistic, indicates the unique effect of that variable with the effects of *all* the other variables in the equation removed. The beta −.20 for education, for instance, means that for each increase of one standard deviation in education there is a decrease of .20 standard deviation in time spent watching television; the effects of age, job satisfaction, and newspaper readership are held constant. The betas for age, job satisfaction, and newspaper readership are all weak or negligible, suggesting that education is the most important variable for explaining television watching.

Multiple regression analysis thus (1) rank orders the variables in terms of their contribution to the variance explained in the dependent variable, (2) indicates the contribution of each variable to the variance explained, and (3) yields betas as indicators of the unique effects of each variable on the dependent variable.

Path Analysis

Path analysis is simply an extension of multiple regression analysis. The major difference is that path analysis involves a time-ordered specification of a causal model. This causal model is developed on the basis of previous research and theory and on the basis of the researcher's reasoning regarding the variables being analyzed. Path analysis allows the calculation of both direct and indirect effects. A direct effect is much the same as the beta noted above: it presents the unique relationship between one variable and another. An indirect effect is the effect of a variable on another variable as carried indirectly through other variables occurring between the two in time order. Both of these effects will be illustrated.

In order to perform path analysis, two criteria must be met. First, there must be a clear, one-way time ordering of the variables. Second, the variables must make sense in terms of the causal model; the fact that sports participation in high school comes before current voting behavior is not reason enough to include it in the causal model. It must also make sense theoretically.

I have calculated a path model of background factors related to college graduation for a large set of data compiled by Sewel and Shah (1968) and have presented these models separately for males and females in Figure 3. Glance through the table before reading further. Notice first the time ordering of the variables. Socioeconomic status (SES) background and I.Q. come first; we assume that they are the initial variables in the model and, for our purposes, are not caused by other variables. Both SES and I.Q. precede and are thought to contribute to parental encouragement to attend college. All three of these variables are thought to influence plans to attend college; all four of these variables are thought to be causally related to attendance at college; and all five of these variables are thought to influence graduation from college.

The values on the arrows are the betas from the multiple regression analysis; they are called *path coefficients*. Looking at the path diagram for males, we observe a path coefficient of .20 for SES to encouragement; a weak positive unique effect is illustrated. Compare this with the same path coefficient for females, which is moderately positive (.26); SES is somewhat more strongly associated with parental encouragement for females. A similar analysis for I.Q. and encouragement indicates I.Q. to be more salient for males (.31 and .25). Let's keep going through the model. For plans to attend college, parental encouragement has about the

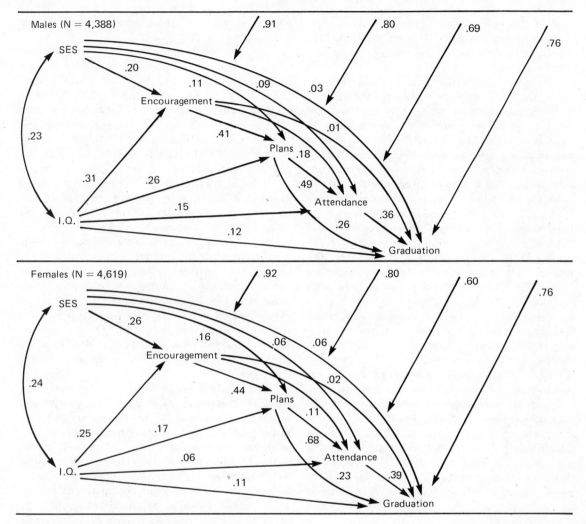

Variables:

    SES = father's highest level of education

    I.Q. = Henmon-Nelson Test of Mental Agility

    Encouragement = perceived parental encouragement

    Plans = intention to enroll in college (asked in 1957)

    Attendance = actual enrollment between 1957 and 1964

    Graduation = receipt of B.A. or not (by 1964)

Source: Path diagrams calculated by the author based on data found in "Parents' education and
           children's educational aspirations and achievement," William H. Sewell and Vimal P. Shah,
           American Sociological Review 33 (April 1968): 191–209.

Figure 3 Path analysis of factors related to
college graduation among men and women, 1964

same moderately positive effect for both males and females (.41 and .44 respectively), but I.Q. has a greater effect for males than females (.26 and .17 respectively) and SES has a slightly greater effect for females than males (.16 and .11 respectively). We can conclude that I.Q. is more relevant for parental encouragement and plans for males than they are for females and SES is more relevant for parental encouragement and plans for females than for males.

Things get a little more complicated as we proceed since there are more antecedent variables to consider. Examining attendance at college, we note the considerably stronger effect of plans for females than males (.68 and .49 respectively): once females plan to attend college, they are much more likely to actually enroll than males. Parental encouragement has a slightly larger effect on attendance for males than females (.18 and .11 respectively), I.Q. has a larger effect on attendance for males than females (.15 and .06 respectively), and SES has a negligible effect in both cases. A reminder: each path coefficient represents the unique effect of one variable on another; the effects of all other antecedent variables have been controlled.

Examining the final dependent variable, actual graduation, we note that attendance has a moderately positive effect on graduation for both women and men (.39 and .36 respectively), plans to enroll has a moderately positive effect on graduation for both women and men (.23 and .26 respectively), both parental encouragement and SES have negligible direct effects on graduation for both women and men, and I.Q. has a weak direct effect on graduation for both women and men (.11 and .12 respectively). In sum, most variables have similar effects on college graduation for males and females; actual enrollment and plans to attend are more relevant than SES, I.Q., or parental encouragement.

Since both plans and attendance are so important for explaining college graduation, it is important to consider possible causal variables for *these* variables. The results indicate the importance of parental encouragement for planning to attend college and the importance of SES and I.Q. for the generation of parental encouragement. Hence, we cannot conclude that SES and I.Q. and encouragement are unimportant for explaining college graduation, even though their direct path coefficients to graduation are low. Instead, we conclude that their effects on graduation are *indirect* through plans and enrollment in college. I have not presented calculations for the indirect effects, but they could easily be calculated to yield a more complete statistical portrait of both the direct and indirect

effects of each of these variables on college graduation.

You may be thinking at this point that a host of other unconsidered variables may help explain college graduation, including money, proximity to home, time spent studying, peer relationships, or marriage. The sum total of all these other variables is represented in the arrows coming from nowhere. If you square the value on this arrow, you have the proportion of that variable left *un*explained by the preceding variables in the model. For both males and females, the amount of the variation in college graduation left unexplained after considering SES, I.Q., parental encouragement, plans to attend college, and actual enrollment is 57 percent; we've explained only 43 percent of the variation in college graduation with this model. Similar calculations for the other variables indicate that we can explain about 52 percent of the variance in college attendance with SES, I.Q., encouragement, and plans for males (and 64 percent for females), 36 percent of the variance in plans with SES, I.Q., and encouragement for both sexes, and about 16 percent of the variance in encouragement with SES and I.Q. for both sexes.

Path analysis is obviously a very useful technique for specifying causal models. In comparison to multiple regression analysis, it allows us to examine the causal interrelationships *between the independent variables* in the model as well as the independent-dependent variable relationships. In effect, each variable becomes a dependent variable for each part of the analysis. And path analysis indicates indirect as well as direct linkages, a very useful advantage when we wish to find out exactly how a group of variables influence some other variable.

Factor Analysis

Factor analysis is a multivariate analytical technique used to ascertain any underlying dimensions in a set of variables. It is a data reduction technique. It differs from other multivariate approaches we have examined in two major respects. First, the goal is different. Instead of trying to explain the variation in a dependent variable in terms of some independent variables, factor analysis seeks to explain how a series of variables are interrelated. Factor analysis helps answer the question "What fundamental characteristics or qualities might the variables have in common?" Second, whereas the other approaches typically focus on a few variables, factor analysis generally is used to examine many variables, often a hundred or more.

I have reported an example from some research a colleague and I did on teacher morale (Wagenaar and Jennings, 1978). We were interested in the existence of any underlying factors in a set of 42 items measuring teacher morale. A subset of the results of our factor analysis are reported in Table 7. The values reported in that table are *factor loadings,* which simply indicate the association between that item and the factor. Using .40 as a criterion for a substantively significant association, we can see that items 1, 6, 7, 10, and 12 load highly on, and therefore comprise, Factor 1; items 2, 4, 8, 9, and 13 load highly on Factor 2; and items 3, 5, and 11 load highly on Factor 3. For the entire set of 42 items there were actually nine factors. A computer can indicate how items load on individual factors, but it is up to the researcher to determine what these items have in common. All the items loading highly on Factor 1 reflect positive reactions to the principal; hence we labeled this factor "satisfaction with principal." We labeled Factor 2 "satisfaction with teacher cooperation" since all the items loading highly on this factor reflect this concept, and we labeled Factor 3 "satisfaction

with teaching as an occupation" since all the items loading highly on this factor reflect positive feelings about teaching. We then performed an analysis of how teacher morale relates to various structural features of schools by using our nine factors as dependent variables. So, instead of using all 42 items separately or just combining them into one scale called "teacher morale," we were able to specify how the various school structure variables related to *each* of the nine statistically separate dimensions of teacher morale.

This illustration shows the advantages of factor analysis for reducing data (from 42 items to 9 factors in the example) and for determining the separate underlying dimensions in a set of variables. Factor analyses yield a large number of statistics other than the loadings described above, but the essence of factor analysis is contained in these loadings and the use made of them.

STATISTICAL INFERENCE

The descriptive statistics commonly used in the social sciences help us to describe the nature of one variable or the relationships between two or more variables. Each statistic tells us something

Table 7. Factor Analysis of Selected Teacher Morale Items* (N = 280)

Item	Factor 1	Factor 2	Factor 3
1. My work is appreciated by my principal	.73	.13	.16
2. Little arguing occurs among teachers	.19	.76	−.04
3. Teaching gives me personal satisfaction	.18	.03	.75
4. Teachers cooperate in our school	.17	.78	.11
5. I love to teach	.16	−.01	.81
6. My principal makes my work easier/ more pleasant	.83	.17	.09
7. My principal recognizes good teaching procedures	.77	.19	.14
8. Our teaching staff is congenial to work with	.25	.79	.01
9. My colleagues are well prepared	.20	.64	.01
10. I discuss problems with my principal	.80	.07	.14
11. If I could choose over, I would choose teaching	.10	.10	.74
12. My principal is interested in me	.85	.11	.11
13. Teachers in this school work well together	.25	.87	.01

*Contains only a subset of the complete list of 42 items.

Source: "Organization Structure, Role Orientation, and Teacher Morale." Paper presented at the annual meeting of the North Central Sociological Association, May 1978, Cincinnati.

about the data; the one we use depends on what we wish to know about the data and on the nature of the data itself, especially the level of the variables.

But describing data is not enough. Since most data come from samples, we must also note the degree to which the data accurately represent some larger population from which the sample was drawn. We must find some way to indicate this level of accuracy; this question can be answered through the use of inferential statistics. *Inferential statistics* allow us to make certain inferences about the nature of descriptive statistics as applied to the larger population from which the sample was taken.

In this section I will present a lengthy excerpt from Kimble's excellent introductory statistics book (1978:10–16) and then I will discuss a few common inferential statistics.

Benjamin Franklin is supposed to be responsible for the observation that nothing is certain in this life but death and taxes. I would like to add a third certainty to the list, the certainty of uncertainty. We live in a probabilistic world, and most of the decisions we make entail an element of risk. If I am a merchant, what proportion of dresses with long and short skirts shall I stock? Some women will wear long skirts, some short, but in what ratio? If I am a gambler, shall I draw to the straight, keep a kicker, bet on the favorite, or finesse the queen? If I am a student taking a multiple-choice test, shall I pick choice "b" or "d"? I don't really know the answer but I suspect that one of them is right. If I am a sick man, shall I submit to surgery? The doctor says that it will probably cure me but there is some chance that I will not survive the operation.

Obviously, there is more to consider in such cases than just the odds, and certainly statistics cannot solve important human problems. But in many cases statistics can provide considerable clarification and a basis for decision. That is what inferential statistics is all about. In this section, I shall develop the essential ideas in this area, beginning with a frivolous example.

The Riddle of the Neglected Lover

To the best of my knowledge, the following puzzle is the invention of Harvard statistician Frederick B. Mosteller.

The scene is a large city and the point of the story involves its subway system. This system is in the form of a continuous loop on which a single train travels, always in the same direction. In general layout the system re- *sembles a figure eight or a dumbbell. . . . The main station in the system is at the point where the two sides of the loop are close together. At this point, by going to one side of the station or the other, a traveler can catch the train going in either direction. Other stations are located at intervals along the rest of the track; two of these other stations figure in the events to be described now.*

Our concern is with three people who are served by this system: Mr. Z, whose office is near the main station, and his two lovers, Ms. A and Ms. B, who live on opposite sides of the city in different sections of the system.

Mr. Z has a problem. Ms. A and Ms. B are equally attractive to him. He visits one or the other of the women on a daily basis, but the choice of which one to visit is always difficult. His solution to the problem is to "leave things up to chance." When he can get away from work (which happens at times that vary unpredictably from day to day), he goes to the station and boards the train whenever it comes. If the train is going east, he visits Ms. A; if it is going west, he visits Ms. B. On the assumption that the probability of catching the east-going train is about the same as that of catching a west-going train, the visits should even out in the long run.[1]

But things do not work out that way: after a period of several weeks Ms. B complains that she is being neglected. Somewhat in disbelief Mr. Z puts Ms. B's complaints to a test and keeps a record of his visits for a month. The data support Ms. B's allegations. There were 21 visits to Ms. A during the month but only 9 to Ms. B.

Was It the Fickle Finger of Fate? How could such an unfair outcome happen? Before offering a possible explanation for the unjust way in which chance has dealt with Ms. B it will be important to look at the puzzle a little more closely. Although this fact cannot be clear to you yet, by the time you finish this book you will understand that Mr. Z's dilemma presents the basic structure of the problems handled by the standard methods of testing statistical hypotheses. The only difference is that the quantitative aspects are minimal in this example.

---

[1] I hope that you will not be put off by the male chauvinistic, heterosexual character of this example. If it offends you, the genders of the players in my little drama can be altered to suit your preferences. The logic of the argument will still hold and that is what I want you to get from this section. Another way of thinking would have Ms. A making the complaint. Again, however, the statistical reasoning I am about to describe will work.

Consider first Mr. Z's reasoning when he decided to leave the choice of visits to chance. In the long run, he argued, the number of visits to Ms. A and Ms. B should be the same because of the equal probability of catching a train going in either direction. There should be no difference between the number of visits. This hypothesis of "no difference" technically goes by the name of the null hypothesis. For the specific test that Mr. Z decided to carry out, the null hypothesis would be that he would make 15 visits to Ms. A and 15 visits to Ms. B.

Exactly 15? Well probably not. Our intuitive sense of the "law of averages" leads us to expect something other than an exact 50–50 split. How about the 21–9 split that actually occurred? Probably most readers will be inclined to reject the idea that such an unequal division would happen under circumstances where the expected split is 15–15. To put the point more technically, such readers reject the null hypothesis and conclude that something must have been wrong with Mr. Z's assumptions.

To develop this point just a bit further, suppose that the visits had been split 17–13. What would you make of that? Probably that such an outcome is within the bounds of chance. How about 18–12 or 19–11 or 20–10? Somewhere you find yourself saying, "Too much already! I doubt that this could happen by chance. I reject such an hypothesis. There must have been some bias in favor of taking the A train."

Making Wise Decisions in the Face of Uncertainty. *But when such seemingly unlikely outcomes force you to such a conclusion, is the conclusion the right one? This is a question that we cannot answer with a definite yes or no. What we can say is of fundamental importance, however.*

The 21–9 split could have occurred by chance even if the true odds of catching Ms. A's train or Ms. B's train were exactly the same. If you were to toss 30 fair coins, it could happen that 21 of them would turn up heads and that only 9 of them would turn up tails. Such happenings are rare. It can be calculated[2] that 21 of 30 coins will come up heads (or tails) less than 5 times in 100. But such rare events do occur, and this is why an absolute yes–no decision is never possible in a case like Mr. Z's.

There is always a choice between two interpretations:

1. *The situation is not what it was originally assumed to be (the null hypothesis is wrong) and the results obtained are a better reflection of the true state of affairs.*
2. *The situation is what it was originally assumed to be (the null hypothesis is right) and we are faced with one of the rare chance occurrences just discussed.*

Types of Error. *Faced with the alternatives just presented for his particular problem, Mr. Z could argue this way: If the chances of catching an east-bound or a west-bound train actually are 50–50 (if the null hypothesis is true), a split as extreme as 21–9 would happen by chance only 4 or 5 times in 100. Since such an outcome is so unlikely, it makes better sense to consider alternatives to the 50–50 null hypothesis (to reject the null hypothesis) in favor of other possibilities.*

What could some of these possibilities be? In general, anything that keeps the train in Ms. B's part of town longer than Ms. A's would increase the probability that when the train came it would be going in Ms. A's direction. Possibly the two segments of the route are unequal in length.... Possibly the segments are of the same length but there are more stations and thus more time-consuming stops in one section.... Possibly the track is inferior in Ms. B's segment and the train must go more slowly. Given these possibilities and the data at hand, Mr. Z would be in good statistical company if he were to decide that his 50–50 null hypothesis must be wrong and that it must be rejected. Pushed on the point Mr. Z could even reject the null hypothesis at a certain level of confidence. He could reason this way: "Well, I could be wrong, but the chances are only 4 or 5 in 100 that I am wrong. So I will reject the null hypothesis at what I will call the 4 or 5% level of confidence."

But, as he recognized himself, Mr. Z could be wrong. This could be one of those rare chance occurrences. If that were the case, Mr. Z would have made what we will call a Type I error. Although with good reason, he has rejected the null hypothesis when it is, in fact, true.

[2]You will find as you get further into this book that I have not the slightest interest in explaining the computational procedures that are commonly used to bolster statistical arguments. I have avoided such explanations whenever I could on the general philosophy that there are other ways to get my ideas across. On the other hand, the reader has the right to be sure that I am not just pulling the numbers out of thin air. For that reason I have included a computational appendix that presents formulas and makes many of the calculations mentioned in the text.

Now consider another possibility. Suppose that the true situation actually is one of those [noted above] . . . but, for whatever reason, such possibilities do not occur to Mr. Z. Unable to think of the alternatives, he reasons that the null hypothesis is true (the probability of catching one train actually is the same as the probability of catching the other) and that his pattern of visits is just one of those rare chance happenings. In this case Mr. Z has made a **Type II error:** *he has accepted the null hypothesis when it is false.*

In common with many of us, Mr. Z might go on to reason that after such a long string of trains that took him to Ms. A, the "law of averages" will take care of things and there will be a succession of trains to Ms. B that would even the number of visits out. If he does take this further step in his thinking, Mr. Z has fallen prey to a very different kind of error: the "gambler's fallacy."

To Put It Briefly

Believe it or not, the ideas presented in the past few pages take you through about half of a first course in statistics. One thing I hope you see is that the ideas are not very difficult. Another thing I hope you see is that statistics is not so much about mathematics, formulas, and calculations as it is about ways of reasoning. In this section, I would like to summarize such reasoning as it applies to the making of inferences from data. The summary involves a series of steps that apply to a wide range of statistical tests. Now, with the aid of our example, the steps:

1. State the hypothesis in null form: *Except for the accidents of chance, there is no difference between the number of visits to Ms. A and Ms. B. In 30 days they should divide 15–15.*

2. Obtain data of the kind identified in the null hypothesis. *Twenty-one visits to Ms. A, 9 to Ms. B.*

3. Determine the chance probability of occurrence (4 or 5 times in 100) of the data obtained if the null hypothesis is true. *This is the step in reasoning where the example left procedures pretty vague. I will explain them more fully [later]. . . . The probability in question, however, is only 4 or 5 in 100.*

4. If the chance probability of the obtained result is small, reject the null hypothesis with a level of confidence that is the probability of obtaining the result by chance: *4 or 5 times in 100. If the chance probability is high, accept the null hypothesis.*

5. Recognize that either rejecting or accepting the null hypothesis involves a gamble. *The null hypothesis allows the occurrence of the 21–9 split 4 or 5 times in 100. If the statistician rejects this null hypothesis because of long odds against an outcome in spite of the fact that unknown to him the null hypothesis is true, he has committed a Type I error. But if he accepts the null hypothesis when it is false, the statistician commits a Type II error.*

Probably the most unfamiliar concepts in this section are those of Type I and Type II error, and it may be worth enlarging our review of them. One way to get the distinction across is by analogy to the decision of a jury in a criminal case. By our laws a defendant is innocent (null hypothesis, he did not do it, step 1 above) until proved to be guilty (by evidence or data, step 2) beyond a reasonable doubt (with a strong level of confidence, steps 3 and 4). Now think of the two possible mistakes that a jury can make. It can find an innocent person guilty (Type I error) or a guilty person innocent (Type II error). The other two decisions the jury can make are correct decisions and, therefore, just ones.

This interpretation leads to still another way to make the distinction. Table 1 presents the true status of the null hypothesis in its columns and the statistically arrived at decision in its rows. The cells produced by crossing rows with columns contain an indication of the significance of each of the four possible outcomes. If the table is unclear, one way to straighten things out would be to make a similar table for the decisions of juries, with the columns representing "truly innocent" and "truly guilty" and the rows representing jury decisions of "acquittal" and "conviction." The meaning of the four cells will then correspond to the meanings I have put in the table in this book.

Table 1. Correct Decisions and Types of Error in Hypothesis Testing

Statistical Decision	Real-World Status of the Null Hypothesis	
	True	False
Accept null hypothesis	Correct decision	Type II error
Reject null hypothesis	Type I error	Correct decision

Research Hypotheses

Looking ahead, it seems important to add one brief point before we leave this topic. Actual research usually begins with what is called a research hypothesis. *The investigator believes that some condition he can control will have an effect on some phenomenon that he is interested in. He collects data hoping that the expected difference will occur. In order to obtain support for this research hypothesis, the investigator actually tests the null hypothesis. If the null hypothesis can be rejected, the research hypothesis gains in credibility.**

A more simplistic way of looking at statistical significance is to view the level of significance as an indicator of how sure you can be that the results are real differences and not the result of sampling error. This approach indicates how much confidence you can place in your results. The statistic itself is the probability that your results are *not* real; hence the lower the figure the better. With a significance level of .05, you can be 95 percent sure the results are real; with a significance level of .01, you can be 99 percent sure the results are real; and with a significance level of .001, you can be 99.9 percent sure the results are real. These three levels are the most commonly used ones.

A very important point should be noted: because your results are highly likely to be real is *no* assurance that the results reflect importance. The level of significance indicates *only* how sure you can be that your results are real; it says *nothing* about the presence or strength of any relationships. In other words, be sure to distinguish *statistical significance* from *substantive significance*. The first is based on inferential statistics, while the second is based on such descriptive statistics as measures of association.

Another cautionary note: Since the level of statistical significance is directly related to sample size, a very large sample may yield statistically significant differences when in fact the differences observed are not very large. Early research on the effects of birth control pills, for example, indicated a statistically significant difference between pill-users and non-pill-users in blood-clot related deaths. But given the extremely large samples in-

*From Gregory A. Kimble, *How to Use (and Misuse) Statistics*, © 1978, pp. 10–16. Reprinted by permission of Prentice-Hall, Inc., Englewood Cliffs, New Jersey. Footnotes renumbered.

volved, the substantive differences were not very large at all (example taken from Johnson, 1977: 239). The basic issue, once again, is that of statistical versus substantive significance. When you see a finding reported as being statistically significant, be sure you go back to the descriptive statistics used to determine the substantive significance of the finding.

Common Inferential Statistics

Perhaps the most common inferential statistic is *chi square*. Chi square is used with tabular data and is therefore most frequently used with nominal level variables. The basic principle of chi square is the comparison of the results actually obtained with the results one would expect to occur if no relationship existed between the two variables.

Let's use the data in Table 6 relating sex to note-leaving among suicide victims and proceed through Kimble's steps. The null hypothesis states that there are no differences between men and women regarding the leaving of suicide notes (step 1). The data gathered to test this hypothesis are reported in Table 6 (step 2). Using chi square as the test of statistical significance, we see that the level of significance is less than .05, meaning that the probability of finding the differences in the table strictly on the basis of sampling error is less than 5 percent when the null hypothesis is true (step 3). Since this chance probability is small, we reject the null hypothesis. Or to follow the more simplistic approach noted above, we are at least 95 percent sure that the differences between men and women regarding note-leaving are real differences (step 4). Finally, we recognize that we may have erred in rejecting the null hypothesis; this instance may be one of those four or five times in 100 that the results would occur as they do when the null hypothesis is in fact true (step 5).

This example also nicely illustrates the point made previously regarding statistical significance and substantive significance. The statistical significance analysis indicates a high level of certainty that the differences between men and women are real differences. But the measure of association employed indicated a negligible association (.08), suggesting that although the relationship is a real one, it does not amount to much substantively. These results may both be a product of the large sample size; with large samples even small differences can be real.

Other inferential statistics involve comparing mean scores on an interval or ratio level dependent variable across categories of a nominal level independent variable. Since each of the means is subject to a certain degree of sampling error, the question becomes: Are the means in fact different or is it possible that the observed differences between the means are simply a function of sampling error? (see Sudman's article on sampling in Section 2.3). Note that we are making inferences about the populations from which the samples were taken: Are these respective population means the same or different?

The two statistics relevant for answering these questions are the t test and analysis of variance. The *t test* is used for independent variables with only two categories, whereas *analysis of variance* is used for independent variables with more than two categories. For both, the independent variable must be nominal and the dependent variable must be interval or ratio. Let's look at a few examples.

Macdonald (1977) compared male nurses with males who were not nurses in terms of their empathy, reasoning that males who went into nursing were more empathetic. Using a 64-item empathy scale, he found that male nurses had a mean score of 41.5 while the mean for other males was 35.8. The question becomes: Is this difference a real difference or is this difference due to sampling error? To answer this question, Macdonald used the t test, resulting in a t value of 3.55 and a statistical significance level of less than 5 percent. For our purposes you can ignore t values and simply focus on the significance level. This level of significance means that there is less than a 5 percent chance that the difference in empathy between male nurses and other males was a result of sampling error. More directly, we are more than 95 percent sure that this difference is a real difference and not a product of sampling error.

The NORC data noted earlier contained six abortion support items. I created an abortion support scale by counting the number of items that people agreed with. I then compared persons of various religious affiliations on this scale. Protestants had a mean score of 4.1, Catholics a mean score of 3.7, "other" religions a mean score of 5.3, and those with no religious affiliation a mean score of 5.4. Analysis of variance employs the F statistic, which was 24.8 in this case, but again we can ignore this value in preference to the significance

level. It was less than 1 percent, which means that there is less than a 1 percent chance that the differences among the mean abortion support scores of the different religious affiliations were the result of sampling error. I am 99 percent sure that the differences were real differences. Knowing this, I can state with confidence that Catholics were, in fact, far less supportive of abortion than persons of other or no religious affiliation and that people with no religious affiliation were more supportive of abortion than were those with a religious affiliation. (These types of analysis can also be done as part of multivariate analysis.)

I have noted only a few of the statistics used to assess statistical significance. A number of others also exist. But their interpretations follow the same pattern as found in those statistics just reviewed.

CONCLUSION

You have just completed a short course in statistical interpretation. In this course we have reviewed descriptive and inferential statistics as well as univariate, bivariate, and multivariate analyses. The statistics reviewed in this article comprise most of those you will encounter in the social science literature.

By now you undoubtedly realize that numbers have no intrinsic meaning; the meaning they have is contingent on the goals of the research and the nature of the topic and variables. That is why it is important to understand all the various aspects of research design, including statistics.

REFERENCES

Cohen, Stuart L. and Joanne E. Fiedler
    1974   "Content analysis of multiple messages in suicide notes." Life-threatening Behavior 4(Summer):75–95.

Davis, James A.
    1971   Elementary Survey Analysis. Englewood Cliffs: Prentice-Hall.

Foreit, K. G. and J. R. Foreit
    1978   "Correlates of contraceptive behavior among unmarried U.S. college students." Studies in Family Planning 9(June):169–74.

Johnson, Allan G.
    1977   Social Statistics without Tears. New York: McGraw-Hill.

Kimble, Gregory A.
  1978 How to Use (and Misuse) Statistics. Englewood Cliffs: Prentice-Hall.

Macdonald, Malcolm R.
  1977 "How do men and women students rate in empathy?" American Journal of Nursing (June):998.

Macht, Mary W., Frederick W. Seidl, and D. Richard Greene
  1977 "Measuring inmate morale." Social Work 22(July):284–89.

National Opinion Research Corporation
  1978 General Social Science Survey, Codebook. Chicago: National Opinion Research Center.

Runyon, Richard P.
  1977 Winning with Statistics. Reading: Addison-Wesley.

Sewell, William H. and Vimal P. Shah
  1968 "Parents' education and children's educational aspirations and achievements." American Sociological Review 33(April):191–209.

Wagenaar, Theodore C.
  1978 "School structural composition and achievement: an empirical assessment." Sociology and Social Research 62(July):608–25.

Wagenaar, Theodore C. and Paul D. Jennings
  1978 "Organization Structure, Role Orientation, and Teacher Morale." Paper presented at the annual meeting of the North Central Sociological Association, May, Cincinnati.

SECTION 4.2

Causal Analysis

Causal analysis lies at the heart of social scientific investigation. The major goal of most research in the social sciences is to assess the causal links between selected independent variables and dependent variables. This emphasis on causal analysis has been repeatedly illustrated in this volume.

Causal analysis contributes to explanation and understanding (as opposed to exploration and description). Basically, explanation helps answer the question "Why?" The answer to this question lies in determining which of the many possible variables are linked to the selected dependent variable.

PREREQUISITES OF CAUSALITY

One of the prerequisites for establishing causality is time order. Obviously the causal variable must precede in time the caused variable. In many instances, however, the time order of the relationship is not clear. We might analyze the relationship between alcohol consumption and marital discord, beginning with the assumption that the alcohol consumption causes the discord. But the cause-effect relationship may be the reverse—the discord may cause the alcohol consumption. The only way to definitely establish time order is to do a longitudinal study. Cross-sectional studies (data gathered at one point in time) impose severe limitations on making causal assertions; the laboratory experiment is perhaps best suited to making causal assertions because of its high level of control over the timing of the independent variable.

The second prerequisite for establishing causality is a statistical relationship between the two variables. That is, variation in the dependent variable is related to variation in the independent variable. You might gather data to demonstrate statistically that as education increases, liberalism increases, or as emphasis on rules within an organization increases, innovation rates decrease (see Zetterberg [1965] for the various forms relationship statements can take).

The third prerequisite is that the relationship between the two variables must not be the result of some third variable influencing both the independent and dependent variables. Earlier we noted that as emphasis on rules increases within organizations, innovation rates decrease. If a third variable, such as size, is held constant, we may find that the original relationship disappears. Hence, large organizations may have more rule emphasis and a lower innovation rate while small organizations may have less rule emphasis and a higher innovation rate. We conclude that there is no causal relationship between rule emphasis and innovation rate; size is more crucial.

Note that even if we have dealt with these three issues, we still cannot be sure that the independent variable causes the dependent variable. All we can say is that we are *more* sure of a causal relationship. Social scientists generally do not say they have "proved" that causality exists, only that they are reasonably certain that a probabilistic causal relationship exists.

A FEW CAVEATS

Causal analysis demands caution. The researcher must keep in mind first that no one phenomenon is caused only by one other phenomenon. Our job as social scientists is to determine which of the possible independent variables are the most relevant for a dependent variable. Second, all these independent variables may operate separately or may operate jointly; our job is to determine how they influence the dependent variable. Third, we cannot say for sure that an independent variable completely causes the dependent variable. We speak in terms of probabilistic rather than completely deterministic relationships.

Fourth, no matter how many independent variables are considered, we will never completely explain a given dependent variable; there will always be a portion of the variation in the dependent variable that can be attributed to chance variation and other unexamined variables. Fifth, since measurement error is usually present in operational definitions, we will be unable to completely explain the dependent variable. And sixth, potentially causal variables should always be derived from theory and previous work on a subject, not from a haphazard selection of variables.

MULTIVARIATE ANALYSIS

Eliminating the possible effect of a third variable is by far the most troublesome of the prerequisites for establishing causality. In the final analysis, we can never be sure that all relevant control variables have been held constant; we can only keep trying until we have developed what can be considered an efficient causal explanation. For this reason multivariate analysis comprises the bulk of social scientific research.

Multivariate analysis can involve a number of different procedures, such as use of tables, partial correlations, analysis of variance, multiple regression analysis, and path analysis. The choice of procedure is largely contingent on the nature of the variables; see Section 4.1, Social Statistics and Data Analysis, for further discussion of these procedures.

No matter what procedure you use, the logic is the same: what happens to the original independent variable–dependent variable relationship when the control variables are introduced? This analysis process is often called elaboration; see the statistics section for further discussion of elaboration.

Multivariate analysis has two primary applications. One involves assessing the effect of control variables as we examine the original independent variable–dependent variable relationship. The other involves selecting a number of independent variables for simultaneous analysis in terms of their relationships with the dependent variable. In the first, the primary emphasis is on the single original relationship; in the second, the primary emphasis is on the combined analysis of the several independent variables. Or, to put it another way, in the first we deal with other variables as control variables, while in the second we deal with other variables as additional independent variables.

THE READINGS

In the first article Janet Hunt and Larry Hunt, having done research on the effect of father absence on sons, examine the effect of father absence on daughters. Most multivariate analyses involve one dependent variable and a number of independent variables; this analysis involves six dependent variables reflecting three dimensions (personal identity, current activities, and future orientation) and two independent variables (father absence/presence and race); the main control variable is social class, since social class effects may be tied to race effects. It is interesting to note (in Table 6) that they even use four of their dependent variables as controls to examine the unique relationship between father absence and the two remaining dependent variables (esteem and sex role, both reflecting the personal identity dimension). Note how their selection of variables is related to the current theoretical literature in the area.

The Hunts use several statistical procedures in their analysis. Because most of their operational definitions produce ordinal level measures, they have chosen to use gamma as a measure of association (and partial gammas for some of the multivariate analyses). They also used t tests to compare mean scores and test the significance of the differences between father-present and father-absent scores. Cross-tabulations were also employed.

The Rubin and Shenker article on self-disclosure among college students (Section 3.5) also reflects the use of multivariate analysis. Note how these authors used multivariate analysis to analyze the separate and combined effects of the independent variables (friendship, proximity, sex) on the dependent variable (disclosure in four areas).

Be sure to apply what you have learned in other sections of this volume to these articles. Look at the operationalization of the concepts. Note, for example, that the Hunts excluded a variety of family types in their operationalization of father absence. Note also the use of statistical significance to ascertain the credibility of the relationships (the p value) and the differing levels of statistical significance accepted for interpretation.

Hunt and Hunt were asked to write a special article for this volume reporting on their experiences with secondary analysis; i.e., using someone else's data. Secondary analysis is becoming increasingly popular because of the rising costs of research, increasing saturation of the population with surveys, and reduced response rates. The major purpose of this article, as with other personal journal articles in this volume, is to provide a more accurate picture of how research is actually done.

You may recall that one principle of research is formulating the hypotheses before gathering the data. This is obviously not possible with secondary analysis. Note the Hunts' analysis of this aspect of secondary analysis, particularly how the data limit the research questions that can be asked. In fact, a typical problem is that the secondary analysis researcher becomes swamped in the data; the Hunts experienced this as well. Note too the role of pragmatic considerations in doing social research—topics are chosen in terms of data availability, data becomes available through personal contacts, computer output can be destroyed in a flood. The major difficulty with secondary analy-

sis is that the researcher must work within the operational definitions, sampling procedures, and similar other constraints imposed by the original researcher. The Hunts
discuss how they dealt with these problems.

The discussion on the separate boys and girls studies is particularly interesting. It
illustrates how answering some questions and dealing with one category of the sample
leads to other questions and the desire to apply the analysis to other categories of the
sample. This discussion also shows how the lack of previous work in an area (father
absence effects on girls) may lead researchers to temporarily ignore the subject, but as a
topic (sex roles) receives more popular attention researchers move into the "growing
market." Perhaps most significant is that this reading reveals the thought processes of
the researchers as they "made sense" of the data. Once again, the research process is
portrayed as a "two steps forward, one step backward" process, not as a simple direct
process.

The last article, on the effects of rock music on becoming pregnant, is included
primarily for fun. But ask yourself: What variables should be controlled to demonstrate
the artificiality of the relationship? This piece also shows how journalistic accounts of
research often are distorted. And finally, it reminds us that we must be wary of any
assertion of causality until other relevant variables have been controlled.

REFERENCE

Zetterberg, Hans L.
    1965 On Theory and Verification in Sociology. Totowa, N.J.: Bedminster Press.
          See especially Ch. 4.

RACE, DAUGHTERS AND FATHER-LOSS:
DOES ABSENCE MAKE THE GIRL GROW STRONGER?

Janet G. Hunt

Larry L. Hunt

Inquiry into the effects of father absence on
children has documented a wide range of negative
outcomes—from disturbed sex-role identification
and low self-esteem (Burton and Whiting, 1961;
Heatherington, 1966) to impaired school performance and delinquency (Miller, 1958; Carlsmith,

Authors' note: We should like to thank Morris
Rosenberg and Roberta G. Simmons for making
available the survey data used in this research.
Computer time was provided by the Computer Sci-
ence Center of the University of Maryland, College
Park.

1964). In recent years concern has been extended,
largely inferentially, to presumed connections between this feature of family structure and intergenerational patterns of low achievement among
American blacks (Moynihan, 1965; Parker and
Kleiner, 1969). While the scope of research has
been broad in terms of potential consequences, it
has been addressed largely to effects on male children, with little genuinely comparative investigation by race. We know little, therefore, about the
implications of father absence for girls, and even
less about possible race differences for these chil-

From Social Problems, October 1977, pp. 90–102. Reprinted by permission of the
Society for the Study of Social Problems and the authors.

dren. The present research explores the impact of father absence on some dimensions of the identities, orientations, and activities of white and black adolescent girls, and is organized to parallel our analysis reported earlier on adolescent boys (Hunt and Hunt, 1975). While the results are inconclusive and the conclusions tentative, they point to the potential import of both racial and sexual inequality in conditioning the consequences of family structure.

THE PROBLEM

Father Absence and Female Children

The expectation that father absence generates personal and social pathologies assumes that the family plays a crucial role in shaping the destinies of children by providing essential economic and psychic resources. Charged with the responsibility of meeting children's basic material needs and being the primary agency for their socialization, the family may determine children's eventual achievement and placement in the status order. The significance of father absence for male children, from this perspective, is clear. Father absence means possible economic deprivation, with the loss of the family breadwinner. Equally important, it means the loss of a male role model and possibly the necessary parental supervision and discipline required for normal gender-identity formation and character development, without which boys "flounder and fail" (Moynihan, 1965:37).

Beyond creating possible economic hardship, it is less clear how father absence might affect female children. In a society in which sex roles severely limit the participation of women in the public-productive sphere, assigning them primarily to domestic-supportive functions, the family is not the same resource for the achievement and status-attainment for girls as for boys. Rather, the nuclear family, as an embodiment of an instrumental/expressive division of labor, socializes girls for a sex-role destiny that largely precludes high levels of personal achievement (Maccoby, 1963; Horner, 1971; Papanek, 1973). It is not surprising, therefore, that what scant attention has been given father-absence effects in girls has focused primarily on possible sex-role disturbances. Specifically, father absence may result in the girl's "loss of skills" for interacting with males in general (Biller and Weiss,

1970); may lead to either extremely shy and withdrawn or "inappropriately assertive" behaviors relative to male peers (Heatherington, 1972), especially during adolescence (Heatherington and Deur, 1971); and may result in trouble with the law (Toby, 1957; Monahan, 1957), typically in the form of delinquency involving "sexual misconduct" (Glaser, 1965)—a pattern Wilkenson (1974) observes is clear and consistent in the "broken home and delinquency" research.

While the emphasis on sex-role problems in girls is understandable in light of the traditional place of women in American society, the potential achievement consequences of father absence for girls are just as intriguing, if more subtle. Inasmuch as mothers *and fathers* routinely sex-type children (Goodenough, 1957; Johnson, 1975), father absence, in conjunction with modifications of the mother role, may remove some of the conventional barriers to female achievement. Thus, although father absence may have a dampening effect on the achievement of male children, it may work to free female children for stronger attachment to personal achievement goals. Thus when both sex-role and achievement effects are considered, father absence may have mixed implications for the development of female children.

The Factor of Race

We have considered how patriarchal dimensions of American society may structure the implications of family variation for female children. We now want to consider how racial stratification may further complicate this picture. Race differences in the meaning of father absence for boys are increasingly noted in the research literature. Largely unexamined, however, is the question of how racial inequality may interact with sex roles in shaping the experience of girls.

There is a growing sensitivity among researchers to the complexities involved in assessing the role of the often father-absent and typically "matriarchal" or "mother-headed" black family in patterning the achievement of male children. There was for some time both preceding and following the publication of the "Moynihan Report" (1965) a tendency to assume black boys are obviously handicapped by the frequent absence of father figures in the home, and that this accounts for much of the difficulty of successive generations of black males in assuming breadwinner roles. This view is now beginning to yield to one which emphasizes structural factors beyond the family as most crucial in shaping the destinies of male children in the black community. This shift is due both to evidence that socioeconomic variables are better predictors of male status problems than family-structure variables (Willie, 1967; Duncan and Duncan, 1969; Berger and Simon, 1975), and to recent comparative studies that find father absence less damaging to black than white boys (Kandel, 1971; Gordon, 1972; Hunt and Hunt, 1975).

In our own comparative research on father-absent black and white boys, we found esteem, sex-role, and aspiration costs for white boys only (and, indeed, some hint of slight sex-role gains for black boys). From this we concluded that the stratification system determines substantially the resource potential of fathers for boys, and hence the import of father absence. It is at higher status levels that intact families can most effectively transmit "success" from one generation to the next. In this context, fathers are central figures in family life, and are important as providers and role models for the development in boys of orientations and identities suited to the pursuit of success goals and eventual movement themselves into breadwinner roles. At lower status levels, where there are structural barriers to personal achievement, family socialization cannot have this advantageous "status transfer" function. Under conditions of structurally-induced poverty, men cannot be effective providers, families cannot be as father-oriented, fathers cannot be positive resources for sons, and thus the presence or absence of fathers in the household cannot be as critical for the biographies of boys.

If this reasoning is correct, how might it apply to father-absent girls, for whom the resource implications of fathers is conditioned by sexual as well as racial stratification? Because of the general allocation of women to domestic-supportive (expressive) rather than public-productive (instrumental) roles, the father, as we have already observed, probably tends to be less of a resource for the *personal* achievement (as distinct from sex-role adjustment) of girls than boys in American society. While their eventual marriages may reflect their status origins, girls do not tend to be direct benefactors of whatever "father-son connection" might be operating in the status order. At issue is how

this pattern of status transfer, via the transmission of achievement opportunities to boys rather than girls, and therefore the resource potential of fathers for girls, might vary by race.

If it is among whites that intact families can most effectively socialize boys for successful achievement and their sex-role destiny of family breadwinning, it is probably also among whites that girls can most effectively be socialized for ideal-typical "feminine" roles, at the expense of personal achievement. Thus, it is under high-status conditions where a single breadwinner can effectively provide for a family that a clear division of labor by sex is most possible. And it is under these conditions that parents—as controllers of resources, role-models, and role-definers—can most clearly socialize boys and girls differently to repeat this pattern. Conversely, the realities of low-status life mean greater numbers of women perform breadwinning roles, blurring any instrumental/ expressive division of labor by sex—a pattern quite prevalent among American blacks (Beal, 1973). Where this is the case, parents cannot socialize children for sharply differentiated roles, and intact families are less obviously a critical resource for the "normal" development of girls. Consequently, father absence may imply neither the resource "loss" relative to sex-role socialization, nor the perhaps enhanced opportunities for personal achievement that it might in the white world.

The Research Questions

Given prevailing systems of both racial and sexual stratification, power, prestige, and wealth are controlled heavily by white males. This means that it is in the white world that resources are most concentrated, that there is the greatest sex difference in the control of resources, and that intact families routinely transfer personal status advantages to sons rather than daughters. From this vantage point we are interested in two major questions in the study of father-absence effects in girls: (1) whether there are some achievement implications as well as sex-role socialization effects attendant with father absence, and (2) whether effects in girls are more marked among whites than blacks, due to a greater sex-role differentiation in the white world.

To investigate these questions we have selected measures from data originally collected by

Rosenberg and Simmons (1972) that permit examining both sex-role and achievement aspects of the identities, activities, and orientations of father-present and father-absent white and black girls. Pertaining to sex role, we have included measures of sex-role identification, dating activities, and marriage plans. More pertinent to achievement, we have used measures of self-esteem, grades in school, and perceived efficacy or destiny control. We move next to a consideration of the sample and variables in greater detail.

THE SAMPLE

The data reported here are taken from a large-scale investigation of the self-images and perceptions of school children conducted by Morris Rosenberg and Roberta Simmons (1972). Employing a combination of cluster and stratified sampling procedures, Rosenberg and Simmons selected a sample of 1,917 students enrolled in grades three through twelve of the public school system of Baltimore, Maryland during the spring of 1968. Trained interviewers using a series of pretested questions—both structured and open-ended—obtained information on self and related attitudes, values and orientations, and family background. All students interviewed participated voluntarily (with parental consent) in two or three interview sessions after school and were paid for their role in the research project. (For more detailed information on the sample and methods of data collection, see Rosenberg and Simmons, 1972.)

From this original data base, female students enrolled in junior and senior high schools (N = 462; 282 blacks and 180 whites) were selected for analysis. Elementary school students were eliminated owing to the lack of key information on sex-role identification and dating behavior obtained only from older students.

THE VARIABLES

Father Absence

Students were classified as having "father-present" or "father-absent" families on the basis of their descriptions of the composition of their households at the time of the interview. A student was classified as "father-present" if her natural parents were currently living together. A student was classified as "father-absent" if she was living with her natural mother and the mother was the only reported adult in the household. The decision to exclude all other varieties of household composition other than the intact parental unit and the "mother-only" type was based upon two considerations: (1) the fact that prior research shows that family and identity dynamics are markedly affected by the presence of step-parents (Rosenberg, 1965) and (2) the concern that the present analysis of girls be comparable to the previously reported research on boys (Hunt and Hunt, 1975).

Examination of the distribution of this variable by race shows that the stable, two-parent unit is more prevalent among whites (84%) than among blacks (68%). This reflects the fact that the rate of father absence is over twice as high among blacks (32% as compared to 15%) and the fact that the number of respondents unclassifiable as either "father-present" or "father-absent" was double for blacks (16% compared to 8%).

Social Class

To assess the importance of social class in generating observed effects, students were classified into middle-, working-, and lower-class categories on the basis of the Hollingshead scheme, which utilizes the occupational and educational characteristics of the head of household. Due to the small Ns the detailed status categories of "upper," "upper-middle," and "lower-middle" were collapsed into a general middle-class category. Whites tended to be concentrated in the middle and working classes (34% and 46% respectively), whereas blacks were concentrated in the working and lower classes (44% and 42% respectively). The distribution of father absence by race and class indicates that father absence is more prevalent among blacks at each class level. (Percent father absent for whites and blacks respectively is: middle class—18, 40; working class—15, 29; and lower class—18, 43.)

Personal Identity: Esteem and Sex-Role

The self-images of the girls were examined by employing two Guttman-type scales designed to measure different components of personal identity. As a measure of a girl's global attitude toward herself in positive or negative terms, a recent version of the Rosenberg self-esteem scale was used. To assess attitudes toward the sex-role component of personal identity, we constructed a four-item scale tapping feelings about and evaluation of self as a girl. Both these scales directly parallel those used in the research on boys (see Hunt and Hunt, 1975, for the precise items included in these scales) with the minor difference of substitution of sex-appropriate words in the case of the items defining the sex-role scale.

Current Activities: Academic Performance and Dating

As measures of selected activities of adolescent girls we used indexes of academic performance and dating behavior. Academic performance is a key variable in the earlier research on boys. Dating has been added because of the emphasis on this variable in past research on father-absent girls. Both measures rest upon the girls' self-reports.

Academic performance in school was indexed by responses to the question "What marks do you usually receive on your report card?" Although all schools did not use the conventional "A" through "F" marking system, norms of conversion were available and answers were coded into the conventional letter categories by the original investigators. Because of the distribution of scores, we collapsed "A" and "B" grades into a "high" category, used "C" grades for a "medium" category and collapsed "D" and "F" into a "low" category. Race differences on this variable indicate higher academic performance by the white girls, with 51% of the whites as compared to 35% of the blacks classified as "high" on academic performance.

Information on dating behavior was obtained by asking the girls "How many times have you gone out on a date in the past month?" Responses were coded into three categories: (1) high, once a week or more—26%; (2) medium, from one to three times a month—24%; and (3) low, no dates in the past month—50%. There were no race differences in dating frequency.

Future Orientation: Marriage Plans and Destiny Control

To assess orientations toward the future, we examined the girls' projected plans to marry and their sense of personal efficacy regarding success in life. Marriage plans were also analyzed among the boys, while efficacy has been substituted in the case of girls for the variable of educational aspirations. The reason for this shift is that the educational aspirations measure was not found to be a discriminating index among father-present and father-absent girls, perhaps because higher educa-

tion has a more ambiguous place in females' lives—i.e., it can be a route to personal achievement as with boys or, alternatively, simply a "finishing" and marriage-marketing process. Efficacy, on the other hand, responds more to variation in family structure and is more readily interpretable as reflecting feelings of *personal* control of one's fate.

Orientation toward marriage was tapped by a single question embedded within a set of questions concerning what the students want to have or be like when they reach adulthood. Within the general set of inquiries, each girl was asked, "Would you like to be married when you get older?" A simple "yes" or "no" response provided the basis of classifying students with respect to marital aspirations.

Orientation toward control of one's personal destiny was measured by a three-item index based upon responses to questions asking subjects whether: (a) luck is more important than hard work in getting ahead, (b) something or somebody stops their efforts to get ahead, and (c) they have any chance for success in life. These items closely parallel those employed in the Coleman Report (1966) to measure "sense of control over environment" and figure as major components of Gordon's (1972) index of self-determination.

The predictive adequacy of both these measures of future orientation with regard to the eventual experience of these adolescents is, of course, problematic. Our purpose, however, is not to determine ultimate futures but to assess the impact of father absence on attitudes toward different possible outcomes in life.

Correlations among the Dependent Variables

The selection of dependent variables in this study was aimed at tapping both sex-role and achievement dimensions of the identities, activities, and orientations of girls. The underlying assumption was that the instrumental/expressive division of labor by sex in American society makes sex role and achievement largely incompatible for girls and probably differentially responsive to father absence. The further assumption that these dimensions are more dichotomized and unsynthesizable for white than black girls underlies our reasoning with respect to possible race differences in father-absence effects in girls. In Table 1, the corre-

Table 1. Intercorrelations among
Dependent Variables for Whites and Blacks (Gammas)

		Sex Role	Dating	School Grades	Marriage Plans	Destiny Control
Esteem	Whites	.09	−.20**	.33**	.06	.40**
	Blacks	.37**	.11*	.06	.06	.25**
Sex Role	Whites		.10	−.08	.38**	.05
	Blacks		.22**	−.14*	.25**	.02
Dating	Whites			−.10	.06	−.01
	Blacks			.06	.45**	.22**
School Grades	Whites				.38**	.17
	Blacks				.05	.07
Marriage Plans	Whites					.18
	Blacks					−.06

*p < .05
**p < .01

lations (gammas) among the outcome measures are presented as a means of identifying how far the worlds of white and black girls do in fact appear to be bifurcated along instrumental and expressive lines.

Table 1 suggests that our reasoning is largely accurate. The gammas for the white girls show that esteem is associated with instrumental competence, being positively correlated with school grades and destiny control and negatively correlated with dating. Conversely, sex-role identification appears to have essentially expressive connotations, being significantly correlated only with marriage plans, and revealing some tendency to be associated positively with dating and negatively with grades. Moreover, examination of the direct correlation be-

Table 2. Personal Identity by Father Absence for Whites and Blacks (Means[1])

Father Absence		Whites Esteem			Blacks Esteem		
	X̄	N	Diff.	X̄	N	Diff.
Present	2.81	(131)		4.04	(142)	
Absent	3.28	(25)	−.47*	3.77	(88)	.27*

		Sex Role			Sex Role		
	X̄	N	Diff.	X̄	N	Diff.
Present	2.27	(113)		2.37	(125)	
Absent	2.16	(25)	.11	2.36	(80)	−.01

[1]High means indicate positive identities.
*p < .10

tween esteem and sex-role identification shows these two terms of personal identification to be unrelated. There is, therefore, a fairly clear indication of dimensionality to the experience of white girls along anticipated lines. The only obvious exception to this pattern is the strong positive correlation between grades and marriage plans. Black girls, on the other hand, show somewhat different patterns. While sex-role identification is positively associated with dating and marriage plans and negatively associated with school grades, esteem is also associated positively with dating, as well as destiny control, and esteem and sex-role identification themselves are strongly correlated. These gammas suggest that sex role integrates both expressive and instrumental spheres for black girls more so than for white girls.

THE FINDINGS

When black and white girls are compared with respect to the impact of father absence on esteem and sex-role identification, different racial patterns emerge. The means for these identity scales, presented in Table 2, show that sex-role identification is slightly lower, but esteem is significantly higher, for father-absent than father-present white girls. Among the black girls, the effects are weaker but indicate tendencies that reverse the white experience: for these black girls father absence has no perceptible impact on sex-role identification but is associated with significantly lower esteem.

In order to examine how much the race differences in Table 2 might be attributable to the different social-class characteristics of the two racial groups, we have presented in Table 3 the family-

Table 3. Personal Identity by Father Absence within Class Levels for Whites and Blacks (Means[1])

Social Class	Father Absence	Esteem			Sex Role		
		$\bar{X}$	N	Diff.	$\bar{X}$	N	Diff.
				Whites			
Middle	P	2.86	(43)	.11	2.16	(39)	−.17
	A	2.75	(9)		2.33	(9)	
Working	P	2.79	(59)	−.84*	2.28	(53)	.08
	A	3.63	(11)		2.20	(10)	
Lower	P	2.79	(28)	−.54	2.45	(22)	.62**
	A	3.33	(6)		1.83	(6)	
		$\bar{X}$	N	Diff.	$\bar{X}$	N	Diff.
				Blacks			
Middle	P	3.47	(17)	−.45	2.63	(16)	.27
	A	3.92	(11)		2.36	(11)	
Working	P	4.15	(71)	.56**	2.25	(63)	−.05
	A	3.59	(29)		2.30	(27)	
Lower	P	4.06	(52)	.03	2.43	(46)	−.04
	A	4.03	(39)		2.49	(35)	

[1]High means indicate positive identities.

*p < .10

**p < .05

structure effects on the identity scales within class levels for both whites and blacks. Although the small Ns of some of the subsamples generated by this procedure make interpretation precarious, the within-class means pretty clearly rule out a social-class explanation of the distinctive racial patterns observed. Thus, the white pattern is not essentially a middle-class one, nor is the black pattern most pronounced at lower-class levels. Rather, we find that the distinctive esteem effects of father absence are most apparent in the working class for both racial categories, and the only significant within-class effect on sex-role identification is the negative sex-role imagery of lower-class, father-absent white girls. Nor does social class improve specification of race differences on other measures; we have reported analysis of the remaining dependent variables by the race and family-structure variables only.

Moving to the activity measures, Table 4 compares the school grades and dating behavior of father-present and father-absent girls within the black and white subsamples. The figures in this table give no clear indication that father-absent girls of either race have more difficulty in school or in forming heterosexual relationships than their father-present counterparts. In fact, what effects there are tend to be in a positive direction. Among white girls, there is an under-representation of father-absent girls in the "high dating" category,

but the gamma summarizing family-structure differences in dating indicates no significant overall tendency for father-absent girls to date less frequently. In contrast, there is a dramatic tendency for father-absent girls to have higher grades. Among black girls, the presence or absence of the father appears to have no impact in either direction on school performance, but a strong effect on dating, with father-absent girls engaging in significantly more frequent dating activity.

The comparisons in Table 5 indicate the association between father absence and two types of future orientation: destiny control and marriage plans. Noteworthy is that all effects are negative and are similar rather than different for whites and blacks. Father-absent girls of both races have lower senses of efficacy than father-present girls, although the effect is significant only for the white girls. They also plan significantly less often to marry—though, again, this tendency is stronger for the white girls.

Taken together, the data on the six outcome measures suggest complex and racially distinctive patterns of effects of father-absence in female children. The white girls seem to benefit considerably in instrumental areas, as evidenced by higher esteem and school grades. However, these gains are not productive of enhanced senses of destiny control, but instead occur in conjunction with lower efficacy than is experienced when fathers are

Table 4. Academic Performance and Dating Frequency by Father Absence for Whites and Blacks (Percents)

Father Absence	Whites School Grades					Blacks School Grades				
	AB	C	DF	N	Gamma	AB	C	DF	N	Gamma
Present	47	47	8	(122)	−.49**	38	48	14	(128)	.00
Absent	71	29	0	(24)		36	54	11	(84)	
	Dating					Dating				
	High	Med	Low	N	Gamma	High	Med	Low	N	Gamma
Present	32	17	51	(127)	.08	19	25	56	(134)	−.29**
Absent	12	44	44	(25)		31	30	39	(84)	

**p < .01

Table 5. Future Orientation by Father Absence for Blacks and Whites (Percents)

| Father Absence | Whites | | | | | Blacks | | | | |
| | Destiny Control | | | | | Destiny Control | | | | |
	High	Med	Low	N	Gamma	High	Med	Low	N	Gamma
Present	72	18	10	(115)	.23**	58	29	13	(132)	.11
Absent	60	28	12	(25)		51	35	15	(81)	
	Marriage Plans					Marriage Plans				
	Yes	No	N		Gamma	Yes	No	N		Gamma
Present	90	10	(134)		.38*	83	17	(141)		.17*
Absent	81	19	(26)			78	22	(85)		

*p < .10
**p < .05

present. In areas more directly relevant to sex-role adjustment, father-absent white girls reveal some, but not dramatic costs. Sex-role identification and dating are slightly lower when fathers are absent, but only marriage plans are significantly reduced. Father-absence effects in black girls are, as anticipated, not as strong as in the white girls, but take some unanticipated forms. For these girls, father absence means not only somewhat diminished marriage plans, but both lower esteem and efficacy. Only dating frequency is enhanced when fathers are absent, while sex-role identification and school grades are essentially unaffected.

To clarify somewhat the "meaning" of these patterns, we have conducted one additional line of analysis presented in Table 6. This analysis is designed to identify the extent to which the effects of father absence on the various outcome measures are interrelated. The partial gammas presented for the relationship between father absence and the identity measures have been computed by using the activity and orientation variables as test factors.

Table 6. Personal Identity by Father Absence,
Zero–order and Partial Correlations (Gammas)

	Whites		Blacks	
		Father Absence By		
	Esteem	Sex Role	Esteem	Sex Role
		Zero-order Gammas		
	−.23*	.20*	.17*	−.06
Controlling for:		Partial Gammas		
School Grades	−.03	.19	.17	−.07
Dating	−.29	.20	.19	.07
Destiny Control	−.35	.35	.03	−.01
Marriage Plans	−.29	.19	.15	−.01

*p < .10 (Significance levels were not computed for the partial gammas. The "significance" of these statistics must be assessed using the zero-order effects as a reference point.)

This procedure reveals how much these latter factors "explain" or "suppress" the relationships between father absence and the esteem and sex-role dimensions of personal identity.

The results of partialing, as would be expected from the zero-order effects, are more pronounced for the white than black girls. The procedure shows clearly that the esteem gain of father-absent white girls is produced, in part, by their higher school grades. When grades are controlled, the gamma for father absence and esteem (−.23) is reduced almost to zero (−.03), indicating that without their higher grades, father-absent white girls would not evidence higher esteem than father-present white girls. By contrast, all other test factors result in a larger partial than zero-order gamma, meaning that these factors suppress the esteem gain of father-absent white girls. This is most marked in the case of destiny control (partial gamma = −.35), indicating that were it not for the loss of efficacy attendant with father absence, the esteem differential between father-absent and father-present white girls would be even greater than we have observed.

The more negative sex-role identification of father-absent white girls (for which the zero-order gamma, .20, is significant at the .10 level) is altered only by the destiny control factor (partial gamma = .35). Again the effect of this factor is to suppress the father-absence effect on identity. Without the lowered efficacy, the sex-role "costs" of father-absent white girls would be greater. Apparently these girls' lack of optimism regarding personal destiny control, while dampening self-esteem, salvages a measure of positive sex-role imagery that would otherwise be lost.

The partial gammas in Table 6 for the black girls show smaller effects but some noteworthy shifts produced by controlling for the test factors. These figures suggest that the slight sex-role gain of the father-absent black girls is to a degree a function of their higher dating level, without which they might experience some sex-role costs with father loss. On the other hand, the esteem disadvantage of father-absent black girls (gamma = .17) appears to be explained in considerable measure by their lower sense of destiny control (partial gamma = .03). This means that, given comparable levels of efficacy, father absence would have essentially no impact on the esteem of black girls.

CONCLUSIONS

In a society in which the female sex role cannot be effectively synthesized with instrumental competence, we reasoned that father absence may leave girls without a key parental resource for normal sex-role adjustment, but at the same time may dispose them toward greater instrumentality. Moreover, as the tension between femininity and achievement is probably greater in the white world, we expected these implications of father absence to be more apparent among white than black girls. The data reported here support these expectations in broad outline, but suggest some further complexities which we address in these concluding remarks. By considering our data patterns in relation to earlier findings on boys, we discover some distinctive features of the situation of father-absent girls.

Among whites as a status group there has been a longstanding tradition of stable breadwinning on the part of males and clear sex-role differentiation within the family. In this context, male children derive important benefits from the "father-son connection," and our research has shown the disruption of this relationship to have an adverse affect on the identities and orientations of white boys (Hunt and Hunt, 1975). On the other hand, family patterns occasioned by father absence appear to release white girls from some of the inhibiting implications of conventional sex-typing with respect to achievement. The extent, however, to which the achievement advantage of these girls registered in the context of school can be translated into the realization of personal success goals in adulthood is questionable. Indeed, their lower sense of personal destiny control, which limits their esteem gain but strengthens their sex-role identification, suggests their own lack of optimism regarding their futures, despite current performance levels.

The low efficacy of father-absent white girls probably reflects the fact that release from sex-typing does not itself remove structural barriers to sex-role change. Particularly where modification of gender socialization has resulted from father absence, its positive effects on girls' achievement may be offset by the generally negative impact of father loss on the financial status of the family, which in turn limits children's educational and occupational attainment. And even more important in the case of father-absent white girls, who are likely to be provided for through such mechanisms as life-insurance and child-support, are the broader structural circumstances that work to "keep them in their place." Institutionalized routes to careers in the public order are neither well-established nor highly visible to female children in American society. Girls, compared to boys, are less frequently recruited and sponsored and often find their own efforts to gain access to these roles ineffectual. Moreover, there is no clear national commitment to a social policy designed to alter the opportunity structure for females comparable to the commitment to (or at least the rhetoric of) the eradication of racism. This may mean that academically competent and currently high-achieving white girls experience a particularly severe form of anomie when they contemplate their futures. If this is true, father absence may have the immediate implication of altering sex-role orientations and behaviors in white girls, but may have little impact on adult patterns of sex-role differentiation without more general structural supports for achievement among women.

In contrast to the white-world pattern of stable male breadwinners and differentiated sex roles, the status realities of blacks have meant greater exposure to conditions that fragment families, making father absence a more frequent and "normal" feature of black life. Our research on boys (Hunt and Hunt, 1975) suggests that under these conditions male children are not negatively affected by the absence of the father and may actually be beneficially insulated from some of the harsh implications of racism. A different picture, however, emerges in the case of black girls. Compared to both white girls and black boys, black girls without fathers evidence consistently negative effects, with the exception of their more frequent dating. This suggests that the experience of father-absent black girls neither "releases" nor "insulates," but may instead involve exposure to demoralizing circumstances. The reasons for this may lie in the fact that, despite some blurring of sex roles, black males and females stand in quite different relationship to the family.

When black men face structurally-imposed "failure" and cannot fulfill the role of family provider, there is a measure of escape and redemption offered by the streetcorner society of lower-class black males. Here men can avoid daily confrontation with their deprived families, rationalize their circumstances, and attain a version of manliness in the terms of a subculture of "shadow values" (Liebow, 1967). But there is no "Tally's Corner" for black women, who are left to cope with the problems of both nurturing and providing for their families without the requisite resources (Stack, 1974). Because females inherit this responsibility for the disrupted family, father absence, while it may lower the visibility of structurally-conditioned adult destinies for boys, probably raises the visibility of these destinies for girls. Our data alone are not sufficient for this inference, but the future orientations and related esteem costs of the father-absent black girls suggest that they are acquainted in some manner with the problematic features of black women's family roles.

In sum, our research suggests that both racial and sexual stratification condition the implications of father loss, such that the greatest costs may be felt by white boys and black girls, while some possible, if limited, gains may be experienced by black boys and white girls. While the magnitude of these effects is small, and they do not by themselves indicate policies that would "liberate" either blacks or females, they illumine some of the processes which sustain patterns of social inequality. In so doing, they underscore the limitations of past policies which have probably focused too heavily on "normalizing" black family life, and stress the importance of addressing the subtle barriers to female status-attainment created by both "normal" and "disorganized" family life in formulating policies aimed at women.

REFERENCES

Beal, F.
1973 "Double jeopardy: to be black and female." Pp. 138–142 in Ronald Hogeland (ed.), Woman and Womanhood in America. Lexington: D. C. Heath and Company.

Berger, A. S. and W. Simon
1975 "Black families and the Moynihan report: a research evaluation." Social Problems 22 (August): 145–161.

Biller, H. B. and S. D. Weiss
1970 "The father-daughter relationship and the personality development of the female." Journal of Genetic Psychology 116 (March): 79–93.

Burton, R. V. and J. W. M. Whiting
    1961 "The absent father and cross-sex identity." Merill-Palmer Quarterly 7 (April): 85–95.

Carlsmith, L.
    1964 "Effects of early father absence on scholastic aptitude." Harvard Educational Review 34 (Winter): 3–21.

Coleman, James S., Ernest Q. Campbell, Carol J. Hobson, James McPartland, Alexander M. Mood, Frederic D. Weinfeld and Robert L. York
    1966 Equality of Educational Opportunity. Washington, D.C.: Office of Education, U.S. Department of Health, Education, and Welfare.

Duncan, B. and O. D. Duncan
    1969 "Family stability and occupational success." Social Problems 16 (Winter): 273–285.

Glaser, D.
    1965 "Social disorganization and delinquent subcultures." Pp. 27–62 in H. C. Quay (ed.) Juvenile Delinquency. New York: Van Nostrand.

Goodenough, E. W.
    1957 "Interests in persons as an aspect of sex differences in the early years." Genetic Psychological Monographs 55 (May): 291–323.

Gordon, Chad
    1972 Looking Ahead: Self-Conceptions, Race and Family as Determinants of Adolescent Orientation towards Achievement. Washington, D.C.: American Sociological Association.

Heatherington, E. M.
    1966 "Effects of paternal absence on sex-typed behaviors in negro and white preadolescent males." Journal of Personality and Social Psychology 4 (July): 87–91.
    1972 "Effects of father absence on personality development in adolescent daughters." Developmental Psychology 7 (November): 313–326.

Heatherington, E. M. and J. L. Deur
    1971 "The effects of father absence on child development." Young Children 26 (March): 233–248.

Horner, M. S.
    1971 "Femininity and successful achievement: a basic inconsistency." Pp. 97–122 in Michele Hoffnung Garskof (ed.), Roles Women Play: Readings Toward Women's Liberation. Belmont: Brooks/Cole Publishing Company.

Hunt, L. L. and J. G. Hunt
    1975 "Race and the father-son connection: the conditional relevance of father absence for the orientations and identities of adolescent boys." Social Problems 23 (October): 35–52.

Johnson, M. M.
    1975 "Fathers, mothers, and sex typing." Sociological Inquiry 45: 15–26.

Kandel, D. B.
    1971 "Race, maternal authority, and adolescent aspiration." American Journal of Sociology 76 (May): 999–1020.

Liebow, Elliot
    1967 Tally's Corner. Boston: Little, Brown and Co.

Maccoby, E. E.
    1963 "Woman's intellect." Pp. 24–38 in Seymour M. Farber and Roger H. L. Wilson (eds.), The Potential of Women. New York: McGraw-Hill.

Miller, W. B.
    1958 "Lower class culture as a generating milieu of gang delinquency." The Journal of Social Issues 14 (Summer): 5–19.

Monahan, T. P.
    1957 "Family status and the delinquent child: a reappraisal and some new findings." Social Forces 35 (March): 250–258.

Moynihan, Daniel
    1965 The Negro Family: The Case for National Action. Washington, D.C.: U.S. Government Printing Office.

Papanek, H.
    1973 "Men, women, and work: reflections on the two-person career." Pp. 90–110 in J. Huber (ed.), Changing Women in a Changing Society. Chicago: University of Chicago Press.

Parker, S. and R. J. Kleiner
    1969 "Social and psychological dimensions of the family role performance of the negro male." Journal of Marriage and the Family (August): 500–506.

Rosenberg, Morris
    1965 Society and the Adolescent Self-Image. Princeton: Princeton University Press.

Rosenberg, Morris and Roberta G. Simmons
    1972 Black and White Esteem: The Urban

School Child. Washington, D.C.: American Sociological Association.

Stack, Carol B.
1974 All Our Kin: Strategies for Survival in a Black Community. New York: Harper & Row.

Toby, J.
1957 "The differential impact of family disorganization." American Sociological Review 22 (October): 505–512.

Wilkenson, K.
1974 "The broken family and juvenile delinquency: scientific explanation or ideology?" Social Problems 21 (June): 726–740.

Willie, D. V.
1967 "The relative contribution of family status and economic status to juvenile delinquency." Social Problems 14 (Winter): 326–335.

SECONDARY ANALYSIS: A PERSONAL JOURNAL

Janet G. Hunt
Larry L. Hunt

In secondary analysis the data has been collected before the research begins. Hence, the data will rarely fit the purposes of the secondary investigator as well as would original data collected with the specific research questions in mind. Moreover, in instances where the data set is selected prior to precise formulation of the research problem, major departures from the conventional logic of research are necessary. While social science training teaches one to think from problem to data, from concepts to variables, and from hypothesis to test, beginning with precollected data requires, at least initially, that one think from data to problem, from variables to concepts, and almost abandon the notion of formulating hypotheses before starting data analysis. We have tried to trace this process as it worked in our case.

DISCOVERING THE DATA AND FINDING A PROBLEM

When we first moved to the Washington, D.C. area, Larry had taken a position at the University of Maryland and Janet taught part-time and had a dissertation to write. After a couple of years, a sense of urgency about completing the dissertation began to develop. She still had not selected a specific topic but knew she wanted a project "that had something to do with self-concept" and would utilize data available in the D.C. region. The advantages of secondary analysis, both from the standpoint of the quality of the data (compared to what might be collected by an inexperienced and unfunded graduate student) and potential time-saving it could mean, seemed clear. The issue was finding a suitable data source.

We decided to contact some people at the National Institute of Mental Health and were advised by some of our colleagues to seek out Morris Rosenberg, who was head of one of the research sections there. We arranged to meet with Dr. Rosenberg to explore various research possibilities. At that time he had just finished writing a book reporting findings from a large-scale interview project among Baltimore school children (Rosenberg and Simmons, 1972) and commented that that particular study had considerably more data than he was ever going to be able to analyze. He indicated an interest in having others work with the data and generously offered a copy of the data set to us.

It wasn't long before what seemed so fortuitous and straightforward became quite overwhelming. Janet began to discover the difficulties of working from a vast data set (containing information derived from three hours of interviewing with nearly 2,000 children ranging from third through twelfth grade) to a specific research problem. One does not want to formulate the research questions before becoming familiar with the strengths and limits of the data. But achieving focus—moving to the selection of a definite subset of items in the interview schedule that connect logically to some issue—can be exceedingly difficult after immersing oneself in the details of the data set. For some time poring over the codebooks lead only to a proliferation of questions. These ranged from the nature of the general issue to be addressed (should it be a theoretically oriented one, such as the dimensionality of the self, or a more policy-oriented one, such as the effects of school integration on black self-image?), to whether the items and scales available provide appropriate operational definitions of the concepts central to these issues, to a host of particulars such as the age groups and/or grade levels to include.

While Janet was searching for a decision on a dissertation project, Larry was exploring the data from another angle. Impressed with its richness, he was trying to formulate a grant proposal to use the data in connection with some of his own research interests. Finally, we both decided that the best blend of our own interests and backgrounds with the virtues of the data at hand would involve examining race differences in self-attitudes from the general theoretical perspective of symbolic interactionism (a school of social psychology associated with George H. Mead, Charles H. Cooley, and more recently Herbert Blumer and Erving Goffman in which we had both been trained as graduate students in the sociology department at Indiana University). The frame of reference for racial inequality would be informed particularly by the in-depth ethnographic studies of the black community by investigators such as Elliot Liebow (1967) and David Schulz (1969). The dissertation ultimately concentrated on race differences in the structure (i.e., interrelationships between self-attitudes) as well as content of the self-concept, and the grant proposal concerned family structure as a potential mediating factor in race differences in self-image. The grant proposal was funded and the research reported in the article reprinted in this volume eventually grew out of that project.

The grant proposal was aimed at a prevailing assumption of the times: that the prevalence of father-absence in black families has detrimental effects on the personalities and self-images of children, especially boys, for whom it means the loss of a gender-appropriate role model. In the period following publication of the Moynihan Report (1965), this presumed family "pathology" was considered to be a central dynamic sustaining the intergenerational pattern of "low achievement" among black males. It bothered us that while social policy was heavily predicated on this view, the validity of this explanation of black status difficulties had never really been demonstrated. The dearth of evidence seemed especially serious since the emerging ethnographic studies of the black community strongly suggested that the black family—while technically often not "intact"—was viable and hardly "disorganized" and its more female-centered structure was better understood as an adaptation to structurally induced poverty than as a causal factor in the perpetuation of low-status circumstances.

We knew already that there was some basis in the Rosenberg/Simmons data for questioning the Moynihan view, for it was reported in *Black and White Esteem* (Rosenberg and Simmons, 1972) that "broken homes" were less damaging to self-esteem in black than white children. The grant proposal called for more extensive comparative analysis, including more outcome variables and consideration of male and female children separately. We argued largely on theoretical grounds that father absence per se was probably not as important a factor for the development of children as was widely assumed. Critical to the argument was the idea that children learn conventional sex-typed behaviors and acquire gender identities (establish sex-role identification) not only from experience with same-sex significant others who serve as role models but also from interacting with opposite-sex significant others who serve as altercasters (Weinstein and Deutschberger, 1963). Children not only emulate role incumbents but fashion their behaviors and self-images from the cues and expectations communicated by persons in counterroles. The major goal, then, was to try to identify the importance of mothers as significant others and potential altercasters in offsetting the effects of father-absence.

THE BOYS STUDY

Things, however, soon took a different turn. We started out by making a series of zero-order comparisons between the self-attitudes of children in father-absent and intact homes within the black and white subsamples. Our selection of dependent variables was guided by our familiarity by now with the questionnaire items and many of their scale properties gained from exploratory phases of Janet's dissertation research. Specifically, we used the esteem scale developed by Rosenberg, a sex-role identification scale we developed ourselves, educational aspirations, and grades (marks) in school. The esteem scale included items used previously by Rosenberg in his work on self-image that have become quite standard as indicators of esteem. For our study we also wanted a sex-role measure because the issue of male sex-role identification is so central to the father-absence literature. The scale we used was constructed from a series of parallel items for boys and girls tapping ideas and feelings about being male or female. We began by considering all of them—even an open-ended question asking how boys and girls differ. We soon discovered considerable difference in black and white responses to normative items identifying particular behaviors as masculine or feminine and therefore decided to work only with those aimed at evaluations and feelings with respect to sexual identity that did not imply specific criteria (e.g., "How masculine—or feminine—are you?" and "How important is it not to act like a boy—or girl?"). We examined several combinations of these items and selected the set with the best scale properties. To try to explore mothering as an intervening variable, we included items bearing on mother identification (in the sense of mother being a significant other whose approval/disapproval counts) and styles of mothering (involved, indifferent, punitive, supportive, etc.).

What we found was puzzling. Among the boys we discovered a substantial race difference: only white boys seemed to be adversely affected by father absence. Most of the literature had suggested that black boys would be most demoralized by this form of family "breakdown." We had guessed that this view probably exaggerated the case for blacks, but we had not expected white boys alone to incur marked costs. We found nothing in the mothering information to explain the difference. And we found no significant effects for the girls.

At that point we elected to concentrate further analysis on the boys. This was in part because of the more extensive literature on father-absence ef-

fects on boys and also because we had found more in the way of zero-order relationships among the boys. We had concluded that the mothering items were not adequate for investigating our ideas about altercasting, in as much as they did not permit us to differentiate the process of altercasting from the more general phenomenon of mother involvement. Nor could we control on the availability of male role models for father-absent boys in the form of other males in the household or vicinity. We could not, therefore, make intelligent inferences about the specific socialization dynamics affecting our subjects. We had also ruled out social class as an explanatory variable. While the white and black boys were concentrated at the high and low ends of the class spectrum, respectively, controlling for class on early runs had not eliminated race differences in father-absence effects—differences were observed at each of the three class levels on which we stratified the sample. It was thus clear that our original lines of analysis were at a dead end and we would have to look in other directions.

We began to rethink the issues to try to find a plausible explanation that could be explored through some form of further analysis of this data. What finally emerged, providing the basis for the specific research questions formulated for that study, was a perspective on the family and its role in the stratification process that saw the impact of the family on children as *relative* to the broader structural context. The family, we reasoned, mediates the flow of resources to children only when the family itself is in a favorable resource position. When it is in such a position (as is more often the case among whites), intact families can give children, especially boys, benefits both practical (e.g., costly higher education and network connections) and psychic (e.g., role models of high-status behavior, direction, and support). But when the family is relatively resourceless (as is more often the case among blacks), it can give little to children that will be an asset to them in the status-attainment process. Father absence under these conditions is thus not a resource loss and not highly detrimental. In fact, father *presence* where there are employment and income difficulties may actually be more demoralizing for children than father absence. We also reasoned that where there has been a caste dimension to the stratification system, these differences over time become normative and institutionalized and cannot be reduced to the social-class circumstances of a particular family within a status group at any given time.

What we needed now was a way to nail down, at least in part, the validity of this resource interpretation of the differential impact of father-absence for white and black boys. It occurred to us that the resource reasoning applied rather specifically to sons' "achievement" or status-attainment—as opposed to other possible values or indicators of well-being (relative to which the white family may be no better equipped to provide than the black family). Therefore the race difference in self-evaluation by family structure should be most apparent among boys who were achievement-oriented. Conditional analyses of the effects of father absence on esteem and sex-role identification by achievement orientation revealed that it was in fact the high achievement oriented white boys who were adversely affected and the black boys in this category who were slightly positively affected by father absence.

Satisfied that we now had a meaningful "package," we were ready to write it up. The delicate issue that faced us at this stage was how to present the findings so as to counter the family pathology view without being polemic and fostering the most probably unwarranted impression that father absence presents no problems to the black community. Our concern here stemmed from the belief that while the policy implications of a single study are not really clear, they are to some degree inevitably implied in any discussion of findings that bear on social issues as salient as race relations. We wanted to tilt our presentation in a direction supportive of the view that perhaps too much emphasis has been placed on "normalizing" the black family instead of restructuring the availability of economic resources. We did not, however, want to irresponsibly minimize family factors on the basis of so little real information about family processes. We tried to handle these concerns by avoiding firm conclusions about family socialization and stressing instead that the findings indicated the importance of looking beyond the family for the key causal factors sustaining racial stratification.

We submitted our report for publication and also presented it in the form of a paper delivered at the national meeting of the American Sociological Association in the fall of 1975. The published version appeared shortly thereafter in *Social Problems* (Hunt and Hunt, 1975). In the months that followed, this study received a lot of play in the form of write-ups in *Psychology Today* and *Behavior Today*, a media interview, and a great number of reprint requests. (We even received several requests to be expert witnesses at divorce trials for white fathers wanting to bolster their cases for custody of sons—an end, of course, to which our research could not legitimately be put.) This apparent high interest level in the issues raised by the study was an important basis for our decision in late 1975 to retrieve the girls in the original analysis, who had been shelved in favor of concentration on the boys. If through further analysis we could find any pattern of father-absence effects in the girls, we might be able to capitalize on the boys study with a follow-up on the girls.

THE GIRLS STUDY

There were other reasons for taking a second look at the girls. The academic climate had begun to change since our original decision to "throw out" the girls. At the time we made the decision, it was standard procedure to eliminate females from most areas of research if they did not fit male patterns (and, indeed, Janet had done so in her dissertation project). Moreover, the father-absence literature was typical in that it focused on matters relating most directly to male children (e.g., the loss of a male role model) and was a source of many more items and expectations regarding the boys than the girls in these families. But since that time this bias in the social sciences has been criticized extensively and there is a growing market for research on females.

Finally, on a more personal level we now had a clearer basis for studying the girls. Janet had finished her dissertation in 1973 and had also taken a position at the University of Maryland, where she was teaching a course on the sociology of women. This experience had stimulated a great deal of reading and thought about women in society and sex stratification, and she was beginning to evolve a more extensive frame of reference to draw on in the search for some pattern in the data on the girls. This was especially significant, because Larry, who had taken primary responsibility for directing the analysis on the boys, had basically "given up" making sense out of the girls. (The destruction of stacks of computer output we had generated on the girls by a flood of our basement also had a discouraging effect.) So Janet, who now had more time and perspective to bring to the task, played a central role in analyzing the girls.

In order to formulate research questions for the girls, two ideas had to crystallize. The first was that perhaps our thinking on the place of black institutions in mediating black achievement—based both on our study of family-structure effects and another line of research we were pursuing on black religion—applied better to males than females. While we were still convinced that it was appropriate to downplay the causal significance of black institutions in favor of more emphasis on discriminatory and allocative processes inherent in white-controlled institutions (Kerckhoff, 1976), we had probably slighted the consequences of the black family for females. Racism promotes male abandonment of families, which leaves females to cope as best they can and absorb the demoralizing effects. Costs associated with family disruption, therefore, may be registered more clearly in female than male children. Our second important realization was that while racial stratification is probably perpetuated primarily through public institutions, sex stratification occurs *within* the family as well as beyond it. It is mainly boys, not children in general, who are sponsored by families for personal status attainment. Girls, on the other hand, are socialized for status attainment through marriage. As a result, the gender identities of girls, compared to those of boys, are probably less identified with personal achievement. We further reasoned that this intrafamily differentiation (stratification) should be most pronounced among whites who have more resources to allocate differentially. Father absence should reduce white family resources and parental roles differentiation. This in turn should have mixed implications for girls, whose conventional sex-role orientations might be weakened but whose achievement orientations might be strengthened. Father loss in the black world, where family resources are frequently already severely strained, should have more uniformly negative implications.

In order to examine these ideas, we had to separate sex-role from personal status- or achievement-related outcomes more explicitly in the girls study than in the boys. The need to distinguish these outcomes resulted in slight shifts in instrumentation in the girls study (to include information on dating and personal destiny control). With

the inclusion of additional variables, we anticipated problems of containing our report within the space normally allotted for a journal article. To present important conditional effects in tabular form as we had done with the boys would clearly be uneconomical, so we decided instead to adjust effects statistically with partial gammas. We felt that our independent variable, family structure, could legitimately be considered ordinal (intact families have more, not just a different kind of, parental presence than father-absent ones, making the categories asymmetrical and therefore not really nominal) but not interval. Gamma and partial gamma thus seemed appropriate and interpretable statistics. Their use also permitted us to retain more categories on our control variables than a dummying procedure required to perform a multiple regression analysis.

In analyzing the girls we tried roughly to parallel the logic of the boys study by looking at effects of family structure on identity and orientation, specifying effects by social class, and then examining identity controlling for orientation. The partial gammas, like the conditional analyses performed on the boys, helped to clarify the causal relationships between father absence and girls' esteem and sex-role identification by identifying the role of orientational factors in elevating or suppressing the zero-order relationships. Most strategic in mediating these effects, it turned out, was the low level of destiny control perceived among father-absent girls, which somewhat diminished esteem but enhanced sex-role identification.

SOME CONCLUSIONS

A common "off the record" question asked of researchers after a study has been completed is, "Knowing what you do now, what would you do differently if you could do the study over again?" Addressing this question might seem an appropriate way to conclude this commentary. Yet perhaps one of the best indications of the difference between secondary analysis and more conventional research strategies is that secondary analysis does not lead one to ask or answer this question. If one starts with a clearly formulated question or specific hypothesis, it may be natural to return at the end of the work to the original question or hypothesis and ask how it might better have been answered or tested. But when the research issues are articulated in an ongoing process of exploring existing data relative to an evolving frame of reference, the assessment is more consistently forward-looking. The question is not how something might have been done better, but what should be done next. This is not to say that one does not discover mistakes and deficiencies along the way but to say that what is learned is not so much applied to the idea of improving the original study as it is incorporated into a changing sense of the research issues. Our final comments, therefore, concern the direction our work has taken since the completion of the study of father-absent girls and what we have learned in general about secondary analysis.

By the time we finished the two studies on father-absence effects, we had little interest in trying to find better ways or better data with which to study socialization dynamics and the phenomenon of altercasting, for what we had learned had led us to deemphasize the importance of socialization in maintaining systems of stratification. Particularly with respect to males, our interest has shifted from altercasting (within the family) to allocation (the assignment of roles and identities in the public sphere) as being the important process to learn to operationalize. Including females in our scope of interest has meant a growing concern for the need to clarify conceptually and empirically the intersection of racial and sex stratification. To this end we have completed a study of male and female black adults, comparing their educational attainment by family background (Hunt and Hunt, 1978). This research includes the variable of mother absence as well as father absence and has enabled us to validate and expand some of our ideas about the family-linked costs of racism and their heavy impact on females. We are currently searching for data that would permit us to examine the differential sponsorship of male and female children within families—that would permit us to document more directly our ideas about intra-family stratification by sex. Our interest in racial stratification has also resulted in continued work on black religion as well as the black family. Our concern with sex stratification has involved work on dual-career and dual-worker families.

We have pursued all of these lines of research primarily through secondary analysis of existing data sets (including the Gary Marx 1967 data, Campbell-Schuman 1968 data, and the NORC annual surveys from 1972 to 1977)—a style of research with which we have become far more comfortable than back when we first began sifting through the Rosenberg/Simmons codebooks. If there is a general point we can make from the experience, it is that while we were initially struck by the discrepancies between "how research really gets done" and textbook norms of research, we later realized that in an abstract sense our experience was in fact probably the norm. We were not really working entirely "backward," as it at first seemed, but in a manner involving thesis-to-verification steps not so different from those identified by the conventional format of research reports. Whether one calls the specific ideas that are formulated and examined in the course of secondary analysis "hypotheses" or simply poses them as questions, issues, or possibilities, the logic of research is always fundamentally that of hypothesis testing, regardless of the source and timing of data acquisition. What we had to discover was how to plug into that formalized process with concrete data we had found and how to hit on theoretically interesting and substantively important ideas to pursue. As we progressed we were able to eliminate much of the aimlessness of our first attempts by developing a clearer sense of our research interests and coming up with a general strategy of scanning zero-order relationships, formulating specific hunches, and checking them out through conditional analysis. But what we learned is probably impossible to codify to the point that a novice researcher could proceed simply by applying the formula. Such is the case in the more idiosyncratic and intuitive aspects of any form of research.

REFERENCES

Hunt, Larry L. and Janet G. Hunt
    1975   "Race and the father-son connection: the conditional relevance of father absence for the orientations and identities of adolescent boys." Social Problems 23:35–52.
    1978   "Family structure and educational attainment: sex differences among urban blacks." Paper delivered at the 73rd Annual Meeting of the American Sociological Association, San Francisco.

Kerckhoff, Alan C.
    1976   "The status-attainment process: socialization or allocation?" Social Forces 55:368–81.

Liebow, Elliot
   1967   Tally's Corner. Boston: Little, Brown.
Moynihan, Daniel
   1965   The Negro Family: The Case for Na-
          tional Action. Washington, D.C.: U.S.
          Government Printing Office.
Rosenberg, Morris and Roberta G. Simmons
   1972   Black and White Esteem: The Urban

School   Child.   Washington,   D.C.:
American Sociological Association.
Schulz, David A.
   1969   Coming Up Black. Englewood Cliffs:
          Prentice-Hall.
Weinstein, E. and P. Deutschberger
   1963   "Some   dimensions   of   altercasting."
          Sociometry 4:454–66.

MUSIC TO GET PREGNANT BY

Mike Royko

Because of my interest in rock music, the following news item out of Tallahassee, Fla., caught
my eye:

*Damning rock music for its "appeal to the flesh," a
Baptist church has begun a campaign to put the torch to
records by Elton John, the Rolling Stones, and other rock
stars. Some $2,200 worth of records were tossed into a
bonfire this week after church officials labeled the music
immoral.*

*The Rev. Charles Boykin, associate pastor and youth
director at the Lakewood Baptist Church, said he had
seen statistics which showed that "of 1,000 girls who
became pregnant out of wedlock, 986 committed fornica-
tion while rock music was being played."*

It was the last part—the amazing statistic—
that intrigued me. I considered getting a portable
radio and blasting rock music at the first 1,000
women I met.

But first I decided to get further details from
Mr. Boykin. I phoned him and we had the following interview:

Where did that statistic come from, the one
about all those girls getting pregnant while listening to rock music?

"I want to be accurate, so let me correct you.
They didn't all listen to it *during* the sex act. I was
speaking of listening to it as a prelude to fornica-
tion, as well as during."

I see. But rock music was involved in all but 14
pregnancies out of 1,000 cases?

"That's right. It was sort of like a Gallup Poll of
unwed mothers."

And who provided the statistics?

"This man. He's from West Virginia. Or maybe
Virginia. He stopped in our church one day and
gave us the statistics."

He's a professional poll taker?

"Uh, no. He's an evangelist. He travels all the
time."

And you believe his statistics?

"Oh, yes. There's a definite relationship between illicit sex and any music with a syncopated
beat. That covers rock and country music and even
some gospel music."

Goodness, a decent girl has got to walk around
with earmuffs on. Tell me more.

"Well, the low bass tones of the bass drum and
the bass guitar make people respond sexually."

(They make me put my fingers in my ears. Am
I strange?)

But the syncopated beat has been around a lot
longer than rock music, hasn't it?

"That's right. And the debauchery began when
Benny Goodman introduced swing music."

Benny Goodman caused debauchery?

"That's right. His music had a syncopated
beat."

Then why weren't lots of girls getting pregnant because of his music?

"They were, but it was covered up. When
Goodman had a concert in Los Angeles in 1938,
there was open sex."

Reprinted by permission of the author. Originally published in the *Chicago
Daily News.*

In 1938?

"That's right. The syncopated beat did it."

How about Glenn Miller, Lawrence Welk?

"When they used the syncopated beat, yes."

Remarkable. I wouldn't have thought Lawrence Welk capable of such rascality. It makes me wonder what really goes on in all those nursing homes.

"It doesn't matter whether a song is slow or fast. It is the syncopated beat. You can trace it all the way back to the jungle, where the beat was introduced. It is primitive, pulsating, hypnotic."

How alarming! Then what kind of music should a nice girl listen to if she doesn't want to be swept up by a jungle, animal instinct?

"Well, the syncopated beat is not predominant in patriotic songs or in most gospel music."

How about classical music?

"I'm not advocating all classical music. In his later music, Bach introduced some syncopated beats."

Aha! I suspected as much of Bach. The old hipster fathered twenty children.

Have you conducted any other scientific research, besides the Traveling Evangelist Poll?

"Well, we made some tests with plants. We played classical music for one group of plants, and rock music for another group, and we didn't play any music for a third group.

"The plants that were exposed to classical music grew in the direction of the speakers. The plants that weren't exposed to any music grew straight up."

And—let me guess—the plants that listened to rock music fornicated and all but 14 of the plants became pregnant, right?

"No, the plants that were exposed to rock music just grew away from the speakers. Then they died."

Well, that's better than breaking your daddy's heart.

Appendix: Readings Correlated with Chapters of Widely Used Social Research Texts

Readings

Text	Section 1.1 Social Scientific Inquiry	Section 1.2 Ethics	Section 2.1 Theory & Research Design	Section 2.2 Measurement	Section 2.3 Sampling	Section 3.1 Field Research	Section 3.2 Other Designs	Section 3.3 Experiments	Section 3.4 Evaluation Research	Section 3.5 Surveys	Section 4.1 Statistics/ Data Analysis	Section 4.2 Causal Analysis
Babbie	1, 2	3	4	5, 6	7	8	9	10	11	12	13, 14, 15, 18, 19	16, 17
Bailey	1, 2	17	3, 19	4, 16	5	10	11, 12, 13	9	18	6, 7, 8	14, 15	
Black/Champion	1, 2	11	3, 4, 5	6, 7	8	9	12			10, 11		
Denzin	1		2, 3, 10			7	8, 9	5		4, 6		
Eckhardt/Ermann	1, 8, 18	24	1, 2	4, 6, 7, 8, 14	11, 12, 13	17, 18	19, 20	21, 22, 23		15, 16	3, 5, 9	10
Lin	1, 8, 18	19	2, 3, 4, 11	10	9	12	12	14		13	5, 6, 7, 15, 16, 17	
Mannheim	1, 2, 3, 4	5, 9	6, 7	8, 10	14	12	13	9		11	15, 16, 17	
Nachmias/Nachmias	1, 2		3	4	12	5	7			6	8, 9, 10	11, 13
Olson	1, 2		4	5	9	3	6, 7	1, 2, 3, 4	12	3, 8	10	11
Orenstein/Phillips				8	6	9, 10, 11, 12				5, 7		
Phillips	1, 2, 3, 15		4, 5	6	13	10	8, 11	7		9	12, 13	14
Seltiz et al.	1, 2, 15	7	3, 4	6, 12	Appendix A	8	10, 11			9, Appendix B	13, 14	5
Simon	1, 8, 18, 33		3, 4, 5, 6, 7, 21, 22	2, 15, 16	9, 24, 31		14	10, 11, 12		13, 19, 20	17, 25, 27, 28, 30	23, 26, 29, 32
Smith et al.	1, 2	3	4	4, 7	5		8			6	9, 10	
Smith		1	2, 3, 12	4, 7	6	9, 10	11	5	13	8	14	
Walizir/Wienir	1, 17, 18	6	2, 3, 5	14	15		12	9		10	4, 7, 8, 13, 16	11
Williamson et al.	1	4	12, 13	3	5	8	10, 11	9	14	6, 7	12, 15	

Texts Used in Appendix Chart

Babbie, Earl R.
1979   The Practice of Social Research. 2nd ed. Belmont: Wadsworth.

Bailey, Kenneth D.
1978   Methods of Social Research. New York: Free Press.

Black, James A. and Dean J. Champion
1976   Methods and Issues in Social Research. New York: John Wiley.

Denzin, Norman K.
1978   The Research Act: A Theoretical Introduction to Sociological Methods. 2nd ed. New York: McGraw-Hill.

Eckhardt, Kenneth W. and M. David Ermann
1977   Social Research Methods: Perspective, Theory, and Analysis. New York: Random House.

Lin, Nan
1976   Foundations of Social Research. New York: McGraw-Hill.

Manheim, Henry L.
1977   Sociological Research: Philosophy and Methods. Homewood: Dorsey Press.

Nachmias, David and Chava Nachmias
1976   Research Methods in the Social Sciences. New York: St. Martin's Press.

Olson, Sheldon R.
1976   Ideas and Data: The Process and Practice of Social Research. Homewood: Dorsey Press.

Orenstein, Alan and William R. F. Phillips
1978   Understanding Social Research: An Introduction. Boston: Allyn and Bacon.

Phillips, Bernard S.
1976   Social Research: Strategy and Tactics. New York: Macmillan.

Selltiz, Claire, Lawrence S. Wrightsman, and Stuart W. Cook
1976   Research Methods in Social Relations. 3rd ed. New York: Holt, Rinehart and Winston.

Simon, Julian L.
1978   Basic Research Methods in Social Sciences: The Art of Empirical Investigation. 2nd ed. New York: Random House.

Smith, Barbara Leigh, Karl F. Johnson, David Warren Paulsen and Frances Shocket
1976   Political Research Methods: Foundations and Techniques. Boston: Houghton Mifflin.

Smith, H. W.
1975   Strategies of Social Research: The Methodological Imagination. Englewood Cliffs: Prentice-Hall.

Walizer, Michael H. and Paul L. Wienir
1978   Research Methods and Analysis: Searching for Relationships. New York: Harper & Row.

Williamson, John B., David A. Karp, and John R. Dalphin
1977   The Research Craft: An Introduction to Social Science Methods. Boston: Little, Brown.

CONTRIBUTORS

Kenneth D. Bailey, Associate Professor of Sociology at the University of California at Los Angeles, is the author of *Methods of Social Research* and has published in the areas of theory construction and sociological methodology.

Robert M. Baumgartner is a Ph.D. candidate in the Department of Sociology/Rural Sociology at the University of Wisconsin at Madison. His research interests include environmental attitudes and behavior, recreational crowding, and mailed questionnaire research methodology.

John J. Berman is Director of the Social/Personality graduate program and Associate Professor of Psychology at the University of Nebraska in Lincoln. His areas of research interest are program evaluation and the interface of law and social psychology.

Murray Blumenthal is Professor of Law at the University of Denver. He is a psychologist and is concerned with the analysis of social power.

George W. Bohrnstedt, Professor of Sociology at the University of Indiana, is editor of the *Social Psychology Quarterly*.

Edgar F. Borgatta is a member of the faculties of Sociology and Social Psychology and Personality at the Graduate Center of the City University of New York, and the director of the CUNY State Data Service. He is co-editor of *Research on Aging*.

Thomas J. Bouchard, Jr. is Professor of Psychology at the University of Minnesota and Director of the Minnesota Study of Twins Reared Apart. His major areas of research interest are industrial organizational psychology and human individual differences.

Donna R. Brogan, Professor of Statistics and Biometry at Emory University School of Medicine in Atlanta, has published several articles on the role of women in the health professions and the education of women students in medicine and nursing.

Amuzie Chimezie, Associate Professor of Afro-American Studies at the University of Cincinnati, has published several articles on Black psychology and the development of Black children.

Jean M. Converse is a Research Associate at the Institute for Social Research, University of Michigan. She is currently preparing a manuscript on the history of survey research in the United States.

Gerald S. Ferman, formerly Associate Professor of Political Science at Western Illinois University, is Executive Director of the Jewish Federation of the North Shore in Marblehead, Massachusetts.

John S. Fitzpatrick, Deputy Budget Director for the State of Montana, is responsible for development and execution of the state budget, planning and evaluating statewide programs, and policy research. His professional interests include industrial, political, and applied sociology.

William Griffitt is Professor of Psychology at Kansas State University. His research interests are in the general area of interpersonal attraction.

Lucille Grow is Assistant Professor at the Wurzweiler School of Social Work, Yeshiva University. Her areas of research include unmarried parenthood and transracial adoptions.

Thomas A. Heberlein is Associate Professor of Sociology/Rural Sociology at the University of Wisconsin at Madison. His research interests include recreational crowding and environmental attitudes and behaviors.

Janet G. Hunt, Associate Professor of Sociology at the University of Maryland, College Park, is currently studying the impact on the family of women's participation in the labor force.

Larry L. Hunt, Associate Professor of Sociology at the University of Maryland, College Park, is presently analyzing sex differences in occupational attainment.

Jonathan Kellerman, a pediatric psychologist, is Associate Clinical Professor of Pediatrics and Psychology at the University of Southern California School of Medicine, and Director of the Psychosocial Program at Children's Hospital of Los Angeles. His current research focuses on behavioral approaches to pain and anxiety in pediatric cancer and hematologic disease.

Gregory A. Kimble, Chairman of the Psychology Department at Duke University, has published in the journals of professional psychology and has contributed to the *Encyclopedia Americana* and the *Encyclopedia Britannica*.

Douglas Klegon is Research Coordinator at the Center for Applied Research, Henry Ford Hospital, Detroit. He has published in the area of the sociology of professions.

Eric S. Knowles is Professor of Urban Studies, Professor and Chairman of Psychology, and a Fellow of the Research Council at the University of Wisconsin, Green Bay. He has made numerous contributions in the areas of environmental and social psychology.

Nancy G. Kutner is Assistant Professor of Rehabilitation Medicine at Emory University School of Medicine in

Atlanta. Her publications include articles on sex-role stereotyping, sex discrimination in education, and professional orientations of medical students.

Jack Levin, Professor of Sociology and Anthropology at Northeastern University, is the co-author of *Ageism: Prejudice and Discrimination Against the Elderly.*

David F. Luckenbill is Assistant Professor in the Departments of Criminal Justice and Sociology at the University of Illinois, Chicago Circle. His research focuses on interpersonal coercion, the social organization of deviance, and deviant careers.

Janet Moursund is Associate Professor in the Division of Counseling and Educational Psychology at the University of Oregon and Director of counseling at Aslan House Counseling Center. Her current interests focus on personality and psychotherapy.

H. Laurence Ross is Professor of Sociology and Adjunct Professor of Law at the State University of New York at Buffalo. His research is focused on the study of deterrence and of law in action.

Mike Royko is a columnist for the *Chicago Sun Times.*

Zick Rubin is Louis and Frances Salvage Professor of Social Psychology at Brandeis University. His research focuses on liking and loving as well as on children's friendships.

Howard Schuman, Professor of Sociology and Program Director at the Institute for Social Research, University of Michigan, is currently completing a book on attitude surveys.

Deborah Shapiro is Professor of Social Work at Rutgers University and Director of the Masters Program at the Camden College of Arts and Sciences in Camden, New Jersey. She has published in the fields of foster care, child abuse and neglect, transracial adoption, and unmarried parenthood.

Stephen Shenker was a member of the freshman seminar at Harvard University that conducted the research reported in "Friendship, Proximity, and Self-disclosure." He later pursued graduate studies in physics.

Seymour Sudman is Professor of Business Administration and Sociology and Research Professor at the Survey Research Laboratory, University of Illinois at Urbana-Champaign. His research focuses on sampling, response effects, and the use of panels to collect data.

Richard R. Troiden is Associate Professor of Sociology at Miami University in Oxford, Ohio. He has published in the areas of crime, homosexuality, and drug use.

Russell Veitch, Associate Professor of Psychology at Bowling Green State University, has published in the areas of interpersonal attraction and environmental psychology.

Theodore C. Wagenaar, Associate Professor of Sociology at Miami University in Oxford, Ohio, recently served as Program Analyst for the National Center of Education Statistics and is active in the American Sociological Association's Projects on Teaching Undergraduate Sociology. He has published articles on teacher militancy, organizational contexts of schools, and attitudes toward abortion and homosexuality.

Walter L. Wallace, Professor of Sociology at Princeton University, is editor of *Sociological Theory,* co-author of *Black Elected Officials,* and author of *Student Culture.*

Donald P. Warwick is an Institute Fellow at the Harvard Institute for International Development and a Lecturer on Sociology and on Education at Harvard University. His research focuses on ethics and the social sciences.

William Foote Whyte is Emeritus Professor of Industrial and Labor Relations and Sociology at Cornell University. He is also Director of the New Systems of Work and Participation Program at Cornell. He continues to do research on rural development in Latin America.

Adam Yarmolinsky is Ralph Waldo Emerson University Professor at the University of Massachusetts and a counselor at the United States Arms Control and Disarmament Agency.